THE WPA GUIDE
TO WASHINGTON, D.C.

THE WPA GUIDE
TO WASHINGTON, D.C.

THE FEDERAL WRITERS' PROJECT
GUIDE TO 1930S WASHINGTON

WITH A NEW INTRODUCTION
BY ROGER G. KENNEDY

*Written and compiled
by the Federal Writers' Project
of the Works Progress Administration
for the District of Columbia*

PANTHEON BOOKS · NEW YORK

THE BOARD OF COMMISSIONERS OF THE
DISTRICT OF COLUMBIA
JOHN RUSSELL YOUNG, *President of the Board*
Sponsor of the District of Columbia Writers' Unit

FEDERAL WORKS AGENCY
PHILIP B. FLEMING, *Administrator*

WORK PROJECTS ADMINISTRATION
FRANCIS H. DRYDEN, *Acting Commissioner*
FLORENCE KERR, *Assistant Commissioner*
JOHN D. NEWSOM, *Director, Writers' Program*

Library of Congress Cataloging in Publication Data

Washington, D.C.
The WPA guide to Washington, D.C.
Reprint. Originally published: Washington, D.C.
New York: Hastings House, 1942. (American guide series)
Bibliography: p.
Includes index.
1. Washington (D.C.)—Description—Guide-books.
I. Federal Writers' Project.   II. Title.   III. Title:
W.P.A. guide to Washington, D.C.   IV. Series: American
guide series.
F192.3.W323   1983   917.53'044   83-42843
ISBN 0-394-72192-6 (pbk.)

Display design by Naomi Osnos

Manufactured in the United States of America

First Pantheon Paperback Edition

Preface

Washington, D. C.: A Guide to the Nation's Capital is a revision and condensation of *Washington: City and Capital* (Washington, Government Printing Office, 1937), second volume issued in the American Guide Series. Though it is but half the size of the original, the present guide contains much new information. It cannot be said of this book, as one reviewer wrote of its four-and-a-half-pound progenitor, that "not even Samson would carry it from depot to hotel"; yet we doubt that the severest critic will find much of importance omitted in this revised "portable" edition. Also, the experience accumulated by the Writers' Program since the publication of the earlier volume has made possible a more usable arrangement of the material.

Numerous mistakes have been rectified in compiling the new volume, yet we are not so sanguine as to hope for complete freedom from error. Substantiated corrections will be appreciated for incorporation in a possible third edition.

Many persons, officially and individually, have contributed to this work of revision, and we wish to express our gratification for their generous help, especially those officials of the governmental departments and agencies who supplied information and personally checked the pages. We are indebted to Mr. Elbert Peets, Chief of the Site Planning Section, U. S. Housing Authority, for the essay on architecture; to Mr. Delbert Clark, manager of the *New York Times* Washington Bureau and author of *Washington Dateline,* for revision of the journalism essay; to Mr. Harold Rosenberg, of the Central Office of the WPA Writers' Program, for the essay on art and the piece on the National Gallery; and to Mr. Darel McConkey, of the National Office, for his editorial supervision of the book as a whole.

MERLE COLBY
Writers' Program

Contents

Part I. The General Background

Part II. Points of Interest

Part III. In the Environs

Part IV. Appendices

Illustrations

xiii

HISTORY—*continued*

President Wilson at the Head of the Victory Parade down Pennsylvania Avenue, February 1919
U. S. Army Signal Corps

King George VI of England Visits President Roosevelt in Washington, 1939
Washington Daily News

The Nation's First Third-Term Inauguration — Franklin D. Roosevelt Takes Oath Before a Huge Crowd, 1941
c Harris and Ewing

SEAT OF GOVERNMENT   *Between 144 and 145*

The Capitol—Statue of Chief Justice Marshall in Foreground
Farm Security Administration: Rothstein

The White House
Farm Security Administration: Delano

Supreme Court Building
Farm Security Administration: McMillan

Treasury Building
W. Lincoln Highton

State Department Building
W. Lincoln Highton

British Embassy
Washington Daily News

Lincoln Memorial
Washington Post

National Archives Building and the "Imperial Facade" of the Federal Triangle Along Constitution Avenue
W. Lincoln Highton

Pan American Union
W. Lincoln Highton

Washington Monument
c Pat Sanford

ART IN WASHINGTON   *Between 82 and 83*

National Archives Building
Richard B. Stewart

Jackson, First Equestrian Statue in the United States, Lafayette Square
Farm Security Administration: Vachon

Navy and Marine Memorial, Mount Vernon Highway
National Park Service

Adams Memorial, "Grief," by St. Gaudens in Rock Creek Cemetery
W. Lincoln Highton

Indian Mural and Indian Office Employees, 8th Floor Cafeteria, South Interior Building
U. S. Indian Office

Outdoor Art Fair, Lafayette Square
National Park Service

Children's Gallery
District of Columbia Art Project, WPA

Artist and Cherry Blossoms
International News Photo

"Major Powell Exploring the Colorado River," Limestone Bas-Relief by Ralph Stackpole, South Interior Auditorium
Section of Fine Arts, PBA

"National Park Service in Alaska," Mural by Gifford Beal, South Interior Building
Section of Fine Arts, PBA

"Conservation of Wild Life," Detail of Mural by Henry Varnum Poor, South Interior Building
Section of Fine Arts, PBA

"Contemporary Justice and the Child," Mural by Symeon Shimin, Department of Justice Building
Section of Fine Arts, PBA

Introduction by Roger G. Kennedy

I T is easier to find one's bearings in Washington than in other
American cities. The Capital pivots around a huge obelisk, the
Washington Monument. In New York, Houston, Chicago, or even,
now, in Boston, we may find ourselves in gridlocked bafflement before
any one of many nearly identical steel-and-glass office warrens, wonder-
ing where to find that one which is our destination. But in Washington
we need only look to the horizon for the Monument, set, appropriately
for the Nation's leafiest city, in the midst of an expanse of green.

We think of it now as our ultimate statement of republican
simplicity, eighty thousand tons making a single point. It does so quite
contrary to the original intentions of the Congress and of Robert Mills,
often described as its architect. What we now see is a tribute, instead,
to the researches of a Foreign Service officer, George P. Marsh. Marsh
instructed the Congress about the architecture of obelisks, and at the end
of the nineteenth century Mills's incomplete stub of a tower, teetering
and off-plumb, was completed according to Marsh's recommendations.

What Mills originally had in mind would, in truth, have been a
better symbol than Marsh's obelisk for the real nature of Washington
the city, though not for Washington the man. It was to be not just
international but shamelessly eclectic. The Egyptian shaft would emerge
from a Babylonian base surrounded by a Greek temple, housing a
statue of Washington in a Roman toga, "sitting in a Greek chariot
drawn by Arabian steeds driven by an Etruscan Winged Victory," in
the immortal words of the 1937 edition of the WPA Guide.

Even in its present, much simplified form, the Monument is a more
complex sign than it appears. It is, of course, a reminder of a person, our
chief father figure. It is also a political statement: it creates an un-
commonly political skyline. The older European capitals were not
created, like Washington, for political purposes. They were the outgrowth of commerce, and most were also cathedral towns. Rome and
Istanbul are rounded; they give us domes. London and Paris are spiky;
they give us spires (despite St. Paul's, one thinks of London's skyline
more for Wren's pinnacles than his domes). Except for the Monument,
our city is squared off, because, in the nineteenth century, the city
fathers set a height limit to match the capacity of fire companies to
reach upward from the street, and found such limits so important
aesthetically that they retained them. Despite a popular belief to the

xvii

contrary, it was not the Monument that set those limits, but it has been their beneficiary—and so have all of us who without the Marsh-Mills obelisk would lose our way.

Let us start at the Monument: many visitors do. Standing at its huge base, we feel the imposition of order, lapidary, constitutional order, upon nature—including human nature. Washington is beautiful not so much because of the site of the city, which is unremarkable, but because it is the result of the operation of will upon circumstance, as is our political system. Washington appears to be serene and remarkably clean. Its architecture is predominantly rational, not romantic (unless one thinks of any aspiration to rational order as romantic). So one can begin at the base of the Monument, and take a breath, and be proud—even in this querulous time.

Then we can walk down the little hill toward Constitution Avenue, where shines, white and superb at a distance, the imperial façade of government offices which shows another kind of pride, which long ago replaced republican simplicity. It is a bold person indeed who does not cower before that front; there is no place on (relatively) dry land where one can sympathize more easily with the feelings of an Eskimo paddling a kayak under the overhang of a Greenland glacier.

The difference between such a glacier and the columnar massif along Constitution Avenue is that the latter is intended to impress. Like the other artificial cities created to be capitals, ours was meant to be awe-some. This was true for the first Government building in the neighbor-hood, the White House. Very early on, George Washington rejected Thomas Jefferson's suggestion that it be of a domestic scale, preferring instead that it denote the power of a rising nation. Jefferson complained that it was "big enough for two emperors, one pope, and the grand lama into the bargain." Others did not find it offensive, because it did not, after all, house emperors or kings, but merely an elected chief magistrate, who could be un-elected every four years. The White House was the Nation's house, not the President's.

The whole official city is like that, grand as much for what it represents as for what it actually is—especially grand, in fact, when one realizes it is set in a swamp. Achieving grandeur in a swamp re-quires a lot of money and a lot of determination. Only on one other occasion was a capital deliberately placed in a site more than half of which was a bog.* That was St. Petersburg, staked out in the delta of the Neva by Peter the Great. Eighty years later, our founding fathers settled upon the area between the slow, tobacco-colored Anacostia River and Rock Creek. Through the site meandered the mosquito miasma called Goose Creek, which they solemnly renamed Tiber Creek.

* There are such claims for Mexico City, but they are mythical.

To this day, if we cleanse our eyes of the rotogravure familiarity of the Federal City and look only at its topography, we can see how tidal basins and reflecting pools have been scooped out to collect the runoff, how the level of the water in those artifices rises and falls with the tide in the Potomac. With a little Spielbergian imagination, we can conjure up a vision of the Jefferson Memorial, set only recently upon filled land, or the Lincoln Memorial, so weighty and so white, disappearing into the ooze with barely a plop. The Jefferson rotunda might leave only a dome exposed, like a white bowler hat floating in the Potomac.

This outcome would not be very desirable. These are two of the most effective pieces of architecture in Washington, which express what can be done in difficult terrain. They are, in this way, parables of our political experiment, which aspires to order—equal justice—despite all our confusions. They are perhaps, like us, a little solemn, but, like us, they are respectful of solid engineering, like that which put museums in the bed of the "Tiber Creek." After its brief Roman apotheosis, that stream is now reduced to an underground river. On rare occasions it has its vengeance, rising in its subterranean bed to send directors and curators scurrying about the basements of museums along the Mall to rescue artifacts from their dampening depositories below sea level.*

Outside the retaining walls, encrusted in the streambeds, are the remains of predecessors who scarcely ever scurried. Too bulky to move very rapidly, dinosaurs and, later, mammoths crossed the Potomac where Washington now reposes. Some remained, as we can determine from the boneyards found recently.

Other, later migrants, also gone now, are revealed by mansions rather than middens. Washington is no longer what it was before the Depression of 1931–41, a wintering colony for the international rich, who built palaces along New Hampshire and Massachusetts Avenues, near Dupont Circle, and out 16th Street, most of which now house legations. Beaux-Arts mansions were built in the same period—1890–1920—by silver and copper kings who once came to Washington in order to keep an eye on how Congress, through its currency policy, was pricing their assets. Because there are more "sovereign nations" in the world today than at any time since the Holy Roman Empire, Washington has made good use of its palatial legacy. It is today the temporary home of an unusual number of ambassadors and ministers, with or without portfolio, plenipotentiary or powerless, from people's republics and imperial potentates around the world.

Since 1700 or so, capital cities seem to have been born international. The first of them in modern times, now called Leningrad, was after

* An alluvial sandbank protects the site of the Smithsonian's truly underground museum, the "Quadrangle," under construction at this writing.

all christened first with a Dutch name, "Puitersburg," and its most famous buildings are the products of a Scottish architect (Cameron) and a French one (de Thomon). One of the latest to be built, Chandigarh in the Punjab, is a museum to the genius of the Swiss-French Le Corbusier. New Delhi was primarily designed by the great British architect Sir Edwin Lutyens, which is not so strange given the date of its composition, 1910–20. But it is worth remembering how offended were both the British and American Institutes of Architects when the Australians decided that only Australians would serve on the jury that selected the architect for their capital city, built at the same time. That jury had difficulty deciding between an American, Walter Burley Griffin, and a Finn, the elder Saarinen. It settled on the former; the international community need not have worried.

In Washington, too, the first architects spoke in many accents. Washington and Jefferson, both gifted designers, spoke the Virginia variety of eighteenth-century English, which apparently sounded a little like present-day Australian. Major Pierre Charles L'Enfant, a military engineer who was laying out avenues 400 feet wide through the swamp, talked in French with Etienne Hallett, architect for the Capitol, and so did Jefferson. The Capitol's first design came from the West Indian physician William Thornton, and its construction was supervised by George Hadfield, who was born and received much of his education in Italy.

The White House was the product, initially, of the Irishman James Hoban, who made it look very like the Duke of Leinster's house in Dublin, with details suggested by several country houses in Ireland. Other improvements, including the porticos and colonnades, were added by Jefferson and by Benjamin Henry Latrobe, whose father was a Huguenot-Irishman and whose mother was Pennsylvania Dutch.

Though all this international talent was assembled at the outset, nobody, as Hadfield lamented, was in charge of any single project, Capitol, White House, or office building, very long. The Capitol was in the 1820's given greater coherence, and a huge cast-iron dome, by Thomas U. Walter. Though Washington has summoned a succession of celebrated designers, it remains true that it is not in Washington that one should look for the highest reaches of America's achievements in architecture. It does have two or three monuments of a world class, of which one, the East Building of the National Gallery, is recent and bears the indelible signature of genius. By comparison, say, to Chicago or Columbus, Indiana, the best one can say for the general tone of Washington architecture is that it is competent. Yet somehow the ensemble is not bland; its controlled scale and its green spaces—releases from the insistent works of man—make it remarkably hospitable, taken all in all.

The internationally trained architects who could rise to a high standard in America in the eighteenth and early nineteenth centuries are not well represented in Washington. Latrobe never had a large commission here. His Decatur House, on Lafayette Square, is polite, but not nearly on the same level as two other Washington houses of his design, disgracefully destroyed. His masterpiece is the Cathedral in Baltimore, not so far away. Latrobe's church work in Washington shows him at Christ Church on Capitol Hill working uncomfortably in the Gothic.

Hadfield's Arlington House, above the Cemetery, is the most conspicuous private house in America, and a very effective residential reliquary for the Washington artifacts collected by his client, George Washington Parke Custis. Most Americans probably associate it more with Custis' son-in-law, Robert E. Lee, than with Custis, but it took its shape as a second Washington Monument. Hadfield's City Hall, now District Court, is probably the most fastidious classical exercise in town, though it was not completed; his design called for a great shallow dome, which would have made it the grandest, regardless of size.

Washington once had the Hay and Adams houses designed by Henry Hobson Richardson, America's midcentury genius, but they are gone. The titans of the Beaux-Arts style, Daniel Burnham, John Russell Pope, and the firm of Carrère and Hastings, all have left to us their recollections of older styles, highly competent and very big. Washington was not the beneficiary of the work of American originals like Frank Furness, Louis Sullivan, or Frank Lloyd Wright. Canberra got Walter Burley Griffin, who studied under Wright, but Washington had nothing of the Prairie geniuses until the Pope-Leighey house was trucked onto the grounds of Woodlawn, a pleasant secondary plantation built by George Washington near Mount Vernon. Washington himself is represented at Acquia Church and Mount Vernon, and Jefferson's Monticello, Poplar Forest, and the University of Virginia are not too distant.

The *Encyclopaedia Britannica* said in 1911—rather severely, perhaps —that St. Petersburg (soon to be renamed Leningrad) had "no traditions, no history beyond that of the palace conspiracies, and there is nothing in its past to attract the writer or the thinker." A recent study of the city in American life tells us that "only Bonn, being the seat of government, yet generating few of the country's heartbeats of finance, commerce, education, or cultural ferment, has some of the same characteristics" as Washington.* People who want all capitals to consolidate all power, in the manner of Paris or London or Rome, are hard on places like Washington, Canberra, Brazilia, Bonn, or New Delhi, which

---

* James Sterling Young, "The Washington Community, 1800–1828," in *The City in American Life: A Historical Anthology*, ed. Paul Kramer and Frederick L. Holborn (New York: Capricorn Books, 1971), p. 57.

concentrate on one kind of power only. These critics are wrong to ask these cities to be something they were intended not to be. When Congress gave up on Philadelphia as a national capital, it was because it was generating too many heartbeats; it was a turbulent commercial city, an exciting intellectual center. The legislators thought it might be quieter where there were fewer mobs and, perhaps, fewer distractions by scientific and technological experiments.

Washington was intended to be a seat of government. Some of the founding fathers, George Washington for one, expected rightly that it would be a great commercial city, which it is. But none thought of it as full of engines, as Manchester was, or as Pittsburgh and Stalingrad became—primarily interesting for what they make. This is also true for intangibles: even today, after the creation of Wolf Trap, the Kennedy Center, and the Arena Stage, Washington is not a place where a deluge of drama or dance is originated. It consumes culture, as New York consumes industrial products.

But it has always attracted writers and thinkers; it is a pleasant place, despite the testimony of politicians. President Kennedy once said that Washington was a city of Southern efficiency and Northern charm. Like many things said about the Capital, this was a handy way of separating the speaker from the subject. Every Presidential candidate since John Quincy Adams has pretended to an aversion to Washington. People who are running hard toward Washington find it expedient to pretend that they are running away from it, or, in fact, against it.

We are a people with a strong anti-urban bias, and Washington is not only a big city but an international city. Politicians tend to speak about it as if it were a sink of international iniquity, like Shanghai in the 1930's. They suggest, further, that it is depraved because it is a place where is done the work of government, work they very much enjoy but must pretend to loathe. So it is part of the liturgy of American public life to say nasty things about Washington.

It is in this context that we can come to the strange story of the two WPA Guides to Washington. Franklin Roosevelt expressed horror at the 1,041 pages of the 1937 edition. He ordered it cut to the half you hold in your hand. There are a number of good reasons why it was cut. Perhaps it offered too easy an example for the charge that the WPA Writers' Project shared his government's propensity for surplusage. More likely, its chief liability was that all those pages were about Washington.

The 1937 edition was impractical; no tourist could have used it as a guide; as the pruners of 1942 said of it, "not even Samson would carry it from depot to hotel." And it was rough. In the words of its preface, it had been "a training ground for the editorial staff. In compiling the volume they learned how the job should be carried on." But sometimes roughness is a virtue. This portable, 1942 version is by far the better guide to Washington, but it is a little bland.

We have already observed the loss of the mild irreverence in the 1937 version about the Washington Monument of Robert Mills. Other cuts showed something more deadly was occurring than the deletion of fun. There was also a systematic elimination of references to discrimination against Negroes. Some such references remain, but the roughest and most eloquent were cut.

Why was this done? Perhaps the New Deal reforming zeal had diminished. Perhaps it had declined into bureaucratic shrewdness. By 1941 the Writers' Project was, to some extent, a patronage system; its editorial staff might have had in mind a domestic political objective. The Roosevelt administration, and its patronage, had faced a severe test, the third-term campaign of 1940: further victories required sustaining the coalition of the segregationist South and the liberals of the Northern cities. And, "there was a war on."

In any case, when the 1942 Guide emerged, its differences from the 1937 version began on the very first page of text. This sentence went out: "And always there are the myriad dark-skinned children of the South upon whom the city is largely dependent for the performance of its manual work." We are led to skip to the chapter on the Negro in Washington. We find it a shred of what it had been. Gone are the discussion of "the shabby contrast between the profession of democracy and the practice of slavery," the details of the race riot of 1919, and sections on Washington as "the very seat and center of the domestic slave traffic"; on attempts by Negroes to flee slavery and laws intended to prevent their escape; on the alleys ("disease-infected sties"); on Negro fraternal clubs; on Negro heroism in the First World War; on discrimination in housing and employment; and on the fraud of "separate but equal" schooling.

We would be the poorer for the loss of material like this in the 1937 volume, and it is good that Pantheon has included the pithiest of it in an appendix to this reissue of the 1942 Guide. Other changes between the two versions were for the better. The anonymous and rather rambling essay on architecture of 1937 was replaced by a feisty but good-humored one by Elbert Peets, now so long departed from newspaper memories that his Dickensian name might persuade us he was a mild man. Peets was a model of restrained passion; he was a critic and urban designer who loved the town, and knew it well.

One of the virtues shared by both editions is that they afford us an opportunity to compare the city they describe with the city we inhabit, and then to pursue the paths they suggest on a tour of our own, filling in the new places and noting what has been added and what subtracted.

When the 1937 Guide was being revised into the 1942 version, the

Pentagon was being built. Its original site was right across the Memorial Bridge, but President Roosevelt heeded the advice of his architect uncle, Frederick Delano, and ordered it moved to a less conspicuous place. It contrives to be remarkably demure, considering the fact that each of its five sides is the length of Britain's largest house.*

Not yet had the highway engineers made the Pentagon inaccessible by land at rush hour; the Shirley Highway had not yet become Washington's closest invocation of Los Angeles. (In 1983, it is a good thing the generals have helicopters, as alternatives to the Fourteenth Street Bridge.) The Guide reported that only 50,000 to 75,000 people commuted to Washington in 1941; a million or more do today. In 1942, 1 in 3 adults in Washington owned a car, a fact thought remarkable because the national average was 1 in 5.5. Today, the average family in the region owns more than 1 car (1.2, to be exact); this probably translates into about 1 for every 2 adults.

The city itself had about the same population it has today, around 650,000, but the automobile has created suburbs that have grown from 300,000 people in 1937 to over 2 million. We should not see in that number a vast ooze of Government workers spreading across the countryside. Half the people in Washington and its suburbs worked for the Government in 1942, and only about a third do today; more work on the Government than for it. As everybody knows, the great growth of government in the past two decades has been at the state and local level; the growth of the Washington area from eleventh largest metropolis in the nation to eighth largest occurred during the war years just after the Guide was written. It is a fair guess that since that time, despite its status as a sunny city (it ranks not far behind Los Angeles in days of sunshine, and ahead of Chicago, for example), Washington has not blossomed much with the Sunbelt cities.

The absence of a great university in Washington has meant that it has not benefited, as have Boston and Palo Alto, from high-technology urbanism. Springfield is not yet Silicon Valley; the Beltway is not yet Route 128. The District has no MIT or Harvard, Stanford or Berkeley.

On the other hand, it has a remarkably high level of education, spread very widely. A glance through *Who's Who* suggests that Washington's intellectual qualities are like its architectural qualities. The "rules statistics have laid down for our guidance"† instruct its citizens to be commendable, comfortable, and competent, but not extraordinary. The Board of Trade tells us that 38 out of 100 of us have college degrees. If travel educates, we are doing a lot of continuing education.

---

* This is Wentworth Woodhouse, still owned by the family of the Marquess of Rockingham who persuaded King George III to accede to the military skill of the predecessors of the Pentagon's tenants, and agree to our independence.

† Lady Bracknell's principle (*The Importance of Being Earnest*).

We take more air trips and hold more passports than the citizens of any other city.

We average out impressively; we are an averaging, civil-servicy kind of place, enlivened by a few redeeming eccentrics. We have the Nation's highest after-tax household income (twice the national average), though we have well below the national average number of millionaires per thousand. Nearly three times as many of us pay rents over $500 a month as the national average; twice as many of us have mortgage payments over $750. The average value of our homes is twice what it is for the nation, yet we have only half the national average of deposits over $100,000.

That image you may have of lots of handsome young people bustling about on Capitol Hill and sipping exotic drinks in Georgetown has some legitimacy. We have 6 percent more men and women eligible to marry than the national average, though our number of divorced people is right on the national mean, and so is our average age. And our per capita consumption of alcohol is twice the national average—second only to Nevada. Despite all this toping we seem to remain in good enough shape to win twice as many Presidential Health Awards as the national average, though, curiously, the number of those who walk to work is not much above average.

We do have a cultural life. Upstream from the Pentagon is another post-1942 addition, the Kennedy Center. It is a tribute to the pertinacity of a group of public entrepreneurs led by Roger Stevens, still its presiding tycoon. Much of what is called the "Washington Renaissance" is due to the organizations that inhabit the Center; there is no doubt that this is a place in which the performing arts are thriving. Since 1942, as well, Mrs. Katharine Shouse has created Wolf Trap, an al fresco cultural center. Another remarkable woman, Zelda Fichandler, is the primary engine behind the Arena Stage, one of the few regional repertory theaters surviving from the great Ford Foundation endeavor to diversify the theater in the 1960's.

All these aspects of our lives were created since the WPA Guide went to press. The Folger Library and the Library of Congress were here then, but in the interval, their energetic leaders have made them centers of the performing arts as well as of literary life.

The Secretary of the Smithsonian, S. Dillon Ripley, like Roger Stevens, has the satisfaction of being able to see millions of people benefit from his exertions every year. A whole new set of Smithsonian Museums on the Mall are new since the Guide—all products of the Ripley administration.

Architecture in the Capital City has acquired two major monuments since 1941, the Jefferson Memorial and the East Building of the National Gallery. As an admirer of classicism of the Jeffersonian, Latro-

bian, and Hadfieldian sort, I am grateful for the deference offered by
I. M. Pei, architect of the Memorial, to these predecessors, and by the
East Building to the Memorial and to the preceding building of the
National Gallery.

The Jefferson Memorial harkens back to Jefferson's love of Palladian
rotundas with porticos, and so does the "old" West Building of the
National Gallery. This is not strange, since both were designed by
John Russell Pope and completed, after his death, by his partners Otto
Eggers and Daniel Paul Higgins. The Guide says rightly that one of
the supreme pleasures of Washington is to stand before the Gallery in
the late afternoon, after the rain has passed, watching the delicate
gradations of its marble, from white to light strawberry, take the
caresses of the sunset.

Then you can turn and watch the sun break right through the
stone prisms of the East Building. Pope offered a reverberation of the
rounded romantic classicism of Latrobe and Hadfield and Thornton,
echoing the expression of the moment when the city was founded. Pei
did something considerably more subtle. He gave us a careful, linear
contrast, a cleansing of the eye, yet at the same time a twentieth-century
variation on the same theme.

That subtlety speaks most readily to joggers on the Mall, who see
both buildings at a pace that forces each structure to comment on the
other. Subtlety speaks again when one enters the East Building to find
a huge open space, with galleries all about, and a great deal of
pedestrian escalating here and there. That space is, of course, an abstraction of a rotunda without roundness, severely linear, but composed
of the same elements. Like the entrance hall at Monticello, like the
rotunda of the National Gallery, like any of the great central, airy
spaces around which one can hang balconies or extend wings, the East
Building evokes feeling—awe, amazement—by the use of disciplined
geometry. It is, therefore, like the central rotunda of the National
Gallery, an example of romantic classicism—revisited.

In the East Building you will probably get an exhibit worth your
attention, but the space is exhibit enough. Save the main portion of the
Gallery for leisurely moments; save the basement for cooling off later,
if you can find a table in the grotto by the underground waterfall. Go
next to see what the Smithsonian has done since this Guide was written.
There are good small pamphlets available in the Smithsonian "Castle"
on all the Mall museums, and on the National Portrait Gallery and
the National Collection of American Art. On the way you can imagine
what the Mall was like when the Castle stood romantically Romanesque
amid the verdure planned by Andrew Jackson Downing.

The Mall has been rectilineated since Downing's time; it has lost
his ponds and bosky dells, his glades and copses, but the Park Service

elsewhere in the city has kept his fructifying spirit alive. The cherry trees need no celebration in these pages. They are what they were in 1941, a springtime glory. Daffodils and forsythia and cultivated grasses of wondrous simplicity make Washington in the spring the sort of place a horticulturist like Downing could visit with some pride. Let there be heard a cheer for the Park Service, and for the committee of the House of Representatives that appropriates for daffodils!

There are other gardens, some of the best open to the public but not dependent upon the Congress or the Park Service.

At the other side of Georgetown from the Mall is Dumbarton Oaks. Its garden is described by Henry Mitchell, who knows about such things (and writes about most things better than anyone else in town), as "one of the best places in Washington to be quiet and happy in"—acres of forsythia and old boxwood, formal parterres, and even a small Oriental garden. The main house, an enlarged version of the bricky, sedate Georgetown style, is a warren of Byzantine scholars from Harvard, but the public is invited into a polished little crystal of a museum by Philip Johnson.

Do not expect to get there quickly. Georgetown is no longer the "quaint, romantic suburb" it was called in the 1937 Guide; in fact, it had ceased to be so by the time the line was cut for the 1942 version. It still had "old warehouses—relics of a once extensive commerce" crumbling along the waterfront, but by now an even more extensive commerce has replaced many of them with boutiques and condominia. Georgetown has some back yards to be romantic in, but M Street is about as quaint as Third Avenue in midtown Manhattan, and as difficult to traverse in a hurry.

Other changes are less easy to describe but, perhaps, more important to the life of the city. During the last forty years Washington has been radically altered by a combination of the top-down impact of what was called "urban renewal" and by the bottom-up movement of hundreds of thousands of relatively poor people, most of them black, out of the dispersed poverty of the rural South into the compressed poverty of the city. About one-third of the city's population was black in 1937, about two-thirds in 1982.

The arrival of hundreds of thousands of people from farms and villages into a great city was not made easy by the policies of the authorities who managed that city. Stable black communities were bulldozed aside to accommodate huge residential buildings, parking lots, and freeways. Urban renewal was one of a series of social experiments on a large scale for which the Nation's Capital served as a testing ground in the years before home rule. In Southwest Washington alone, 800 acres were redeveloped. Population movements wracked the life of the city, which was, at the same time, catching up more rapidly than most of the Nation with the delays of justice and the imperatives of the Constitution: the District of Columbia schools were integrated in 1953, before the Supreme Court made integration a national imperative in the Brown decision.

During the late 1960's social tensions accumulated that burst into flame in the riots of 1968. The riots marked the nadir in the life of the community; whites and affluent blacks emigrated to the suburbs; whole reaches of the central city were burned out; the schools were described as jungles; things seemed bleak. But the tide turned, and by the early 1980's there was discernible movement, on the part of those who had the resources for choice, back into the city. The subway system, finest in the Nation, was tying the city together, and creating villages like Capital Hill from which people actually commuted to the suburbs.

Architecturally, the subway entrances (especially that at Dupont Circle) provided some of the most exciting processional spaces in town; and at the edge, twentieth-century transportation called forth a masterpiece: Eero Saarinen's Dulles Airport Terminal Building. One of the virtues of the Dulles Terminal was that it prompted a respectful reappraisal of Daniel Burnham's older entrance to the city, Union Station, an instance of the Architecture of Great Expectations—early in the century, all seemed possible to those who thought largely and were unafraid.

Uphill from the station, symbols appeared in the 1960's and 1970's of other, even larger expectations: the imperial role of the United States was expressed in huge white adjuncts to the Capitol, which itself was given a larger façade. There appeared two new Senate Office Buildings and one for the House. A new palace for the book was added to the Library of Congress, and the Roman spirit was made even more explicit in facilities for circuses: Kennedy Stadium and the Convention Center.

Yet all was not imperial in scale. In fact, great architectural conglomerates like Skidmore, Owings and Merrill put their best designers to work on an intimate scale to provide for the redemption of Pennsylvania Avenue, and for an equally diffident provision for Lafayette Park, the front yard of the White House. All along, Washington's virtues had been intimate virtues, behind its colossal façades. As the subway made it possible to live without an automobile, people rediscovered residential neighborhoods in the city itself. The powerful black middle class continued to live as it had for three generations, quietly and confidently "up 16th Street," and "Northeast." Adams-Morgan grew into a subculture like New York's Upper West Side. Georgetown, of course, had always been there, though at times even Georgetown was creaky. A combination of a new transportation system and the accumulating sense of loss, nurtured by the historic preservation movement, sent back into the center of the city a flow of people and of money. In the nick of time, people noted the destruction of fine nineteenth-century housing between the White House and Dupont Circle, and lamented its replacement by a clutter of developers' boxes glowing putrescently with blue-white fluorescents. Regret is not always debilitating, and nostalgia does not always sap the will; in Washington, historic preservation has been a powerful affirmative force, which has led to a recrudescence of neighborhoods.

These are sometimes the same neighborhoods to which the Guide refers, though the use of individual buildings has changed. The condominium has replaced the boarding house. Many office workers, in the thirties and forties, lived in boarding houses, like the founding fathers. (It is said that when Thomas Jefferson was elected to the Vice Presidency his fellow boarders did not even offer him a place closer to the fire.) When the Guide was written, "the big-but-homelike boarding house" was still a happy accommodation for those who "must live economically but are used to living moderately well." The author of those words, the redoubtable Elbert Peets, obviously preferred a boarding house to "ducky little FHA love-nests" or the apartment buildings which "began to grow like popcorn when the New Deal came to town . . . machines for that way of living."

The boarding houses so beloved of Peets have gone. I am told by one senior citizen that the last, Hartnett Hall, was closed in 1972, and that the building is now occupied by one of Washington's larger gay bars. The suburbs have sprawled, and the condominium has divided the airspace of Washington into as many compartments as the boarding houses did, but at higher altitudes. Rosslyn has bristled with a demonstration of what might have happened to Washington itself if the fire companies had had longer ladders or high-pressure hoses when the height limits were set.

The skyline is the worse for Rosslyn, and there have been, as one might expect, some changes in forty years, but not so many as to make this Guide of mere antiquarian interest. What it says is still true, by and large, and well said. Elbert Peets was right: "Washington . . . is a beautiful place, as American cities go, made beautiful by its trees, skies, fogs, rivers, and low green hills, even by the rich chaos of its buildings, a chaos subdued by its magnificently ordered plan." The chaos has been subdued, somewhat, in the center of town, squeezed out to the edges, where it presents an effulgence of the unplanned. The suburbs act as a transition from Washington's artificial order to the rich chaos of the rest of America. The classical impulse, represented in much of Washington's architecture and in the very artificiality of its plan, is the same impulse toward order that leads us to make constitutions, to demand equal justice, to struggle for self-control, and to rejoice in a seemly order of sentences, like those offered in many places in the WPA Guide. They describe a city whose physical appearance at least attempts some conformity with its political—and, therefore, moral—reason to exist.

General Information

Altitude: 0—420.

Area: 69 sq. mi.

Population: 663,153.

Information Service: Washington Board of Trade Information Bureau, Star Building, 11th St. and Pennsylvania Ave. NW., also maintains a booth in Union Station, supplying information concerning street-car and bus services, hotels, boarding houses, apartments, and sightseeing trips. Travelers' Aid Society, 612 E St. NW., has a booth in the Union Station, assisting travelers in need of information and financial aid. U. S. Information Service, a Government bureau, 14th St. and Pennsylvania Ave. NW., furnishes information on Federal activities, personnel, public buildings, and Government departments; inquiries may be made in person, by telephone, or by mail. Automobile clubs include District of Columbia Motor Club (American Automobile Association), Pennsylvania Ave. and 17th St. NW., and the Keystone Automobile Club (American Motorists Association), 1643 Connecticut Ave. NW. For the latest weather forecast for Washington and vicinity (all hours) dial WEather 1212.

Railroad Station: Union Station, Massachusetts and Delaware Aves. NE., for Atlantic Coast Line RR., Baltimore & Ohio RR., Chesapeake & Ohio Ry., Norfolk & Western Ry., Pennsylvania RR., Richmond, Fredericksburg & Potomac RR., Seaboard Ry., and Southern Ry.

Bus Terminals: Greyhound Terminal, 1110 New York Ave. NW., for Greyhound, Blue Ridge, and Peninsula Transit Corp. lines. Safeway Bus Center, 1201 New York Ave. NW., for National Trailways System.

Commercial Airport: Washington National Airport, 3½ miles S. of downtown Washington, on Mount Vernon Memorial Highway, for

xxxi

American Airlines, Eastern Air Lines, and Pennsylvania-Central Airlines.   Taxi 60¢; bus 10¢.

Steamship Pier: Norfolk & Washington Steamboat Co., Maine Ave. and 7th St. SW.

Streetcars and Local Busses: Fare 10¢, 6 tokens for 50¢, weekly pass $1.25; transfers, interchangeable on streetcars and busses, must be requested at time fare is paid.   A free guide map showing streetcar and bus routes in the District is issued by the Capital Transit Co., 36th and M Sts. NW.   The company also maintains a telephone information service.

Taxis: 4 zones; fare, based on 2 passengers, 20¢, 40¢, 60¢, and 80¢, with 10¢ for each additional passenger.   Extra charge for waiting time, more than 2 bags, trunk, and trips out of the District.   First zone covers downtown section.

Interurban Streetcars and Busses: Capital Transit Co., 36th and M Sts. NW., has extensions of local lines into Arlington County, Va., and Montgomery and Prince Georges Counties, Md., co-operating with Washington Rapid Transit Co., in portions of Maryland north and northeast of the District.   Alexandria, Barcroft & Washington Transit Co., 1001 D St. NW., for busses to Alexandria and Mount Vernon, Va.   Washington, Marlboro & Annapolis Motor Lines Inc., Star Building, shows its destinations in its corporate name.   Arnold Operated Bus Co., 11th St. between E and F Sts. NW., for northern Virginia points.

Sightseeing Busses and Limousines: Tours of the city and environs start from the Union Station and central points in the downtown section.   Licensed guides for visitors using their own cars may be found on Pennsylvania Ave. in the vicinity of the Capitol and White House.

River Excursions: Potomac River Line, 7th St. and Maine Ave. SW., and Wilson Line Inc., 7th St. Wharves, SW.

River Tours: Yacht *Betsy Ross,* 900 Maine Ave. SW., for 2-hour trips (2, 5, and 8 p.m. daily) up the Anacostia River to the Navy Yard and up the Potomac River to Georgetown.

"Flightseeing":   Washington National Airport, 3½ miles S. of downtown Washington, on Mount Vernon Memorial Highway, for 20-

minute blimp trips ($3 per person) and 5-minute plane trips (usually $1.50 per person) over Washington. The following near-by airports also have commercial "flightseeing," passenger, and charter services: Beacon, Alexandria, Va.; Capitol; Congressional, on US 240 S. of Rockville, Md.; Hyde Field, Clinton, Md., on State 5; Queens Chapel, on Queens Chapel Rd. NE. of Catholic University; Schrom, Greenbelt, Md.

Accommodations: The majority of the higher-priced hotels and restaurants are in the vicinity of the White House and on Connecticut Ave. NW., south of Cathedral Ave. Many moderately priced hotels are grouped near Union Station. Cafeterias and popular-priced restaurants are available throughout the business district. Washington Tourist Camp, under supervision of the Government, East Potomac Park, has 144 cabins, 40 heated, with tent sites, trailer sites, and other services.

Street Arrangement: Washington is divided into four sections— Northwest, Northeast, Southwest, and Southeast—by North Capitol, East Capitol, and South Capitol Sts., and an imaginary line through the Mall, each extending out from the Capitol. North-south streets are numbered, east-west streets are lettered (omitting J Street and ending with W Street). The "second alphabet," containing the next alphabetical series of streets in the Northeast and Northwest, is composed of two-syllable names, the "third alphabet" of three-syllable names, and "fourth alphabet" streets are named for trees and flowers. Diagonal avenues are mainly named for States, "Roads" follow few rules of direction or straightness, "Places" are short streets through blocks.

Traffic Regulations: Speed limit, 25 m.p.h., except where otherwise indicated. No right turns on red lights except where marked; at some congested downtown intersections, street-light arrows indicate right and left turns. Parking is parallel to the curb, and within 6 inches of it, except where angle parking is specifically designated; parking meters downtown, 5¢ an hour. During rush hours several streets, such as 11th and 13th, and the Rock Creek and Potomac Parkway, marked with orange-and-black or white-and-black arrows, are confined to one-way traffic. Copies of principal traffic regulations are obtainable from the Department of Vehicles and Traffic, 453 Pennsylvania Ave. NW., or from automobile associations.

How to Leave Washington: Northeast via US 1-50—NE. on Maryland Ave., New York Ave., or Rhode Island Ave. Northwest via

US 240—W. on Pennsylvania Ave. and M St. to Georgetown, N. (right) on Wisconsin Ave. through Bethesda, Md. North via US 29— N. on 16th St., right at N. end of 16th St. through Silver Spring, Md. South via US 1—S. on 14th St., crossing Potomac River on Highway Bridge; US 1 Alternate, S. across Highway Bridge, taking second right ramp down to Mount Vernon Memorial Highway. South-west via US 29-211—W. on Pennsylvania Ave. and M St., left on Key Bridge, then right on Lee Highway. South via Md. 5—E. on Pennsylvania Ave., across John Philip Sousa Memorial Bridge, through Anacostia. West via US 50—W. on Constitution Ave., left around Lincoln Memorial, right across Arlington Memorial Bridge, then right on US 50 through Arlington, Va.

Theaters and Motion Picture Houses: Washington has more than 60 licensed theaters, including the National Theater (legitimate drama), 1325 E St. NW., the Gayety (burlesque), 513 9th St. NW., two vaudeville and motion picture houses, and several first-run movie theaters in the downtown area; the rest are neighborhood movie houses. There are night clubs and restaurants specializing in after-dinner entertainment.

Concert Halls: Constitution Hall, 18th and D Sts. NW., and Coolidge Music Auditorium, Library of Congress.

Radio Stations: WMAL (630 kc.), WRC (980 kc.), WOL (1260 kc.), WINX (1340 kc.), WWDC (1450 kc.), and WJSV (1500 kc.).

Recreation

Washington's spacious public parks system provides every recreational facility from marble rings to polo fields, and all major sports and athletics are represented by amateur, professional, collegiate, and scholastic teams. The city and its environs have facilities for nearly all types of recreation, whether for spectators or participants.

Archery: Two public archery greens are maintained on the Monument Grounds, and the Chevy Chase Ice Palace, 4461 Connecticut Ave., has four archery courts that are open the year around. There are several private ranges in and around Washington to accommodate about 10,000 devotees of this sport, and targets are set up on Sundays in Rock Creek and the Potomac Parks for fair-weather practice. Most of Washington's colleges and universities have archery teams.

Baseball: Washington's American League "Senators," winners of three league pennants (1924, 1925, 1933) and of one World Series (1924), occupy the spotlight in the Nation's Capital. Griffith Stadium, 7th St. and Florida Ave., NW., is the scene of a season's opening each year at which the President traditionally tosses out the first ball in the presence of officials and diplomats. The stadium, seating 32,000, is also used for professional football games, wrestling, prize fights, and other outdoor attractions.

Four colleges and universities have a collegiate baseball season, playing games at the following fields: Catholic University, 7th St. and Michigan Ave. NE.; Georgetown University, 36th and O Sts. NW.; George Washington University, games on the Ellipse and at Griffith Stadium; Gallaudet College, 7th St. and Florida Ave. NE. The American Amateur Baseball Championship is played here each year. Nearly all Government agencies have teams that play on the city's public diamonds, and compete in the fall for the governmental championship. Many commercial organizations have baseball teams that play in amateur and semiprofessional leagues. In addition to collegiate and high school fields there are 18 municipal diamonds: 5 in Anacostia Park, 4 each on the Ellipse and Monument Grounds, 1 each at Brentwood Recreation Center, Fort Mahan, Rock Creek Park, Turkey Thicket Recreation Center, and Whitehaven Parkway. Public diamonds are under the supervision of the Community Center and Playground Department, 1740 Massachusetts Ave. NW., from whom permission may be obtained to use the fields.

Badminton: Three municipal courts, at Fort Bayard Park, on the Grounds Southwest of the Commerce Building, and in Rock Creek Park.

Basketball: In addition to collegiate and scholastic teams, Washington is represented in the National Professional Basketball League by the Christian Heurich Brewing Co. team ("The Brewers"), who play home games at Riverside Stadium, 26th and D Sts. NW. Numerous Government agencies have teams, which compete in elimination tournaments, and there are commercial and amateur teams in considerable numbers; games are played in gymnasiums of Federal buildings, the YMCA, the Jewish Community Center, Turner's Arena, the Uline Ice Palace, and Riverside Stadium. Municipal courts are operated at Fort Bayard Park and Turkey Thicket Recreation Center.

Bicycling: Single and tandem bicycles can be rented from park concessionaires in the vicinity of the Tidal Basin and around the periphery of the various parks. Prices range from 15¢ to 25¢ an hour for single bikes to 50¢ an hour for tandems. A portion of the roadway in the Potomac Parks is marked off for cyclists, and this is a popular area for the sport, including the loop around Hains Point.

Boating, canoeing, sailing: The President's Cup Regatta, for small sailboats and outboard boats, held in the Potomac River off Hains Point each autumn, is Washington's premier boating event. It attracts contestants from all over the country, and is attended by more than 250,000 people. The yacht basin at 12th St. and Maine Ave. NW. is a center for mooring, repairing, and accommodating small boats, and the Washington Channel is an area where sailboats, outboards, yachts, launches, and cabin cruisers find harbor. Boundary Channel near Old Washington Airport has mooring space for boats of all description, and for a few small seaplanes, and Alexandria has a historic yacht club. The Washington Canoe Club and the Potomac Boat Club, on the Potomac River at Key Bridge, have produced notable amateur scull and shell teams. Above Key Bridge, on the north side of the river, are several boathouses that rent canoes and rowboats, at reasonable hourly and daily rates. The reconditioned Chesapeake and Ohio Canal and smooth upper stretches of the river are popular for such small-boat trips. Boats of almost every size and description can be rented in the Washington Channel, including launches and cabin cruisers equipped with captain and crew, for short or extended trips, and a yacht for a tour of Washington's water front. Steamers make excursion trips to Marshall Hall and Mount Vernon, and weekend runs to Colonial Beach, Virginia.

Bowling: Washington is headquarters of the National Duckpin Congress, and has two major competitions each year—the *Evening Star* handicap tournament during the Christmas holidays, with gold medals and a $500 stake, and the Dixie Meet, paying about $1,800 to the winner in the men's division and more than $400 to the topflight bowler in the women's division. Bowling is largely confined to commercially operated alleys, some 800 in number, which are constantly crowded by members of the city's 4,500 teams in 325 leagues.

Boxing: One or more professional bouts are fought each summer in Griffith Stadium, 7th St. and Florida Ave. NW., and fighters of all divisions perform in Turner's Arena, 1341 W St. NW.; Uline Ice Palace, 3rd and M Sts. NE.; Riverside Stadium, 26th and D Sts. NW.; and the National Guard Armory, E. end of E. Capitol St. Local colleges have their boxing teams, and boxing has been made a major sport in the local National Guard unit. Government departments, law schools, business colleges, and even schools of accountancy have boxing teams.

Croquet: Washington has 9 public croquet courts, 6 of which are in Meridian Hill Park, 16th and Euclid Sts. NW. Two of these courts can be used for roque, a game that combines croquet with cushion play similar to billiards. There is one court each at Anacostia Park, Montrose Park, and Palisades Field House.

Cricket: This English version of baseball is played at a few of the local country clubs, but the wickets are set up only on such rare occasions as teams from other cities visit here.

Dog Shows and Field Trials: The National Capital Kennel Club holds an annual show in January or February, usually in Riverside Stadium, which attracts pedigreed entries from every part of the country. The spring meeting of the Old Dominion Kennel Club, in Alexandria, also open to all breeds, draws many Washington entries.

The National Capital Field Club holds two annual field trials at

Bradley Farm, 7 miles out River Road in Maryland. Date of the trials is dependent on the weather, but the fall events are generally held in November, the spring trials in March or April. Three stakes are usually involved, one for puppies or novices, a shooting-dog competition, and an open or all-age stake.

Fencing: An annual fencing tourney is held at the YMCA, 18th and G Sts. NW., which also serves as a clearing house of information on fencing teams and matches in the city. Government agencies, diplomatic groups, educational institutions, and military branches have fencing teams; classes are conducted at the YMCA.

Fishing: Captain John Smith, exploring the lower Potomac in 1608, reported an "abundance of fish, lying so thick with their backs above water—for want of nets, we attempted to catch them with a frying pan, but we found it a bad instrument to catch fish with; neither better fish, more plenty, nor variety, had any of us seen in any stream."

Fishing is not that good today in Washington and vicinity, but it remains one of the premier sports of the region. No license is required for salt- and tidewater fishing, but State licenses are necessary for angling above the tidewater area of the District. Launches for salt-water fishing trips can be rented in Washington Channel, equipped with everything but beer and fisherman's luck, and sometimes with the latter. Parties often rent a boat for Chesapeake Bay fishing excursions, and take good catches of sea trout, bluefish, channel bass, and the sluggish but delicious hardhead. In tidewater around the city are large-mouthed bass, crappie, catfish, and mullet. In the spring, whitefish, perch, shad, herring, and striped bass gather here to spawn. Above tidewater the fishing is usually good for pike and smallmouthed bass. In the fresh waters of near-by Maryland and Virginia there is usually good fishing for bass, brook trout, and rainbow trout. Fishing regulations and license fees change frequently, and it is advisable to get up-to-date information from the motor clubs, from dealers in fishing equipment, or from sports departments of local newspapers.

Fly-casting: The Izaak Walton League and the Amateur Athletic Union sponsor several fly-casting exhibitions each year at the Lincoln Memorial Reflecting Pool, on the Mall. Information is available from the Superintendent of National Capital Parks, South Interior Building, 18th and C Sts. NW.

Football: The spectacular Washington "Redskins" of the National Professional Football League have held the center of the Washington football stage since 1937, when they made their debut here, and won the national championship. They have won a division title, and usually have had a high standing in the "pro" football world. Their home games are played in Griffith Stadium, 7th St. and Florida Ave. NW. Catholic University, which plays home games at its own field, 7th St. and Michigan Ave. NE., won over Mississippi, 20-19, in the 1936 Orange Bowl game at Miami. Georgetown and George Washington Universities play home games in Griffith Stadium. Georgetown, in the 1940 Orange Bowl game, lost to Mississippi 14 to 7. There are a number of other college and high school fields, and 11 municipal fields in the city.

Golf: In addition to country club courses, Washington has five public golf links and a Tom Thumb course:

Anacostia Park, 18 holes; Langston course, 9 holes, Oklahoma Ave. and Benning Rd. NE.; East Potomac Park, 36 holes; midget course, East Potomac Park, open summer; Rock Creek Park, 18 holes; West Potomac Park, two 9-hole courses, one for Negro golfers.

Greens fees: Mon.-Fri., 15¢ for 9 holes, 25¢ for 18 holes. Sat., Sun., and holidays, 25¢ for 9 holes, 50¢ for 18 holes.

Handball: There are 4-wall courts at the YMCA, 18th and G Sts. NW., and a 4-wall court at the Jewish Community Center, 16th and Q Sts. NW. Elimination tournaments and A.A.U. meets are held at the "Y." By making advance arrangements and paying a small fee, these courts can be used by the public. One-wall courts (free) are numerous in public playgrounds and public school grounds.

Hiking: One of the most popular hikes in the Washington region leads up the towpath of the Chesapeake and Ohio Canal, north and west from Georgetown, 4.5 miles to Cabin John Bridge, whence there is streetcar transportation for the return. A 13.4-mile round trip can be taken on the towpath from Cabin John Bridge to Great Falls, with return transportation at Cabin John Bridge. Favored hikes within the District include the 5-mile loop around Hains Point, a walk of a mile or two around the Tidal Basin, especially popular when the cherry trees are in blossom, and there are miles of trails in Rock Creek Park. A 40-mile motor or bus trip on Virginia Highway 7 connects at Bluemont with the Appalachian Trail along the summit of the Blue Ridge; 15 miles north is Harpers Ferry, West Virginia, whence train transportation is available to Washington. The trail can be reached at many other highway points, for long or short hikes north or south.

Hockey: The National Capital has two ice hockey teams, the "Ulines" of the American Professional Hockey League, playing home games at Uline Ice Palace, 3rd and M Sts. NE., and the "Eagles" of the Eastern Amateur Hockey League, playing home engagements at Riverside Stadium, 26th and D Sts. NW. There are also facilities for hockey at the Chevy Chase Ice Palace, 4461 Connecticut Ave. Field hockey is played by girls' school teams on two fields in the Ellipse and one in Rock Creek Park.

Horseback Riding: More than 30 stables in and near the District provide mounts and instruction in riding (see telephone directory for list of riding academies). There are many miles of bridle paths in the Washington park system, through Rock Creek and the Potomac Parks, and a 9-mile path parallels the Mount Vernon Memorial Highway between Washington and Alexandria.

Horseshoes and Quoits: There are 34 horseshoe courts (free) in the public parks: 22 in Grounds South, 6 in Anacostia Park, 6 in West Potomac Park.

Marbles: Four regulation rings are maintained in Grounds South.

Picnicking: The National Capital Park Police, with offices in the South Interior Building (outside entrance on 18th St. just north of C St.), issue free permits for the use of more than 100 picnic sites, with fireplaces, in the National Capital Park system. Applications must be made in writing, and the permittee has a right to the assigned picnic site. Wood for use in fireplaces must be provided by picnickers. There are many charming picnic places in Rock Creek Park, along the Mount Vernon Memorial Highway, at Fort Dupont and Fort Hunt, and elsewhere in the park system. For cold picnic lunches there are scores of tables, with water and toilet facilities near, that may be used without a permit.

Pigeon Racing: The National Capital Racing Pigeon Concourse Association sponsors spring and fall matches over courses ranging from 100 miles for younger birds to a maximum of 600 miles for more experienced racers. The city has about 10 racing pigeon clubs.

Polo: At the polo field in West Potomac Park, local teams, including the Army team from Fort Myer, compete in games sponsored by the United States Polo Association. The season is from May 1 through

Acme Newspictures, Inc.

JULY 4 FIREWORKS AT WASHINGTON
MONUMENT, WHITE HOUSE IN FOREGROUND

EASTER MONDAY EGG-ROLLING AT THE WHITE HOUSE

THE PRESIDENT LAYS AN ARMISTICE DAY WREATH AT THE TOMB
OF THE UNKNOWN SOLDIER, ARLINGTON NATIONAL CEMETERY

CROWDS AMONG THE CHERRY
BLOSSOMS, WASHINGTON TIDAL BASIN

Washington Daily News

NAVY BAND CONCERT IN FRONT OF THE CAPITOL

"SUNSET SYMPHONY" AT THE WATER GATE

Underwood and Underwood

Richard B. Stewart

PARADE OF THE SCHOOLBOY PATROL

"GRAY HORSE BATTALION" OF
FORT MYER IN ARMY DAY PARADE

U. S. Army Signal Corps

TOURISTS IN STATUARY HALL

©*Harris and Ewing*

WASHINGTON CORRESPONDENTS—PRESS
CONFERENCE AT THE WHITE HOUSE

SENATE SESSION, COMPLETE FROM PAGE BOYS TO GALLERY

WASHINGTON NATIONAL AIRPORT

October; schedules are given in local papers. Games are played at Fort Myer (*free*) on Wednesday and Saturday afternoons.

Shooting: The headquarters of the National Rifle Association of America, 1600 Rhode Island Ave. NW., is a clearing house for information on pistol and rifle shooting. The NRAA range, 10 G St. NW., is open to the public 5-11 p. m. Mon.-Fri., at 50¢ an hour per target. Washington has many shooting clubs, including Boy Scout, high school, Government agency, police, military, collegiate, and women's groups.

Shuffleboard: Permits for use of the two shuffleboard courts on Grounds South are issued by the Community Center and Playground Department, 1740 Massachusetts Ave. NW.

Skating: Washington has three commercial rinks—Chevy Chase Ice Palace, 4461 Connecticut Ave.; Riverside Stadium, 26th and D Sts. NW.; and Uline Ice Palace, 3rd and M Sts. NE. In winter, when the ice is thick enough for safety, the Lincoln Memorial Reflecting Pool is opened for public skating. There are several roller-skating rinks, including the Coliseum Roller Rink, 510 26th St. NW.; the Armory, Silver Spring, Maryland; and the Barn Dance Auditorium, Alexandria, Virginia.

Sledding: When the snow is deep enough on the city streets, about 40 of Washington's best hills are roped off for sledding, after school hours and on Saturdays and Sundays.

Soccer: There are three municipal fields in the Monument Grounds and one in West Potomac Park. Nearly every playground has its soccer team, and elimination tourneys are held each year for the playground championship.

Softball: All branches of the Government, most business houses, and many clubs have men's or women's teams that play on the 30 municipal diamonds or in Griffith Stadium. There are 12 diamonds in West Potomac Park, 6 in Anacostia Park, 4 in Monument Grounds, 4 in Rock Creek Park, 2 on the Mall, 1 at Fort Bayard Park, and 1 in the Turkey Thicket Recreation Center.

Speedball: This game, a combination of football, soccer, and basketball, is played on two fields in West Potomac Park. Permits for use of the fields are obtainable at the D.C. Community Center and Playground Department, 1740 Massachusetts Ave. NW.

Swimming: Because of the pollution of Potomac waters, Washington relies mainly on artificial pools for swimming. The D.C. government operates the following pools free for public use: Georgetown Playground, 33rd St. and Volta Place NW.; Rosedale Playground, 17th and Kramer Sts. NE.; Hains Point, 4th and Van Buren Sts. NW.; 2nd and T Sts. NE. (two pools); Georgia Ave. and Barry Place NW. (two pools for Negroes); 24th and N Sts. NW. (two pools for Negroes).

The leading commercial pools are Chevy Chase Pool, Chevy Chase Lake, Md. (out Connecticut Ave.); Airport Pool, S. end of Highway (14th St.) Bridge; Glen Echo Pool, Glen Echo, Md. (out Massachusetts Ave. Extended); Maryland Club Gardens, Marlboro Pike, Md. There are also pools at athletic centers such as the YMCA and Jewish Community Center, and at various hotels. Some high school and university pools are open to the public in summer.

The nearest salt water swimming is on the Chesapeake beaches, about 40 miles eastward.

Tennis: The Community Center and Playground Department, 1740 Massachusetts Ave. NW., issues free permits for use of 50 tennis courts in the city: 17 on the Mall, 10 in Anacostia Park, 8 at the Turkey Thicket Recreation Center, 4 at Langdon Park, 4 at Montrose Park, 3 at White Lot, 2 in Rock Creek Park, 1 at Garfield Park, and 1 on the Monument Grounds. Many courts are maintained privately or by organizations.

Track: Three nationally known marathons are run here each year —the *Evening Star* national championship marathon, with an international roster of contestants, over a course of 26 miles 385 yards; the District Playgrounds 10-mile race, sponsored by the Takoma Park Citizens' Association, drawing contestants from the eastern United States and Canada; and the 3½ mile Trans-city Race for Negro contestants. Collegiate and high school track and field meets are held in the spring at the various educational institutions.

Trapshooting and Skeet: There are a number of trapshooting and skeet ranges in the Washington area. Information on these sports may be obtained from the Washington Gun Club, the Kenwood Skeet Club, the National Capital Skeet Club, the Skyline Gun Club, and the Alexandria Skeet Club.

Volleyball: There are 6 publicly maintained volleyball courts in the city: 2 in Grounds South, 2 in Rock Creek Park, 1 in Fort Bayard

Park, 1 in the Turkey Thicket Recreation Center. Free permits for the use of courts may be obtained from the Community Center and Playground Department, 1740 Massachusetts Ave. NW.

Wrestling: Professional shows are staged weekly at Turner's Arena, 14th and W Sts. NW. Sports centers such as the YMCA and Jewish Community Center have mats that are available to the public at a nominal cost. Local schools and colleges have wrestling teams that compete with each other and with visiting teams.

Calendar of Annual Events

The Washington year ordinarily is bright throughout with official celebrations and festivals of many kinds. During the national emergency, beginning in 1940, however, a more restrained and serious atmosphere prevailed in the Capital. Formerly the official year opened with a series of receptions and dinners at the White House. The following functions occurred during January and February, on dates fixed by the President in the order named: Diplomatic Reception, Cabinet Dinner, Vice President's Dinner, Judicial Reception, Speaker's Dinner, Diplomatic Dinner, Congressional Reception, Dinner to the Chief Justice and the Supreme Court, Reception to the Officials of the Treasury, Post Office, Interior, Agriculture, Commerce, and Labor Departments and Federal agencies, Army and Navy Reception. In 1941, of the customary January-February functions, only the Judicial and Army and Navy Receptions were held. The long-established New Year's Day Reception at the White House has not been observed during President Franklin D. Roosevelt's administration. Embassies and legations observe royal birthdays, independence days, and other holidays of their native countries; but, during periods of emergency, representatives of countries at war omit many of the customary observances.

On special days services are held around the city's many memorials, in memory of illustrious men and women. The churches celebrate religious festivals frequently, and have excellent musical programs. In addition to official and commemorative occasions, there are seasonal pilgrimages to historic places—houses, churches, gardens; and there are a number of flower shows, at the Botanic Garden and elsewhere. Numerous conventions of national associations; sports events, water carnivals; musical and educational affairs of importance, occur throughout the year.

Outstanding annual events of fairly general observance are included in the following list:

JANUARY

Third (unless it falls on Sunday)	at the Capitol	Congress convenes
Seventeenth	city-wide	Benjamin Franklin's Birthday observed by various societies
Nineteenth	city-wide	Robert E. Lee's Birthday observed by Confederate societies
Twentieth (every fourth year)	at the Capitol	Inauguration of the President of the United States
Thirtieth	at principal hotels and city-wide	Series of President's Birthday Balls, for benefit of Infantile Paralysis Fund

FEBRUARY

Twelfth	at Lincoln Memorial	Lincoln's Birthday Services; the President places the memorial wreath
Fourteenth	at Douglass Memorial Home	Frederick Douglass' Birthday observed by Negro children. The Musolit Club observes the Friday nearest to Lincoln's and Douglass' birthdays
Fifteenth	at Arlington Cemetery	Memorial Services for victims of Battleship *Maine* explosion
Twenty-second	at Mount Vernon; in Congress; at Washington Monument.	Washington's Birthday pilgrimages, special services, and laying of wreath by the President at the tomb of Washington
Last week	Cathedral of SS. Peter and Paul	Pilgrimage to Woodrow Wilson's Tomb
No fixed date	variable	Midwinter Dinner of Washington Board of Trade, attended by the President and other celebrities

MARCH

Seventeenth	city-wide	Saint Patrick's Day observed by churches and celebrated by Irish societies

MARCH—*Continued*

| No fixed date | at Willard Hotel | Gridiron Club Dinner, usually attended by the President and other high officials |
| No fixed date | at White House | "Gridiron Widow's" party |

MARCH OR APRIL

No fixed date	at the Tidal Basin	Cherry Blossom Festival
Easter Monday	White House South Grounds, Zoological Park, and Washington Monument Grounds.	Easter-egg rolling
No fixed date	in near-by Maryland and Virginia	Wanderbirds' Hiking Club opens hike season

APRIL

Sixth	city-wide	Army Day parade by military organizations, units from Fort Myer, public-school cadets, Army, Navy and Marine bands
Twenty-eighth	at Pan American Building and other places	Birthday of James Monroe, celebrated by Pan American Union and patriotic societies
First week (usually on the third)	city-wide	American Creed Day
Third Friday	city-wide	Arbor Day; tree-planting
No fixed date	city-wide	D.A.R. Convention
No fixed date	at Griffith Stadium	President throws out the first ball to open baseball season
No fixed date	Georgetown, Maryland, Virginia	Spring tours of historic gardens
No fixed date	variable	National Capital Kennel Club, annual dog show

MAY

First	city-wide	May Day festival and services in parks and playgrounds
Thirtieth	at Arlington Amphitheater	Memorial Day Parade and services; the President lays wreath at Tomb of Unknown Soldier
Thirtieth	city-wide	Schoolboy Safety Patrol Parade
First or second week	at Bradley Farms	National Capital Horse Show, three days
Second Sunday	at Arlington	Mother's Day services
No fixed date	city-wide	Community Center May festivals for children
No fixed date	District waters	Fishing season opens for perch, bass, and salt-water fish; herring snagging season begins on fifteenth
No fixed date	in near-by Maryland	Spring racing season opens

MAY AND JUNE

No fixed date	District and near-by Virginia	Pilgrimages to historic churches

JUNE

Fourteenth	city-wide	Flag Day
Fifteenth	Tidal Basin and Anacostia River	Fishing season opens, continuing until November fifteenth
No fixed date	at Monument Grounds	Sylvan Summer Theater opens for amateur performances
No fixed date	at high schools	Cadet reviews
No fixed date	city-wide	4-H Club National convention

JULY

Fourth	Monument Grounds and city-wide	Independence Day Parade, fireworks in evening on Monument Grounds
First week (usually)	at Fort Myer	Horse show and polo games

July and August

No fixed date	at Arlington Bridge Water Gate	National Symphony Orchestra gives series of eight outdoor concerts

August

No fixed date	in Washington and environs	Potomac Appalachian Trail Club hikes begin

September

Seventeenth to twenty-second	city-wide	Constitution Week, observed by American Bar Association
First Monday	city-wide	Labor Day celebration
No fixed date	on the Potomac	President's Cup Regatta, three days

October

Twelfth	city-wide	Columbus Day, observed by Knights of Columbus, Italian societies, and other groups
Twenty-second to twenty-fifth	at Meadow Brook Saddle Club	Inter-American Horse Show
Twenty-fifth	at Constitution Hall	National Symphony Concert Season opens
Twenty-seventh	city-wide	Navy Day, air show, parade, concerts; Navy Yard usually opened to the public
Thirty-first	city-wide	Halloween parade
First week	at Supreme Court Building	Supreme Court convenes
No fixed date	at National Museum	Potomac Rose Show

November

Seventh	variable	League of American Pen Women, Celebrity Breakfast
Eleventh	at Arlington Cemetery	Armistice Day exercises; wreath laid by the President

NOVEMBER—*Continued*

Last Thursday	city-wide	Thanksgiving Day
No fixed date	Maryland and Virginia	Duck-hunting season opens

DECEMBER

Twenty-fourth	city-wide	Christmas Eve; National Community Christmas Tree in Ellipse is lighted by the President; choral singing in Ellipse and elsewhere
Twenty-fourth	at Franciscan Monastery	Midnight mass
Twenty-fifth	city-wide	Christmas Day; children of embassies and legations greet children of the world in International Children's Christmas Broadcasts
No fixed date	at Willard Hotel	Gridiron Club semi-annual dinner

PART I
The General Background

Washington: City and Capital

THROUGHOUT at least the first half-century of its existence, Washington was little more than a southern village, centering about Lafayette Square and straggling off to the Capitol on the east, Georgetown on the west, and the hills and river to north and south. For several decades after its transition to city status, it retained a rather definite Southern character. Even in the great composite community of today—a synthesis or microcosm, as it were, of all America —no little of this original aspect survives, coloring the city's physical background and pervading its life.

Not only in old Georgetown, but scattered through the District, are isolated houses which belong scarcely less distinctively to the ante bellum South than do the early habitations of Richmond and Savannah. Many of these houses are now used for business purposes or as the headquarters of national organizations, but a few still shelter a private existence almost as detached and aristocratically aloof as that of some mansion in Charleston "befo' de wah"; while in others the strenuous domestic and social life of today is superimposed upon the old background.

Everywhere in the Capital one hears the indolent cadence of Southern speech, and encounters that admirable though (to some) irritating southern characteristic—the innate aversion to hurry and worry. In springtime the blossoms of magnolia, azalea, honeysuckle, rhododendron, and other typically Southern vegetation in parks and private grounds vie with the Japanese cherry trees of Tidal Basin and river in glorifying the city with color and fragrance.

The fundamental fact about Washington is that it was created for a definite purpose and has been developed, with many modifications, according to a definite plan. Therein lies its unique distinction among American cities, and among all existing capitals in the western world. The purpose was to provide a permanent seat of National Government; the plan was formulated by a French architect and military engineer, Pierre Charles L'Enfant, who had served in the Continental Army. Europe's foremost capitals are vast amorphous growths which have their independent character and existence as great communities, quite apart from and more or less obscuring their character as governmental centers. But the character of Washington as a nation's capital is basic, determining in largest part not only the city's outward aspect and prevailing atmosphere but the routine pattern of life for most of its inhabitants.

The natural situation of Washington has dignity, distinction, and beauty. The city's governmental and main business section lies between a long reach of the Potomac River on the south and the west and that river's so-called Eastern Branch—the Anacostia. From the confluence of these streams, the land diverges northward in a fairly level plain, to meet and merge into a downward-bending ellipse of low hills, forming altogether a kind of great amphitheater, roughly triangular in shape. From north to south through this amphitheater runs Rock Creek, bedded for most of its course in a rocky glen which, with a broad strip of wooded land along each of its sides, constitutes Rock Creek Park— the chief natural attraction of Washington, with the wide wooded reach of the Potomac as a close second. Sir James Bryce knew "of no great city in Europe (except Constantinople) that has quite close, in its very environs, such beautiful scenery as has Washington in Rock Creek Park and in many of the woods that stretch along the Potomac on the north and also on the south side, with the broad river in the center and richly wooded slopes descending boldly to it on each side."

Within an area of about 70 square miles, which may be called either Washington or the District of Columbia (or "D.C.") as one pleases, for the city and the District are now virtually coextensive, reside more than 600,000 persons. The suburban area, in Maryland and Virginia, contains an additional 300,000 or so, of whom probably at least a fourth journey to and from the city each day by private motorcar or public bus. Inside the District the tide of urban population has long since overflowed the northern limits of L'Enfant's plan and spread to the Maryland Line on three sides, engulfing in its course a number of provincial villages, the names of which survive in most cases as regional designations. Georgetown, lying along the northern shore of the Potomac west of Rock Creek, is the oldest and most densely populated outlying section of the city.

Because of the absence of large-scale industry within the District, its population is racially homogeneous to an exceptional degree. But with respect to regional origin within the United States, probably no other large urban population is less homogeneous; and a composite portrait of all Washingtonians would doubtless be as true a portrait of the average or typical present-day American as could be obtained.

When the seat of national government was transferred from Philadelphia to Washington in 1800, the entire staff of Federal employees numbered about 130 clerks, with a due proportion of higher officials. Even at the close of the Civil War this total had increased only to about 7,000. Today, Government workers in Washington (exclusive of the legislative, judicial, and military services) number more than 200,000 and with their families constitute more than half of the Capital's entire population. It is this huge army of Federal employees—drawn from every part of the country and organized in scores of separate units, but deriving its livelihood from a common source and therefore held together by a common bond—which chiefly affects the city's routine life, its economic life in particular. A majority of the Federal employees now in Washington (1942) have been taken on during the administration of President Franklin D. Roosevelt.

Only four other cities in this country have a larger Negro population than Washington, and these four (New York, Chicago, Philadelphia, and Baltimore) are all considerably larger. More than one-fourth of the Capital's inhabitants are Negroes.

The other distinctive population groups in Washington are diverse and relatively small. There are the embassy and legation people from every land, without whom formal society in the Capital would lose most of its color and variety. There are retired officials of every sort—ex-Senators and ex-Representatives; Army and Navy men, to whom Washington is the only fixed point in an unstable universe; former heads and subheads of departments and bureaus; and an occasional ex-Cabinet member. There are the scientists and scholars, some in Government service, some "free lancers" who live and work here because of the unrivaled research facilities the Capital affords. There are lobbyists, tax experts, patent attorneys, "go getters" and "go betweens" of every sort, many of them former Government employees. There are journalists and press correspondents, probably the largest group of its kind in the world, who mirror and echo Washington life for the Nation. There are the wealthy winter sojourners, who fill the expensive hotels and apartment houses or occupy luxurious homes of their own for a part of each year. Finally there are the perennial job-hunters and supplicants for political baksheesh, a group ever shifting in personnel but ever the same in mass and purpose.

Within the city's residential section, and to some extent in its business section, there is a profusion of shade trees bordering all main thoroughfares and scattered thickly in the open squares. Had Washington no other attraction or distinction, it would still be notable as the best-shaded city in America. But though they enjoy this notable blessing of trees, Washington streets suffer under the curse of a motor-car traffic relatively far greater and seemingly if not actually more congested and perilous than that of even New York. Washington had, in 1940, one car to every three and a half persons, with an annual registration of about 200,000 in all. (The national average is 5.5 persons per car.) In addition, to obtain a complete picture, one must take into account the "foreign license" cars of Maryland and Virginia suburbanites who drive into town daily, and of transient motorists from other States—doubtless altogether a daily average of anywhere from 50,000 to 75,000. The ratio of taxicabs and busses to population is considerably higher than in any other large city.

Considering its physical equipment for cultural purposes, including scores of libraries, five art galleries, and half a dozen universities, Washington might well be regarded by a stranger as the Athens of America. Perhaps it is, as far as any city deserves such a title; certainly it ought to be, if cultural equipment really made for a cultured community. "Legitimate" drama, however, has a single remaining shrine. The city's galleries and museums are visited almost wholly by tourists; its unexcelled library facilities are utilized mostly by high school and college students, and by research workers from other States. In truth, apart from the cultural equipment maintained or directed by the Federal Government and other agencies for the country at large, culture in Washington stands at about the same general level as in most other American cities of comparable size.

As an appendage and ward of the Government, Washington lives and has its being in an atmosphere predominantly political. Both for local consumption and for export to the country at large, politics is its principal commodity. As some one has remarked, it is the "issue" and "slogan" manufacturing center of the United States. In this national stadium the big teams contend not for a single afternoon but throughout the year. The contest lags when Congress is not in session, though the coaches and water boys of the two big party headquarters are only a little less active than usual. In Presidential campaign years, when the rest of the country is at fever heat, civil-service Washington takes the pointing with pride and viewing with alarm in a spirit of relative calm. Most Government employees send their absentee ballots home, and observe the contest with interest. After election the city strikes a new pace, settles down to a new tempo. The battle between the Ins and Outs assumes a new phase, under different war cries. But, as the French say, the more it changes, the more it is the same thing.

Every minute phase of this intensive political warfare is reported to the country and the world by a prodigious "press gallery." Some 300 newspapers throughout the United States, as well as a good many in foreign cities, maintain bureaus or special correspondents of their own in the Capital. The rest are abundantly supplied by the national or international press associations. At a rough average, about half a million words of political news and comment are telegraphed out of Washington daily. There is perhaps an equal volume of mailed material—daily and weekly "letters" and "columns," special feature articles, along with an oral flood of speeches, debates, and whatnot poured from local broadcasting stations directly into the Nation's homes. Finally, there is the presentation of political events, personalities, and interviews in the newsreels of at least four national motion-picture producers, and in the "stills" of many press photographers.

Washington has, besides many specialized press bureaus in other fields (science, finance, commerce, agriculture, geography, education), scores of national publicity or propaganda agencies for every sort of enterprise and activity, whose daily or weekly "releases" drift down over the country like an incessant snowstorm. It has, too, its many free-lance writers and photographers who supply the popular periodicals with material about every phase and feature of the Capital. Probably no other city in the world is kept so prominently and continually in the public eye and the public mind.

As a result, most literate inhabitants of the United States are scarcely less familiar with Washington, its politics, personalities, and public buildings, than they are with their own communities; and sooner or later most of them come to the tangible city. They are thoroughly at home here in a historic and political atmosphere which they have breathed vicariously since childhood, and amid surroundings which they have seen pictured countless times. They come by train, motorbus, airplane, and in their own cars, from every section of the country; and collectively, with their fellow tourists from other lands, they comprise a visiting contingent of about 2,000,000 persons every year. Sightseeing is the Capital's chief industry—indeed, its only large-scale industry, if politics be excluded from such a category.

If Washington were not the Nation's Capital, its formal social life would not differ greatly from that of any other American community of similar size. In other words, virtually all that gives society here its distinction, its special color and variety, its individual code, arises in the city's character as the abode of high governmental officials, originating from every section of the United States and from every country of the world. These high officials and their wives constitute the central and supreme hierarchy of formal society in the Capital. The White House is its Sinai, and its commandments are an imposing body of ritual as sacred to all true believers as any bible. The code of this inner hierarchy is handed down, as it were, to a secondary social order which, while nonofficial in character, more or less impinges upon and has frequent access to the higher body. Thence it seeps forth and in some degree permeates the Capital's formal social life in general.

The all-important essence of this code or ritual is precedence—the relative ranking of high officials, American and foreign. In European capitals precedence is fully and definitely formulated in governmental documents called "protocols"; but in this country we have only a body of unwritten and more or less tentative law, based on established or prevailing custom in official circles. Reduced to practice, this law has chiefly to do with the order in which public functionaries and their wives are seated at dinner—and woe betide the host or hostess who ignores it! During several administrations preceding the Coolidge era, guests at White House dinners were "seated" by the official social secretary; then the whole ticklish business was tossed into the State Department's lap, where it remains. The Department "will give out certain rules and regulations, though refusing to be quoted as authority and supplying no written lists."

It might well be supposed that, in view of its median geographical position between the northern and southern extremities of the Atlantic coast, Washington should enjoy a climate exceptionally favorable to open-air sports and recreations throughout the year. And so, perhaps, it does—for all its torrid midsummers and slushy midwinters. At any rate, one may safely say that the inhabitants of few other large American cities play more numerously and habitually and variously in the open. This is mostly a development of the past quarter century or so. Viewing the Capital's recreational facilities in 1902, the McMillan Park Commission reported that "the positive dearth of means of innocent enjoyment for one's leisure hours is remarkable." Today those means are abundant, and abundantly utilized. There are many miles of bridle paths in Rock Creek and Potomac Parks; numerous fine golf courses and country clubs within or conveniently near the District; the broad river leading down into Chesapeake Bay for yachting and motor-boating; outdoor swimming pools; a polo field or two. There are baseball, football, and hockey fields, tennis and badminton courts—on the Ellipse, in Potomac Park and elsewhere. The Potomac and Anacostia Rivers provide fishing and boating facilities for everyone; hikers pursue a score of well-worn trails into neighboring Virginia and Maryland woods; bicyclists throng the less traffic-burdened boulevards; in winter there is usually skating on the Reflecting Pool, and occasionally on the river.

Those to whom statistics are important will be interested in knowing that with respect to population Washington ranks eleventh among cities of the United States, according to the 1940 census. The assessed value of its taxable realty was $1,193,499,086, and the cost of its municipal government was $45,128,921 in 1939. It is one of only three cities in this country which have no funded indebtedness. With respect to cost of living, it is among the first on the list of all American cities. The total value of its manufactured products for 1937 was $74,107,-967; printing is the largest single item. With only 0.48 per cent of the country's total population, it contributed to the Federal Government 0.53 per cent of total internal revenue collections during the fiscal year ending June 30, 1940. Its income tax payment was even higher proportionately, at 0.76 per cent of the country's total—a proportion greater than that of any one of 27 States and Territories

Among cities of comparable size, in addition to the greatest number and largest dollar-total of income tax returns, it boasts the largest annual retail sales per capita, the "highest median rental and home value," and the largest number of homes valued at more than $5,000. On a per capita ratio, it has more telephones than any other city in the world.

In addition to those larger and deeper impressions which the Capital makes upon every intelligent visitor, he is bound to carry away with him the memory of many casual glimpses and fragmentary observations—seemingly trivial, for the most part, yet not without significance of one sort or another. The familiar blimp sailing serenely above the city—a compact silver cloud by day, a shifting constellation of red stars by night; youth, chiefly feminine youth, issuing in a surging late-afternoon tide from some great Government building, as from a college stadium; Rochambeau in bronze, at a corner of Lafayette Square, pointing a sternly accusing finger at the gingerbread State Building diagonally opposite his pedestal; the flashing color and harsh cry of a bluejay darting out of a tree; panhandlers pleading for dimes in the shadow of buildings where billions of dollars are being disbursed; an elderly Congressman, in wide-brimmed hat and cape-overcoat, trying to look like Daniel Webster; a tree-lined vista opening from one of L'Enfant's circles and closing in the filtered light of sunset over Georgetown; the hubbub of huge cafeterias, filled largely with Government employees; wet-nosed children, holding the supreme right of entry for once, assessing childless adults 25¢ for taking them to the White House Easter egg-rolling; the centrifugal motion of traffic on Washington's many circles; streets in a constant state of repair; scores of externally pompous Victorian boarding houses; pay-day newspaper editions, fat with advertising; Federal wives jamming the streetcars on these same days, and other evidences of a city operating on a Government pay-day economy; a flower or fruit stand's splash of vivid color against the drab background of a downtown street corner. Of such various small change as this, no less perhaps than of the large currency of noble architecture and rich historical associations, will the sum of one's Washington memories be made up.

Natural Setting

VIEWED from the air or from the top of the Washington Monument on a clear day, salient topographical features of the District stand out: to the south, the Potomac, nearly a mile wide at this point, low marshy lands along its borders; the Anacostia River to the south and east, edged by reclaimed flats; the Potomac Parks and, across the river, Washington National Airport, on filled-in swamplands; the artificially created Tidal Basin; Rock Creek winding down through magnificent scenery from the northwestern plateau region; and a gentle roll of hills encircling the city to the north. Wooded suburban areas, parks, and tree-lined avenues merge softly with each other in a seemingly continuous mass of vegetation.

The Capitol, at the head of the Mall, dominates the scene not only because of its striking contour and height, but also because it was erected on the brink of a natural rise which contrasts sharply with the long low-lying expanse that ends with the Lincoln Memorial on the shore of the Potomac. The elevation on which the Capitol is built averages about 90 feet above the Potomac; while the lower land, on which stands the series of public buildings from the National Museum to the Washington Monument, averages only 40 feet or less and has been inundated on occasion by freshets from the river. These two levels represent the lower members of a succession of terraces carved out by the Potomac and other streams in a prehistoric age when, possibly augmented by glaciers in the north, they rushed with great momentum and volume through widening channels.

Older than either of these terraces is one extending from Meridian Hill Park through the Mount Pleasant section at an elevation averaging about 200 feet; and highest and oldest of all is a terrace of which fragments remain at Soldiers' Home, Tenleytown (near the District's NW. line), and Good Hope Hill (east of the Anacostia River); it slopes from an elevation of 500 feet at Freedom Hill (15 miles west of Georgetown) to 170 feet at Upper Marlboro (10 miles east of Anacostia). The terraces are of the Coastal Plain formations which occupy the surface of most of the District's area except that lying west of Rock Creek, a picturesque stream flowing through the city's wildest and largest park area and emptying into the Potomac just below Georgetown. Rock Creek marks the dividing line between the older, harder Piedmont Plateau and the softer Coastal Plain deposits, which have tended to wear away, making the demarcation constantly more abrupt.

The Coastal Plain formation consists of sands, gravels, boulders, loams, and clay in various successions. They are 10 in number and all but one seem to have originated through invasion and deposition by the ocean and subsequent washing and redistribution of the deposits by streams. The single exception is the oldest Coastal Plain formation, known as the Potomac, which was formed by the washing down of soil and rocky debris from the Piedmont Plateau by successive inundations of the sea. Fossil leaves, lignitized tree trunks, and occasional dinosaur bones found in the Potomac formation are evidences of its continental origin. The remains of a cypress swamp, formerly extending from M Street to 17th and K Streets, uncovered in excavating for the Mayflower Hotel, indicate something of the prehistoric appearance of the Washington region.

Finding substantial footing for the great public buildings has proved a difficult engineering problem, especially in the instance of the Washington Monument. A resurvey in 1854 revealed the necessity of introducing a subfoundation of concrete to distribute the weight of this structure over a greater area than originally had been planned. When the Post Office was erected at 12th Street and Pennsylvania Avenue the marshy ground made it difficult to get proper foundation, and it was not until immense piles were driven deep that the work could go on. Beneath the National Archives Building huge pumps operate to safeguard the foundation from waters of the old Tiber Creek.

The northwest area of the District, in striking contrast with the low Coastal Plain formation, lies among the crystalline rocks of the Piedmont Plateau. At Key Bridge, Georgetown, the river narrows rather abruptly, while its banks become higher and more precipitous. This point marks the descent of the stream from the crystalline rock region of the plateau into the soft sands and clays of the plain. From here almost to the intersection of the river and the northwest District Line the character of the banks is such as to justify the name commonly given them, "the palisades of the Potomac."

Above Chain Bridge, not far below the District Line, there occurs a further abrupt narrowing of the stream and the waters race through a gorgelike channel with banks ranging up to about 250 feet. At the District Line are the Little Falls. The gorgelike character of the stream increases as one approaches Great Falls, about 15 miles west from Chevy Chase.

The narrowing banks of the Potomac tend to conserve tidal effect. Despite the distance of Washington from Chesapeake Bay, the river has an average tidal rise and fall of 2.9 feet, as compared with 1.1 feet at Baltimore and 1.3 feet at Key West.

The climate of Washington, product of its topography and geographic location, is commonly criticized because of the frequency of stifling days in summer and the mild but depressive winters. Lying at the confluence of the Potomac and Anacostia (or Eastern Branch) Rivers, nearly 100 miles upstream from Chesapeake Bay, Washington is built for the most part on a peninsula of low marshy land formed by the meeting of these streams. Humidity is high, and the winds, mainly from the south, have low average velocities the year around. The mean summer temperature over a period of 50 years is 75° F. Dense humidity and langorous winds, however, occasion frequent periods of wilting heat. During the winter months wet, unpleasant, slushy days result from the combination of relatively high average temperature and unusually high humidity. During a 50-year period the mean winter temperature was 35° F. The extremes of temperature during the period, including both summer and winter, were exceptionally far apart, ranging from —15° to 106° F. Precipitation throughout the year is evenly distributed, averaging about 42 inches. The United States Weather Bureau records a remarkable snowfall in January 1922, when 25 inches fell in 24 hours. This surpassed the records for the same length of time in Boston, New York, Chicago, and St. Paul.

The edges of four different zones of plant and animal life extend over the District and its environs, giving the area a singularly abundant and varied wildlife. There are approximately 1,800 varieties of flowering plants and 250 different native shrubs and trees; more than 300 varieties of birds, 94 of fishes, and 68 amphibians.

Washington's thousands of trees, though many of them are native, probably include a higher percentage of exotics than those of any other American city. Many a Government official traveling abroad has contributed to the number of introduced specimens, but most exotics have been provided by Federal plant introduction agencies. The best known exotics are the Japanese cherry trees, around the Tidal Basin. In any event, whether native or introduced, the trees intercept, with green aisles and arches, and intervals of shade, the hard white light reflected from limitless façades of stone.

Although L'Enfant's original sketches included plans for tree planting, little attention was paid to this or to the preservation of natural groves until the beginning of the nineteenth century. Thomas Jefferson, while President, was outraged by the cutting of trees on the Mall, and did much to save and restore the natural beauty of the city. He planted Lombardy poplars, because of their "most sudden growth," along Pennsylvania Avenue, and often gathered and planted seeds and seedlings in other spots. In 1815, the city made its first appropriation expressly for trees, stipulating 400 English elms to replace the poplars along Pennsylvania Avenue. These, in turn, were replaced by lindens, oaks, maples, sycamores, and other varieties.

Until the middle of the century, small appropriations were made annually for tree planting, and Washington began to be known as one of the few capitals of the world distinguished for sylvan beauty. No really important step, however, was taken after Jefferson's time until about 1872, when the first systematic municipal tree planting was begun under Alexander R. Shepherd.

Many native shade trees may be seen at their best in the parks, squares, and gardens of Washington, and along the principal streets. American elms on Q Street, New Hampshire and New Jersey Avenues, around the Ellipse and Lafayette Square, and arching over several sections of New York Avenue; sycamores on Florida Avenue and approaching the White House; the pin oak and red oak, colorful in all seasons, along upper Connecticut Avenue and on Pennsylvania Avenue, SE.; Massachusetts Avenue's American lindens; and old willows around Hains Point and by the Potomac.

The Oriental ginkgo, found in innumerable places, dates back farther than any other tree. With its fan-shaped leaves and gesturing branches, it is scarcely changed from what it was in the age of the dinosaurs. Ginkgos are planted along Lafayette Square, 5th Street, 14th Street, and elsewhere. Other exotics are the ailanthus, acacia, locust, cedar of Lebanon, European elm, willow, hornbeam, holly, and linden; and the Asiatic magnolia, in the wood between the Tidal Basin and the Lincoln Memorial. The Japanese Paulownia, with lilac blossoms, is naturalized throughout the region and, likewise, the Chinese scholar or pagoda tree, with greenish-yellow flowers.

There are several varieties of magnolia, perhaps the handsomest being the great-flowered, with lustrous dark leaves and large lemon-scented ivory blossoms. This tree is in flower late into the summer in Lafayette Park, the Cathedral Close, the grounds of the Department of Agriculture, around the Capitol and other public buildings, and in many private gardens. Another and smaller magnolia blooms in early spring even before it is in leaf.

The squat Camperdown elms in Thomas Circle and a great copper beech in Lafayette Park are of unusual interest. Over Lafayette Park's 7 acres are planted 97 varieties of trees, including spruce, fir, basswood, hornbeam, redwood, bronze beech, magnolia, cherry, ash, holly, yellowwood, yew, Japanese cryptomeria, the Paulownia, sawtooth zelkown, and bald cypress.

Evergreens are numerous; American holly, of which there are fine stands in the Capitol Grounds, in Cathedral Close, and at St. Elizabeths Hospital; boxwood, around the Supreme Court and the Lincoln Memorial; English yew, in Meridian Hill Park, the White House grounds, and Grant Circle; and Irish yew in the grounds around the Smithsonian Institution and the White House, and in two groupings in front of the lodge in Lafayette Park.

Dogwood in profuse bloom, especially in Rock Creek Park, is one of the sights of the Capitol, rivaling the cherry blossoms around the Tidal Basin and at Hains Point. The native wildcrab flowers along the sea-wall drive, and fragrant native honeysuckle covers uncared-for areas in an almost tropical tangle.

In Rock Creek Park, along the Potomac trails, and in other wooded areas, all the native species are represented and many naturalized ones, such as the Paulownia and white-flowered black locust. In Rock Creek Park alone, 63 out of 66 kinds of trees are native. The soaring black walnut with its bright green crown of leaves, the ample sycamore, the basswood, cottonwood, pignut, willow and various oaks, beeches, and pines, make the splendor of these groves, with honeylocust, wildcrab, dogwood, and hawthorn flowering among them.

The trees of the District contribute a bright procession of flowers, beginning with those which bloom before or with the leaves, like the early magnolia, dogwood, white June-berry, and the exquisite Judas-tree. The red cedar, golden with catkins in early spring, the red and silver maple, white ash, and boxelder, the fragrant linden and white-flowered locust, the Paulownia in purple panicles, the catalpa, horse-chestnut, and persimmon, and the tuliptree with greenish-yellow flowers, are conspicuous.

Although the flora of two distinct regions meets along the fall line, several species, such as the arum, are common to both. In general, the plants adapted to acid soil seek the bogs and tide-flats of the Coastal Plain, while asters and scores of species accustomed to higher elevations predominate in the Piedmont Plateau. Seeds of mountain plants and trees, white pine, sweet birch, laurel, and rhododendron, are carried down the Potomac and establish themselves along its bank, along Rock Creek and in near-by ravines. Within Rock Creek Park is much of the original flora of the District, including a colony of *Pinus pungens*. In deep ravines, on half-wild hillsides, and level groves, and along old rock ledges spring flowers abound.

Marshes of wild rice extend over much of the Anacostia River estuary, and, along the lower Potomac, wild celery, Peltandra, and various waterweeds. In the dry sterile woods of the Coastal Plain, sassafras, sweetgum, and evergreen laurel grow at the foot of pines, oaks, and chinquapins. Here, too, blueberries and huckleberries flourish. On both the Piedmont Plateau and the Coastal Plain are found the scrub pine forests with sparse undergrowth of Pipsissewa and moccasin flowers.

Among the birds, Washington's three most conspicuous specimens are all introduced—the pigeons, loved and fed by many habitues of the city's parks; the ragamuffin English sparrow; and chattering hordes of starlings (both of the latter species, the English say, were well-behaved before they left home). Rock Creek Park, in addition to being a natural woodland well suited as a habitation for native birds, draws an additional increment of bird-dwellers through a strange, but apparent, feeling of kinship for the captive birds in Rock Creek Zoo. Seagulls wheel gracefully about the water front. To the waterfowl sanctuaries at Roaches Run, Rock Creek and elsewhere, come gallinules, herons, bitterns, coots, egrets, sandhill cranes, and numerous ducks and geese. The District is generally the habitat for songbirds native to the region.

Washington's greatest panhandlers, the gray squirrels, have adapted themselves to a sleek and lucrative existence, garnering peanuts begged from park-bench people, and nesting comfortably in large-boled trees. Cottontail rabbits survive on the lawns and in the hedges of suburban Washington, having apparently learned the nuances of escape from neighborhood dogs. There are numerous chipmunks, a few opossums, and an occasional skunk. The remaining small mammals of the District come mostly in the class for which traps are set at night.

Twenty-three species of snake are known in this region, but only the garter, the ring, green, black, and banded water-snake are often encountered. Once in a while a plump and poisonous copperhead moves across the towpath along the canal, or among tangled undergrowth. Painted, spotted, and streaked tortoises wander about quite generally; the box tortoise is common in the woods; the snapping turtle is found occasionally in slow marshy streams; and, in any boggy place, may be seen the small mud-turtle, or spine-tailed terrapin.

The streams of the District support three widely different types of fish: Those entering with the tide and ascending the Potomac to spawn; fresh-water fishes of the Coastal Plain; and upland varieties. Some 94 species have been recorded in all. Of the salt-water fishes that come far enough upstream to be included in District fauna, three species of the herringlike alewife, come up as far as Little Falls; the shad, striped bass or rockfish, and white perch to Great Falls. The shad runs far less abundantly than in former days. Other salt-water fishes found near by are the silver-gar, pipefish, pig fish, spot, whiting, angelfish, sea-robin, and flounder. Eels, having spawned in the ocean deeps near Bermuda, find their way in great numbers into many streams. Fourteen food fish have been introduced into the Potomac, including two kinds of crappie, largemouthed and smallmouthed black bass, catfish, wall-eyed pike, goggle-eye, tench, carp, and at least one variety of sunfish. In addition to these, bream, pickerel, and calico bass are found. Five species of the "whiskered" catfish are common, especially the fork-tail Potomac cat. Twenty or more species of minnow and carp make up the largest local family, and the unprepossessing suckers are also common.

Grasshoppers, locusts, and crickets are myriad in summer, and by night the woods are lit by fireflies and full of the reiterant katydids. Not so pleasant are the ticks, "chiggers," and mosquitoes.

The Indian Background

UNDER a bronze beech in the Congressional Cemetery is the grave of Push-ma-ta-ha, Choctaw chief and commissioned officer in the United States army during the War of 1812, who died in Washington in 1824, while treating with the Government for his people. On the sandstone shaft are Push-ma-ta-ha's words, "When I am dead, let the big guns be fired over me." Here, in the Capital City, the grave is a reminder of a lost culture and of extinguished council fires.

The 30 or 40 principal and subordinate Indian tribes of the Chesapeake Bay region were mainly of Algonquian linguistic stock. The confederacy welded by Powhatan in the Virginia tidewater region probably did not extend north of the Potomac; and the peninsula between the river and the bay was occupied by the Piscataway. Traditionally, the Piscataway originated among the Nanticoke, the second important tribal group, who held the Eastern Shore country in Maryland.

Captain John Smith, who explored the Chesapeake region in 1608, writes of the tidewater Indians: "Their houses are in the midst of their fields or gardens; which are small plots of ground, some 20 (acres), some 40, some 100, some 200, some more, some less. Sometimes from 2 to 100 of these houses are together, or but a little separated by groves of trees. Near their habitations is little small wood, or old trees on the ground, by reason of their burning them for fire." The villages were usually encircled by palisades and placed within easy access to sea food and waterfowl.

On the Anacostia River, from Giesboro Point almost to Bladensburg, there was such a riparian village, which Smith recorded as Nacothtant (Nacotchant and Nacochtank are variants); opposite, on the west bank, was a smaller settlement. Within the present city of Washington, near Carroll Place, was a similar village, and a number have been traced along the south shore of the Potomac and near Little Falls. The valley at the foot of Capitol Hill was, according to tradition, used for fishing grounds, and Greenleaf Point near by as a council gathering place.

At the present Mount Vernon, Smith indicated an important village called Taux or Tauxemont; and opposite, in Maryland, Mayaones. On this latter site, 20 miles south of Washington, the remains of three layers of Indian settlement have been discovered on the Ferguson estate. About 2,000 skeletons and numerous artifacts have been unearthed, including two of the largest skulls ever found. At the time of Captain John Smith's visit, about 100 warriors lived in the third settlement on this spot. Charred post holes show that the village was later burned, probably by Virginians.

The Algonquians, as a whole, were less aggressive than the neighboring Iroquois, and not so highly developed politically; but in the peaceful arts they reached a certain distinction. Traits common to the tidewater region included idol ceremonies to the supernatural *Okee* (Powhatan name) or *Ochre* (Nanticoke name), cleaning the bones of dead chiefs before preserving them in ossuaries, and a special fire rite. Priest-doctors, or medicine-men, were esteemed among the tidewater Indians. The Nanticokes were noted for their skill in sorcery and in the manufacture and use of poisons.

"During the 62 years following the settlement of Jamestown," wrote Thomas Jefferson, "two-thirds of the Indians of 40 tribes disappeared because of smallpox, spirituous liquors, and abridgement of territory." In addition to pressure from the colonists, the lower bay tribes were harried continually by the Conestoga (or Susquehannock) Indians, an Iroquoian tribe at the northern end of Chesapeake Bay. In 1673, the Piscataway were forced to abandon their village and remove to what is now Washington and, in 1675, they were again on the move up the Potomac. The Nanticoke suffered much the same fate. At war with the white settlers from 1641 to 1648, when the Susquehannock also turned on them, they drifted westward with the Piscataway. At this point the Iroquois League, noted for relentlessness and cruelty, was moved to rescue the tidewater Indians along with their own kinsmen, the Susquehannock, from extinction at the hands of the white man.

The archeological importance of the village Nacothtant, and of the District region as a whole, can be gathered from this summary by Dr. W. H. Holmes: "The greatest aboriginal bowlder quarry known, and the most important implement shops yet observed on the Atlantic slope are located [in Rock Creek Park] two and one-half miles from the White House. . . . One of the most important soapstone quarries in the great series extending . . . from Massachusetts to Georgia is on Connecticut Avenue . . . and the most important village site in the whole tidewater province is situated on Anacostia River within the city."

The principal quarry workshop is west of 16th Street at its juncture with Arkansas Avenue, about on a line with 18th Street extended. Few completed specimens of primitive craftsmanship remain but much rough work can still be found. At the National Museum the technique of shaping stone implements and weapons is illustrated in a life group and, in a similar group, modeled after the Indians of Catalina Island, California, is shown the art of making vessels of steatite or soapstone in which the District was rich.   The largest soapstone quarry ever found in this country exists in its original condition on a hillside above Gum Branch of Bull Run, near Clifton, Virginia, 22 miles from Washington.

The Rose Hill, or Dumbarton rock quarry, the most important within District borders, is covered by an apartment building opposite the Connecticut Avenue entrance to the Zoological Gardens.   The Naval Observatory stands on a soapstone quarry site.   Of other widely distributed quarries, there are sites at Riggs Mill, Four Corners, and Olney in near-by Maryland, and another at Clarendon, Virginia. Near Benning, Maryland, and within what was Nacothtant, is a paint quarry, discovered in 1879.   Here, rocks containing oxides yielding crimson, carmine, orange, and purple, were broken in mortars and the pigments extracted.

The pottery of the tidewater Indians was almost entirely utilitarian in function, with rudimentary decoration.   Often the pot was shaped within a basket or net, and the impressions either left on the clay or partially smoothed off.   The decoration, usually confined to the neck and rim, consisted of geometrical patterns impressed by means of cords or thongs stretched over the finger tips, or run lengthwise.   From these textile-impressed fragments and from other evidence, it is known that the Potomac Indians wove wattled material for shelter and fish-traps, mats for coverings and hangings, nets for fishing, baskets, pouches, bags, and other articles.

The band of Indians nearest Washington is the Potomac tribe, numbering about 150, with a settlement on the banks of Potomac Creek some 8 miles north of Fredericksburg, Virginia, and 45 miles from Washington.

Various place names are of Indian origin; Potomac, Piscataway, Mattawoman, Accokeek, Accotink, Pohick.   Anacostia appeared first as Acoughtank on an old map thought to have been carried by Captain Smith, who himself called the village Nacothtant.   Captain Henry Fleete named the Indians Nascotines, a word later latinized by the Jesuits to Anacostia.   Analostan, the old name for Theodore Roosevelt Island, probably derived from the same source.

Since its founding, the Capital has received Indian delegations in almost continuous processions, sometimes to make treaties, more often to protest or petition.   The sight of such delegations is not uncommon today on Washington streets, made up of men wearing full feathered and beaded regalia, or ten-gallon hats, cowboy boots, and braided hair. The Indian Office employs a number of Indian men and women, including those with names such as Audrey Warrior (a Sioux, appropriately), O. K. Walkingstick, and Timothy Iron Teeth. The Indian Arts and Crafts Board maintains shops, in the South Interior and Commerce Department Buildings, selling authentic Indian craftwork. Individuals of Indian blood have occasionally held high places in the Federal Government, an outstanding example being Charles Curtis, whose mother was a Kaw Indian, and who was elected Vice President in 1928.

Mount Vernon Ladies' Association of the Union
MOUNT VERNON, HOME OF GEORGE WASHINGTON

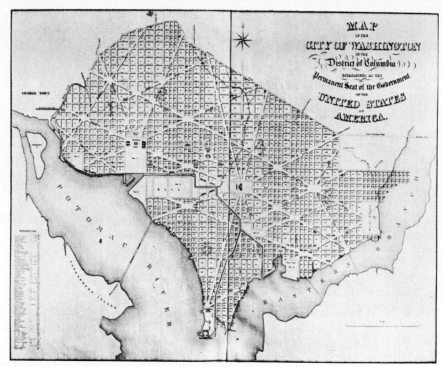

L'ENFANT PLAN, ACCORDING TO A LATER DRAFT

"BIRD'S-EYE" VIEW OF WASHINGTON BY E. SACHSE ("DRAWN FROM NATURE AND ON STONE"), 1853

THE BURNING OF WASHINGTON BY THE BRITISH IN 1814, BY A BRITISH ARTIST

Fine Arts Division, Library of Congress

LINCOLN MEMORIAL STATUE, BY DANIEL CHESTER FRENCH

Brady Photo, U. S. Army Signal Corps

ANACOSTIA BRIDGE, 1862, OVER WHICH JOHN WILKES
BOOTH ESCAPED AFTER LINCOLN'S ASSASSINATION

UNION SOLDIERS GUARDING CHAIN
BRIDGE DURING THE CIVIL WAR

Federal Works Agency

GRAND REVIEW OF FEDERAL TROOPS ON
PENNSYLVANIA AVENUE AFTER THE CIVIL WAR

©Harris and Ewing

THE BONUS ARMY OF 1932, BURNED
OUT AND DRIVEN OUT BY SOLDIERS

PRESIDENT WILSON AT
THE HEAD OF THE
VICTORY PARADE DOWN
PENNSYLVANIA AVENUE,
FEBRUARY, 1919
U. S. Army Signal Corps

Washington Daily News

KING GEORGE VI OF ENGLAND VISITS
PRESIDENT ROOSEVELT IN WASHINGTON, 1939

**THE NATION'S FIRST THIRD-TERM INAUGURATION—FRANKLIN
D. ROOSEVELT TAKES OATH BEFORE A HUGE CROWD, 1941**

©*Harris and Ewing*

History

WASHINGTON history necessarily begins on the Potomac River—known to early aborigines as the Co-hon-go-roo-ta, to the Spanish as the Espiritu Santo, to the first English explorers as the Elizabeth, and to Lord Calvert's pilgrims as the St. Gregory. "White men were on the Potomac River in the first half of the 16th century," says the Catholic historian Shea. But the earliest explorer who is known to have sailed for any considerable distance up the river was the Spanish admiral, Pedro Menendez, founder of St. Augustine (1565) and governor of Spain's Florida possessions. He ascended, in 1571, as far as Aquia Creek—possibly as far as Occoquan Creek, about 25 miles below Washington. His departure, in the same year, marks the end of Spanish connection with Potomac history.

Captain John Smith explored the Potomac River in 1608, possibly as far as its falls. He was the first white man to reach the river's navigable head, though some authorities think he did not actually land upon what is now Washington soil. From 1608 to 1622 no other white man is known to have reached the upper tidewater Potomac region. Then a foraging party from Jamestown, aided by friendly Indians from the Virginia side, crossed from Potomac Run to the Maryland side of the river, and raided the Indian town of Nacothtant, in what is now the Anacostia region.

George Calvert, the first Lord Baltimore, came to Virginia in 1629, "to plant and dwell." But, as a devout Roman Catholic, he would not take the Protestant oath required of all colonists, and Governor Hervey ordered his return to England. In the homeland, Lord Baltimore received a royal grant of that part of Virginia north and east of the Potomac River between 38° and 40° north latitude. The tacit understanding between King Charles I and Lord Baltimore was that in this proprietary domain, christened "Maryland," the persecuted Catholics from the homeland might find refuge. The first Lord Baltimore died in 1632, but his son and heir, Cecil Calvert, sent his younger brother, Leonard, with "very near 20 gentlemen of very good fashion and 300 laboring men," with two Catholic fathers, Andrew White and John Altham, to begin the Maryland colonization.

They arrived in Chesapeake waters in March 1634, coming to anchor near the mouth of the "Potomeack"—or, as they renamed it, the "St. Gregory"—at Blakistone's Island. Soon, however, Calvert hurried upriver in the smaller of his two ships. The ruler of the native tribes on the Maryland side was the "emperor" of the Piscataway Indians. To gain the latter's good will was Calvert's mission in sailing up the river to Piscataway Creek, about a dozen miles below Washington. He took with him as interpreter, Henry Fleete, a fur trader who had spent 2 years in the region—according to A. R. Spofford the first white man authentically known to have trodden upon what is now Washington soil. The Indians were hostile to Calvert, so he returned with Fleete down the Potomac to its mouth and settled a short distance inland north of the river, where "the Cittie of St. Mary," first capital of Maryland, developed.

From that point settlement rapidly and peacefully spread up the river. Grants of land to gentlemen planters were in most cases large. The manorial system prevailed—an estate of 1,000 acres or more became a manor and its master a lord. Settlement seemed sparse, yet by the beginning of the eighteenth century most of the land on both sides of the Potomac had been taken up and the upper tidewater region peopled by some of the most aristocratic families of Virginia and Maryland.

Opposite Mount Vernon, at the mouth of Piscataway Creek, stands Warburton Manor, granted in 1641 to the Digges family. A little south of this is Marshall Hall, granted to William Marshall in 1651. Bordering on "the freshes of Piscataway" was Mount Airy, the seat of Benedict Calvert, son of the fifth Lord Baltimore; here General Washington often stayed, and Calvert's daughter Eleanor married John Parke Custis, son of Martha Washington. Nearer the present city of Washington was another historic mansion, Oxon Hill, home of the Addisons. Between Oxon Creek and the Eastern Branch (or Anacostia River) was Blew Playne, a tract of 1,000 acres granted in 1662 to George Thompson. In 1663 Thompson was granted three other tracts; Duddington Manor, 1,000 acres; Duddington Pasture, 300 acres; and New Troy, 500 acres. In 1670 he leased his tracts for 1,000 years to Thomas Notley, who in 1671 patented them as Cerne Abbey Manor. At his death in 1679, his godson Notley Rozier inherited the manor. In 1716 it was again given its original name of Duddington Manor; and in the last decade of the eighteenth century, this manor (then, by intermarriage, owned mainly by the Carroll and Young families) was the largest and most valuable estate within what then became the District of Columbia.

West of what is now Capitol Hill was a tract called Rome, granted to Francis Pope in 1663, and wrongly supposed by many writers to include the high land upon which the Nation's Capitol now stands. In 1660 James Langworth, of Charles County, Maryland, bequeathed to his son John his rights in 670 acres "yet to be taken up"; this, it is thought, was the 600-acre tract granted to John Langworth in 1664—the so-called Widow's Mite, lying to the northward. It changed hands many times during the next 130 years. A tract known as Vineyard, in what became the Georgetown area, was patented to William Hutchison in 1696; part of it was owned by Robert Peter in 1791. In 1703 Colonel Ninian Beall, of Upper Marlborough, acquired much land in the same vicinity—the so-called Rock of Dunbarton (or Dumbarton), and that recorded as Beall's Levels. Part of the latter passed to the Burnes family, including much of the land now in the White House area and along Pennsylvania Avenue to the east.

The "10-mile square," which in 1791 became the Federal area, was fringed with many notable manors—Riversdale, belonging to the Calverts; Northampton, manor of the Fairfaxes of Cameron; the Darnall homes, including Woodyard; the Carroll manors, including Rock Creek Mansion, where Father (later Archbishop) John Carroll lived; Chillum Manor, where one branch of the Digges family lived; Clean Drinking Manor, which passed from Colonel John Courts to Charles Jones; Friendship, one of the Addison manors; Rosedale, the Beall properties, and others.

Long before towns began to have any importance in the region, the social life of the great landowners was varied and delightful. Tobacco had brought vast wealth to the gentlemen planters of Virginia and Maryland, and the abundance of slaves had given them ample leisure. The gentlefolk lived much in the saddle, "thinking little of riding five, ten, even more miles to pay a social call, or to dine, with a neighbor." "Every house was a house of entertainment," says Spofford, "for hotels were almost unknown. Any decent stranger was sure of welcome." Card parties, horse races, shooting matches, athletic sports, fencing, and other gentlemanly tests of alertness and skill, river parties, hunting meets, riding matches—all were popular in their season. The tables of gentlefolk gave evidence of abundance and good taste. Liquors were to be had in every variety, and hospitality was so open and sincere that it was a rare day when some stranger did not sit at the family table. George Washington records that his family did not once sit down to dinner alone for 20 years.

But these landed proprietors, with their affluence and leisure, by no means comprised the whole of humanity in Colonial Virginia and Maryland. There were many small planters who worked the less fertile land themselves—sometimes with a slave or two, sometimes alone; and some of the great Maryland landowners made fortunes by settling German immigrants on their plantations as tenant farmers. These small growers could not, like the rich proprietors, profitably consign their crops to English agents. "The large planters, therefore, became traders, buying the tobacco of their poorer neighbors and opening plantation stores in which the small farmers bought necessary merchandise." There was also a rather considerable artisan, mechanic, and laborer class, mostly persons sent over from England under indenture to Colonial employers, whom they were required to serve for a period of from 3 to 5 years, as recompense for the cost of their passage and a commission to the agent or shipowner who had arranged the transaction. To all of these economically oppressed classes, the western "back country" offered a promised land toward which they pushed in ever-increasing numbers. But no path of escape in any direction stood open to the hordes of Negro slaves, who constituted by far the largest population group in the tidewater region, and upon whose labor the imposing structure of plantation prosperity in that region was chiefly based.

Thirty years after the coming of the Calverts, St. Mary's City near the mouth of the Potomac was still the only place in the province that could be called a "towne." Indeed, under the manorial system there was little need of towns. Tobacco was king, and each manor was a community in itself. Counties began to be organized as well as minor divisions called "hundreds," the Washington region being known as "New Scotland Hundred." Prince Georges County, which originally included what is now the District of Columbia, was organized in 1695, taking in all of Charles County north of Mattawoman Creek, near Glymont, its territory reaching to the Blue Ridge Mountains and including all the *terra incognita* beyond.

The first communities in the upper tidewater Potomac region were those little hamlets that gradually came into being at the river landings, where the manorial lords had their tobacco warehouses. The first town of appreciable size to develop in this region was Upper Marlborough, the legal seat of Prince Georges County (which then extended to the Potomac River, Montgomery County not being created until 1776). Upper Marlborough was a small village when laid out in 1706; but it grew rapidly in urban importance, and when chartered or rechartered in 1744 it was fast emulating Annapolis as a center of fashion and gaiety. Bladensburg, at one time designated Garrison's Landing, became a town in 1742. Alexandria, earlier known as Belle Haven and earlier still as Hunting Creek Warehouse, was laid out in 1749. Georgetown, between which and Rock Creek lay an old shipping point known as Saw Pit Landing, was organized in 1751. Alexandria and Georgetown, in the second half of the eighteenth century, became the principal ports of the region, both hoping in time to compare favorably with New York and Philadelphia.

But until the end of the Colonial period, life centered chiefly in the manors. Only on gala occasions did the urban influence draw from the manorial. All the elite from both sides of the Potomac attended the plays at Upper Marlborough, where every season for 20 years after 1752 the players from Annapolis displayed their artistry for the Potomac gentry.   Then, and during the race weeks, every manor house over a wide radius was crowded, each a brilliant social center in itself.

This was the region in which President Washington, in 1791, decided to set the National Capital.

During the Revolutionary period the Continental Congress was a somewhat nomadic body.   At different times within a single year (1777), Baltimore, Philadelphia, Lancaster, and York had the distinction of being the seat of Congress.   In 1783 the delegates were comfortably settled in Philadelphia, and might have stayed there indefinitely had not mutinous Continental soldiers come upon them suddenly, while in session, demanding their long overdue pay.   Affronted and alarmed, Congress removed to Princeton, New Jersey, a small place soon deplorably overcrowded.   The need for a permanent seat of national government, preferably some place of virgin territory wherein a "Federal town" might be built, became imperative.

The Continental Congress, while still at Princeton, considered offers from various sections; so many were made, and such rivalry was shown, that prudent Congressmen began to see in the "Federal town" question a most dangerous issue.   Before very long the matter was looming ominously as a major source of contention between North and South, and a compromise was suggested.   On October 7, 1783, Congress called for surveys of land near Georgetown on the Potomac River and land near Trenton on the Delaware River, the resolution being later modified to provide for the building of *two* "Federal towns," one on each river.   The surveys were made, but in October 1784, while in session at Trenton, Congress ignored the Potomac site in arranging that three commissioners should "lay out a district of not less than two nor more than three miles square on the banks of the Delaware," near its falls, "for a Federal town."   In December of the same year it resolved "to take measures for suitable buildings to be erected" on this site; but the last of the three commissioners was not appointed until 3 months later, when the temporary seat of government had been transferred to New York City.

It was now apparent that the South had not yet given up the fight to secure the "Federal town."   A motion to substitute the Potomac for the Delaware site was defeated, but dissension was so acrid, and the waning of interest in Federal union itself was so obvious in some of the States, that the Trenton project was permitted to become inactive. Until the confederated States had become a constitutional entity, it seemed wiser for the national body to drift along in a temporary seat of government.   In May 1787, delegates called "to revise the articles of confederation" met in convention at Philadelphia, and during the next 4 months drafted the Constitution of the United States. It was adopted by the Convention on September 17, 1787, and ratified by a sufficient number of States by the end of the following June.

On March 4, 1789, the First Congress of the United States convened in New York City. On April 6 both houses of Congress went into joint session to "open and count the electoral vote for President and Vice President." By unanimous vote, General George Washington of Virginia was elected President; and James Adams of Massachusetts, who received the next highest number of votes (each elector being required to vote for two names), was declared Vice President. The question of choosing a permanent seat of government seemed to pivot on these two opposite temperaments. In them the South and the North clashed. The South had won the Presidency; but within a year John Adams himself, by virtue of his deciding vote as President of the Senate, had brought seeming victory to the North in the bitter battle to secure the "Federal city." He voted for Germantown, Pennsylvania.

When Congress reconvened, in January 1790, Southern members moved to reconsider the "Federal town" bill. Six months of bitter conflict followed. By the end of May, Philadelphia had won a partial victory in being made the temporary Capital for a decade from December 1790; and a House vote to place the permanent Capital on "the easterly bank of the Potomac" was lost, 15 to 9. The South was offended, and might secede from the Union. However, it could rejoice in one triumph—by a narrow margin it had defeated Hamilton's "assumption bill," by which the Nation would assume the war debts of the individual States. Hamilton appealed to Jefferson, who in truth was alarmed at the possibility of a "dissolution of our Union at this incipient stage." The next day Hamilton was Jefferson's guest at dinner. So, too, were Congressmen White and Lee of Virginia; and the savory viands and mellow Madeira proved softening influences upon the guests. The two Virginia Congressmen agreed to change their "assumption" votes, after Hamilton had promised to secure sufficient northern votes to win for the Potomac region the permanent Capital. So both bills eventually became law. The so-called Residence bill, approved July 16, 1790, authorized the selection of a site "not exceeding 10 miles square" somewhere in the Potomac region, and the establishment therein of the permanent seat of government of the United States. The President was to choose the site, acquire the tract, and appoint building commissioners.

Thus was born the Capital City. Much was expected of this "only child of the Nation," but little was done to nurture it. Congress had no money to invest in such a project, which would require at least a million dollars. Maryland and Virginia agreed to provide $120,000 and $72,000, respectively, for public buildings, and to cede to the

Nation their jurisdiction over the area chosen for the Capital. The rest would depend in the main upon what arrangements President Washington, as agent for Congress, might succeed in making with owners of land within the area. But before he had attempted any negotiations, a new and important figure appeared upon the scene.

Pierre Charles L'Enfant, of French birth and military training, had followed Lafayette to America and won repute as an engineer in the Revolution. Civil work in the post-war years brought him closer to General Washington. After the Constitution's ratification, L'Enfant realized that a great nation had been conceived. To design a Capital worthy of such a nation became the absorbing ambition of his life, and in September 1789 he wrote to President Washington, begging for "a share in the undertaking." Fortunately, he addressed a man no less idealistic than himself, though one with a larger experience of practical limitations. L'Enfant's offer of assistance in creating a Capitol "magnificent enough to grace a great nation" was accepted.

In October 1790, President Washington took up his role of agent. He inspected many Potomac sites—from Conococheague, about 80 miles above the present city, to Oxon Hill, several miles below; and in January 1791 he made his decision, choosing the land in Maryland which is now the District of Columbia, and a small section across the Potomac in Virginia, including the town of Alexandria. In the same month he appointed Daniel Carroll, Thomas Johnson, and David Stuart as commissioners to select favorable sites for public buildings. He was now ready to employ L'Enfant to lay out the city and another surveyor, Andrew Ellicott, to survey the bounds of the tract, 10 miles square. Ellicott came in February and L'Enfant in March. During the latter month the President met the local landowners at Suter's Tavern in Georgetown, and persuaded them to sell at £25 ($66.66) an acre any land the Nation might need as sites or grounds for public buildings, and to permit the remainder of the proposed city area to be divided into lots and sold, the proceeds from every other lot to go to the Government. It was further agreed that no charge should be made for the land needed for highways.

All seemed well. But, as L'Enfant proceeded with his planning, the landowners opened their eyes in amazement. Streets 100 to 110 feet wide, avenues 160 feet wide, one grand avenue 400 feet wide and a mile long! This crazy Frenchman was literally throwing away good real estate. But they still had time to curb his extravagant use of what rightly was half theirs. They might even get back the whole, for they had not yet signed away their titles to the land. Trouble was brewing for the agent, resting at Mount Vernon, and he was doubtless aware of it.

However, he let L'Enfant go on. This the latter did, oblivious to all private considerations. In the distance eastward from the site selected for the President's House, was a commanding rise—Jenkins Hill. Upon this eminence L'Enfant placed the Federal House, or Capitol, and to connect it with the President's House he planned a highway 160 feet wide, later designated as Pennsylvania Avenue. He was practical enough to see "that the Capital City's nourishment, unlike that of other cities, would come out of its public buildings rather than out of its trade centers." So he made his highway plans subordinate to these features. "Thus," he concluded, "in every way advantageously situated, the Federal City would grow of itself and spread as the branches of a tree does toward where they meet with most nourishment." Alas, he was but the planner; he could not control the growth. A decade later it was apparent that each of the many landowners had striven to divert to his own land the development that should have grown steadily and compactly out from the center. Hence, Washington for 50 years seemed to be little more than a number of straggling villages more or less remote from the public buildings.

In June 1791 President Washington faced his most difficult task, that of securing from the disgruntled landowners title deeds for the land required. L'Enfant's first draft of the city plan, which he now had to show them, confirmed their earlier forebodings. Of their 6,111 acres within the plan, 3,606 would be required for highways. The land to be purchased by the Government for public building sites and grounds or "reservations" amounted to 541 acres. The remaining 1,964 acres were to be divided into city lots (20,272 in all) and sold for the equal benefit of Government and landowners—the former paying for the public building sites and grounds from its half of the proceeds. But unpromising as it appeared upon first glance, the arrangement was in truth an excellent one for the landowners—their share in the city lots was estimated to yield about 10 times what the original acreage could be sold for as plantation land. The deeds were signed.

Although supposedly subordinate to the commissioners, L'Enfant was allowed to proceed unhampered for a while. In September 1791 the commissioners instructed him to number and letter his streets according to the simple system which has remained in effect ever since. They also asked for a copy of his plan, to be used in connection with a public sale of the city lots. L'Enfant indignantly refused to comply with this latter request. He would do nothing to aid "speculators to purchase the best locations in his vistas and architectural squares and raise huddles of shanties which would permanently disfigure" his creation. The sale of lots was a failure, and the commissioners blamed L'Enfant, but the President did not reprimand him.

Soon, however, another incident occurred which Washington felt he could not condone.   The manorial lord of Duddington, Daniel Carroll, the largest landowner of the Federal region, had begun to build a new manor house.   Unfortunately, it obstructed one of L'Enfant's vistas, and the indignant planner ordered the squire to demolish it.   He would not, so L'Enfant did.   The commissioners complained to the President. The planner was peremptorily dismissed (in January 1792), and Ellicott was asked to complete his work.   For his services in planning the Federal City, L'Enfant was offered $2,500 and a lot near the White House, both of which he refused.   He died, impoverished and broken-spirited, in 1825.   Eighty-four years later his body was removed from an obscure grave in Prince Georges County, Maryland, and given the belated honor of military burial in Arlington Cemetery.

For nearly two years after L'Enfant's dismissal little progress was made.   Then it was announced that on September 18, 1793, the corner-stone of the north wing of the Capitol would be laid by the President of the United States.   An important feature of the day would be a sale of city lots.   The cornerstone ceremony was impressive, but the sale was a failure—even though President Washington set an example by buying a few lots for himself.   The Capital City had palled upon the investing public.

A few days later a young man, sent by the President himself, came into the commissioners' office.   He was "of good repute" and "of much money"—a young Bostonian related to Vice President Adams.   "If," concludes the President's letter to the commissioners, "you can find it consistent with your duty to the public to attach Mr. Greenleaf, he will be a valuable acquisition."   The commissioners found it quite consistent; and within a few days they had sold James Greenleaf 3,000 city lots at $66.50 each.   But no money changed hands; payment was to be spread over a period of 7 years without interest!   Two months later a greater figure came into the realty picture—Robert Morris, the Philadelphia financier.   He also would purchase 3,000 of the lots, and he would now stand openly as a partner of Greenleaf in the local venture.   The commissioners were quite willing to cancel Greenleaf's first purchase, inasmuch as the two now made a joint purchase of 6,000 lots at $80 each.   Under the new agreement, however, the buyers could secure title even before they paid for the lots; and there were other conditions that hopelessly confused the situation.

Within a year or two, these speculators held such a monopoly of local realty and were asking such prohibitive prices that sales entirely ceased.   Worse troubles followed, and in 1797 the commissioners realized that the building fund would have to be replenished from other sources than the sale of city lots.   They borrowed $100,000 from the State of Maryland, and Congress was induced to make an appropriation of a like amount.   By the end of 1798 the exterior of the President's

House was completed, the Senate wing of the Capitol was under roof, and a contract placed for the first departmental building—the Treasury. The new activity in public building brought a return of courage to investors, and much private construction was carried through.

At the time of George Washington's death, on December 14, 1799, Congress was in session at Philadelphia, and had received President Adams' reminder that under the provisions of the Residence Bill of 1790 Congress should convene in the permanent seat of government on the first Monday in December 1800. On May 15, 1800, Congress having adjourned, Adams directed his Cabinet so to arrange their departmental affairs "that the public offices may be opened in the city of Washington . . . by the 15th of June." This was done, and Philadelphia ceased to be the seat of national government on June 11, 1800. The removal was not a stupendous task; according to the historian Bryan, the Government personnel consisted of only 126 persons. Their private effects came by road; the state papers and national archives were shipped by water. President Adams arrived on June 3, staying until the 14th. By then most of his Cabinet had appeared.

ADOLESCENT CAPITAL

Secretary of the Treasury Wolcott painted a doleful picture of local conditions as he found them upon his arrival:

"There are few houses in any one place, and most of them small, miserable huts, which present an awful contrast to the public buildings. The people are poor, and as far as I can judge, they live like fishes, by eating each other. You may look in almost any direction, over an extent of ground nearly as large as the city of New York, without seeing a fence or any object except brick-kilns and temporary huts for laborers."

President Adams' wife Abigail, one of the most forceful women of her time and a great letter-writer, came in November, to find the "President's Palace" an unfinished and largely unfurnished building in the midst of brickyards and litter. "We have not the least fence, yard, or other convenience without, and the great unfinished audience-room [the present East Room] I make a drying-room of, to hang the clothes in."

Washington's first great political excitement was occasioned by the election of 1800, in which President Adams, confident of a second term in office, went down to defeat, and the electoral tie between Jefferson and Aaron Burr was decided by the House of Representatives in Jefferson's favor. Bitterly chagrined, Adams worked on at the President's House far into the last night of his term, and then drove out of

Washington at dawn to avoid attending Jefferson's inauguration. As a Virginia gentleman, a member of George Washington's Cabinet, and Vice President under Adams, Jefferson was invested with a certain degree of respectability in Federalist eyes; but the new party which he headed was regarded by Hamilton and his followers as a rabble certain to lead the country to ruin.

Jefferson and his anti-Federalist friends "had laughed at Adams' coach-and-six and at attempts of Americans to ape the ceremonials of European courts." On the day of his inauguration, March 4, 1801, the President-elect walked to the Capitol from his boarding house, two blocks away, and then strolled back again after the ceremony—not in the least perturbed that he should have to rub shoulders with his fellow boarders for another fortnight, while workmen prepared the President's House for his coming. Upon taking possession of the "great stone house, big enough for two emperors, one pope, and the grand lama into the bargain," as he described it, Jefferson did away with the frequent formal "levees" of his predecessors, and announced that he would receive on New Year's Day and the Fourth of July all who cared to visit him. But there were still some social occasions which could not be avoided or which could not be handled with Jeffersonian simplicity; and for these Mrs. Madison, wife of the Secretary of State, proved a tower of strength to the widowed President. Long before her husband succeeded Jefferson in 1809, "the incomparable Dolly" had become the acknowledged queen of Washington society; and during the eight years of Madison's regime she overshadowed in some respects her able but personally rather unprepossessing husband.

In 1801, a temporary chamber known as "the Oven" was built on part of the foundations of the south wing of the Capitol. Here the sessions of the House of Representatives were held until 1804. Then "the Oven" was razed and the building of the south wing of the old part of the Capitol was begun. The latter was ready for occupancy in 1807. It had been and still was an anxious time for Washingtonians. A strong movement to retrocede the District area to Virginia and Maryland developed. Many held that it would be far better to move the seat of government at once to some established city and forget this experiment. "All around are premature symptoms of decay," cried one agitator in 1808, "so many houses built, not inhabited, but tumbling into ruins." That last forlorn effort of the bankrupt land speculators, Morris Village (a row of dwellings on South Capitol Street between N and O Streets), was like "the ruins of Palmyra." Even friends of the Potomac city were critical. In 1809, the British minister Francis Jackson likened the American Capital to the British, yet spoke about Washington's "wild, desolate air from being so scantily and rudely cultivated." All were agreed, however, that Washington was charming during "the season." Mrs. Madison's drawing room would be filled with "gallants immaculate in sheer ruffles and small clothes," exchanging delightful small talk with "dainty belles in frills, flounces, and furbelows." But during the congressional recess even President Madison thought the city was "a solitude." "You cannot imagine," wrote Washington Irving in 1811, "how forlorn this desert city appears to me, now that the great tide of casual population has rolled away."

Had Irving visited the Capital 3 years later, after the British invasion of August 1814, he would have found it somewhat more forlorn even than a "desert city." Madison had sought ineffectually to curb the young Republican "War Hawks" in Congress who were clamoring for aggressive action against England, and in 1812 the country entered upon a war for which it was in no way prepared. On August 19, 1814, British regulars under General Ross, with marines under Admiral Cockburn from the latter's squadron in Chesapeake Bay, landed at Benedict on the Patuxent River in Maryland, and began a leisurely 40-mile march upon Washington. Five days later they were met near Bladensburg, just outside the District line, by a hastily assembled force of militia and marines commanded by General Winder. In the ensuing engagement the American troops were soon routed, and retreated in partial disorder to Georgetown, leaving the Capital undefended. Ross and Cockburn entered the city late in the same day (August 24). That night and next morning they burned the Capitol, the President's House, and all other public buildings except the combined Post Office and Patent Office. Very little private property was destroyed. There was a terrific windstorm during the afternoon of the 25th, and fearing a surprise attack by reinforced troops in the resulting confusion, the British withdrew that evening. Three days later a small British fleet appeared before Alexandria, levied a heavy tribute of food and merchandise from the town, then sailed down the Potomac to join Cockburn's squadron in attacking Baltimore.

With the Executive Mansion in ruins, President and Mrs. Madison took up temporary quarters in Colonel Tayloe's Octagon House. Congress convened in the one remaining public building, the Post and Patent Office. In 1815 a structure which came to be known as the "Brick Capitol" was erected by private subscriptions on part of the site now occupied by the Supreme Court Building. Here Congress held its sessions from December 1815 to December 1819, while the original Capitol was being rebuilt; and on an "elevated portico" in front of this structure James Monroe took the oath of office as President on March 4, 1817. Before the end of the latter year, Monroe and his family were installed in the rebuilt President's House, and official society in Washington again assumed its wonted stateliness and formality—as witness this "elegant extract" from Mrs. E. F. Ellet's *Court Circles of the Republic:*

"The court circle in Monroe's administration still had the aristocratic spirit and elevated tone which had characterized the previous administrations. Its superiority was universally acknowledged, and nothing vulgar entered its precincts. Elegance of dress was absolutely required. On one occasion Mr. Monroe refused admission to a near relative who happened not to have a suit of small-clothes and silk hose in which to present himself at a public reception. . . . The female society at Washington during the administration of Monroe was essentially Southern. Virginia, proud of her Presidents, sent forth her brightest flowers to adorn the court circle. The wealth of the sugar and cotton planters, and of the vast wheatfields of the agricultural States, cultivated by negroes, enabled Southern Senators and Representatives to keep their carriages and liveried servants, and to maintain great state. Dinners and suppers with rich wines and the delicacies of the season, had their persuasive influence over the minds as well as the appetites of the entertained."

In the course of his triumphal tour of the United States 1824-25, General Lafayette paid several visits to Washington, receiving here (as everywhere throughout the country) public and private honors such as seldom before had been accorded a foreigner in any land. President Monroe welcomed him upon the first of these occasions, in September, 1824; President John Quincy Adams bade him Godspeed upon his final departure, a year later.

Partisan politics, that strong meat upon which official Washington has ever since fed with keen relish, came into its own toward the close of Monroe's 8-year "era of good feeling." Conservative opposition to Jackson and his "western Democrats" in 1824 was no less bitterly aggressive than to Bryan and his "western Populists" in 1896. John Quincy Adams, defeated by popular vote but elected by the House of Representatives, succeeded Monroe in 1825 and gave the country one of its ablest administrations. Then, 4 years later, he went down to overwhelming defeat against the man whom he had once characterized as a "brawler from Tennessee." The control of national government by "eastern gentlemen of the old school in wigs, ruffles, knee breeches, and silver buckles" had definitely ended, and democracy was in full power. Some of the scenes attending Jackson's inauguration have been thus described by an eye witness:

"The whole of the preceding day, immense crowds were coming into the city from all parts, lodgings could not be obtained, and the new comers had to go to George Town, which soon overflowed and others had to go to Alexandria. . . . A national salute was fired early in the morning, and ushered in the 4th of March. By ten o'clock the Avenue

was crowded with carriages of every description, from splendid Bar-
ronet and coach, down to waggons and carts, filled with women and
children, some in finery and some in rags. . . . The day was warm
and delightful, from the South Terrace we had a view of Pennsylvania
and Louisiana Avenues, crowded with people hurrying towards the
Capitol. . . . At the moment the General entered the Portico and
advanced to the table, the shout that rent the air still resounds in my
ears. When the speech was over, and the President made his parting
bow, the barrier that had separated the people from him was broken
down and they rushed up the steps all eager to shake hands with him.
It was with difficulty he made his way through the Capitol and down
the hill to the gateway that opens on the avenue. Here for a moment
he was stopped. The living mass was impenetrable. After a while a
passage was opened, and he mounted his horse which had been provided
for his return (for he had walked to the Capitol) then such a cortege
as followed him! Country men, farmers, gentlemen, mounted and
dismounted, boys, women and children, black and white. Carriages,
waggons and carts all pursuing him to the President's House." (Margaret Bayard Smith, *Forty Years of Washingon Society*.)

The list of Jackson's Cabinet appointments, given out shortly before
his inauguration, included the name of his intimate friend, Senator
John H. Eaton of Tennessee, as Secretary of War. Three months
earlier, Eaton had married the young and beautiful Peggy O'Neale
Timberlake, widowed daughter of a Washington hotel keeper, and
feline gossip was busy with Peggy's name when Jackson announced her
husband's appointment. At once the Capital's chaste matrons, led by
the wife of Vice President Calhoun, instituted a rigid social boycott
against Mrs. Eaton. President Jackson, recently widowed and still
smarting under campaign aspersions made against his wife, rushed
angrily to Peggy's support, and before long came to associate Calhoun
with what he regarded as a conspiracy to discredit his administration.
Secretary of State Van Buren, free of wifely influence, joined his chief
in championing the Eaton cause. For two years this imbroglio held
the center of the stage in Washington, disrupting political and social
relations, deranging public business, and permeating the local atmosphere with bitterness. It provided the groundwork for political developments which eventually led Calhoun to withdraw from the
Democratic Party and gave Van Buren the Vice Presidency in 1832
and the Presidential nomination in 1836.

George Washington's dream of a trade route by water connecting
the Ohio River country with Chesapeake Bay by way of the lower
Potomac River began to take tangible form when, before a distinguished
company at Georgetown on July 4, 1828, President John Quincy
Adams turned the first spadeful of sod for the Chesapeake and Ohio

Canal. Believing that the canal would make Washington a great trade center, the city pledged itself for a million dollars' worth of stock in this enterprise, in addition to the heavy investments of private citizens. But construction of the canal lagged; even by 1850, when work was discontinued, it had been completed only to Cumberland, Maryland. Long before that time the pinch of an unwise investment began to be felt. The problem of raising a million dollars from a purse which did not contain even the interest on that sum was furrowing the brows of the city fathers; and their overlords on "the Hill" were bringing them to book. "There is danger, emphatically, that the city will be sold to the Dutch," declared an angry Senator in 1834; "agents of the foreign creditors," he said, were actually in town, "ready to purchase the property of these citizens of Washington under the hammer." The city extricated itself temporarily, but soon was floundering in one of the country's most severe depressions. Van Buren in 1837, like Hoover in 1929, was the inheritor of disaster—a national "morning after" headache induced by wild speculative carousing; and except for his advocacy of a measure creating national subtreasuries, adopted a few months before he left office, he "simply drifted about offering no measure of reform or public assistance to the suffering people." As a result, the opposing Republican (or, as it now called itself, the Whig) Party swept to easy victory in 1840, under "Tippecanoe" Harrison's banner. Within a month after his inauguration, Harrison died of pneumonia, and the Vice President, John Tyler, was sworn into office. Washington weathered the depression fairly well, but seemed somewhat threadbare in the last years of the poor times, little money having come from Congress or the taxpayers for city maintenance, and none for improvements.

British visitors to the Capital in its adolescent era were not favorably impressed. Harriet Martineau, with her silver ear trumpet, came here early in 1835 from Philadelphia. There she "had found perpetual difficulty in remembering that I was in a foreign country," but "at Washington it was very different.

"The city itself is unlike any other that ever was seen, straggling out hither and thither, with a small house or two a quarter of a mile from any other; so that in making calls 'in the city' we had to cross ditches and stiles, and walk alternately on grass and pavements, and strike across a field to reach a street. . . . Then there was the society, singularly compounded from the largest variety of elements; foreign ambassadors, the American government, members of Congress, from Clay and Webster down to Davy Crockett, Benton from Missouri, and Cuthbert, with the freshest Irish brogue, from Georgia; flippant young belles, 'pious' wives dutifully attending their husbands, and groaning over the frivolities of the place; grave judges, saucy travellers, pert newspaper reporters, melancholy Indian chiefs, and timid New England ladies, trembling on the verge of the vortex; all this was wholly unlike anything that is to be seen in any other city in the world; for all these are mixed up together in daily intercourse like the higher circle of a little village, and there is nothing else."

"Everybody knows that Washington has a Capitol," wrote Captain Marryat in 1838, "but the misfortune is that the Capitol wants a city. There it stands, reminding you of a general without an army, only surrounded and followed by a parcel of ragged little boys, for such is the appearance of the dirty, straggling, ill-built houses which lie at the foot of it." To Charles Dickens, Washington in 1842 consisted of "spacious avenues that begin in nothing and lead nowhere; streets a mile long that only want houses, roads, and inhabitants; public buildings that need but a public to be complete; and ornaments of great thoroughfares which only need great thoroughfares to orna- ment. . . . One might fancy the season over, and most of the houses gone out of town with their masters." Washington was "a Barmecide feast," a "monument raised to a deceased project." And so it would remain, thought he.

For any marked improvement in its shabby physical appearance, the Capital had a long time to wait. But in at least one important particu- lar, its social life was undergoing definite change in the mid-century decades. That life had hitherto centered chiefly in the Presidential and diplomatic groups, but now members of Congress, in ever-increas- ing numbers, were bringing their families to the Capital and taking an independent lead in its social activities. Those officials who could afford to do so were building homes of their own, instead of sharing the common "messes" in boarding houses and hotels. In its fundamental *mores,* however, Washington society underwent little change. Its exalted sense of the proprieties could be no less wantonly outraged in the fifties, when Mr. Corcoran displayed to public gaze the marble nudity of Powers' *Greek Slave,* than in the twenties, when John Quincy Adams installed a billiard table in the President's House. Its romantic dovecotes could be no less violently fluttered in 1860, when Albert Edward, Prince of Wales, came to town, than in 1840, when a fat and elderly and wealthy Baron de Bodisco, Minister from Russia, married a Georgetown schoolgirl. And certainly there was little change, then or later, in the basic composition of official Washington society—that strange heterogeneous and disconsonant mixture of every sort of element from every section of the country, gathering and dispersing with each change in party fortune like iron filings under the alternate impulses of a magnet.

The first railway to reach the Capital was completed in 1835—the Baltimore and Ohio, which began with a service of four trains daily between Washington and Baltimore and a running schedule of only a little more than two hours (half the usual stagecoach time). Three years later it was possible to make an all-rail journey from Washington to New York. The telegraph came in 1844 when, after a decade of vain appeals to Congress for an opportunity to demonstrate his instrument, Samuel F. B. Morse sent out over a wire to Baltimore the famous words, "What hath God wrought."

The town of Alexandria, looking forward hopefully to a great future in trade after the completion of the Chesapeake and Ohio Canal, believed it would have freer scope for developing that trade under Virginia, which had a large stake in the canal enterprise. In response to an appeal in 1846, Congress drowsily acquiesced in the retrocession to Virginia of all of the District of Columbia south of the Potomac. Georgetown also desired to return to its parent State, and for the same reason, but Maryland was more interested in railroad enterprises than in the canal, and Georgetown was unsuccessful in this effort.

The District was now growing rapidly in population. In 1840 nearly 44,000 persons were living within its boundaries—as against only about 14,000 in 1800. By 1850, notwithstanding the retrocession to Virginia of some 30 square miles, the population had increased to 51,687; in 1860 the figures were 75,000.

The *Princeton* disaster of 1844 was the severest tragedy that befell official Washington between Admiral Cockburn's incendiary visit and Abraham Lincoln's death. The *Princeton* was one of our first attempts at a propeller-driven warship; its armament included a tremendous Paixhans gun of special design, heralded far and wide as the "Peacemaker." It was also one of the first steam warships to reach Washington; hence the excitement when this triple novelty anchored off the Navy Yard in February 1844. On the last day of that month an elaborate official excursion was planned, to demonstrate the prowess of the *Princeton* and the "Peacemaker." President Tyler and his family, his Cabinet, ex-President John Quincy Adams, the leaders in both houses of Congress, and a number of foreign diplomats were included in the party that was ferried to the *Princeton* off Alexandria for an excursion to Mount Vernon, with feasting and music punctuated by demonstration shots from the "Peacemaker." On its final discharge, the gun burst at the breech, scattering mangled guests and crew upon the *Princeton's* decks. Secretary of the Navy Gilmer was killed, as were Secretary of State Upshur, Congressman Maxon of Maryland, Commander Kennan of the Navy, and President Tyler's father-in-law, David Gardiner of New York.

At the time of Polk's administration, Washingon had become an important station on the Underground Railroad, by means of which Southern slaves were smuggled northward to freedom. A spectacular

attempt at slave-running was made in April 1848, when 76 house-
servants belonging to prominent local families were carried off at night
on a small vessel, which reached the river's mouth before being captured. In the resulting public clamor, a mob stormed the office of Dr.
Gamaliel Bailey's abolitionist weekly, the *National Era,* demanding that
the editor remove his press. Although no violence ensued, the Capital
was more thoroughly alarmed than it had been since the British invasion
of 1814. This, however, was but a mild outburst of mob spirit in
comparison with an incident of 9 years later, when a band of armed
ruffians came over from Baltimore to assist the "Know Nothing"
candidates in a local election, terrorizing the city until dispersed by
United States Marines in a conflict near the present Public Library.
Six men were killed in the rioting and more than twice that number
wounded.

The unsuccessful slave-running incident of 1848, with its attendant
disorders, was only a local straw indicative of a national storm, which
had long been gathering around the issue of slavery, and which overshadowed all else in Washington after the subsidence of jingoistic
fervor aroused by the Mexican War in Polk's regime. The Presidents
who succeeded Polk, from Taylor to Buchanan, were either powerless
or incompetent to allay that storm. At the National Capital, more than
anywhere else, it soon became apparent that the "irrepressible conflict"
was indeed irrepressible, for it was here that Northern and Southern
sentiment collided with greatest force. Disruption of the Union might
well make Washington a dead city—each of the nations would undoubtedly establish its own central capital. John Brown's raid on
Harpers Ferry, 65 miles away, caused consternation among Washingtonians, hemmed in as their defenseless city was by two slave States.
On Capitol Hill, in the last angry clashes of legislators, one Senator
suggested "that the city might remain the Capital—but of the Southern
Confederacy," and the galleries greeted this sally with approving
laughter. Southern sympathy was strong in Washington; indeed, the
Capital was overrun by Southerners. Their "blue cockade" was
flaunted even at the President's New Year's Day reception in 1861.
Washington was tragically divided against itself.

In the last year of his administration, Buchanan sought to organize
the Washington militia, but Congress would not act. Winfield Scott,
the aged General in Chief of the small United States Army, had almost
no troops at hand, and he doubted the loyalty of the citizen soldiery.
Still, the militia must be used. A survey showed that, although there
were four local regiments, in actual strength these comprised only 150
men. A militant political organization of Southerners, the Jackson
Democratic Association, had 800 members who were drilling at night,

and who might at any moment seize the Capital, without aid from the slave States. The local militia was reorganized as quickly as possible. Before the end of February 1861, one thousand Washingtonians were under arms and in uniform. Trouble had been feared on February 13, the day of the electoral count; but that day passed quietly, and Abraham Lincoln was declared President-elect. On Washington's Birthday marching militia displayed the Stars and Stripes; ex-President Tyler protested to President Buchanan, and the latter apologized.

President-elect Lincoln entered Washington quietly a few days before the inauguration and went to Willard's Hotel. On Inauguration Day, almost hidden by an escort of soldiers, Lincoln drove swiftly down Pennsylvania Avenue. Perched on housetops, other troops with pointed rifles watched the thronged sidewalks and windows. At the Capitol all the windows bristled with guns, while a deep cordon of soldiers was drawn up around the inaugural platform. The city was virtually under military occupation, though after the inauguration the citizen soldiery went back to their civilian pursuits for a while.

On April 9, while Virginia was still hovering on the brink of secession, President Lincoln ordered the Washington militia into Federal service. That mobilization saved the Union Capital, perhaps even the Union itself; for, 8 days later, Virginia threw in its lot with the South, and the cry "On to Washington!" rang through all the near-by Southern States. Virginian troops swarmed into Alexandria. They could not yet attack, but it was rumored that they only awaited the arrival of artillery from Richmond.

Lincoln issued his first call for Northern troops on April 15. Seventy-five thousand would soon be under arms, but many anxious days must be endured before their arrival, with the defense of the city resting almost entirely upon its citizens. The first Northerners to arrive were Pennsylvanians, in civilian clothes and almost unarmed. While passing through Baltimore they were stoned. The next day several members of a Massachusetts regiment, the Sixth, were killed in that city. "No Abolitionists should cross Maryland to attack our brothers in the South," Baltimoreans declared grimly. But many more Northern soldiers must reach Washington very soon, or the Confederate flag would fly over the Capitol. A New York regiment which had been rerouted by water was anxiously awaited. The enemy outside the city was gathering strength enough to overwhelm the defending force, and the ever-present enemy within loomed even more ominously. At last the New York regiment arrived, by way of Annapolis. "Those who were in the Federal Capital on that Thursday, April 25, will never during their lives forget the event," wrote John Hay. "An indescribable gloom had hung over Washington nearly a week, paralyzing its traffic and crushing out its life." But as the Seventh New York Regiment marched up Pennsylvania Avenue hope returned to the besieged Capitol. "The presence of this single regiment seemed to turn the scales of fate," said Hay.

At least two other occasions of grave danger to the seat of national Government came later. The first of these was in July, 1861, following the battle of Bull Run, when the Confederates might well have occupied the Capital had they realized the thoroughness of their victory over the demoralized Union forces. The second was 3 years later, when a strong Confederate force under General Early crossed the Potomac some 80 miles above Washington, and after a wide flanking march appeared suddenly at Silver Spring, about 6 miles north of the city, on the afternoon of July 11, 1864. Had he pressed on at once, it is probable that Early might have taken the Capital. But delaying until next morning, he gave Grant time to rush up reinforcements, and in the engagement of July 12 (during which President Lincoln watched the fighting from a parapet at Fort Stevens), Early was repulsed and later recrossed the Potomac into Virginia.

During the 4 years of conflict, Washington was virtually base headquarters of the Northern armies. All its activities centered about the war. Its parks and squares were camping grounds; its churches became hospitals. Hosts of Negro refugees poured in from adjoining States, adding tremendously to the public burdens. The city as it appeared to one of its residents in 1862 is thus pictured by Mary Clemmer Ames, in her *Ten Years in Washington:*

"Capitol Hill, dreary, desolate and dirty, stretched away into an uninhabited desert, high above the mud of the West End. Arid hill and sodden plain showed alike the horrid trail of war. Forts bristled above every hill-top. Soldiers were entrenched at every gate-way. Shed hospitals covered acres on acres in every suburb. Churches, art-halls and private mansions were filled with the wounded and dying of the American armies. The endless roll of the army wagon seemed never still. The rattle of the anguish-laden ambulance, the piercing cries of the sufferers whom it carried, made morning, noon and night too dreadful to be borne. The streets were filled with marching troops, with new regiments, their hearts strong and eager, their virgin banners all untarnished as they marched up Pennsylvania avenue, playing 'The girl I left behind me' as if they had come to holiday glory—to easy victory. But the streets were filled no less with soldiers foot-sore, sun-burned, and weary, their clothes begrimed, their banners torn, their hearts sick with hope deferred, ready to die with the anguish of long defeat. Every moment had its drum-beat, every hour was alive with the tramp of troops going, coming."

SINCE THE CIVIL WAR

Late in the evening of April 14, 1865, less than a week after Lee's surrender at Appomattox, the Capital and the country were stunned by the news that President Lincoln had been shot while attending a performance at Ford's Theater. All that night and through a dismal rainy dawn, the city was in a blaze of excitement. Then, at half-past seven, the church bells tolled and a hush fell over the streets—Lincoln was dead. Two months later, following a drumhead trial in the old Arsenal (present Army War College), four persons (including a woman) charged with complicity in the crime were hanged in the adjoining prison yard. Meanwhile, on May 23, Meade's veterans had marched down Pennsylvania Avenue 60 abreast, before dispersing to their homes. The mighty column was 6 hours in passing before President Johnson and General Grant in the reviewing stand. Sherman's men made an even longer procession the next day. Not until the end of the World War in 1918 did the Capital see such another military display.

"The 12 tragic years that followed the death of Lincoln," says Claude G. Bowers, "were years of revolutionary turmoil. . . . Never have American public men in responsible positions, directing the destiny of the Nation, been so brutal, hypocritical, and corrupt." President Johnson, seeking to carry out Lincoln's conciliatory policy toward the conquered South, fought a courageous battle; but the real control was in Congress, where a coalition between Southern "loyalists" and Northern "radicals" had its vengeful and bitter way. The rabid debates in Senate and House, the all but successful impeachment proceeding against Johnson, the sordid maneuvering and plotting and bickering in every quarter, kept the Capital pitched to a high key of excitement.

Owing to a bitter quarrel between the two men in 1867, Johnson refused to ride with General Grant in the latter's inaugural parade of 1869, or to witness his induction into office. But the country at large placed unbounded confidence in the reticent little general with the perennial black cigar. By the end of his first year as President, every intelligent observer had come to realize, with Henry Adams, that "a great soldier might be a baby politician." During Grant's 8-year regime, Washington and the country were shaken by a series of scandals, involving at least two Cabinet members, a number of prominent national legislators, Grant's private secretary, and his brother-in-law. The catastrophe of "Black Friday" in September, 1869, resulting from an attempt by Jay Gould and Jim Fisk to corner the gold market, was followed by the Credit Mobilier revelations, and these in turn by other developments which if less important were scarcely less unsavory. The lobbyist, first prominent in the early days of Johnson's regime, when many claims arising out of the Civil War were being pressed against the Government, now blossomed into full flower as a Washington institution.

Grant, with his plain ways, his incessant smoking, his fondness for horses, brought to the White House something of the free and rough atmosphere of a headquarters tent. But in the fashionable hotels and private mansions of Washington, society reveled in a newly acquired splendor, with "diamonds in every hotel parlor, equipages on the Georgetown Road, capitalists in the Senate, state dinners unsurpassed among officials."

Graft and glitter, however, by no means comprised all of Washington life in "the gilded age." Ristori appeared in her greatest roles, Edwin Forrest in Shakespearean plays, Joe Jefferson in *Rip Van Winkle*. Good music and interesting lectures were usually available; and, for those privileged to enter them, there were many homes in which high thinking and memorable conversation held sway—such homes, for example, as those of Charles Sumner and George Bancroft. The little group, including Whitman and Burroughs, which met at William Douglas O'Connor's house, Henry Adams' and Horatio King's literary dinners, Dr. Spencer F. Baird's Sunday evening gatherings—these, no less than the furtive conferences at Welcker's restaurant or Cooke's banking office, the fashionable hotel "hops" and sumptuous state dinners, have their places in any true picture of the Capital in Grant's time.

In this period, also, Washington underwent a physical regeneration which transformed it from a shabby, overgrown village to something like a modern metropolis. As a civic entity it had struggled along somehow since the beginning, a hapless stepchild of the Federal Government, with little help and much hindrance from Congress, developing slowly in a sprawling shiftless fashion and getting on as best it could with only the barest modicum of municipal improvements. Something was done during the Civil War—a few streets paved, an inadequate water supply brought down from Great Falls, horse-drawn streetcars installed to replace the old rickety omnibusses. But the ebb and flow of wartime activities had, in general, left the city in far worse condition than before. "The curtailment of the army camps about only offered a better view of the ravages wrought. The surrounding forts, deserted now, were crumbling to decay, and the shedlike corrals for army horses and wagons were abandoned to the town toughs, who found them a convenient rendezvous." The dust-choked thoroughfares were bogs of mud after every rain. The primitive sewage system was a menace to health and an affront to the nostrils.

Prominent among the Washingtonians who were unwilling that

such conditions should continue indefinitely was Crosby Stuart Noyes, on the staff of the Washington *Star*. In 1863 Noyes was elected to the city council; in 1867 he acquired control of the *Star,* becoming its editor in chief. Associated with him in the city council and also in the ownership of the newspaper was Alexander Robey Shepherd, a prosperous local builder, who early became the advocate of an extensive modernization program. Through his newspaper, Noyes waged an effective campaign for civic improvement, while Shepherd developed a concrete plan of action in the field of public works, to be put into effect when the time was ripe.

For many years Washington had been governed by a mayor and city council, elected by popular vote. In 1871 Congress instituted for the District a territorial form of government, to be administered by a governor, a board of public works, and a legislative council of 11 members, all appointed by the President; together with a lower legislative body of 22 members (the "house of delegates"), and a voteless delegate to Congress, elected by the District. The new law permitted the District to increase its funded debt, then standing at about $4,-000,000, to not more than $10,000,000. Under President Grant's appointments, the banker Henry D. Cooke became Governor of the District, and Alexander Shepherd a member of the board of public works. As vice president and executive officer of the latter, Shepherd then had his long-awaited opportunity. "Openly, courageously, and with dictatorial abandon" he embarked upon a tremendous task of civic improvement.

"With czarlike zeal, he tore up the tracks of the railroad which crossed Pennsylvania Avenue at the foot of Capitol Hill near the Peace Monument. Before the dew was off the grass in the morning, he supervised the tearing down of the old Northern Liberties Market House on the square where the Carnegie Public Library now stands. One Saturday night, he nearly buried the depot of the Baltimore and Ohio Railroad at the corner of New Jersey Avenue and C Street by building up the street preparatory to grading and surfacing it." (George Rothwell Brown, *Washington: A Not Too Serious History.*)

He constructed many miles of sewers, paved many streets, laid sidewalks, provided adequate water facilities and spacious parks, put in street lights. City taxpayers began to raise their voices when his road-building reached out into the "cow pastures" beyond city limits. When he began to plant trees along the new roads the cries against his "waste of public funds" became a continuous clamor.

But Shepherd had entrenched himself well. He had powerful friends, President Grant among them. Many Congressmen had full confidence in him. However, forces beyond the control of Shepherd or Congress or the President swept over Washington and other American cities in 1873—another Nation-wide financial panic. Governor Cooke, a brother of Jay Cooke, deemed it wise to resign from city office, his own bank having been drawn into the cataclysm. Shepherd was made Governor, but the poor times greatly aided the opposition to him; and finally, in June, 1874, Congress substituted a temporary form of commission rule for the territorial plan of government, thus abolishing the office of Governor, and conducted an investigation into Shepherd's operations. Although he was found innocent of personal dishonesty, the Senate refused to confirm his later appointment as commissioner in view of the fact that he had increased the District debt far beyond the $10,000,000 legally authorized—to $22,000,000 in fact! This debt was later funded on a 50-year basis, under Federal guarantee as to principal and interest, the final installment being paid in 1922.

On June 11, 1878, the so-called "organic act," by which the District of Columbia has ever since been governed, was approved; under this measure the District became a municipal corporation, managed by three commissioners appointed by the President of the United States. The census of 1880 showed a population of 177,624, as against 131,700 in 1870. Many new suburban areas were being developed. The city's first apartment house was built in 1879. The telephone was introduced in 1877, and a year later it was reported that 119 "electric speaking telephones" had been installed in Government offices. The first electric light appeared in 1881, and the first electric streetcar in 1888.

An event which stirred the city more than any other since Lincoln's assassination occurred on July 2, 1881, when President Garfield was shot and mortally wounded by Charles J. Guiteau, a disappointed office seeker, in the Baltimore and Potomac station at 6th and B Streets, the site now occupied by the National Gallery of Art. Following his death about 10 weeks later, the President's body lay in state in the rotunda of the Capitol, and was then taken to Cleveland for burial. The assassin Guiteau was later hanged in the old Washington Asylum and Jail.

Apart from the ever ebullient concerns of national politics, the late eighties and early nineties constitute a relatively placid interlude in local history, with nothing more calamitous in their record than the flood of early June, 1889, when water on Pennsylvania Avenue reached the level of streetcar floors. President Cleveland's marriage at the White House, in his first year of office, provided a 9-day wonder for the Capital; the doings and sayings of Benjamin Harrison McKee, "baby of the White House," were of perennial public interest during the next Presidential administration. Then, breaking rudely into the tranquil scene, came "Coxey's army" in 1894—a ragged troop of unemployed workers, some 300 in number, who had tramped from Mas-

sillon, Ohio, to "petition the Government for a redress of grievances."
They reached Washington on April 29; two days later "General"
Coxey and some of his followers attempted to speak on the steps of
the Capitol, but were promptly carried off into the enforced retirement
of 20 days in jail. The rest of the "army" departed.

For a few months in 1898, during the war with Spain, martial
spirit of a sort once more pervaded the Capital. Camp Alger, just
south of Fort Myer, served as the local rendezvous for volunteer troops
in this brief conflict. A great military parade in honor of Admiral
Dewey took place in the Capital on October 3, 1899. In December
of the following year, Washington celebrated the completion of its
first hundred years as the seat of national government, the commemorative exercises being attended by many distinguished guests, American and foreign.

Following President McKinley's assassination at Buffalo in September, 1901, the rough-riding hero of the Spanish-American War,
Theodore Roosevelt, moved into the White House. To that storied
mansion, grown somewhat stuffy with the odors of late Victorian
sanctity, and to the Capital's official life in general, he brought the
dispersive and sanative qualities of a somewhat riotous breeze.

"He filled the White House with all sorts and conditions of men:
Western bull-whackers, city prize fighters, explorers, rich men, poor
men, an occasional black man, editors, writers; and around his festal
board gathered three times a day, from early morn until night, men
whose faces never had been seen in the White House before. . . .
Party managers were disturbed at the motley crew which Roosevelt
called in. . . . In the White House his life as a father, as a hun-
band, as a citizen, as a politician, was most interesting, but almost
primitive in its simplicity. Few forms were observed. He cut red
tape. He talked state secrets in a loud voice to statesmen in the presidential workroom, so that reporters could hear. He went on long
walks through the parks in the environs of Washington, taking fat
military officers with him, who panted along a step or two behind.
He tolerated no sacred cows." (William Allen White, *Masks in a
Pageant.*)

The tumult and the shouting to which Washingtonians had become accustomed under Theodore Roosevelt's energetic regime died
away at last, to be succeeded by the somewhat lethargic calm of Taft's
single term—a calm disturbed only by the Pinchot-Ballinger controversy of 1909-10. And then came Woodrow Wilson and his idealistic strivings toward a "new freedom" in our national economic life;
followed by the years of troubled neutrality in the great European
conflict, and on April 6, 1917, the declaration of war against Germany.
For more than a year and a half thereafter, Washington was domi-

nated by a single overwhelming purpose—the successful prosecution of the war. Workers from every walk of life swarmed into the city by tens of thousands to staff the various war bureaus; stucco buildings to house those bureaus sprang up almost overnight. Men in uniform filled the flag-decorated streets; parades and "drives" were almost everyday occurrences. From all the allied nations came statesmen, military experts, financiers, business executives, to consult with public officials here on various phases of the war. Washington was the center not only of an embattled nation but to some extent of an embattled world. Then at last came the celebration of Armistice Day, the welcoming home of war veterans, the return of General Pershing, the many divisional parades, and finally the honors paid to the Unknown Soldier.

After what has been termed "the outbreak of peace," late in 1918, the political scene in Washington promptly reverted to its wonted status. Wilson's physical breakdown, in September, 1919, while it did not terminate the ruthless fight in Congress against his policies and purposes, created a situation which the Capital had never known before. Looking back over the last year and a half of Wilson's second term, Edward G. Lowry wrote:

"For a long time the social-political atmosphere of Washington had been one of bleak and chill austerity suffused and envenomed by hatred of a sick chief magistrate that seemed to poison and blight every ordinary human relationship and finally brought to a virtual stoppage every routine function of the Government. It was a general condition of stagnation and aridity that had come to affect everybody here. The White House was isolated. It had no relation with the Capitol or the local resident and official community. Its great iron gates were closed and chained and locked. Policemen guarded its approaches. It was in a void apart. Almost from the beginning it had seemed to the sensitive local intelligence to exhale a chill and icy disdain for the chief subordinate figures and personages.who under the President comprise the personnel of the Washington community. This may have been imagination, but it had the full effect of a reality. It all made for bleakness and bitterness and a general sense of frustration and unhappiness."

Into this dismal scene, on March 4, 1921, walked the new President Warren G. Harding, apostle of "normalcy." At once the atmosphere of Greek tragedy dispersed in a radiant glow of jolly good fellowship. "We are just folks," announced the President's wife; it was Old Home Week, after a long exile. The Capital relaxed, yawned, became careless and open-handed. But disturbing cloud-shadows soon drifted across the sunny landscape. The story of Washington during this period—the story of the Teapot Dome and Elk

Hills oil scandals, of corruption and extortion on the part of several Government officials—all this is of relatively recent and familiar memory. Welcome relief in the record of these years is afforded by the important Disarmament Conference of late 1921 and early 1922, which brought to the Capital large delegations of high officials from eight foreign countries.

Under President Coolidge, who succeeded Harding upon the latter's death in 1923, was inaugurated the huge Federal Triangle development program, involving the purchase of about 70 acres of land between Pennsylvania and Constitution Avenues east of 15th Street, the demolition of many old buildings, and the construction of several great public edifices. Private building during the twenties achieved in Washington its greatest and most rapid expansion up to that time. In the period between 1900 and 1930, population within the District increased from 278,718 to 486,869.

Acute economic distress throughout the country was brought home to the Capital in unpleasantly direct fashion by several "hunger marches" during the latter part of President Hoover's administration. The first of these reached Washington early in December, 1931; its members were kept under strict police surveillance while guests of the city for two days, but were allowed to present demands for Federal relief to Vice President Curtis and Speaker Garner. A much more formidable army, led by the Reverend James R. Cox of Pittsburgh, arrived about a month later. Father Cox presented a plea to Congress, interviewed the President, and then led most of his ragged cohorts back to Pittsburgh. The last of these demonstrations occurred in December, 1932. This time the marchers came into Washington under police escort, and although given shelter they were not permitted to present their demands directly to Congress or the President. After marching past the Capitol and holding a mass meeting, they departed —minus 14 members of the vanguard, who had been jailed for parading before the White House.

Meanwhile, in the summer of 1932, a "bonus army" caused far more serious concern. Unemployed veterans from various parts of the country began arriving early in June, by motor truck and on foot, to petition Congress for immediate payment of a war bonus. Organized in semimilitary fashion, they set up crude camps in and near the Capital. A group that had taken possession of several condemned buildings on Pennsylvania Avenue resisted an effort of District police to evict them. In the ensuing affray one man was killed and several injured. Later in the same day President Hoover ordered Federal troops to drive the veterans from their Pennsylvania Avenue billets and their camp on the Anacostia flats. The unarmed defenders were quickly routed, their huts and tents burned, and themselves scattered upon their homeward paths. At least one other invasion by "bonus marchers" occurred later, in President Franklin D. Roosevelt's first term, but there was no disturbance.

During President Roosevelt's first two terms, the physical aspect of Washington continued to change. The tip was placed on the Federal Triangle with the dedication of the Apex Building in 1937; the opening of the National Gallery of Art in 1941 brought to the Capital the greatest collection of old masters in the Western Hemisphere, and, with its other galleries, made Washington a great city for its exhibitions of fine arts; the Mall was almost entirely cleared of buildings; the Jefferson Memorial, on the south side of the Tidal Basin, was all but completed (not without an *opéra bouffe* touch when protesting ladies chained themselves to Japanese cherry trees to prevent their being uprooted for the initial excavation); the War Department Building rose rapidly, west of the Interior group; and the Washington National Airport, three-fourths of it dredged from the Potomac River, was put in shape for commercial flying. Other structures, less monumental perhaps, or less related to the municipal plan, were erected to house an expanding Government—Federal Office Buildings No. 1 and No. 2, the Social Security Building, the Federal Loan Building.

The Roosevelt administration brought to Washington many persons who had been accustomed to commute to suburban residences from other metropolitan centers, and Federal workers showed a greater tendency than ever before to reach out into the environs for places to live. This movement took many new residents to Alexandria and Arlington, in Virginia; to Silver Spring and Takoma Park, in Maryland; and into many other adjacent areas. The era of small houses, ushered in by Federal housing agencies, contributed to the settlement of Washington's peripheral area. The population of the District of Columbia, during the 1930's, showed a gain of more than 176,000, figures for 1940 giving the District population at 663,153. Because of the movement of population to the surrounding areas, however, this figure does not reflect the actual population increment in the Washington area. Motor traffic increased in proportion to the regional growth, and, since there were few corresponding developments to care for traffic and parking, these problems became increasingly acute. "Staggered hours" for Government workers in the various agencies, inaugurated in 1941, provided some relief from traffic congestion.

In pageantry and public show, the Capital City continued to mirror the national picture, and at the same time assumed a unique position among the world's capitals—it became the center of the only major democracy existing as such. Washington's elaborate reception to the King and Queen of England in 1939 was indicative of an Anglo-American rapprochement that has developed rapidly since. A similar reception at almost the same time, with about the same show of military pomp, to President Somoza of Nicarauga, was an indicator of increased emphasis on Pan American friendship. When, in the fall of 1940, the Gravelly Point Airport was dedicated by President Roosevelt, Washington saw the precise maneuvering of more than 400 military planes—one of the greatest air shows the country has ever staged. This "flexing of the national muscle," as the President termed it, provided Washington with a contemporary glimpse of the Nation's preparation for defense. Washington as a refuge for dethroned European royalty was underlined with the arrival of Crown Princess Martha of Norway, in 1940, to take a residence in near-by Bethesda, Maryland.

Meantime, "New Deal" workers of the first two Roosevelt terms, eager to defeat depression and create a better social and economic Nation, made their vital, democratic mark on the Washington social scene. If, as contemporary observers believed, they gradually settled into the ways of "old-line" Government workers, they have only repeated a process the Capital City has seen before. There was, however, an infusion of new blood beginning with 1939, when National Defense agencies and the military branches brought industrial and production experts, military and naval workers, to Washington, creating another change in the social complexion.

January 20, 1941, was an historic day for Washington, and for the Nation, marking the first third-term inauguration—that of Franklin D. Roosevelt—in the history of the country. The inaugural address was brief, lasting about 12 minutes. The parade, less grandiose than many others, stressed military preparedness. A 15-minute air show brought more than 200 military planes into maneuvers over the city, including 35 four-motored "flying fortress" bombers, more than had assembled for one show before. Three weapon-carrying men were arrested (one of them had a sword), and taken under observation for their zeal in "defending the President." Inauguration and parade were witnessed by probably a million people.

Washington, like the rest of the Nation, was stunned by the Pearl Harbor attack of Sunday, December 7, 1941. That night, the White House was ablaze with lights. A few people gathered in Lafayette Square, north of the Executive Mansion. Others came, and others, until there were perhaps a thousand. They said little. They stood quietly, their faces toward the White House. The building had more lights than they had ever noticed before. There was a sad kind of cheerfulness about it. They could see people coming out and going in. Newsmen, diplomats, Cabinet members, generals and admirals perhaps. Somebody doing something about it. The crowd stood silently, reaching out for comfort. They derived a certain solace from the lights and the comings and goings. Then, gradually, they went away.

The next morning Washington emerged as an armed camp. Helmeted and bayoneted soldiers guarded strategic buildings, utilities, bridges. Officers of the Army, Navy, and Marines, who had been going to work in mufti, went that day in uniform. Every second man in tailored khaki seemed to be a major or a lieutenant colonel. The blue-overcoated Navy men all seemed young, as if fresh from Annapolis. The city, like every other coastal municipality in the country, prepared for air raids. Fighter planes buzzed hornetlike above the city, night and day. "National defense" changed overnight to "the war effort." Wartime alphabetical agencies sprang up; one of them, War Production Board, narrowly escaped the title of War Production Administration—and the initials WPA. Thousands of new employees came to Washington. Traffic increased. Housing vacancies dropped quickly to the irreducible fraction of 1 per cent. Tire rationing, sugar shortage, higher prices, longer hours, War Time, Winston Churchill's visit . . . the rest is national history, accented perhaps more heavily in Federal Boomtown than elsewhere.

The Negro in Washington

THE Negro, from the start, has exerted a profound influence upon the city of Washington. Benjamin Banneker, a Negro mathematician, was appointed by George Washington to serve on Major L'Enfant's commission for surveying and laying out the city. The lot of Banneker's fellows, however, even in our times, has hardly been so auspicious. Viewing Washington in its early years Thomas Moore found:

> Even here beside the proud Potomac's streams . . .
> The medley mass of pride and misery
> Of whips and charters, manacles and rights
> Of slaving blacks and democratic whites. . . .

Although conditions hardly deserved to be called ideal, still the cook, coachman, and artisan, in Alexandria, Georgetown, or Washington, and the truck farmer in the adjacent rural areas, was generally better off than the field hand in the Deep South. But, because of its situation, the District of Columbia served as a natural outlet for coastwise slave ships and overland slave caravans. There were slave pens in what is now Potomac Park, one in the Decatur House, fronting on what is now Lafayette Square, and several others, even more notorious. Distressful conditions among the Negroes impelled the slaveowner John Randolph to the use of bitter invective: "You call this the land of liberty, and every day that passes things are done in it at which the despotisms of Europe would be horror-struck and disgusted. . . . In no part of the earth—not even excepting the rivers on the Coast of Africa, was there so great, so infamous a slave market, as in the metropolis, in the seat of government of this nation which prides itself on freedom."

A chorus of voices rose in harmony with Randolph's. The struggle for abolition in the District recruited such men as Benjamin Lundy, Salmon P. Chase, Charles Miner, Charles Sumner, William Lloyd Garrison, Henry Wilson, William H. Seward, and Congressman Abraham Lincoln. The forces led by men like Calhoun, however, were too strong, and Congress refused to act. The District remained slave territory until the Compromise of 1850. The Negroes of Washington, free and slave, sometimes took matters in their own hands. The Underground Railroad had important stopping places in the city. It is probable that Harriet Tubman, "the Moses of her people" and the greatest underground agent, worked around Washington as well as on the Eastern Shore of Maryland.

In 1830 there were 6,152 free Negroes in the District of Columbia, compared with 6,119 slaves; in 1860, 11,131 compared with 3,185 slaves. Thus, in 30 years, the free colored population was nearly doubled, while the slave population was halved. Stringent regulations affecting free Negroes were written by the District Common Council. No Negro, slave or free, could testify against whites. Meetings for any other than fraternal and religious purposes were forbidden. After Nat Turner's Virginia insurrection in 1831, Negro preachers were banned. Curfew rang at 10 o'clock for all Negroes. Though forbidden by law, many succeeded, through friendly whites, in running hotels, taverns, saloons, and restaurants. Negroes held a monopoly on barbering, and free colored boys were porters and bootblacks. Waiters were numerous and comparatively well paid. There were skilled carpenters, bricklayers, shoemakers, stonemasons, wheelwrights, blacksmiths, plasterers, printers, cabinetmakers, cab drivers, and draymen. For free colored women the opportunities were limited to dressmaking, laundering, nursing, and housework.

Chances to gain a livelihood were scanty for many Negroes, however, and some were driven to petty larceny. Some Negroes ignored or violated the curfew. Race riots developed in spite of the fact that a Negro striking a white man was subject to having his ears cropped (a legal penalty in the District until 1862). Mulattoes sometimes set up self-defeating distinctions against their darker brothers. There were examples of Negroes serving as informers, as catchers of runaways, as hat-in-hand seekers of personal favors, and as slave-kidnapers.

Negro education got its start in 1807, shortly after the first schoolhouses for white children had been built. Three freed Negroes who could not read or write hired a white teacher and set up the first school. John F. Cook, a shoemaker, opened a school in 1834. Myrtilla Miner, a white woman, driven from place to place in her effort to establish a Negro school, finally purchased two city squares. Harriet Beecher Stowe donated $1,000 and Johns Hopkins was one of the trustees. The buildings were stoned and set on fire, but Miss Miner stood her ground; intruders were given a tacit warning when Miss Miner took up a pistol practice in the school grounds. By 1860 there were more than 1,200 free Negro children in District schools.

Church was the solace of free Negroes. Methodism started among them in 1820, when a group of free Negroes withdrew from Ebenezer Church and formed a separate congregation. After 1831, other Negro groups withdrew from established congregations. At St. John's an outside stairway leading to the gallery was called "the nigger's backstairs to heaven." Colored members decided that there must be other ways to get there, and left the church. Sabbath schools were popular among adults and children, because they furnished instruction in the three R's. The free Negro frequently left Jonah waiting, and the walls of Jericho standing, while he fathomed the sequences of the alphabet.

Negro houses ran the gamut from hovels to commodious homes. Some crouched behind the imposing dwellings of employers, or were grouped in hidden alleyways. The homes of the well-to-do were scattered here and there, and separate Negro communities existed. Many free Negroes were poverty-stricken, but others had homes on 16th Street; a feed dealer, Alfred Lee, purchased the mansion on H Street which had been the British Embassy. At the time of the Emancipation Act, Negroes in the District of Columbia were paying taxes on $650,000 worth of real estate.

In 1862, the year in which slavery was abolished in the District, President Lincoln authorized the enlistment of Negroes for the Army. Two regiments served with honor at Fair Oaks, Petersburg, Fort Taylor, and elsewhere. Negro contrabands, male and female, had earlier crowded to the camps, eager to serve "Marse Lincum's boys." The mustering out of Negro regiments at the close of the war further increased their number in the District. By 1880 there were 59,696 in the city and its environs, representing one-third of the population. At their best, these people were intelligent and eager to help themselves; at their worst they showed, in the words of a Federal chaplain, "cringing deceit, theft, licentiousness, all the vices which slavery inevitably fosters." President Lincoln favored colonization for them, and several hundred former slaves were shipped to Haiti. When their plight became desperate a warship was sent for them, and they were settled in Arlington.

As the flood of refugees swept in, McClellan's Barracks housed them, and numerous barracks were built in Washington and Alexandria. Two hundred tenements were fitted up at Campbell Hospital. Real estate agents floated a project that resulted in Washington's "alley system." The deep back yards, and even the front yards, promised higher returns from rentals than from formal gardens. By 1897 there were 333 alleys, inhabited by 19,000 people, and more than three-fourths of them Negroes. Here, sometimes in $10 shacks, ex-slaves got their first taste of freedom. Negro communities acquired such names as Goose Level, Vinegar Hill, Foggy Bottom, Swampoodle, Bloodfield, and Cowtown.

For new arrivals, accustomed chiefly to manual labor in the fields, there was little employment in a city predominantly governmental and residential. Pauperism forced many to eke out a living by pickings on the dumps. Others took to pilfering, and the crime rate was high. In 1891 the Superintendent of Police attributed much of the crime to neglect of Negro children. The death rate for Negroes that year, largely increased by infant mortality, was nearly double that of the whites. The Freedmen's Bureau, missionary organizations, and Negroes themselves, through their lodges, churches, and schools, waged a determined battle against poverty, poor health, and ignorance. Freedmen's Bureau was created by Congress in 1865 for "relief work, education, regulation of labor, and administration of justice." It exerted its greatest influence in establishing Freedmen's Hospital, Howard University, and a number of schools for Negroes. An Act of Congress ruled that Washington and Georgetown allocate to the trustees of Negro schools a proportionate part of all moneys received, but the corporation of Washington refused to do so until 1867, after which the Negro schools fared better.

An old Negro preacher in Georgetown said of the freed Negro, "Fifteen years after he came out of slavery, what did he do? Sat down by the River of Babylon and sang, 'Peace at home and pleasure abroad,' and went to sleep by the weeping willows for twenty-five years." He was, perhaps for emphasis, overstating the case. There was definite, if gradual economic advance. Many made their living as domestics, barbers, cobblers, grocers, dry-goods merchants, artisans, contractors, real estate dealers, hucksters, saloonkeepers, and hotel proprietors. Others inherited property, made prudent investments, and became prosperous. Negro firemen were appointed on a full-time basis in 1870; colored policemen have been on the force since the Metropolitan Police was organized in the sixties. Many Negroes found employment in the Government service, most of them as laborers or messengers, a few as clerks. Certain political plums fell to Negroes, such as the positions of fourth auditor, register of the Treasury, and recorder of deeds. There was an increasing class of doctors, lawyers, preachers and teachers.

Though politically articulate, the Washington Negro in this period exerted little force. His newly acquired suffrage was swept away by disfranchisement of the District in 1874, an act said to have been definitely influenced by the fact that Negroes made up one-fourth of the population. Negro political figures, however, were numerous. There were a score of Representatives, including Robert Brown Elliott, John M. Langston, and John R. Lynch. Negro Senators were Hiram R. Revels and Blanche Kelso Bruce, both of Mississippi. And there was Frederick Douglass, the anti-slavery orator, marshal and recorder of deeds for the District, and Minister to Haiti.

For many years after the Civil War, Washington was said to have "the most distinguished and brilliant assemblage of Negroes in the world." The reputation was sustained by cultural societies such as the Second Baptist Lyceum, the Congressional Lyceum, and the Bethel Literary Society. The National Negro Academy had upon its roster such scholars as W. E. B. DuBois, the Grimke brothers, W. S. Scarborough, J. W. Cromwell, and Kelly Miller. At the close of the century Paul Laurence Dunbar, Negro poet, lived here. In 1897-98 he was assistant to Daniel Murray, another Negro, who held a responsible position in the Library of Congress. Will Marion Cook, who was distinguished in music, was for a number of years a resident of Washington. The two leading Negro newspapers of the period, W. Calvin Chase's *Washington Bee* ("Watch the Sting") and E. E. Cooper's *Colored American,* are valuable as indices to social life, and refreshing because of occasional highly personal editorial exchanges between the proprietors. G.A.R. encampments provided excuses for lavish hospitality. Emancipation Day ceremonies were popular turnouts, until rivalries terminated them. Inaugural balls for Negroes, held on March 5, after the official ball, and other balls and banquets were numerous and prodigal. Churches and clubs had frequent excursions down the river. Political dignitaries at times had to yield to a visitor like Peter Jackson, heavyweight champion of Australia, or Isaac Murphy, noted Negro jockey of the eighties. Major Taylor, "the champion colored bicycle racer of the world," defended his title and defeated all comers at the Washington Coliseum.

Musicals were popular. A Negro opera company founded in 1872 gave several performances at Ford's Treater. Williams and Walker, and Cole and Johnson, "in the brightest ebony offering, *A Trip to Coontown,*" were viewed by Washington Negroes. Sissieretta Jones, "Black Patti," sang in 1892 for President Harrison's White House reception. The biggest musical event in years was the first all-Negro oratorio, *Emanuel,* directed by J. Henry Lewis. The Fisk Jubilee Singers and other choruses sang frequently in Washington.

The first decade of the twentieth century was marked by a consolidation of some gains, and a loss of others. Negro leaders, attracted by the period's visions of reform, turned more hopefully to the "race problem." There was a conference, in 1903, on "How to Solve the Race Problem." Militant members of the conference, dissatisfied with commissions and committees, joined forces with liberal groups and in 1910, in New York City, organized the National Association for the Advancement of Colored People.

Washington's First Separate Battalion, the Negro National Guard unit, was brigaded overseas during the World War with the "Red Hand" Division of the French Army. Of nearly 600 Washington Negroes in the outfit, more than 200 were wounded and 33 killed. A score of Washington Negroes received the *Croix de Guerre.* More than 5,000 Negroes from the District came into service through the operation of the selective draft. World War veterans were later organized in two American Legion posts.

A race riot took place in Washington in 1919. Headlines announced a wave of assaults on white women by Negroes. White soldiers, sailors, and marines beat up several innocent Negroes. Colored people retaliated by beating up several innocent whites. Street fighting was fierce, if sporadic. Regular troops, and a rainstorm, helped authorities to disperse the mobs. A year later, a Negro charged with murder confessed to the attacks for which two Negroes were serving sentences.

An extensive migration from the South, accelerated in the years of the war because of lowered quotas for European immigrants, and by the demand for industrial labor in the North, stranded many Negroes in Washington. Other cities were prepared for the mass invasion of industrial centers, but Washington, even though it was growing by leaps and bounds, had little work for the newcomers to do. There was an aggravation of the post-Civil War problems of housing, health, and employment.

Negroes of Washington (as shown by the 1940 census) total 27 per cent of the population. In July, 1940, 69 per cent of relief cases were Negro, almost in inverse ratio to the racial distribution of the population. Many of the unemployed live in the 170 alleys, occupied by 7,000 people. The Alley Dwelling Authority, with a program of providing new low-rental housing units and razing an equal number of alley dwelling units, was established in 1934, with a ten-year program to clear these slums. Employable Negroes make a living generally in domestic and personal service, and as unskilled laborers. A large number are in various Government departments, but only a few have a rating as clerks or foremen. About 4,900 are listed in the trades, and 3,400 in the professions. Prosperous Negroes live in all sections of the city, but Negro expansion into "white" areas is often sharply contested.

The health situation remains grave in crowded areas. Only one city in the United States has a higher death rate from tuberculosis than Washington; more than half of the tubercular cases in 1940 were Negroes. Infant mortality is high, and cases of social diseases and disintegrated home life are frequent. Negro patients are received in colored wards at most Washington hospitals, but some have private clinic service only. Freedmen's Hospital, administered by the Federal Security Agency, is the Negro general hospital, and there are private hospitals conducted by leading surgeons of the race. In comparison with the rest of the country, Washington has a heavy concentration of Negro medical practitioners.

Areas found to be dense in disease are classed in police reports as dense in crime. The "numbers" game is popular in the alleys, as it is on the avenues. Money that dribbles away to the numbers "baron" could well be spent for bread, milk, and shoes, but these poor people look upon the number slip as a sesame to monetary affluence.

Social agencies include two active branches of country-wide organizations—the National Association for the Advancement of Colored People (usually abbreviated to NAACP), and the National Urban League, organized here as the Washington Urban League in 1939. The NAACP, staffed entirely by Negroes, acts in a broad field to discourage discrimination and to advance the status of the Negro. The Urban League, having a half-white and half-Negro board of directors, seeks to integrate Negroes into the work-life of the community. Shortly after its inception in Washington, the league was instrumental in having a Negro-staffed telegraph office installed in the U Street business community. It, too, works on a broad social-economic front for better racial understanding and better economic opportunities for Negroes. The 12th Street YMCA, erected in 1912 in Hell's Bottom, supports boys' clubs and summer camps. The Phyllis Wheatley YWCA, founded in 1905, aims at similar community service for women and girls, with Camp Clarissa Scott operating in summer months. Community centers, playgrounds, and settlement houses have programs of a wide variety. Athletic activities are popular. Howard University and Miner Teachers College have heavy schedules in football, basketball, and track with many Negro collegiate teams.

Baptists are the most numerous churchgoers in Washington; second to them are the Methodists, divided into several branches. There are several other denominations, and many independent churches. Storefront churches attract attention with crudely lettered signs, their unconscious humor modified by their patent sincerity. In one backward section a little church given over to noisy "rousements" and "gravy-giving" sermons is neighbor to a chapel of quiet, dignified services, pastored by a devoted and scholarly man who has left a deep impress upon the community.

Of nearly $12,765,000 appropriated (1940-41) for public schools in the District of Columbia, more than one-third was devoted to Negro schools. Educational facilities for Negroes include 3 senior high schools, 4 vocational schools, 7 junior high schools, and 37 elementary schools, with 1,083 teachers and 36,340 students. The teachers are unusually well prepared, and salaries are on the same scale as those of white teachers. Howard University is called by some "the capstone of Negro education." Miner Teachers College has received high rank from accrediting agencies. Frelinghuysen University gives college instruction to night-class students. The National Training School for

Women and Girls is known as the school of the three B's: the Bible, the Bath, and the Broom. The *Journal of Negro Education* is edited at Howard University, and the *Journal of Negro History* is published in Washington. The weekly *Afro-American,* with a Washington edition, and the semiweekly *Washington Tribune* are the city's Negro newspapers.

In 1903 the British Negro composer, Samuel Coleridge-Taylor, sponsored by a society named for him, conducted in Washington the first American performance of his *Hiawatha* trilogy. The Washington Conservatory, under the direction of Mrs. Harriet Gibbs Marshall, was an important factor in musical education. Roland Hayes sang in Washington churches during his long struggle for recognition. Lillian Evans Tibbs, later known in opera as Madame Evanti, was one of Washington's well-known soloists. The Howard University Glee Club is nationally popular, under the direction of Roy W. Tibbs and Todd Duncan. The latter carried the role of Porgy in Gershwin's opera, *Porgy and Bess.* Washington Negroes were not admitted to the all-Negro spectacle, *Green Pastures,* when it showed at the National Theater in 1933. When Marian Anderson, Negro contralto, was refused the use of Constitution Hall in 1939, Secretary of the Interior Harold L. Ickes arranged for her to sing an Easter program on the steps of the Lincoln Memorial (*see Music*). Miss Anderson also sang at the White House on several occasions. Edna Jones, another Philadelphia Negro woman, who sang at Mrs. Roosevelt's reception for the cabinet ladies in 1940, was hailed as a find comparable to Marian Anderson.

Washington's many Negro dances range from "house shouts" to "bals masques" of the Negro "400." Social clubs are legion, and Washington Negroes are great "joiners"; the largest orders are the Elks, Odd Fellows, Knights of Pythias, and Masons, but some with an ancient history like "Love and Charity" linger on. The movie houses attract great crowds of colored people. Three theaters are on U Street, the thoroughfare of Negro businesses and pleasure-seekers. Howard Theater, an institution offering movies and musical shows, attracts an audience of both races. Poolrooms, cabarets, beer gardens, and eating places do an apparently thriving business. Yet much of the gaiety represents only an escape from economic realities.

The Negro's story is not his alone. White humanitarians have protested his enslavement and abuse, and statesmen have worked for his integration into the American pattern. The contribution, however, has not been all in one direction. In his largely anonymous role as laborer, craftsman, domestic, and personal service worker, the Negro has contributed, and continues to contribute, very largely to the building, maintenance, and operation of the Nation's Capital. In the field of scholarship, a number of Howard University teachers and scientists have done work that transcended racial lines. Mordecai W. Johnson, first Negro president of Howard, is an eminent educator. Kelly Miller, who died at an advanced age in 1940, was widely known in the fields of sociology and education. Other Howard professors who have done significant work include Ernest E. Just, in the natural sciences; Ralph J. Bunche, Charles E. Burch, E. Franklin Frazier, Abram L. Harris, Alain Locke, Rayford Logan, Charles H. Thompson, and Charles S. Wesley, in the humanities and social sciences.

Contemporary Negro writers who have produced book-length works are not numerous but their literary productions in some cases have been acclaimed by critics. Sterling A. Brown, Washington-born poet and critic, has been much quoted as a result of his *Southern Road,* a volume of poetry published in 1932; he was awarded a Guggenheim fellowship six years later. Georgia Douglass Johnson is known for her poetry, and Alain Locke for his writings on art and music; Locke edited a collection, *The New Negro,* published in 1925, and *The Negro in Art,* issued in 1941. Jean Toomer is best known for his *Cane,* a volume of poems and short stories.

The L'Enfant and Later Plans

MAJOR PIERRE CHARLES L'ENFANT'S plan for Washington is justly considered America's most notable achievement in municipal planning. There is a continuing contemporary legend that it has been revived and reapplied in the development of Washington since the beginning of the twentieth century. Actually, the passage of time, the influence of the Chicago Exposition of 1893, the growth of Government, and the advent of the machine age have modified L'Enfant's concept to a larger extent that it has been followed.

The site chosen for the city lay within the Y formed by the junction of the Potomac River with the Eastern Branch (Anacostia River). As a point of connection between seagoing craft and inland canal and highway routes, the site had a certain geographical logic, though it was chosen in a political deal (*see History*). A relatively flat, gently undulating tract of land rose gradually from these rivers to a range of encircling hills. In area it covered about 10 square miles, or approximately one-tenth of the District area. The eastern part of this tract was marked by a plateau 80 feet above the river, with a knoll at its western end known as Jenkins Hill—the site of the Capitol. Goose Creek, also called Tiber, flowed along the base of this knoll, turning sharply westward through a marshy woodland. This practically uninhabited woodland area was the geographic base upon which L'Enfant was to apply his "grand plan."

More astonishment is shown in the twentieth century about L'Enfant's plan than in his own day. Laying out cities was no novelty in Colonial and pioneer America, and the cultural background for such work (mostly based on centuries of European experience) was well known to George Washington, Thomas Jefferson, and others of L'Enfant's contemporaries. L'Enfant himself was not ill-prepared by background for the task. He was the son of an applied artist and tapestry maker in Paris, and he was an able artist and draftsman. He fought in the Revolution, where he received his military title. He drew pencil portraits of officers at Valley Forge, designed a medal for the Society of the Cincinnati, arranged a patriotic pageant in New York City, rebuilt the old city hall there, and had some repute as an engineer, according to the easy standards of his day.

First and foremost, however, L'Enfant considered himself an artist, and he put a high monetary valuation on his services—so high that his refusal to accept modest remuneration eventually reduced him to penury. As to city design in general, L'Enfant was acquainted with the plans for such American cities as Annapolis, Savannah, Williamsburg, Philadelphia, and New York. Jefferson sent him the plans of a dozen European cities. His plan for the Capital City was a work of art according to the recognized style of his period. As adapted to the site, it was unique.

The gridiron pattern of L'Enfant's streets was a design favored in frontier America, where it stood as a geometric proof that the tough, ominous, round-edged wilderness had been subdued. L'Enfant's, nonetheless, is no stiff grid with uniformly sized city-block meshes. Rather, it is a rhythmic pattern, the work of an artist, in which the size of the blocks varies in relation to the main and median axes of the plan. Clearly, L'Enfant had in mind some kind of city zoning that would capitalize on the "Grand Squares" for public purposes, while the smaller blocks were apparently intended for residential use. His basic gridiron pattern remains today, accounting for the "long" and "short" blocks in Washington.

"Lines or Avenues, of direct communication . . . devised to connect the separate and most distant objects with the principal, and to preserve through the whole a reciprocity of sight" account for Washington's present-day diagonal avenues. Widespread planting of trees in later years, however, has destroyed much of the "reciprocity of sight" so highly prized by the planner. Some students of L'Enfant are convinced that the designer of Washington's layout acquired this principle of imposing diagonals on a chessboard directly from Evelyn's plan for London. At the point where these "divergent Avenues" connected with north-south and east-west streets, L'Enfant placed "the different Squares or Areas . . . proportional in Magnitude to the number of Avenues leading to them."

In making use of the Renaissance *patte d'oie* (or goose's foot), whereby three streets radiating from a single point would permit a simultaneous vista along all three, L'Enfant laid the groundwork for Washington's numerous "traffic circles," which have been roundly berated by many a driver since the advent of the automobile. Such "reciprocity of sight" had been useful to ancient planners laying out hunting preserves for noblemen, by which the furtive darting of poachers might be thrice more readily seen, and to militarists planning cities for uneasy royalty, whereby cannon placed in squares or circles "most advantageously and reciprocally seen from each other" could command thoroughfares in several directions. To L'Enfant this type of layout was a matter of wide vistas, and perhaps more than a little nostalgia for Versailles. To those of the internal combustion engine era there re-

mained nothing to do but burrow under them, as the city has done
(1940) at Thomas Circle and (1941) at Scott Circle. Happily for
the repose of L'Enfant's artistic soul, this development came more
than a century after his death, for there is very little "reciprocity of
sight" from a tunnel.

L'Enfant's basic plan for placing the "Congress House," the
"President's palace," and "the equestrian figure of George Washington" was triangular. For this scheme he apparently owed much to
the Trianon in Versailles, the scale of the Washington group running
almost exactly a third more than the scale of the Trianon. "The
positions for the different Grand Edifices," L'Enfant explains, "were
first determined on the most advantageous ground commanding the
most extensive prospects." More subtly, and more artistically, he
planned a pleasing optical triangulation whereby the eye, perceiving the
placement of each major unit, would apprehend the disposition of the
whole. The present Pennsylvania Avenue would provide the vista
between the Capitol and the President's House, the open "President's
park" would allow for a view of the Washington statue "voted in
1783 by the late Continental Congress." The present obelisk was
later erected instead of the equestrian figure, and a portion of the Treasury Building was allowed to cut off the vision between the White
House and Capitol, but otherwise this segment of the L'Enfant layout
exists much as he planned it. Where the Mall is now, L'Enfant
originally laid down a "Grand Avenue, 400 feet in breadth, and about
a mile in length, bordered with gardens, ending in a slope from the
houses on each side." To him this concourse was to be traveled on,
homes would line its edges (including "spacious houses and gardens,
such as may accommodate foreign ministers, etc."), and people would
look out pleasantly across the public gardens.

Issuing from the hill west of the Capitol, L'Enfant planned a
"Grand Cascade, formed of the water from the sources of the Tiber."
On each side of this grandiose fountain, public gardens would provide
a way for carriages and people to pass from the upper to the lower
levels of Capitol Hill. Around the square east of the Capitol, and
along East Capitol Street, L'Enfant postulated a wide avenue, and
"the pavement on each side will pass under an Arched way, under
whose cover, Shops will be most conveniently and agreeably situated."
This portion of the L'Enfant blueprint is an expression of the easy democracy of the French, who feel no sense of *lèse majesté* while haggling
for carrots in the shadow of a cathedral or Government edifice. The
east plaza has since been planted to grass and trees, which as one architect remarks "has been a jolly thing for the squirrels." The monumental Library of Congress has risen across one diagonal leading out
from L'Enfant's plaza, the even more monumental Supreme Court

Building has gone up, asymmetrically from the planner's point of view, alongside another. Practically none of his plan for this part of town has been realized. In the present Lincoln Square he would have erected "An historic Column, also intended for a Mile or itinerary Column, from whose station . . . all distances of places through the Continent are to be calculated." The nearest approach to this idea is the Zero Milestone, placed much later in the Ellipse, south of the White House. Continuing eastward, L'Enfant's East Capitol "Avenue" would have led to a bridge crossing the Anacostia River. The three spans since erected across this affluent, the Anacostia Bridge at the foot of 11th Street SE., the bridge at the eastern end of Pennsylvania Avenue, and the bridge on Benning Road, have carefully avoided the site indicated by the Capital's first planner. Early development of the eastern "grand approach" to Washington and the Capitol is said to have been effectively halted by excessive prices put on real estate, but this may have been only one of the factors involved.

L'Enfant intended the Supreme Court Building to stand in the present Judiciary Square, at present 4th Street, one of the important cross-axes of his plan. Generously sized "Grand Squares" at this median axis still survive. Eighth Street was a median cross axis, having a grand place in the L'Enfant scheme. At the site of the Civil Service Building (Old Patent Office), L'Enfant proposed a nonsectarian "Church intended for national purposes, such as public prayer, thanksgivings, funeral Orations, &c."—a sort of Westminster Abbey as "likewise a proper shelter for such monuments as were voted by the late Continental Congress, for those heroes who fell in the cause for liberty." South of it, in the present Market Space along Pennsylvania Avenue, was to be a fountain, and, where the Archives Building stands, a public market in connection with the Tiber Creek canal. The vista, now blotted out by the Archives Building, the Federal Warehouse, and the Thomas Jefferson Memorial Junior High School, was to extend to the Potomac water front, where L'Enfant proposed to erect "A Naval itinerary Column . . . to celebrate the first rise of a Navy, and . . . to consecrate its progress and Achievements." Twelfth Street south of the present Mall was plotted as a great avenue 250 feet wide, tapering to 200 feet at the Potomac shore. L'Enfant must have climbed a tree before he planned this wide thoroughfare, otherwise he could scarcely have known that there was a straight stretch of the Potomac reaching due south for 12 miles. Here was a vista to rival the best at Versailles, given a greater effect of depth by the tapering sides of the avenue. This view, with many another L'Enfant planned, has been lost, and Hains Point has been dredged up to fill in the foreground.

Then, there was the canal. The planner and his contemporaries in no way foresaw that Government would become an industry of sufficient size to support a city. Georgetown and Alexandria were already seaports of some importance, and they visualized Washington as a busy maritime port, tapping the hinterland by means of canal connections, which were to extend to the Ohio River. Far from creating a sacrosanct monumentality to house the Government, L'Enfant found a certain fitness in carrying his utilitarian canal through the heart of the city. His "Canal through Tiber Creek" was plotted to follow the approximate line of present-day Constitution Avenue, on the north side of the present Mall. It widened into a sort of lagoon south of the "President's park," creating a lovely place for water pageants, a form of show with which L'Enfant was acquainted. Wharves were plotted in a widening of the canal at 12th Street, to allow for the development of a small market, and more ambitious wharves were planned at the projected 8th Street market. (Here again, on the canal, L'Enfant laid down the rhythm of his cross-axes, at 16th, 12th, and 8th Streets.) The canal was to cross the present Mall area at the foot of Capitol Hill, then to continue southerly along the course of present Canal Street to the Anacostia River east of the present Army War College, where L'Enfant apparently had in mind a transshipping center and a busy market. Another branch of the canal was projected to extend to the Anacostia west of the present Navy Yard. The canal was dug, and developed to a certain extent. Jefferson sometimes shopped at a market along the waterway, and old photographs of 1860 show its stone-lined banks. The old Lock Keeper's House at 17th Street and Constitution Avenue NW., and the name of Canal Street are all that remain of L'Enfant's canal. Never, presumably, did it attain to the gentle utility and decorativeness L'Enfant planned for it.

"This mode of . . . improving the whole district," said L'Enfant, "must leave to posterity a grand idea of the patriotic interest which promoted it." In these lines he wrote a justification for his plan, which has certainly given Washington a spaciousness characteristic of the Renaissance, and, read in these latter years, a pathetic sort of obituary for those parts of it that have been lost. A stormy and impetuous young man (he was 37 when he designed the city), L'Enfant lived to see his plan considerably altered and all but forgotten. While he was in Philadelphia, late in 1791, quarreling with Andrew Ellicott about the redraft for engravings, he received a query as to whether he would subordinate himself to the commissioners in carrying out the details of his plan. He replied that he would not, and was discharged the following February. At George Washington's suggestion he was offered $2,500 for the job, but he refused disdainfully. In subsequent years L'Enfant endlessly petitioned Congress for the payment of nearly $100,000, what he thought his artistic services were worth. Congress eventually gave him about $3,000. He died in 1825, in the home of a friend near Washington.

During the ensuing years the most pertinent departure from L'Enfant's concept was the development of the city westward, rather than eastward, from the Capitol. High prices for real estate to the east may have hastened this trend, but "miasmas" rising from the canalized Tiber Creek probably contributed. The railroads came, trains steamed along the broad avenues, and there was an unsightly station on the present Mall. This central park area received its present name early in the 1850's, when it was laid out as a promenade in the English landscape style. Thereafter, Washington "just grew" until the Chicago Exposition of 1893.

The Exposition's "Court of Honor," surrounded by buildings of an even height and containing statuary and fountains, had much to do with what happened next to Washington. The Capital City celebrated its first centennial in 1900, and the American Institute of Architects held a symposium on the esthetic condition of the city. There was a crying need for a new railroad terminal, and prevailing prosperity encouraged the assumption that something ought to be done about the Nation's Capital. Senator James McMillan of Michigan, chairman of the Senate District Committee, in 1901 sponsored a resolution authorizing the employment of a committee of experts to make "plans for the development and improvement of the park system of the District of Columbia." Those appointed to the committee were Daniel H. Burnham and Charles F. McKim, architects; Frederick Law Olmsted, Jr., landscape architect; and Augustus Saint-Gaudens, sculptor. Their report, published in 1902, did not confine itself to parks, but presented a plan for the development of the whole Mall area. It purported to "restore the original plan and to adapt the principles of its design to new and enlarged conditions," but more largely it redefined L'Enfant's Renaissance plan in the light of the Beaux Arts tradition.

The Washington Monument, for the sake of a better foundation, had been placed on a knoll some 300 feet southeast of the intersection L'Enfant had figured for the Capitol-Monument and White House-Monument axes. The McMillan Commission shifted to the new axis and extended the Capitol-Monument line due west to the proposed site of the Lincoln Memorial. It then extended the north-south axis from the White House through a proposed Monument garden to the site of a recreation center they planned on the site of the present Jefferson Memorial. It placed the Union Station on a diagonal from the Capitol, and proceeded to lay out the currently popular "Court of Honor" around the Mall. Federal buildings were to surround the Capitol area on three sides, north, east, and south. A solid phalanx of Federal buildings was to rise on each side of the Mall, and most of the present Federal Triangle was to be filled with buildings. Others were to rise around Lafayette Square and hem it in. The Commission proposed the Arlington Memorial Bridge in a line with the Arlington mansion south of the Potomac, construction of a parkway connecting Potomac and Rock Creek Parks, a memorial highway between Washington and Mount Vernon, reclamation of the Anacostia Flats and their transformation into a public park, and other developments, many of which have been since accomplished.

At the time of its publication there was considerable opposition to the McMillan Commission's report. Gradually, however, it found such favor in influential quarters that "piece by piece, without being adopted as a whole, its main elements were fixed." The reputation of its authors had more than a little bearing on general acceptance of the plan. One modification was an added concentration of departmental buildings in the Federal Triangle, following the intrusion of several private and semipublic buildings around Lafayette Square and the natural reluctance to remove such historic landmarks as St. John's Church and the Decatur House.

The success of the McMillan Commission stimulated Congress to set up other commissions and planning bodies in later years. The Fine Arts Commission was established in 1910, the Public Buildings Commission and Board of Architectural Consultants in 1919, the Zoning Commission in 1920, and the National Capital Park and Planning Commission in 1924. The constantly amended plan for Washington has been built up by these various bodies, often with the "advice" and "assistance" of non-official pressure groups, such as chambers of commerce, merchants' and manufacturers' associations, citizens' associations, and traffic councils.

In 1929 a proposal was made to develop East Capitol Street as an Avenue of States, more or less along the line of L'Enfant's proposal for development of the eastern part of the city. The East Capitol Street development terminates in Anacostia Park, where the construction of a sports center is (1942) well under way, including a National Guard armory, a stadium, and an athletic field. Several monumental buildings have gone up south of the Mall. A Federal Rectangle is being constructed west of 17th Street and north of Constitution Avenue, including the two Interior Department buildings, the War Department Building, and others. Additional plans call for extensive development of park areas in and adjacent to the District, extension of Rock Creek and Anacostia Parks into Maryland, park improvements along Sligo and Cabin John Creeks, maintenance of a riverside parkway with a rejuvenated Chesapeake & Ohio canal between Georgetown and Great

Falls, and construction of a Fort Drive to encircle the city and connect many outlying Civil War forts.

Opinion of the Washington city plan, especially that part of it growing out of the Chicago Fair "Court of Honor," has been by no means unanimously favorable. City planners and architects have said that the Federal Triangle concentration, and others surrounding the Mall, have created an unholy traffic situation without attempting to apply a remedy, that the departments have been grouped in the lowest and hottest part of the city, that employees must for the most part cross the congested business district to reach them, that the tendency is to create sacrosanct department areas instead of building the Government into the life of the city, that the monumental edifices are actually office buildings and purport to be what they are not, that monumentality has been carried beyond the point of diminishing return, that it would be better to build decentralized departmental buildings and encourage the development of villages around them for departmental employees, that it would be better to build places to work in the surrounding hills than places to play, and so on.

Yet, even the most acrimonious critics of Washington planning, those most nostalgic for the canal and for the lost vistas of L'Enfant, find it hard to sustain their anger to the end. The magnificent Mall and the view of the Capitol from Pennsylvania Avenue would never have existed except for the breadth of L'Enfant's vision, and certainly no American city can offer a more just relationship between the flow of space and the scenic impact of Washington's principal monuments. The generally spacious character of the Capital City unquestionably goes back to L'Enfant and his plan. If most of L'Enfant's "goosefoot" vistas and his long perspective down the Potomac River have been lost, many of them have been blotted out by trees, which have a cool green virtue of their own. L'Enfant's successors have provided a panorama of Washington from the Mount Vernon Memorial Boulevard that is one of the finest general views of a city in the Nation. Then, too, there is always the possibility that if L'Enfant's plan had survived entire, there would be hundreds of critics to pick it to pieces —architecture and city plans lend themselves to disagreement and debate. L'Enfant, for instance, would probably have built the White House with a dome. As it is, the first planner and his successors have contributed greatly to the city, which takes a creditable place among the capitals of the world.

Architecture

By Elbert Peets

T HIS chapter has to do with the buildings of the city, primarily as visible things—their appearance and how they came to be given the external form they have. This chapter is written to help you enjoy Washington, to guide you toward high adventure of the spirit as you ride and walk through the Capital City of these States. Or, if at such times your spirit be not set a-singing, this chapter wants you at least to have the experience of viewing curious things, of accounting for them in some degree, and of comprehending their place in the flow of architectural form.

To keep the buildings of Washington from impinging upon the mind as a chaos of unrelated phenomena is not easy. Because, although Washington has a certain totality of expression, very few buildings contribute much to the peculiar feel of the city. The soul of Washington is in its plan, its streets and squares and radiating avenues. Without this mastering plan the buildings, in the first view, would be a bedlam. But beyond the conspicuous variety of the first impression lies a mass of substantial uniformity—the red-brick row houses that form the city's great pool of human habitation. This is not true of the shopping-and-theater blocks along F Street nor of lower Connecticut Avenue—in smart streets such as these everything is yellow brick, stucco, enamel, glass, and gray stone. And everywhere through the city there are a few houses of stone and many brick houses painted buff, white or gray. Whole suburbs are built of single houses. But a sampling of the city, at random, including all its four sections, will prove that it is a city of row houses, and that a warm dark red is its basic color.

There is good clay in the region, rich in the iron that makes bricks red. And the row house is the ancient English folkway of urban residence. To a visitor from Detroit or Los Angeles, talk of brick houses will arouse expectations of quaintness and Colonial charm. As a general picture, these hopes will be disappointed. Washington was born in the fine afternoon of the Georgian style, but it was born poor; most of the lovely houses of "circa 1800" were built in such truly Colonial towns as Charleston, Philadelphia, and Salem. Yet here and there, throughout the older regions of the city, there are veterans that

have the unmistakable distinction of Georgian building.   Many are fat
bourgeois houses with big chimneys, honest pitched roofs, and well-
proportioned windows of small panes.   A few are really distinguished
town houses, worthy of Savannah or New Castle.   The yellow-and-
white Blair House near Lafayette Square is one of the best.   Another,
on Eye Street near 20th, is now the home of the Arts Club.   This
about the paucity of Colonial architecture in Washington obviously
does not apply to Georgetown, where one can stroll for an hour without
leaving the eighteenth century.   The feel of the Georgetown streets
is quite unlike Washington.   The Post Office Department draws no
line between the two communities, but to the town planner they are
wholly apart.   Poetically speaking, Washington is like an oak in its
prime that stands beside a beautiful old dogwood, always in flower.

In the Capital's third or fourth decade new forms crept in.   The
swing from Georgian began with taller windows, jamb mouldings
carried around arched openings without a break at the impost, orna-
mentations suggesting foliage forms—all details shifting slightly toward
medieval motifs, perhaps a good deal affected by baroque.   In much
the same way the latest Gothic buildings shifted toward grotesque
classic details.   Cornices increased in projection, modillions developing
into brackets enriched with details that exhibited the powers of the
new woodworking machinery.   Some of these first frontier fruits of
styles already sophisticated in London and New York have much charm
of pattern, like a perfectly designed sampler or title page.

Contemporary with this softening of the Georgian was another
movement, almost contrary in spirit.   This was the Greek Revival, of
which not many strongly marked creations survive in the residential
architecture of Washington.   The first considerable growth of the city
was at the time of the Civil War and it fell within an architectural
era more influenced by pressed brick than by any of the historical styles.
The invention of pressed brick (always deplored by persons of a nostalgic cast) changed quite radically the face of Washington's houses.
It came at a moment when, simultaneously, the nineteenth century
group-soul yearned for good mechanical finish, for fancy workmanship,
and for a flavor of medieval picturesqueness.   Pressed brick made all
of these things possible.   They could be laid with narrow joints, forming a neat smooth wall; their uniform size and sharp edges made possible all sorts of picturesque patterns—picturesqueness was thought to be
essence of medieval art—that would have been lost in the crude approxi-
mations of the old handmade bricks.   The skilled bricklayers of Washington took full advantage of the qualities of the new material.   They
built a prodigious quantity and variety of bay windows, corner towers,
dormers, parapets, corbelled cornices, porches, entrance arches, window

enframements, string courses, mouldings, ornamental panels, and many things for which orderly architecture has no recognized designation.

Externally, the conspicuous thing about these nineteenth-century row houses is their bay windows. For this, there is a particular reason. Washington streets are wide and the city-owned right of way goes right up to the front wall of the buildings. The sidewalk is from 5 to 30 feet away from the house. The front yard, therefore, although normally used as if it were private property, is part of the street. The city permits lot owners to erect porches projecting 5 feet and bay windows projecting 4 feet beyond the property line. A great majority of the older houses accordingly have projecting bays extending from the ground to the roof, or beyond it. A few of these are half-round, like the Bulfinch bow windows of Boston; most are square or half-octagonal. They catch sunlight and afford long views along the street, but they rob Washington of the reposeful street-walls that are so pleasant in many row-house towns.

During the 1870's and 1880's, square miles of these brick row houses were put up by speculative builders. Most of them are three stories, plus a high basement. Very often there is a service entrance under the porch or iron steps. The kitchen is often in the basement with dumb-waiter service to a butler's pantry. Or the kitchen is on the main floor, in an ell. The stairs are against a side wall. There is often an alcove (above the entrance hall) in connection with the front bedroom. The bathroom is often attenuated in plan. There is rarely need for a second stairway because Washington maids usually go home in the evening.

These streets of quaint-to-ugly—but fairly comfortable—row houses form the bulk of the city's shelter. They should not be high-hatted by wandering citizens of western towns in which everyone lives in a white-painted vine-covered cottage. No wood houses and landscaped lawns could give 60 years of use at moderate rentals and come through looking as neat and decent as most of the Washington row houses do.

The expression row house does not necessarily imply identity in the row. It is applied also to contiguous houses built separately, as the finest row houses in Washington were built. Until about 1920 quite expensive residences of the row-house type were still being erected, such as the house Secretary McAdoo built on 16th Street just above Scott Circle. On Massachusetts and New Hampshire Avenues and on all the streets around Dupont Circle are other specimens of the genre worth coming upon. The best of these houses are not invariably the latest to be built nor the most expensive. Scattered through the city there are row houses of all periods—most often dating from the eighties and nineties—that are sincere and sympathetic architecture. Perhaps some of them were influenced by the houses Richardson built for Hay and Adams on Lafayette Square and by LaFarge's scholarly brickwork in St. Matthew's Church and its parish house. Some of them embody delightfully both the dignity and the geniality of comfortable living. Many are by unknown masters, in styles long left behind. But these houses, along with the happy blunders and strange antics of less thoughtful designers, give to the old and middle-aged streets of Washington a fascination that few cities can equal.

It is fortunate for Washington that the mass of its residential construction has been done in permanent materials and that most of its workers are of the white-collar class—and, further, that so many of them are single and that so many want to live within walking distance of their work. These circumstances, shielded by an intelligently enforced zoning law, have preserved the prosperity of large sections which, in Cleveland or Chicago, would have degenerated into slums or blighted areas. It is quite possible, in Washington, for a street to change in type of occupancy without conspicuous evidence of physical and aesthetic decay. In most cities the aesthetic decay of a street begins with an invasion of boarding houses. In Washington the boarding houses do not necessarily have that result. Government clerks must live economically but are used to living moderately well. The big-but-homelike boarding house is for such as these a happy compromise. They may occupy, with a friend or two, a bedroom designed by a fashionable architect (in 1904) to meet the tastes of the wife of a millionaire Senator. They listen to the radio in the senator's parlor and dine comfortably in his basement billiard-room. By cutting a few doors through party walls, this profitable co-operation can spread into two or three adjacent houses. And the only outward sign of the changed occupancy is a brass plate letting you know that this is the Wyoming Club.

In recent years the new residences in what might be called the upper brackets have been built as free-standing houses, though rather closely grouped. In the Kalorama district, for example, and in other neighborhoods lying northerly and westerly of the city, there are hundreds of sumptuous homes. And in other suburbs, as in Chevy Chase and Takoma Park, there are even larger areas of free-standing houses occupied by people of moderate means. Around the outer fringe there are now the usual clusters of ducky little FHA love-nests with red or blue shutters tacked up beside the windows. Yet the brick row house has not been abandoned. There are broad areas of new brick rows near the city—notably around the outlying section of New Hampshire Avenue. Most of them have become "group houses"—each unit in the row is tricked out with a half-timber gable end or a patch of stone to give it "individuality."

Then there are the apartments. Relatively few in number until the "other war," they began to grow like popcorn when the New Deal came to town. Some of them are of a magnitude and completeness that make them impressive machines for that way of living. Take West-chester Apartments, for example. And more recently the outlying apartment groups—as Falkland, at the end of the 16th Street, Colonial Village and Buckingham across the Potomac in Arlington—have developed a new manner of suburban living in which the ameni-ties of space and pleasant environment compensate for relative remote-ness from urban bright lights. The formula, one sees, is based on car ownership and cheap land.

In these apartment groups a sophisticated Rip van Winkle, just awakening, would note something passing strange. The side and rear walls of these buildings are made of the same brick as the front! Since the Civil War it has been the American custom to build apartments on the Queen-Anne-Mary Ann principle—yellow-brick front and red-brick for the rest, or vice versa in towns where red brick costs more than yellow. The decay of that custom is a major architectural phe-nomenon. To explain this change some observers say it was pioneered by Government housing projects. These, since they must be built of the cheapest permanent material, are built, all four sides, of one thing, usually a hard common brick. Perhaps the current fashion in windows also has some bearing on the phenomenon; you really have to design in three dimensions if you use corner windows. Which reminds one that the city has lately been peppered with smart and likable apart-ment house creations in yellow brick with corner windows and glass doors. This is the chic of 1942. Which is true, doubtless, of every other city in the country.

Washington is not like other cities, however, in respect to two sorts of buildings, the headquarters of national organizations and the em-bassies of foreign countries. In each of these classifications a numerical majority occupy quarters built originally as sumptuous private resi-dences. In recent decades, however, many countries have erected embassy buildings—those of Great Britain and Japan are pointed out to every tourist. In material and style the proud-yet-gracious British group is perhaps a reminder that the word "ours" at one time did not dissociate English ways from American. The fascinating little home of the Venezuelan delegation is a tactful reminder that our South American neighbors know as much as we do about what goes on in the world of shelter-construction.

The commercial buildings of a city traverse in their evolution the same cultural valleys that the road of residential construction passes through. But the ways in which they are alike are often hard to see. And, as time passes, the bifurcation widens. The early shops and offices of Washington have not survived well—nothing like as well as they have in Frederick and Annapolis. There have been such constant remodelings and rebuildings here, and whole regions of old commercial buildings—such as the site of the Triangle—have been razed. There is no building in Washington to match the old Iron Block in Milwaukee. Indeed there is probably not in the city a good specimen of the castiron store fronts that Bogardus of New York sold by the yard in the 1870's. Of the beetling rococo pediments that flourished in those days only a few gallant examples still exist.

The passing of these old store fronts is a loss to American street architecture. The modern stores, all trying to be unlike their neighbors, each purposely singing in a different key, are inimical to all civility and community expression. At least so it seems when the transvaluation begins. A fashionable retail street, after the stores have built up their own smart society, has its fetching qualities. As examples: three or four blocks in the vicinity of F Street and 14th, various uptown shopping centers, and scattered gatherings of chic modern shops.

Washington's office buildings are not high; none of them would rate as skyscrapers in New York or Chicago. They tend, rather, to have great bulk. That is conspicuously true of the Federal Loan Building (1940), one in which simple bulk is given dramatic value. It is utterly plain, the surest way to attain distinction in an environment somewhat overrich in architectural insistency. There is a fine view down 15th Street (from the east sidewalk, well up toward Massachusetts Avenue) in which this geometric mass composes with the Washington Monument. The building seems, in this view, quite contemporary in form-feeling with the Monument.

The Longfellow Building (1941), Connecticut and Rhode Island Avenues, is so modern that it has a horizontal flagpole. It is also noteworthy as the first radically modern office of a Government agency. Its design is clearly iconoclastic; the building might be thought of as a favorable portent if the location were favorable from any point of view but its advertising value. It is at a busy and noisy corner; land in the vicinity is too expensive to clear for car parking. Incidentally, the concentrated bulk of the building makes it what should be technically known as a bomber's delight.

Half this chapter has been written and hardly a word has been said about marble and granite and limestone, about domes and columns and porticos. Surely it is time, in Shakespeare's Shakespearean phrase, for us to feed our eyes upon the monuments and things of fame that do renown this city! It seems to be a tenet of American opinion—at least of Washington official opinion—that all governmental buildings should be monumental and, further, that monumental means built of stone. That is not at all logical but it does give a shade of sense to the statement that in Washington brick is the building material of the people and stone the building material of the Government. In any case, the history of Government building in Washington has paralleled pretty closely the evolution of stone architecture through the same years.

Architecture is as international as music. The story of Government building through the century and a half from Dr. Thornton's Capitol to the latest defense office building, has continuity and reason only when it is correlated with the flow of architecture in the world outside Washington. Buildings are preceded (and followed!) by thinking. Colonial thinking about architecture was based on European ideas— with a certain lag in time. Palladio and Vignola, in 1791, were a little old-fashioned in several European capitals, but they still ruled architectural thought in the young United States. In detailing the general style of the Capitol, Thornton and the rest had the good sense to play safe. What is astounding about it, even as it was first built, is the Capitol's great size. That was not merely a good guess that the country would grow in population. It was part of the architectural thought of such men as Jefferson to do things on a large, open, and dignified scale. They lived in the Renaissance tradition.

While the Capitol was being completed, new ferments were at work in the architectural world. The Greek Revival came; to it the new States of the west owe many buildings—among them the beautiful State Capitol of Ohio. In Washington, Elliott made the south portico of the old Patent Office a copy of the Parthenon front. In 1836 Robert Mills did the first section of the Treasury—the east side, with its 30 lovely Ionic columns. The next great work was the construction of the wings of the Capitol, carried through by Thomas Walter. Quite consciously he respected and followed the style of the old building, just as he respected Mills' work in his completion of the Treasury. Walter was quite aware of the new ways that were coming in. He saw the growing vogue of the Gothic Revival—in some of its forms an unwitting revival of baroque—of which the first nonecclesiastical work in this country, the old Smithsonian, was completed in 1856.

Thomas Walter saw also the development of a technical means of producing cheaply the foliage forms and medieval motifs for which people were asking. This was cast iron. It was also used in the manufacture of beams, columns, and plates for building construction. Cast iron made it possible to build a high dome over the Capitol. In designing it, Walter was not controlled by any existing work, as he had been in designing the wings, and he used, on the dome, a good deal of tactful ornamentation of the wreath and garland type. Walter knew how to weave in the new forms without offense to his Renaissance dome.

But our luck could not continue. By the 1870's the universal romantic taste had taken possession of the new building materials and the new machines for cutting wood and stone.   In the buildings that resulted there was often confusion between purpose and means, but there was at least restless experimentation—the dead hand of the past lay more lightly on the period than is supposed.   The old National Museum, built in 1879, was presumed to be Byzantine, but essentially it was a fairly efficient enclosure of space for the exhibition of a lot of things to a lot of people.

Thus always the streams of thought swirled around the beloved past and the exciting present.   A vigorous eddy was caused by the physical as well as creative bulk of H. H. Richardson.   His cousins of the spirit turned granite quarries into post offices—one of them stands alongside Pennsylvania Avenue.   The planners of the Triangle hatched a clever scheme to get this building torn down.   They laid out a circular plaza which cannot be completed while the Old Post Office stands.   But the plaza forms a rather pleasant setting for the huge old veteran, whose demolition does not seem imminent.

Another architectural current that caused important erosions along these shores was the French École des Beaux Arts.   It brought Washington the Library of Congress, begun in 1886.   Before it was completed, came the Chicago Fair.   The World's Fair of 1893 was Beaux-Arts too, but it had the advantage of being done by such men as Charles Follen McKim and the further advantage of being executed in plaster of Paris, a beautiful material.   Louis Sullivan said, "The damage wrought by the World's Fair will last for half a century from its date."   Adding 50 to 1893 gives 1943.   We are at the end of the prophesied period.   In Washington, at least, Sullivan has proved to be right.   With but few exceptions, every piece of official architecture built in this city during that period has had some of the Chicago plaster of Paris at its core, though over each has been laid a pretty veneer in some acceptable style.

The Commission of 1901, which laid down the lines on which modern Washington has developed, included in its membership the principal designers of the Chicago Fair.   Their tenets were these: (1) "Classical" style; (2) uniform cornice height; (3) concentration of buildings in the Triangle, along the Mall, and around the Capitol and White House.

The Senate and House Office buildings were the first result of the program.   They were handsome adaptations of Gabriel's Garde-Meuble on the Place de la Concorde.   The Lincoln Memorial and Cass Gilbert's Treasury Annex, first section of the intended frame around Lafayette Square, were started during the World War.   Then there was a pause; the Triangle plans were initiated about 1925.   By that time architects had learned and unlearned.   The San Francisco Fair had taught the beauty of enclosed courts.   More was known about the

French plaza designs of the eighteenth century. Charles Platt had designed skyscrapers that were Florentine palaces. The Federal Reserve Banks had explored new ways to give office buildings the appearance of being stone and not steel. And the Beaux-Arts clichés, as painfully illustrated by the now-disdained District Building, had definitely shifted to the shady side of the ledger. So, when the Triangle plans appeared, they were very different from the plans that would have been made two decades before. Of course there was no disloyalty to the three basic rules of 1901. No one questioned the importance of making the Triangle symbolize America by building beautiful Italian palaces for our file clerks. None of the first-flight architects questioned the architectural taste of the Secretary of the Treasury, nor did he question theirs. So the Triangle was built. It contains a pair of plazas in the French mode of 1760 (Contant d'Ivry made a somewhat similar plan for a proposed town hall in Paris) and the buildings are done in delicately modulated French and Italian palatial styles, the precise identification of each being a matter that could interest only a professor of architecture. One of them, to be sure, the Justice Building, is modern—in the sense of using a Greek style more primitive than the standard.

Though still pointed to with official pride, the Triangle has had in recent years a very poor press. The location is usually described as atrocious city planning and the common attitude toward the monumental office buildings is simply satirical. The cost, also monumental, is mentioned with chiding.

Perhaps the Triangle ought never to have been built, but there it is, and any pile of stones has within it certain fundamental verities which no stupidity of client or architect can quite take away. That melodramatic group of porticos on Constitution Avenue—how easily, on a foggy evening, can be imagined the incredulous joy of some long-future Hugo Robert, searching the ruined city for scenes to paint, when he should first come upon those ingratiating, vainglorious columns and cornices. . . . While its red-tile roofs were still being laid, the Triangle became a landmark, a thing of the past. Waddy Wood's South Interior Building was designed in an avowed mood of "No more Seicento, no more Louis Seize, no more enclosed light courts." So the style of the building is a stripped-down Patent Office or Treasury; the few columns are purified by being square and lacking entasis.

The new burst of office construction has still further high-lighted the Triangle as the-thing-to-do-it-different-from. The new buildings south of the Mall, around 4th Street SW., are about as modern as they could be without being Modern. Since the Renaissance tradition of wall-membering is easily adapted to long vertical openings but not to horizontal ones, simplicity in the glass area has been attained by

carrying vertical windows through three or four stories. A large simplicity of scale results; whether that is a good thing is less a matter of
architecture than of town planning.

The War Department Building (1941) is still a little farther post-
Triangle. It disclaims any controlling cornice-height. It is not a
composition carried out upon flat facades but a masculine composition
of great masses mortised together. This building truly looks like a
war department; if its functions were something like the Battle Abbey
in Richmond—if it contained the sacred things of the Department, the
maps, rosters, and records of wars, old weapons, stands of frayed battle
flags; if it had a distinguished place in the street plan of the city; if,
further, the clerks and typewriters and desks and ash trays were housed
somewhere else in well-oriented offices—this would be a first-rate
building.

As every new building has been planned and built it has become
more and more clear that the town planning factors are becoming
absolutely crucial to the success of new buildings in Washington. There
are already so many huge buildings around the Mall, with many more
sites not yet filled, that each new construction finds itself with numerous inevitable relationships—and if these relationships are not well
managed, the whole group suffers. Then too, the law of diminishing
returns operates to destroy the value of purely individual architectural
effects. From now on, in Washington, the effort to give strong and
independent character to a building will be useless. The only large
satisfactions must come from position, logical environment, relationships, and the embracing totalities of town planning. Architects who
disregard this condition will go down in defeat and will carry their
friends with them.

The Mellon Gallery—as people persist in calling the National
Gallery of Art—can be used to illustrate some of these relationships.
The Gallery has as its central element a large saucer dome. Considered
in detachment from the function of the building and from the social
responsibilities of art, it is a very lovely dome. If the plan of a large
garden and a little town were organized under the control of that
dome, the whole composition might be magnificent. But here it is a
secondary mass and stands near another dome, that of the National
Museum (now called the Natural History Building), which is somewhat suppressed in character (though vigorously detailed), with the
evident purpose of deferring to the Capitol. Approaching the Capitol
now, along the Mall, one is extremely conscious of the domes of the
Museum and the Gallery, so different in color and in feel of contour.
They are obviously unfriendly, and the Capitol suffers from this feud
within its guard of honor. If other buildings set down along the Mall
continue to be of the egocentric sort, each piping its own tune, the

result will be pandemonium. The first law of aesthetic town planning is that the many must efface themselves so that the few may stand forth in dignity and dominance.

By way of technical comment on the Mellon Gallery, something should be said as warning against calling it "pure Greek." The building is more Roman than Greek, but more Renaissance than either. The use of shallow rectangular niches at a corner of various wall-surfaces—the purpose being to destroy secondary symmetries in order to strengthen the dominant axis—is a baroque conception. If the building must be ticketed with a style, it might be called Beaux-Arts in the purity of death.

Mr. Pope's other Pantheon, the Jefferson Memorial, has one great advantage over its sister on the Mall—it will have a fine garden of its own to stand in. It will in fact be a jewel of garden art, a very gracious thing as you see the dome, in the afternoon, from across the Potomac—likable, yet a little soft. Perhaps we have here a materialization of the cherry-blossom sentiment which hangs heavily upon the site. But inevitably, in this garden Pantheon, one questions the use of a portico with a circular colonnade. It is normally, as in the Pantheon itself, the contrast of the columns of the portico against the solid wall of the rotunda that gives the portico its contrast, its "value." That Mr. Jefferson, standing within, will be comfortably illuminated, is the anxious prayer of the Society for the Prevention of Cruelty to Statuary.

Since all these capitoline structures were the fruits of ideas, things that were first built in the ever-wandering faith of men, it may be well to mention two buildings that are as yet (1942) only images. One is Frank Lloyd Wright's fairy-land design for a "crystal city" on a fine site near the intersection of Connecticut and Florida Avenues. There would be a hotel, shops, recreation. The land cost compels high buildings—which the District authorities refuse to authorize.

The other is the Saarinens' plan for the proposed new Smithsonian. At the instigation of Edward Bruce, Congress in 1938 authorized a competition for the design of the building. To no sophisticated surprise, the award went to a "modernistic" design. No money has been appropriated for the building, but the plan hovers over the Mall, an angel of hope to some, an evil ghost to others.

These words were caught together as Washington seethed with defense work and workers. A chapter about buildings in Washington is being assembled in more lasting stuff than words. Every day there are rumors of new buildings, temporary and permanent, to be located downtown, uptown, or across the Anacostia River. Persons of optimistic temperament are saying that the incubus of monumentality will be thrown off and that no more office buildings will be designed and located to ornament the Mall. Persons of more realistic temperament base similar hopes upon the purifying effect of budgetary limitations. Well, the pendulum was swinging back, long before defense crept upon us. The flight from plaster of Paris has now become a race. We shall see. . . .

Washington, however, is not, even in defense time, a place exclusively of work and conferences and air-conditioning. It is a place of recreation also, where people walk or drive on a summer evening, and a place of pilgrimage, where hundreds of people go late at night to the Lincoln Memorial. It is a beautiful place, as American cities go, made beautiful by its trees, skies, fogs, rivers, and low green hills, even by the rich chaos of its buildings, a chaos subdued by the city's magnificently ordered plan. To gain these values of the spirit and the eye, the visitor to Washington should explore persistently, should go into all parts of the city, wander through unknown streets and famous ones, go to the terrace of the Capitol before sunset until the lights are on, walk up Meridian Hill during a snowstorm. Upon all this material the lights and shadows play, giving golden moments of beauty equally to true and false, old and new. Washington has inexhaustible resources for those who have the gift of fashioning dramatic experiences out of architecture.

Art

ART in the "Federal Town" is primarily, of course, the paintings and sculpture of its public buildings and the monuments in its streets, squares, and parks. Here statues, busts, architectural carvings, historical panoramas, portraits, have been accumulating since the birth of the Nation; so that the city offers on its surface a permanent display reflecting the history of American art—from the repetitious Italianate sculpture of the early nineteenth century to the many-styled native creations sponsored today by the Government art projects.

Always a center of American art, Washington has, since the opening of the National Gallery in 1941, also begun to take its place as an art capital of importance. With its many rooms of Italian, Flemish, Dutch, Spanish, French, British, and early American masters, the National Gallery, constantly augmented by gifts and loans, has raised the city's rank as a museum center. But even before the inauguration of the "Mellon Gallery," the city was already rich in museums and collections. The Corcoran Gallery provides a wide coverage of the chief schools of paintings and sculpture in nineteenth-century United States, and has interesting groups of French canvases and statuary, with an especially important representation of Corot and the sculptor of animals, Antoine Barye; Dutch, Flemish, and English masters, noteworthy Renaissance drawings, and objects of art are among the items of its well-known W. A. Clark Collection. The Phillips Memorial Gallery has one of the finest collections in the country of modern paintings and of works exemplifying the influences that shaped them—by Goya, El Greco, Daumier, Renoir, Ryder—and in addition conducts an important program of temporary exhibitions, such as that of the first retrospective display in the United States of paintings by the great French contemporary, Rouault, held in the winter of 1940-41. In the Freer Gallery is a good collection of Oriental art, including Japanese and Chinese paintings, porcelains, and statuary. There are also many fine canvases by Whistler.

The National Collection of Fine Arts, in the Natural History Building of the Smithsonian Institution, is extremely broad in scope—from American Indian and European artifacts, through a miscellany of European and American masterpieces, to contemporary art of the United States. Crowded with fossils, skeletons, mineralogical specimens, pianos, dioramas, the museum recalls American galleries of the first half of the nineteenth century where portraits of famous men, panoramas of Heaven and Hell, and an occasional landscape hung among stuffed birds, Indian arrowheads and tomahawks, and curiosities of all sorts.   Here also is one of the largest and most comprehensive collections in the world of American aboriginal pottery, and excellent examples of the powerful sculpture of primitive peoples.   And here too in the Gellatly Collection is the finest group of the paintings of Albert Pinkham Ryder, one of America's greatest masters.

Just as American students and amateurs of Italian art now find it necessary to visit the Mellon and Kress collections at the National Gallery, scholars of antiquity will be drawn to Washington in order to examine the Bliss Collection of Byzantine, early Christian, and Medieval art, and to make use of its 10,000-volume library on these subjects.   Harvard University, to which Mr. and Mrs. Bliss turned over their acquisitions in 1940, hopes to make Dumbarton Oaks a research center for advanced investigators in the Medieval Humanities. Another specialized institution of importance to researchers is the Textile Museum of the District of Columbia, founded by George Hewitt Meyers in 1925.

These institutions have made Washington a great storehouse of. European, Oriental, and American art.   But the essential character of the art of the city lies not so much in the masterpieces deposited in it by collectors as in the work created here since its beginning.   To the capital came in its first years the painters of "The American School" of Benjamin West, who had left the Colonies before the Revolution to live in London and had become president of the British Royal Academy.   The painters of the early Republic, with some few exceptions, owed much of their training to West.   Theirs was perhaps the only movement in American art inspired directly by political events.   Their ideal was to depict in the grand manner the personages and happenings of the Revolutionary War.   John Trumbull's panels, *Signing of the Declaration of Independence, Surrender of Burgoyne, Surrender of Cornwallis,* and *Washington Resigning His Commission as Commander in Chief of the Army,* at the Capitol, Gilbert Stuart's and Charles Willson Peale's portraits of Washington and other personages, as well as the many portraits by Thomas Sully, are among the canvases in the capital associated with the teachings of West.

In general, the pupils of West experienced a disappointment similar to that of L'Enfant, planner of the city, as the heroic conception they had formed abroad of the Revolution for Freedom collided everywhere with the indifference or self-seeking of people going about their daily business in a raw country.   The commissioning of works of art was often attended by haggling, political maneuvering, and arbitrary control of subject matter.   It must also be confessed that, whatever the will of the idealists, the artistic talents of America were seriously limited. Charles E. Fairman's much-detailed *Art and Artists of the Capitol* (1927) is especially fascinating in the chapters which refer to the processes whereby the early decorations of our major public buildings came into being. In 1805 Benjamin H. Latrobe, architect of the Capitol, wrote to an Italian friend of Thomas Jefferson for his "assistance in procuring for us the services of a good sculptor in the erection of public buildings in this city, especially of the capitol." Latrobe pointed out to his correspondent that "the wages given by the day to our best carvers are from $3.00 to $2.50. . . . They are considered good wages, but the workmen who receive them are very indifferent carvers and do not deserve the name of sculptors." It was further indicated by Latrobe that the United States Government would pay for the sculptor's transportation back home, but he urged that "this stipulation should not be made unless absolutely demanded."

Giuseppe Franzoni, the sculptor who arrived from Italy in response to Latrobe's appeal, was the first of a long troupe of craftsmen from that country whose work appears in Washington's public places. Prominent among these men who interpreted America to Americans in plaster were Luigi Persico, Enrico Causici, Giuseppe Valaperti, Antonio Capellano, and Carlo Franzoni, brother of Giuseppe.

Horatio Greenough, the first American sculptor to add his work to that of the Italians at the Capitol, modeled in the same classic-revival tradition and, in spite of the frontiersman subject matter of his *Rescue* group, failed to strike a native note. From his time on, commissions for sculpture at the Capitol were awarded only to Americans. The Italian style persisted, however, in the pediments, figures, and doors of Thomas Crawford, creator of the statue of *Freedom* on the dome of the Capitol; and Randolph Rogers, designer of the bronze doors for the eastern entrance to the Rotunda, also adhered rigidly to his Italian training. So, too, did Hiram Powers, whose statues of Jefferson and Franklin are in the Capitol. A replica of Powers' *Greek Slave,* a nude figure which set off much moralistic head-shaking in the 1840's, and even more enthusiasm in the 1850's, is now a popular attraction at the Corcoran.

John Frazee and Clark Mills, pioneers of American realistic sculpture, are both represented in Washington; a bust of John Jay by the former is at the Capitol, the latter's famous statue of Andrew Jackson, the first equestrian group in the United States, is in Lafayette Square. These artists emerged from the artisan tradition of the American makers of ships' figureheads, weathervanes, and decorative carvings, and their work, despite its relative crudity, is acknowledged today to be more powerful in character and sound in execution than most of the facile creations of the Italianates. Mills erected a foundry at

Richard B. Stewart

NATIONAL ARCHIVES BUILDING

Farm Security Administration: Vachon

JACKSON, FIRST EQUESTRIAN STATUE IN
THE UNITED STATES, LAFAYETTE SQUARE

NAVY AND MARINE
MEMORIAL, MOUNT
VERNON HIGHWAY
National Park Service

W. Lincoln Highton
ADAMS MEMORIAL, "GRIEF," BY ST. GAUDENS,
IN ROCK CREEK CEMETERY

U. S. Indian Office

INDIAN MURAL AND INDIAN OFFICE EMPLOYEES,
8TH FLOOR CAFETERIA, SOUTH INTERIOR BUILDING

CHILDREN'S GALLERY
*District of Columbia
Art Project, WPA*

OUTDOOR ART FAIR, LAFAYETTE SQUARE

ARTIST AND CHERRY BLOSSOMS

"MAJOR POWELL
EXPLORING THE
COLORADO RIVER,
LIMESTONE BAS-
RELIEF BY RALPH
STACKPOLE, SOUTH
INTERIOR
AUDITORIUM

*Section of Fine Arts,
PBA*

"NATIONAL PARK SERVICE IN ALASKA," MURAL
BY GIFFORD BEAL, SOUTH INTERIOR BUILDING

"CONSERVATION OF WILD LIFE," DETAIL OF MURAL
BY HENRY VARNUM POOR, SOUTH INTERIOR BUILDING

"CONTEMPORARY JUSTICE AND THE CHILD," MURAL BY
SYMEON SHIMIN, DEPARTMENT OF JUSTICE BUILDING

Bladensburg, and here he cast his *Jackson* and other works.   Hezekiah Augur, also working in this tradition, executed the portrait bust of Chief Justice Ellsworth in the old Supreme Court room at the Capitol.

Chester Harding and John Neagle, both largely self-taught, wandered as portrait painters through the Kentucky and Ohio territories before their character studies came to be sought by Washington leaders of taste.   George Catlin, also self-taught, covered the farthest reaches of the country sketching and painting Indians of many tribes; in 1846 his invaluable record of Indian life was purchased by the Government and was later deposited in the National Museum.

Among the French who contributed to Washington statuary before the Civil War were Nicholas Gevelot, designer of *Penn's Treaty with the Indians,* over the north door of the west entrance to the Capitol, and Pierre Jean David d'Angers, whose statue of Jefferson and bust of Lafayette are much admired by art critics.   Jean Antoine Houdon spent two weeks at Mount Vernon making studies of Washington from life; casts of his celebrated *Washington* are in the rotunda of the Capitol.

Adjoining the panels by Trumbull in the rotunda are four historical scenes, by John Vanderlyn, W. H. Powell, John G. Chapman, and Robert Weir, teacher of Whistler at West Point.   Vanderlyn, painter of the much-reproduced *Ariadne,* was perhaps the best artist of the group.   Unlike his contemporaries, who worked in the rather stiff British manner, Vanderlyn had been thoroughly trained in France. Unfortunately, however, his commission at the Capitol came after many difficulties and delays and was executed in the declining years of his life.

Portraits and historical subjects have been painted in every period of American art, but as a movement the school of West was soon superseded by the panoramic landscape of the "Hudson River School" and genre subjects in the style developed in Düsseldorf, Germany.   The quiet photographic country scenes of the Hudson River painters— Thomas Cole, Asher Durand, Thomas Doughty, and others—are exceptionally well represented at the Corcoran Gallery and appear in other Washington collections and public displays.   Of the Düsseldorf painters perhaps the best known in this city is Emanuel Leutze, painter of the huge *Westward the Star of Empire Takes Its Way* and other historical subjects and portraits at the Capitol.   His work, dry, literal, overdetailed, is typical of the Düsseldorf handling.

The first frescoes in America were painted by Constantino Brumidi, a naturalized Italian, who for twenty-five years (1855-80) was employed at the Capitol, covering its walls with portraits, historical scenes, and allegories, mostly at the rate of $10 a day.   Brumidi, a decorative painter of mediocre talent, worked in what was left of the tradition of Raphael and Corregio.

A good deal of dissatisfaction had developed among American artists and their friends concerning the manner of awarding commissions for public art and the type of work that had resulted. An art commission was appointed by President Buchanan in 1859 with three eminent artists as members. They were Henry Kirke Brown, sculptor, John F. Kensett, a leading Düsseldorf-trained landscapist, and James R. Lambdin, portraitist. In their report estimating the art that had been done at the Capitol, these artists criticized Brumidi and the foreign treatment of American themes, attacking the use of classical draperies in portrait statues of eminent Americans, and expressed themselves in favor of realism and historical accuracy. The art commission, was however, disbanded the following year. On this event Dr. Fairman quotes *The Crayon* as follows: "We are not surprised at it, the act being in keeping with the usual course of the Government to the arts. . . . The causes of the repeal of the law providing for the Art Commission are characterized with the coarseness, ignorance and cunning which are always brought into play. . . . They are due both to the craft of politicians and to the impassive state of opinion in relation to the art that prevails throughout the country." Not unil 1910 was the need for an art commission again officially acknowledged: in that year the present National Commission of Fine Arts was established by an Act of Congress to pass upon plans for all new structures in the District of Columbia and all matters of art with which the Federal Government is concerned.

In the years following the Civil War, a regeneration of the city was begun under "Boss" Shepherd; streets were paved, parks graded and fenced, an elaborate sewage system installed. A period of great movement and expansion was under way in American life, as the country lifted itself out of its agricultural and mercantile past and entered its industrial phase. It was the time when the first great American museums were organized; the incorporation of the Corcoran in 1870 coincided with the establishment of New York City's Metropolitan and the Boston Museum of Fine Arts. With improved communications with Europe, styles in painting succeeded one another at a rapid rate. Out of the Hudson River and Düsseldorf manner had developed the painting of spectacular scenery by such artists as Albert Bierstadt, Thomas Moran, and Frederick Church. Huge sums were paid by America's new millionaires for the Herculean canvases turned out by these artists. Moran, generally accepted as the most talented of this group, is represented in the Capitol by the *Chasm of the Colorado* and *The Grand Canyon of the Yellowstone*.

From the Barbizon school in France came the impulse towards a new, more mellow naturalism in landscape painting, and this was reflected in the paintings of George Innes, Homer Martin, and many others whose work appeared in the capital at this time. Alexander Wyant, showing the influence of British landscapists, produced scenes related to those of the Hudson River group but richer in tone. With the great realists, Winslow Homer and Thomas Eakins, and the romantic mystic, Albert Pinkham Ryder, American art reached its first mature and independent expression. Mural painting took on a new significance in the studied compositions of John La Farge and his teacher, William Morris Hunt. The works of these men may be seen in the National Collection of Fine Arts in the Smithsonian, the Phillips Memorial Gallery, the Corcoran, and the Library of Congress.

Historical painting and portraiture in Washington's public buildings had tended to become rather drily academic. French Impressionism and the brush drawing of the Munich School brought refreshing innovations in handling displayed in the compositions of Whistler, Mary Cassat, Childe Hassam, and J. Alden Weir, hung in capital galleries.

In sculpture Henry Kirke Brown, who despite his five years of study in Rome had succeeded in retaining a native flavor, showed rugged originality in his statues of Washington and General Winfield Scott and in his pieces in Statuary Hall. The work of John Q. A. Ward, American trained and a thorough craftsman, was a landmark in United States sculpture, and his General Thomas, in Thomas Circle, and his monument to Garfield, at First Street and Maryland Avenue, Southwest, are among his most important figures.

The names of the decorators of the Library of Congress constitute a roll call of the chief artistic reputations in the United States at the time of its completion in 1897. Augustus Saint-Gaudens, whose statue, *Art,* is in the central reading room, and Olin Levi Warner, designer of two of the doors to the main entrance, enriched American sculpture with the verve and emotional subtlety of French romantic realism. (Saint-Gaudens, regarded by many as America's greatest sculptor, is best known in Washington for his *Adams Memorial* in Rock Creek Cemetery.) Other carvers of the library's decorations, as well as of pieces seen throughout the city, are Frederick MacMonnies, Daniel Chester French, John T. Flanagan, Paul W. Bartlett, John Donoghue, Cyrus Dallin, F. W. Ruckstuhl, E. Hinton Perry, J. Scott Hartley, Bela L. Pratt, Philip Martiny, Theodore Bauer, E. C. Potter, Charles H. Niehaus, and Louis Saint-Gaudens. The mural painters of the library, led by Edwin Blashfield, Elihu Vedder, Kenyon Cox, Gari Melchers, and George W. Maynard, are equally representative.

Among popular works in Washington by sculptors of this generation are the buffaloes at the Q Street Bridge, by A. Phimister Proctor; the colossal marble *Lincoln* in the Lincoln Memorial, and the *Dupont*

Memorial Fountain in Dupont Circle, by Daniel Chester French; Gutzon Borglum's equestrian statue of General Philip H. Sheridan in Sheridan Circle; the *John Ericsson Memorial* in Potomac Park by James Earle Fraser. The much-admired *Puck* at the Folger Shakespeare Memorial Library is by Brenda Putnam, a leading modeler of the succeeding period; she studied under Pratt, Fraser, and Charles Grafly—the last designed the elaborate *General Meade Memorial* in Union Square.

Founded in 1897, the Library of Congress Division of Fine Arts presents several important collections of drawings, prints, and books, including etchings by Whistler and Pennell, Japanese prints, original drawings by American illustrators, and 70,000 volumes, periodicals, and pamphlets on art subjects.

Though Washington art is chiefly a matter of things done in connection with public places, there has been a great deal of unofficial and semi-official activity. The Society of Washington Artists, organized in 1890, has held annual exhibitions of living American painters and sculptors. The seventeenth biennial exhibitions of contemporary American painting conducted to date at the Corcoran Gallery have aroused national interest, and the generous prizes have been sought by leading artists. The Public Library of the District of Columbia has an important circulating collection of books, magazines, and prints, and frequently exhibits the work of local art groups and individual craftsmen. The Washington Society of Fine Arts, organized in 1905 to advance art and its appreciation, and the Arts Club of Washington (1916), which promotes cooperation among those interested in each of the arts, have programs of lectures, exhibitions, and other services. Four days a year, usually in May, an outdoor art fair, which brings out much native talent, is held in Lafayette Square under the sponsorship of the *Times-Herald*. The Children's Art Center, organized in 1937 by the WPA as the Children's Art Gallery, now carried on by a citizen's group, gives free instruction to children in painting and sculpture, and organizes exhibits of works by and for children. Washington also has numerous art schools for adults, some private, others connected with its museums and universities.

During the past decade Government buildings in Washington, as elsewhere, have been the scene of a creative surge in mural painting and, to a slightly lesser degree, in ornamental sculpture. Commissions for the decoration of Federal buildings are now awarded by the Section of Fine Arts of the Public Buildings Administration through anonymous competitions open to all. The winning designs are chosen by juries of artists and critics. Politics in the selection of artists have thus been reduced to a minimum. Murals in public buildings of the District of Columbia have been executed by the members of the Art

Program of the Work Projects Administration, which has also allocated easel paintings to offices of Federal buildings.

A new realism is the predominant style of these recent murals and sculptures. As an esthetic movement it owes much to that revolt against academic standards initiated by the "Henri Group" at the beginning of the twentieth century. Impressionism, post-Impressionism, abstract art—all had been absorbed into American art by the time the new program was started in the 1930's. Many of the WPA artists and competition winners of the Section of Fine Arts have been younger men whose compositions have been approved on the basis of merit alone, so that fresh strains have been introduced in a steady flow.

Scenes from life in America, past and present, are favorite themes of the new decorations. The contemporary appears in such compositions as *Mail Box at the Crossroads,* by Doris Lee, *The Family Letter,* by Alexander Brook, *Post Office Interior,* by Reginald Marsh, all at the Post Office Department building, and William Gropper's exciting composition *The Construction of a Dam,* in the South Interior Building. The same dynamic realism is evident in the historical and allegorical subjects of Boardman Robinson, Leon Kroll, and George Biddle, in the Justice Department Building, and in John Steuart Curry's *Land Rush in Oklahoma* in the South Interior Building. In sculpture, too, the same note is struck by Attilio Piccirilli, Chaim Gross, Heinz Warneke, and Louis Slobodkin, among many others. Paul Manship, William Zorach, and the painter Rockwell Kent represent a formalistic emphasis associated with architectural forms. An interesting variation is found in the murals by Indian artists in both the main cafeteria and in the eighth-floor cafeteria of the South Interior Building.

In 1868, in his report to the Senate, the Commissioner of Education declared: "In selecting works of art to decorate the Capitol our effort should not only be directed to their [the people's] entertainment and improvement but to giving them what they can readily understand and appreciate." This principle of aiming at the general level of appreciation has always guided those who have made Washington art an anthology, in the past not too well compiled, of the painting and sculpture of the Nation. Officials have sought a popular reflection of America's plastic genius—but in deciding what other people could understand they also reflected their own limitations. The new, enlightened method of awarding commissions, which provides a freer, more direct channel to the artists of America, is certain to have far-reaching effects on Washington art, as well as on that of the Nation as a whole.

Music and the Theater

FROM the Civil War to the beginning of the twentieth century Washington shared with other large cities all that was great in American and European theaters. The seven famous playhouses flourishing here at the beginning of the century with one exception live now only in memory and the few pages of history that have been allotted to them.

Washington's music, on the other hand, is greater in contemporaneity than in history. To the history of music Washington has given significantly only the service bands and some of their scores, which reflect in music the fanfare of national politics and patriotism, and one well-known native musician, John Philip Sousa. Today, however, a local symphony orchestra and the offerings of the Library of Congress are significant factors in American music.

DRAMA

As early as 1790 McGrath's Company of Comedians, headed by the so-called "King of American Strollers," presented *The Beggar's Opera* at Georgetown. In 1799 bands of strolling players visited Georgetown, giving theatrical performances in candle-lit halls, taverns, and even stables. They carried no scenery and their costume and make-up was meager.

The early period of the theater in Washington was marked by heroic and often futile managerial struggles for financial and artistic success. A small playhouse, in Blodgett's Hotel at 8th and E Streets, impressively named the United States Theater, opened as Washington's first theater in 1800, playing *Venice Preserved* and *A Spoiled Child*. Here Wignall and Reinagle, Philadelphia opera impresarios, brought their 20-piece orchestra, and stayed for a brief season. The United States Theater was a financial failure, closing less than a month after the opening, with a curiously appropriate play—*A Cure for Heartache*.

In 1804 this notice appeared in the *National Intelligencer:* "The public are respectfully informed that the Washington Theater will open on Wednesday evening, November 14, 1804, with a Grand Medley of entertainments by the celebrated Mr. Maginnis from London, who has performed in most capital cities of Europe and

America." The advertisement was illustrated with a cartoon and carried the additional instruction: "No Segars are to be smoked during the performance." During the next 16 years the Washington Theater offered every variety of theatrical fare from light comedies and farces to Shakespeare and the classics. The first record of a Presidential visit to the theater was in 1819, when James Monroe attended a charity benefit performance.

In 1820 the Washington Theater was partly destroyed by fire. A second Washington Theater, seating 700, was erected in 1821, with improvements and innovations. Stoves were installed, reserved seats inaugurated, acoustics improved, liquor was excluded from the box lobbies, and separate boxes were provided for Negroes. A year later Junius Brutus Booth appeared there in *Hamlet, Richard III, The Iron Chest,* and other plays. Lafayette visted the theater in 1824. Among the well-known actors who played there, in addition to the elder Booth, were Burroughs, Cooper, and Mrs. Barnes. Enlarged again in 1831, the Washington was reopened under the management of Joseph Jefferson (the second). Its decline began, however, with the opening of the rival National Theater in 1835. Further improvements, and the changing of its name to the American Theater, merely delayed its demise, in 1836.

During these years various notables of the foreign operatic stage visited Washington. As in the late Colonial period, grand opera began to have presentations in America at the same time the premieres occurred in Europe. Washington heard a few of these operas, including Mozart's *Marriage of Figaro* in 1836, Bellini's *La Sonnambula* in 1837, Rossini's *Barber of Seville,* Auber's *Fra Diavolo,* and Beethoven's *Fidelio* in 1838.

The rough, unpaved, unlighted streets of that time made attendance at the theater a difficult task. In bad weather Pennsylvania Avenue was an extended quagmire. During heavy snows and rains it often cost as much as $10 to go by hack from the residential areas to the theater. Despite these difficulties hopeful promoters opened the new National Theater in 1835, on the site where the present National Theater stands. James Henry Hackett played Falstaff here in 1838, and many other noted actors appeared at the National between then and 1845, when the theater was destroyed by fire.

The National, rebuilt in 1850 on the same site, was renamed New National Hall. Following the tragic collapse of one of its walls during a performance, it was rebuilt and reopened in 1852, as the New National Theater, the President and his Cabinet attending. Between that time and 1922, when the present theater was opened on the original site, the National was destroyed by fire and rebuilt four times. The season of 1866-67, when Joseph Jefferson first appeared in Washington as Rip Van Winkle, was one of the most brilliant the city ever witnessed. A list of plays and players that were thereafter presented at this theater would constitute an accurate index of much that was best and most significant in American theatrical history. Today the National is the last remaining refuge of the legitimate theater in the city.

A Baptist Church on 10th Street was converted, in 1861, into Christy's Opera House. It was remodeled the following year and opened as Ford's Athenaeum, with Lucille Weston in *The French Spy*. The theater burned in December, and in the fall of 1863 it was rebuilt and reopened as Ford's Theater. It was here that Abraham Lincoln was shot by John Wilkes Booth, on the night of April 14, 1865. Edwin Booth, who had appeared in Washington during the early 1850's, was so heartbroken by his brother's act that he never returned to the Capital thereafter.

Soldiers quartered in Washington during the Civil War were entertained at a variety house over Wall's carriage shop at 9th and C Streets. A number of other theaters, built during the seventies and eighties, were razed in the early 1930's, in the course of clearing ground for the Mall. In Chase's Vaudeville House, Bioscope moving pictures were introduced to Washington in 1899.

With several playhouses flourishing in the eighties, Washington theaters reached a high point, which was sustained well into the twentieth century. Programs and performers reflected all that was great on the American and European stage of the time. C. W. Couldock, Lily Langtry, Kate Claxton and Charles Wyndham, Sarah Bernhardt, Ellen Terry, and later the third of that immortal group of dramatic actresses, Eleonora Duse, led the trek to the Capital City for breath-taking performances—many of them American premieres.

Washington during the nineties outdid itself in theatrical activity. Seven playhouses presented, in scintillating succession, the idols of the world's theater. In addition to the reappearance of those who had come in the eighties, there appeared Henry Irving, Lillian Russell and her husband, Perugini, Adelina Patti, Maude Adams, and many others. It is reported that the ghost of John McCullough, who had died in 1885, was haunting his favorite theater, the National, where he turned up at the prompter's table one night in 1896, in the garb of Hamlet. Variety gave place to vaudeville, and ministers delivered sermons against the theater as female stage stars became noted for their legs! Motion pictures gave faint promise in "peep shows," or "store shows" with Edison's Kinetoscope in nickelodeons. Metzerott's Music Hall entered the upper brackets by moving into a new building on F Street in 1892. Four years later it became the Columbia Theater, an opera house, and under the same name was one of the first legitimate houses to install motion pictures.

Of the theater buildings standing today, the Belasco ranks second only to the National in historical importance. Erected in 1895 facing Lafayette Square, it was originally known as the Lafayette Square Opera House. In 1905 the theater was taken over by David Belasco and the Shuberts, and the name changed to the Belasco. Sarah Bernhardt, David Warfield, Mrs. Fiske, DeWolf Hopper, and Mrs. Leslie Carter were among the great performers appearing at the Belasco in the days before it became a motion-picture house and, in 1940, a warehouse for Government records.

The legitimate theater was on the wane during the first dozen years of the twentieth century, yet this period brought the opening of two of the three remaining "legitimate" theaters in Washington, and contributed to the development of Washington dramatic stars who achieved success elsewhere; they include Wilton Lackaye, Billie Burke, Nat Wills, Ina Claire, Ruth Chatterton, and Helen Hayes. The Gayety Theater, playing burlesque to this day, opened in 1907. The Howard, a Negro theater with a program of motion pictures and vaudeville, supported by jazz orchestras, retains some of the quality that, in its halcyon days, made it one of the important theaters of the country. Since its opening in 1911 with S. H. Dudley's *Smart Set,* the Howard has introduced to its audiences many performers who became Broadway stars. Black Patti, musical comedy star, and Tutt Whitney and J. A. Shipp, of *Green Pastures* fame, are remembered from this early period. Florence Mills cakewalked across the Howard stage before she triumphed in *Shuffle Along* and *Plantation Revue*. Other noted Washingtonians who have graduated from the Howard are Will H. Vodery, musical arranger for the Ziegfield Follies, Ada Ward of *Brown Buddies,* popular singer of mammy songs, and Claude Hopkins and Duke Ellington, jazz band leaders.

Today the commercial theater is almost exclusively the cinema. The legitimate theater presents companies which play here before their Broadway openings, and touring companies making one-week stands. The tradition of the legitimate stage is carried on, aside from the National Theater, by numerous Little Theatre and amateur groups. Catholic University's Department of Speech and Drama has attracted national attention since 1937 with its experimental work in writing and producing original plays and classics. Leo Brady's *Brother Orchid,* first produced here, has since had national distribution. *God's Stage,* at the university, seeks to trace the course of drama with religious motifs from Aeschylus to the present day. Howard Players, a Negro organization connected with Howard University, presents plays at the university and at Garnett Patterson Junior High. The Pierce Hall

Players, organized in 1931, having its own theater seating 500, produces about six plays each season. There are several dramatic organizations within Government departments, and the Washington Civic Theater produces several plays a season at the Wardman Park Theater. The Roadside Players, a semiprofessional troupe presenting old comedies and melodramas during the summer season, in an old red barn six miles out the Rockville Pike, in Maryland, is Washington's pioneer barn theater. The Crossroads Theater, its counterpart on the Virginia side of Washington, presents summer performances of modern plays and mystery thrillers in a haymow. The National Sylvan Theater, on the Washington Monument grounds, has an outdoor stage with trees and shrubs for a backdrop, where plays, light operas, and other productions are given in summer; audiences sit on chairs or recline on the lawn. The Shakespeare Society, one of the oldest amateur groups, meets in the Universalist Church on 16th Street for the presentation of scenes from Shakespeare and other Elizabethan dramatists. Bess Davis Schreiner's dramatization of Henry van Dyke's *The Other Wise Man* has been presented annually during Christmas week, since 1925, at the Luther Place Memorial Church on Thomas Circle.

MUSIC

Music was originally brought to Washington by the Government. The Marine Band, the oldest military band in the United States, made its official debut at the White House in 1801. Thereafter it provided music for the President's New Year's Day receptions and other social and patriotic events.

The first public song recital is thought to have been that of Mrs. Oldmixon in 1803. The first auditorium suitable for opera was the Washington Theater, opened in 1822. Two years later Sir Henry Bishop's opera, *Clari, or the Maid of Athens,* was produced in this hall. It is remembered today because its libretto, by John Howard Payne, contained the song "Home Sweet Home." John Quincy Adams, better known as a President of the United States (1825-29) than as a hymnist, wrote a complete metrical version of the Psalms. *The Christian Psalter,* published at Quincy, Massachusetts, in 1841, contains 22 of his hymns and psalms.

Jenny Lind appeared at the New National Hall in 1850; at the "Swedish Nightingale's" second performance her audience included the President, Vice President, members of the Cabinet, and the Justices of the Supreme Court. In the same year, Mario, the tenor, and Giulia Grisi, the dramatic soprano, held a sensational joint recital, with tickets at $10 and boxes at $50 to $75. A returned "forty-niner" is said to have paid $1,000 for a box.

John Philip Sousa, a native Washingtonian and leader of the Marine Band from 1880 to 1892, is best known for his stirring "The Stars and Stripes Forever," "Liberty Bell," and "Semper Fidelis." Sousa also wrote light operas, which were popular in their day, and organized the Washington Musical Assembly, an orchestra of 85 members, which gave several concerts at Albaugh's Opera House in 1887.

During the eighties music flourished throughout the city, especially in the churches. At the Congregational Church were heard the best in home talent and the great visiting artists, including the Boston Symphony Orchestra under the baton of Wilhelm Gericke. J. W. Bischoff, resident organist and choir director of the Congregational Church, wrote the music for a number of songs, though he was blind from the age of two.

In the "gay nineties," Jeannie Winston, an Australian prima donna noted for her male roles, was the city's operatic favorite. Gustav Heinrich's Grand Opera came to the Academy of Music spring after spring, with casts including singers of international repute. Josef Hofmann and Fritz Kreisler—at that time child prodigies—played in Washington, and Paderewski, Rafael Joseffy, Ethelbert Nevin, Eugene Ysaye, Ap Tomas, Emma Juch, and Nellie Melba were all heard here.

The Dvorak Musical Association, a Negro society, was organized at the turn of the century. The Samuel Coleridge-Taylor Society, named for the British Negro composer, was founded in 1902 and presented its first concert the following year. Coleridge-Taylor visited Washington in 1903 and directed the first presentation of his *Hiawatha* trilogy, with the Marine Band accompanying a Negro chorus of 200.

Community opera and "sings" were popular during the World War and rose to a climax in the great "sing" of June 1, 1918, in which 10,000 persons participated. National Music Week, an outgrowth of this movement, has grown steadily in importance since its inception in 1921; this music festival is now celebrated during the first week in May by thousands of professional and amateur musicians and by the public at large throughout the country. In Washington, church choirs give concerts, contests are sponsored by the music clubs, and the public schools present various kinds of musical entertainment.

The United States Army Band is a direct descendant of the musical organization of the American Expeditionary Forces, formed by General John J. Pershing at Chaumont, France, during the World War. The United States Navy Band was formed in 1923 by enlarging an earlier organization, and was made a permanent institution by act of Congress in 1925. The annual tours, local free concerts, and radio programs of the Navy, Army, and Marine bands have brought them national repute. They also give concerts in the Pan American

Union auditorium in winter, and in the Union's Aztec Garden in summer, to further cultural understanding between North and South America. The three services, during the early 1930's, augumented their musical activities with symphony orchestras.

The Music Division of the Library of Congress has the largest music library in the United States, ranking with the great collections abroad. The chamber music concerts given under its auspices are known throughout the world. They are supported by the Elizabeth Sprague Coolidge Foundation and by the Gertrude Clarke Whittall Foundation, established in 1925 and 1937 respectively. With the encouragement of chamber music as its major purpose, the Coolidge Foundation subsidizes and sponsors American composers and concerts of American and other music throughout the country. Each year a gold medal is presented at the Founder's Day Concert here to the musician who has done most for chamber music in the preceding 12 months. Every four years a prize of $1,000 is awarded for the best composition for four stringed instruments. Festivals, featuring the Nation's foremost ensemble groups playing their own instruments are held biennially. In the Coolidge Auditorium at the Library, designed for the presentation of chamber music, such noted ensembles as the Pro Arte, Coolidge, Roth, and Kolish quartets have given concert series. A nominal fee of 25¢ is charged for admission.

The Whittall Foundation is a Washington benefaction. Mrs. Whittall donated to the Library of Congress her priceless collection of Stradivari instruments, the Whittall Pavilion (*see Library of Congress*) where they are exhibited, and an additional fund for concerts. The collection includes a cello, three violins, and a viola, and is the largest frequently played group of instruments by Stradivarius. Among the well-known chamber ensembles who play the "Strads" at Whittall concerts are the Budapest, Gordon, Roth, and Stradivarius quartets; admission is the same as for Coolidge concerts. The Whittall Pavilion, with its amplifier, is used to seat the overflow attendance at Coolidge and Whittall concerts. An annual chamber music concert is also given at the Library of Congress under the sponsorship of the Nicholas Longworth Foundation, established in 1933.

The Washington Philharmonic Orchestra, first symphonic group in the city, was conducted by William H. Santelmann for a short time in 1900-01. The Washington Symphony Orchestra, under the baton of Reginald de Koven, American composer of *Robin Hood* and other light operas, began a three-season career in 1902. The orchestra was reborn in 1907 but perished after its third concert. Another local orchestra, formed by Heinrich Hammer in 1911, was equally short-lived. Finally, the National Symphony Orchestra was established in 1931 by Hans Kindler, cellist of the Philadelphia Symphony Orchestra and one of the world's ranking virtuosi. Potential symphony players had left Washington during the years of musical drought, and Kindler found it necessary to combine local talent with musicians imported from New York, Philadelphia, and Boston. A remarkable growth in popularity and prestige has since given the orchestra a solid standing among the leading musical organizations of the country. The orchestra tours the East from Canada to Florida and the Middle Atlantic States as far west as Ohio. During the winter season it gives 20-odd concerts at Constitution Hall, and, for eight weeks in summer, presents two concerts a week at the Potomac Watergate. Many noted guest soloists and conductors appear with the orchestra. Student concerts at the public schools bring music to thousands of local children.

There are two civic orchestras, the Washington Civic Orchestra, conducted by Kurt Hetzel, and the orchestra of the Washington Sinfonietta Society, conducted by Van Lier Lanning. A number of Government departments have symphonic groups, the most active being that of the Department of Agriculture, under the direction of Dr. Walter Bauer.

In addition to these symphonic and chamber concerts, Washington offers other good and even great music. Among the visiting orchestras are the Philadelphia, Boston, and New York Philharmonic. Soloists include Szigeti, Horowitz, Hofmann, Rachmaninoff, Flagstad, Tibbett, Pons, Crooks, Spalding, and Menuhin. The series of Musical Mornings at the Mayflower Hotel, presenting guest soloists, and the Candlelight Concerts (chamber music) at the Phillips Memorial Art Gallery add to the social as well as the musical life of the Capital.

Perhaps the most dramatic event in the musical history of Washington was the Easter Sunday (1939) recital by Marian Anderson on the steps of the Lincoln Memorial. Thousands of listeners, white and Negro, filled the wide expanse from the Memorial to the Reflecting Pool. As the vibrant voice of the American Negro contralto rose in song, applause, said one critic, "seemed a futile intrusion." The occasion was spotlighted by the controversy that preceded it, in which Miss Anderson's manager had sought unsuccessfully to rent Constitution Hall from the D. A. R. for a performance. The case had all the excitement, publicity, and bitterness of a *cause célèbre*. Instead of Constitution Hall with its 4,000 ticket holders, Miss Anderson had for her performance the setting of the impressive Memorial, the Reflecting Pool, and spacious grounds. It was a sunny day, and an audience of 75,000 heard her sing Schubert's "Ave Maria," the Negro spiritual "Nobody Knows the Trouble I've Seen," and "America."

The committee of sponsors was composed of Cabinet members, Senators, Representatives, and other men and women of national distinction headed by Mrs. Roosevelt and Chief Justice and Mrs. Hughes.

Secretary of the Interior Harold Ickes, in presenting Miss Anderson, said: "Genius, like justice, is blind. For genius has touched with the tip of her wing this woman who, if it had not been for the great mind of Jefferson, if it had not been for the great heart of Lincoln, would not be able to stand among us today a free individual in a free land. Genius draws no color line. She has endowed Marian Anderson with such a voice as lifts any individual above his fellows."

The Music Division of the District of Columbia WPA has about 10 performing units, those better known including the Negro Community Chorus of 40 mixed voices, the 16-piece Chamber Orchestra, and dance bands for whites and Negroes. In addition to these units, the Music Division's 16 teachers do auxiliary educational work, available to schools, community centers, and institutions for underprivileged children. Its workers also carry on research in American folksong at the Library of Congress.

Churches play an active part in the musical life of the city, particularly in organ and choral work. Among the organists and directors who give recitals are Paul Gallaway, Washington Cathedral; Arthur Howes, St. John's Episcopal Church; Sterling Wheelwright, Church of Jesus Christ of Latter-day Saints; R. Dean Shure, Mount Vernon Place Methodist Episcopal Church; and Theodore Schaefer, Church of the Covenant-First Presbyterian. Among the many church choirs are the adult male choir of St. Matthew's; the boys' and men's choirs of the Cathedral, St. John's, and St. Stephen and The Incarnation; the mixed choirs of the Immaculate Conception, First Congregational, and Covenant-First Presbyterian. The A Cappella Choir of the First Congregational Church, under the direction of Ruby Smith Stahl, is also well known.

The Washington Guild of Organists sponsors an annual week of organ recitals, and brings to the city many notable organists. The Washington Choral Society, directed by Louis Potter, is an active group. The Capital has a few notable contemporary composers, including La Salle Spier, whose *Symphonic Visions* has been played by the National Symphony Orchestra; Mrs. Mary Howe, best known for two orchestral tone poems, *Sand* and *Stars;* and R. Dean Shure, who has published more than 100 compositions for the symphony orchestra, the organ, piano, and voice.

Literature

I N RECALLING an incident of his first visit to the Capital in
1850 Henry Adams remarks that a certain aunt of his "could
not guess—having lived always in Washington—how little the
sights of Washington had to do with its interest." Similarly, no one
who has not delved beneath the subject's surface aspects could guess
how little those writers most commonly identified with Washington,
especially its few native writers, have to do with its literary interest.
In literature, as in other fields, the city's cultural characteristics are
for the most part acquired rather than inherent, exotic rather than
indigenous. The authentic children of light who at one time or another
resided here were not born on the premises, so to speak; nor in most
cases did they die on the premises. They are native to other habitats,
rooted by birth or affinity in other soils, essentially aliens in a community
which drew and held them for a while but could seldom assimilate them.

But for all this, few American cities surpass Washington in respect
to an abundance of literary associations. The creators of those associations were in largest part persons who came here not primarily to
pursue a literary calling, but in various other capacities—as political
appointees or seekers of political appointments, as newspaper correspondents, research workers, teachers, lecturers, and what not. Federal
officeholders far outnumber those in any other category. They come
and go with every new administration; each receding tide, however,
leaving on the beach a few stragglers, who for one reason or another
choose (or are obliged) to remain. These latter, with a sprinkling
of private residents, comprise the only relatively static elements in a
scene which is predominantly kinetic. In brief space, one can do
no more than focus attention here and there upon the more significant
or conspicuous figures, as they appear and dissolve in the ever-shifting
procession.

In 1801 there appeared the first book printed in the new "Federal
City"—Samuel Blodgett's *Thoughts on the Increasing Wealth and
National Economy of the United States*—copies of which no longer
enthrall the bibliophile. A more substantial figure in this early literary
landscape is that of the many-sided and energetic Yankee, Joel Barlow—
lawyer, diplomat, financier, philosopher, wit, poet (of a sort), the
intimate friend of Jefferson and Tom Paine and Robert Fulton and
many another then famous or destined for fame. In 1807, two years

97

after his return from a sojourn abroad, Barlow purchased a large estate bordering on Rock Creek, a mile or two north of the Potomac; and here at Kalorama he presided for several years over the first real cultural oasis in the "ten-mile square," until he went abroad once more, in 1811, as Minister to France, and died a year later in Poland. While living at Kalorama, Barlow published the work which gave him for a time the character of a great national poet. This was *The Columbiad,* an ambitiously conceived epic of America, in 10 books and 3,675 rhymed couplets. Hawthorne's comment on its "ponderosity of leaden verses" has been echoed in varying phrase by a host of later critics, and Barlow's reputation as a poet is negligible today.

Several bombastic "historical" dramas by George Washington Parke Custis, a step-grandson of the first President, and some equally bombastic verses by Thomas Law, the talented but eccentric English land speculator who married Custis' daughter, belong to this arid early period, as do three or four books with a background of Washington life and scenery written by George Watterston, an early Librarian of Congress. Much better known than these men, however, is William Wirt, for 12 years (1817-29) Attorney General of the United States, biographer of Patrick Henry and author of *The Letters of a British Spy*—a book almost as widely read in its day as Barlow's *Columbiad.* During his long term as Attorney General, Wirt lived in a fine brick mansion on G Street, a little east of 18th, built and previously occupied by Tobias Lear, the last of George Washington's private secretaries and himself an author in a modest way. Lear published in 1795 a volume of *Observations on the River Potomack, the Country Adjacent, and the City of Washington.* Lear died by his own hand in the garden adjoining this home.

A later literary resident in the Lear mansion, John Pendleton Kennedy of Baltimore, wrote a biography of the former occupant, William Wirt; though he is best known as the author of *Swallow Barn* and two later novels—which enjoyed in their day a wide popularity. Kennedy twice held political office in the Capital, first as Congressman from 1838 to 1842, then as Secretary of the Navy in 1852-53. Those familiar with Poe's life in Baltimore will recall the aid given by Kennedy to the struggling poet, and the latter's statement that to Kennedy he owed "life itself." The author of *Swallow Barn* numbered Washington Irving also among his intimates; and on the last and longest of Irving's several stays in the Capital, he was Kennedy's guest in the old Lear mansion for the first 3 months of 1853.

James Kirke Paulding, an earlier crony of Irving's and his collaborator in the *Salmagundi* venture, served in Washington from 1815 to 1823 as secretary of the Board of Navy Commissioners, and again during 1837-41 as Secretary of the Navy in Van Buren's Cabinet, living for a part of this latter term in the historic old Rodgers House on Lafayette Square. Paulding's historical novels, especially *The Dutchman's Fireside* and one or two others with a background of Colonial life in New York, were long a popular staple of American fiction. He wrote much else besides—poems, essays, critical sketches, and with John P. Kennedy, his successor in the Cabinet after a decade's interval, he contributed very largely to the creation of such literary culture as Washington could legitimately claim in the first half of the nineteenth century.

Another distinguished man of letters who served as Secretary of the Navy in the course of this half century is the historian George Bancroft, a member of Polk's Cabinet for 18 months in 1845-46 while he occupied the Blair House on Pennsylvania Avenue. Thomas H. Benton, also a historian of note, was at the Capital from 1821 to 1850, as United States Senator from Missouri, and for a few years thereafter, while he was writing his *Thirty Years' View,* as a private citizen.

Peter Force—historian, editor, publisher, and onetime mayor of Washington—was a force in fact as well as name in the city's early life. During John Quincy Adams' administration (1825-29) he edited and published *The National Journal,* Adams' political organ. Then, with Congressional authorization, he tackled the huge task of editing and publishing a series of *American Archives,* embodying all important national historical documents, in chronological arrangement. Nine volumes of this series, covering the years 1774-76, were eventually issued. Force's personal collection of rare Americana has long been available to research workers in the Library of Congress. He also published, in 1845, *A Picture of Washington,* and "attached to the back a Washington Guide."

Though he wrote and published several volumes of poetry in the grand manner, Henry Rowe Schoolcraft is famous not as a poet but as an early scientific explorer of the West, and as author of a monumental work on the Indian tribes of this country. For several years preceding his death in 1864 Schoolcraft lived in Washington, and here his wife wrote a pro-slavery novel entitled *The Black Gauntlet,* which enjoyed a mild vogue just before the Civil War.

Charles Lanman's explorations, as described in his *Tour to the River Saguenay* and *Letters from the Allegheny Mountains,* were of a limited and amateur sort in comparison with Schoolcraft's. Lanman came to Washington in the late forties as Daniel Webster's private secretary. He was connected with *The National Intelligencer* for a time, and held various library positions here throughout five or six decades. Of his many publications in various fields, the most widely read were the two travel books.

Although this is a causerie of literature rather than of journalism, it seems essential to give something more than incidental mention to at least one Washington periodical—*The National Era,* established in 1847 and edited by Dr. Gamaliel Bailey, an ardent Abolitionist. The names of Bryant and Whittier figured in its list of contributors; Mrs. Sara J. C. Lippincott (Grace Greenwood), a minor literary light of Washington for nearly half a century, was one of its early staff editors; the first of those innumerable lush novels composed by Mrs. E. D. E. N. Southworth in her Georgetown cottage adorned its pages as a serial in 1849; and Mary Abigail Dodge (Gail Hamilton), who later became a permanent Washingtonian, turned her clever pen to its advantage in the late fifties—serving meanwhile as governess of Dr. Bailey's children. But *The National Era* is chiefly famous as the medium for the first publication of *Uncle Tom's Cabin,* which ran as a serial in its pages in 1851-52.

For a year or two in the decade just preceding the Civil War, the Abolitionist cause was also forcefully championed from the pulpit of the old First Unitarian Church by Moncure D. Conway—best known perhaps for his standard biography of Thomas Paine, though he wrote much else. So uncompromising, indeed, was his stand against slavery that a timorous board of trustees dismissed him from the pastorate. Dr. Conway was but one of several prominent men of letters associated at one time or another with the Unitarian Church. Ralph Waldo Emerson, on his way back to Boston from a health-seeking sojourn in the South, preached one of his earliest sermons here—in the late 1820's. Samuel Longfellow, whose fame as a poet has been obscured by that of his more illustrious brother, occupied its pulpit for a short time, at the beginning of his career; as did also Edward Everett Hale, author of *The Man Without a Country* and many other books in various fields. Returning to Washington about a half-century later, in 1903, Dr. Hale served as chaplain of the United States Senate until just before his death in 1909.

Key Bridge, over the Potomac River at Georgetown, testifies to the enduring fame of one who wrote the words of an enduring song. Francis Scott Key, for whom the bridge is named, came to Georgetown as a young lawyer in 1805, and lived there for 20 years in a house on M Street. He wrote little else than "The Star-Spangled Banner," and the circumstances under which that *tour de force* was written, in 1814, are familiar to every proper American school child. But it was the ironic fate of Key's contemporary, John Howard Payne, to father a long list of ambitious plays and operas, along with much journalistic writing, only to be remembered afterward as the author of a single song—"Home, Sweet Home"—composed abroad in 1822. Payne visited Washington or resided here at various times from 1809 to 1851, as actor, dramatist, journalist, and seeker of diplomatic posts—always, it would appear, harried by acute ill-fortune. He died in 1852, while serving as American consul at Tunis; some 30 years later his remains were brought here and given burial, with a commemorative monument, in Oak Hill Cemetery, Georgetown. A nationally popular song, which, unlike those by Key and Payne, had its actual origin in Washington, and which ranks far higher than theirs as poetry, is Mrs. Julia Ward Howe's "Battle Hymn of the Republic." It was written in Willard's Hotel, on the night following its author's return from witnessing a review of Union troops near the Capital, late in 1861. Within a few weeks its stirring rhythms, wedded to the tune of "John Brown's Body," were sounding throughout the North and in every camp of Union soldiers on the Southern battle fronts.

Though Mrs. Howe's "Battle Hymn" has led us into the Civil War period, it seems desirable to turn back for a moment and mention a few among the many literary notables, American and English, who were merely passing visitors to the Capital in the first half century or so of its existence, and who thereby made some contribution to its literary associations. First in point of time is Thomas Paine, the noted pamphleteer (*Age of Reason, Common Sense, The Crisis*), who for several days was Jefferson's honored guest in the Presidential mansion, directly after Paine's return from abroad in 1802; his appearance on the streets arm in arm with the President scandalized official Washington, and led one extremist to suggest that Jefferson and his "blasphemous crony" should be hanged on the same gallows. The poet Thomas Moore, elegant and patronizing, paused for a week or so at the British Legation here, on a grand tour of America in 1804, and composed his much-quoted satiric fling at "the embryo Capital." Washington Irving, in the course of four sojourns between 1812 and 1853, seems to have done more than any other visitor to oxygenize the rarefied early literary atmosphere of Washington. The popular English writer of sea yarns, Captain Marryat, came in the thirties and recorded his impressions with a severe yet not wholly unsympathetic pen.

Caustic Mrs. Trollope, whose *Domestic Manners of the Americans* so fluttered the young Republic's dovecotes for years after its publication in 1832, evinced a somewhat surprising partiality for the Capital. Writing in 1831, she says: "I was delighted with the whole aspect of Washington; light, cheerful, and airy, it reminded me of our fashionable watering places. . . . The total absence of all sights, sounds, or smells of commerce adds greatly to the charm." Her illustrious son Anthony, coming 18 years later (and again in 1861), liked the city rather less than did his mother. Charles Dickens, on the occasion of his first visit in 1842, liked it not at all—as certain passages in his

American Notes abundantly testify. That other great Victorian, William Makepeace Thackeray, who lectured here in 1853, and 1856, was more lenient; as was also the clever and sprightly Harriet Martineau, a mid-century guest at Mrs. Elizabeth Peyton's select boarding house on Pennsylvania Avenue, where into her silver ear-trumpet flowed the conversation of Clay, Calhoun, Webster, John Marshall, and other notable persons then subject to Mrs. Peyton's domestic care. The English poet commonly known as "Owen Meredith" was in Washington as private secretary to his uncle, Sir Henry Bulwer, British Minister to the United States in 1849-52, and extremely improbable tradition has it that he composed his famous novel in verse, *Lucile,* in the old Matthew St. Clair Clarke House on H Street, then occupied by the Legation. Nathaniel Parker Willis seems to have devoted most of his time throughout at least three extended stays in the Capital to writing for various New York periodicals; the first of these stays was in 1836-37, the second in 1846, the third in 1862-63. Although Edgar Allan Poe was frequently in Washington, his most famous visit was in March 1843, when he came to lecture and be received at the White House but remained to imbibe too deeply with several convivial friends here—to the discomfiture of the local literati who had sponsored his visit.

Against the turbulent background of political and military Washington in Civil War days moved a humble figure (then unknown to all but a little circle of friends and disciples) whose reputation has since emerged as conspicuously in the field of literature as has that of Lincoln in the field of statesmanship. Walt Whitman came down to Washington from Brooklyn, late in 1862, on his way to the Virginia front, where his brother George had been wounded. Returning to the Capital, he settled down here, and for the succeeding year and a half he devoted most of his time and energy to personal ministrations among the sick and wounded soldiers quartered in the city, eking out the barest living for himself meanwhile by part-time work in the office of an Army paymaster. Then, after a physical breakdown, he was ordered home for 6 months of rest. Returning to Washington in February 1865, he secured a clerkship in the Indian Bureau of the Interior Department, from which he was summarily ousted a few months later by Secretary James Harlan, following a chance discovery that the clerk had once written a disreputable book called *Leaves of Grass.* It was not long before the efforts of friends had found for him another governmental berth, this time in the Attorney General's office. That position he held more than 7 years—until his sudden paralytic stroke of January 1873, which led to his departure for Camden 5 months later.

Whitman's methods of nursing during the Civil War days were

as unorthodox as his poetry. He came and went at will through the squalid emergency hospitals, letting the tonic of his exuberant and generous personality do duty for bedside training. Of the triumph of this peculiar technique there is no question. A "well-known correspondent of the New York Herald," quoted in John Burroughs' book on Whitman, testifies:

> I saw him, time and again, in the Washington hospitals, or wending his way there with basket or haversack on his arm, and the strength of beneficence suffusing his face. His devotion surpassed the devotion of woman. . . . Never shall I forget one night when I accompanied him on his rounds . . . there was a smile of affection and welcome on every face, however wan, and his presence seemed to light up the place as it might be lighted by the presence of the God of love. From cot to cot they called him, often in tremulous tones or in whispers. They embraced him; they touched his hand; they gazed at him. To one he gave a few words of cheer; for another he wrote a letter home; to others he gave an orange, a few comfits, a cigar, a pipe and tobacco, a sheet of paper or a postage stamp . . . from another he would receive a dying message for mother, wife or sweetheart. . . . As he took his way toward the door, you could hear the voices of many a stricken hero calling, 'Walt, Walt, Walt! Come again! Come again!'

The chief scene of his ministrations seems to have been the Armory Square Hospital, 6th Street and what is now Independence Avenue. However, he ranged the city far and wide, caring for the sick and wounded, gathering impressions and facts for his newspaper letters, and never failing to leave the imprint of his unique personality wherever he went. John Burroughs describes him in those days as "a large slow-moving figure clad in gray, with broad-brimmed hat and gray beard. . . . He had a hirsute, kindly look, but far removed from the finely-cut traditional poet's face."

In the catalog of Whitman's creative work during his Washington decade, first place must be given to the great threnody in commemoration of Lincoln, "When Lilacs Last in the Dooryard Bloomed." This, with the other poem inspired by Lincoln's death, "O Captain, My Captain," and a few less notable pieces, was published as a sort of sequel to the volume of war poems entitled *Drum Taps,* which though chiefly written before the end of 1863 did not appear until 1866. A small group of miscellaneous poems, issued in pamphlet form with the title of *Passage to India,* also belongs to this period, throughout the whole of which Walt was intermittently revising and reshaping the 1860 edition of *Leaves of Grass.* His prose work of the time includes the essay, "Democratic Vistas," and two volumes of letters—*The Wound Dresser,* descriptive of his hospital experiences during the war; and *Calamus,* embodying his correspondence with Peter Doyle, the young Irish streetcar conductor who for several years had been Walt's most intimate friend in the Capital.

Whitman's presence in Washington was the magnet that drew thither in 1863 a young man named John Burroughs, then an impecunious country school teacher in New York State, with definite literary ambitions. Burroughs was one of those to whom *Leaves of Grass* had spoken a compelling personal message, and he had heard much about Whitman the man in letters from his Washington friend, E. M. Allen. He decided to try his fortune in the Capital, hoping to secure a Government position which would give him some leisure for writing and for association with Walt and his circle. For a month or so after his arrival he did part-time work in the Quartermaster General's department, lodging meanwhile in a back room of his friend Allen's army supply store. Here, in the autumn of 1863, he first met Walt Whitman. Thereafter the two were much together, discussing the soul and immortality and many lesser things on long country jaunts, over a mug of ale and a peck of oysters at Harvey's, or in company with a few other chosen spirits at William Douglas O'Connor's house (1015 O Street NW.). The more tangible results of this communion were a magazine article by Burroughs entitled "Walt Whitman and His Drum Taps," printed in *Galaxy* for December 1866, and a little volume of *Notes on Walt Whitman as Poet and Person* published the following year. In 1864 Burroughs secured a clerkship in the Treasury Department; and by 1868 he had a home and a garden of his own—at 1332 V Street NW. (the house, occupied by Negroes, is still standing). Many of the essays which went into his first two nature books, *Wake Robin* and *Winter Sunshine,* were written here, and owe their inspiration to scenes or impressions or experiences in Washington and the neighboring countryside. By the end of 1872 Burroughs had grown weary of city life, and returned to his native State.

William Douglas O'Connor, in whose home Whitman lived for several months after his arrival at the Capital in 1862, was a brilliant, high-minded, and eloquent Irish-American journalist, in Government service from 1861 until his death in 1889. His forceful anti-slavery novel, *Harrington,* was issued in 1860 by the Boston publishing firm which also sponsored the 1860 edition of *Leaves of Grass,* and the two writers had met in their publisher's office. This casual friendship soon ripened into intimacy after Whitman's coming to Washington. When Walt was summarily discharged from the Indian Bureau, in 1865, O'Connor wrote and published a fiery pamphlet entitled *The Good Gray Poet,* which was the first widely circulated defense of *Leaves of Grass* and its author. A few stories and poems, with some writings in support of the Baconian theory, make up the rest of O'Connor's literary output.

Among several now more or less prominent writers who, like

O'Connor, appeared upon the local scene in 1861, one was a young man named John Hay. Another, Louisa M. Alcott, served as a nurse in the Union Hospital at Georgetown during the early Civil War period, gleaning thereby the material for her earliest published book, *Hospital Sketches*. Edmund Clarence Stedman, after several months here as a war correspondent, was appointed in 1861 to a clerkship in the Attorney General's office, which he held until returning to New York some two years later. For a considerable part of this time, Stedman shared living quarters with a fellow poet, John James Piatt, a clerk in the Treasury Department from 1861 to 1867, and (1871-75) librarian of the House of Representatives. John Burroughs' letters from the Capital frequently mention "poet Piatt" and his gifted wife, Sarah M. B. Piatt, whose 17 volumes of verse include at least 2 early titles written in collaboration with her husband. Along with Stedman and Piatt should be mentioned a less youthful Apollo in the service of Admetus at this time—John Pierpont, poet, Unitarian clergyman, and reformer, for 5 years (from 1861 until his death at the age of 81) a clerk in the Treasury Department.

Among the few distinguished men of letters whose residence in Washington for any considerable term of years was (to outward appearance) self-chosen, Henry Adams stands out by far the most conspicuously. His first visit to the Capital was as a boy of 12, in 1850; he stayed with his grandmother, the widow of John Quincy Adams, and his father took him to the White House, where "all the boy's family had lived" and where he "took for granted that he should some day live." A decade later, in the winter of 1860-61, he was here again, this time as private secretary to his father, who had just been elected to Congress, finding then, as in 1850, "the same rude colony camped in the same forest, with the same unfinished Greek temples for workrooms, and sloughs for roads."

With his father's appointment as Minister to England, in 1861, young Adams went abroad for a 7-year sojourn, at the end of which he once more returned to Washington, working here as a newspaper correspondent until the beginning, early in 1870, of another 7-year cycle spent elsewhere. Finally, in 1877, he came back with the definite intention of settling down in the Capital—"partly to write history, but chiefly because his seven years of laborious banishment, in Boston, convinced him that, as far as he had a function in life, it was as stable-companion to statesmen." From that time until his death in 1918 (though with frequent and sometimes long intervals of travel) Henry Adams was the foremost private citizen of Washington, sharing more than any other in its various higher activities, and viewing with a keen and philosophic eye its crowded cavalcade of men and events.

Few salons in this country, then or since, could rival those presided over by Adams and his wife, before the latter's death in 1886. The Adams breakfasts were a local institution in the late eighties. But with all the rest, including an immense correspondence, Adams found time for a surprisingly large and diverse literary output—the nine-volume *History of the United States During the Administrations of Jefferson and Madison,* biographies of Albert Gallatin and John Randolph, two novels, the study of medievalism entitled *Mont-Saint-Michel and Chartres,* and that singular autobiography *The Education of Henry Adams,* which in less than two decades since its posthumous publication has become a classic of American literature. Adams' first novel, *Democracy,* appeared anonymously in 1880, and created a mild sensation in its day; it is a skillful presentation of Washington life and affairs in the decade following the Civil War, with especial reference to the financial and political scandals of Grant's administration. *Esther,* published 4 years later under the pseudonym of Frances Snow Compton, proved much less popular with the public, although Adams himself thought it a better novel than *Democracy.*

While in Washington as private secretary to his father, just before the Civil War, Henry Adams chanced to meet John Hay, a young man of his own age who had lately come to the Capital as one of President Lincoln's secretaries. "From the first slight meeting . . . he recognized Hay as a friend, and never lost sight of him at the future crossing of their paths." Hay left Washington at the close of the war, to occupy diplomatic and journalistic posts until 1878, by which time he had married into a fortune and had won literary fame as the author of *Pike County Ballads* and *Castilian Days.* Then he returned, to serve for a year or so as Assistant Secretary of State, resigning that position to enter with John G. Nicolay (his friend of the old Pike County days in Illinois and his fellow-secretary in Lincoln's service) upon the task of preparing a historical biography of Lincoln. As Walt Whitman had drawn Burroughs to the Capital in 1863, so in 1879 Henry Adams was the determining factor that led Hay to make his home here. After 5 years of intimacy, the two friends commissioned the Boston architect, H. H. Richardson, to build them adjoining houses on H Street, facing Lafayette Square and across Sixteenth Street from old St. John's Church. Hay's home on the corner, executed in Richardson's best "donjon keep" style, vied with its companion to the west as a center of cultural and political light for 20 years, until the death of its owner (then serving as Secretary of State) in 1905. While this luxurious mansion was under construction, Hay wrote and published *The Bread Winners,* an anonymous diatribe (in fictional form) against labor unions, which with literary charm and skill ration-alized the possessive instincts of upper-class America in the prosperous eighties. By 1890 he had completed, in collaboration with Nicolay, the 10-volume *Abraham Lincoln: A History,* and in the same year he issued a volume of collected poems.

Clarence King, though he wrote but one non-scientific book (that climbers' classic, *Mountaineering in the Sierra Nevadas*), was the closest intimate of Adams and Hay for nearly a quarter century. When the United States Geological Survey was established in 1879, he became its first Director, resigning 3 years later to practice as a private mining engineer. Thereafter he was occasionally in Washington, living with one or another of his two friends on Lafayette Square. He died in 1901. Henry Adams knew nearly every great American of his time, but to none does he give higher praise in his autobiography than to Clarence King: "The best and brightest man of his generation, with talents immeasurably beyond any of his contemporaries."

Next to King, the friend closest to Adams and Hay throughout their Washington period seems to have been the perennial Senator from Massachusetts, Henry Cabot Lodge, whose home at 1765 Massachusetts Avenue was a social, political, and literary rendezvous during most of the quarter-century just preceding the Coolidge era. In his Harvard days Lodge had studied history under Henry Adams, and later he won his own spurs in the field of historical scholarship with biographies of George Cabot (his great-grandfather), George Washington, Alexander Hamilton, and Daniel Webster.

A less intimate though more distinguished friend of Henry Adams, and his close neighbor for a long period, was George Bancroft. From 1874 to 1891, for the last 17 years of a life which began when the National Government was moving into the new Capital, Bancroft occupied a home on H Street between Connecticut Avenue and 17th— a modest squarish dwelling with a large garden, now obliterated. Here the elderly historian and diplomat laboriously revised his 10-volume *History of the United States* for two separate editions, published nearly a decade apart, and completed two new works—a *History of the Formation of the Constitution* and a biography of *Martin Van Buren to the End of His Public Career.* For all his scholarly preoccupations and his advanced age at this time, Bancroft was a devotee of social pleasures, of gardening, and of the bridle path. In the garden adjoining his H Street home he achieved fame among horticulturists by originating, from parent European stock, the popular "American Beauty" rose.

Of several western writers who made more or less transitory appearances upon the Washington scene after the Civil War, the earliest is Mark Twain, who arrived here in the late autumn of 1867, directly after landing from his first journey abroad. He came to take a position with Senator Stewart of Nevada, whom he had known in the West. Owing to what may be mildly described as temperamental differences between the two men, this connection was short-lived; and for the greater part of his few months' stay, Mark was chiefly engrossed in publication arrangements for *The Innocents Abroad* (his first nationally popular book) and in conducting with William Swinton what he described as "the first Newspaper Correspondence Syndicate that an unhappy world ever saw." An amusing chapter of Senator Stewart's autobiography is devoted to this brief phase in Mark Twain's life.

No element of humor lightens the story of the next western visitant. Early in 1877, John James Piatt (the Ohio poet) undertook to establish here a literary periodical called *The Capital*. Conceiving that Bret Harte's name on its masthead would be a drawing card, he offered the editorship to Harte at a salary of $5,000 a year. Then as always impecunious, Harte jumped at this alluring bait, and hastened forthwith to Washington, where he spent several anxious months (July to October, 1877) at the old Riggs House, while Piatt's plans slowly petered out for lack of adequate financing. At the end, with the publication in bankruptcy, Harte was left stranded here. Through the aid of political friends, he secured a Government position, as commercial agent at Crefeld, Prussia, and left the Capital on this mission.

Near the present 16th Street and Crescent Place, on Meridian Hill, stood for some 30 years the log cabin built and occupied by "the poet of the Sierras," Joaquin Miller, during his residence in Washington— from 1883 to 1885. Miller came here seeking political office, but disappointed in this quest he remained to carry on some literary work and to edify the Capital with frequent glimpses of his picturesque person, clad in a frock coat and corduroy trousers tucked into high-heeled boots, with a great tasseled sombrero rising above his long yellow hair and bristling mustachios. His log-cabin home was moved to Rock Creek Park in 1912 by the California State Association, and presented to the Nation.

The gifted but never adequately appreciated author of *South Sea Idyls,* Charles Warren Stoddard—long prominent with his friends, Bret Harte and Joaquin Miller, in San Francisco's Bohemian group of the seventies and eighties—appeared upon the Washington scene in 1889. He came to teach English literature at the Catholic University of America, remaining in that connection until 1902. Unusual personal charm and wide experience of life made Stoddard a great favorite in local literary and social circles during his 13 years' stay here. At least four of his published books were written in the house he occupied on Capitol Hill.

Still another literary San Franciscan who figured for a time in Washington life is the inexplicable and mordant Ambrose Bierce. When Collis P. Huntington's notorious "refunding bill" was before Congress in 1896, William R. Hearst sent Bierce here to report the bill's progress for his newspapers and to aid in its defeat. With this purpose accomplished, Bierce returned to California for two years. In 1898 he was in Washington again, as local oracle and feature writer for Hearst. He pursued that occupation, with occasional intervals of travel, for a decade thereafter. Then he turned to independent writing and the preparation (for a Washington publisher) of his *Collected Works,* hobnobbing meanwhile with a few congenial cronies in "newspaper row," or acting as cook and host at brilliant Sunday breakfasts in the Olympia Apartments, where he lived until the autumn day in 1913 when he set out upon the mysterious journey to Mexico from which he never returned.

Alfred Henry Lewis, a contemporary laborer with Bierce in Mr. Hearst's Washington vineyard, is the last in this little group of men from the West. Coming to the Capital from Kansas City in 1891, he served as correspondent for the Chicago *Times* until that journal's demise in 1894; then he became head of the Hearst bureau here. The first of his inimitable "Wolfville" stories related in the picturesque lingo of an old western cattleman, appeared in the Washington *Post* for July 7, 1895, opening up a vein of pay-ore which Lewis tapped with success almost to the time of his death in 1914.

Three names particularly prominent in the Capital's later literary-social annals are those of Frances Hodgson Burnett, Thomas Nelson Page, and Maurice Francis Egan. Appearing upon the Washington scene in 1877, Mrs. Burnett soon established a more than local reputation as talented writer and gracious hostess. At one of her afternoon receptions at 1219 I Street (the house in which she wrote *Little Lord Fauntleroy*) Oscar Wilde made a memorable appearance during his American lecture tour of 1882, arrayed in "black silk clawhammer coat, fancily flowered dark waistcoat, knee breeches, silk stockings, and patent leather pumps with broad buckles." From 1886 to 1890, Mrs. Burnett lived at 1730 K Street; then, from the proceeds of *Fauntleroy's* phenomenal success as book and play, she was able to build the home at 1770 Massachusetts Avenue which she occupied until her death in 1924.

Thomas Nelson Page was associated with Washington life and letters over a period of nearly 30 years, although his actual residence here was interrupted by a 6-years' absence abroad (1913-19) as Ambassador to Italy. For a time after coming to the Capital from Richmond in 1893, he lived at 1708 Massachusetts Avenue; but by 1897 he had built and was occupying the handsome Colonial mansion at 1759 R Street, where many of his best known books were written and where he died in 1922. Under the genial and lavish hospitality dispensed here, this home became in a sense the chief literary-social center of the South—its only formidable rival hereabouts being the historic

Fairfax House in Alexandria during the several years just preceding 1920 when Mrs. Burton Harrison presided there.

Like the author of *Marse Chan* and *Red Rock,* Maurice Francis Egan had a home in Washington for nearly 30 years but was abroad in diplomatic service for a considerable part of this period. He held a professorship in English literature at the Catholic University of America from 1896 to 1904, when he was appointed United States Minister to Denmark. Returning from abroad to his home on Capitol Hill in 1918, Dr. Egan spent the remaining 6 years of his life in quiet literary work and in social intercourse with a host of friends.

The picturesque figure of Albert Pike—lawyer, ex-Confederate general, exponent of Freemasonry, as well as poet—adorned the Capital from 1868 until his death in 1891. Richard Hovey's boyhood days were spent here, and after his graduation from Dartmouth in 1885 he studied drawing and painting for a year in the Art Students' League of Washington. John Hay's daughter Helen (later Mrs. Payne Whitney) evinced unusual poetic ability in the small volume modestly entitled *Some Verses* issued in 1898. The Negro poet Paul Laurence Dunbar held a minor position in the Library of Congress for about 15 months, in 1897-98. One of the most gifted of recent American poets, Eleanor Wylie, lived in Washington from the time of her first marriage in 1906 until 1911. Harriet Prescott Spofford, like Miss Wylie a novelist as well as a poet, spent many winters here before her death in 1921. Still another poet-novelist, Miss Grace Denio Litchfield, has made her home in the Capital for nearly half a century.

With the possible exception of Thomas Jefferson, the early "literary Presidents" are so called chiefly because their names are attached to rather more than the usual Presidential quota of state papers, journalistic articles, personal correspondence, diaries, and political pamphlets. Not until the advent of Theodore Roosevelt and Woodrow Wilson was any occupant of the White House a creator of what (for lack of a better term) is often referred to as "pure literature"—or, as the specialist sometimes puts it, "mere literature." They, too, were specialists in a way, so far as their predilection for history is concerned but even their historical writing has a definite literary flavor. Of the two, Roosevelt was the more prolific and versatile, Wilson the more scholarly and finished writer. Throughout their respective terms of office (Roosevelt's from 1901 to 1909 and Wilson's from 1913 to 1921) they imparted to the White House, and in some degree to official Washington life in general, a distinctive literary atmosphere.

Scarcely less important than theirs was the contribution, as a leavening literary influence in the Capital during the same general period, made by two distinguished foreign diplomats and men of letters, J. J. Jusserand and James Bryce. The former's service in Washington, as French Ambassador to the United States, extended through nearly a quarter century, from 1902 to 1925; and something more than the first half of this period is charmingly commemorated in his reminiscent volume, *With Americans of Past and Present Days*. Bryce's term of office as British Ambassador was for the relatively much shorter period from 1907 to 1913; but he had made three previous visits to this country, and had spent much time in Washington, while engaged in the preparation of his authoritative work on *The American Commonwealth*.

Not often regarded as literary productions, Government reports take their place in the Washington cultural scene, since they are published here, and often written here. Buried in the disheartening format of the Government publication, literary works of a high order occasionally emerge. The best early examples seem to occur in volumes on exploration, geology, and ethnology. A few are mentioned, more as an aperitif than as a full-course menu, to demonstrate that the Government writer does not invariably adhere to a dull, bureaucratic formula.

Major John Wesley Powell, in his *Exploration of the Colorado River* (1875), produced a narrative as full of suspense, action, and color as a novel, and set the pace for a series of rich narrative and descriptive reports in the 1880's. Clarence Edward Dutton's *Report on the Geology of the High Plateaus of Utah* (1880) and his *Tertiary History of the Grand Canyon District* (1882) have only in recent years been recognized for their vivid descriptive quality. The Smithsonian Institution has published the *Scientific Writings* of Joseph Henry, its first secretary, in which Henry's capabilities as an author are well demonstrated. W. T. Hornaday's *Extermination of the American Bison* (1887), a scientific source volume and a clarion literary message in one, was also published by the Smithsonian Institution. A galaxy of forceful writers gathered in the Bureau of American Ethnology in the eighties and nineties, and contributed to the volumes of the Bureau, in addition to writing notable individual works. Among these men were W. H. Holmes, whose *Pottery of the Ancient Pueblos* (1886) is a well-penned work; Frank H. Cushing, who distinguished himself with *Zuñi Creation Myths* and other works on the Zuñis; W J McGee, Walter Hough, J. Walter Fewkes, Neil Judd, and others.

It should be said in closing that this brief chronicle makes no pretense of dealing exhaustively with its subject. In particular, though a few prominent later names are mentioned, no thoroughgoing effort has been made to deal with Washington writers of the past quarter century. That task belongs more properly to some commentator of the future.

Journalism

S INCE the *Times and Potowmack Packet* began to appear weekly in Georgetown in 1789 about a thousand newspapers and periodicals have been established in the District. The majority lasted but a brief time. Many were issued as temporary campaign publications; many more began bravely and ended in financial difficulty. This unequaled record of failures made Washington a "journalistic graveyard." And yet, during the first 30 or 40 years of the nineteenth century, before the invention of the telegraph, Washington newspapers, as administration organs and with almost complete monopoly of Washington news, were as important as the strong New York dailies. From the Civil War until the present, the development of the Washington correspondent elevated journalism in the Capital to a position of exceptional importance and power.

More than 300 newspapers in the United States and many in foreign cities maintain bureaus and special correspondents in Washington. Added to these are the national and international press associations, special bureaus, press photographers, and innumerable free-lance writers. Washington correspondents transmit governmental news to other parts of the country, and often directly affect the shaping of policies through the information they bring to the Capital on conditions elsewhere. Some of the most brilliant newspaper men and women have been numbered among them, with an influence comparable to that of the great editors in foreign capitals.

In the spring of 1795 an enterprising Norfolk printer named Thomas Wilson piled his printing press and other paraphernalia on a large wagon and drove into the wilderness area on the Potomac which had been designated to become the Capital in five years. Wilson thought it wise to launch a newspaper on a small scale, and to be on hand for Government business when it started. He was not deterred by the fact that, across Rock Creek in Georgetown, three papers had been started in the past six years, two of which were then dead and the third moribund. Wilson set up his plant on Greenleaf Point near the present Army War College and on May 22, 1795, issued the first newspaper with a Washington imprint. It was a quarto-sized eight-page pamphlet graced with the title, *Impartial Observer and Washington Advertiser*. Overweighted with this masthead, the paper did not prosper, either as a semiweekly or as a weekly. Sideline sales of

"Carey's war maps, writing paper, writing ink, ink powder, etc." were not sufficient to save the enterprise. Wilson died the following February, and his paper followed him to the grave scarcely three months later.

In June 1796, Benjamin More, owner of a Washington general store, founded the *Washington Gazette,* a four-page weekly. It suspended publication after a year, was resuscitated a few months later, and finally gave up the struggle in 1798. When the seat of government was transferred to Washington in 1800, the "city" had no newspaper. Georgetown and Alexandria had one paper each—the four-year-old *Sentinel of Liberty,* and the twelve-year-old *Virginia Journal and Alexandria Advertiser,* which still exists as the Alexandria *Gazette.*

The editor of the *Virginia Federalist,* a supporter of Hamilton's party at Richmond, moved to Georgetown and on September 25, 1800, published the first issue of the triweekly *Washington Federalist.* Less than a week later the *National Magazine and Cabinet of the United States* took up the cause of Jefferson from the heights of Georgetown, the publisher of this paper having also removed there from Richmond. The semiweekly *Washington Museum,* representing the Federalist Party, appeared in November 1800.

More important to the administration than any of these was the triweekly *National Intelligencer,* the first issue of which appeared in Washington October 31, 1800. It had a more or less assured success from the beginning. The young editor, Samuel Harrison Smith, on the advice of Jefferson came here from Philadelphia, where he had edited the *Universal Gazette.* He continued the *Gazette* as a weekly edition of the *Intelligencer.* Smith's paper became the official organ of the administration, with access to Government printing as patronage. When Congress assembled, Smith asked permission to report proceedings, which the Federalist majority denied him. At the second session, the Republicans—or Democrats, as they came to be called—issued orders that reporters be admitted to the floor. Smith was a good stenographer and his reports were, for some time, the only printed records of congressional proceedings. When Smith resigned the editorship in 1810, Joseph Gales, Jr., and William W. Seaton, new owners of the *Intelligencer,* continued to report the proceedings of the Senate and House respectively.

From 1824 to 1838 the reports were published in book form under the title of *Register of Debates,* the ancestor of the *Congressional Globe* and *Congressional Record.* The earlier publications were issued at private risk, though Congress subscribed to a certain number of copies; the *Record* has been printed entirely at Government expense. In 1843, Gales and Seaton were permitted to undertake publication of debates prior to 1824, based on stenographic notes, condensed journals of proceedings, and newspaper accounts.

During the War of 1812 the *National Intelligencer* appeared as a single sheet while the editors were helping to guard the city. The British sacked and burned the newspaper office, occasioning a few days' delay in publication. The *Intelligencer* continued publication, however (as a daily after 1813), until Gales' death in 1860.

Many papers, begun during the first decade of the century, did not survive. The *Atlantic World,* for instance, first issued by John Wood in 1807 in the interest of Aaron Burr, lasted only a few months. For the first three decades, newspapers were written for the classes rather than the masses, published less domestic than foreign news, and were not sold on the streets. Communication was limited to slow-going coaches and sailing boats. Washington newspapers were generally popular, as sources of governmental news and as the organs of administration and opposition parties. This period produced the first special correspondence from Washington, as early as 1825. Some authorities, however, date the beginning of the Press Gallery as early as 1823.

During the 1830's two labor papers, the *American Mechanic* and the *Washingtonian,* appeared in the District, and newsboys and carriers were introduced. Until the Civil War, various administrations continued to maintain so-called official papers, to which printing and other patronage would go in exchange for editorial approval of policies. Changes in official organs usually followed changes of parties in power. A noted series of such shifts reflects the tempestuous character of the administration of Andrew Jackson. Coming into office in 1829, Jackson abandoned support of the *National Journal* (established by Peter Force to advocate the candidacy of John Quincy Adams) and gave official approval to the pro-Jackson *United States Telegraph.* The editor, Duff Green, was in favor for a brief period, until he supported Vice President John C. Calhoun in his political differences with Jackson. Thereupon the President brought Francis Preston Blair to Washington to found the *Globe* and to become a member of Jackson's "Kitchen cabinet." Blair began publication of the *Congressional Globe* in 1832, a record of debates in book form, partially subsidized by governmental subscriptions. Propagandist and muckraking periodicals of the ante bellum era include Mrs. Anne Royall's weekly *Paul Pry* (1831-36) and its successor, *The Huntress* (1836-54). Mrs. Royall, who was stolen by the Indians when a child and lived among them for 15 years, was a queer, unattractive, but intelligent woman. The period also produced certain abolitionist papers, including the *Genius of Universal Emancipation* and Gamaliel Bailey's *National Era,* in which *Uncle Tom's Cabin* appeared as a serial in 1851. Contributors to the Washington journals of the day included such literary figures as Whittier, Lowell, Hale, Wendell Phillips, and others.

About 1838, because of the slowness of communicating news, daily papers in New York, Philadelphia, and Baltimore established a pony express for the transmission of news. It also served Washington, but the need for it was brief. The railroads developed, and the telegraph came into practical use in 1844. The New York Associated Press, founded in 1848, began to serve papers of the Middle West and Far West. Washington papers then fell into a decline, for they no longer held a monopoly on news originating in the Nation's Capital. The *Globe* was succeeded by the *Madisonian,* which gave place to Ritchie's *Union,* but none of these or their successors had the power of the old *Telegraph* and *Globe.* Political support ceased to be an important factor. The success of a paper depended upon its ability to mobilize a reading public for its advertisers. The oldest newspaper in Washington, the *Evening Star,* dates back to 1852, when this changing trend began to take definite form.

The institution of Washington correspondent, the most important phase of journalism in the Capital, was an outgrowth of letter-writing. Visiting editors, who came to Washington for political reasons, were accustomed to write letters to their papers back home, giving their personal views on legislative and other matters. One of the first of these was James Cheetham, English-born radical and vigorous Jeffersonian who edited the *American Citizen* in New York from 1800 until his death in 1809. William Duane, gifted young Irish-American editor of the *Philadelphia Aurora,* was a letter-writing contemporary of Cheetham; both were expert in vituperation and attack. Elias Kingman came to Washington from Rhode Island in 1822, and for the next 40 years operated a news bureau, contributing to leading papers all over the country, and in a sense establishing the profession of correspondent distinct from that of visiting editor and occasional letter-writer. Colonel Samuel L. Knapp, representing the *Boston Galaxy,* came about the same time and soon began to furnish news to other papers than his own.

Not until 1832, however, was the Washington correspondent as such given general recognition. In that year James Brooks came here to represent the Portland *Advertiser;* to him is generally credited the idea of regular correspondence from the Capital to the press. The elder James Gordon Bennett the same year left Washington to establish the New York *Herald.* As a Washington reporter for the New York *Courier,* Bennett had written letters full of intimate details about the lives of prominent people, sparkling news items similar to those in popular columns of today. News value above all else was his criterion, and it is said of him that he freed the press from party control. Forerunners of the gossip columnists were present among these early correspondents. Matthew J. Davis, biographer of Aaron Burr, wrote as "The Spy in Washington," and Nathan Sargent as "Oliver Oldchild." Writing fearlessly from behind their pseudonyms, valuable channels were opened to them, and they quickly revealed important political information. The decade before the Civil War produced an outstanding group of correspondents. Ben: Perley Poore, editor of the Boston *Bee,* came to Washington in 1854, served a short time in the Army, and was made clerk of the Senate Committee on Printing Records. His *Reminiscences of 60 Years in the National Metropolis* presents an excellent picture of the period. E. A. Pollard, correspondent for the Charleston *Mercury,* was later an unflagging critic of Jefferson Davis, during the war.

Notable Civil War correspondents included Horace White, who, as a reporter, accompanied Lincoln during his campagin against Douglas, and who later edited the Chicago *Tribune* and the New York *Evening Post;* John Russell Young, correspondent with the Army of the Potomac; Henry Villard, who was later a railroad builder and controlling owner of the New York *Evening Post;* A. R. Spofford, Librarian of the Library of Congress from 1864 to 1869; Whitelaw Reid, afterward publisher of the New York *Tribune* and Ambassador to Great Britain; and Walt Whitman, who was a reporter for the New York *Times* while serving as a nurse in the Union Army. Mrs. Emily Edson Briggs, who won her record as a war correspondent during the Lincoln administration, was probably the first woman admitted to the White House as a press representative. Her letters, signed "Olivia," were also printed in England.

The personal interview, according to Francis A. Richardson, originated with J. B. McCullagh's interview with Alexander H. Stephens about the Confederacy. McCullagh was a Washington correspondent and editor of the St. Louis *Globe-Democrat.* President Andrew Johnson later permitted himself to be quoted by McCullagh. Richardson, who was one of the 26 telegraphic correspondents in the press gallery during the Reconstruction period, tells in his *Recollections of a Washington Newspaper Correspondent* how Senators, Cabinet members, Representatives, and other Government officials sought out correspondents during this era. Confidences were regarded as inviolate. Correspondents represented three to six newspapers each, and realized a large income, sometimes $10,000 to $20,000 a year. De B. Randolph Keim, another prominent correspondent of the time, was favored by President Grant, who succeeded Johnson.

Except for a few favored individuals, from Fillmore's administration to that of President Wilson, correspondents depended for White House news on Cabinet officers and personal secretaries. Cleveland would see no reporters. McKinley, almost as silent, had as friend and counselor Marcus Alonzo Hanna, whose residence on Lafayette Square drew swarms of newspapermen. A few correspondents were privileged to print Theodore Roosevelt's fervid convictions at the risk of immediate repudiation by their author. "T. R." initiated the custom of releasing stories for Monday papers, when news is ordinarily light. During Taft's administration, Gus Karger covered Washington for the Cincinnati *Star,* which was owned by the President's half-brother, Charles P. Taft. Karger was permitted many interviews with the President, the results of which he shared with his newspaper friends.

President Wilson inaugurated conferences with the entire corps of Washington correspondents, and in lieu of direct quotation he sponsored the concept of an "official spokesman." Information was printed as having a source such as a close friend of the President, some high authority, or a White House official. These thrice-weekly conferences were discontinued during the World War, but the precedent had been set, and Harding revived them. Himself a newspaperman, President Harding was popular with correspondents, talked to them frankly and simply, and assumed the blame for any misstatement. During the Conference on Limitation of Armaments, Harding made an erroneous statement about the status of Japan in the Four-Power Treaty. A diplomatic furor followed, and the President issued a personal statement, shouldering the blame for the mistake. Charles Evans Hughes, then Secretary of State, suggested that questions be submitted in writing before each conference. This plan was adopted and continued through the Coolidge and Hoover administrations, but was abruptly ended by the second Roosevelt, who from the outset permitted free oral interrogation. During President Coolidge's administration the "White House spokesman" came into disrepute; often there were as many different versions of a story as there were reporters at the conference, the "spokesman" having talked to many anonymous interviewers and inexpert reporters. This resulted, in 1927, in the death of the term as a figure of speech. The journalistic ghost, however, reappeared during the Presidency of Herbert Hoover but was promptly laid, perhaps forever, by Franklin D. Roosevelt.

The press conferences of President Roosevelt have set a standard which his successors will probably find difficult to abandon. While the office of President and the deference it commands preclude completely frank discussion, and while President Roosevelt has not hesitated to cut off the pursuit of an embarrassing topic, the "wide-open" character of his meetings with the press is without parallel in presidential history. His predecessors frequently canceled press conferences, but President Roosevelt has seldom done so. Even when away from Washington he holds conferences at the customary time for the handful of correspondents who accompany him.   Mr. Roosevelt early in his first term laid down the rule that he would not grant private interviews to individual correspondents, and there have been few exceptions to this rule.   Press relations generally under the New Deal have become highly standardized, with most of the Cabinet officers and heads of important agencies following the President's example of regular conferences.   Each agency maintains a full-dress press relations staff, working under the name of "information section."   The Office of Government Reports, created in 1939 and nicknamed "OGRE," is a sort of clearing house for Government press agents.   Lowell Mellett, former editor of the Washington *Daily News,* is chief of the OGR, and is responsible only to the President.   Many of the leading press agents are former members of his newspaper staff.

Washington correspondents, or journalists who have at one time or another been Washington correspondents, are now and then elected or appointed to important Government posts.   Notable among them are Arthur Capper and Carl Schurz, elected to the Senate; James Rankin Young of Pennsylvania, Horace Greeley of the New York *Tribune,* William E. Barrett of the Boston *Advertiser,* Amos Cummins of the New York *Sun,* Erasmus Brooks, and Louis Ludlow of Indiana, all of whom were elected to the House; Robert J. Wynn, Postmaster General under Theodore Roosevelt; Whitelaw Reid, Ambassador to Great Britain; John Russell Young, Minister to China; William C. Bullitt, Ambassador to Soviet Russia and to France; and Leo R. Sack of the Scripps-Howard Newspaper Alliance, Minister to Costa Rica. Mr. Ludlow at the time of his election was the Washington correspondent of the Columbus *Dispatch,* and claims the distinction of being the only man ever to go directly from the press gallery to a seat on the floor.   A larger number have held positions in various Government departments, or have served as Commissioners of the District of Columbia.

The more strictly local phase of journalism, that of the daily newspaper, is represented (1942) by one morning paper, two evening papers, and one that publishes editions around the clock.   Oldest of these is the *Evening Star,* established in 1852, during the Pierce-Scott Presidential campaign.   The editor, Joseph B. Tate, gave up political partisanship with the defeat of General Scott, and attempted to make the *Star* an authoritative news organ.   He was a poor business man, and the paper passed out of his hands the following year.   Crosby S. Noyes and his associates bought the *Star* in 1867 and added the Sunday edition in 1905.

The Washington *Post,* owned by Eugene Meyer, formerly Governor of the Federal Reserve Board, is a morning paper, founded in 1877 by Stilson Hutchins.   Started as a Democratic organ, the *Post* under Meyer has followed an independent policy.   The afternoon *Times,* founded in 1894 by a group of unemployed printers, was purchased by Frank A. Munsey, who in 1917 sold it to Arthur Brisbane. William Randolph Hearst purchased the paper in 1922, the same year in which he bought the morning *Herald,* which was established by Washington business and professional men in 1906.   The *Times-Herald* represents a merger of the *Times* and *Herald,* which Mrs. Eleanor Patterson bought from Hearst after having served as his publisher of the *Herald* for a number of years.   The *Times-Herald* is perhaps the only newspaper in the world that publishes editions around the clock.   Independent in politics, many of its other-than-local editorials are reprinted from the New York *Daily News,* of which Mrs. Patterson is a part owner.   The *Daily News* was established in 1929 by the Scripps-Howard chain and has been published since in tabloid form; it takes an independent editorial attitude on local and national affairs.

A new type of journalistic experiment was attempted in 1926 by David Lawrence, a Washington correspondent, when he launched the *United States Daily,* devoted exclusively to news of the Federal Government.   Publication was suspended during the depression in the early thirties, but Lawrence later revived the paper as the weekly *United States News;* it is now published in magazine format.

The National Press Building, 14th and F Streets, contains the offices of many Washington correspondents and a majority of the Washington news bureaus.   On the thirteenth floor is the headquarters of the National Press Club, a working organization established in 1908 and open to all Washington journalists as well as to a large contingent of "associate" and "inactive" members.   It has a ticker service and the facilities of a club, sponsoring entertainments and social affairs to which many guests are invited.   The Press Building was planned for 12 floors, to keep it within the restrictions of the District building code. When another story and a half appeared necessary, Congress enacted a special amendment to the code to permit construction of the additional space, now occupied by the club.

The Gridiron Club is an organization of Washington correspondents with a resident membership limited to 50.   It meets twice a year for dinners to which statesmen, scientists, diplomats, and other eminent men are invited.   Ben: Perley Poore was one of its organizers in 1865 and its first president.   The established custom of the club is to present satirical skits of current public affairs, with jokes more often than not aimed at distinguished members and guests.   The President of the United States is always invited and must take his share of the ribbing.   The stunts are given voluminous publicity, but speeches of the honor guests are entirely off the record.   The place of Gridiron dinners in Washington political life was summed up by President Taft, when he commented on the "surprise and embarrassment of foreign ambassadors at their first Gridiron dinner and their subsequent whole-hearted appreciation of the spirit of these occasions."

Mrs. Franklin D. Roosevelt in 1933 inaugurated the custom of giving a "Gridiron Widows" (or, more smartly, "Widiron") party at the White House at the same time as the Gridiron dinner. Guests for the occasion are the women of the press and the wives of newspapermen and officials who are dining with the club that evening. Press photographers are invited to "Widiron" parties, but otherwise the women follow the precedent of the men in maintaining secrecy about the speeches of honor guests.

The Overseas Writers Club, one of the most exclusive clubs in Washington, is composed entirely of American journalists who have seen service as foreign correspondents. It meets irregularly, not oftener than once a week, at luncheons to hear prominent diplomats, returned correspondents, or other distinguished speakers. Few guests are invited, the speakers talk and answer questions freely, and the meetings are never publicized.

The Women's National Press Club, organized in 1919, is a social and educational luncheon club with strict membership requirements; its nonactive list is composed entirely of formerly active members. Honor guests have included ambassadors and their wives, distinguished statesmen, writers, artists, and scientists. The club had the President of the United States as a guest speaker in February 1941. The wife of the President is always the ranking guest.

Science

I T IS related that Albert Einstein, when he was forced to find employment in the Swiss patent office and was thrown into intimate contact with problems of scientific technology, abandoned some of the preconceptions of the pure scientist and came to recognize that applied science, while concentrated on the solution of practical problems, often uncovered facts and theories of high value in the advancement of pure science. A critical judgment on Washington science and scientific life must start with the recognition that the vast army of Government scientists is concerned largely with problems of applied science; problems set by the multiplying social and economic concerns of the Government. However, the critic must realize, with Einstein, that this is far from dismissing the importance of their work for theoretical science. Notwithstanding their predominantly practical orientation, governmental and private scientific organizations in Washington constitute the most important scientific center in the United States.

The influence of Washington scientific activity is, however, far different from what it would have been had the Government planned a great theoretical scientific center, or even a practical center coordinated with theoretical instruction and research. Like Topsy, the present broad activities "just grew." However, with great laboratories and research programs in the various government departments, and with the development of local institutions of higher learning, the National Capital has become a training ground for the young. Expert scientists are attracted from all parts of the country to accept positions in scientific bureaus. Young people with an interest in science as a career are drawn here to sit at the feet of scientific masters. Between the employment opportunities within the Government, the extensive facilities of laboratory, museum, and library, and the day and evening courses in universities and colleges, it is possible for students to gain an excellent theoretical and practical education while earning a livelihood. This advantage, however, is not readily available to natives of Washington, because of the limited Civil Service quota governing the District of Columbia. A number of scientific societies, both local and national, have meetings and conclaves throughout the year for the discussion of technical and general subjects. These gatherings are usually open to the public, and students are welcomed; scarcely a night passes during the midwinter season without at least one such meeting.

The "graduation" of trained personnel into private and commercial scientific enterprise is a normal expectancy in Government work. Federal salaries are low. The top grades are few in number and offer much less monetary compensation than comparable positions in private industry, or even in schools and universities. Despite this fact, many Government scientists turn down desirable outside offers for a stable, unhurried Government career, following their chosen bent. Many others, especially the younger people, leave each year for other employment. The heads of research and experimental organizations, however, have gradually adopted the philosophical view that their personnel losses should be considered a service to the country.

The idea of creating a Federal educational and scientific center at the seat of the Government occurred to more than one person during the early period of the Republic, but the compromises necessary in drafting the Constitution, coupled with the poverty of the Government in its early years, prevented the realization of any such ambitious plan. At the Constitutional Convention, James Madison, probably acting at Washington's suggestion, proposed to include among the powers of Congress the right to establish a national university and the right to encourage the advancement and dissemination of scientific knowledge. The proposition was lost, and the only clause in the Constitution directly relating to science is that providing for the issuance of patents by the Federal Government.

Although, under the ambiguous general-welfare clause, the right to establish a national university and to encourage science has been frequently asserted, it was found easier, for economic and political reasons, to invoke that power cautiously for the establishment of some seemingly insignificant bureau rather then boldly to demand that the Government set up a Federal educational center. In proportion as the Federal Government grew stronger and more prosperous, the interests opposing Federal education grew stronger as well. During the period immediately preceding the Civil War, the slavery-States' rights issue stood in the way of Federal encouragement of science and education. Since then, privately endowed universities have not seen fit to encourage the establishment of a national department of education or of a central university in Washington.

Under the circumstances, the wonder is not that Federal scientific activities in Washington have not developed according to a co-ordinated plan, but rather that they have developed to the extent they have. The development has taken place largely by a series of friendly conspiracies; conspiracies which have sought either to introduce a tiny camel's head into the Federal tent or, once the head was in, to introduce the rest of the body without too alarming rapidity. Occasionally these friendly conspiracies have been aided by happy accidents, such as Napoleon's sale of half a continent to the United States, which compelled the Federal Government to send out scientific surveys to discover how big a bargain it had bought; or the bequest of a fortune for scientific purposes by Smithson, an Englishman who had never even visited the United States.

The events in Washington's administration are typical of the whole history of Federal scientific development. Washington recommended to Congress the adoption of patent legislation and the establishment of a patent office. As this proposal was in conformity with a Constitutional provision, it was immediately accepted and the Patent Office was instituted under the Secretary of State in 1790. At the same time Washington repeatedly recommended that Congress develop scientific services for agriculture and establish a national university. Neither of these recommendations was accepted. But neither Washington, nor anybody else at the time, realized that out of the Patent Office there would develop a scientific department of agriculture. After 12 years, the duties of the Patent Office became too complex for the Secretary of State to handle alone, and in 1802 Secretary of State Madison appointed Dr. William Thornton superintendent of the Patent Office. Thirty-seven years later, the head of the Patent Office—his dignity now grown to the title of Commissioner—managed to persuade Congress to appropriate $1,000 a year for the purchase of seeds and for the collection of scientific information on agriculture. This modest step on the part of Commissioner Ellsworth was the beginning of the Department of Agriculture, and before the Civil War the Commissioner of Patents had specialized assistants working on economic entomology, chemistry, and botany. Further important steps awaited the Civil War and the decline of States' rights opposition.

The next episode in Washington scientific history begins with Thomas Jefferson; he astounded and irritated his contemporaries by carrying on original researches in geology and paleontology during his entire term of office. The youthful William Cullen Bryant in his poem, "The Embargo," wrote bluntly of him:

> Go, wretch, resign the Presidential chair;
> Disclose thy secret measures, foul or fair.
> Go, search with curious eyes for horned frogs
> 'Mid the wild wastes of Louisianian bogs,
> Or where the Ohio rolls his turbid stream
> Dig for huge bones, thy glory and thy theme.

Had Jefferson been more in favor of extending Federal powers, it is likely that the dream of a national university would have been realized in his administration. But as an extreme partisan of States' rights he hesitated even over the purchase of Louisiana. In the end he closed the bargain and sent out three scientific expeditions to explore the territory—Lewis and Clark to the northwest, Zebulon Pike to the southwest, and William Dunbar to the Red and Washita River valleys. These exploratory expeditions, which were followed by numerous others during the next half century, set the precedent for the scientific exploration of the national domain, and ultimately led to the creation of the United States Geological Survey in 1879.

Another scientific achievement of the Jefferson administration was the founding in 1807 of the Coast Survey, later renamed the Coast and Geodetic Survey. Albert Gallatin, Secretary of the Treasury, is credited more than anybody else with inaugurating this Survey which, by expansion of duties, has passed from charting the coast line to the determination of fundamental land positions, the study of gravitation, magnetism, earthquakes, and a whole range of related scientific fields. This Survey is today one of the most important scientific bureaus in the Government.

For 30 years after Jefferson, the further development of scientific services by the Federal Government was at a standstill. In Madison's administration, war problems tended to preclude other concerns. After Madison's time, the change in the cultural character of the Government personnel tended to eliminate scientific inquiry. John Quincy Adams was, however, an exception to the rule; but all his valiant labor on behalf of science, his agitation for a national university, his backing of the proposal for a national observatory, and his great scientific report on weights and measures (written in 1818 while he was Secretary of State), had almost no effect. The report on weights and measures did result in the creation, 12 years later, of an Office of Weights and Measures in the Coast Survey. But this Office, though it was the precursor of the Bureau of Standards, created in 1901, was a routine administration, like some of the State offices with the same name today, without scientific functions.

There were vain attempts to get Congress to establish a national observatory, and such a station was finally bootlegged into existence as part of the Naval Depot of Charts and Instruments. Of all the Government scientific institutions, the Naval Observatory approaches nearest to the field of pure science. With the advent of Professor Simon Newcomb during the Civil War period, the Observatory quickly rose to first rank among the astronomical observatories of the world and has remained there ever since.

During this same period of congressional indifference to science, news came that James Smithson, who died in 1829, had left his entire fortune of $500,000 to the United States for the diffusion of scientific knowledge. The bequest became available in 1835, **after the death of**

Smithson's nephew, but it took Congress 11 years to make up its mind what to do with it. There was disagreement as to the purposes for which the fund should be used. Some favored a university; some an agricultural college; John Quincy Adams favored an observatory, either with or without a university; others favored a museum and publications, such as had been developed by the privately founded Columbian Institute and its successor, the National Institution. There was even opposition in many quarters to the Government's acceptance of a private gift. In 1846 Congress at length took action and founded the Smithsonian Institution as a governmentally managed foundation, with broad powers including that of custodian of all national museum collections.

The first secretary of the Institution, Joseph Henry, who shares honors with Faraday for the discovery of electromagnetic induction, fought for many years to devote Smithsonian funds exclusively to research purposes, but was overruled by his associates. As an institution centering around a museum, the Smithsonian eventually developed. Nevertheless, research was not neglected, and the Smithsonian began a number of lines of research later financed by the Federal Government. The most important of these are the researches in Indian ethnology, which developed into the Bureau of American Ethnology; and the experiments in solar radiation, now carried on by the Astrophysical Observatory. Both these organizations, though governmentally maintained, are managed by the secretary of the Smithsonian Institution. In addition, since the Government took over the financial responsibility for the museum established by the Smithsonian, the latter has been able to devote its own funds to research and publication in connection with museum work.

The Smithsonian Institution has served for many years as a training ground for scientists, particularly in the biological and ethnological fields. The secretaries—Joseph Henry, Spencer F. Baird, and Samuel P. Langley—all exercised a personal influence on the development of scientific ideas which is difficult to describe precisely, but which is admitted on all sides to have been considerable. The Smithsonian Institution has served as national headquarters for the great federation of American scientific societies known as the American Association for the Advancement of Science (organized in 1848). The meetings of the association, however, are seldom held in Washington, rotating from year to year in the various cities of the country.

Next in the line of milestones of governmental scientific development is the Civil War. It may seem strange that a war fought to free the slaves should have an epochal significance in the development of the Government's scientific bureaus. Yet, the legal issue of the Civil War was the question of National versus States' rights. In the fifties Representative Justin Morrill of Vermont several times sought to introduce his bill for the creation of agricultural and industrial land-grant colleges. One of the prime ideas behind the plan, as it afterward turned out, was to use these colleges as agricultural experiment stations—an idea that is said to owe its origin to Captain Alden Partridge, of the United States Army. The Morrill bill was repeatedly voted down because of the opposition of Southern Congressmen, who feared Federal domination in agriculture and education. In fact, Morrill had to wait until the secession of the South before the bill could be enacted, early in 1862. The same year the Department of Agriculture was organized under an independent commissioner, without a Cabinet seat.

Thus, the Department of Agriculture was at last launched on its career, a career which made it in a very short time the largest governmental department except the Treasury, and the largest scientific organization under Government auspices. The experiment stations, foreseen by the Morrill Act and further developed by the Hatch Act of 1887, became the center of the scientific services provided by the Department. The Department itself acquired Cabinet status in 1889. Several scientific bureaus, developed in other departments, were transferred to it because of a connection, direct or indirect, with agriculture. Still other scientific bureaus developed by fission from those already in the Department.

The national crisis of the Civil War was directly responsible for the creation of the National Academy of Sciences, designed as a consultative organization on matters of science and technology. The Academy, comprising by intention the leading scientists in the country but having its headquarters in Washington, has been of some benefit to Washington science through the opportunity it affords for exchanges of scientific ideas, between visiting scientists of national prominence and those located in Washington, whether members of the Academy or not.

After the Civil War there was no longer any hesitancy on the part of Congress in establishing Government scientific services whenever the need for them was effectively presented. In 1866 the Naval Observatory, which had been functioning as part of the Depot of Charts and Instruments, was made an independent organization, and the service of charts became the Hydrographic Office of the Navy. In 1869 plans for a national weather service under the direction of the Signal Corps of the United States Army were formulated by Cleveland Abbe, director of the Mitchell Observatory at Cincinnati, who had organized a regional weather service in the Midwest. Abbe became identified with the service in 1871. Experiments in organized weather reporting had been started several times before—notably by the Commissioner of the Land Office in 1817, by the Patent Office in 1841, and by the Smithsonian Institution in 1847—but the effective beginning of a national weather service dates from 1869. The weather service was removed in 1891 from the Signal Corps and made into an independent Weather Bureau functioning under the Department of Agriculture; it was made a bureau of the Department of Commerce in 1940, because of its close relationship with the Civil Aeronautics Authority, which was moved into the Department at the same time. In 1871, largely through the efforts of Spencer Baird, secretary of the Smithsonian Institution, a Fish Commission was created, to study methods of conserving American fisheries. This Commission, which developed into the Bureau of Fisheries of the Department of Commerce, and in 1940 became a part of the Department of the Interior's Fish and Wildlife Service, studies the biology of commercial fishes and co-operates with State institutions in scientific measures to conserve and develop the supply of edible fish. It is also responsible for the protection of the Alaskan seal herds.

The greatest post-Civil War scientific development, however, was the creation in 1879 of the United States Geological Survey as part of the Department of the Interior. With the close of the Civil War four separate geological surveys of western lands were undertaken by the War and Interior Departments, and it became apparent that this vast work could best be handled by a unified organization. After a great deal of preparatory agitation, including a report from the National Academy of Sciences, the Geological Survey was finally established, with Clarence King as the first director. The Survey, originally confined to the public domain of the West, was extended by subsequent legislation to include all parts of the country. At the same time the subject matter of its investigations was intensified and extended. No study that borders on geology has been neglected, and the Survey has passed from economic phases of geology to problems of paleontology and stratigraphy. Topography and hydrology have been taken over by specialized divisions. In addition it has been responsible for the development of programs which have resulted in the creation of the Bureau of Reclamation, the Bureau of Mines, and the Forest Service. A program of experimental geology—that is to say, of creating artificially, under controlled conditions, the physical and chemical reactions responsible for geological formations—was developed by the Survey, but due to lack of appropriations it was taken over and carried out by the Geophysical Laboratory of the Carnegie Institution.

Passing over the great scientific development of the Department of Agriculture in the closing decades of the nineteenth and opening decades of the twentieth century, we come to the remarkable event represented by the creation of the National Bureau of Standards in 1900. On the initiative of the Secretary of the Treasury, the old Office of Weights and Measures in the Coast Survey was transformed into a vast Government testing laboratory as well as a laboratory for technical and scientific research in physics and chemistry. In this way the scientific program of the Federal Government may be said to have been properly rounded out, for while the Department of Agriculture handles all phases of applied biology, and the Geological Survey handles the broad field of the mineral and extractive industries, until 1900 there was no similar agency to develop the scientific services necessary for general industry.

The Bureau of Standards, whose first director was Samuel W. Stratton (later called to head the Massachusetts Institute of Technology), has brilliantly justified itself. It has been responsible for a large number of discoveries in pure science and in technology. The savings in governmental purchasing costs through the testing work of the Bureau have exceeded the cost of its maintenance, so that its benefits to industry and science are in the nature of a donation.

Two years after the creation of the Bureau of Standards, the Treasury Department again managed to create a first-class scientific service from an insignificant germ. This was the Public Health Service, which traces its origin to the Marine Hospital Service created in 1798. This hospital service was originally placed in the Treasury Department because the customs agents could most easily collect hospital fees from sailors to sustain the Service. The United States Public Health Service, under the direction of the Surgeon General, conducts scientific research in public-health matters, collects statistics, and enforces quarantine laws affecting interstate and foreign commerce. It has, however, no regulatory powers over public-health matters within States, and can help local health bodies only when its assistance is solicited. Under the Social Security Act the Public Health Service distributes about $11,000,000 a year to States to assist State and local agencies in maintaining public-health programs, in addition to some $6,000,000 to assist the States in the control of venereal diseases. It also has smaller sums for investigating diseases and public-health problems.

Among the so-called New Deal agencies, that of chief scientific importance is the National Resources Planning Board, which functions largely through technical experts, and is charged with drawing up a program and plan of procedure for the wise utilization of technical, human, and natural resources. It also co-ordinates the similar activities of the State Planning Boards. Thus, for the first time, the Government is taking an interest not merely in the greater scientific exploitation of natural resources, but is consciously associating this exploitation with social and economic policies.

This review covers the main lines of development of the Government's scientific services in Washington. A few words should be added about the private institutions. Although Washington is served by five universities, none of them has large facilities for scientific research. Georgetown University is, however, famous for its seismological laboratory, operated as one of the stations of the Jesuit Seismological Service. In 1902 Andrew Carnegie established the Carnegie Institution of Washington to promote scientific research. After a few years of experimentation with subsidizing scientific research by existing institutions, the institution decided to establish its own research organization. Three of its 10 units were set up in Washington, and two of these— the Division of Terrestrial Magnetism and the Geophysical Laboratory—are devoted to natural science.

After the World War there was a further development of foundation interest in science at Washington. Carnegie and Rockefeller philanthropic foundations collaborated in endowing the National Academy of Sciences and its war baby, the National Research Council. The latter was turned into an agency for distributing scientific grants-in-aid and research fellowships in natural science. As the research has for the most part been done elsewhere, this development of the council has not greatly affected the role of Washington in science.

The absence of a common organization in which the personnel of the various scientific groups are associated—such as is furnished, for example, by a university organization—stimulated the formation of a scientific club in Washington during the Civil War period. This was succeeded in 1878 by the Cosmos Club, which has served as the favorite rendezvous of scientific men for more than half a century.

Of less exclusive and more academic character are the special societies which came into existence mostly between 1870 and 1890, and which meet to hear papers on scientific subjects, and otherwise promote the interests of their particular branches of science. Eighteen such societies, with a combined membership of more than 5,000, were federated in 1898 into the Washington Academy of Sciences, with headquarters at the Cosmos Club. The academy publishes a monthly journal and conducts semipopular lectures under the auspices of the constituent societies. These lectures constitute one of the principal channels for the popularization of scientific ideas in Washington. Other popular lectures are conducted under the auspices of the Carnegie Institution and the Smithsonian Institution.

The National Defense Advisory Commission in 1940 organized the National Defense Research Committee, to co-operate with scientific branches of various Federal and private agencies in the fields of physics, chemistry, and engineering. The National Inventors' Council, organized by the Secretary of Commerce, acts as a clearing house for inventive genius, carrying much the same role as the National Consulting Board during World War I. Whenever Uncle Sam needs an invention, specifications are sent to the Council and a group of trained scientists and engineers decide which registrant will get the assignment. If the Council is unable to find the required person on its own registry, it may refer to the National Roster of Scientific and Specialized Personnel, largest of its kind in the world; when completed it will contain more than half a million names.

PART II
Points of Interest

Capitol Hill

Streetcars: Lincoln Park, Navy Yard, 17th & Penna. SE., Union Station, Brookland, Catholic University, 13th & D NE.
Busses: Congress Heights, Bolling Field via Portland, and Trinidad.
Taxis: First zone.

Capitol Hill is one of the most commanding eminences in this Coastal Plain city, rising 88 feet from tidewater at the Potomac River. Once known as Jenkins Hill, it is today familiarly referred to as "The Hill." Centered by the Capitol, the Hill area is a focal point for legislative and judicial activities of the Government—in the three-way system of Federal checks and balances the Hill has two of the weights, the other being at the White House a mile and a half away. Northeast and southeast of the Capitol, and symmetrically placed in relation to its grounds, are the green-roofed, white marble Senate and House Office Buildings. Just west of the Old House Office Building is the narrower, porticoed white marble mass of the new, built on lower ground but rising to a line with the roof of the old.

East of the Capitol is the cobwebby gray mass of the Library of Congress, with green-trimmed dome and cupola; back of it is the modern white marble Library Annex; and to the northeast is the modest white marble cube of the Folger Shakespeare Library—two city blocks containing the greatest concentration of library materials in the Nation. Along Independence Avenue, south of the Library, is a clutter of restaurants, souvenir shops, and small business establishments.

North of the Library stands the glittering white Supreme Court Building with its Corinthian portico and tall white flagpoles. North of that is the five-story buff Methodist Building, and a row of brick and clapboarded dwellings and small hotels extending along 1st Street NE., past the four-story Senate Office Building, to border Union Station Plaza beyond. Northwest of the Senate Building, in the spacious, landscaped Plaza, is a fountain and reflecting basin, designed by Bennett, Parsons, and Frost, and erected in 1934. Its white dome of water, illuminated by yellow lights at night, provides a motif in keeping with that of the Hill's most prominent building. Under a portion of the Plaza extends a streetcar underpass and the entrance to the subterranean Senate garage.

On the north side of the Hill looms the hangar-shaped, black-roofed Union Station, with its three cavernous entrance arches and three tall white flagpoles. West of it is the long white marble mass of the green-roofed City Post Office and the red-brick bulk of Government Printing Office buildings. At the northwest corner of the Plaza is a cluster of six- to eight-story buff brick hotels, and almost due west of the Senate Office Building is the six-story Indiana limestone Acacia Insurance Building, its entrance flanked by falcon-headed sphinxes.

West of the Capitol extend broad, traffic-filled Pennsylvania and Constitution Avenues, and the green sweep of the Mall.

THE CAPITOL

The impressive Capitol (*open 9-4:30, Mon.-Sat.; closed Christmas and New Year's Day; open after 4:30 when Congress is in session*), dominating all Washington, stands in spacious grounds on the crest of a hill, where the north-south and east-west axes of the Federal metropolis intersect.   By day, the sun shines brilliantly on its white walls and flags fly continuously east and west of the central dome; a flag is raised over each house while it is in session.   By night, floodlights throw the huge central dome into extraordinary prominence and a single light gleams from the lantern above, indicating the meeting of one or both houses.   Visitors from most States see here the inspiration of their own State capitol, and recognize in the dome a symbol of Federal Government.

On the steps of the Capitol's east front, Presidential inaugurations have been held since James Monroe's time, with the exception of that of President Taft, which was held in the Senate chamber because of inclement weather.   On a specially built platform over the central flight of steps, the Chief Justice of the United States administers the oath of office in the presence of his colleagues, legislators, governors, the uniformed diplomatic corps, and thousands of spectators.   This ceremonial is followed by the inaugural address and the procession to the White House.

The Capitol Grounds, 120.6 acres in area, are landscaped with 2,000 trees and 5,000 shrubs, besides fountains, terraces, and balustrades, and are traversed by broad, sweeping walks and drives.   The grounds were given their present general appearance by Frederick Law Olmsted, landscape architect, in the last decades of the nineteenth century. Several trees are of historical interest.   The Washington Elm, a magnificent specimen more than 100 feet high, is said to have shaded the first President while he discussed plans for the Capitol.   The Cameron Elm, near the southwest corner of the House wing, was saved from the ax in 1870 by Senator Simeon Cameron of Pennsylvania; rather than have the tree demolished he persuaded the Senate to have a sidewalk laid around it.

The selection of a site for "the Congress House" or Capitol was one of the initial problems before Major L'Enfant when, at President Washington's direction, he began to lay out the Federal city.   Jenkins Hill, overlooking the entire area, seemed to him "a pedestal waiting for a monument"; he placed it here, and the hill subsequently assumed the name of the monument.   The Commissioners of the city in 1792 announced a prize competition for Capitol plans, and the award was given to Dr. William Thornton, amateur architect, whose design impressed Washington by its "grandeur, simplicity and convenience"; Jefferson found it "simple, noble, and beautiful." On September 18, 1793, music sounded and there were artillery salutes as Masons in full regalia stood by, and George Washington, wearing an apron embroidered by Madame Lafayette, declared the cornerstone "well and truly laid."

Several architects appointed to superintend construction were dismissed for attempting to alter the Thornton plan, and finally its creator was placed in charge. Collaborating with James Hoban, designer of the White House and official architect of the Government, he proceeded with the work. When Federal funds gave out in 1796 the State of Maryland supplied money raised by a lottery. Subsequently the Federal Government again assumed the financial burden. In 1800 the north wing, known for a long time as the Senate wing and later as the Supreme Court wing, was completed. Congress, removing from Philadelphia, met here on November 17, 1800, for the first time in the new Capital City, and was addressed by President Adams the following day. The Senate, the House, and the Supreme Court (which met infrequently), convened for a time in this rectangular building.

In 1801 there was erected within the half-completed House wing an elliptical one-story brick structure, which, because of its arched roof and high inside temperature, was known as "the Oven." Six years later the House of Representatives moved into the south wing, upon its completion by Benjamin H. Latrobe, appointed Director of Works by President Jefferson in 1803. At this time the two stone wings were joined by a wooden arcade where the rotunda now stands. The city was so undeveloped in 1809 that the British Ambassador "put up a covey of partridges about 300 yards from the House of Congress, yclept the Capitol." Between the wings were two wells of drinking water.

Observing that weather and souvenir hunters had damaged the uncompleted building, Congress urged upon the President the necessity of speeding its completion, but an unexpected setback ensued. As an incident in the War of 1812, the British expeditionary force under the command of General Robert Ross, aiming to wipe out "this harbor of Yankee democracy," set fire to the unfinished Capitol, destroying the wooden roofing, the interior of the House wing, the west side of the Senate interior, and many marble columns. When Congress reassembled, it convened in a cramped space in Blodgett's Hotel, 7th and E Streets, then in use by the Patent Office. Removal of the seat of government from Washington was discussed. To allay this agitation, a private building was hastily erected by a group of citizens and offered to Congress for its meeting place at a rental based on cost. This building, "the Brick Capitol," stood on the site of the Supreme Court Building, and served as the home of Congress until the war-scarred Capitol was restored by Latrobe in 1819. Eight years later, under the direction of Charles Bulfinch, who succeeded Latrobe, the link between the two wings was completed and crowned with a low wooden dome, according to the Thornton plan.

Congress in 1850 authorized the construction of two extensions. The plans of Thomas U. Walter, of Philadelphia, were adopted, including replacement of Thornton's old dome by a larger one of metal. On July 4, 1851, the cornerstones of the extensions were laid by President Millard Fillmore. In one of the stones Daniel Webster deposited a document which declared that "the Constitution still exists unimpared . . . growing every day stronger and stronger." The House extension was completed and occupied in 1857, the Senate extension two years later. In 1860 the Supreme Court moved into the old Senate chamber, and in 1864 Congress transformed the old House wing into Statuary Hall. Not even the Civil War halted work on the Capitol—workmen went quietly on, assembling the huge iron dome.

A patriotic crowd assembled on December 2, 1863, to witness the placing of the statue atop the lantern of the dome. When a field battery fired the national salute of 35 guns at noon that day, the Capitol was complete in its main lines as it stands today. Minor renovations have been made since, to permit the introduction of steam heating (1865), elevators (1874), fireproofing (1881), electric lighting (1882), a modern drainage system (1893), and replacement of dangerously antiquated roofs over the House and Senate chambers (1941).

The $18,000,000 building is 751 feet 4 inches long and 350 feet wide, covering about 3.5 acres. As seen from the east or west, it is composed of seven units. In the center, directly under the dome, is the rotunda, the walls and floors of which are built of Aquia Creek, Virginia, sandstone, painted white to harmonize with the marble portions of the building. Flanking it are rectangular wings, topped with flat domes and cupolas, rising to a level with the base of the dome. These wings, once joined by a wooden arcade, constitute the central section, which from 1827 to 1857 was the entire Capitol. South and north of these original wings are short passageways connecting the extended wings at each end, the northern occupied by the Senate, the southern by the House.

The cast-iron central dome, which cost more than $1,000,000, is painted white to harmonize with the masonry. With its special trusses, bolts, and girders supporting a weight of 8,909,200 pounds, its construction was a remarkable engineering feat. The dome has a base diameter of 135 feet 5 inches and rises 285 feet above the eastern plaza. It is composed of two shells, one imposed upon the other, expanding and contracting with temperature variations; between the two shells winds a stairway. The cap of the dome springs from a drum modeled after that of St. Peter's at Rome. Around the base of the drum is a peristyle colonnade of 36 fluted Corinthian columns, representing the States of the Union at the time the dome was completed, and above the colonnade is an exterior gallery. Surmounting the peristyle is a clerestory penetrated by tall arched windows. A row of console brackets forms a transition from the clerestory to the ribbed surface of the cap, with medallion windows set between the ribs. Surmounting the cap is a lantern, decorated with a colonnade of 13 fluted Corinthian columns, representing the original States, with a lookout gallery at its base. Atop the lantern is Thomas Crawford's 19-foot bronze *Freedom*, the plaster model for which was almost lost at sea during its journey from Italy. Jefferson Davis who, as Secretary of War, was in charge of construction of the Capitol, compelled Crawford to alter the headgear on his statue, lest there be raised above the Capitol such a portent as a Phrygian or liberty cap, the symbol of liberated slaves. Crawford substituted a crested helmet, with the result that the elevated figure is often mistaken for a feather-decked Indian warrior. The bronze statue was cast by Clark Mills at his state-subsidized foundry in Bladensburg.

The walls of the main structure consist of a rusticated base supporting Corinthian pilasters, which rise two stories and are surmounted by an entablature and a balustraded parapet. The eastern façades of the central section and of the House and Senate wings are dominated by double porticos of monolithic 30-foot Corinthian columns, and each is approached by a monumental stairway. Flanking the central stairway on the north is Horatio Greenough's marble group, *The Rescue,* a tableau of a frontiersman saving his wife and child from massacre by an Indian, and Luigi Persico's *Discovery of America* on the south, characterized by Senator Charles Sumner as "a man rolling ninepins." Within the portico, in wall niches, are Persico's *Ceres as Peace* and *Mars as War,* and above the main entrance is Antonio Capellano's bas-relief of Washington between *Fame* and *Peace.*

The central pediment on the east façade is decorated with Luigi Persico's *Genius of America,* the Senate (north) pediment by Thomas Crawford's *Progress of American Civilization and the Decline of the Indian,* a good example of early American sculpture, and the House (south) pediment by Paul Bartlett's *Peace Protecting Genius,* unveiled in 1916 and considered among the better works in the Capitol. The 10-ton bronze doors leading from the central portico to the rotunda, modeled by Randolph Rogers at Rome in 1858 and cast by von Müller of Munich, tell the *Story of Christopher Columbus* in eight panels and a lunette. They are said to compare favorably with the Ghiberti doors in Florence. The west façade, like the east, has as its dominant architectural note a renaissance neo-classicism. Colonnaded loggias or porches extend out from the central section and the two extended wings, and there is an esplanade along the ground-floor level, approached by a series of balustraded stairs. On the lower level, between the stairways, is a heroic bronze of Chief Justice John Marshall, seated, perhaps with unintentional symbolism, with his back to the "Congress House." Behind the statue, which was executed by W. W. Story, son of Justice Story, is a white marble fountain.

Official guides conduct one-hour tours of the building for 25¢ per person, though anyone is free to see it without guides; the guide fee is 15¢ each for high school students in groups, 10¢ for graded school students in groups.

The interior is copiously ornamented, with tiled and mosaic floors, variegated marbles, great corridors and staircases, and about 300 pieces of sculpture and painting. Mark Twain's exclamation that here may be found "the delirium tremens of art" was no doubt unduly acrid, but Senator Charles Sumner declared on the Senate floor that the rule to bar bad art from the Capitol had been "too often forgotten." Here and there is a beautiful mantel, a well-executed row of columns, a vivid fresco. Some of the oil paintings, especially those of Gilbert Stuart, Peale, Vanderlyn, Sully, Trumbull, and other early American artists, are of great interest; some of the statuary was done by notable sculptors, including Elisabet Ney, Jo Davidson, Daniel Chester French, and Gutzon Borglum. One of the least known decorative features is the most original and successful—the so-called American order of capitals, Corinthian in type, in which the traditional acanthus leaves are partially replaced by tobacco leaves, and by ears of corn.

The principal floor of the Capitol is entered from the eastern central portico, through the Columbus Portal into the GREAT ROTUNDA. This immense circular hall, 95 feet 8 inches in diameter, beneath the central dome, rises more than 183 feet to the canopy or under-side of the dome. The Virginia sandstone walls are broken by four doorways on the principal axes of the rotunda. North and south doors lead to the Senate and House wings, respectively, and the east and west doors are exits, leading to the two fronts of the building. The circular walls are divided by fluted Doric pilasters into eight large and four small panels; the large panels are occupied by murals, the small by statuary. The oil paintings on the east side of the building, which are accompanied by keys, are (from north to south) Robert Weir's *Embarkation of the Pilgrims,* John Vanderlyn's *Landing of Columbus* (which has been reproduced in many school histories), W. H. Powell's *Discovery of the Mississippi,* and John G. Chapman's *Baptism of Pocahontas.* The four murals of the Revolution on the west side of the Rotunda were done by Colonel John Trumbull, who, after serving through the Revolution, traveled from New Hampshire to South Carolina to gather material for his pictures, and had such national leaders as George Washington and Thomas Jefferson as models. Trumbull's *Signing of the Declaration of Independence,* nearest the south door, was roundly criticized by John Randolph of Roanoke in 1828, when he called it a "shin-piece," because it exposed gentlemen's legs in small clothes. The others, from south to north, are *The Surrender of Burgoyne, The Surrender of Cornwallis,* and *Washington Resigning his Commission.*

The statues, beginning at the east door and circling the rotunda clockwise, are as follows: George Washington, two copies after Houdon; Edward D. Baker, by Horatio Stone; Thomas Jefferson, by David d'Angers; Alexander Hamilton, by Horatio Stone; Ulysses S. Grant, by Franklin Simmons; Abraham Lincoln, by Vinnie Ream; Abraham

Lincoln, colossal head, by Gutzon Borglum; James A. Garfield, by C. H. Niehaus; Andrew Jackson, by Belle Kinney and L. F. Sholz; Marquis de Lafayette, by David d'Angers; George Washington, bronze bust, by David d'Angers.

Over the four doors are high-relief panels, all on Indian themes. That over the east door is Enrico Causici's *Landing of the Pilgrims;* that over the south door, Causici's *Conflict Between Daniel Boone and the Indians,* is said to have caused a delegation of Winnebago Indians to flee from the building when they saw the white man's representation of an Indian being vanquished in battle; that over the west door is Antonio Capellano's *Rescue of Captain John Smith;* and that over the north door is *Penn's Treaty with the Indians,* by Nicholas Gevelot.

The pilasters of the rotunda support an entablature and cornice surmounted by an encircling coffered band and a frieze in chiaroscuro fresco, 300 feet in circumference and 9 feet high, encircling the rotunda about 75 feet above floor level. Not intended as a permanent decoration, but as a sample to resemble relief, the frieze was executed by Constantino Brumidi, who, having suffered mortal injuries from a fall off the scaffolding, died after completing seven panels. Filippo Costaggini carried on the work from Brumidi's sketches, crowding nine panels into seven to make room for two of his own design. These he never completed, one panel remaining blank, except where it contains an unapproved sample of a later artist's work. Historical tableaux, from the landing of Columbus to the discovery of gold in California, constitute the subjects treated in the frieze.

Light is admitted to the Rotunda through windows around the peristyle drum. Above the windows is a gallery, and above that the coffered domical ceiling and the canopy, by Brumidi, portraying the *Apotheosis of Washington,* a huge canvas more than 6,000 square feet in area, though it appears much smaller from the floor. The first President is attended by Liberty and Victory, and grouped around him are female figures representing the Thirteen Original States, and six allegorical groups typifying War, Agriculture, Mechanics, Commerce, Marine, and Arts and Sciences.

In 1825, officers of the House and Senate were charged with keeping order in their respective sections of the Capitol. Between the two, in a sort of twilight zone, lay the Rotunda, for which neither house would make any rules. As a result, enterprising merchants offered for sale here, under the guise of manufacturing exhibits, "stoves, stew pans, pianos, mouse traps and watch ribbons," while an impresario set up a "Panorama of Paris, Admission 50 cents."

Funeral rites of many noted persons have been held in the Rotunda. Abraham Lincoln's was the first body to lie in state here; others have been those of Thaddeus Stevens, Charles Sumner, James A. Garfield, John A. Logan, William McKinley, Pierre L'Enfant (on the occasion of reinterment at Arlington), Admiral George Dewey, the Unknown Soldier of the World War, Warren G. Harding, and William Howard Taft.

The north door of the Great Rotunda leads to the NORTH SMALL ROTUNDA, an oval colonnaded hall with a domical ceiling topped by a cupola. This, the oldest part of the Capitol, is notable for its columns having capitals decorated with tobacco-leaf motifs, designed by Benjamin H. Latrobe, in 1816. The Roman mosaic floor surrounds an open well, with a view of the ground floor below. A door leads north to the Supreme Court Section.

The foyer of the SUPREME COURT SECTION contains statues of two Revolutionary generals—John Stark (of New Hampshire), by Carl Conrads, and Nathanael Greene (of Rhode Island), by H. K. Brown. These and other life-size statues of State notables in the Capitol constitute the Statuary Hall collection and its overflow. The original intention was to place statues from each State in this hall, but owing to overcrowding and the concentration of too much weight on one floor, it was necessary to confine this group to one statue from a State; the others are distributed elsewhere in the building.

East of the foyer is a semicircular room—the Senate Chamber from 1819 to 1859, and the Chamber of the United States Supreme Court from 1860 to 1935. The room, remodeled (after the fire of 1814) by Latrobe along the lines of a Greek amphitheater, has been preserved as it was when the Supreme Court sat there. A low half-domed ceiling with central skylights is decorated with square coffers. Ionic columns of gray-green Potomac marble form a loggia and support a small gallery, once the Senate gallery. Behind the dark-red draperies, which made a rich background for the Supreme bench, the Justices formerly lunched, one at a time, warmed by a wood blaze in the fireplace. In front of the bench is a space formerly reserved for clerks, reporters, counsel, and spectators. About the walls are busts of former Chief Justices.

In this room, in 1804-05, was held the Federal impeachment trial of Associate Supreme Court Justice Samuel P. Chase. For that occasion the Senate Chamber, at the direction of Vice President Aaron Burr, was decorated to resemble Westminster Hall, where the British Parliament had recently tried Warren Hastings. The setting was highly dignified, but the Vice President, who was himself under indictment in New Jersey "for the murder of Alexander Hamilton," was frequently obliged to request the Senators to be more quiet when apples and cakes were passed around. Chase was acquitted. In this room the Senate confirmed the treaty which provided for the Louisiana Purchase, and ratified the treaties of peace that ended the War of 1812 and the Mexican War. Here, too, Webster, replying to his rival Hayne, declared for "liberty and union, now and forever, one and inseparable." In this atmosphere the Supreme Court decided some of the most momentous cases of its history, including the income-tax suit, in which its ruling against the Government brought about the Sixteenth Amendment. The Electoral Commission met here while deciding the disputed Hayes-Tilden election in 1876, which was decided in favor of Hayes by one electoral vote.

Along an arcaded passageway between the Supreme Court Section and the Senate Extension are statues of two noted physicians and of two American statesmen: Ephraim McDowell (Kentucky), first physician in America to perform an ovariotomy (1809), by C. H. Niehaus; Crawford W. Long (Georgia), first doctor to use ether as an anesthetic (1842), by J. Massey Rhind; John Hanson (Maryland), first presiding officer of the Continental Congress, by R. E. Brooks; John M. Clayton (Delaware), Secretary of State during Zachary Taylor's administration, by Bryant Baker. At the north end of the corridor is the south door of the Senate Chamber, over which there are three white and three red lights; the Senate is in public session when the white lights are on, in executive session when the red bulbs are lighted.

The SENATE EXTENSION is a rectangular wing placed at right angles to the main longitudinal axis of the Capitol. The Senate Chamber, occupying the center of the wing, has corridors on each of its four sides, and is like a building within a building, the outer shell being composed of the offices of Senate officials. The South Corridor is paved with bright English minton tiles, as are most of the Senate corridors. Along its walls are busts of Vice Presidents, supplementing a series in the Senate galleries, and an excellent oil portrait of Washington by Gilbert Stuart. An American-made clock in this corridor has been in operation since 1802.

In the East Corridor, occupying a niche opposite the East Grand Stairway, is Hiram Powers' heroic statue of Benjamin Franklin. Over the landing half way up the stairway is W. H. Powell's *Battle of Lake Erie,* the largest oil painting in the Capitol. Employees of the Capitol are said to have posed for the artist while he was painting this mural to commemorate the occasion on which Commodore Oliver Hazard Perry sent the message, "We have met the enemy and they are ours." The East Elevator Foyer, opening off the East Corridor, is paved with black and white marble, and its walls are of gray-green marble, flanked with fluted white marble Corinthian columns. The column capitals are carved in a combination of acanthus-leaf and tobacco-leaf design. Busts of Vice Presidents occupy a portion of this foyer. Of two elevator shafts, one is marked "Senators Only," an indication of the exclusive atmosphere that pervades the Senate wing. Entering and exiting by private elevators and stairways, members of "the greatest deliberative body in the world" are seldom seen by the public, except on the floor of the Senate. Numerically less than one-fourth the size of the House, and occupying essentially an equal space, the Senate has more room for the appurtenances of dignity.

Several rooms along the North Corridor of the Senate Extension, open to the public when the Senate is not in session, are richly furnished and decorated. The SENATORS' RECEPTION ROOM, reached from the north end of the East Corridor, is notable for its Brumidi frescoes. The VICE PRESIDENT'S ROOM, at the corner of the North and East Corridors, contains an antique French clock, Rembrandt

Peale's portrait of Washington, several busts of Vice Presidents, and a gigantic crystal chandelier. The MARBLE ROOM, next west in the suite, has walls veneered with variegated Tennessee marble, and the paneled Vermont marble ceiling is supported by Corinthian columns of Italian marble. In this room Senators receive distinguished guests. The PRESIDENT'S ROOM, at the west end of the suite, is one of the most richly appointed rooms in the building. Its massive chandelier was gold-plated at a cost of $25,000. The walls are adorned with carved gilt mirrors, which repeat the gold accents of the chandelier and window valances. The room has a tiled mosaic floor, red window drapes, and red mahogany doors. The Brumidi frescoes, requiring 6½ years to complete, include medallion portraits of Washington and his first Cabinet, symbolic groups, and portraits of Columbus, Vespucci, Franklin, and William Brewster, the Plymouth colonist.

The GALLERY FLOOR of the Senate wing is best approached by the East Grand Stairway a massive balustraded stair in mauve-brown marble. At the head of the stairway, in the East Gallery Corridor, is A. G. Heaton's oil mural, *The Recall of Columbus*. In the East Gallery Elevator Foyer is an idealized mural portraying *Leif Erickson Discovering America*. Thus, within a few feet of each other, the pretensions of northern and southern Europe to have produced the discoverer of the New World, are both recognized. In this foyer are a number of busts, including that of Thomas Crawford, sculptor of the crowning figure on the Capitol dome; Senator Charles Sumner, abolitionist leader and critic of Capitol art; Presidents Abraham Lincoln and Zachary Taylor; Thaddeus Kosciuszko and Casimir Pulaski, Polish officers who fought in the Revolution; Viscount James Bryce, British Ambassador to Washington and student of American life; Flat-Mouth and Be-sheck-kee, Chippewa chiefs, by Francis Vincenti. In the East Gallery Corridor is Cornelia Adele Fassett's oil mural, *The Florida Case Before the Electoral Commission*. Along the North Gallery Corridor are workrooms, telegraph offices, and other facilities for Senate newspaper correspondents. Entrances from these corridors lead to the Senate galleries.

The SENATE CHAMBER, 113 feet long, 50 feet wide, and 36 feet high, has served as a meeting place for the upper House since shortly before the Civil War, and has been little changed since then, except to provide modern lighting, heating, and air conditioning. The Vice President of the United States, or the President *pro tempore* of the Senate, sits in a carved chair on a dais in the form of a classic marble niche, while other chairs on the dais are occupied by the sergeant at arms, secretaries, and clerks. Seated about the dais are page boys, who carry messages and run errands for the Senators. These boys come from all parts of the country, and spend part of each day in school. Facing the dais are the desks of Senators, arranged in semicircular rows, Democrats to the right of the presiding officer, Republicans to his left.

The Chamber walls, under the galleries, are divided into panels by slender pilasters grouped in pairs, and each panel is decorated with arabesques and shields. Doors leading to the floor and galleries are of bird's-eye maple, embellished with bronze appliques. The flat ceiling is a glazed and paneled skylight with occasional stained-glass medallions. A series of busts of the first 20 Vice Presidents decorates the gallery walls. A unanimous Senate resolution in 1884 prohibited the display of portraits, paintings, or mural frescoes in the Chamber. In this great hall, all Vice Presidents since 1861 have been inaugurated in the presence of the President, President-elect, and Members of Congress, just before the new President takes the oath in front of the Capitol.

Galleries on the east and west are in part reserved for holders of special cards obtainable from Senators, and in part open to the general public; the same holds true for the House galleries. The north gallery, behind the chair of the presiding officer, is open to the general public, except for the raised central Senate press gallery. On the south, facing the chair, is a gallery reserved for members of the diplomatic corps and for members of the Senators' families.

At the top of the West Grand Stairway, which leads down from the gallery floor, is one of Charles Willson Peale's noted portraits of Washington. Above the landing, half way down the stairs, is James Walker's oil mural, *The Battle of Chapultepec*. At the foot of the stairway, in the West Corridor of the principal floor, is Horatio Stone's marble statue of John Hancock, whose elaborate signature stands at the head of those on the Declaration of Independence.

The stairway continues to the West Corridor, Ground Floor, which is elaborately decorated with Brumidi frescoes. Here are vividly executed arabesques, lunettes, and medallion panels of animals, allegories, portraits, and historic scenes, done in the Renaissance manner. The north end of this corridor, particularly, is known as the "Pompeiian Corridor" because of the color and treatment of its decorations. The Senators' Refectory and Dining Room are on the east side of the Senate v ing. No alcoholic liquors are sold here, though the House Restaurant sells beer.

A long central corridor running from north to south connects the Senate Extension with the House Extension. Beneath the North Small Rotunda it opens into an OVAL HALL, containing a circle of piers supporting the colonnade on the floor above. Through the light well there is an upward view of the interior of the northern small dome.

A door on the southeast leads to the CORN FOYER, containing Latrobe's columns, in which the flutings are made by representations of cornstalks, and the capitals are carved with ears of corn. Latrobe wrote to Jefferson in 1809 that this work had won him "more applause from members of Congress than all the works of magnitude or difficulty that surrounded them." The foyer gives access to the LAW LIBRARY on the north, where the Supreme Court met before it was moved to the principal floor above. Its similarity to a grotto gave point to a famous sally of John Randolph—he called the courtroom, where Chief Justice Marshall was handing down his historic constitutional opinions, "the cave of Trophonius," for the subterranean chamber of the reputedly omniscient oracle of Lebadea.

The central corridor continues along the main axis of the building to the CRYPT, an immense circular hall directly under the Great Rotunda, divided into concentric circular aisles by sturdy paired columns, and having a groined arched ceiling. The room reveals the ponderous medieval substructure of the building. A model of the Capitol, 12 feet long, is on the north side of the Crypt. Northeast of the Crypt is Adelaide Johnson's sculptural work in which the busts of Lucretia Mott, Susan B. Anthony, and Elizabeth Cady Stanton, noted early suffragists, seem to emerge from a massive marble block. An unusual concept for memorial statuary, this piece has earned the nickname of "Three Old Ladies in a Bathtub." Below the Crypt, in "the tomb," is kept the black-draped catafalque used for those who lie in state in the Capitol. The key to this room is kept in the Capitol Architect's office on the basement floor; visitors may see the catafalque. In this basement chamber it was planned, after 1799, to keep the bodies of George and Martha Washington, but the family in 1832 objected to their removal from Mount Vernon.

South of the Crypt is the HALL OF COLUMNS, sometimes called "Tobacco Hall" because of its brownstone walls and Latrobe's tobacco-leaf capitals, serving as a monumental foyer to the south portal of the building. Between the fluted columns are statues of State notables, a part of the overflow from the Statuary Hall collection. Reading south, on alternate sides from the northeast corner, they are: E. Kirby Smith (Florida), last Confederate general to surrender, by C. A. Pillars; Charles B. Aycock, North Carolina governor and educator, by Charles Keck; George W. Glick, Kansas governor and one-time national leader of the Democratic party, by C. H. Niehaus; Zachariah Chandler (Michigan), Secretary of the Interior under President Grant, by C. H. Niehaus; James Z. George, Mississippi jurist and Reconstruction leader, by Augustus Lukeman; James Harlan (Iowa), Secretary of the Interior under Lincoln, by Nellie V. Walker; John E. Kenna, Confederate soldier, West Virginia Senator, and proponent of Federal aid for slack-water navigation, by Alexander Doyle; Francis P. Blair (Missouri), Free-Soil editor and Union general, by Alexander Doyle; Philip Kearney (New Jersey), Civil War general, by H. K. Brown; James Shields, Illinois Senator and Civil War general, by Leonard Volk; John Winthrop, governor of Massachusetts Bay Colony, by R. S. Greenough; James P. Clarke, governor of Arkansas, by Pompeo Coppini; Oliver P. Morton, Indiana's Civil War governor, by C. H. Niehaus; J. L. M. Curry, Alabama educator and author, by Dante Sodini; Thomas Starr King (California), Unitarian clergyman, author, and lecturer, by Haig Patigian; Jacob Collamer, Vermont Senator and personal adviser of Lincoln during the Civil War, by Preston Powers; Julius S. Morton (Nebraska), originator of Arbor Day, by R. Evans.

On the Ground Floor just south of the West Grand Stairway is

THE CAPITOL — STATUE OF CHIEF
JUSTICE MARSHALL IN FOREGROUND

Farm Security Administration: Delano

THE WHITE HOUSE

Farm Security Administration: McMillan

SUPREME COURT BUILDING

W. Lincoln Highton

TREASURY BUILDING

W. Lincoln Highton

STATE DEPARTMENT BUILDING

BRITISH EMBASSY

Washington Daily News

Washington Post

LINCOLN MEMORIAL

W. Lincoln Highton
NATIONAL ARCHIVES BUILDING AND THE "IMPERIAL FACADE"
OF THE FEDERAL TRIANGLE ALONG CONSTITUTION AVENUE

PAN AMERICAN UNION

W. Lincoln Highton

WASHINGTON MONUMENT

©Pat Sanford

the HOUSE AGRICULTURE COMMITTEE ROOM, containing Brumidi's first allegorical frescoes, done in 1856. They include *Cincinnatus Called from the Plough to Become Dictator of Rome* and *Putnam called from the Plough to Join the Revolutionary Forces.* Representative Lovejoy in 1859 disapproved these pictures, stating that he would have preferred "the picture of a western plow with its polished steel moldboard, with the hardy yeoman . . . holding a span of bays with arched neck and neatly trimmed harness" and at the other end "a Negro slave with untidy clothing, with a slouching gait, shuffling along by the side of a mule team. . . . Thus we should have a symbol of the two systems of labor now struggling for ascendancy."

East of the Hall of Columns are the House Dining Rooms and barber shops. Stairways and elevators lead up to the principal and gallery floors.

The SPEAKER'S LOBBY, at the south end of the House Extension on the Principal Floor, open only when the House is not sitting, is richly decorated with frescoes and hangings, and with portraits of former Speakers, including John S. Sargent's notable portrait of Thomas B. Reed. At the east and west ends of the lobby are private stairways leading to the ground floor, as in the Senate Extension; over the west stairway is Albert Bierstadt's oil mural, *Viscaine Landing at Monterey,* and over that on the east is his *Discovery of the Hudson River.* A large map, painted on glass, shows by means of lights the current condition of weather all over the country.

The East Grand Stairway, opening off the East Corridor, leads to the gallery floor. At the foot of the stair is Powers' marble statue of Jefferson, and on the landing half way up the stair is Francis P. Carpenter's mural, *First Reading of the Emancipation Proclamation,* only painting in the Capitol commemorating the Civil War. Along the South Gallery Corridor are rooms for House newspaper correspondents; various entrances to the House galleries open from this floor.

The HOUSE CHAMBER, central hall of the House Extension, is similar to the Senate Chamber, in size and decoration. The paneled skylight is embellished with medallions containing the coats of arms of the 48 States. On the south wall is Vanderlyn's fine copy of Stuart's portrait of Washington, and a portrait of Lafayette by Ary Scheffer, presented by the French artist in 1824, at the time of Lafayette's visit to Washington. The fresco on the same wall, signed "C. Brumidi, Citizen of the U. S.," portrays Cornwallis suing for peace.

The Speaker of the House sits on a marble dais, facing the 444 seats of the House, arranged in semicircular rows. Unlike the Senators, the 435 Representatives have no desks or reserved seats. On a malachite stand at the Speaker's right is the great mace of the United States, a bundle of 13 black rods surmounted by a silver globe and eagle. When the House meets as a Committee of the Whole, the mace is removed from its pedestal.

In this room, because of the multiplicity of legislators, clerks, and page boys, and throughout the House Extension, there is, when Congress is meeting, a lively sense of representative Government in action. In the Capitol, within an architectural atmosphere recalling ancient times, operates an institution which, with modifications, resembles the public forum of old. At this center of Washington's leading industry (Government) the tools in use—thought, voice, and pen—are ancient tools. The products of legislation, bills and resolutions, are carried from place to place by boys, recalling the methods of medieval guilds. If the superficial trappings of writing, movement upstairs and down, speech at a distance, and the transfer of persons, have been mechanized, these things make little difference in the operation or atmosphere of the forum-by-representation.

In the House Chamber, both branches of the national legislature meet to listen to messages from the President. Thomas Jefferson interrupted the practice of delivering Presidential messages in person on the ground that such a practice savored too much of "speeches from the throne," and had his messages read by clerks of the Senate and House. Jefferson's method was followed by all Presidents until Woodrow Wilson revived the older form, which has since been followed with few lapses.

The West Grand Stairway leads down from the gallery floor to the principal floor. At the head of the stairs is R. N. Brooke's portrait of John Marshall, and over the landing half way down the stairs is Emanuel Leutze's composite mural, *Westward the Course of Empire Takes Its Way*. At the foot of the stairway is Joseph Lasalle's bust of Be-sheck-kee, Chippewa chief, modeled after the bust by Francis Vincenti.

From the North Corridor an arcaded passageway leads north, along the main axis of the building, into a windowed loggia. A critic has said of C. B. Ives' statue of Jonathan Trumbull, Colonial governor of Connecticut, within this space, that of all the dead then in and around Statuary Hall, it seemed "most conscious of being dead and most solicitous to appear alive." Here are also statues of William King, first governor of Maine, by Franklin Simmons; Jacques Marquette (Wisconsin), French Jesuit who, with Jolliet, discovered the Mississippi River, by Gaetano Trentanove; Wade Hampton, Confederate general from South Carolina, by F. W. Ruckstuhl; and Will Rogers (Oklahoma), the humorist, by Jo Davidson.

The corridor leads into STATUARY HALL, a semicircular room 96 feet in diameter, extended on the flat side by a colonnaded bay, and surrounded by life-size bronze and marble statues of notables from the various States. The Corinthian colonnade on the north side of the hall, and the screen of columns on the south, are monoliths of variegated Potomac marble, with capitals of white Italian marble. The dome-like ceiling is decorated with coffers and surmounted by a cupola. The eagle over the south door, by Guiseppe Valaperti, is his sole work in the Capitol. Latrobe was dissatisfied with the original design, which resembled a Roman more than an American bald eagle. Fearing that "any glaring impropriety of character will be immediately detected by our Western members," Latrobe asked Charles Willson Peale to help the Italian with the design. Valaperti subsequently disappeared, and it was thought that he drowned himself. Enrico Causici did the *Liberty* above Valaperti's eagle. Over the north door is a gallery decorated by Carlo Franzoni's marble *Car of History* clock. The room has an odd acoustical property; a person standing on a brass marker in front of the Robert E. Lee statue can hear a loud whisper from a corresponding point on the opposite side of the room. This acoustical peculiarity has been somewhat deadened by changes in the interior arrangement of the room.

From 1807 to 1857 this hall was the Representatives' Chamber. When it was completed, John Randolph of Roanoke remarked that it was "handsome and fit for anything but the use intended." To smother its many reverberations, great curtains were hung between the columns on the south side. In front of the curtains were couches upon which Members might recline. Henry Clay presided over the House in this room from 1811 to 1820 and from 1823 to 1825; he was the first outstanding presiding officer of the House, and set many precedents that are still followed. The Missouri Compromise was debated here in 1819, in the presence of many ladies, and Clay did much to force its passage. In the course of this debate John Randolph was moved to point to the gallery and exclaim: "Mr. Speaker, what, pray, are all these women doing here, so out of place in this arena? Sir, they had much better be at home attending to their knitting." This "misery debate" lasted so long that the House was exhausted by it, and one member fainted while attempting to speak.

Here, in 1824, the House heard two addresses by Robert Owen, the Scotch Utopian Socialist, then on his way to found a colony at New Harmony, Indiana. Here, ten years later, was announced the death of John Randolph of Roanoke, by a colleague who himself fell dead as he spoke. In this room the aged ex-President, John Quincy Adams, was stricken with paralysis during a roll call in 1848; a metal plate in the floor, 10 paces in front of the Jefferson Davis statue, marks the spot where he fell. The room became so crowded, toward the end of its tenure as the House Chamber, that those seated in the front rows of the galleries found it impossible to push their way out for refreshment. The practice then evolved of passing food from the floor to the galleries by means of a long pole. Ladies, and members of the diplomatic corps, once permitted seats on the floor, were subsequently banished to the galleries with the other spectators.

From 1857 to 1864 the room was empty except for "cobwebs, apple cores, and hucksters carts." Toward the end of this period a Representative complained about the condition of the room. "I look around to see where the venerable John Quincy Adams trembled in his seat and voted and I see a huckster woman selling ginger bread. I look to see . . . where Clay sat, and I find a woman selling oranges and root beer." In 1864 the room was dedicated as a National

Statuary Hall, to which each State might send statues of two distinguished deceased citizens. The number in this room was decreased in 1934 to one from each State. Beginning east of the north entrance and going clockwise the statues are as follows:

Daniel Webster, New Hampshire orator and statesman, by Carl Conrads; John C. Greenway, Arizona copper miner, by Gutzon Borglum; Samuel Adams, Massachusetts Revolutionary patriot, by Anne Whitney; Charles Carroll of Carrollton, Maryland, signer of the Declaration of Independence, by Richard E. Brooks; Robert Livingston of New York, negotiator of the Louisiana Purchase and sponsor of Robert Fulton's steamship venture, by E. D. Palmer; Dr. John Gorrie of Florida, inventor of the artificial ice machine, by C. A. Pillars; Frances E. Willard, Illinois temperance leader, the only woman so honored, by Helen F. Mears; Hannibal Hamlin, Maine, Vice President under Lincoln, by C. E. Tefft; Thomas H. Benton, Missouri Senator and proponent of the frontier point of view, by Alexander Doyle; Samuel J. Kirkwood, Iowa's Civil War Governor and Secretary of the Interior under Garfield, by Vinnie Ream; Roger Sherman, Connecticut signer of the Declaration of Independence, by C. B. Ives; Zebulon Z. Vance, Civil War governor of North Carolina, by Gutzon Borglum; Alexander H. Stephens, Georgia, Vice President of the Confederacy, by Gutzon Borglum; Ethan Allen, a virile portrait of Vermont's hero of the Revolution, by Larkin G. Mead; George L. Shoup, Idaho's first governor, by F. E. Triebel; John C. Calhoun, South Carolina orator and statesman, by F. W. Ruckstuhl; Henry Clay, Kentucky orator and statesman, by C. H. Niehaus; Lewis Cass, Territorial governor of Michigan and Secretary of State under Buchanan, by Daniel Chester French; Caesar A. Rodney, Delaware signer of the Declaration of Independence and major in the Revolutionary War, by Bryant Baker; William Allen, Representative from Ohio and author of the campaign slogan of 1844, "Fifty-four-forty or fight," by C. H. Niehaus; Uriah M. Rose, Arkansas jurist, legal writer, and member of the Second Peace Conference at The Hague in 1907, by F. W. Ruckstuhl; Jefferson Davis, Mississippi, President of the Confederacy, by Augustus Lukeman; Robert E. Lee, Virginia, commander-in-chief of the Confederate Army, by Edward V. Valentine; Roger Williams, founder of Rhode Island, by Franklin Simmons; Junípero Serra, Spanish Franciscan missionary and founder of a number of early California missions, by E. Cadorin; Robert Fulton, Pennsylvania, inventor of the first commercially successful steamboat, by Howard Roberts; Joseph Wheeler, Alabama, Confederate and Spanish-American War general, by Berthold Nebel; Henry M. Rice, Minnesota pioneer, Senator, and Indian Commissioner, by F. E. Triebel; William H. Beadle, South Dakota educator and legislator, by H. Daniel Webster; Robert M. LaFollette, liberal statesman from Wisconsin, by Jo Davidson; Huey P. Long, Louisiana's "share-the-wealth" governor and Senator, by Charles S. Keck; William Jennings Bryan, Nebraska, thrice-nominated "free-silver" candidate for the Presidency, by R. Evans; John Sevier, governor of the "State of Franklin" and first governor of Tennessee, by Belle Kinney and L. F. Sholz; Francis H. Pierpont, governor of the "Reformed State of Virginia," which gave "legal" permission to West Virginia to secede from the Old Dominion, by Franklin Simmons; Lew Wallace, Indiana, author and Union general, by Andrew O'Connor; John J. Ingalls, Kansas Senator, by C. H. Niehaus; Sequoyah, Oklahoma, inventor of the 85-letter Cherokee alphabet and leader of the Cherokee people, by Vinnie Ream and G. J. Zolnay; Sam Houston, frontiersman, soldier, and first president of the Republic of Texas, by Elisabet Ney; Richard Stockton, New Jersey signer of the Declaration of Independence, by H. K. Brown. Nine States—Colorado, Montana, Nevada, New Mexico, North Dakota, Oregon, Utah, Washington, and Wyoming—are (1942) unrepresented in Statuary Hall.

North of Statuary Hall, opening out as a part of the main north-south corridor, is the SOUTH SMALL ROTUNDA, a circular room with domical ceiling and cupola. Here, in the sandstone walls, columns, archways, ornamental ceilings, and age-worn spiral stairway opening off the southwest corner, can be studied the texture and scale of the original masonry of the Capitol. This rotunda contains three statues: George Clinton, "father of New York State" and its governor for seven terms, six of them in succession (1777-95), by H. K. Brown; Stephen F. Austin, colonizer of Texas, by Elisabet Ney; and John Peter Gabriel Muhlenberg, Lutheran clergyman, Revolutionary general, and Pennsylvania Congressman, by Blanche Nevin. A corridor on the north connects with the Great Rotunda.

The INTERIOR OF THE DOME, approached by a stairway on the southwest side of the North Small Rotunda, is open to visitors in normal times. It was closed in 1939, for the duration of the national emergency. The stairway, which runs between the two shells of the dome, providing a view of their inner structure, has 365 steps, representing the days of the year. It leads up to the gallery just below the Brumidi fresco, under the dome cap, whence there is a view of the echoing Great Rotunda below. The stairway continues to the two exterior dome galleries, that just below the lantern being the highest point to which the public is admitted. From this vantage there is a view of the city and its surroundings inferior only to that from the Washington Monument or from an airplane.

Below the Capitol's ground floor are the basement and sub-basement. From the basement radiate three subways—a monorail car passage from the Senate wing to the Senate Office Building, a pedestrians' passage from the House wing to the two House Office Buildings, and a mechanized book conveyor to the Library of Congress. The office of the Architect of the Capitol is on this floor, in addition to storerooms, repair shops, and service rooms. On this level, in a room at the west front of the terrace, is a school for page boys. The sub-basement is devoted entirely to service facilities for the huge building.

GOVERNMENT PRINTING OFFICE

The Government Printing Office (*open, free, 10-3 Mon.-Fri.; conducted tours at 10 and 1, beginning at Room 802, Building 3; no smoking except in cafeteria and Harding Hall*), largest printing plant in the world, occupies four buildings close to the mailing and shipping facilities of the City Post Office and Union Station. Three of them are massive red-brick structures west of North Capitol Street, between G and H Streets, and the other is a three-story-and-basement building east of the same street; they have a total floor space of 33 acres, where GPO employees work in shifts 24 hours a day. In 1940 the GPO's 7,200 employees, receiving $1,250,000 pay each month, produced published material for which $25,000,000 was received. This included 2,000,000,000 postal cards, 268,000,000 money orders, 650,000,000 book-pages (2,000,000 pages a day), and 5,000,000,000 pieces of job work (such as letterheads and forms), to mention only a few. Among the materials used in one year for this vast publishing job were 83,000,-000 pounds of paper, 10,000,000 pounds of type metal, and 322,130 pounds of printing ink. Methods range from quiet handwork by artisans, reminiscent of medieval craft practices, to the manipulations of noisy twentieth-century machines, almost human in the complexity of their operations.

Fewer than 7,000 persons visit the plant each year, possibly because a mistaken notion prevails that it is not open to the public, possibly because guards are required to question each person entering the buildings concerning his business. Educationally, there are few places affording a more complete view of book-making, from manuscript to bound volume. From the standpoint of the onlooker, some of the processes are spectacular, some are beautiful in their simplicity, and the entire plant is a lesson in human ingenuity applied to the graphic arts. Most of the floors, in order to decrease the rumbling of heavy supply trucks, are paved with wooden blocks. As a consequence this is one of the few Washington points of interest in which visitors do not acquire "museum feet."

Building No. 1, NW. corner North Capitol and G. Streets, built in 1901, is an ornate red-brick structure eight stories high; the Office of the Superintendent of Documents is in the southwest corner of this building. Building 2, often called the GPO Annex, completed in 1928, connects with the old building on the west side. Building 3 is an eight-story red brick building adjoining Building 1 on the north. It was completed and occupied in 1940, and though its architectural lines are in keeping with the oldest building, the lines run more to verticals and horizontals than to the arches and colonnades of an earlier architectural period. Building 4, on the east side of North Capitol Street and facing Buildings 1 and 3, completed and occupied in 1938, is commonly designated as the GPO Warehouse.

Conducted tours begin at the INFORMATION ROOM on the eighth floor of Building 3, and visitors are taken into portions of Buildings 1,

2, and 3, all of which adjoin. Guides do not attempt to show the operations of the entire plant, but most of the book-making processes are covered. Additional trips may be arranged to include other parts of the buildings.

Among the offices on the eighth floor are those of the Public Printer, who has charge of the entire plant; the Purchasing Division, which buys the enormous quantity of materials needed to operate this gigantic publishing house, and sells such by-products as wastepaper; the Production Manager, who has immediate supervision over all printing; the Planning Division, which has the responsibility of planning the layout, design, and physical progress of the work; the Comptroller's Office, which computes the exact amount of time spent by each of the 7,200 employees on each piece of work; and the Disbursing Office, which handles the enormous monthly pay roll.

On the seventh floor, in the northwest corner, are 100 monotype keyboard machines, upon which the first step is taken in preparing type by the "mono" or single-type method. Each machine has a keyboard similar to that of a typewriter, and the machine, operating by compressed air, punches holes in a narrow roll of paper, preparing a record similar to a player-piano roll. On the same floor, in an adjoining room, are 130 monotype casting machines, upon which the "roll" is "played" and the type is cast, one character at a time. The casting machines consume 7 tons of type-metal daily. The metal is an alloy of lead, tin, and antimony, and has the virtue of solidifying almost instantly. It is cast into 25-pound "pigs" each having an eye at one end by which it is suspended over the melting pot on the machine and fed in as needed. Visitors see piles of these pigs in the casting-machine room. Monotype is used mostly for work where many different characters are needed, where rules need to be inserted, as in tabular material, and to simplify correction, since it is easy to replace any character. Monotype requires careful handling, since a hopeless "printer's pi" would result from spilling any portion of the assembled type.

On the same floor is the SORTS SUPPLY ROOM, which keeps on hand 300,000 pounds of type, more than 11,000 pounds of which are distributed to the workrooms daily. Metal-type sizes range from 4- to 72-point, the former less than one-sixteenth of an inch in height and used mostly for imprints. Wooden type, in larger sizes, ranges as high as 360 points, 5 inches tall. The supply room also keeps about 70 different kinds of rules and borders, and a supply of metal "furniture," used in locking page forms. On the same floor are the CORRECTING AND ASSEMBLING ROOM, where most of the galley and page corrections are made. The PROOF ROOM, also on this floor, has a staff of about 25 copy editors for each shift, their desks surrounded by standard works of reference. The proofreaders on this floor are part of a staff of about 300 employed by the GPO. Many of them are experts in various fields, including foreign languages. One of their many duties is to proofread the *Pan American Bulletin* in editions issued in three languages—English, Spanish, and Portuguese, and the many languages employed in international treaties.

On the sixth floor are the 78 line-casting machines—linotype and intertype, differing very little except that they bear separate trade names. These machines, fascinating to many people for their complex and continuous operation, cast type in solid lines. The hands of speedy and accurate operators play over the large keyboards, there is the tinkle of dropping type mats, the operation of levers and shafts, as the machine sorts and replaces the matrices in the magazine, and the ceaseless appearance of shiny new slugs of type. Most type for ordinary jobs is set by line-casting machines. Corrections involve the resetting of entire lines, but the handling of a line type requires less time and care than that of the monotype product. The HAND SECTION, on this floor, is the room in which the type is assembled in pages and locked in rectangular metal frames or "chases." Margins are provided by the use of metal "furniture," against which metal keys and wedges are turned tightly.

The STEREOTYPE SECTION, smelling of steam and heated paper, is the area in which type is plated for printing. Much of this work is done by the wet-mat process but is being replaced by a later method employing dry mats. The "mat" is made of layers of blotting and tissue paper pasted together, and is kept moist before an impression is made on it. A wet mat is placed over a page of type and subjected to a pressure of 200 pounds to the square inch. It is then dried in an electric dryer. Plates are cast flat or curved, depending on the kind of presswork involved. The Stereotype Section has two groups of casting "boxes" each ranged around a central vat of molten metal. Eight of the "boxes" are for making curved plates, four for flat, an indicator that the greater portion of the GPO's printing is done on rotary rather than flat-bed presses. The dried mat is placed in the "box" and held in place by air suction. A workman pours in a ladle of molten metal, which cools sufficiently in one minute to remove it as a page-size plate. The plates are shaved and beveled to fit the press for which they are intended. Stereotype plates are of sufficient durability to make about 75,000 printed impressions without too much wear.

The ELECTROTYPE-MOLDING SECTION, also on the sixth floor, is an area of the Government's publishing plant which combines the work of artisans, electrochemists, and operators of twentieth-century machines. The rooms have a pleasantly pungent odor of hot wax and acid solutions, two of the ingredients most important in electroplating. The process begins with a wax plate, sized and shaped similar to an unframed wall mirror. Impressions of type pages are made by machine pressure in the wax, a process shown to the visitor. Some wax is squeezed up by this pressure and the wax tablet is passed under a large blade, which trims the plate to a uniform thickness. A flame is run quickly over the wax impression to re-round the edges of the type. The plate is then dusted with graphite, the same material as that used in pencil lead. Graphite is a conductor of electricity, a fact of importance in the next step. The wax plate is suspended in a solution of copper sulphate, through which an electric current is run. Within an hour, by a process of electrolysis, a copper shell seven or eight thousandths of an inch thick is deposited on the wax tablet. The shell is removed from the wax and "fried" like a pancake on a restaurant hot plate while sheets of tinfoil melt into the hollow back. It is then moved in front of twin spouts from which molten metal pours into and around the shell, to give it "backing." A bell similar to that of an alarm clock rings when the metal reaches the desired thickness. The "backed" plate is scrubbed with kerosene by an automatic rotary brush, and is later finished to fit the press for which it is intended. Electrotype plates represent a finer grade of work than stereotype plates, and they have sufficient durability to make more than 500,000 impressions. The Electroplating Section has smaller facilities for nickel-plating, which makes plates capable of about 1,000,000 impressions, and for making chromium plates, which will print indefinitely.

The GPO's six-bed Emergency Hospital, maintained principally for employees injured or taken suddenly ill while on duty, is on the fifth floor. Also on this floor are the office of the Superintendent of Platemaking, the Finishing Room, and the Patents Section, where specifications for patents are printed. The conducted tour does not ordinarily include this area.

On the fourth floor is the MAIN PRESS ROOM, occupied by many of the GPO's 196 presses. These are of various kinds—rotary, flatbed, cylinder, horizontal, vertical, platen, embossing, envelop, and offset. Presses in a wire cage opposite the east elevator are used for confidential printing—Civil Service examinations, passports, military codes, examinations for West Point Military Academy and the Naval Academy at Annapolis and the like. The public is not admitted here.

The visitor is bewildered and amazed by the variety and mechanical ingenuity of the presses in this area. Some presses print in two colors while making a single run. Some presses, usually pointed out by guides, pick up sheets of paper by means of suction cups and deliver them for printing. When coming off the press the sheets pass over a gas flame, which has the double virtue of partially drying the ink and removing static electricity from the paper. This curious force makes sheets of paper stick together as if magnetized. There are "bob-tail" presses which print bills and forms at the rate of 2,200 an hour. There are rotary presses printing both sides of postal change-of-address cards from copper plates—printing, cutting, and delivering more than half a million cards a day. There are copper-plate presses that print, perforate, slit, count, and deliver money-order blanks at the rate of more than 40,000 a day. And there are many rotary presses used for book and pamphlet work.

On the same floor, conveniently situated with regard to the presses, are machines for folding, assembling, trimming, and stitching pamphlets and books. One machine folds and pastes, in one operation, such small items as eight-page pamphlets. Strings of ordinary Christmas-tree tinsel dragging over completed pamphlets as they come from the machine, absorb static electricity. Pamphlets of 12 or 16 pages are "saddle-stitched" by means of wire staples inserted at the fold. Automatic stitching machines, requiring only one operator, or gang-stitching machines, requiring a row of girls to feed folded pamphlets to the stapling-machine conveyor, are used in this process. There are folding machines and machines that assemble book signatures of 16 pages each, keeping them in proper order for stitching. There is an indexing machine, which cuts and prints index margins in one operation; the operators are highly skilled, counting the number of pages assigned to each letter of the alphabet with such speed that they keep pace with the rapid-fire machine. There is a "three-way trimmer," a large and noisy machine that slices uneven edges from assembled book signatures in a dual operation. Its giant blades are changed every four hours, and the constant increment of paper strips is carried by suction to the basement, where it is baled and sold as waste. Scores of publications of all kinds and sizes are in process of publication at all times, and the visitor picks up random titles—*Infant Care,* Uncle Sam's perennial best-seller, issued by the Department of Labor; *Consumers Guide; Maximum Hours,* also a Labor Department publication; *30,000 Urban Youth,* issued by NYA; *Camp Life,* the CCC periodical; the *Basic Field Manual* of the U.S. Army; *The U.S. Government Manual,* an informational bulletin prepared by the Office of Government Reports; *Florida Oranges,* one of many Department of Agriculture bulletins; the *Naval Directory;* the *Nautical Almanac;* and many others.

An island of quiet craftsmanship in a sea of machines is in the REBUILDING UNIT on this floor, where books are rebound by hand for the Library of Congress and for Government department libraries. An object of constant visitor-interest is the artisan who places gold lettering on the rounded shelf-edge of "recased" books. A thin coating of vaseline is rubbed over the rounded edge of the cover, to hold strips of 23-karat gold leaf, thinner than tissue paper. Using a handled "stick" of type, the workman makes the impression on the strips of gold leaf with manual pressure, aided by the already heated type. Two sticks of type are sometimes required to impress the name of the author, title of the book, library number, place and date of publication, and the library medallion. The residue of gold leaf is taken off with a piece of crude rubber, from which the gold is later recovered. The newly lettered binding is then ready to resume its place on the library shelves. Other steps in the rebinding process can be seen on this floor.

The third floor, on which the ruling machines operate, is not ordinarily included in the conducted tour.

On the second floor is the CONGRESSIONAL RECORD PRESS, a specially constructed web press for printing the daily issues of the *Congressional Record*—it is one of the most remarkable machines in the Government Printing Office. The *Record,* containing the daily utterances of Congressmen on the floor of the Senate and House, is printed with the speed of a daily newspaper. Its length runs from 3 to 300 pages daily, depending on the length of the sessions and the volubility of Congressmen; the average is 64 pages. Copy for the *Record* must be delivered to the GPO by 11:30 p.m. Type is set, irrespective of length, and stereotype plates are on the press by 2:30 a.m. The press runs off 12,500 copies an hour, and delivers them printed, folded, gathered, and stapled. The usual circulation of the *Record* is 43,000 copies, all of which are in the mail by 8 a.m. The MAILING MACHINE, just next, assists in this final operation. Flat copies of the *Record* are fed into this machine, which folds, turns and pastes them in addressed wrappers and delivers them to an endless belt, which drops them into mail bags. As filled, the mail bags are dropped down a convenient chute, which carries them to the basement and launches them on an endless belt running under North Capitol Street to the City Post Office.

Among these and other mechanical processes on the second floor, an artisan works noiselessly, using an old, old, method, marbling the edges and endpapers of books. Not so much used today as in former years (though it is still the badge of a ledger), marbling is the process of applying veined or variegated colors to the exposed page-edges of books and sometimes to the endpapers, or those directly inside the covers. A material basic to this process is gum hog, a fluid gum imported from India. Into a tray or trough of gum hog the artisan drops water color from a brush—favored colors are red, yellow, and blue. The bright colors spread into oval blobs on the gum, interspersed with smaller drops of contrasting colors. A simply-constructed "comb," made by driving nails through a strip of wood, is run rapidly through the surface of the solution. An amazing and colorful change takes place— the colors interweave in scalloped lines, and a pattern of brilliant color is produced in a twinkling. Another "comb," operated with a weaving motion, turns a portion of the solution into a pattern similar to that of a peacock's tail. A sheet of paper laid on the surface of the solution, or the edge of a book lightly dipped, comes away bearing the color and pattern. This is one of the most memorable processes—simple, vivid, combining color and motion—that the visitor sees in the entire GPO plant.

The BINDERY on this floor completes the process of bookmaking, using many ingenious machines. One machine sews assembled book signatures with cotton thread. The product looks like an impossibly thick book, since it sews all signatures indiscriminately, but end "sigs" are marked with a dot of ink, so the threads can be cut to separate the signature groupings into books. The book then goes to the round-ing machine, which applies pressure to round the hinged edge of the book. The back-lining machine applies, consecutively, a coating of glue, a strip of cloth, another coat of glue, and the end-papers, to which the back is later glued. The back of a book, in this atmosphere, is a "case," and the machine for making cloth bookbacks is a "casemaker." A roll of cloth feeds into the machine, on one side of which glue is auto-matically applied. The machine places cards of stiff board on the glued cloth, a strip of paper between, cuts and folds the cloth around the boards, and presses the whole between rollers to iron out the wrinkles. Inked titles are printed in a highspeed press, but gold and gold-foil titles are printed on a manually-operated press, using the same basic method as that employed by the craftsman who prints gold titles by hand—heat and pressure are applied simultaneously by a machine press. Excess gold leaf and gold foil are removed with a mechanical rotary brush, operated by a man wearing a gauze mask to prevent him from inhaling particles of gold. This is one of the few places in the world where a human being takes steps to protect himself from gold. Pieces of gold foil and gold leaf are swept up from the floor and sent away for recovery of the metal. The casing end machine completes the binding process. This mechanism takes the book as it comes from the back-lining machine, with attached endpapers, runs a glue-coated roller over the outside of the endpapers, and clamps on the completed "case." Piles of newly cased books are put under hydraulic press exerting a pressure of 80 pounds to the square inch, and locked between brass-bound boards for 12 hours to adhere and dry. They are then ready for delivery to the Government department for which they are printed and to the Superintendent of Documents for public distribution and sale.

Conducted parties usually return to the eighth floor of Building 1, on the elevator. On this floor are the CAFETERIA, seating 900 people and serving more than 1,000,000 meals a year at an average cost of 22¢, and HARDING HALL, an auditorium and recreation room seating 1,700. Dances, banquets, movies, and other employees' functions are held in this hall, which is also a repository of cups and trophies won by GPO athletic teams. Only in these two rooms, and only when off duty, are GPO employees permitted to smoke. The APPRENTICE SCHOOL, also on this floor, trains Civil Service appointees between the ages of 17 and 20 years in printing, bookbinding, presswork, stereotyping, electrotyping, and photoengraving. Started in 1922, its enrollment is limited to 200 at a time. These low-salaried apprentices work at production during their in-service training, and after 5 years of apprenticeship they become journeymen and are given permanent employment in the GPO. Few students in technical schools have an equal opportunity for professional study in such a well-equipped laboratory of printing.

The conducted tour ends at the INFORMATION ROOM on the eighth floor of Building 3.

In addition to the divisions of the GPO plant visited on the regularly conducted tour, a number of correlated divisions carry on significant work. The Maintenance Division, for instance, in order to maintain the building and equipment, has machine, electrical, carpentry, plumbing, sheet-metal, blacksmith, automobile, paint, and boxmaking shops. It also maintains an underground tunnel mail-conveyor system which carries up to 2,000 mail bags a day between the GPO and the City Post Office. The Division of Tests and Technical Control analyzes paper, ink, type-metals, and all other materials used in the

GPO to determine their chemical and physical suitability for printing and bookbinding processes. The type-metal foundry of this Division remelts type metal returned from the printing presses and restores it to standard formulas so it can be used again. The Ink Section manufactures the various types of inks used in this Office and all other Government Departments. Laboratory chemists and experts sometimes assist other Government departments in detecting forgeries, through their technical knowledge of inks and papers. The Roller and Glue Section manufactures rollers used in all the different kinds of printing presses and makes a variety of glues and pastes for bookbinding.

The SALESROOM OF THE SUPERINTENDENT OF DOCUMENTS (*open 9-4 Mon.-Fri.; no smoking*) 45 G Street NW., the retail outlet of "the largest bookseller in the world," has racks holding free catalog lists by subjects, bookshelves displaying typical Government publications, and a long counter over which GPO publications are sold. Behind the counter is a row of locker-like shelves containing books and bulletins most in demand. Back of the unassuming face it presents to the public, the Office of the Superintendent of Documents distributes annually more than 700 million copies of books, bulletins, leaflets, periodicals, and forms of all types. Of the average distribution, 70 million public documents, 18 million are sold to the public at cost of production plus 50 per cent, as required by law. Three million publications are sent to 500 Federal depository libraries throughout the country, and the Documents Division Library maintains about 900,000 books, pamphlets, and maps.

The WAREHOUSE (Building 4), N. Capitol Street and Jackson Alley, is a long rectangular three-story gray cast-stone building facing the main GPO group, and extending back to the railroad tracks behind Union Station. The building is 467 feet long and 87½ feet wide, its floors designed to carry a load of 500 pounds to the square foot. A spur of trackage enters the third floor of the Warehouse, and there is space for 16 freight cars on this floor. Seven hundred carloads of paper, each weighing 40,000 pounds, can be stored in the warehouse at one time. Thousand-pound rolls of paper are unloaded from the freight cars and carried by an automatic "lowerator" to the floor below. Electric trucks, tractors, trailers, heavy-duty cranes, elevators, and other rolling stock are necessary in the movement of paper between the warehouse, through a two-way underground tunnel 30 feet beneath North Capitol Street, and the several floors of the main plant.

CITY POST OFFICE

The City Post Office, NE. corner North Capitol Street and Massachusetts Avenue, occupied in 1914 and remodeled in 1933, at a total cost of $7,000,000, was designed by Daniel H. Burnham, architect of the Union Station, to harmonize with that building. Successor to the first local postal station, placed on F Street in 1795, and others, it is a four-story structure of white Italian marble on a granite base. The principal façade, on Massachusetts Avenue, consists of a central three-story Ionic colonnade with slightly projecting entrance pavilions at each end. The deeply recessed portals, flanked by Ionic columns and massive bronze lamps, are adorned with bas-relief panels bearing the shield and eagle of the United States. The inscriptions for the east and west cornices were originally composed by Charles W. Eliot, president of Harvard University; they were edited as inscribed by President Woodrow Wilson, without his knowing the identity of their author.

The interior is planned to avoid congestion in the major working space and in the public area. The public corridor, extending the full width of the building parallel to Massachusetts Avenue, is decorated in buff marble and bronze, in the manner of a Roman hall of state. The colonnades of the public lobbies are executed in richly veined gray-green marble, with monolithic shafts having white caps and bases.

In the working space, representing most of the building, practically all facilities for transporting and assorting mail are mechanically operated. North- and west-bound mail is handled on the street level, south- and east-bound mail on the lower or tunnel level. Incoming mail is automatically distributed on huge belt conveyors, and a subterranean conveyor 1,000 feet long transports the huge bulk of mail handled daily by the Government Printing Office, on the opposite side of North Capitol Street. An enclosed bridge over 1st Street, at the east end of the building, connects the post office with Union Station, providing direct connection with the train shed. In addition to this main office, 72 branch stations throughout the District assist in serving a city with a population of well over 600,000, and in handling the postal messenger service between Government agencies.

A cafeteria on the third floor and a recreation room in the basement are maintained for the convenience of employees.

UNION STATION

Union Station, facing south at Massachusetts and Delaware Avenues, serves all railroads entering Washington: the Atlantic Coast Line, the Baltimore & Ohio, the Chesapeake & Ohio, the Pennsylvania, the Richmond, Fredericksburg & Potomac, the Seaboard Air Line, and the Southern. An information desk is on the west side of the central waiting room. Station service includes telephones and telegraph, newsstands, drugstore, restaurant, and other conveniences.

Designed as a gateway appropriate to Washington, Union Station serves to introduce the visitor to the grand scale and imposing architecture of the city. Monumental in conception, the building was designed in the manner of Roman classic architecture by Daniel H. Burnham, Chicago architect and director of works for the Columbian Exposition of 1893. The central pavilion of the main façade is based upon the theme of three great triumphal arches, and the main waiting room is conceived in the manner of the central hall in the Baths of

Diocletian. The vast structure is balanced in composition, the main waiting room constituting the central motif, with symmetrically disposed elements on each side. The great concourse, extending the entire length of the station, affords direct passage to trains.

The south or main façade, of white Vermont granite, consists of a monumental central loggia with three arches flanked by long arcaded wings accented at the ends by arched pavilions. The loggia, through which the Capitol can be seen, is adorned with massive Ionic columns supporting colossal allegorical figures placed against an unusually high attic. The figures, by Louis Saint-Gaudens, represent *Fire, Electricity, Freedom, Knowledge, Agriculture,* and *Mechanics.* The inscriptions on the attic story of the loggia and the end pavilions were selected by Charles W. Eliot, president of Harvard University.

Inside the entrance loggia is the huge waiting room, approximately 220 feet long exclusive of the transverse colonnades, and 120 feet wide, with a barrel-vaulted ceiling, paneled with deep coffers, 95 feet above the floor at its highest point. Five great archways, 30 feet wide and 50 feet high, afford access to the concourse. The transverse colonnades and those within the archways are surmounted by ornamental standing figures. Waiting passengers are accommodated by long rows of high-backed benches. Semicircular windows above the archways, and a similar opening more than 70 feet in diameter in the east wall, admit light into the enormous room. West of the waiting room are ticket offices and baggage rooms; east of it are dining rooms and a suite of rooms reserved for the use of the President and other distinguished guests; there are vehicular entrances at each end.

The great concourse, which serves the train shed, is 760 feet long and 130 feet wide. This immense space was designed to accommodate unusual traffic during Presidential inaugurations and other special events in Washington. The arched ceiling of the concourse is 45 feet high at the center, and is lighted from above. East of the concourse are gates and stairways, leading below to the subway tracks of southbound roads, which pass through a 4,000-foot tunnel, emerging south of New Jersey Avenue and D Street.

Union Station was completed in 1907 at a cost of about $4,000,000, though the cost of the entire development (tunnel, plaza, landscaping, rerouting of tracks, and so on) exceeded $21,800,000. The station covers more than 25 acres and is served by 20 tracks on the upper level and 12 on the lower, carrying about 40,000 passengers and upward of 220 trains daily. The yard equpiment includes a power plant, a roundhouse and repair shop, and one of the most complete intercommunication systems ever designed.

Immediately in front of the station are three giant flagstaffs, 110 feet high, painted white and surmounted by the conventional gilt ball and eagle. Directly in front of the station building is the COLUMBUS MEMORIAL FOUNTAIN, by Lorado Taft. Figures representing the Old and New Worlds flank the central, globe-surmounted marble shaft, from the base of which a ship's prow emerges, bearing the figure of Columbus.

Union Station was the first building constructed under the impetus of the McMillan Commission's plan for a more harmonious and beautiful Capital. One of the first great union terminals, it was also one of the first to which the municipality contributed funds in excess of the bare cost of the terminal to insure architectural distinction as well as utility. During the last decades of the nineteenth century, railroads cut across the Mall and ran down the streets of the city, each with its shabby and inconvenient terminal. Out of the agitation against grade crossings there grew a movement for a union terminal, linked with a reconsideration of the original plan of the city as laid out by L'Enfant (see *The L'Enfant and later Plans*). Favorable legislation was passed by Congress in 1903, and the central terminal was completed four years later.

SENATE OFFICE BUILDING

A quadrangular (but not square) five-story white marble structure, the Senate Office Building, northwest corner 1st and B Streets NE., designed by Carrère and Hastings, was begun in 1906. Three sides were finished by 1909, and the fourth, the work of Wyeth and Sullivan, was finished in 1933. The north and south façades of the building are lined with a high rusticated base and Doric colonnades, and are crowned with a heavy classic cornice and balustraded parapet, Four corner pavilions, with massive piers and deep loggias, relieve the severe horizontality of the exterior. On the east side, under a central pavilion forming a portico, a triple archway provides a vehicular entrance to the landscaped inner court.

On the southwest corner of the building a broad flight of steps rises to the main doorway, which opens on the second floor of the building into an octagonal marble rotunda, two stories in height. The rotunda has a domical ceiling and is adorned with pilasters and arches, affording access to the gleaming white, echoing corridors of the second and third floors. Opening from the rotunda on this upper floor is the caucus room, largest in the building, paneled with marble and hung with four enormous crystal chandeliers. The room was first used in 1912 for the Senate hearing on the sinking of the *Titanic*. Room 224C was the scene of the drawing for the military draft of 1917. Other rooms in the air-conditioned building are reserved for meetings of standing Senate committees, but the majority of the space is given over to impressively furnished office suites, of at least three rooms each, for the 96 Senators. It also contains a restaurant, barber shop, post office, gymnasium, and underground garage.

Immediately below the rotunda is the terminus of the only rapid transit subway in Washington. The monorail electric cars, held upright by a trolley working on a steel beam, serve Senators and visitors traveling between Senate offices and the Capitol.

SUPREME COURT BUILDING

The Supreme Court Building (*open 9-4:30 Mon.-Fri., 9-1 Sat.*), northeast corner East Capitol Street and 1st Street NE., designed by Cass Gilbert, is a glittering white marble temple with flanking wings and an imposing central portico. A short flight of steps flanked by tall candelabra leads to the marble plaza at the front of the building; near each end of the plaza is a tall flagpole with a sculptured bronze base. In its center, monumental entrance steps lead up to the central portico. Twin rows of elaborately modeled Corinthian columns, surmounted by a sculptured pediment, suggest a Roman temple, its form of worship announced by the inscription below the pediment, "Equal Justice Under Law."

The building stands out as a low square mass with a central nave-like section, higher and longer than the rest, leading from the great front portico to a similar but less elaborate pavilion at the rear. The wings rise one story and basement above ground, an arrangement shown by small windows below and high windows above, flanked by engaged Ionic pilasters. The central section has two additional stories and an attic. The entire structure is roofed with gleaming white tile, and is surrounded by a white marble terrace and a low balustrade of the same material. It was completed in 1935.

On each side of the entrance stairs are enormous cheek blocks supporting allegorical statues by James E. Fraser. The meditative female figure on the north block symbolizes deep contemplation of the problems of justice, the powerful and vigilant male figure on the south block typifies execution of the laws. The nine figures in the pediment, by Robert Aitken, reflect the same general theme of authority. The *Goddess of Liberty,* with the scales of justice in her lap, is enthroned in the center. She is flanked by two guardian figures, *Order* and *Authority,* represented by Roman soldiers, and on either side of these guardians are groups of two figures each, representing *Council.* Finally, at each extremity of the pediment, is a recumbent youth with a book, symbolizing *Research.* For the four *Council* figures, and for the two *Research* figures, the sculptor has followed the medieval tradition of incorporating historical and living personages in the midst of symbolic types. The *Council* figures on the spectator's right are likenesses of Chief Justice Hughes and the sculptor himself; those on his left are the architect, Cass Gilbert, and the noted constitutional lawyer, Elihu Root. The *Research* figures depict John Marshall (right) and William Howard Taft (left) as students.

The theme of the rear or eastern pediment, by Herman A. MacNeil, is suited to its place on the building—it emphasizes the contributions of Eastern and Mediterranean civilizations to the development of the law. The central figure is that of Moses, bearing the tablets of Hebraic law; to the left is Confucius, the great lawgiver of China; and on the other side is Solon, master codifier of Greek law. The central group is flanked by symbolical figures, and smaller figures at the ends represent the fable of the hare and the tortoise.

The great bronze doors at the western entrance, each of them weighing 3,000 pounds, have bas-relief panels designed by John Donnelly, in collaboration with the architect. The doors are rolled out of sight when the building is open, but may be seen when it is closed. Each of the eight panels has two figures, representing an episode in the evolution of justice: *Left door, bottom to top:* Shield of Achilles, showing two men in debate, and the man speaking the "straightest judgment" is to receive two gold pieces on a stone; Praetor's Edict, proclaiming judge-made law in Rome; Julian and the Scholar, portraying the development of law by the scholar and advocate; Justinian Code, showing Justinian publishing *Corpus Juris,* the first code of laws. *Right door, bottom to top:* Magna Carta, showing King John signing the document that gave legal rights to the freemen of his realm; Statute of Westminster, wherein the Chancellor publishes the statute in the presence of King Edward I; Coke and James I, in which Coke bars King James from sitting in the "King's Court," making the court independent of the executive; Marshall and Story, showing Chief Justice Marshall delivering the *Marbury* vs. *Madison* opinion, and setting the precedent for the Supreme Court to invalidate acts of Congress (there is an anachronism in making Story a figure in this panel, for he never participated in a decision invalidating an act of Congress, and became a member of the court eight years after Marshall's history-making decision).

MEMORIAL HALL, inside the entrance, is lined with Doric columns and wall niches, and has a sumptuous beamed and coffered ceiling. On decisions days (Mondays when court is in session) this hall is filled with long queues of visitors waiting for admission to the crowded courtroom.

The COURTROOM is the principal point of interest in the building, and the focal center in the organization of the main floor plan. Designed with exacting symmetry, the Court chamber possesses unusual power and majesty, surpassing in sheer impressiveness perhaps any public room in the country. The unity of the room depends upon a measured regularity in the treatment of the walls and a fine sense of scale and color. Open Ionic colonnades with flanking side aisles set off by bronze grillwork screens contribute to the dramatically solemn setting. Above the simple, continuous entablature is an impressive Attic frieze, the work of A. A. Weinman, decorated with historical and allegorical figures. High windows in the aisle walls, originally intended to afford vistas upon the formal inner courts, have been covered with Venetian blinds to shut out the brilliant light reflected from the walls, and the room is artificially illuminated. Rich velvet curtains behind the colonnade at the farther end of the room furnish an imposing background for the Justices' bench. Elaborately carved chairs were designed for the nine Justices, but they preferred to retain the old leather chairs they had occupied in the previous courtroom.

The Supreme Court is the tribunal of last resort on Federal laws, and the final court of appeal on State laws, in cases involving the United States Constitution.

Two sections of long benches, in the central portion of the room, provide seating for the audience. Government attorneys occupy the front benches on the right side, and private attorneys, including candidates for admission to the Supreme Court bar, are seated in front benches on the left. For the press, special seats with tables are reserved next to the side aisles. The tables are equipped with pneumatic tubes through which reporters send their notes to the basement press rooms. The side aisles, on decision days, are crowded with standees. The courtroom is open to the public within the limit of accommodations while court is in session—during alternate fortnights from the first Monday in October to the last week in May.

Also on the main floor are suites of offices for the Justices, a private conference room in which the court meets for deliberations, two large and impressively decorated chambers intended for international conferences, offices of the marshal and clerk of the court, a room for members of the bar, and suites for the Attorney General, the Solicitor General, and other Government attorneys. The Justices' suites have three rooms each, whereas in their old home in the Capitol, the entire court had only three rooms in addition to the courtroom. The suites are similar, except that the Chief Justice's rooms are larger, and occupy a central position directly behind the courtroom, with windows opening on the east portico. The Justices' offices are finished in American oak and equipped with wood-burning fireplaces. They are "assured of complete privacy, not only in the building, but upon their arrival and departure. Their automobiles proceed directly down a ramp into the basement and are parked there, while the Justices ascend in private elevators to a corridor closed to the public, connecting all the suites and the courtroom itself. Their dining room [also private] is on the second floor."

On the basement floor are storage and filing rooms, the cafeteria and kitchen, rooms for minor officers of the Court, and two press rooms—one for correspondents of individual papers, one for the press associations—each equipped with chairs, tables, lounges, lockers, telephones, and bookcases.

Two beautiful cantilever marble staircases of spiral form lead from the main floor to the second and third floors, but they are closed to the public, access to the library being by elevator only.

The LIBRARY OF THE SUPREME COURT, occupying the whole of the third floor and most of the second floor, is administered by the Law Library of Congress. The library, which has a capacity of 350,000 volumes, including stack room on the fourth or attic floor, had in 1940 more than 74,000 volumes. Other legal collections are stacked in the old Supreme Court library in the Capitol and in the Library of Congress. The Supreme Court Library is open only to Justices, members of the Supreme Court bar, Members of Congress, and law officers of the various Government agencies. The oak-paneled Main Reading Room, on the third floor, is equipped with stack alcoves containing State reports, directly accessible to the reader. Exhibit cases in this room contain a number of rare documents, including a handwritten brief by Henry Clay and the first volume of printed records of cases from the lower courts. The Elbridge T. Gerry Collection, bequeathed to the Supreme Court in the early 1930's, is housed in a special room on this floor. The Justices' Reading Room and Library is on the second floor, with other reading rooms for members of the bar, and stacks shelving complete sets of bound records and briefs in all cases filed with the Court from 1832 to date.

LIBRARY OF CONGRESS

The Library of Congress (*open, free, 9 a.m.-10 p.m. Mon.-Fri., 9-6 Sat. [9-1 in summer], 2-10 Sun. and holidays, closed Christmas and July 4; free guide service on request; no smoking except in smoking rooms*) is housed in two massive buildings east of the Capitol, the three-story gray sandstone Italian Renaissance Main Building and the five-story modern setback Annex directly behind it, across Second Street SE. The grandiose Main Building, with its triple-arched entrance, twinned columns, low dome, and lantern cupola, was built during the period 1889-97. It was constructed by Thomas L. Casey, Chief of the U.S. Army Engineers, on the basis of the design by John L. Smithmeyer, Paul J. Pelz, and Edward Pearce Casey, Washington architects, and was, at the time, the largest structure in the world devoted to library purposes alone. The white marble Annex, designed by Pierson and Wilson of Washington with Alexander G. Trowbridge as consultant, completed in 1939, is designed in the modern manner, to conform to the plan of the near-by Folger Shakespeare Library and the Supreme Court Building. Planned with much greater economy of space, the Annex is primarily a large central core of shelf-space surrounded by an outer hollow crust of offices. Covering 2 acres of ground as against the Main Library's 3½ acres, it is designed to shelve 10,000,000 books, twice as many as the older building. The two buildings, erected at a cost of $18,747,000, have a total of 414 miles of shelves, containing nearly 6,000,000 books and pamphlets, nearly 1,500,000 maps and views, more than 1,150,000 pieces and volumes of music, more than 500,000 prints, nearly 1,000,000 bound volumes of newspapers, and separate manuscripts running to such numbers (probably into the millions) that a separate count is not feasible. This Library of the Nation is a part of the legislative establishment, supported mainly by annual appropriations from Congress, but the librarian is appointed by the President, and the facilities of the institution are as accessible to students as those of any public library. There are 11 reading rooms, other accommodations for study in 13 divisions handling specialized material, 200 study tables in the stacks, and 226 study rooms for research workers. The library has the largest collection of aeronautical books in the world, the largest collection of Chinese books outside the Orient, the largest Russian collection outside Russia, and many of its other collections are preeminent in their field.

The Library of Congress was started by legislative enactment in 1800, accompanied by an appropriation of $5,000, and arrangements to set up library space in the Capitol. John Beckley of Virginia was the first librarian. By 1814, when the Capitol was burned by the British, the library contained little more than 3,000 volumes and 50-odd maps and charts. To replace the loss Thomas Jefferson offered the Government his private library of 6,487 volumes at $23,950—an offer that was accepted in 1815 in the face of accusations of extravagance and protests against the irreligious character of many of his books. The collection was gradually increased until 1851, when it comprised 55,000 volumes. A disastrous fire that year destroyed the library quarters and all but 20,000 books, including two-thirds of the Jefferson collection. Ainsworth Rand Spofford, Washington newspaper correspondent, built the library rapidly after his appointment as librarian in 1864. Two years later an act of Congress transferred the library of the Smithsonian Institution, about 40,000 scientific publications, to the Library of Congress. In 1867 the present system of international exchange of public documents was adopted, whereby 150 copies of each Government document are exchanged for similar publications of foreign countries. The same year the Peter Force collection of Americana, some 60,000 items, was acquired by purchase. An amendment to the copyright law in 1870 required that two copies of every published item be deposited in the Library of Congress to perfect copyright, and the development of international copyright in 1891 added many more volumes to the library's shelves. The library of Dr. Joseph Toner (27,000 books and 12,000 pamphlets and periodicals) was presented to the Library of Congress in 1882, and the Hubbard collection of engravings was presented in 1898.

Meantime, after 1872, the most serious problem confronting the Library was the question of new quarters. Many wild schemes were advanced, including one to honeycomb the dome of the Capitol with bookstacks. After much wrangling in Congress, and many delays, the present Main Building was occupied in 1897. In subsequent years two of the original interior courts were filled with bookstacks to alleviate crowding. Part of another court was filled in 1925 by the Coolidge Chamber Music Auditorium, and an extension was made on the east of the Main Building in 1934 to house the Rare Book Room. The Whittall Pavilion, adjoining the Coolidge Auditorium, was built in 1938, and the following year the Annex was completed and occupied, providing a space surplus for the first time in more than 30 years. The Library of Congress Trust Fund Board, created in 1925, has handled gifts and bequests valued at approximately $2,200,000.

The massive MAIN BUILDING, hailed as a masterpiece of architecture in its day, seems today over-lavish in ornamental detail, though it stands as an authentic period piece of the 1890's. The main façade consists of a great central pavilion with flanking wings and end bays. Rising above the rest of the building is a ribbed copper dome which terminates 195 feet above the ground in a lantern and finial torch, symbolizing the Flame of Knowledge. A grand stairway, rising on either side of an elaborate fountain, leads to a broad open terrace before the arched entrance doors. The heroic fountain group, the *Court of Neptune*, by Roland Hinton Perry, is centered around a muscular bronze figure of Neptune, flanked on each side by nymphs riding prancing sea horses. The semicircular basin contains bronze frogs and turtles spouting jets of water from their mouths, and the pool is appropriately inhabited by goldfish. Sculptured heads, modeled to illustrate the chief ethnological types of mankind—European, Near Eastern, Negro, Amerindian, and Asiatic—serve as decorative keystones over the arched first-story windows. Circular windows in a gallery at the second-floor level frame an assortment of portrait busts of great literati —Demosthenes, Scott, and Dante, by Herbert Adams; Goethe, Franklin, and Macaulay, by F. Wellington Ruckstuhl; Emerson, Irving, and Hawthorne, by J. Scott Hartley. Beneath this gallery are three heavily carved entrance archways with spandrel figures by Bela L. Pratt, representing *Literature, Science,* and *Art*. Decorations on the three bronze entrance doors portray, respectively, *Tradition,* by Olin L. Warner, north door; *The Art of Printing,* by Frederick MacMonnies, center door; and *Writing,* by Warner and Adams, south door.

The magnificent MAIN ENTRANCE HALL is floored with a geometrically patterned mosaic of white, brown, yellow, and red marble, centered with a conventionalized sunburst and compass of polished brass, with rays pointing to brass signs of the zodiac in the periphery of the hall. The balustraded white marble stairways ascending from the main hall, the work of Philip Martiny, are decorated with male cherubs carved in high relief; each represents some art or science, such as the physician with his mortar and the electrician with his telephone. Amusing groups of cherubs perched on the stair piers symbolize the continents. The eastern wall is broken by a commemorative arch, with spandrel figures by Olin L. Warner representing the student in youth and age. Short arcaded corridors surrounding the Main Entrance Hall are decorated with rich mosaic vaulted ceilings and floors inlaid with white, blue, and brown marble, and the walls are adorned with a series of lunette murals.

The East Arcade contains six panels by John W. Alexander to illustrate the *Evolution of the Book:* Prehistoric man builds a pile of boulders in the *Cairn;* an Oriental storyteller relates his yarn in *Oral Traditions;* Egyptians chisel a tomb in *Hieroglyphics;* an Indian makes drawings on a buffalo skin in *Pictograph;* a monk prepares an illuminated parchment in *The Manuscript Book;* and Gutenberg stands beside his machine in *Printing Press.* In a small lobby at the entrance to the Reading Room are five lunette murals by Elihu Vedder symbolizing *Government* in its best and worst aspects. In the South Arcade are eight lunette murals on *Lyric Poetry* by Henry O. Walker: The six smaller paintings represent boy subjects of poems: *Ganymede* (Tennyson), *Endymion* (Keats), *There Was a Boy* (Wordsworth), *Uriel* (Emerson), *Adonis* (Shakespeare), and *Comus* (Milton). Large group paintings treat symbolically the subjects of *Joy and Memory* and *Lyric Poetry*.

The North Gallery contains seven lunettes on *The Family* by Charles Sprague Pearce: *Religion, Labor, Study, Recreation, The Family,* and *Rest*. Left (west) of the entrance to the North Corridor is the Library's OFFICE OF INFORMATION, where visitors may obtain advice about the institution.

Along the North Corridor are nine lunettes by Edward Simmons portraying *The Muses:* Melpomene (tragedy), Clio (history), Thalia (comedy), Euterpe (music), Terpsichore (the dance), Erato (poetry of love), Polyhymnia (oratory and sacred poetry), Urania (astronomy), and Calliope (epic poetry). At the north end of this corridor is the entrance to the MAP DIVISION READING ROOM. The division has nearly 1,500,000 maps and views, and 10,000 atlases. Its collection is especially rich in maps of the American continents. The globe collection includes Völpel's manuscript 4-inch armillary sphere made in 1543, and other collections include such items as an original manuscript of L'Enfant's plan for the city of Washington, Champlain's map showing parts of New England and Canada (1608), 13 manuscript maps attributed to Lewis and Clark (1804-06), and 8 maps made or annotated by George Washington. Current publications in the cartographic field are available in the reading room.

Along the South Corridor are nine lunettes of the *Greek Heroes* by Walter McEwen: *Paris, Jason, Bellerophon, Orpheus, Perseus, Prometheus, Theseus, Achilles, and Hercules*. In the richly decorated CONGRESSIONAL READING ROOM (*not open to public*), on the west side of the South Corridor, are two remarkable mosaic murals by Frederick Dielman, *Law* over the north fireplace and *History* over the south fireplace. Seven ceiling panels, *The Spectrum of Light,* by Carl Gutherz, include a panel of Pegasus, the winged horse of Greek mythology, facing the beholder, by an odd optical illusion, from any angle; school children have written in that this panel impressed them more than anything else in the Library of Congress. The Southwest Pavilion is occupied by the office of the Legislative Reference Division (*not open*). Formerly the Senate Reading Room, this richly decorated room, with its dark-oak paneling and gold ornamentation on the ceiling, was once used for a reception to the Prince of Wales; the sculptured panel above the marble fireplace was executed by Herbert Adams. The South Gallery is occupied by the LEGISLATIVE REFERENCE SERVICE. This is the only Division of the Library exclusively devoted to the service of Members of Congress, for whom it performs research especially in the fields of law, history, economics, political science and legislative history.

The grand stairway from the Main Hall (*open July 4 in addition to regular times*) leads to the second floor. On the east side of the stair well, in a specially constructed case attended by an armed guard, is kept the GUTENBERG BIBLE, one of three perfect copies on vellum known to exist, the others being in the British Museum at London and in the Bibliothèque Nationale at Paris. It was published by the inventor of printing at Mainz, Germany, about the year 1455. A part of the Vollbehr Collection of Incunabula, it was purchased by Dr. Otto H. F. Vollbehr in 1930 for $350,000, the largest price ever paid for a single printed book. Congress in 1930 appropriated $1,500,000 to purchase the entire Vollbehr Collection, including the Gutenberg Bible and 3,000 incunabula (books printed before 1501), covering the whole field of fifteenth-century thought.

In addition to this regular display, may be seen the Lincoln Cathedral copy of the MAGNA CARTA, the first great document of human rights, signed at Runnymede, England, in 1215. This closely-written parchment manuscript, unreadable except by scholars of ancient Latin script, was deposited in the Library of Congress by the British government in 1939, after being displayed at the New York World's Fair, to remain for the duration of World War II. The appropriateness of displaying this document on the same floor with the Declaration of Independence and the American Constitution has been pointed out by no less a person than the Marquess of Lothian, British Ambassador, who turned it over to the Library for safekeeping. This is the finest copy of the original Magna Carta, or Great Charter, two others being in the British Museum and one in the Salisbury Cathedral. The barons of King John forced the monarch to grant them a charter of liberties following his defeat in a disastrous war with France. Intended originally to relieve wealthy barons from unjust demands by the monarchy, it has taken an important place in defining human rights, as shown in the following short quotations: "No scutage or aid [taxes] shall be imposed on our kingdom, except by common counsel of our kingdom." "No freeman shall be taken or imprisoned or disseised or exiled or in any way destroyed . . . except by the lawful judgment of his peers or by the law of the land." "To no one will we sell . . . right or justice."

On the west side of the Main Hall is the white marble SHRINE, designed by Francis H. Bacon, in which, under protective yellow glass, the original Declaration of Independence and Constitution of the United States have been exhibited since 1924. These precious documents are attended by armed guards day and night. The birth certificates of the Nation are somewhat faded, but distinct facsimiles are kept in near-by cases. John Hancock's bold signature on the Declaration, however, is still plainly legible. In cases to the north of the Shrine are other notable exhibits, including Lincoln's original draft of the Gettysburg Address, the Monroe Doctrine in manuscript, as drafted for President Monroe's message to Congress in 1823, the first message ("What hath God wrought") sent by Samuel F. B. Morse on the original electric telegraph in 1844, letters of the Presidents with their portraits, and other semipermanent or temporary exhibits.

The Main Hall is lavishly decorated; apparently no part of its walls or ceilings have been left unadorned. There are murals, plaques, lunettes, and Pompeiian panels, most of them treating their subjects in some symbolic manner. The four ceilings contain 56 English, Scottish, American, Italian, Spanish, Flemish, German, and French printers' and publishers' marks, including those of Caxton, Aldus, and Elzevir.

The Northwest Gallery, the hall just above the North Corridor on the first floor, contains two murals by Gari Melchers, in addition to the Presidential and other exhibits.

The Northwest Pavilion is occupied by the MANUSCRIPTS DIVISION READING ROOM, where students have access to the uncounted millions of manuscripts in the Library, the largest collection in America. The room is decorated by W. L. Dodge's murals on *Art, Literature, Music,* and *Science.* Papers that are important in the study of American history have been stressed in making this collection, including an almost unbroken series of manuscripts of the Presidents, of the Continental Congress and various Colonies and States, letters of such statesmen as Franklin and Hamilton, and the military papers of American generals. Through a Rockefeller grant and other means the Library has obtained more than 2,000,000 pages of reproductions of documents relating to American history, copied in foreign archives and libraries. The Manuscripts Division sometimes obtains papers with certain restrictions attached, as when it received a collection of Abraham Lincoln letters from Robert Todd Lincoln, which will not be open for examination until 1947. Manuscripts in the division are available for inspection under the supervision of library attendants.

The second-floor space south of the Main Hall, in the Southwest Gallery and Southwest Pavilion, is occupied by exhibitions of library material relating to the fine arts. The exhibits continue along the South Gallery, at the west end of which is the FINE ARTS READING ROOM, in which the public has access to half a million prints (etchings, engravings, lithographs, etc.), more than 70,000 books, and periodicals dealing with various aspects of the fine arts. The division's Pictorial Archives of Early American Architecture, contains plans and photographic negatives of early buildings, including those studied and photographed by the Historic American Building Survey (a Civil Works Administration project when it began in 1933; later a Work Projects Administration project). Prints from these negatives, and plans, are sold at a non-profit price of about 15 cents each. Noteworthy collections received by gift include the Gardiner Greene Hubbard engravings, the George Lothrop Bradley prints, the prints of Joseph Pennell, and the Pennell collection of Whistleriana—letters, etchings, and documents.

A stairway on the east side of the Main Hall leads to a landing, on the wall of which is Elihu Vedder's heroic mosaic mural, *The Minerva of Peace,* which required seven years to complete. The 15½-foot figure of the goddess of wisdom, from the second floor below, has the appearance of a three-dimensional figure.

The stairway continues to the READING ROOM GALLERY, from which it is possible to look down on the great rotunda of the Main Building, used as a public reading room seating about 300 persons. The floor of the reading room forms an impressive picture with its scores of mahogany reading desks arranged in concentric circles about the central distributing desk; just east of this desk, however, two sections of the reading room are devoted to card-catalogue cabinets. The vast rotunda, 100 feet in diameter, is octagonal in shape. At each angle, clustered columns of red Numidian marble support the huge arches sustaining the weight of the dome, the inner shell of which rises to a height of 125 feet. On the first floor, partitions divide the arcade into alcoves for reference books. The coloring in the rotunda shades from deep red through gradations of yellow to the old ivory of ceiling panels and sculptures. It is most striking on certain April and October afternoons, when a beam of sunlight penetrates the rotunda, striking a rosy glow from the Numidian marble columns.

From the visitors' gallery only a glimpse can be caught of Edwin H. Blashfield's allegorical painting of *Human Understanding* in the lantern of the dome, but his mural in the collar between dome and lantern, *Progress of Civilization,* can be seen to full advantage. This giant canvas, 150 feet in circumference, portrays 12 seated figures symbolizing the principal nations and epochs that have contributed to civilization. Several of the faces are portraits, *England* being represented by Ellen Terry and *America* by features similar to those of Abraham Lincoln. Upon the entablatures of the eight marble piers are symbolic figures in plaster, and between them, on the balustrades, are 16 bronze portrait statues. Paul Wayland Bartlett's Michelangelo is considered one of the best pieces of statuary in the Library, while the Homer of Louis Saint-Gaudens and the Shakespeare by Frederick MacMonnies are thought to have exceptional merit. The rotunda clock, ornamented with semiprecious stones, is the work of John Flanagan.

The attic story, reached by elevators from the Main Hall, contains a smoking room and a CAFETERIA (*smoking permitted*), from which there is an excellent close-up view of the Capitol dome and a view westward along the Mall. The Levantine character of the Mall is curiously emphasized from certain windows, when a low dome on the Capitol is aligned with the domes of the National Gallery of Art and of the National Museum, and the minarets of the Smithsonian Institution and the Egyptian obelisk of the Washington Monument come readily into the same vista. The cafeteria serves lunches only, 11:15-2:15 Monday through Friday.

The basement floor, entered from the west at the ground level, has a CHECKROOM (*free*) to the left (north), and an exhibit of Chinese maps to the right. On the east side of the North Corridor is the WHITTALL PAVILION, a rectangular hall built (1938) in a portion of the inner court through the benefaction of Mrs. Gertrude Clarke Whittall to house the Stradivari instruments she had donated to the

Library, and to accommodate the overflow from chamber music concerts in the adjoining Coolidge Auditorium. The room is decorated with a Beauvais tapestry (c.1700) of *Apollo and the Muses,* is furnished with specially selected antique chairs, some of which have built-in lyre motifs, and the iron grille doors are decorated with violin motifs. The principal display in the pavilion, however, is the windowed case in the west wall containing the five Stradivari instruments and the bows by François Tourte (1747-1835) "the Stradivari of the bow." The Betts violin, made by Stradivari in 1704 and valued at $125,000, is named for its earliest recorded owner, Arthur Betts. The Ward violin was made in 1699, and the Cassavetti viola in 1727. The case is specially air-conditioned to prevent deterioration from contact with ordinary air, and a steel door closes behind the glass, when the Library shuts its door at night. The instruments, to keep their tone sweet, are played frequently at Whittall concerts in the Coolidge Auditorium (*see Music*).

The COOLIDGE AUDITORIUM, just north of the Whittall Pavilion, is an intimate hall seating 511, built in 1925 with funds provided by Mrs. Elizabeth Sprague Coolidge for the presentation of chamber music concerts by the Coolidge Foundation (*see Music*); it has since been used for Whittall and other concerts. In the lobby entrance is a portrait of Mrs. Coolidge by John Singer Sargent, and display cases show the music of such composers as Haydn, Brahms, and Mozart.

The MUSIC DIVISION READING ROOM (*open 9-4:30 Mon.-Fri.. 9-1 Sat.*), in the North Gallery of the basement, makes available to the public the Library's enormous resources for study and research in music. Its collections include almost 1,500,000 volumes and pieces, among them the most complete collection anywhere of musical publications since 1890. Works in the handwriting of the great composers—Bach, Hayden, Mozart, Beethoven, Wagner—are numerous, and the manuscript collection includes items that are landmarks in the development of music in America. In 1935 the only daughter of Victor Herbert deposited in the Library about two-thirds of the manuscript scores of the American composer, and more recently, through the bequest of Mrs. Elise Fay Loeffler, all of the manuscript scores of Charles Martin Loeffler and much of his correspondence became part of the collection here. The Archive of American Folk Song, now a part of this division, includes hundreds of phonographic records of hill-billy, cowboy, Indian, Creole, Negro, and other native songs. The division sponsors field trips to out-of-the-way places for the collection of recordings, including the penitentiaries of the South, where the Negro sings out his tragedy, to the little-investigated Sea Islands of Georgia, to the turpentine country of Florida, and into the bayous of Louisiana's Cajun country. The division has a little soundproof room equipped with piano, phonograph, music stands, and a radio, where records man be heard and musical scores tried by performers.

In the Southwest Basement Pavilion is the BOOKS FOR THE BLIND UNIT, a branch of the Library financed by Congressional appropriation. From this unassuming room, more than 40,000 volumes of raised-type books and "talking books" are mailed free of postage to blind users throughout the Nation. Blind readers may also make use of the Library's facilities here, through the special unit of the Library, Service For the Blind.

The CURRENT PERIODICAL ROOM, in the South Gallery of the basement, has seats for about 200 readers, who have direct access to current issues of about 290 "home-town" newspapers from all over the country, to about 165 foreign newspapers, and to more than 1,000 current magazines. This is one of the best patronized reading rooms in the Library.

The Main Library Building is so constructed, with elevators at front and back, and access through the building only by way of the Main Reading Room and a basement corridor, that visitors normally prefer to see first those exhibits in rooms accessible from the west side of the building.

The office of the PHOTODUPLICATION SERVICE, facing the east-west basement corridor near the center of the building, is the public's access to a service that provides duplicates of book, map, manuscript, and other materials, at non-profit prices. Established by a Rockefeller grant, this division makes reproductions by photostat, photograph, microfilm, blueprint, multilith, and ozalid processes. Having spacious quarters in the Annex, it turns out more than 500,000 microfilm exposures a year.

Just east of this office it is possible to see, through large windows, the control room for the pneumatic tube service to the Annex and some of the machinery used in the slower continuous-belt conveyor service to the Capitol. Books are carried, by the pneumatic system, in oval metal cases with a capacity of eight average-sized volumes. The cases weigh 27 pounds each, and, with their load of books, travel the 700 feet between this control room and that on the fourth floor of the Annex in 28 seconds. Contents of the cases are saved from damage by a cushion of air at the receiving end. The slower conveyor system to the Capitol, once considered a marvel of mechanical speed and efficiency, travels a little faster than a man normally walks. Parts of this system can be seen at the cellar level, below the basement.

On the main floor, the MAIN READING ROOM CATALOG (*open to readers only*) extends from the rotunda of the Main Reading Room into the next room to the east. The catalog contains more than 10,800 trays, containing card listings of 6,000,000 books. Behind this catalog extends the UNION CATALOG, established through a Rockefeller grant, containing more than 10,500,000 listings of book and periodical items in 100-odd American libraries. This central and several subsidiary catalogs constitute the most extensive bibliographic repertory in the world.

The Northeast Corridor, main floor, is occupied by a spacious SOCIAL SCIENCE REFERENCE ROOM, containing reference works on social science and study tables for research workers. The Southeast

Corridor is occupied by the DOCUMENTS DIVISION, the function of which is to acquire, arrange, and assist in the use of national, local and municipal government publications. Since 1910 this division has issued a *Monthly Check-List of State Publications,* and it publishes other bibliographic works.

On the second floor, the Southeast Corridor is occupied by the HISPANIC ROOM (*open 9-4:30 Mon.-Fri., 9-5 Sat.*), designed by Paul P. Cret in the spirit of seventeenth-century Spanish and Portuguese interiors and opened to the public in 1939. In the entrance vestibule hangs a heraldic Columbus coat of arms on tapestry. The 130-foot arched gallery has tables and chairs to accommodate 50 readers, and display cases in which rare maps, documents, books, and pamphlets are shown. The room is lighted by tall arched windows on the east side, over each of which is the name of an important historic or literary figure in one of the Hispanic or Latin American countries—Cervantes, Magellan, Columbus, Loyola, El Cid, Bolivar, and so on. The opposite side of the room has a corresponding series of inscribed arches over balconied and gold-curtained reference alcoves. Three silver chandeliers provide central lighting, and the lower walls are covered with a wainscoting of white and ultramarine tiles from Puebla, Mexico. The south end of the long hall, over a commemorative tablet, is decorated with a painting on stainless steel by Buell Mullen, unveiled in 1940. The richly colored painting, having a three-dimensional effect on its background of burnished steel, is a reproduction of the coat of arms conferred on Columbus by Queen Isabella following his return to Spain from America. The surface of the steel was routed with hand tools before the colors were applied, and the pigments are protected by a special varnish. About 100,000 volumes on Hispanic and Latin American subjects are shelved adjacent to the Hispanic Room, and many other divisions of the Library have valuable Hispanic materials. A catalog and reference room adjoining serve as a guide and source for materials in this broad field.

The air-conditioned RARE BOOK ROOM (*open 9-4:30 Mon.-Fri., 9-5 Sat.; no pens may be used in this room*) occupies a central position on the east front of the Main Building, on the second floor. Entered between heavy, three-paneled bronze doors bearing the insignia of famous printers, this dignified Colonial chamber is used partly as an exhibit hall and partly as a reading room. The display cases contain a changing exhibit of rare books. The adjoining white-tile stacks, on which more than 100,000 rare items are stored, resemble a bank vault for safety, a scientist's laboratory for cleanliness. On air-cooled shelves is material ranging from 1,083 rare Bible items to the first issue of Edward Wheeler's *Deadwood Dick.* Here are kept more than 4,000 incunabula, Colonial newspapers, magazines, almanacs, and broadsides, and a diverse collection of rare and fine books. Noteworthy items are the first editions of Greek classics, printed before 1501, the first edition of Milton's *Paradise Lost,* the 1550 edition of *Piers Plowman,* a copy of Waldseemueller's *Cosmographie* of 1507, the first book to substitute the name America for Columbia, and, among its collection of tiny New England primers, the book containing the first printing of the child's prayer, "Now I lay me down to sleep." Books in this collection are for use in the Rare Book Room only.

The LAW LIBRARY READING ROOM, in the East-North Curtain, is the workshop of the largest general legal research library maintained by the Federal Government. Just inside the entrance is an exhibition room in which are displayed rare legal items from the United States, Latin America, and foreign countries. The reading room, seating 75 readers, contains a three-deck book stack in which is shelved a working library of more than 30,000 Anglo-American law books. Included among these are full sets of Federal, State and English reports, digests, and citators; statutory compilations of the Federal and State governments with all subsequent session laws; a large collection of Anglo-American legal treatises and reference books; and sets of the leading Anglo-American legal periodicals.

Adjoining the reading room are stacks in which are shelved most of the Law Library's collection of nearly half a million books. These include the reports of judicial decisions and the legislation of every dominion and colony of the British Empire and of practically every country in the world. This primary source material is supplemented by digests, legal treatises and reference books, and legal periodicals.

There are several special collections, among them the Russian collection, of which 600-odd volumes came from the libraries of the Czars. There are representative collections of Oriental material covering the law of China, Japan, Siam, and Tibet, 20,000 volumes of general law, Roman law, canon law, medieval law, Mohammedan law, and miscellaneous groups, such as trials, bibliography, criminology, and legal curiosa.

Facilities are provided in the Northeast Pavilion and North Curtain for the consultation and use of foreign collections and legal rariosa. In that section are shelved the *Records and Briefs of the Supreme Court of the United States.* Near by is one of the most valued collections in the Law Library, that of the English Year Book, and other early English legal material printed prior to the seventeenth century. The Law Library has probably the largest collection of legal incunabula in the United States, containing many rare volumes from the Vollbehr and Thacher collections. Among the notable collections acquired by gift or purchase are those of Thomas Jefferson, James Louis Petrigu, Justice Oliver Wendell Holmes, and Paul Kruger of the University of Bonn.

In addition to printed books the Law Library has rich holdings of manuscripts, among them fourteenth- and seventeenth-century English items, fourteenth-century Venetian statutes, 46 Russian scrolls of the seventeenth and eighteenth centuries, a large number of seventeenth- to nineteenth-century English legal documents, Justice Samuel P. Chase's notebooks on pleading and practice, and the Jefferson collection on Virginia law.

The Law Library of Congress, created by act of Congress in 1832, has occupied its present position in the Main Building since 1902. Its principal collections, approximately 375,000 volumes, are in this building. The old Supreme Court Chamber in the Capitol, however, contains a working library of 25,000 volumes for the use of Members of Congress, their staffs, and members of the bar in attendance at the Capitol. In the Supreme Court Building are two collections—the general collection of about 30,000 volumes, and the conference collection of 20,000 volumes for the exclusive use of the court. The "judges' sets," about 6,000 volumes, are distributed as required to the Justices. A small reference collection is maintained just off the floor of the House of Representatives, and a larger one is kept in the House of Representatives Library. Perhaps the outstanding center of legal record and reference in the Nation, the Law Library maintains an expert reference staff to handle its collections and to assist readers in their use.

DECK A, on the top floor of the east section of the Main Building, reached by elevators, has an excellent general reference collection, study rooms for special researchers, and the Library's SEMITIC DIVISION, with collections of Hebraica and Judaica (books written on Jewish subjects in other languages than Hebrew and Yiddish) that compare favorably with those of other great national libraries. DECK B, on the level below, has the collections of the ORIENTALIA DIVISION, and the SLAVIC DIVISION, in addition to study rooms for researchers. The Orientalia Division has the largest collection of Chinese and Japanese books outside the Orient, upwards of 200,000 volumes. It also administers smaller collections in Korean, Tibetan, Manchu, Mongolian, and other Far Eastern languages. The Slavic Division, with more than 170,000 titles exclusive of periodicals, has as its base a Russian collection that is probably the largest outside Russian boundaries.

From the cellar level, reached by elevators, a tunnel leads under Second Street SE. to the Annex. There is an air of industrial activity about the cellar, which contains machine, carpentry, and electrical shops, in addition to an auxiliary power plant. The twin pneumatic tubes for carrying books run along the ceiling of the tunnel, which dips downward and at a given point the pedestrian steps consciously into the air-conditioned atmosphere maintained in the Annex.

The rectangular white marble ANNEX BUILDING is an excellent example of the appropriateness of modern architectural design applied to a public building. Vertical projections, sparingly used on the sheer lift of the first four stories, relieve this portion of the building from an appearance of too great massiveness. The fifth story, set back 35 feet from the main façade, covers the same space as the central core of bookstacks in the floors below. A lesser setback above completes the exterior design of the building.

Bronze doors, identical at the east and west entrances, are decorated with bas-relief figures designed by Lee Lawrie, New York sculptor, to symbolize the legendary inventors of the various alphabets employed in the art of writing: Ibis-headed *Thoth,* Egyptian divinity of wisdom and amanuensis of the gods; four-eyed *Ts'ang Chieh,* Chinese patron saint of pictographic letters, who is credited with inventing written language after seeing bird tracks on the seashore; curly-bearded *Nabu,* Sumero-Accadian god of the stylus and supposed founder of the first institutional library; *Brahma,* supreme god of the East Indian trinity, who is supposed to have given a knowledge of letters to the human race; the Phoenician *Cadmus,* who is said to have brought the art of writing to Greece; *Tahmurath,* Persian hero who is supposed to have conquered demons and forced them to teach him "some 30 scripts"; wing-footed *Hermes,* messenger of the Greek gods, inventor of the alphabet and numbers; horn-hatted *Odin,* Norse deity who looked down from Yggdrasil, "the wind-stirred tree," saw written runes, and fell out of the tree; shillalah-bearing *Ogma,* inventor of letters in prehistoric Ireland; feather-decked *Itzamna,* Maya inventor of writing and books; *Quetzalcoatl,* source of Aztec culture; and *Sequoyah* (1770-1843), the only historic character in this even dozen of deities, inventor of the Cherokee syllabary of 85 characters. Another Lawrie door, at the south entrance, is decorated with the seals of the United States and of the Library, a male figure symbolizing physical labor, and a female figure symbolizing intellectual labor.

Elevators within the east and west portals give access to the fifth floor, with its elevator lobbies richly decorated with Missouri marble. From the west lobby windows is a view of the Main Building, bringing the ribbed copper dome closer than from any other point in the city. On sunny winter days buzzards gather on the balustrade around the base of the dome to sun themselves, a curious circumstance that has produced many a quip.

The central room on this floor is the richly appointed CARD INDEX ROOM, with more than 13,000 trays for catalog entries. Entrances on each side provide access to the North and South Reading Rooms, each measuring 60 by 100 feet and providing table space for several hundred readers. The reading rooms are flanked on each side by three spacious alcoves containing reference materials. The NORTH READING ROOM, specially equipped with reference works on genealogy and American history, is ornamented with four murals by Ezra Winter, inspired by the works of Geoffrey Chaucer (c. 1340-1400). A lunette on the south wall, over the control desk, portrays three "olde gentil Britons" playing their instruments and singing their lays. The north wall mural recalls "that Aprille with his shoures soote" when "longen folk to goon on pilgrimages." The pilgrims of the *Canterbury Tales* are portrayed in two long canvases on the east and west walls. Leading them, on the west wall mural, is the Miller, and Chaucer is fifth in the procession, which is completed on the east wall.

The SOUTH READING ROOM, identical with the North except that its walls have (1942) no murals, is equipped with reference materials on science and technology. The SMITHSONIAN DEPOSIT of nearly 600,000 volumes on scientific subjects, is available to readers through this room. This collection, with that of the Library of Congress, represents one of the richest collections in existence on science, including memoirs and transactions of scientific bodies, accounts of scientific expeditions, and proceedings of international scientific congresses. The materials of the AERONAUTICS DIVISION, organized in 1930 and having more than 25,000 volumes, the world's largest collection on aeronautics, is also available through this reading room. Current periodicals and latest books are included, and the division has technical advisers to assist serious students of the subject.

The outer space on the fifth floor is occupied by 172 small study rooms for the use of special researchers.

The fourth floor, at which elevators do not ordinarily stop, is occupied by stack space, storage room, and some of the building's air-conditioning machinery.

Offices on the third floor are devoted entirely to the CARD DIVISION, which conducts a catalog card distribution service, selling about $300,000 worth of printed Library of Congress cards each year to 6,500 libraries, in addition to firms and individuals. The south office is one long sunny room, with dozens of lengthy tables, along which clerks glide on wheeled stools, filling orders. Adjoining storage rooms have space for 350,000,000 cards.

Second floor offices include those of the Classification and Shelf-Listing Division, the Catalog Division, the Co-operative Cataloging and Classification Service, the Accessions Division, and the Publication Division.

The first floor is occupied entirely by the COPYRIGHT DIVISION, entered by the south door. An information office, open to the public for information on copyright matters, is in the southwest corner of the building. Copyrights are issued for periods of 28 years, at a nominal charge of $2 for printed works and $1 for photographs, prints, and other unpublished items. Since its inception as a branch of the Library of Congress in 1870, the Copyright Division has entered more than 5,500,000 copyrights, and has received more than 9,000,000 articles for deposit in the Library. In its handling of foreign material for copyright, the Division has a large turnover of foreign stamps; in 1940 a Library of Congress stamp collection was started to preserve these philatelic materials for public use.

The NEWSPAPER REFERENCE ROOM, just north of the west entrance to the basement or ground floor, is equipped with tables and large easels for the reading of bound volumes of newspapers. About 340 American and foreign newspapers are available in bound volumes, the total holdings of the Periodicals Division reaching almost 1,000,000 volumes. Most of the remaining space on the basement floor is taken up by the Bindery, around the northern half of the building, and the Printing Office in the south and southeast portions; both are branches of the Government Printing Office.

The sub-basement floor is occupied mainly by air-conditioning equipment, but also houses darkrooms and other facilities of the Photoduplication Service, and quarters of the engineering, housekeeping, and custodial staff. Ramps on the north side of the building give access to an underground parking space at this level.

The cellar level connects with the tunnel from the Main Building, and it is necessary to ascend two floors from here to the basement—one of the few places in Washington where this curious relationship exists. At the east end of the tunnel is a SMOKING ROOM, and a short distance west from the elevator foyer, in the tunnel, is a LUNCHROOM, serving sandwiches, pastries, and beverages. The cellar extends under a portion of the building, and has room for storage and mechanical equipment.

FOLGER SHAKESPEARE LIBRARY

Just north of the Library of Congress Annex, in small, formally landscaped grounds on East Capitol Street between 2nd and 3rd Streets SE., is the modern, rectangular, white marble Folger Shakespeare Library (*open, free, 9-4:30 weekdays*), housing more than 145,000 volumes of Shakespeareana and original editions of English Renaissance books—a collection that can be matched nowhere in the Western Hemisphere. The founder and donor, Henry Clay Folger, millionaire Standard Oil executive, hoped to house the library in a building of Elizabethan design, but zoning requirements defeated this plan. Paul P. Cret, the architect, handled a difficult assignment with consummate skill—he produced a graceful and rather dazzlingly white modern exterior to coincide with plans for Capitol Hill architecture, and (a bit surprisingly, to some visitors) created a high-beamed and rather gloomy interior to reflect the spirit of Elizabethan architectural styling.

The north or Capitol Street façade is approached at each end by a low flight of marble steps, leading to the two main entrances. The two tall doors are flanked by block carvings of Pegasus, symbol of poetry, and over each portal is one of the twin masks of Tragedy and Comedy. Between the two end doors are nine tall two-story grilled windows, lighting the exhibition room indoors. Beneath the windows are bas-relief panels by John Gregory, depicting scenes from nine of Shakespeare's plays. The façade is crowned by a simple attic, inscribed with the following commentaries on the playwright:

THIS THEREFORE IS THE PRAISE OF SHAKESPEARE
THAT HIS DRAMA IS THE MIRROUR OF LIFE
Samuel Johnson

HIS WIT CAN NO MORE LIE HID THAN IT COULD BE LOST
READE HIM, THEREFORE; AND AGAINE AND AGAINE
John Heminge Henrie Condell

THOU ART A MONIMENT WITHOUT A TOMBE,
AND ART ALIVE STILL, WHILE THY BOOKE DOTH LIVE,
AND WE HAVE WITS TO READ, AND PRAISE TO GIVE.
Ben Jonson

The high grilled windows of the west or 2nd Street façade look out on a small formal garden and white marble fountain centered by Brenda Putnam's exquisite *Puck,* his hands raised in mock horror, seeming ready to repeat the inscription on the statue's base, "Lord, what fooles these mortals be!" On 3rd Street the walls of the east wing are broken by the aluminum doors of the theater entrance, surmounted by twin masks representing Tragedy and Comedy. The double doors are ornamented with floral bands in low relief.

The interior is wholly in the style of seventeenth-century England. The vaulted entrance halls are finished in rough plaster with flagstone floors and rich decorations in stone and wood.

The EXHIBITION GALLERY is a paneled hall of exceptional scale and dignity. The high vaulted ceiling is elaborately decorated with strapwork designs in plaster relief, the floor is of mosaic tile, and the grilled wooden doors bear coats-of-arms carvings dating from the Elizabethan age in England. Hanging on the oak-paneled walls are paintings of Shakespeare and of scenes from his plays, including Sir John Lawrence's picture of John Philip Kemble as Hamlet, the George Romney painting of Shakespeare as an infant attended by Nature and the Passions, and, in a showcase, the *Ariel and Caliban* of William Blake. In other cases are examples of the handwriting and seals of noted Elizabethans, and their books, with note-crowded margins. There is a faded letter written by Queen Elizabeth in 1593 to James VI of Scotland, and a brief document bearing the signature of Henry VIII.

In another case are examples of the four First Folios of Shakespeare. The First Folio, nearest rival to the Gutenberg Bible in the esteem of collectors, is the earliest printed collection of Shakespeare's works. The Folger Library has 79 of the world's 250 First Folios, the nearest approach to an original, since none of the plays exist in Shakespeare's own hand; they are thought to have been destroyed by printers or lost in the London fire of 1666. The Library displays George Washington's London edition of 1793, the set owned by Lincoln, a copy of the first American edition of 1795, once owned by John Adams, and an old volume bearing this inscription, "James Boswell, 1766." The diary of the Reverend John Ward is shown, bearing this entry, well known to Shakespeare scholars: "Shakespeare, Drayton and Ben Jonson had a merry meeting and it seems drank too hard for Shakespeare died of a feavour there contracted." The oldest document shown was written in 1435 at Rouen, France, by the King's Treasurer, John, Bastard of Orleans; it mentions Sir John Fastolf, who, in name though not in character, became Shakespeare's Falstaff.

The rarest editions and manuscripts are kept in air-conditioned vaults, to prevent them from decomposition because of exposure to air, and the vaults are deep in the ground to save them from possible destruction by bombs—a precaution taken several years before the emphasis on bomb destruction was demonstrated by European and Asiatic wars in the late 1930's. These precious documents include a copy of the First Quarto of *Titus Andronicus* (1594), first of Shakespeare's published works, and the Vincent Folio, called by Folger "the most precious book in the world." In another section of the vault, away from public eyes, is a unique relic—one of Queen Elizabeth's corsets.

The READING ROOM, in the southwest corner, entered from the Exhibition Gallery or from the Catalog Room, is designed in the manner of a traditional English great hall, having a high hammer-beam ceiling hung with three bronze chandeliers. Light enters through three large bays along the south wall and through a stained glass window in the west wall, copied from a church window at Stratford upon Avon. The work of Nicola D'Ascenzo, it depicts the *Seven Ages of Man*. The walls are lined on three sides with a high oak wainscot and bookshelves in two tiers with a continuous gallery, approached by a double stairway over the west door. On the north wall is a stone-canopied fireplace set with marble inlays. At the east end a hall screen forms a frame for the entrance to the Folger burial crypt, flanked by portraits of Mr. and Mrs. Folger. The donor of the library became interested in the works of the Bard of Avon in 1879, while he was a student at Amherst College, after hearing a lecture on Shakespeare by Ralph Waldo Emerson. His collection started with a cheap 15-volume set of Shakespeare's plays and poems. From this time he began to gather literature of the Elizabethan period. In 1930, two weeks after the cornerstone was laid in President Hoover's presence, Mr. Folger died, and was later buried in this crypt. By the terms of his will, the institution is administered by the trustees of Amherst College. The building was dedicated April 23, 1932, on what is generally considered to be the 368th anniversary of Shakespeare's birth.

The THEATER, seating 262, is entered from the east lobby through a door surmounted by a bas-relief portraying children acting in a masque. Although it does not pretend to be an exact reproduction of any particular Elizabethan theater, the plan is inspired by the inn courtyard theaters of seventeenth-century England, with balconies enclosing three sides and a threefold red-draped stage at the end. The stage, flanked by oriel bays, consists of an outer, an inner, and an upper stage. To carry out the impression of an open courtyard, the walls are finished in half-timbers and plaster. The "open ceiling" is draped with a colorful canopy.

HOUSE OFFICE BUILDINGS

The OLD HOUSE OFFICE BUILDING, SE. corner Independence and New Jersey Avenues, almost identical with the Senate Office Building, is symmetrically placed on the south side of the Capitol grounds, to conform with the landscape plan for the area. Designed by Carrère and Hastings, the building was completed in 1908, to accommodate the 391 Representatives then in Congress. The census of 1910 increased the apportionment of Representatives to 435, and it was necessary to add another floor. Ornamental details of this building are more simplified than those of the Senate Building, and its floor plan is divided into two- rather than three-room suites, in addition to which there are several committee and caucus rooms. The two House Office Buildings provide office space for Representatives from the States, the delegates from Alaska and Hawaii, and the commissioners from the Philippines and Puerto Rico; these delegates and commissioners sit in House sessions but have no vote.

The NEW HOUSE OFFICE BUILDING, SW. corner Independence and New Jersey Avenues, designed by Allied Architects, Inc., of Washington, and completed in 1933 at a cost of $6,500,000, was provided to relieve the crowded condition in the old building. It has offices for 250 Representatives, in addition to committee rooms. This nine-story rectangular structure of marble and granite looms to the west of the older building and encloses a landscaped court around a central fountain.

The approach to the principal Independence Avenue entrance is through an arcaded loggia in the base of the north portico. This deep portico, with its Ionic columns, ornamental railings, and crowning pediment, is the most striking feature of the exterior. The north elevation, with its balustraded terrace and three-story colonnade recalls the design of the south façade of the House wing of the Capitol. The entrance foyer is designed with fine restraint, its buff limestone walls accented at each end with graceful colonnaded bays. Beneath the ceiling line is a frieze composed of the seals of States, Territories, and possessions of the United States. The adjoining elevator lobby and the flanking corridors are decorated with low-relief panel ornament.

Largest and most imposing of the five major committee rooms is that of the Ways and Means Committee, approached through a spacious lounge with decorations after the manner of the early nineteenth century. Within the committee room the major decorations are pilasters, columns, plaster eagles, and gold brocaded draperies. A bronze chandelier is suspended from a central sunburst framed in a circular panel. In the basement is a large gymnasium with showers, massage and locker rooms for the use of Representatives. A pedestrian subway connects with the Old House Office Building and the Capitol.

CAPITOL POWER PLANT

The Capitol Power Plant (*closed to the public*), occupying a fenced-in city block at New Jersey Avenue and E Street SE., is a large red-brick building with a red-tile roof, arched windows, and a white flagpole, its entrance façade looking more like a conventional YMCA building than a power and heating plant. Connecting with a railroad at the rear, the plant's coal bunkers are piled high with stacks of coal, and an enclosed incline carries the fuel far up into the interior of the building. This and other central heating plants in Washington explain an oft-observed peculiarity of life in Washington—the fact that no coal trucks back up at the base of public buildings to disgorge their loads. Because of such units as this, the principal groups of buildings in the city are saved a dusty and noisome business.

When built in 1910, the power plant served the Capitol, the Senate Office Building, the House Office Building, and the Library of Congress with electrical power, light, and heat; since then its service has been extended to other buildings. Air-cooling equipment was added in 1938. In the approximately 170 days the refrigeration apparatus is in operation each year, more than two billion gallons of water are used, and the refrigeration is equal to the melting of a block of ice 105 feet square and as high as the Washington Monument. Fuel to generate power and to provide heat and cooling costs about $300,000 a year.

U. S. BOTANIC GARDEN

Administered by the Architect of the Capitol, the United States Botanic Garden (*open 9-4 Mon.-Fri., 9-12 Sat.*), Maryland and Independence Avenues SW., has several collections of plants that are unrivaled in the world. Surrounded by a flat terrace, the aluminum-and-glass shell of the conservatories rises above the modified classic façade of the one-story front. An arcaded vestibule carries across the full width of the building, with a large colonnaded pavilion at the center and a minor pavilion at each end. The massive glazed archways are high enough to permit the transference of tall subtropical plants from the conservatory to the outer terrace when weather conditions permit. The keystones of the arches are sculptured with heads of mythological deities—Flora, Pan, Pomona, and Triton. The inner vestibule opens into a parallel conservatory, 262 feet long, behind which is a large glass rotunda having a domical roof rising above the rest of the building and affording adequate height for palms planted inside.

The Botanic Garden's collections of orchids, azaleas, cycads, hardy chrysanthemums, Erabu and Creole lilies, citrus plants, and cacti rival those of any conservatory in the world. The American-developed azalea group, 90 varieties and 400 plants, is rated by experts as the finest in the world. The cycad collection of 12 varieties is the finest known; these plants, survivors of prehistoric times, have been hybridized in the Botanic Garden since 1938, and their seeds, the size of hens' eggs, have been made to reproduce artificially for the first time. The orchid collection contains more than 500 types of this exotic flower. The collection of hardy chrysanthemums, having more than 300 varieties, is the largest and best in the world. Combining steam-created equatorial heat and damp mixtures of heavily organic Washington earth, specialists here have produced excellent examples of tropical and subtropical plants of many kinds. Plants developed here have been used on the grounds of the Capitol Power Plant and Library of Congress Annex.

Across Independence Avenue, south of the Botanic Garden, is the bronze BARTHOLDI FOUNTAIN, executed by Frederic Auguste

Bartholdi, sculptor of the Statue of Liberty.   Known to nearly every Washington visitor, this work consists primarily of three graceful female figures holding on their fingertips a heavy circular basin into which dainty jets pour hundreds of pounds of water.

Federal Triangle

Streetcars: Those operating on Pennsylvania Ave., 14th St., and 7th St. run along the Triangle or cross it.
Busses: Pennsylvania Ave., 9th, 11th, 12th, and 13th Sts. Constitution Ave. busses during rush hours only.
Taxis: First zone.

The Federal Triangle is a group of 12 massive Government buildings east of the Ellipse. The geometric figure into which these structures fit, like a set of try-blocks, has its base line at 15th Street and extends to an apex at 6th Street, with Constitution Avenue defining the south limits and Pennsylvania Avenue the north. Except for the northwest corner, cut off by D Street, the geometric figure is a perfect right triangle, with Pennsylvania Avenue as the hypotenuse. Most of the buildings are eight stories in height, but their huge dimensions and the evenness and horizontality of their roof- and cornice-lines make them appear much lower. Of modern classic design, they are constructed of limestone in varying tones of buff and gray. Red-tile roofs form an almost unbroken line of color along the nine blocks of the Triangle.

On Pennsylvania Avenue this group of monumental buildings, with their 400 columns, their ornamental entrances, pedimented loggias, and row upon row of office windows, faces a motley line of shops across the way. On the Constitution Avenue side, the open spaces of the Mall are in contrast with the imposing façades of the buildings. Each block presents some grand entrance, some elaborate portico, some sculptured pediment, some series of classic columns.

Nine of the buildings in the Triangle were erected between 1930 and 1937 (*see The L'Enfant and Later Plans*). Antedating these are the Old Post Office, the District Building, and the utilitarian Farm Credit Building. The cost of these structures, not counting land and furnishings, is approximately $78,000,000—enough to buy each employee a modest cottage costing almost $3,000. Each weekday morning 30,000 workers leave their homes, converge on this area, and disappear into the monumental buildings. Each weekday afternoon, at almost the same hour, they reappear on the streets, and fight their way across the business section toward home. Underground parking facilities in some buildings are not nearly sufficient, and the flood of humanity clogs the transportation systems, all of which operate above ground. The buildings were designed to meet the normal growth of their respective agencies for 20 years, but several of the larger organizations have grown so rapidly that they have overflowed the inflexible boundaries of the Triangle to find office space elsewhere.

Heat for the Triangle buildings comes from the Central Heating Plant, and four-foot mains buried under Constitution Avenue draw water from the Tidal Basin to produce an air-conditioned atmosphere in the offices and corridors.

APEX BUILDING

The Apex Building, which houses the FEDERAL TRADE COMMISSION (*open 9:15-5:45 Mon.-Fri., 9:15-1:15 Sat.*), occupies a triangular plot on Pennsylvania and Constitution Avenues NW. between 6th and 7th Streets, and forms the apex of the Federal Triangle. Of modified classic design, the seven-story and attic structure was designed by Bennett, Parsons, and Frost, Chicago architects, and completed in 1938 at a cost of $3,277,000. It is commandingly situated, being the part of the Triangle first seen from the east, and its distinctive rounded portico is appropriate to this conspicuous position. The limestone structure, built on a granite base, has a floor area of nearly 3½ acres, divided into offices, hearing rooms, an air- and sound-conditioned cafeteria for the 580 employees, and a special dining room for the commissioners. An interior light court, 76 by 107 feet, is faced with brick of a color to harmonize with the limestone.

The outstanding architectural feature of the building is the 6th Street façade, semicircular in plan, with a monumental colonnade forming a portico from the third-floor level through three floors to the cornice line, above which is the attic (cafeteria) floor, and the red-tile roof. On each side of the portico is a square plinth, upon which stand heroic sculptured figures symbolizing *Man Controlling Trade,* sculptured in limestone by Michael Lantz and unveiled in 1942. The monumental figures portray a workman in two stances, controlling a spirited stallion. Mr. Lantz' composition was chosen by a jury consisting of Paul Manship, Lee Lawrie, and Adolph Weinman, sculptors, elected, for the first time in a Government competition, by the artists submitting work.

The building has two entrances on the Pennsylvania Avenue side and two on Constitution Avenue. Over-door decorations in relief on the Pennsylvania Avenue side are by Chaim Gross, showing workmen engaged in steel construction, symbolizing *Industry,* and by Robert Laurent, depicting seamen at work with pulleys and ropes, symbolizing *Shipping.* Over the Constitution Avenue entrances the bas-reliefs are by Concetta Scaravaglione (*Agriculture,* a man binding and a woman gleaning grain), and by Carl Schmitz (*Trade,* a mariner bartering with an African for an ivory tusk). The four ornamental grill doors, made of aluminum, are decorated with panels of sailing ships, freighters, and airplanes, illustrating the growth of communication and trade. Eagle medallions on the west or 7th Street side are the work of Sidney Waugh. Automobile and service entrances on this side of the building lead to basement parking and utility areas.

The five-member Federal Trade Commission has operated since its creation in 1914 to prevent immoral interstate trade practices and those tending to monopoly or restraint of trade.

NATIONAL ARCHIVES BUILDING

The National Archives Building (*open 9-7 Mon.-Fri., 9-5 Sat.*), Pennsylvania and Constitution Avenues between 7th and 8th Streets NW., designed by John Russell Pope and completed in 1935 at a cost of $8,578,000, is among the most imposing structures in Washington. An example of pure classicism in the grand manner, the Archives Building has large unbroken wall surfaces, enriched by superb colonnades and sculptured porticoes, the whole surmounted by an immense attic of solid masonry, and giving an impression of enduring purpose and august character. The sculptured decorations are confined to allegorical rather than realistic themes, in keeping with the classical treatment of the building.

The deep Corinthian portico on the Constitution Avenue side, with well-proportioned and crisply modeled columns 57 feet high, is approached by a monumental flight of steps, flanked at the street level by two heroic statues, the work of James Earle Fraser—a female figure symbolizing *Heritage,* and a watchful male figure representing *Guardianship.* The figures in the huge pediment, one of the largest in the Nation, also by Fraser, symbolize the act of transferring historic documents to the *Recorder of the Archives,* the central figure. The scale of the colonnade is maintained in the main entrance portal— colossal bronze outer doors, said to be the largest in the world, are 49 feet high, 9 feet wide, and a foot thick. Weighing 10 tons each, they are mechanically operated. Four medallions in the frieze on this façade represent the Federal Departments of War, State, Treasury, and Navy.

The north or Pennsylvania Avenue façade, through which entrance is usually made, has a pedimented portico above a high granite base containing the entry doors. The pediment sculpture on this front, by Adolph Alexander Weinman, portrays a central figure of *Destiny* flanked on each side by the *Arts of Peace* and the *Arts of War.* The griffins at the end symbolize the *Guardians of the Archives.* On each side of the central doorway, carved in high relief on single slabs of granite the full height of the door, are figures in Roman armor representing the *Guardians of the Portal.* These and the heroic pedestal figures flanking the doorway are by Robert Aitken. The aged male figure with the closed book, west of the doorway, symbolizes the *Past;* the female figure on the east, with the open book, represents the *Future.* Five medallions in the frieze on this façade represent the Labor Department, the House of Representatives, the Nation (center), the Senate, and the Post Office Department (mail bag and winged sphere). On the west or 9th Street façade are two medallions symbolizing the Department of Agriculture and the Department of Justice. The frieze is completed on the 7th Street front, with medallions representing the Departments of Commerce and the Interior.

Within the Constitution Avenue entrance is a great foyer, paved with rose and gray Tennessee marble, on the second or principal floor. The circular floor inlay in bronze represents the four major divisions of the archives—Legislation, History, the Judiciary, and War and Defense. Beyond the foyer is a semicircular hall with a half-dome rising 75 feet from the floor. This hall was designed to house the Declaration of Independence and the Constitution, which, however, remain in the Library of Congress. Two murals by Barry Faulkner portray the historic figures associated with the signing of the Declaration and adoption of the Constitution. Cases ranged along the walls exhibit documents of national interest. On each side of the rotunda a curved corridor leads to a large council chamber designed in the manner of an eighteenth-century drawing room and decorated with French gray walls, walnut woodwork, and furniture upholstered in green leather. Three SEARCH ROOMS (*no smoking; no tracings may be made; no pens may be used in these rooms*) on this floor, decorated in the manner of the early Italian Renaissance with cross-beam ceilings and painted decorations, seat about 100 research workers, each of whom is required to have an admission card issued by the Archivist upon written application.

Above the search rooms, on the third floor, is the acoustically perfect AUDITORIUM (*no smoking*), seating 216, in which motion pictures and sound recordings are seen and heard. Groups desiring the use of such auditory or visual archival material are required to make application through an authorized spokesman at least one day in advance. Adjoining the Auditorium are specially equipped cabinets for the storage of inflammable film.

This building was the first adequate depository for important Federal documents, though the need for such facilities had been felt since the meeting of the First Continental Congress in 1774. The building has one of the most efficient burglar alarm systems known, and it is thoroughly air-conditioned, to protect documents against the humidity and the chemical damage that would result from long-time contact with outside air. The inner shell of the building is windowless, protecting archival materials from outside light.

DEPARTMENT OF JUSTICE BUILDING

The huge eight-story Department of Justice Building (*open 9:30-6 Mon.-Fri., 9:30-1:30 Sat.*), Pennsylvania and Constitution Avenues at 9th and 10th Streets NW., giving an impression of massive squareness, has nevertheless a triangular segment on the Pennsylvania Avenue side, and is lighted and aerated within by four courts—a triangular court on the north side, a great rectangular central court, and two square areas within the south walls. Combining archaic Greek and modern forms, the building was designed by Zantzinger, Borie, and Medary, Philadelphia architects, and completed in 1934 at a cost of $10,000,000. The exterior walls, faced with limestone, are adorned on two sides with three-story Ionic colonnades, and there are pedimented loggias at each of the four corners. The attic story, above the cornice line, is roofed with polychromatic terra-cotta tile. Central entrance doors on Constitution and Pennsylvania Avenues are of aluminum grillwork, decorated with wheat and lion motifs. The corner doors are of solid aluminum with striking black surface designs. Each entrance is flanked by aluminum torcheres. A series of mottoes, on the subject of justice, appears over entrances and above second-story windows on all four sides of the building.

Colonnaded driveways, entered through grilled gates, lead into the landscaped central court from 9th and 10th Streets. In the center of the court, on a terraced platform, is an aluminum-bowl fountain. From the fountain platform can be seen the "four winds" sculptures on the attic story by Carl Paul Jennewein. Ramps lead under the fountain to a parking area below the court.

The principal entrance, from Constitution Avenue, leads into a circular lobby, richly decorated with bas-relief panels representing scenes in legal history from early Egyptian to early American times. The interior finish of the building is of plaster, Mankato stone, and limestone. Floors are of tile mosaic or terrazzo. Lobbies and principal corridors are illuminated by cove, or indirect, lighting. The prevailing color scheme is blue and silver, with a liberal use of aluminum trim on doors, stair railings, and elevator cars.

Directly north from the entrance lobby is the first floor elevator lobby. In the stairwell, left, is Emil Bisttram's oil mural, *Contemporary Justice and Woman,* portraying Modern Justice severing the chains that have bound woman to man-made traditions. A bottom panel depicts woman as the slave of ancient times, and eight side-panels depict her as sculptor, student, scholar, executive, dancer, sportswoman, voter, and scientist.

Due north from the Constitution Avenue entrance, in a spacious lobby opening off the central court, is a series of 18 tempera murals by Boardman Robinson, presenting *Great Codifiers of the Law.* In addition to the signing of the Magna Carta and the ratification of the Constitution of the United States, the artist provides a series of panels with idealized portraits of great lawgivers from Menes and Moses to Justice Oliver Wendell Holmes. Robinson spent more than two and a half years painting this series, which extends from the main floor to the head of the stairs.

A great reception hall opens near the head of the stairway, at the south end of which, on a small stage, are two symbolic figures, a female *Spirit of Justice* and a male *Majesty of Justice,* executed by C. P. Jennewein and cast in aluminum. Narrow stairs beside the stage lead to the second floor lobby. Here, in a position corresponding to the Bisttram mural on the first floor, is the second in this series—John Ballator's tempera mural, *Contemporary Justice and Man.* Men in the foreground are represented as unwanted and unhappy in a period of national depression, while in the middle foreground and background they are shown planning and building cities, dams, model communities, and terracing their land.

On the third floor, directly above the Ballator painting, is Symeon Shimin's tempera canvas, *Contemporary Justice and the Child.* The central figure is that of a boy, his eyes burning with ambition, about to go forth from his mother to take up the foreground symbols, triangle and compass, to plan and build in the world. Direful conditions in the shadow of a factory are shown on the left, while on the right children are seen at study, in the laboratory, and on the playing field.

On the fifth floor, in the corresponding elevator foyer, are three frescoes by George Biddle, portraying *Society Freed Through Justice.* Workers are shown laboring under the worst conditions, and under conditions of contentment realized through social justice. On the same floor, at the opposite ends of the elevator corridor, are fresco lunettes by John Steuart Curry, depicting *Justice of the Plains—Movement Westward,* and *Justice Versus Mob Violence.*

The JUSTICE DEPARTMENT LIBRARY, northward along the elevator corridor, is two stories in height, finished in plaster, curly maple, and walnut. The library, with about 100,000 volumes, is used mainly by Department of Justice attorneys. The walls are decorated by 20 oil-on-board panels by Maurice Sterne, under the general title of *The Search for Truth.* In the pauses of the main corridor, parallel to Constitution Avenue, are 12 fresco murals by Henry Varnum Poor. An oil mural by Henry Bouché at the west end of the corridor depicts various activities of the Department of Justice.

FEDERAL BUREAU OF INVESTIGATION EXHIBITS (*open in normal times; conducted tours; 9:30-3:30 Mon.-Fri.; 9:30-11:30 Sat.*), Room 5633, and in adjoining rooms, include cases of trophies taken by G-men in dealing with criminals of Nation-wide notoriety. Organized in 1908 as the investigating unit of the Department of Justice, the FBI has developed into a co-operative clearing house and crime-solution agency for the Nation. The Bureau's criminal jurisdiction was greatly enlarged by laws enacted between 1932 and 1934, permitting it to act in cases involving the crossing of State lines. The FBI has jurisdiction over all matters relating to espionage, counterespionage, sabotage, and similar activities affecting the internal security of the United States and its possessions.

Visitors take a great interest in the Division of Identification, with its 15,000,000 fingerprint cards supplied by more than 11,000 law enforcement agencies all over the world, including the Bureau's 53 field offices in the United States. Fingerprints sent in for identification can often be matched in two minutes by means of a mechanical sorter. More than 2,000,000 additional fingerprint cards are in the civil identification file, to be used for ready identification in case of accidents, loss of memory, and other eventualities. The nickname or "moniker" file contains more than 15,000 nicknames, of value in identifying criminals known only by aliases. This list includes such descriptive nicknames as Banjo Eyes, Big Lipped Louie, Garbage Can Johnny, Babbling Bess, and Butcher Knife Liz. Even more alluring to the detective-story reader is the Bureau's crime laboratory, where chemists, physicists, ballistics experts, and other scientists examine guns, scrapings from boots and tires, hair, lint from pockets, and many seemingly insignificant objects to trace clues and apprehend criminals. The FBI National Police Academy, established in 1935, has "graduated" more than 86,000 State, county, and municipal police officers since it began. These men, having taken their course at the "West Point of Law Enforcement," establish training schools in their home departments.

In addition to its work as an investigation and enforcement agency, the Department of Justice serves as the Federal Government's legal staff, suing and defending suits in the name of the Government, and giving legal opinions and advice to the President and to heads of Federal departments.

INTERNAL REVENUE BUILDING

The large seven-story Bureau of Internal Revenue Building (*open 8:15-4:45 Mon.-Fri., 8:15-12:15 Sat.*), Constitution Avenue between 10th and 12th Streets NW., with a northern extension along 10th Street and Pennsylvania Avenue, was the first Triangle edifice, started in 1930. Giving an outward appearance of rectangular solidity, the main, or southern, portion of the building is nevertheless lighted and ventilated from within. The plan is that of a cross within a square, creating four square courts inside the outer and larger square. The extension northward on 10th Street and northwestward on Pennsylvania Avenue was completed in 1935. This extension, obviously unfinished, is barred by the Old Post Office Building, and the northwest façade, with a curved front to match the east façade of the Post Office Department Building across 12th Street, awaits completion. Designed by the Office of the Supervising Architect, then in the Treasury Department, and erected at a cost of $11,940,720, this enormous building has a floor space of almost 29½ acres and houses about 1,750 office rooms.

The monumental Constitution Avenue façade, with a white marble Doric colonnade of 20-odd columns, contrasts with the warmer tone of the limestone walls. The three bronze main entrance portals, on this side, are flanked by sculptured urns. Within the entrance is a spacious marble lobby with a coffered ceiling. From this lobby, marble corridors extend to offices in the various wings. The Bureau, a branch of the Treasury, collects all Federal taxes except customs, and enforces laws relative to internal revenue. The building, occupied almost exclusively by offices, has a top-floor cafeteria for the 5,000 employees. Three of the inner courts are landscaped, and a fourth, approached from a vehicle entrance on 12th Street, is a service area and provides access to parking facilities under the building.

OLD POST OFFICE BUILDING

Thrusting its dark granite bulk and square clock-tower in stubborn nonconformity above the general level of other Triangle buildings, and determinedly blocking completion of the grand circular plaza planned for opposite façades of the Internal Revenue and Post Office Department Buildings, the Old Post Office Building (*open 9-5:30 Mon.-Fri., 9-1 Sat.*), Pennsylvania Avenue between 11th and 12th Streets NW., is a Romanesque landmark that Washington is slow to give up for the sake of a plan.

The moon-colored clock-faces, looking out from their 315-foot tower in four directions over Washington, is the most elevated public timepiece in the city. Its hands, 5½ feet and 7½ feet long, originally weighing 75 pounds each, in the early life of the building gathered such weights of ice and sleet in winter storms that they stopped the clock. Thanks to subsequent researches in lighter materials, the weight of the hands has been reduced to 14 pounds each, and the timepiece is more accurate.

The medieval-type structure was considered an outstanding building when it was completed at a cost of $2,585,000 and turned over to the Post Office Department in the fall of 1899. Soon after, it was the scene of a tragic accident—City Postmaster James P. Willett fell through an unguarded elevator door and was killed. The building, with some 350 marble-lined office rooms around a central skylit court, became rapidly overcrowded, and was superseded for postal use when the adjacent Post Office Department Building was occupied in 1934. The first-floor walls are paneled in blue-veined brown marble, and the guards point out such configurations as "the smiling cat," "the borzoi dog," and "the white-faced cow." Four feet high, formed by blue veining in the quartered marble, the sleek smiling tabby and the shaggy dog sit on their haunches on either side of the door leading into Room 23, right of the 12th Street entrance. The cat is much the better of the two figures. The cow's head, about the size of a half-dollar, is in the east corridor right of Room 10.

Triangle planning and the decline of Romanesque architecture in public favor have relegated the venerable building to transient occupancy by various Government agencies, pending arrangements for more acceptable quarters elsewhere. Yet, the gray granite hulk commands a continued if not very vociferous admiration because, fortresslike, it holds out against the Triangle invasion, because it adds a time-tried variant to Washington's conformist skyline, and because it has a clock.

POST OFFICE DEPARTMENT BUILDING

The Post Office Department Building (*open 9-4:30 Mon.-Fri., 9-1 Sat.*), SW. corner Pennsylvania Avenue and 12th Street NW., with a floor-plan in the shape of an hourglass, was designed by Delano and Aldrich, New York architects, and completed in 1934 at a cost of $10,800,000. An integral part of the Triangle plan, the building's central semicircular units face eastward on 12th Street, to form half of a projected circular plaza which will be completed by demolition of the Old Post Office Building and erection of a facing semicircular unit in the Internal Revenue Building, and westward on a landscaped grand plaza to occupy the central area of the Triangle to 14th Street. The "grand plaza," its monumental north side incomplete, is now filled with close-packed ranks of parked cars, giving some validity to one planning director's conceit that the plaza could be "laid out to black beetles" instead of fountains and greenery.

The east or 12th Street façade, adorned with Ionic colonnaded pavilions and central portico, a sidewalk arcade, and a mansard roof, is designed to conform to the French treatment implied in a circular plaza. Above the central portico of this façade is an elaborately sculptured pediment, designed and executed by Adolph Alexander Weinman, who designed all the exterior sculpture on this building; the central female figure, *the Spirit of Progress and Civilization,* is flanked by allegorical sculptures symbolizing various types of transportation and communication. The façades of the semicircular units are pierced at the center by three monumental arches, which lead into a central vaulted arcade, providing vistas into each adjoining plaza. The west façade has Doric colonnades and pedimented porticoes in harmony with the architectural treatment of buildings fronting the Great Plaza. The curved attic parapet bears a monumental inscription and a Doric frieze, which presents primitive methods of communication in a series of bas-relief panels. Flanking this series are winged figures, executed by Anthony de Francisci, one accompanied by an owl, the other by an eagle, symbolizing the transmission of the mail by night and by day. Two pediments on this façade represent intercommunication between the continents; the north pediment, executed by Sidney Waugh, portrays Europe and Africa; the south pediment, done by George Snowden, represents America and Asia; above each pediment are two eagles, the work of F. G. R. Roth. The Pennsylvania Avenue pediment, executed by Walker Hancock, symbolizes the bond of world postal union.

Enclosed courts, approached from the east and west through arched driveways, are centered by circular fountains. Within the North Court, over an arch west of the central fountain, is the LIZARD ON THE KEYSTONE, a perfectly sculptured high-relief about 8 inches long, which was not included in specifications for the building. Several explanations have been offered for the presence of the decoration. Some say that one of the architects, rolling some modeling clay between his hands, threw it away, that it stuck on a block of uncarved stone, and that the mason, thinking it a part of the design, carved the lizard beneath the keystone scroll. Department guards think it was put there by the co-architect Delano, as an insignia from a family coat of arms, much as Whistler used a butterfly on his paintings. No one has accepted responsibility for this example of adventitious art, and no one has advanced the most plausible theory—that it was put there for fun.

The BENJAMIN FRANKLIN POSTAL STATION (*open 24 hours a day; closed on Christmas*) is a long service hall with a complete series of postal windows, extending the length of the first floor on the Pennsylvania Avenue side of the building. It is entered by two doors, one on the avenue near 12th Street, the other near 13th Street. A vividly colored tile map of the world is inlaid in the floor of the entrance near 12th Street. Opposite the entrance are oil murals by Alexander Brook portraying two simple scenes, *Writing the Family Letter* and *Reading the Family Letter*. At the western end of the Station, near the 13th Street entrance, is Tom Lea's sculpturesque oil mural, *The Nesters,* a Texas farm scene with a rural delivery mail box placed inconspicuously in the background.

The LIBRARY (*open 9-12, 1-4 Mon.-Fri.*), in Room 1315, reached by the corridor south from the 12th Street entrance, has on its shelves about 20,000 books and pamphlets relating to the history and functions of the postal establishment. It also maintains original records of mail routes from the earliest days, including those relative to mail passage on river steamboats. A departmental library, this institution receives more than 3,000 requests annually for authentic postal information from other departments, from Members of Congress, and from the public. The library ceiling is decorated by two works of Vahe Kirishjian, the oil-on-canvas *Four Seasons* and the oil-on-plaster *Signs of the Zodiac.*

Art work and other points of interest within the Post Office Building are most conveniently seen from the north and south elevator lobbies, at each end of the single corridor across the waist of the building's hourglass floor plan.

Two tempera murals by William C. Palmer, in the north elevator lobby, seventh floor, depict two frontier American scenes—*Stagecoach Attacked by Bandits* and *Covered Wagon Attacked by Indians.* A spiral marble staircase leads down to the floor below. In the north lobby, sixth floor, are two oil murals by Doris Lee—*Country Post,* a scene showing farm people gathered around rural mail boxes mounted on a wheel, and *General Store and Post Office,* a village scene.

The PHILATELIC AGENCY SALESROOM (*open 9-3 weekdays*), Room 6505, in the northeast (12th and Pennsylvania) corner of the building on the sixth floor, maintains an office for the sale of stamps to collectors. Any United States stamp still in stock may be purchased here. Annual sales of stamps by this agency bring the Department a revenue of well over $1,000,000.

The STAMP EXHIBITION ROOM (*open 9-3 weekdays*), Room 6355, just south of the salesroom, is an important source of philatelic information for collectors. In this room are the original etchings of various United States stamps, and the proofs of every issue printed since 1847, the date of the first stamp issued by the Nation. The exhibits include specimens or proofs of all varieties of stamps and stamped paper, rough sketches, finished drawings, steps in designing commemorative issues, working specimens on steel dies, transfer rolls, flatbed and rotary press plates, powdered dyes and mixed inks, the ingredients of stamp gum, and many other details relative to the processing of stamps. In a corner of the room is the small canceling machine used in the Antarctic post office of Little America. Among the rarest items are full sheets of 4- and 8-cent stamps printed on bluish experimental paper—the only copies known to exist, valued at $200,-000. Also shown are some of the famous inverted air-mail stamps, valued at $4,300 each. In all, there are about 50,000 American specimens, in addition to some 1,800 die-proofs.

The collection also contains about 12,000 foreign stamps from 180 foreign countries, obtained by the Philatelic Agency through the International Postal Union at Berne, Switzerland. Membership in this union makes it possible for the Department to obtain current issues of all foreign countries. Among others, the collection includes almost a complete set of the increasingly valuable King George V Jubilee issues.

In the north elevator lobby, fifth floor, are two oil murals by Frank Mechau, *Pony Express* and *Dangers of the Mail,* the first portraying a change of horses at a pony express station, the second showing Indians torturing a captured pony expressman. On the fourth floor, in the same lobby below, are two frescoes by Reginald Marsh, crowded, rhythmic, muscular representations of *Sorting Mail* and *Transfer of Mail from Liner to Tugboat.*

The POSTMASTER GENERAL'S RECEPTION ROOM, a palatial Georgian chamber with anterooms at the north and south ends, is on the east side of the main third-floor corridor. Having richly carved pilasters and door headings, the walnut-paneled room is an impressive formal hall, and its anterooms provide space for an array of sculptured works. In the north anteroom are Paul Manship's 7-foot marble statue of Samuel Osgood, first Postmaster General (1789-91), and four 4-foot aluminum statues of typical figures in the mail service—Gaetano Cercere's *Rural Free Delivery Mail Man,* Heinz Warneke's *Expressman,* Louis Slobodkin's *Hawaiian Postman,* and the *Alaska Snowshoe Mail Carrier,* by Chaim Gross. Occupying niches within the entrance to the Reception Room are *Contemporary Postman* by Attilio Piccirilli and *Air Mail Pilot* by Oronzio Maldarelli. On the walls of the Reception Room are wood-sculptured medallions by Gleb Derujinsky presenting profile portraits in bas-relief of ten early Postmaster Generals. Within the south entry are aluminum figures of the *Stage Driver (1789-1836)* by Sidney Waugh and *Pony Express Rider*

(1850-58) by Arthur Lee. Four more figures in the south anteroom complete this group—Berta Margoulies' *Postman (1691-1775)*, Stirling Calder's *Post Rider (1776-89)*, Carl L. Schmitz' *Delivery Carrier (1863)*, and Concetta Scaravaglione's *Railway Mail Carrier (1862)*. William Zorach's 7-foot marble statue of Benjamin Franklin, occupying the most prominent position in the south anteroom, is one of the most human and lively sculptures of the much-portrayed "father of the United States postal system."

On the second floor, north lobby, are two oil paintings by Eugene Savage portraying *The Post as a Connecting Thread in Human Life*.

The remaining portrayal of the United States Post through the eyes of mural artists is in the south elevator lobby, on the various floors: Seventh, Karl Free's oil-on-canvas murals, *French Explorers and Indians* and *Arrival of Mail in New Amsterdam;* sixth, George Harding's tempera paintings, *Franklin and His Administration of the Post* and *Carrying of Dispatches in the Revolution;* fifth, Ward Lockwood's frescoes, *Opening of the Southwest* and *Building of the Railroads in the West;* fourth, Alfred D. Crimi's frescoes, *Post Office Workroom* and *Transportation of Mail;* second, Rockwell Kent's oils, *Mail Service in the Tropics* and *Mail Service in the Arctic*.

The basement floor of the building is devoted to a large cafeteria, and mail receiving and dispatching areas.

LABOR-INTERSTATE COMMERCE GROUP

The Interstate Commerce Commission (*office hours 8:30-5:15 Mon.-Fri., 8:30-12:30 Sat.*), the Departmental Auditorium, and the Department of Labor (*office hours 9-4:30 Mon.-Fri., 9-1 Sat.*) are housed in a single monumental building group on Constitution Avenue between 12th and 14th Streets NW. The floor plan of the extended rectangular structure is divided in such a way that the Interstate Commerce Commission and the Labor Department occupy short rectangular sections, with interior courts, at the east and west ends, respectively, of the larger structure, while the Departmental Auditorium is assigned the square central space between. Designed by Arthur Brown, this massive structure was completed in 1934 at a cost of $11,012,538.

Entrance to the central Auditorium is through three square portals in the high base of a pedimented portico rising through three stories. The flanking structures consist of six-story units surmounted by an attic story above the main cornice, a central arched doorway, and pedimented pavilions with colonnades at each end. These pediments are decorated with allegorical figures. The east pediment, on the Interstate Commerce Building, by Edward McCarran, symbolizes *Interstate Transportation;* the west pediment, by Wheeler Williams, represents *Commerce and Communication;* the east pediment on the Labor Department Building, by Albert Stewart, symbolizes *Labor and Industry;* the west pediment, by Sherry Fry, represents *Abundance and Industry*.

The interiors of the two structures are virtually identical, in the style of the French Empire, with paneled walls and ceilings, elaborate bas-reliefs of Roman symbols and trophies, and lighting fixtures in the form of fasces. Offices and corridors are arranged in a rectangle around a large central court, which contains a fountain in the case of the Labor Building, and two large hearing rooms, separated by a central corridor and rotunda, in that of the Interstate Commerce Building. The two buildings house, respectively, the Interstate Commerce Commission, an 11-member board engaged in the regulation of common carriers in interstate commerce, and the Labor Department, youngest executive department in the Government (started in 1913), engaged in promoting the welfare of laboring people and their children.

The high Doric portico of the DEPARTMENTAL AUDITORIUM, forming the central motif of this impressive group, is surmounted with a monumental pediment containing an allegorical sculptural group by Edgar Walter, representing *Columbia*. Under the portico is a bas-relief panel, by Edward Amateis, showing General Washington, with the aid of General Greene and General Sullivan, planning the Revolutionary Battle of Trenton. The interior of this spacious hall, reached through a marble foyer, is designed with unusual splendor. Massive Doric colonnades line the side aisles, and stand in bold relief against the light from tall windows; the ceiling is finished in light blue, and the windows are draped in gold. A spacious stage and rostral platform, at the north end, is framed by a paneled screen wall, set with elaborate gilded bas-reliefs. Huge chandeliers of polished white metal, with plain crystal shades, complete the decorative scheme. The stage and motion picture screen are unique. Bolted together, they are raised and lowered electrically. The screen, measuring 19 by 26 feet, is one of the largest in existence. The Auditorium, including a large balcony, seats 1,325; an additional 1,500 can be accommodated with extra chairs.

Behind the stage, and overlooking the "great plaza" are three large conference rooms, decorated in green and gold leaf, given high praise by many artistically-minded visitors. A huge CAFETERIA is in the basement.

The LABOR DEPARTMENT EXHIBITS, in Rooms 1213-17, Labor Building, include charts showing the development and interdependence of the American people, the growth of cities, and the rise and fall of prosperity in the Nation. Other displays, subject to change, deal with accident prevention, workmen's compensation, working hours for women, employer-employee relationships, unemployment insurance, and child welfare. A display of paintings hangs on the walls of first-floor corridors.

DISTRICT BUILDING

The six-story marble District Building (*open 8:45-4:15 weekdays, 8:45-12:45 Sat.*), SE. corner 14th and D Streets NW., designed by

Cope and Stewardson and completed in 1908 at a cost of $2,000,000, is the "City Hall" of Washington, containing the offices of the District Commissioners and heads of the various municipal departments. This structure and the utilitarian Farm Credit Building, flanking it on the east, are scheduled for eventual demolition in order to complete the monumental northern spur of Triangle buildings to enclose another side of the "grand plaza." District government offices will be removed to the Municipal Center. The District Building faces a small triangular park bordering the south side of Pennsylvania Avenue, in which stands a green-stained bronze statue of Alexander R. Shepherd, who was outstanding in the District's development during the 1870's (*see History*).

Above the main entrance is the seal of the District, set between reclining female figures. Within, there is a broad marble corridor and a grand central stairway. On the walls of the entrance vestibule are plaques commemorating former Commissioners, and the corridor walls are hung with portraits of former District officials. Right of the entrance is a bronze bust, by William Couper, of Crosby Stuart Noyes, major supporter of Shepherd's plans for municipal development.

COMMERCE DEPARTMENT BUILDING

The Department of Commerce, engaged in the promotion of foreign and domestic commerce, is partially housed in the huge seven-story building (*open 8:30-5 Mon.-Fri., 8:30-12:30 Sat.*), one block wide and nearly three blocks long, that extends across the base of the Federal Triangle on 15th Street between Constitution Avenue and D Street NW. The floor plan is that of a long rectangle divided into six equal sections, each built around an enclosed inner court; had the six sections been superimposed upon one another, the Commerce Building would be 42 stories high, covering half a city block. This monumental building, decorated in the Italian Renaissance Palazzo style, was designed by York and Sawyer, New York architects, and completed in 1932 at a cost in excess of $17,000,000. Having a floor space of almost 37 acres—equal in area to a modest farm—the building amply justifies its 15 entrances, 32 elevators, 16 stairways, and 8 miles of corridors. Though simple and right-angled in plan, the sense of geometric precision is missing within its long marble corridors, and the building has the reputation of being the easiest place in Washington in which to get lost.

The exterior walls are of granite through the first two stories, above which they are made of Indiana limestone. At the seventh-floor level, behind a balustraded parapet, is a short setback to an attic story roofed with red mission tile. Variety is achieved on the 14th Street façade by means of a monumental Doric colonnade across the central third of the building, while the flanking north and south units are treated more simply. North and south fronts are also dominated by a central colonnade, while the 15th Street side is broken by four pavilions with colonnaded porticoes and sculptured pediments. Two sets of triple-arched gateways, two stories in height, dividing the general mass into three units, lead into open courts, which give access to a restricted parking area and to service areas in the basement. Magnificent grilled gates hang in the courtyard archways, and bronze Florentine lamps flank the entrance doorways. Carved inscriptions on the various façades were written or chosen by the art critic Royal Cortissoz. Sculptural groups in the pediments, symbolizing various bureaus housed in the building, were designed by James E. Fraser.

The interior, except for special rooms, is frankly an office building. Decorations throughout were designed by Barnet Phillips. The 14th Street lobby, in the center of the building, is classic in design, with rusticated walls, arches, Doric columns, a painted and coffered ceiling, and a terrazzo and marble floor. The INFORMATION OFFICE is on the south side of the entrance lobby, and building guards are liberal with accurate directions.

A series of frequently changed MAIN LOBBY EXHIBITS are placed in cabinets about this central hall. Industrial products are most frequently shown, such as the exhibit of plastics in the winter of 1940-41, ranging from synthetic brooms and football helmets to shoes and radio cabinets. Displays of methacrylate resin revealed how fresh orchids, diseased human organs, and tropical butterflies with their dustlike wing-scales undisturbed, can be preserved in their natural colors within this crystalline substance. An earlier display showed, through models, the evolution of the airplane from the frail Wright biplane of 1903 to the airliner of the 1940's.

The AQUARIUM (*open 8:30-4 Mon.-Fri., 8:30-12:30 Sat., 10-4 Sun. and holidays*), on the basement floor beneath the main lobby, has 48 display tanks and 3 floor pools, in all of which natural conditions are simulated. The collection of game and food fishes includes about 2,000 American fresh-water fish, three-pound bullfrogs from the Louisiana marshes, blackfish from Alaska, and six small aquariums containing brilliantly colored tropical fishes. Aquarium officials, however, are most proud of their trout collection, which has some unusual varieties, including several albinos, one of them marked with a red cross on its forehead. During hatching season, units are set up to demonstrate the incubation of fish-eggs and the successive stages of the animal's growth. The Aquarium is maintained by the Department of the Interior's Fish and Wildlife Service. West of the Aquarium, on the basement floor, is a huge CAFETERIA, with table space for 900 people.

The DEPARTMENT OF COMMERCE LIBRARY, on the seventh floor of the central unit, has more than 200,000 publications covering a wide range of commercial and industrial subjects.

The PATENT OFFICE SEARCH ROOM, main entrance at northwest corner of building, 15th Street side, extends across the north front of the building on the first floor. Desk space is provided to facilitate the work of patent attorneys, inventors, and other serious students, in their research among the 8,000,000 United States patents. Show racks in the search room display facsimiles of many historic patents, including the first issued in America—that granted to Joseph Jenkes by the General Court of Massachusetts in 1646, covering a device for a water mill—the Bell telephone patent, the Edison phonograph and incandescent-lamp patents, that for the Whitney cotton gin, the Morse telegraph, the McCormick reaper, the Howe sewing machine, the Wright flying machine, the De Forrest vacuum radio tube, the Mergenthaler linotype, and many others. The application for Abraham Lincoln's patent on "A Manner for Buoying Vessels," in his own handwriting, describes a method of getting boats over shallow waters. Models of patented machines, in display cases, include those of gas engines, electric motors, an early submarine and torpedo, and models of much less importance, including a device for propelling a sled over snow, and a gas-operated burglar alarm, dated 1871, with a large brass bell to sound a warning.

U. S. INFORMATION CENTER

The U. S. Information Center *(open 7 a.m.-10 p.m. weekdays),* Pennsylvania Avenue between 14th and 15th Streets NW. and extending to D Street, a two-story structure, is in essence a central hall with east and west wings, arranged in a kind of lozenge-shaped space between four streets. The design is uncompromisingly plain, and its few deviations from the straight wall are functional rather than decorative. The main entrance on Pennsylvania Avenue is flanked by red flagpoles and surmounted with Bauhaus architectural lettering, in contrast to the usual Government practice of designating its buildings with titles obscurely chiseled in the architrave or engraved on small bronze plaques at knee level. The building is covered with composition board, unpainted. It cost $530,000, and was erected in 1942, in 36 days flat. Most pretentious of World War II temporary buildings, it is also known as Building V—"for Victory."

The central information hall, reached from Pennsylvania Avenue or D Street, is a two-story room paneled from floor to ceiling with squares of birch and gum wood in natural colors, the beautiful grains of which are blithely unmatched; it is decorated with war posters, which, like travel bills in a railway station, are changed from time to time. The paneling terminates abruptly in corridors beyond the normal use of the public. The hall, which indeed has somewhat the air of a railroad station, is centered by a closed oval counter reaching almost the full length of the room; the counter circumambulates batteries of files which contain a complete picture of the Government's labyrinthine activities. Here the public, and the Federal departments themselves, may obtain "quick and responsible information" on governmental matters from a staff of intensively trained clerks.

Specialists from the various agencies have been loaned to the Center to answer technical questions. The entire periphery of the hall is lined with small glass-fronted consultation rooms occupied by such specialists. In wings adjacent to the hall the Procurement Division, the Civil Service Commission, the War Production Board, the Office of Price Administration, and other agencies maintain liaison officers. Also in close connection is the Defense Housing Registry, and recruiting offices of the Marines and Coast Guard. The Information Center has had at least two requests by newcomers for dates with attractive Government girls, and it must know where to send the man who has invented a reversible airplane. The balance of the building is occupied by a part of the staff of the Office of Government Reports and the U. S. Information Service.

Direct contact is supplemented by telephone service. The number is EXecutive 3300 (the same as the President's).

Along the Mall

Streetcars: Operate on Pennsylvania Ave., 7th St., 14th St., and 19th St. (Potomac Park).
Busses: Run on Constitution Ave., 9th St., 12th St., 17th St., and to Potomac Park.
Taxis: First and second zones.

The rolling, rectangular greensward between the Capitol and the Washington Monument underwent many changes, in plan and in fact, before it became the serene and impressive channel for Washington vistas that it is today. Originally a swampy woodland, often inundated by the Potomac River, L'Enfant planned it as a "Grand Avenue, 400 feet in breadth . . . bordered with gardens, ending in a slope from the houses on each side." By 1848, when the cornerstone was laid for the Washington Monument, L'Enfant's axial plan did not seem important, and the monument site was shifted a hundred yards southeast of the spot he had chosen. Years before the McMillan Commission presented its plan for Washington in 1902, the romantic school of English landscape gardening had invaded America, and the commission laid out the Mall much as it is today. The name, Mall, was also borrowed from England, where it adorned a promenade in St. James's Park, London, and later was used to designate any fashionable promenade. Originally signifying the maul, or mallet, used in the popular seventeenth-century game of pall-mall (or ball-maul), the name was first applied to a pall-mall alley in London, and afterward to the promenade on that site.

Although the Mall covers only that stretch of greensward from the Capitol Grounds to 14th Street, the visitor usually continues across the Monument Grounds between 14th and 17th Streets, and into that part of West Potomac Park which includes the Lincoln Memorial and Arlington Bridge. The area is one of memorials, museums, and art galleries, and throughout its length it presents the best of spacious and monumental Washington. Less visibly, the central line of the Mall divides Northwest and Southwest Washington.

At the eastern end of the Mall, where 1st Street separates it from the Capitol Grounds, its corners are marked by two monuments enclosed in traffic circles. In the northeast corner, at Pennsylvania Avenue and 1st Street NW., is the white marble PEACE MONUMENT, completed in 1877 by Franklin Simmons, working from a design by Admiral David D. Porter. It is a symbolic creation, representing America weeping on the shoulder of History for the loss of Navy men at sea. The statue takes its name from a subordinate figure of

Peace on a pedestal flanking the main shaft. At the southeast corner of Maryland Avenue and 1st Street SW., is the GARFIELD MEMORIAL, a portrait statue by J. Q. Adams Ward, unveiled in 1887. Subordinate figures of a student, a statesman, and a warrior symbolize the President's versatile personality.

Stretching its 252-foot length along 1st Street, across the Capitol end of the Mall, is the GRANT MEMORIAL, designed and partially executed by Henry Merwin Shrady and completed after his death by Edmond R. Amateis. On a central pedestal is an equestrian bronze figure of General Grant, said to be the second largest such bronze in the world. Bronze groups of Union cavalry and artillery in action are portrayed at each end of a long granite base. The monument was unveiled in 1922, on the centenary of Grant's birth. On the north side of the Mall, below the Grant Memorial, is the GENERAL GEORGE GORDON MEADE MEMORIAL, executed by Charles A. Grafly and presented by the Commonwealth of Pennsylvania.

Parallel one-way drives extend the length of the Mall, with stops at all arterial cross-streets. Though a pleasant and uncrowded drive, with splendid views of the Capitol and the Monument, during rush hours the cross-streets are packed with impenetrable traffic.

Many temporary office buildings were erected on the Mall during the First World War. One of the relatively few remaining examples is Building E, on 6th Street, with its dingy brown stucco, white windows, and tall, arched entrances. The advent of World War II brought a new crop of alphabetically lettered temporary buildings, which are considered much more attractive than those of the nineteen-teens. They are modern in line, painted white, fitted with Venetian blinds, and have perky square visors over their unpretentious entrances. These two-story structures mushroomed rapidly during 1941, and by early 1942 had used up most of the letters of the alphabet. Building V, on account of the Second World War slogan, "V for Victory," is more elaborate than the rest.

The gleaming white National Gallery of Art and the similarly domed National Museum are built on the north side of the Mall between 4th and 10th Streets, while the red-brick cluster of the Smithsonian group, and the gray granite Freer Gallery, occupy the south side between 7th and 12th. On the Mall opposite the National Archives Building, between 7th and 9th Streets, was held the first agricultural fair in the United States, in 1804. "It was a decided success," reported the *National Intelligencer,* which said that the exhibits "on the south side of the Tiber" extended from "the bridge at the Center Market to the Potomac." This must have been gratifying to Dr. William Thornton, first architect of the Capitol and first superintendent of the Patent Office, for it was he who first suggested fairs or market days similar to those in his native England. The continuous mass of red-roofed limestone buildings in the Triangle group borders the Mall on the north, between 6th and 15th Streets. On the south side, between 12th and 14th, the white-columned portico of the Department of Agriculture Administration Building gleams out across the greenery.

Within the Monument Grounds, southeast of the Monument, is the Sylvan Theater, with a backdrop of shrubbery, Lombardy poplars, and evergreens, where outdoor dramatic, operatic, and dance performances are presented in Summer.

From the rounded eminence that serves as a pedestal for the obelisk of the Washington Monument, the white marble Pantheon of the Jefferson Memorial gleams through the trees to the south. Westward lies the Reflecting Pool, like a royal carpet before the gleaming classic shrine of the Lincoln Memorial. Impressive monuments, they have nevertheless had their critics. Joseph Hudnut, Dean of Harvard University's Graduate School of Design, has said of this group: "Architecture, which lives by association, has suffered no stranger metamorphosis than that which has transformed an Egyptian Washington, a Greek Lincoln, and a Roman Jefferson into evocative symbols of Americanism."

South of the Lincoln Memorial, the Arlington Bridge reaches in nine low graceful spans across the placid Potomac.

NATIONAL GALLERY OF ART

The long low marble structure on the Mall west of the Capitol is the National Gallery of Art, Constitution Avenue between 4th and 7th Streets NW. (*open, free, 9-5:30 Mon.-Fri., 9-1 Sat., 2-5 Sun.; free bulletin with list of art works at information desk*), which, according to present indications, will become in time one of the leading painting and sculpture museums of the world. Already its collection of Italian paintings is unsurpassed in America, while its masterpieces of the Flemish, German, Dutch, Spanish, French, British, and early American schools contain many items never before made accessible to the public.

The gallery and the nucleus of its exhibit were the gift to the Nation of Andrew W. Mellon, Secretary of the Treasury (1921-32). In 1936 Mr. Mellon wrote to President Roosevelt announcing his plan to create a national museum which, not bearing his name, would "attract gifts from other citizens who may in the future desire to contribute works of art . . . to form a great national collection." Congress accepted the gift the following year, provided a six-and-a-half-acre site for the Mellon building, and instituted the National Gallery of Art as a bureau of the Smithsonian Institution, administered independently by a board of trustees consisting of the Chief Justice of the United States, the Secretary of State, the Secretary of the Treasury, the Secretary of the Smithsonian Institution, and five general trustees. Funds for maintenance of the gallery are supplied by annual congressional appropriation.

At its opening March 18, 1941, the gallery had on display the Mellon Collection, consisting of 126 paintings and 26 pieces of sculpture, and the Kress Collection of 375 paintings and 18 sculptures. The Kress group, all Italian, had been deeded to the Nation in 1939. Since then Joseph E. Widener of Pennsylvania has promised to the gallery his remarkable assembly of more than 100 items, including outstanding Rembrandts, El Grecos, and Vermeers, and important pieces of sculpture. In addition, Miss Ellen Bullard and three anonymous donors have supplied the beginnings of a collection of prints. The impressiveness of this start may be judged by comparing it with that of the National Gallery in London, which opened in 1824 with 38 pictures.

The $15,000,000 building, of pink Tennessee marble, is designed in two windowless block wings stretching from a central rotunda capped with a low dome. It is 785 feet in length, and provides a half million square feet of floor space, of which about half is used for exhibition purposes. Most visitors enter through three doors facing Constitution Avenue on the street level; the principal entrance, however, on the Mall side of the rotunda, is through a classical portico of the type generally adorning Government edifices.

It was natural that the addition of another Classic adaptation to American museum buildings should have aroused strong dissent, particularly from those who have been hoping for progress in gallery construction. The design, however, created by the late John Russell Pope, and carried to completion by his associates of the firm of Eggers and Higgins, was conceived in close conference with Mr. Mellon, and in the opinion of the Mellon trustees is entirely justified by its harmony with the general architecture of the Capital. Regardless of what one thinks of its plan, the building has a special charm: its 800 carloads of rose-white marble have been carefully graded in tone from the ground upward, so that in the sunlight its whiteness does not shimmer, like other new Washington buildings; rain draws out its inner tint until even the pavements surrounding it have a strawberry glow under the wetness. Evergreens around the moat wall add to the quality of softness which the building gains at certain distances under favorable light.

Beyond a flight of steps from the Mall, and through two twelve-ton bronze doors, is an entry into the rotunda, core of the building's design. The magnificence and apparent inutility of this hall, which imitates the Pantheon in Rome, will doubtless arouse many discussions during the "thousand years" the gallery is expected to stand. One hundred feet in diameter and the same in height, the rotunda is centered by a fountain which scatters the sound of flowing water across the marble floor and through the circle of deep-green Italian-marble columns. Reflecting the ripples, the polished bronze *Mercury* of Giovanni Bologna, sixteenth-century Flemish-Florentine sculptor, ascends from the fountain, the left foot resting on a gust blown from the mouth of a wind-god. Above the 24 columns, the dome, faced with limestone, terminates in a glass oculus. It is only here, in this blending of the cold green height of the marble columns, the luster of the bronze, and the creamy austerity of the limestone, that the museum seems deliberately to display its opulence.

East and west of the rotunda stretch two long corridors, 100 by 35 feet; in the west corridor are Jacopo Tatti's (Sansovino) *Venus Anadyomene* and *Bacchus and a Young Faun,* sixteenth-century works, which Napoleon Bonaparte took to Paris as loot from Italy. Other sculpture will be placed in these halls, which end in two gardens, where flowers and potted plants provide a setting for fountains adorned with lead groups executed more than 250 years ago for the gardens at Versailles, and which were displayed at the New York World's Fair.

The ceilings of the sculpture corridors, like those of the galleries, are of laminated glass, which diffuses the sunlight, or the rays of floodlights concealed in the "attic" for use at night or on gloomy days, so that an even light falls on all the pictures, regardless of the weather or hour of the day. This glass is a quarter of an inch thick and very strong; yet if shattered by a blow, it turns at once into dust so that paintings and visitors are protected against injury. The lighting of the National Gallery is said to be the most modern and efficient in the world, which is fortunate in view of the unusually heavy surface of varnish with which the paintings are protected. Another factor in preserving the paintings is the even level of temperature and humidity maintained in the gallery through a vast invisible system of coolers, steam pipes, humidifiers, pumps, and fans.

There are almost 100 galleries on the main floor. Picture hanging arrangements were carefully considered during the building of the museum, and effects have been analyzed since the works were placed on display. Wall decorations in the different rooms recall those in use during the periods in which the paintings were created. Plaster walls with travertine trim form the background for the early Italian paintings, brocade for the later Italians. Dutch and Flemish works are hung upon oak paneling, and the English, French, Spanish, and American upon painted wood. The floors of most of the galleries, in welcome contrast to the stone of the entranceways, are of broad, pegged oak boards. Sofas are provided in some rooms, though the fact that the galleries usually open into one another, resulting in a continual circulation of visitors, detracts somewhat from the pleasure, sometimes found in museums not built in the expectation of such large crowds, of sitting and reflecting upon a masterpiece at leisure. As a compensation, however, the paintings are so ordered that it is possible to start with the earliest period and pass, century by century, to the latest.

The procession of masters opens with Duccio di Buoninsegna, thirteenth-century painter of Siena; his younger contemporary, the great Giotto, founder of the school of Florence, represented by a golden-hued *Madonna and Child;* and Cimabue, mentioned by Dante as the most important painter before Giotto. Works from the Sienese School include the striking *Calling of the Apostles Peter and Andrew* by

Duccio, with its strongly Byzantine cast; four works by Sassetta, among them his *Meeting of St. Anthony and St. Paul* and *Madonna and Child;* five of Giovanni di Paolo; and three by Pietro Lorenzetti, whose work escapes the pietistic formula of most of the Sienese.

Raphael, most celebrated of the Umbrian School, whose lyrical and gracious figure stands at the peak of the Renaissance, is represented by four paintings: the much-publicized *Alba Madonna,* which Mr. Mellon obtained from the Hermitage Gallery in Leningrad at the price of $1,000,000; the *Niccolini-Cowper Madonna;* the charming *Saint George and the Dragon;* and the bust portrait, *Bindo Altoviti.* Among earlier Umbrian masters on display are Gentile da Fabriano, rich colorist and scrupulous painter of nature, whose *A Miracle of St. Nicholas* aroused the enthusiasm of Vasari when he saw it in Florence; Perugino, under whom Raphael studied; Pintoricchio, another pupil of Perugino; Signorelli, and others.

Fifteenth-century Florence, which developed fresco, and where the new Renaissance spirit of scientific clarity manifested itself most strongly, contributes *The Madonna of Humility* and a profile portrait of a young man, by Masaccio, one of the greatest pioneers of Florentine art and a master in the rendering of aerial space; three paintings by Fra Angelico, whose later style was influenced by Masaccio; and two sometimes attributed to Uccello, a leader of the "Scientific School," whose experiments in linear perspective have been of much interest to modern abstract artists. Four paintings illustrate the accomplishments of Fra Filippo Lippi, known to all readers of Robert Browning; the century climbs towards its climax in the work of his disciples, Filippino Lippi and the renowned Sandro Botticelli. The latter's *Adoration of the Magi,* one of his greatest compositions, was acquired from the Hermitage Gallery, for which it had been purchased in 1808 by Czar Alexander I; his *Portrait of a Young Man in a Red Hat* was another prized item of the Mellon Collection. Piero Di Cosimo, whose tremendous panel, *The Visitation with Two Saints,* is more than six feet in height and width, was the teacher of Andrea del Sarto, celebrated in another of Browning's poems. Del Sarto's *Madonna and Child with the Infant St. John,* painted in 1528, is very similar to his composition, executed in the same year, now in the Kaiser Friedrich Museum in Berlin.

From Florence, too, comes sculpture bearing such re-echoing names as Donatello, Mino da Fiesole, Pollaiuolo, the Della Robbias, Verrocchio. The sculpture collection is of an exceptionally high order.

Wonderful golds, reds, and blues stream from the walls hung with masterpieces of the Venetian School. During its lengthy development, this style, reflecting the luxury and gaiety of Venice's palaces and festivals, produced a galaxy of master colorists and lavish painters of drapes, landscape backgrounds, and the human body.

Jacopo Bellini, born at the opening of the fifteenth century, and trained by Gentile da Fabriano and several of the Florentine masters,

INTERIOR VIEW, CATHEDRAL OF SS. PETER AND PAUL

W. Lincoln Highton

SACRED HEART ROMAN CATHOLIC CHURCH
AND STATUE OF CARDINAL GIBBONS

CHURCHES AT 16TH AND HARVARD STREETS—L. D. S. (MORMON) CHAPEL, NATIONAL MEMORIAL BAPTIST CHURCH, AND ALL SOULS' UNITARIAN CHURCH

hotos by W. Lincoln Highton

NEW YORK AVENUE
PRESBYTERIAN
("LINCOLN")
CHURCH

LATE AFTERNOON CLASSES, MANY OF THEM
FOR GOVERNMENT WORKERS, CLOSE AFTER
DARK AT GEORGE WASHINGTON UNIVERSITY

Farm Security Administration: Marion Post

GREENBELT SCHOOL

GEORGETOWN UNIVERSITY

Washington Board of Trade

Farm Security Administration: McMillan

TIDAL BASIN AND JEFFERSON MEMORIAL

W. Lincoln Highton

FEDERAL RESERVE BUILDING

NATIONAL ACADEMY
OF SCIENCES
W. Lincoln Highton

"WHAT FOOLES THESE MORTALS BE" — BRENDA
PUTNAM'S *PUCK*, FOLGER SHAKESPEARE LIBRARY

exerted an all-pervasive influence upon the studios of his native Venice through his own work and that of his sons, Gentile and Giovanni, and his son-in-law, Andrea Mantegna. The style of Mantegna, identified with the Paduan School, is represented in the gallery by the master's *Saint Jerome in the Wilderness,* an early and somewhat unsatisfactory picture, and two others, as well as by a series of six allegorical depictions of Triumphs (of Divinity, Time, Chastity, etc.), by the School of Mantegna, in which are mingled comic, sentimental, and macabre notes. Giovanni Bellini, throwing off in his later years the last restraints of the fifteenth-century manner, achieved new splendors and color harmonies in the recently introduced medium of oil. His serene *Flight into Egypt* has been called by Berenson one of "the earliest landscapes in the modern sense of the word, produced in Italy." Of the five Kress Collection paintings by his pupil Lorenzo Lotto, *A Maiden's Dream* and *Allegory* have passages interestingly suggestive of twentieth-century surrealism.

But two other pupils of Giovanni Bellini, Giorgione and Titian, surpassed even their master in freedom and sensuousness of conception. Giorgione's style so penetrates that of his contemporaries that indentification of particular works has long been a matter of controversy. Completely authenticated Giorgiones are extremely rare, and the Kress Collection's *Adoration of the Shepherds,* subtle in texture and warmly toned, though almost universally attributed to Giorgione, is held by some to have come from the brush of Titian.

In Titian the lighting, pigmentation, and sensuous appeal of the Venetian School reached their highest development, and European art bore the mark of his influence for two centuries. His ample bejewelled nudes, with their pale gold tresses and velvets, furs, and veils, have come to represent a distinct type of feminine beauty. Six canvases by Titian and seven by Tintoretto, who succeeded him as the leader of the Venetians, as well as numerous examples by lesser masters, make this part of the exhibition especially rewarding. Veronese's regal *The Finding of Moses* is in the best manner of the period.

Tiepolo, though born more than a century after Veronese, carried on his tradition. By the eighteenth century, however, Venetian painting had lost much of its creative vigor, diffusing itself in rococo decoration. Yet a good deal of charm survives in the work of Guardi, Canaletto, Magnasco, and Pietro Longhi. Of particular interest to visitors of the National Gallery is the *Interior of the Pantheon,* by Panini, of the eighteenth-century Roman School, which permits a comparison of the gallery's rotunda with the original.

The collection includes many valuable examples of non-Italian art, though nothing approaching the comprehensiveness of the Italian section is achieved. There are nó works by Brueghel, for instance, only one Rubens, and but three French paintings. It is expected, of course, that later gifts will strengthen the museum in this respect.

One of the treasures of the museum is *The Annunciation* by Jan van Eyck, "father of oil painting" and founder of the Flemish School. Petrus Christus, whose works are very rare, appears with *The Nativity,* a highly attractive composition showing much imagination in its detail. Hans Hemling, Holbein the Younger, Van Dyck, Gerard David, and Rogier van der Weyden are other major contributors to the Flemish and German section. The Rubens is a portrait of Isabella Brant, the artist's first wife, and has by some critics been attributed to Van Dyck.

The Dutch group, though comparatively small, is of the highest quality. Nine masterpieces of Rembrandt include a moving *Self-Portrait,* the tragic *Lucretia,* and the psychologically sensitive *A Woman Holding a Pink,* and *An Old Lady with a Book. A Polish Nobleman* shows the master in a more flamboyant mood. Six portraits by Frans Hals are in his characteristically hearty style. Perhaps the rarest items in the Dutch rooms are the three Vermeers, *The Girl with a Red Hat, The Lacemaker,* and *The Smiling Girl.* Vermeer's lucid textures were the result of slow and painstaking labor, and he left relatively few pictures. The Dutch interest in genre subjects is indicated by the titles of his canvases, as well as by those of Aelbert Cuyp—*Herdsmen Tending Cattle, The Maas at Dordrecht;* of Meindert Hobbema, represented by *A Farm in the Sunlight, A Wooded Landscape,* and *A View on a High Road;* and of Gerard Ter Borch, with *The Suitor's Visit.*

The Spanish exhibit is confined to El Greco, Velazquez, and Goya. *Saint Ildefonso* and *Saint Martin and the Beggar* show El Greco's mature style; the former canvas was once owned by the leading nineteenth-century French painters, Millet and Degas, a significant fact in connection with El Greco's influence upon modern art. The realism of Velazquez, which dominated Spanish painting after El Greco's death, is seen in *Pope Innocent X, The Needlewoman,* and *Portrait of a Young Man.* Goya, whose career extended into the nineteenth century, gloriously closed the great period in Spanish art. and his *Marquesas de Pontejos* and three other canvases were among Mellon's most cherished possessions.

British painting of the eighteenth and early nineteenth century was devoted to aristocratic portraits and idyllic landscapes. Reynolds, Gainsborough, Romney, Lawrence, and Raeburn are represented by several of their famous portraits of ladies of the period, and Constable and Turner appear with colorful scenes.

The United States group is restricted to portraits of the early Republican period. The public will perhaps find most interest in the *George Washington* of Gilbert Stuart, and *The Washington Family* of Edward Savage. A Copley, a Trumbull, a Chester Harding, a Benjamin West, and a Mather Brown, suggest rather than constitute a collection of early American art.

The policy of the gallery provides that no work of art shall be added to the permanent collection whose creator has not been dead at least twenty years. On the street floor, however, a special gallery has been provided for loan exhibitions of the works of living artists.

NATURAL HISTORY BUILDING

The four-story gray granite Natural History Building (*open, free, 8:45-5:15 Mon.-Fri., 8:45-12:45 Sat., 1:30-4:30 Sun. and holidays; closed Christmas and New Year's Day*), Constitution Avenue and 10th Street NW., one of the Smithsonian group and usually called the National Museum, contains the National Collection of Fine Arts and the world's largest collections of anthropological, biological, and geological material relating to the United States and its possessions. Displays containing some 17,000,000 specimens are visited by more than 800,000 persons a year. Designed by Hornblower and Marshall and completed in 1910 at a cost of $3,500,000, the neoclassic building is surmounted by a low dome above the columned entrance portico on the south side. North, east, and south wings extend out from the rotunda or south pavilion, while two L-shaped halls or gallery ranges form the outside walls of two inner courts.

The Rotunda, with an inside measurement of 71 feet, and the central portion of the North Wing, contain permanent art exhibits, a part of the NATIONAL COLLECTION, which includes the George P. Marsh collection of etchings, engravings, and books on art; the Harriet Lane Johnston collection of portraits by British masters; the Ralph Cross Johnson collection of paintings by Italian, French, English, Flemish, and Dutch masters; the William T. Evans collection of paintings and wood engravings by contemporary American artists; and the John Gellatly collection of pictures, glass, jewels, oriental specimens, and antique furniture. Outstanding items of the National Collection, on this floor, include works by Francia, Guardi, Maes, Rembrandt, Rubens, Titian, Ryder, George Inness, Winslow Homer, Blakelock, Copley, Duveneck, Gainsborough, Lawrence, Malbone, Romney, Twachtman, Julian Alden Weir, West, and Wyant. Temporary exhibits of art are shown on the basement floor.

In the East Wing, right from the rotunda, are three parallel halls that might have been called the HALLS OF EVOLUTION, exhibiting fossils and reconstructed extinct monsters. In the southernmost hall, facing the Mall, is a case labeled "the most perfect marine fossils ever found," containing Cambrian shellfishes more than 400,000,000 years old. In a case 120 feet long are shown the "dates" of origin and fossil remnants of various plant and animal forms; the last twelve inches only of this exhibit comes within the period of human life.

The central hall in the East Wing exhibits skeletons and restorations of prehistoric monsters. The mounted skeleton of a Diplodocus, 12 feet high and 70 feet long, is flanked on one side by a skeleton of the Basilosaurus, a whale of the Eocene epoch, the only mounted skeleton of its kind in existence, and on the other side by the bones of American mastodons, extinct ancestors of the elephant. There is a restoration of the armored Stegosaurus and of the flying reptile, Pteranodon, among many other exhibits in this enormous hall.

The third parallel hall, facing the eastern inner court, contains fossil plants, including those that contributed to the formation of coal in ,the Carboniferous period. At the eastern end of the East Wing is an exhibit of fossil birds and mammals.

The eastern hall of the L-shaped East Range contains stalactites and stalagmites from great American caverns, geyser deposits from the Yellowstone National Park, the 1,370-pound "ring meteorite" from Tucson, Arizona, and hundreds of other geological specimens. In the northeast corner of this floor is the HERBERT WARD AFRICAN ROOM, containing the English explorer's portrait sculptures of nearly a score of central African types—the chief, the slave, the witch doctor, and others. The collection is rounded out with thousands of weapons and other articles used by African natives.

The northern segment of the East Range has lifelike exhibits of foreign groups, portraying exotic habits of dress; the North Pavilion, directly back of the Rotunda, is devoted to an exhibit of Pell glass. Along the east wall of the North Wing are cases showing Asiatic ethnological materials, and the opposite side of the wing is devoted to Eskimo and Indian groups, with their physical characteristics, customs, and dress portrayed in a series of dioramas; a large collection of Indian baskets and pottery is included. Indian materials occupy the northern portion of the West Range.

The PHYSICAL ANTHROPOLOGY EXHIBIT, in the northwest corner on the main floor, contains a series of human skulls, including casts of such historic finds as the skull of the Heidelberg man, Neanderthal man, the man of Spy, and others. Skulls of Java man and Piltdown man are shown in relation to those of modern man.

The remainder of the first floor is given over to birds and mammals, in cases and dioramas showing the native habitat. The western portion of the West Range contains birds of every country and climate while the west end of the West Wing displays specimens brought back by Theodore Roosevelt from his African expedition of 1910. The three parallel halls in the West Wing show mounted mammals of all sizes and types.

On the second floor, the balcony surrounding the Rotunda is filled with an enormous collection of Worch pianos, while the East Wing, on south, east, and north sides, houses respectively, specimens of gems and minerals, ores, and building stone. The East Range on this floor presents antiquities of aboriginal Americans, including productions in stone, pottery, and metal. Thousands of arrowheads, hammer stones, and chipped flint knives are exhibited, as well as a lifelike group of Indians portrayed at work in a soapstone quarry in the vicinity of Washington. Stone effigies from the Mississippi mounds, pottery from all over the country, and beautiful silver and copper work are displayed.

On the east side of the North Wing is an area devoted to the antiquities of Mexico and Central America. The portal of the Temple of Warriors at Chichen-Itzá (Mexico) is outstanding for its massive architecture; a cast of the great stone Aztec calendar recalls the astronomical and mathematical advances of these ancient peoples, and various examples of Aztec sculpture show their progress in the fine arts. The opposite side of the North Wing contains Eurasian antiquities, including pottery and art objects from ancient Greece and Egypt, and miscellaneous artifacts representing the Stone and Bronze Ages of Europe.

The north portion of the West Range is devoted to a colorful exhibit of art textiles, and the west segment to displays of invertebrate animal life. In the north hall of the West Wing are exhibits of comparative anatomy, including human and animal embryos, skeletons of fishes, reptiles, birds, and mammals arranged to show the course of evolution, and a case in which the anatomy of man and that of the apes and monkeys are compared. The west end of the West Wing has collections of fishes and reptiles, and the south hall, fronting on the Mall, displays a collection of whales, including a 78-foot model of a sulphur-bottom whale and a 75-foot skeleton.

Upper floors are mainly occupied by offices and rooms for scientific study. Tucked away in inconspicuous places are the George Catlin paintings of Indians, made during the first half of the nineteenth century, and examples of Indian pottery and basketry. In the basement is space for temporary art exhibits, unclassified items collected during recent field expeditions, and an auditorium where free lectures on the Museum's work are given.

West of the foyer is the COLONIAL ROOM, with honey-colored pine wainscoting, straight-backed chairs, hooked rugs, and pewter dishes, dating from 1760 to 1780. The room, presented by Mrs. Gertrude D. Webster, is a faithful portrayal of an American living room of the Revolutionary period. Two other rooms in the basement exhibit materials on the flora and fauna of the District of Columbia.

ARMY MEDICAL MUSEUM AND LIBRARY

The Army Medical Museum and Library (*open, free, 8:15-5 weekdays*), among the largest of their kind in the world, are housed in a single red-brick building at the northwest corner of 7th Street and Independence Avenue SW. The museum, with more than 150,000 specimens, 70,000 photographs relating to the field of medicine, and about 300,000 microscopic slides, is visited annually by more than 100,000 persons.

The first floor of the museum contains exhibits on the structure of the human body, and collections of historic instruments and appliances. The historical section contains one of the world's largest collections of microscopes, stethoscopes, opthalmoscopes, and other surgical and medical equipment. Chinese and ancient Roman surgical instruments are shown as well as field sets used by American military surgeons in the Revolution, the War of 1812, and the Mexican War. The collection includes the field case, sword, and uniform of the surgeon of General Custer's command, most of whom were annihilated by Indians in 1876. The section on anatomy contains skeletons, models, dissections, and other specimens showing the normal aspects of human and animal bodies. The collection of human embryos contains specimens ranging from foetuses three weeks old to full-term babies; there are several sets of twins, and the American quintuplets, born in Kentucky in 1896.

The LIBRARY READING ROOM, on the first floor, gives access to the largest working medical library in the world, containing more than 5,000,000 items in all fields of medical science, including dental and veterinary medicine. The collection includes about 400,000 books, 534,000 pamphlets, 9,500 portraits and photographs, and an average of 1,800 current periodicals, 1,100 of them in foreign languages. It also has rare autographs, clippings, engravings, and manuscripts, and maintains a card index file of 2,000,000 items, in addition to special indices. Medical incunabula (printed before 1501) include 460 of some 600 known to exist. Special collections include biographical and bibliographical works in the field of medicine, and Federal, State, and municipal documents on sanitation, public health, and vital statistics. The Library's printed *Index Catalogue* (1880—) is used as a standard medical work throughout the world. Started with a collection of books in the office of the Surgeon General in 1818, the Library reached a maximum of development under the leadership of Surgeon General John Shaw Billings in the years following 1865.

On the second floor is the MUSEUM OF PATHOLOGY, containing specimens of abnormal, diseased, and injured organs. Exhibits illustrate results of cancer, tuberculosis, venereal diseases, war injuries, and diseases of the skin; there is a large display of abnormal babies, and a group illustrating some superstitions of medicine. In the east room, second floor, is a case containing a few tufts of Abraham Lincoln's hair, a plaster cast of his hand, a vertebra of John Wilkes Booth, Lincoln's assassin, and other relics.

The Army Medical Museum was founded in 1862 by Surgeon General William A. Hammond with some 7,000 specimens from the battlefields of the Civil War. The original purpose was to make it a museum for the study of war wounds, but its scope has enlarged with the years to include the whole medical field. It functions as a diagnostic center for the Army in general in studying diseases and injuries. Eggers and Higgins, New York architects, were engaged in 1941 to design a new $3,750,000 building for the Library and Museum, to be erected on a "centrally located" site.

ARTS AND INDUSTRIES BUILDING

The huge, square, red brick Arts and Industries Building (*open, free, 8:45-5:15 Mon.-Fri., 8:45-12:45 Sat., 1:30-4:30 Sun. and holidays*) of the Smithsonian group (sometimes called the Old National Museum), 9th Street and Independence Avenue SW., covering an area of 2⅓ acres, contains a majority of the 132,000 individual specimens owned by the Smithsonian Institution's Engineering and Industries Department, and most of the 508,000 specimens administered by the Division of History. The exhibits in this and the adjoining Aircraft Building are seen by more than 1,000,000 visitors a year.

Entered from the Mall through the central North Tower, the rectangular North Hall contains numerous historic relics—life masks of Lincoln, Admiral Peary's North Polar trophies, Washington memorabilia, medals of honor bestowed on statesmen, soldiers, scientists. On the west wall hangs the United States flag that waved over Fort McHenry in 1814 and inspired Francis Scott Key to write the "Star Spangled Banner." Suspended from the ceiling is the *Spirit of St. Louis,* the airplane in which Charles A. Lindbergh flew nonstop from New York to Paris in 1927.

Under the dome of the Rotunda, which adjoins this hall on the south and continues the historical exhibits, stands the plaster cast from which Thomas Crawford made his bronze statue of *Freedom* atop the Capitol dome.

Right of the North Hall, in the West North Range, is an exhibit of White House gowns, including those worn by "first ladies" from Martha Washington to Mrs. Herbert Hoover. Around this nucleus are other displays of costumes and jewelry illustrating American fashions in the eighteenth and nineteenth centuries.

Just south of this exhibit, in the Northwest Range, are coin collections arranged in cases, and suspended from the ceiling is the *Winnie Mae,* the airplane in which Wiley Post flew solo around the world in 7 days 19 hours (1931), and in which he later demonstrated the value of high-altitude flights.

In the Northwest Court, just east of the *Winnie Mae,* are exhibits relative to naval history, and in the West Hall, west of the Rotunda, are military history exhibits, including Curtiss airplanes suspended from the ceiling. In the Southwest Range, south and west of West Hall, are examples of mineral technology, including the story of white lead, the base of all paints, specimens of grinding materials, outstanding examples of the glassmaker's art, and, hung from the ceiling, the airplane in which C. P. Rogers made the first flight across the continent (82 hours) in 1911. The Southwest Court, just east of this exhibit, demonstrates the technology of coal.

The West South Range, in the southwest corner of the building, is devoted to the mining and processing of various ores and minerals such as copper, sulphur, cement, iron, gold, asphalt, and coal. A model of the giant pit of the Bingham Canyon (Utah) mine gives a realistic picture of open-pit mining methods. From the ceiling of this hall hang examples of gliders made in 1909 and 1930. A steel tower adjoining the halls of mining supports a clock belfry dating from 1797. It reaches to the gallery, where clock and watch exhibits are shown, including a 93-dial display clock. Behind the clock tower is a portion of a Roman aqueduct constructed nearly 2,000 years ago, with cement as hard as when it was set by Roman workmen.

The importance of textiles in human history is demonstrated in the South Hall exhibits, extending into the adjoining East South Range.

First World War bombers hang from the ceiling of the South Hall, and a sail plane is exhibited in East South Range, in which there are also models of early sewing machines invented by Elias Howe, Allen Wilson, and Isaac Singer. In this same hall is a swarm of bees in a glass beehive, seen busily at work during the summer months.

In the Southeast Range are the oldest gasoline automobiles in America, including cars built by Duryea, Haynes, and Olds, and the *Winton Bullet No. 1,* which established the first speed record (68 m.p.h.) at Daytona Beach in 1903. Other exhibits range through early electric broughams to streamlined contemporary cars. The Southeast Court, just west of this hall, is given over to woodworking industries, including examples of techniques in fighting forest fires.

East Hall, adjoining the Rotunda, is devoted to exhibits of land and air transportation. On the floor are the first steam locomotives operated in America, and models of many subsequent locomotives and railway carriages. A portion of the exhibit shows the evolution of carriage transportation from the creaking carts of Mexico and the rickshaws of China through the luxurious carriages of the nineteenth century. In the same room is a cross-section model of Rome's Appian Way, built in 312 B.C. Suspended overhead are aircraft illustrating the accomplishments of Stringfellow (1868), Lilienthal (1894), Gallaudet (1898), and Langley (1896-1903).

Northeast Range exhibits demonstrate the evolution of watercraft. Primitive dugout canoes hang on the walls, and there are beautiful models of sailing vessels of all sorts, and models of the earliest steamboats invented by Fitch, Fulton, Rumsey, and others. In the Northeast Court are exhibits of swords and firearms.

Power contrivances, exhibited in the East North Range, include mechanical and electrical machines basic in modern industry; some of them are arranged so they can be operated by visitors. Overhead is the Wright Brothers airplane, built in 1909, the first aircraft acquired by any government for military purposes; behind it hangs the first autogiro flown in America (1928).

Smaller arts and industries exhibits are assembled in gallery rooms around the building. These include the original telegraph and telephone instruments used by Morse and Bell, photographic equipment, boots and shoes, leather, rubber, clocks, typewriters, talking machines, musical instruments, and ceramics.

AIRCRAFT BUILDING

Adjoining the Arts and Industries Building on the west is the Smithsonian's Aircraft Building, a steel hangar erected in 1917 to provide room for experiments with Liberty engines for airplanes; after the war it was retained to house relics of American aviation.

Exhibits left of the entrance show birds and other flying creatures —the original aviators. There are Chinese kites, illustrations of ancient winged deities, a section of the Bell tetrahedral kite frame, and a Blue

Hill box kite used by the United States Weather Bureau. The development of the balloon by De Lana, Capello, the Montgolfiers, Charles, Blanchard, Wise, and others, is illustrated by pictures and models. More recent balloons are represented by the basket, equipment, and aerostatic apparatus with which Captain H. C. Gray ascended in 1927 to a height of 42,470 feet, and by the gondola of *Explorer II,* the Anderson-Stevens stratosphere balloon which in 1935 established the world's altitude record of 13.7 miles. In addition to the gondola of the *Pilgrim* (1925), the first commercial airship designed for helium gas, there are two models of dirigibles—the C-3, a nonrigid type used for patrol service during the World War, and a rigid Goodyear-Zeppelin of the type used by the United States Navy.

Models of pioneer flying devices are numerous, illustrating the advance of airplane design. They include a quarter-size design by Leonardo da Vinci for a muscle-powered aircraft in his manuscript of 1490; a one-twentieth size model of W. S. Henson's projected airliner of 1842; a model of Sir George Cayley's aircraft, proposed in 1843; the steam aircraft engine which John Stringfellow, first man to demonstrate successfully the principles of dynamic flight, sent to London for the first aeronautic exhibition in 1868; Alphonse Penaud's helicopter and planaphore of 1870-71; several models of Dandrieux' helicopter "butterflies" of 1879; Pichancourt's ornithopter of 1889; Lawrence Hargrave's compressed-air ornithopter of 1891, which flew 312 feet; sections of a model made and flown by Augustus Herring in 1895; a gasoline aircraft-engine built by de Dion Bouton in 1899; and an experimental model made by Dodge in 1900.

Six representative battleplanes of World War I, shown here, are the De Havilland-4, this specimen being the first American-made fighter plane of the war; a French Spad XIII—three American aces flew this plane, and shot down seven enemy ships; a Spad XVI, the observation plane flown by General William Mitchell, commander of the U.S. Air Forces in France; a German Fokker D-7, captured at Verdun in 1918; an F-5-L flying boat, used for patrol and convoy duty; and the 350-pound Martin K-3 of 1917, an extreme in smallness and lightness of construction.

There is a large collection of planes that made historic post-war flights, including the hull and engine of the NC-4, which in its New York-Azores-Lisbon-Plymouth flight of 1919 was the first aircraft to cross the Atlantic; the T-2, one of the first Fokker cantilever-wing monoplanes, which made the first nonstop flight across the continent (27 hours) in 1923; the *Chicago,* flagplane of the Army squadron that first flew around the world in 1924; the Loening amphibian *San Francisco,* one of the "good will" planes that visited 21 American republics in 1926-27; the *Polar Star,* in which Lincoln Ellsworth and Herbert Hollick-Kenyon flew across the Antarctic continent in 1935; and the little black racer which in 1925 won the Pulitzer and Schneider air race trophies. An aircraft of unique technical interest is the Berliner helicopter of 1924, a milestone in the development of a type that ascends vertically.

Other advances in aviation since 1900 are illustrated by more than 100 models, most of them built to the standard scale of 1 to 16. They include the "Early Birds" (1903-16), First World War planes of 1914-18, U.S. Army, U.S. Navy, transcontinental, transoceanic, air mail, exploration, speed and racing, and "flying wing" ships. Fifty engines and more than 100 propellers illustrate the growth of aircraft power.

SMITHSONIAN BUILDING

The red-brick Smithsonian Building (*open, free, 8:45-5:15 Mon.-Fri., 8:45-12:15 Sat., 1:30-4:30 Sun. and holidays*), facing north across the Mall on a line with 10th Street, was designed by James Renwick and built in 1852. Planned after the architect had visited Palestine, the building reflects the character of Near East buildings, having a confusion of towers, turrets, and pinnacles, an arcaded porte-cochère, and panels of red and blue tile set in ochre-colored brick. Besides housing the administrative offices of the Smithsonian Institution, it is the headquarters of the editorial department that issues Smithsonian publications, and of various art and science bureaus administered by the Institution.

The Institution was established by the $550,000 bequest of James Smithson, an Englishman who had never been to the United States, a gift that was not accepted by the Government until 1846, seventeen years after the donor's death. Since the original Smithson endowment other gifts have increased the funds to $2,000,000. In itself a private foundation that became a ward of the United States Government, the Institution is charged with the administration of seven Government bureaus. The National Museum, with exhibits in the Natural History, Arts and Industries, and Aircraft Buildings, is administered by the Institution, which also has charge of the National Collection of Art, housed in the Natural History Building and in the Freer Gallery of Art. The newest bureau of the Smithsonian is the National Gallery of Art, which is managed by a separate board of trustees. The National Zoological Park, the Bureau of American Ethnology, the International Exchange Service, and the Astrophysical Observatory are also administered by the Smithsonian.

In the great main hall of the Smithsonian Building is an "index exhibit," visualizing the Institution's program of diversified activities. In separate alcoves are dioramas, working models, specimens, and pictures showing the organization's work in the fields of astronomy, biology, geology, radiation and organisms, history, anthropology, engineering, industries, and art.

The SMITHSONIAN ROOM, off the main hall, contains a complete set of Smithsonian publications, occupying nearly 140 linear feet of shelf space. These volumes, with the facts and researches contained in them, have had a profound effect on the content of every dictionary, encyclopedia, and textbook published since the 1880's. On the same floor is the SMITHSONIAN LIBRARY, containing more than 900,000 volumes, some of which are shelved in the Arts and Industries Building, and some in the Smithsonian Deposit at the Library of Congress.

The GRAPHIC ARTS EXHIBIT, at the west end of the building, portrays various stages in the history of writing. The pictograph and hieroglyphic stage is represented by Indian and Aztec rock pictures, and by a rubbing of the celebrated Rosetta stone, with its inscriptions in Greek, Egyptian hieroglyphs and Egyptian demotic; this stone enabled Occidental savants to unlock the secrets of ancient Egyptian writings. There are illuminated medieval manuscripts, a page from the Gutenberg Bible (the first printed book), the press of William Bradford (1660-1752), the press used by Benjamin Franklin in 1726, and exhibits of present-day newspaper printing. In addition to writing and printing exhibits, there is a detailed comparative exhibition of the three principal branches of illustration—relief engraving, intaglio or engraving by incision, and lithography. In the section on intaglio etching are specimens by Dürer and Rembrandt.

Upstairs offices include those of the International Exchange Service, the Government's agency for the interchange of scientific, literary, and governmental publications with foreign governments and groups; the Bureau of American Ethnology, engaged in study of Amerindian cultures and the publication of reports and bulletins on their findings; and the National Herbarium, containing hundreds of thousands of pressed specimens of American and other flora, collected for research purposes. The Astrophysical Observatory, in a building adjoining the Smithsonian Building on the south, carries on its work in connection with solar observing stations in Chile, California, and New Mexico.

FREER GALLERY OF ART

The Freer Gallery (*open, free, 9-4 daily except Mon., Christmas, and New Year's Day*), NE. corner Independence Avenue and 12th Street SW., is housed in a rectangular granite building with a high basement and a lofty main story, entered through a central loggia of three arches accented by Doric pilasters, and surmounted by a stone balustrade. Designed by Charles A. Platt, the building was provided by Charles Lang Freer of Detroit to house his art collection, which was accepted by the Government and opened to the public in 1923. In the interior, 19 exhibition rooms are disposed around an arcaded corridor and an intimate central court with low plantings and a graceful fountain. Exhibition spaces are low, and vaulted ceilings are provided with skylights equipped with diffusing glass and adjustable curtains to meet special lighting requirements of the objects shown.

The WHISTLER COLLECTION, in the south corridor, serves somewhat as a preparation for the Asiatic exhibits, since Whistler, fascinated with oriental rules of composition and color tonality, attempted to adapt these rules and combine them with European traditions. Some of his paintings showing the Asiatic influence are *Blue and Gold: Valparaiso, Blue and Silver: Bognor, Blue and Silver: Battersea Reach,* and *The Music Room: Harmony in Green and Rose.*

The PEACOCK ROOM, in the southeast corner of the gallery, is a dining room decorated by Whistler for F. R. Leyland, London shipbuilder, to harmonize the surroundings with his painting *Rose and Silver: The Princess from the Land of Porcelain,* which hangs on one of the walls. The walls and shutters are decorated in turquoise blue and gold, based on the color and form of peacocks. The shelves, built to display Leyland's collection of oriental pottery, are lacquered, and the wall opposite Whistler's painting is decorated with golden peacocks having crystal eyes. The leftward peacock, superb in his dignity and elegance, represents Art. The other, disorderly, irate of countenance, his feathers stamped with the faces of coins, stands for Wealth. Whistler is said never to have considered these decorations as anything but a gaudy prank. Freer purchased the Peacock Room in 1904 for $63,000.

Adjoining the Peacock Room, on the east side of the building, are other Whistler compositions—pastels, water colors, etchings, lithographs, engravings, and drawings. Other artists included in Freer's American collection are Dewing, Thayer, Tryon, Homer, Sargent, and a single item by Ryder.

It has been said of the ASIATIC COLLECTION, in the western portion of the gallery, that it stands in the same important relationship to the art and archeology of the Far East as the collections of the Cairo Museum to that of Egypt. From China are examples of the creative expression of 42 centuries in paintings on album, scroll, panel, and screen, sculptures in wood and stone, ceramics, and bronzes. Among the paintings are works from the two great epochs in Chinese art—the Tang (618-907 A.D.) and Sung (960-1280 A.D.) dynasties. One painting is a portrait on silk of the philosopher Lao-tzu, attributed to Chou Fang, court painter of Emperor Te-Tsung (786-805 A.D.). Another painting, a realistic sketch of quails and grasses attributed to the artist-emperor Hui-Tsung (1100-1126), has attracted the attention of critics for its quiet penetration of the spirit of nature and its imaginative idealism suggesting wider vistas than the subject. Chinese sculptures—stone Buddhas, deities, trinities, and guardians—represent the Han dynasty (206 B.C.-220 A.D.), the Six dynasties (220-618 A.D.), and the Tang dynasty (618-907 A.D.)

The collection of Japanese screens demonstrates an art form distinct in the history of painting—the folding screens functioned as temporary walls in dwellings, but the mural decorator found it necessary to solve the problem of composing them in such a manner that each leaf would share in the harmony of the whole composition, yet stand as a self-sufficient unit when seen alone. One of the screens, *Pines on Wintry Mountains,* by Yeitoku (1543-90 A.D.), is outstanding. There are more screens by the same master, all retaining the luster of pigment and gold leaf characteristic of this artist. The grouping of Koyetsu screens is the largest in any collection. Among the treasures from the Byzantine world are Greek Biblical manuscripts ascribed to the fourth century.

Charles L. Freer, donor of the gallery buildings, its contents, and an endowment for upkeep and accessions, was a successful manufacturer of freight cars. In 1904, at the age of 46, he retired from business and devoted himself to study, travel, and the purchase of art works. His venture into the then unfamiliar realm of oriental culture enabled him to amass a significant collection of Far Eastern works, and his adroitness as a buyer enabled him to gather his outstanding collection of Whistler's works.

WASHINGTON MONUMENT

From its focal position on the Mall between the Capitol and the Lincoln Memorial, the towering marble shaft of the Washington Monument (*open 9-4 daily, except April 15-Oct. 31, when Sat. and Sun. hours are 9 a.m.-10:30 p.m., closed Christmas Day; elevator service at 5-minute intervals; adm. 10¢*) rises sharply against the Capital skyline. It is the tallest masonry structure in the world, rising 555 feet 5⅛ inches above the crest of a rolling knoll in the Monument Grounds. This landmark, visible for miles by day and floodlighted at night, is the first thing many people see in the Nation's Capital.

This immense masonry structure, weighing 81,120 tons, is a hollow shaft without a break in its surface except the relatively tiny east entrance door and the paired windows on each of the four sides at the 500-foot level. Resting on a foundation 126½ feet square and extending nearly 37 feet into the earth, the obelisk at the base has walls 15 feet thick and measures 55 feet 1½ inches on each face. It tapers gradually until the walls at the top of the shaft are 18 inches thick and 34 feet 5½ inches on each face. Built on a sturdy substructure, the Monument is estimated to be capable of withstanding a super-tornado blowing at the rate of 145 miles per hour. The exterior blocks of marble are laid in two-foot courses of squared stone, backed by rubble masonry, up to the 150-foot level. Upward to the 452-foot level the marble is backed with blocks of New England granite, and above that point it is built of through-and-through marble blocks. The pyramidion atop the shaft begins at the 500-foot level, and is surmounted with a 3,300-pound capstone. This stone is tipped with an aluminum pyramid 8.9 inches high, weighing 100 ounces, surrounded by 144 platinum-tipped lightning conductors; at the time it was made in 1884, this was the largest and costliest solid block of aluminum ever cast. It has inscriptions on each of the four sides—names of the commissioners completing the Monument, important dates in the Monument's history, names of the technical staff, and the Latin phrase *Laus Deo.*

The elevator and a flight of 898 steps ascend to a chamber within the base of the pyramidal cap. From the barred windows is a view equal to that from an airplane of the entire District of Columbia and parts of Maryland and Virginia. From these windows red lights shine at night as a warning to aircraft. A peculiarity of the Monument is the fact that it sometimes "rains" inside. Because of the relatively slow response of the stone walls to outside temperature changes, a sudden warm spell following cold causes a condensation of moisture in the upper air within the shaft, and a definite precipitation follows. The "rain" is sometimes so pronounced that attendants wear overshoes and raincoats.

Most visitors prefer to ride up in the elevator and walk down the steps to see the 202 carved tribute blocks within the shaft, but some prefer the more strenuous reverse order. Each State donated a stone, though some were given while present States were territories. Utah was still the Mormon State of Deseret when its stone was given, and this memorial is almost the only physical reminder of that period of its history. California announces itself as the "youngest sister of the Union." The Delaware inscription declares that this State, "First to Adopt, Will be the last to Desert the Constitution." The North Carolina stone commemorates the State's Mecklenburg Declaration of Independence in May, 1776. Indiana, on its inscription, "knows no North nor South, nothing but the Union."

Of 22 stones given by municipalities, 6 are from Massachusetts. The New Bedford stone, dated 1851, bears the carving of a whale, symbolic of the city's economic foundation at that time. One stone was given by American citizens in Foo Chow Foo, China, in 1857, heyday of the China trade and the clipper ship. There are stones sent by the governments of Brazil, China, Greece, Japan, Siam, Switzerland, Turkey, Wales, and the Free City of Bremen. The Turkish stone is engraved with a tribute by the Sultan's court poet. That from Japan, "exported from the harbor of Simoda" in 1853, was brought to Washington by Commodore Matthew Calbraith Perry as he returned from "opening the door" of Nippon. That from Greece puts George Washington on a level with Solon and Pericles. That from China rates the First President above a whole constellation of celestial patriots. One stone was brought by an American from the historic library in Alexandria, Egypt, and one was given by the Cherokee Nation. There are stones donated by churches, Sunday schools, temperance societies, State militias, municipal fire departments, literary and professional societies, labor and fraternal organizations, business organizations, and many others.

The history of the Monument begins in 1783, when the Continental Congress passed a resolution providing for "an equestrian statue of General Washington," and L'Enfant made a place for it in his city plan drawn eight years later. Washington objected to such expenditures from limited Government resources, and the matter was dropped. Nine days after Washington's death in 1799, John Marshall proposed a marble tomb in the city, but no appropriation was made after two years of quibbling in Congress. In 1816, Virginia proposed a tomb in Richmond. Congress then passed an act creating a tomb in the Capitol, which was built, and projected a monument in the city. Attempts to obtain congressional action on a monument were made in 1819 by Senator Goldsborough, in 1824 by Representative (later President) James Buchanan, in 1825 by President John Quincy Adams, and in 1832 by Henry Clay. This last failure led to the formation of the Washington National Monument Society, headed by George Watterston, librarian of Congress. The following year Robert Mills' design for a million-dollar monument won in a general competition. Less than $30,000 was collected by $1 subscriptions, and census-takers were enlisted to aid the drive in 1840, with little success. Early in 1848 Congress finally granted a site for the Monument on public grounds "not otherwise occupied." The President and the board of managers of the society chose L'Enfant's site, but moved it about 100 yards southwest to insure a better foundation. On July 4, 1848, the cornerstone was laid with elaborate Masonic rites, Grand Master French using the same trowel Washington had used in 1793 to lay the cornerstone of the Capitol.

Government approval and returning prosperity brought more contributions, but not enough. Alabama offered to provide a stone in lieu of monetary donation, and the plan was adopted. The call went out, and stones were enthusiastically provided by organizations, States, and foreign powers. A block of marble from the Temple of Concord at Rome was sent as the gift of Pope Piux IX. The anti-foreign, anti-Catholic American Party protested the "Papist" gift. One March night, 1854, a band of masked men overpowered the night watchman, stole the block of marble, and made away with it. It is believed that the "Know Nothings," as members of the American Party were called, smashed it with sledgehammers and dropped the fragments into the Potomac. This act of vandalism outraged the world, and donations of stones and money ceased. The society appealed to Congress for help, and the national legislature agreed that it would, on Washington's Birthday, 1855, appropriate $200,000 to complete the Monument. On the eve of this action, however, on the night of February 21, Washington "Know Nothings" broke into the offices of the society, seized the records and books, held an "election" to put their own members in office, and the next morning announced themselves in possession of the Monument. This monumental act of thievery caused Congress to table the motion giving aid to the society. Partly because of their piracy of the Monument, the "Know Nothings" fell into disrepute, failed to collect funds, and two years later collapsed as a political body. In 1859 the Washington National Monument Society was incorporated by Congress, with its old officers but no appropriation.

Approach of the Civil War caused abandonment of the Monument project when it stood as a square stub 150 feet high, its outer courses finished with Maryland marble. In 1876 Congress finally made an appropriation of $200,000, payable at the rate of $50,000 a year, and Army engineers under the leadership of Lieutenant Colonel Thomas L. Casey took over construction. The substructure was found to be inadequate, and the Monument had tilted from the vertical. The delicate task of shoring up the structure to make it plumb was accomplished, and a new slab of concrete 13½ feet thick was laid under the old foundation. The new base was complete by 1880.

At the time the Government took over the construction, George P. Marsh, United States Minister to Italy, disliking the Mills design, began his researches on the traditional proportions of obelisks. The Mills plan called for a decorated Egyptian shaft 700 feet high, mounted on a conic Babylonian base, and surrounded with a circular Greek temple 100 feet high and 250 feet in diameter. At Marsh's suggestion all decorations and base-plans were omitted, the height of the Monument was reduced to 10 times its baseline, and the squat cap of Mills' plan was replaced with a steeply inclined pyramidion of traditional design.

Unable for a time to obtain Maryland marble, the engineers laid 13 courses, or 26 feet, of matching Massachusetts marble, beginning at the 150-foot level. The Maryland marble, with which the remainder of the Monument is faced, has weathered to a slightly different tone, and is responsible for the "ring" sometimes noticed on the shaft. Work proceeded rapidly, and on December 6, 1884, in a howling gale, the capstone was finally set and the aluminum tip put in place. The story is told that when the aluminum pyramid was exhibited in New York and Washington, visitors requested the privilege of stepping over it, so they might say that they had stepped over the top of the Washington Monument, at that time the tallest structure in the world. The Monument has since been exceeded in height by structures of steel and concrete, but it remains the tallest piece of masonry.

On February 21, 1885, Robert Winthrop, who had delivered the formal address at the laying of the cornerstone 37 years before, dedicated the Washington Monument. It was opened to the public on October 9, 1888. The first elevator was a steam hoist, used until 1900, when the first electric elevator, requiring 5 minutes for the ascent, was installed. It was condemned in 1922 and replaced in 1927 by the present electrically operated car, which makes the ascent in 1¼ minutes, operating on a 5-minute schedule.

The Monument was cleaned for the first time in 1934-35 as a PWA project. A tubular steel scaffolding, said to have been the highest ever built, was erected around the shaft, and the Monument was scrubbed with steel brushes, sand, and water. The work took almost five months, and cost $100,000. While the scaffolding was up, a Richmond Republican on his way to New York saw the Monument, so the story goes, and hastened home to his political colleagues. "Something will have to be done about that man Roosevelt," he told them. "He has the Washington Monument all crated up and is going to ship it away!" A daring thief one night climbed the scaffolding and stole the platinum-tipped rods from the top of the Monument.

The marble obelisk, Washington's most conspicuous landmark and one of its most popular points of interest, visited annually by nearly

1,000,000 persons, was completed at a cost of almost $1,500,000, including society, Government, and other resources.

LINCOLN MEMORIAL

The temple-like white marble Lincoln Memorial (*open, free, 9 a.m.-9:30 p. m. daily, except 9-4:30 on holidays; closed Christmas and Labor Day*) stands at the west end of the Mall, weighting the Mall axis to counterbalance the Capitol at the other end. Although based on the Greek temple form ("coldly cribbed from the Parthenon," says one architect), the monument departs in several respects from the traditional conception. The entrance, in order to accent the termination of the Mall axis with a broad façade, is on the side instead of the end. The recessed attic varies from the classic pedimented roof, and there are other lesser variations.

Set in a circular lawn 1,200 feet in diameter, the Memorial is placed on a 14-foot granite wall and approached by a flight of steps 130 feet wide. The broad stairway is flanked by mammoth cheek-blocks surmounted by classical urns. The superstructure, of white Colorado marble, is approximately 80 feet high, and the walls are enclosed by a peristyle colonnade measuring 118 by 188 feet. Each of the 36 fluted Doric columns, representing the States of the Union at the time of Lincoln's death, is 44 feet high and 7 feet 5 inches in diameter. The names of the States are inscribed in a frieze above the columns between wreaths in bas-relief. On the attic parapet are 48 festoons in bas-relief symbolizing the present States, with their names carved beneath. The columns, entablature, and walls are tilted inward to avoid the optical illusion of bulging at the top.

Throughout the interior, the floors and wall base are of pink Tennessee marble. Walls are of Indiana limestone, and the ceiling is made of thin marble panels, treated with a saturation of beeswax to make them translucent, and supported by a framework of bronze girders. Thus the daylight reaching the inner hall through the eastern opening is supplemented by a quiet glow diffused through the ceiling.

The main chamber, 60 feet wide, 70 feet long, and 60 feet high, is centered by the heroic STATUE OF ABRAHAM LINCOLN, by Daniel Chester French. This realistic figure, seated in a huge chair with fasces adorning the front of the arms, faces out through the colonnade toward the Washington Monument and the Capitol. It is 19 feet high, and the 12½-foot armchair is mounted on a high pedestal. The sculpture, of crystalline Georgia marble, is constructed of 20 blocks so perfectly interlocked that the statue seems one huge monolith; Picirilli Brothers, stone cutters, required 4 years to complete the work from French's model. At night the figure is illuminated from above, endowing the face and figure with impressive highlights and shadows.

In the north and south halls (each 38 by 63 feet) are bronze plaques giving the text of Lincoln's Gettysburg Address and Second Inaugural Address. Mural canvases, *Emancipation* and *Reunion,* painted in subdued colors by Jules Guérin, portray symbolic groups typifying the principles held by Lincoln.

Efforts to erect a memorial to Abraham Lincoln began in 1867, two years after his assassination, when Congress incorporated the Lincoln Monument Association and called upon Clark Mills, American sculptor, for tentative plans. Partly because of political embroilments, nothing came of this effort. In 1911 Congress created the Lincoln Memorial Commission, with former President William Howard Taft as chairman. The Commission chose the memorial site, then a swamp, against the advice of Speaker Cannon, who warned that "the malarial ague from these mosquitoes would shake it to pieces." Henry Bacon was chosen as the architect, and the memorial was erected at a cost of $2,940,000. The cornerstone was laid on February 12, 1915, the 106th anniversary of Lincoln's birth, and formal dedication services were held on Memorial Day, 1922.

The Memorial has had its critics, those who think a cold Greek temple an incongruous monument to a man of Lincoln's warmth and human kindness, and those who find the realistic Lincoln statue out of harmony with the abstractness of the memorial structure. Some think the attic too high for good proportion, and some believe that the rounded mass of boxwood planted around the base detracts from a firm connection with the earth—two observations that may be related. However, the 1,200,000 persons who visit the Memorial each year apparently find no inconsistency in this combination of an abstract ideal with the individual character of a rugged national hero.

The shallow rectangular REFLECTING POOL and the small transverse Rainbow Pool at its eastern end, form a shimmering vista of water nearly 2,000 feet long, in which the tall shaft of the Washington Monument is clearly reflected on still days. The Rainbow Pool is so called by reason of its 200 jets, throwing water upward and inward, breaking into a spray and producing a prismatic effect. Turned on only during special celebrations, the spray is sometimes illuminated at night. The Reflecting Pool, intended primarily for decorative landscaping, has taken its place in the city's recreation—it is used in warm weather for model sailboat races and flycasting contests, and in winter, on the few occasions when the ice is thick enough, it is opened for skating.

NAVY AND MUNITIONS BUILDINGS

The four-story stucco NAVY BUILDING (*open only to pass holders*), Constitution Avenue between 17th and 19th Streets NW., is a factorylike Government building with 10 wings reaching back from Constitution Avenue almost to the Reflecting Pool. Built during World War I as an emergency structure, it continues as the crowded headquarters of the Navy Department. The eight-wing MUNITIONS BUILDING (*open only to pass holders*), stretching between Constitution Avenue and the Reflecting Pool from 19th to 21st Streets

NW., is a War Department relic of the same period. Both are scheduled for demolition when new space can be provided, and this portion of the Mall will be opened.

THE LOCK KEEPER'S HOUSE

On the southwest corner of Constitution Avenue and 17th Street NW., is all that remains physically of L'Enfant's plan for a canal through the Capital City—a diminutive two-story building of dressed fieldstone with end chimneys, a central entrance between two first-floor windows, and twin dormers on north and south façades. Charmingly proportioned, it was built about 1835 and served as residence of the lock keeper. Remodeled inside, it is now used as a lodge for U.S. Park Police and as a public rest station.

ARLINGTON MEMORIAL BRIDGE AND WATER GATE

The low-arched spans of the Arlington Memorial Bridge reach across the Potomac River just southwest of the traffic circle around the Lincoln Memorial. Considerations of safety for airplanes using the Washington Airport, and the desire to assure an unimpaired view of the Lincoln Memorial at one end and the memorial entrance to Arlington National Cemetery and Arlington House at the other, led the architects, McKim, Mead, and White, to make use of low, flowing lines for the entire structure. Classic balustrades, lamp standards placed at sidewalk level, and simple monumental approaches contribute to the design as a whole, and harmonize with the architectural surroundings.

The bridge has nine segmental arches, their spans increasing in length from 166 feet at the ends to 184 feet at the central arch, and in height from 28 feet at the ends to 35 feet at the center, giving the bridge a slightly arched overall appearance. The reinforced concrete framework of the structure is veneered with North Carolina granite, except the central arch, a steel draw-span painted to resemble stone, which opens for the passage of vessels. This operation is performed by a bascule of two leaves, each 92 feet long and weighing 6,000 tons, raised by powerful electric motors in one minute. Siren blasts and the flashing of red lights warn traffic before the draw is opened. The bridge piers on both sides are decorated with bas-relief medallions of eagles, flanked by decorative fasces. These, the conventionalized bison heads ornamenting the keystones of the arches and the eagles on the west pylons are by the sculptor C. Paul Jennewein. The 90-foot roadway, with two 15-foot walks and six 10-foot vehicular lanes, is paved with cobblestones, except the central draw-span, which is covered with light-weight asphalt.

The WATER GATE, due west of the Lincoln Memorial and flanking the Arlington Bridge on the District end, is a segmental arc of 40 granite steps, 206 feet wide at the top and 230 feet wide at the base, forming a decorative buttress between the bridgehead and a curved, balustraded masonry ramp carrying a roadway from the Lincoln Memorial toward Rock Creek Park. A curved portion of Riverside Drive, running under the Arlington Bridge and the Rock Creek Parkway ramp, skirts the Water Gate steps. Opposite the steps, which serve as seats in this convex amphitheater, a barge with an orchestra shell is anchored in summer, and in this setting the National Symphony Orchestra has presented summer evening concerts since 1935. Flotillas of canoes push in around the barge during concerts, and the roadway, the steps, and the surrounding area is filled with seatholders and standees.

The Arlington Bridge and Water Gate, though they have come to occupy a separate place in the thoughts of Washington people and visitors, are a part of a comprehensive larger plan. The bridge, the Water Gate, the Rock Creek Parkway ramp, the extension of Riverside Drive, and the monumental entrance to Arlington National Cemetery on the Virginia side are an integral portion of the plan for completing the Mall and connecting it by a diagonal axis to the cemetery across the Potomac (see *Arlington*). The bridge also connects this portion of the city with the Mount Vernon Memorial Boulevard (US 1 to the south) and with US 50 to the near-by town of Arlington and points west. Daniel Webster proposed such a bridge, and the McMillan Commission drew it into plans prepared in 1901. Construction was started in 1926 and completed in 1932 at a cost of $14,-750,000.

President's Square

Streetcars: Westbound—Rosslyn, N. Y. & 15th NW., Cabin John, Friendship Heights, Potomac Park, Mt. Pleasant, 19th & F NW.   Eastbound—Kenilworth, Union Station, 17th & Penna. SE., Lincoln Park, 13th & D NE., Brookland, Catholic University.
Busses: Westbound—18th & Penna. NW., Chevy Chase Circle, Riverside Stadium, Hains Point.   Eastbound—22nd & Shepherd NE., 4th & E NW., 15th & Penna. NW., Treasury.
Taxis: First zone.

The President's Square, including the White House Grounds, Lafayette Square, and the Ellipse, is flanked on the east by the Greek-Revival Treasury Building and on the west by the Victorian State Department Building. Only the north grounds of the White House, one of Washington's premier points of interest, are open to visitors, and a limited portion of the President's mansion can be seen by the public. The Ellipse, a tree-bordered circle due south of the White House, is mainly a recreational area, with baseball diamonds, hockey and football fields. Park police find it necessary to post "No Short Cuts" signs to prevent Government employees from treading out paths across the Ellipse. On the north border of this circular park is the square stone stub of the ZERO MILESTONE, from which all distances from the Nation's Capital are supposed to be computed. Tennis, badminton, and horseshoe courts occupy park areas east of the Ellipse, within view of the columned Commerce Department Building.

THE WHITE HOUSE

The White House, Executive Mansion of the United States, 1600 Pennsylvania Avenue, is surpassed by none of the world's great residences of state in charm and dignity. In its design and setting, any suggestion of formal display has been deliberately avoided. Its annals, too, lack the highlights and shadows with which more lavish expenditure, hoarier age, and bloody tales of court intrigues have endowed England's Windsor Castle, the Quirinal in Rome, and Moscow's Kremlin. Instead, its century-old walls memorialize the beginnings of a great Republic and the first struggles of its citizens toward self-expression; visitors from all nations find delight in its graceful simplicity and purity of line. The White House, indeed, is one of the few buildings in Washington that have avoided the barbs of architectural criticism. It is the oldest public structure in the Federal City and the most beautiful of its period.

The White House is connected with the Capitol, a mile and a half to the east-southeast, by Pennsylvania Avenue. Across the avenue to the north is Lafayette Square; on the east, the White House is flanked by the Treasury, and on the west by the State Department Building. To the south is the Ellipse, with its girdle of magnificent trees and its four baseball diamonds. From Pennsylvania Avenue, the tip of the Washington Monument is visible above its roof. The American flag flies over the White House except when the President is away from Washington.

The President's Square originally contained approximately 80 acres. It was a rough piece of barren land notable only for its view of the Potomac—long since cut off—and the unhealthy marshes at its southern border. In 1800, the present grounds were marked off, but were not enclosed until the administration of John Quincy Adams. Gardens, in which President Adams spent many hours, took shape, and seedlings were set out. Martin Van Buren, when he became President in 1837, provided for stables, fountains, stone walls, and iron railings. Rich topsoil for flower beds was collected, and enough native and exotic plants were obtained to do credit to a royal English garden. Rare specimens, such as golden madder and enchanter's nightshade, democratically shared space with peas, parsnips, and York cabbage.

By 1849 the ground south of the President's House had been drained, and two years later the Commissioner of Public Buildings, "at the suggestion of several prominent gentlemen of the city and by appropriation of President Fillmore" secured the services of Andrew Jackson Downing, landscape designer, to lay out the White House grounds.

The grounds again profited by an era of prodigal spending when President Grant took office. The ugly iron fences along the walks of the north grounds were removed, to allow for a broad sweep of lawn. East Executive and West Executive avenues were cut through, and the lowlands at the south were filled in and planted with trees and shrubbery; these improvements were made by George G. Brown, known as the "father of the Washington park system."

The present grounds comprise a fenced and wooded park of 18 acres, which the Mansion itself, with the adjoining Executive Office, divides into the North and South Grounds. The main approach is along a curved driveway through the North Grounds, from gateways on Pennsylvania Avenue (*usually open*). The drive passes under a porte-cochère to the central portal of the White House. On visiting days, entrance to the Mansion is by way of the gate on East Executive Avenue; official visitors use the West Executive Avenue entrance. As the South grounds are now considered the private gardens of the President, the two South Executive Avenue entrances are closed to the public except on special occasions.

The south façade of the White House rises from a mass of shrubbery and flowers, at the upper end of a long vista over the "Presidential Ellipse," past the Washington Monument and through Potomac Park to the south, with the Jefferson Memorial in the distance. To the west of the façade are elaborate flower gardens, tennis courts, and clustered trees and thickets, one of which conceals the "President's Walk." On the east are small groves and gardens and an oblong pool, bordered by evergreens. A paved driveway curves from the two gateways up to the south portico.

Prior to the first administration of President Cleveland, the South Grounds were occasionally opened to the public, but now they are seldom open except on Easter Monday for the annual "egg rolling." On this occasion, children bring colored Easter eggs in festive baskets of plaited and dyed straw; the President and his wife appear and greet their young guests, and the United States Marine Band and other service bands furnish music. Grown people accompanying children are admitted to the rolling in the morning; but adults alone, only later in the day.

The festivities consist mainly of rolling eggs down the sloping terraces, so that they will collide with one another on the lawn below, as in marbles or the old game of bowls. Younger children occupy themselves with toy balloons, and, after the rolling, they all eat their lunches on the lawn and run about in popular childish games. Children congregate also in the Zoological Park, where the steep slope below the Lion House permits old-style egg rolling, a perilous descent for the egg, which (being boiled) is eaten as soon as it is cracked. As far back as President Johnson's time, children rolled their Easter eggs on the White House lawn. Others used the eastern lawn of the Capitol Grounds until officials, solicitous for the grass, forbade the performance here.

The White House trees represent some 80 varieties, many of them exotic, and are the careful selection of generations. Three elms beneath which James and Dolly Madison led open-air cotillions still thrive here. Two of the oaks were standing when the British set fire to the White House in 1814. The towering American elm on a knoll at the east end of the South Lawn began life as a sapling at the home of John Quincy Adams in Massachusetts. Near by is a group of magnolias, brought by Andrew Jackson from his Tennessee home and replanted here in memory of his wife. In 1878, Rutherford B. Hayes planted an American elm near the western entrance to the North Grounds. Grover Cleveland's bride planted a blood-leaf Japanese maple—apparently attracted by its rather macabre name, for her husband protested that he "could see no sense of planting a tree for the name of the thing."

Near the north front entrance are scarlet oaks planted by the grandchildren of President Benjamin Harrison. President McKinley also planted a scarlet oak near the present Executive Office. Another oak, from Russia, has a curious history. Senator Charles Sumner once sent to the Czar of Russia some acorns from an oak near the tomb of Washington at Mount Vernon. Many years later, an oak on Tsarina Island in the Neva River in Russia bore the legend that it grew from an acorn from Washington's tomb. American Ambassador Hitchcock sent back some acorns from this tree for planting in the White House grounds, but the resulting tree proved to be of a Russian species.

President Harding planted a European beech; Mrs. Harding an elm and a group of magnolias. Mrs. Coolidge presided at the planting of a weeping birch, a memorial to the mothers of Presidents of the United States. President Hoover assisted in the planting of an American elm, in memory of the two-hundredth anniversary of Washington's birth; and of a white oak from Lincoln's birthplace and a cedar from Washington's boyhood home. A California redwood was Mrs. Hoover's contribution.

The White House stands today practically as its designer, James Hoban, planned it in 1792, on the site designated by Major L'Enfant in his original plans for the Federal City. Hoban's design has many characteristics of the late eighteenth-century Renaissance mansion popular in England and Ireland when this Republic was young.

From its north approach, the White House appears to be a two-story edifice of simplicity and spaciousness, but not of great size. As a matter of fact, the building, exclusive of its terraced galleries at either side, is 170 feet long, 85 feet wide, and 58 feet high. Besides the visible two stories, it has a basement at ground level and an attic concealed by a crowning balustrade.

There has been much speculation as to how the White House first got its name: whether because of its walls of white sandstone from the Aquia quarries of Virginia; from a coat of gleaming white paint, such as it now unvaryingly wears; or from the Southern tradition of the plantation house, frequently a "White House." The President's Palace, as it was first called, and the Capitol, both of sandstone, may have been painted white immediately after completion but, so far, no absolute proof of this has been found. The "shining objects" described by John Cotton Smith, Congressman from Maine, in December, 1800, may have been simply the sandstone structures—as he says, "in dismal contrast with the scenes around them." The white paint applied to the reconstructed "President's house" after the fire of 1814 did not prompt its familiar name, as reference was made to the "White House" in accounts of the fire. When President Madison gave his first New Year's Reception in the repaired edifice, January 1, 1818, he gave it the name of Executive Mansion, which it bore officially until 1901-02, when President Theodore Roosevelt proposed to elevate and dignify the popular name. By authority of an act of Congress, the name "White House" was used thereafter on all executive stationery and documents.

All four sides of the White House were designed to give symmetry and balance, but the northern and southern façades differ in many particulars. The dominant feature of the north front is an impressive Colonial portico with four Ionic columns, which forms a porte-cochère and a porch. The unadorned walls on either side of the portico are relieved by symmetrical rows of windows. This simple architectural device gives the façade, with its regular form and mass, an appearance of unostentatious scale and graceful domesticity. The larger windows on the main floor are alternately crowned with triangular and segmental pediments, with supporting console brackets and bracketed sills. A simpler treatment subordinates the windows of the second story.

The architectural treatment of the south façade is more generous, because of the additional basement story, with its rusticated stone work, and the Ionic pilasters that line the walls between the windows. The façade is broken by a columned portico, semicircular in form, which looks down upon the gardens and gently sloping lawn. The portico is informally furnished and makes an attractive lounging place, with direct access to the Red Room and Green Room on the main floor.

From the east and west façades, at the ground floor, are long, low galleries, whose terraced roofs form spacious promenades at the main-floor level. The façades above the galleries are treated alike, with Palladian windows opening on the terraces and arched or lunette windows at the second story. The roof promenades, known as the East and West Terraces, are miniature formal gardens, with tubbed trees and flower boxes. Beneath the West Terrace is the swimming pool built, partly by subscription, for the use of President Franklin D. Roosevelt.

The two galleries are cleverly constructed to emphasize the difference between the northern and southern fronts of the White House. As seen from Pennsylvania Avenue, they scarcely rise above the crest of the surrounding ground, thus maintaining the rectangular effect of the north façade; from South Executive Avenue, however, they give the impression of low, colonnaded wings added to a rectangular façade. They appear symmetrical, but actually the east gallery extends 215 feet, and the west only 165 feet, from the White House proper. The Executive Office Building, at the end of the west gallery and aligned with it, somewhat minimizes this discrepancy. Both galleries are 35 feet wide. The Executive Office Building is approximately 140 feet long and 100 feet wide. It conforms in design and color with the White House, with which it is connected by a corridor beneath the West Terrace.

At the East Executive Avenue entrance (*open 10-2 Mon.-Fri., 10-1 Sat.*), used by visitors without invitation, is a foyer, opening on the south into a formal rose garden and on the north to the driveway. In this foyer are the first four of a series of Presidential portraits, some of which hang in nearly every room of the Mansion: *John Adams,* by G. P. A. Healy; *James Madison* and *Andrew Johnson,* by E. F. Andrews; and *Ulysses S. Grant,* by Le Clair.

The corridor gives access to four rooms that are used principally for the display of White House curios and relics. Among the Presidential portraits in the corridor are *Benjamin Harrison,* by Eastman Johnson; *Millard Fillmore,* by G. P. A. Healy; and *Rutherford B. Hayes,* by Daniel Huntington.

The LIBRARY, the first of the four rooms, contains books presented to the White House during recent years by American publishers. In the room across the corridor from the Library are displays of White House china used during successive administrations since Washington's time, all appropriately labeled. Here is a set of Mount Vernon Cincinnatus plates; a sugar bowl and coffee saucer of Van Braam china that belonged to Martha Washington; a celery glass used by John and Abigail Adams. A fruit bowl with three supporting figures in French bisque is supposed to have been saved by Dolly Madison when the British burned the White House. Andrew Jackson's great coffee cup is here, and some of his American china decorated with a motif of Southern foliage. Van Buren's table is represented by a water pitcher; Zachary Taylor's by a Sheffield candlestick; and the John Quincy Adams family by some of their Saxonware. The purple-bordered Haviland-Limoges pieces, bearing the arms of the United States, are from the table of Abraham Lincoln. The Woodrow Wilson china is from a set of 1,700 pieces made in New Jersey, the first full dinner service of domestic manufacture to grace the Presidential table.

In the elliptical room on the south side of the corridor, known as the DIPLOMATIC RECEPTION ROOM, is a clock salvaged from the San Francisco earthquake and fire of 1906. From this room President Franklin D. Roosevelt has broadcast many of his fireside chats and other radio messages. Four Presidential portraits are on the walls: *Ulysses S. Grant,* by Henry Ulke; *Zachary Taylor* and *James A. Garfield,* by E. F. Andrews, and *Chester A. Arthur,* by Daniel Huntington. The fourth room, opening from the Diplomatic Reception Room and not directly from the corridor, contains furniture used in the White House by Presidents Johnson and Arthur.

The corridor, which is closed to the public at this point, continues through to the West Terrace, past a private staircase and service rooms. A wide stairway leads from the corridor to the main floor. The East Room, to the right of a small landing, is open to the public, but the Reception Hall, to the left, is closed to visitors.

The kitchens are in the section of the lower floor not open to the public. The original kitchen was in the central part of the basement, directly below the north portico. It had a huge fireplace in its western wall, with cranes for pots and kettles and long-handled skillets hanging ready for use; a great brick oven for roasting simultaneously a small flock of turkeys or a few suckling pigs; a small oven for pastry; and several Dutch ovens. A visitor during Fillmore's day records that "the fine state dinner for 36 people every Thursday" was cooked in the huge fireplace. Later, the Fillmores set up one of the then novel patent cooking ranges to the dismay of the White House cook, who could not master the drafts in the new contraption. Mrs. Lincoln had the kitchen removed to the northwestern part of the basement, presumably because the building of the north portico deprived the old kitchen of daylight. Mrs. Benjamin Harrison had the kitchen floors done in cement and tiles.

During the summer of 1935, the kitchen was extensively remodeled by the National Park Service, Department of the Interior, which has physical supervision of the White House. Funds for the purpose were allocated from the PWA and, at the President's request, relief workers were used as far as possible. The culinary department was completely modernized. Underground storerooms were built beneath the west driveway, with refrigerated compartments for meats and fish and other compartments for staples. A wine vault and a vault for White House silver were constructed. The immense old kitchen is now divided into three rooms, refitted with walls of Carrara glass and work surfaces of Monel metal and stainless steel. Gas stoves have given way to commodious electric ranges, and the rest of the kitchen equipment to electrically operated devices.

A dumb-waiter conveys the prepared food to the butler's pantry, between the two dining rooms on the main floor. After the food is served, the kitchen utensils are returned to the basement, and, at the close of the meal, the dishes go to an electric dishwasher on the third floor. The various units are so arranged that a state dinner or an informal tea may be served with equal efficiency. There is a small but completely equipped kitchen on the third floor for emergencies.

Recent changes include a steward's room and a carpenter shop beneath the west driveway and, on the lower floor, a servants' dining room, servants' restrooms, a furniture storage room, and a housekeeper's office. Across the corridor from the kitchen, the doctor's office has been remodeled and a dispensary put in.

On the main floor, the great East Room occupies the entire eastern wing. Balancing it on the west are the State and private dining rooms, with their attendant services. Between, and opening on the wide front porch, is the Reception Hall. Running from the East Room to the State Dining Room—behind the Reception Hall—is the spacious central corridor, from which open three formal reception rooms: the Red Room, the Blue Room, and the Green Room. The floor of the corridor is of Joliet limestone; its buff and white walls are decorated with pilasters and a classic cornice.

The main RECEPTION HALL, separated from the corridor by six marble columns, is used only by members of the President's family and their guests, and for receiving visitors of state. Inlaid in the floor, in yellow bronze, is the Presidential seal, and in an ellipse of 48 stars are bronze figures giving the dates of the laying of the cornerstone (1792) and of the reconstruction of the Mansion (1902). On either side of the fanlighted main portal are windows hung with red-silk draperies. On the walls are these portraits: *William McKinley,* by W. D. Murphy; *William H. Taft;* and *Woodrow Wilson,* by F. Graham Cootes. In the lobby are Charles Hopkinson's *Calvin Coolidge* and a portrait of *Warren G. Harding.*

The EAST ROOM, the "great hall" in the White House, the scene of major state gatherings, is magnificently proportioned—87½ feet long and approximately 45 feet broad. Three immense crystal chandeliers, with thousands of glittering pendants, hang from an elaborately decorated plaster ceiling. The color scheme is predominantly white and gold. The walls are of paneled wood, enlivened with Corinthian pilasters and bas-relief panels (by the Piccirilli brothers), showing scenes from Aesop's Fables. The floors are of oak parquetry. On the walls are two notable pictures—full-length portraits of George and Martha Washington. The painting of the first President, rescued by Dolly Madison when the British burned the White House, is believed to be a copy of the one by Gilbert Stuart. The portrait of Martha Washington was done by E. F. Andrews.

The East Room is rich in memories of assemblies, festive and tragic. In earlier days many Presidents used it as a reception room for New Year's Day visitors. Here guests were entertained following the marriage of the President's daughter, Maria Hester Monroe, to Samuel Lawrence Gouverneur, in 1820, and here Lafayette was received by Monroe in 1824. Other notable weddings that took place in this room were those of the first White House bride, the niece of Dolly Madison; of Nellie Grant to Algernon Sartoris, in 1874; of "Princess" Alice Roosevelt to Nicholas Longworth, in 1906; and of Jessie Woodrow Wilson to Francis B. Sayre, in 1913. Buchanan received in the East Room the first embassy from Japan, and the Prince of Wales, later Edward VII. During the Civil War, the East Room saw many famous Union generals at the New Year's receptions.

Funeral services were held here for Presidents William Henry Harrison and Zachary Taylor, and here the bodies of Abraham Lincoln, William McKinley, and Warren G. Harding lay in state before being carried to the Capitol.

A doorway in the east wall opens upon the promenade roof of the east gallery. The west wall has three doors, through one of which visitors enter from the basement stairway. The doors to the central corridor and the formal rooms adjoining are closed to the public except by special permission, usually obtained by a card from a Senator or Representative. The rest of the main floor is not generally accessible.

The GREEN ROOM, in Monroe's day a cardroom, is used for informal receptions. Doors of inlaid mahogany lead to the East Room and the Blue Room. The Green Room, some 30 feet long and 23 feet wide, has but one window, which opens by a glass door upon the porch of the south portico. The latest of the Green Room's many redecorations was in the Coolidge administration. It is now furnished mainly in Early American, with green silk damask wall coverings and curtains, and a green Aubusson rug, bearing the coat of arms of the United States. The white marble mantel was brought from England in 1792, for later installation. The portraits are of *James K. Polk, Martin Van Buren,* and *John Quincy Adams,* by G. P. A. Healy; and *Thomas Jefferson,* by E. F. Andrews.

The BLUE ROOM, generally considered the most beautiful room in the White House, is decorated in the style of the First French Empire. It was once widely known as the "Elliptical Salon," because of the ellipse formed by continuing the curve of the southern wall. The walls are finished with white enameled wainscoting and covered with heavy, corded, blue-silk brocatelle. Window draperies are of the same material, with gold fret motifs embroidered at top and bottom, and stars in the valances. Above the valances are poised American eagles. The room is lighted with a crystal chandelier, supplemented by wall sconces. The furniture has white and gold woodwork and blue and gold upholstery. A white marble mantel, decorated with sheaves of marble arrows, tipped and feathered in bronze, dates from 1792. The mantel clock, decorated with a seated figure of Minerva, is said to have been given by Lafayette to George Washington.

The Blue Room is used customarily for state receptions such as the annual Army and Navy, diplomatic, judiciary, and congressional receptions. Ambassadors paying their first formal visits are received in this room. Two doors lead east to the Green Room, one west to the Red Room, and one north to the main corridor.

The marriage of Maria Hester, daughter of President Monroe, took place here in 1820; that of John, son of President John Quincy Adams, in 1826; of Elizabeth, third daughter of President Tyler, in 1842; of President Cleveland and Frances Folsom, in 1886; and of Eleanor Wilson to W. G. McAdoo, in 1914. Here were held the brilliant receptions to the Infanta Eulalia, daughter of the Queen Regent of Spain, in 1893, and to Prince Henry of Prussia, brother of the German Kaiser, in 1902.

The RED ROOM, identical with the Green Room in size and shape, was formerly known as the "Washington Room," because it possessed the famous Washington portrait now in the East Room. The wainscoting is enameled in white; the wall covering is of damask with red draperies; the furniture is upholstered in red damask; and the parquetry floor is covered by a red Aubusson rug. The chandelier is of bronze, and the mantel is similar to that in the Green Room. The two west doors lead to the State Dining Room, and the southern door to the porch.

Under earlier administrations, the Red Room was used as a reception room preceding state dinners, such as those in honor of the Vice President, the Supreme Court, the Diplomatic Corps, the Cabinet, and the Speaker of the House of Representatives. It is now used as a reception room for smaller dinners. President Hayes took the oath of office here late Saturday night, March 3, 1877 (the fourth fell on a Sunday).

On the east wall is the portrait of *Theodore Roosevelt,* by John Singer Sargent; and on the west wall, that of *Grover Cleveland,* by Eastman Johnson.

The STATE DINING ROOM has a great horseshoe table, around which more than a hundred persons may be seated. With the exception of the East Room, this is the largest room in the White House, occupying almost the entire southern end of the main floor, with windows looking out on the south and west. Paneled English oak, after the late-Georgian manner, covers the walls, which are adorned with carved pilasters surmounted by a carved cornice. The ceiling is elaborately decorated in plaster bas-relief, with a central silver chandelier. On the western wall is a great fireplace and chimney piece of cut stone. The velvet window draperies, upholstery, and rug are all of green. The portrait of *Abraham Lincoln,* by G. P. A. Healy, was set on the north wall by President Hoover.

A door in the northwest corner, concealed by a painted screen, leads to the butler's pantry, and another in the northeast corner, to the private dining room. Of the three doors in the east wall, one is the main entrance from the corridor, while the other two lead to the Red Room. The private dining room is a relatively small, square room with a segmental vaulted ceiling and two windows facing north. Against the east wall is a marble mantelpiece with a gold-framed mirror. Walls are of plaster with a white enamel wainscoting. On the south wall is the portrait of *John Tyler,* by G. P. A. Healy. The room furnishings are of mahogany Chippendale, with red-velvet draperies and rugs.

The upper rooms, entered only by members of the Presidential household and their intimate friends, are reached from the east end of the central corridor by a wide stone stairway, screened by a double wrought-iron gate; also by a small elevator, whose oaken panels were cut from rafters of the Old South Church in Boston. Seven bedroom suites, a library, and a study are arranged along a wide hall that runs across the house from east to west. The four corner suites include small dressing rooms. President Jackson was the first to use, as a Presidential suite, the southwest rooms, in one of which the 9-year-old Tad Lincoln was put to bed by a White House guard on the night of his father's death.

The large BLUE BEDROOM, directly above the southern end of the East Room, was Lincoln's study, where he held many Cabinet meetings during the Civil War. In this room, he signed the Emancipation Proclamation on January 1, 1863. Twice he took up his pen, and twice he laid it down. Turning to Secretary of State William H. Seward, he explained that he had been shaking hands at the New Year's reception since 9 o'clock in the morning, and that his right hand was almost paralyzed. "If my hand trembles when I sign," he added, "all who examine the document hereafter will say, 'He hesitated.'" A third time he grasped the pen, and signed slowly but firmly.

From the time of Andrew Johnson to that of Theodore Roosevelt, the Blue Bedroom frequently was used as a personal office for the President. Adjoining it is the "Monroe Drawing Room," for generations used as a Cabinet meeting place. A tablet in the wall states that here President McKinley signed the treaty with Spain that ended the war in 1898.

In the oval room above the Blue Room, now known as the President's Study, the first New Year's Day reception was held in 1801. Here, in his favorite chair, Lincoln read a chapter of the Bible each

Life Photo by Eliot Elisofon

REQUISITIONS, SPECIFICATIONS, PRICE LISTS
. . . AN OFFICE IN THE NAVY DEPARTMENT

U. S. Indian Office

AROUND THE COUNCIL TABLE IN WASHINGTON—SIOUX
CHIEFS CONFER WITH THE INDIAN COMMISSIONER

RESEARCH IN THE LIBRARY OF CONGRESS

Washington Daily News

WASHINGTON AT NIGHT—OLD POST
OFFICE BUILDING IN FOREGROUND

Life Photo by Eliot Elisofon

GOVERNMENT OFFICES, LIKE PENS IN
A STOCKYARD, CLUSTER BENEATH THE
SILENT ORGAN IN THE OLD AUDITORIUM

Washington Daily News

MORNING TRAFFIC FROM VIRGINIA — ARLINGTON CEMETERY
ENTRANCE AND ARLINGTON HOUSE PORTICO IN BACKGROUND

PARKING LOT IN THE FEDERAL TRIANGLE

Farm Security Administration: Myers

WASHINGTON WATERFRONT

NATIONAL GALLERY OF ART

CAVALRY REVIEW, FORT MYER

AIR CORPS MANEUVERS, 1931

THE PRESIDENT THROWS OUT THE FIRST
BALL TO OPEN THE BASEBALL SEASON

day, while the family assembled for breakfast. In the room is Franklin
D. Roosevelt's desk, made from timbers of the *Resolute.*

On the third or attic floor are 14 rooms, including storerooms, sewing room, servants' quarters, and the housekeeper's cedar-fitted room.
In 1833, President Jackson's coachman was ill of smallpox in one of
these rooms. When the panic-stricken servants refused to serve him,
the President shut himself in with the sick man and nursed him to
health.

Distributed over the upper floor are the following portraits:
Franklin Pierce, by G. P. A. Healy; *William Henry Harrison; James
Buchanan,* by Chase; *Zachary Taylor, James Monroe* and *Andrew
Jackson,* by E. F. Andrews; and *George Washington,* by Luis Ca-
dena (Quito, 1877).

The EXECUTIVE OFFICES are in the semi-detached three-story building at the end of the West Terrace. They are entered from the basement floor of the White House through a foyer, which gives access to
the President's suite, a small anteroom, and an oval office. The suite
is flanked by the Cabinet Room and the office of the secretary to the
President. Offices for the executive retinue extend along the west
side. In the northwest corner is the press room, and in the southwest,
a conference room. Along the east side are the offices of Secret Service
men and filing clerks. Public entrance is from the north. Visitors are
received in a large central lobby, the most interesting feature of which
is an immense round table, presented by the Philippine insurrectionary
leader, Emilio Aguinaldo, in 1934. The table, probably made in
Bilibid Prison, Manila, was set up with great difficulty in the lobby
but could be carried no farther on account of its size. From the lobby,
there is a south exit to a colonnaded veranda adjoining the Rose Garden and the "President's Walk."

The offices are thoroughly modern, with indirect lighting, cork
and rubberized floors, and air conditioning. On the upper floor are the
telegraph rooms and a telephone switchboard that centralizes the 150
branch lines in the Mansion and the offices. Here, too, is handled the
White House mail, every item of which is carefully scrutinized and
turned over to the proper authority. Not infrequently, in this way,
letters from the most humble sources are brought to the attention of
the President. In the Cabinet Room are the *Jefferson* and *Jackson* portraits and one of *Woodrow Wilson.*

In addition to the Presidential portraits, the White House has
other fine paintings and several pieces of sculpture: *Mrs. John Tyler,*
by F. Analli; *Mrs. Theodore Roosevelt,* by Theobald Chartran (gift
of the French Republic); *Mrs. Rutherford B. Hayes,* by Daniel Hunt-
ington (gift of the W.C.T.U.); *Dolly Madison; Mrs. Abraham Van
Buren* (daughter-in-law of the President), by Henry Inman; *Mrs.
Benjamin Harrison,* by Daniel Huntington (gift of the D.A.R.);
Mrs. Calvin Coolidge, by Howard Chandler Christie (gift of Pi Beta
Phi); *Mrs. Abraham Lincoln,* by Katherine Helm; and *Signing of the
Treaty with Spain,* by Theobald Chartran (showing President William

McKinley standing). Among the sculptures are the marble busts of *Mrs. Andrew Jackson,* of *Martin Van Buren,* and of *Marquis de Lafayette,* and a small bronze reproduction of the equestrian statue of *Andrew Jackson* in Lafayette Square (*see Lafayette Square*). A contract has been let by the Government for painting President Herbert Hoover's portrait.

* * *

"Heaven bestow the best of blessings on this house, and on all that shall hereafter inhabit it. May none but honest and wise men ever rule under this roof."

This was the prayer written in 1800 by John Adams, the first President to live in the White House, the cornerstone of which was laid on October 13, 1792, just 300 years after the discovery of America.

James Hoban, an Irish-American, won the prize of $500 offered by the District Commissioners for the best design for the "President's Palace." Construction work began immediately, but, because of money, labor, and transportation difficulties, eight years passed before the house was ready for occupancy. Even when John and Abigail Adams took possession, the "Palace" was still unfinished. An attempt was made to remove the shacks of workmen from the grounds, but, there being a housing shortage, the men refused to continue work unless permitted to live in them.

As first mistress of the Mansion, Mrs. Adams was impressed by its grandeur but greatly annoyed by its inconveniences. Although she had sufficient servants, there were no bells in the house. She complained that "promises are all you can obtain." There was insufficient furniture for the great bare rooms, and Mrs. Adams was obliged to use the now sumptuous East Room to hang out the family washing. Firewood, expensive and scarce, was needed in great quantities for drying damp walls.

The first gala day in the White House was under Jefferson on July 4, 1801, when about 100 guests were received in the Blue Room. That day Jefferson started the fashion of shaking hands, instead of merely bowing as had been the custom under George Washington and John Adams.

James Madison Randolph, son of Jefferson's daughter, Martha, was the first child born in the White House, while Esther Cleveland was the first child of a President born there—in September, 1893. The first wedding in the Mansion was that of Maria Monroe, daughter of President James Monroe, and her cousin, Samuel Gouverneur, who had been President Madison's private secretary. The ceremony took place on March 18, 1820, in the Blue Room, "directly on the emblems of 'U.S.' woven into the Aubusson rug." The grand ballroom was lighted for the first time at a reception for the couple when they returned from their honeymoon. William Henry Harrison's was the first Presidential funeral from the White House. It took place 30 days after he was inaugurated on March 4, 1841.

From Monroe's day forward, successive White House regimes have had their own ideas of decoration, so the furniture has been subject to continuous additions and changes. When it became hopelessly scrambled, the whole decorative scheme would be changed to accord with the standards of the period. Thus Monroe began the period of "French furnishings" that lasted until the Civil War. Congress tried in vain to stop this vogue in 1822 with a law that "All furniture used in the President's House purchased for use in the President's House shall be as far as possible of American or domestic manufacture," but Jackson and Van Buren drew upon themselves a heavy fire of congressional criticism by their lavish purchases of "elegant French Furniture." After 1860, however, the White House families went in for heavy ornate mid-Victorian furniture, with a superabundance of marble tops, huge mirrors, black walnut, horsehair, and plush. Lincoln and Johnson favored black walnut. Grant added enormous wardrobes, with mirrors in the doors, and lambrequins over the marble mantelpieces. Hayes contributed massive sideboards of the prevalent imposing type. Then Arthur began all over. He sent away 24 cartloads of this miscellany (some of which dated back to Jackson's time), to make place for his own ideas of Presidential grandeur—gold wallpaper in the dining room, Tiffany glass screens and imitation marble columns in the main reception room, pomegranate plush draperies over windows and mantel, and furniture to match. Harrison went him one better with stained-glass windows in the Blue Room and jigsaw scrollwork over the dining-room door.

In 1902 came the complete structural renovation of the White House, and the Roosevelts seized this opportunity to urge upon the Nation a systematic and dignified scheme of furnishing. Congress allowed $100,000 of its appropriation to be earmarked for furniture and decorations; some years later later it authorized the acceptance of gifts of Colonial furniture. This started a controversy that lasted through the Coolidge administration, between the lovers of Colonial furniture and those, including the American Institute of Architects, who wished to see the furniture harmonized with the style of the White House, which is not Colonial but European Renaissance. Briefly put, the arguments for the Colonial style were that the White House is a Colonial structure; that it symbolizes the Nation's founders, and, therefore, it is the logical place for assembling the best of American craftsmanship. The opposing arguments were that early American furniture varied too much in different regions to make a uniform system of decoration anything but sectional—for New England, Central, and Southern craftsmanship, though all beautiful, varied widely—while the architectural style of the White House offered a basis for uniform decoration that would not be inconsistent with American history. To support this claim, they pointed to the widespread use of French Renaissance furniture in early days.

The result of the controversy is a compromise, by which both schools are represented with great harmony and success, though there are still many inconsistencies. The East Room retains the imperial atmosphere of its design. Mrs. Hoover contributed 50 gold chairs of its style and period, to be used when occasion demanded. The Colonial influence predominates in several rooms. Lincoln's nine-foot four-poster walnut bed remains in the Lincoln bedroom on the second floor, covered with a crocheted bedspread Mrs. Coolidge spent 2 years in making. Mrs. Coolidge also secured many interesting pieces for the several Colonial rooms.

Mrs. Hoover made a permanent restoration of the sitting room on the second floor (once the private parlor of Mrs. Monroe), by having the original furniture in the Monroe Museum at Fredericksburg, Virginia, duplicated. To complete its fittings, the Smithsonian Institution donated an Astor piano.

It was not the furniture so much as the habitability of the White House that perplexed its earlier mistresses. The Adams family had a trying four years, and, by the time Jefferson succeeded Adams, the east walls of the house were still unplastered and the grounds unimproved. Jefferson made the mansion fully habitable, besides carrying through some unrealized features of the Hoban plan. These included terraces in the form of wings extending from the east and west façades, very similar in line to those which Hoban later rebuilt. But Jefferson marred the effect by having long rows of one-story "offices" erected in front of them, to serve also as "meat house, wine cellar, coal and wood sheds and privies."

Jefferson, being a widower, called to his aid as mistress of the White House the inimitable Dolly Madison, whose husband was then Secretary of State, and the annals of White House hospitality began forthwith. Frequent dinners were given for numerous guests, and entertainment was lavish. Jefferson spent $10,000 on fine wines during his eight years in the White House. He did away with the formal daily receptions or dances Washington had instituted in Philadelphia and which the Adamses had striven to maintain. Instead he received persons of all stations at any seasonable hour, often in dressing gown and slippers. He abolished precedence rules, ignored titles, and instituted an etiquette that discouraged aristocratic practices. His informality was widely popular, but John Adams, who was being criticized by implication, remarked that he did not think he was less of a democrat because he preferred to curl his hair, whereas Jefferson wore his straight.

Then James Madison became President, and Dolly Madison was the most brilliant hostess the Capital ever knew. For eight years she exercised her tact and charm to mollify political opponents and win the confidence of provincial and hesitant guests. At the weekly state dinners, she generally took the head of the long table, while the President, preoccupied with administrative problems, sat silent at a place halfway down. Her dinners and balls were reproductions of pre-Revolutionary *soirées* in Paris. At dinner a servant stood behind each guest. Levees were held every week, and grand receptions on New

Year's and Independence Days. On a visit to the Capital in 1811, Washington Irving wrote: "Mrs. Madison is a fine, portly, buxom dame, who has a smile and a pleasant word for everybody. . . . But as to Jemmy Madison—Ah! poor Jemmy!—he is but a withered little apple-John."

Many of Dolly Madison's coreligionists in the Society of Friends, or Quakers, and many democratically minded citizens as well, were offended by the luxury of the Madison household; its mistress drove about in a chariot costing $1,500, and clothed herself in gowns, jewels, shoes, and turbans from New York and Paris. She used rouge, dipped snuff, and played at "One hundred." Mrs. Seaton, the wife of a South Carolina editor, complained of the use of rouge and paint by the wives of the President and Cabinet members, and sarcastically remarked that at receptions "it is customary to pay your obeisance to Mrs. Madison, curtsy to his Highness, then take a seat."

These festivities came to an abrupt halt August 24, 1814, when the British burned most of the public buildings, including the White House. The French Ambassador's servant, seeking out General Robert Ross, the British commander, found him in the White House, piling furniture in one of the rooms, preparatory to burning the building. The fire left little but the outer stone walls, and the greater part of these had to be taken down and rebuilt. Hoban was charged with this task in 1815 and faithfully reproduced his original design. After the fire, the *City Gazette* remarked: "The destruction of the President's House cannot be said to be a great loss in one point of view, as we hope it will put an end to drawing rooms and levees; the resort of the idle, and the encouragers of spies and traitors." Yet Dolly Madison herself prevented the loss from being greater than it was. Gathering together a trunkful of Cabinet papers, silver plate, valuable china, and the great portrait of Washington, she fled the city, bringing her salvage back unharmed after the invaders had left.

President James Monroe occupied the rebuilt Mansion in the fall of 1817, refurnishing the interior with articles especially imported from France and with his own possessions. On New Year's Day of 1818, he gave a great reception in the reconstructed White House and followed it with weekly receptions known as "drawing rooms." Observers recorded that, while the social life of the Monroe administration was less brilliant than when Dolly Madison ruled, it was more stately. One evidence of the stiff formality of White House life in those rather pompous times is the fact that the President's wife could never return calls. No such restriction exists today.

With John Quincy Adams the spirit of New England returned. He records in his diary that he rose regularly at 5 a.m., took a 4-mile walk before breakfast, worked all day, and retired at 11 p.m. The social obligations of his office troubled him. He wrote in 1828, "This evening was the sixth drawing room. These parties are becoming more and more insupportable to me."

When Andrew Jackson, a widower, came to the White House, he

threw his home open to everyone. On March 4, 1829, thousands who had come to Washington to attend the inauguration crowded into the Mansion. "High and low, old and young, black and white, poured in one solid column into this spacious mansion." They brawled, broke glassware, stood on the damask-covered chairs and sofas, treated officials with scant ceremony, and pressed about the President until he fled by a back door.

At Jackson's last public reception there was an even more disorderly scene. Some New York friends, anxious to outshine the Massachusetts farmers who once presented Jefferson with a 750-pound cheese, had sent Jackson a 1,400-pound cheese, which ripened for a year in the cellar of the White House. On Washington's birthday in 1837, the local citizenry was invited to sample the Pride of New York and was joined by a host of visitors from Alexandria, Baltimore, and the surrounding country. The Senate adjourned in honor of the occasion; Martin Van Buren, then President-elect, was present. George Bancroft wrote of seeing in the White House on this occasion "apprentices, boys of all ages, men not civilized enough to walk about the room with their hats off—starvelings, and fellows with dirty faces and dirty manners." When the day closed, the White House was smeared with the sticky cheese.

During the Van Buren administration, the weekly drawing rooms were abandoned, but the display of earlier days was restored—even exceeded. Captain Marryat, the British novelist, praised the President for having "prevented the mobocracy from intruding themselves at his levees. The police are now stationed at the doors." Van Buren drove about in a magnificent coach, dined off silver plate, gave many small dinners prepared by an English chef—though no food was served at general receptions—and lived in conspicuously luxurious fashion. His daughter-in-law, who acted as hostess of the White House, had her guests formally announced. She received them seated on a raised platform, wearing a long-train purple-velvet gown, with a headdress of three feathers. All this was regarded as a flagrant betrayal of the Jackson tradition.

William Henry Harrison, "Old Tippecanoe," had no opportunity to bring his wife to Washington, for he survived his inauguration only one month. His successor, John Tyler, strove to restore a simpler atmosphere to the White House social life. President Tyler's wife died in the White House in 1842, and two years later he married Julia, daughter of David Gardiner, of New York. David Gardiner soon afterward was killed, before the President's eyes, in the explosion on the steam warship *Princeton*.

By the time James Knox Polk was in residence, the atmosphere was again one of "grave respectability." At Polk's evening receptions there were no cards, dancing, or refreshments. Guests were received informally by the long-haired President and his wife and thereafter spent the evening "solemnly promenading around the East Room in pairs." A guest at the White House during Taylor's administration records that a military band played tunes on the lawn, while everybody walked "in and out and about without restriction; the President perhaps strolling over the lawn amidst the company, ready to shake hands with anyone."

President Fillmore introduced the novelty of morning receptions. During his administration, a great state dinner was given to Louis Kossuth, the exiled Hungarian revolutionist.

President Buchanan, who was a bachelor, had spent some years as American Minister at the Court of St. James and at the Court of the Russian Czar. A polished diplomat, he was regarded as an unusually brilliant host in the White House. Two important social events occurred during his occupancy—the reception to the first embassy from Japan and a dinner for the Prince of Wales, later Edward VII.

A great crowd attended Abraham Lincoln's first levee. A new party was in power, and again a new element appeared in the White House. Northern antislavery and Western agrarian sentiment dominated, and many Southerners pointedly stayed away from state receptions. Guests appeared in negligee shirts, slouch hats, and cowhide boots; Indian agents in their beaded buckskins. When the Civil War came, state dinners were abandoned. In the midst of the President's anxieties, one of the Lincoln children died; at once the White House went into mourning, and receptions were discontinued. A cloud settled over the mansion, which deepened with the death of the President and was only gradually dispelled during Andrew Johnson's tumultuous term.

Grant's administration saw another revival of social glitter in the White House, as wealthy manufacturing and banking groups began to dominate in Presidential circles. Many noble and royal foreign guests were entertained by Grant, Hayes, Garfield, and Arthur; among them were two Russian grand dukes, the Italian Duke of Abruzzi, and the Swedish crown prince. The company at some state dinners overflowed into the corridor of the main floor.

During Grover Cleveland's second administration, White House etiquette again had to be revised, for Great Britain, France, Italy, and Germany raised their envoys here from the rank of Minister to that of Ambassador.

President Harding introduced the custom of inviting guests to breakfast. Under Harding and under President Coolidge, many Senators, Representatives, newspapermen, and foreign visitors dined early in the morning on hot cakes and sausage and other dishes that showed no influence of imported chefs.

During the Hoover administration there was held the most elaborate ceremony in recent White House annals, to honor the visiting King of Siam in 1931, one of the few times when a reigning monarch has been in the White House. The King visited the President, and the President immediately returned the call. The same night the President entertained the King at a great banquet in the White House. In the summer of 1939, President Franklin D. Roosevelt and Mrs. Roosevelt entertained, as over-night guests at the White House, King George VI and Queen Elizabeth, of England.

Mrs. Roosevelt established two social precedents at one stroke in 1934, when, on the evening of the Gridiron Club dinner at the New Willard Hotel, she gave the first costume ball in the White House. To this exclusively feminine gathering, she invited the wives of the Gridiron Club's guests and other social leaders; "Widiron" dinners have continued during the Roosevelt administration.

During all this time, additions and alterations to the White House were being continually made. Hoban built the semicircular south portico in 1824, and the colonnaded north portico in 1829. During Andrew Jackson's term, the East Room was finished and furnished. About 1833, water, piped from a spring in what is now Franklin Park, replaced the pumps that had supplied the White House until then. Gas lighting was installed in 1848. Water from the city system was introduced in 1853, in which year provision was also made for central heating. In Benjamin Harrison's administration appeared the novel convenience of electric-light buttons. Bathrooms were installed during President Rutherford B. Hayes' term, 1877-81. During Hayes' term also, one telephone line was brought in; in 1902 the first telephone switchboard was introduced.

Jefferson's "offices" were destroyed during the British invasion; the East and West Terraces were erected in 1815. The original eastern terrace was somewhat out of scale with the western one, and it was replaced in 1869 with a more suitably proportioned structure. More recently the flower pots and oiled paths of the Victorian era gave way to a less formal arrangement of the grounds. The Executive Offices took the space occupied for decades by the greenhouses, and Colonial gardens were laid out south of the terraces.

By 1902 the White House began to show the effects of generations of wear and tear. Moreover, the Executive Offices filled so much of the second story that little remained in the way of comfortable dwelling quarters for the President and his family. Since the east gallery was given over to living quarters for the domestic staff, the only space available for entertainment was on the main floor, which was utterly inadequate. On major occasions, guests entered through the stately main entrance, but had to leave through a window in the East Room by a temporary wooden stairway. Wraps had to be piled in the lobby or in the dining rooms. For large dinners, the State Dining Room had to be supplemented with tables set up in the Reception Hall. At the instance of President Theodore Roosevelt, Congress therefore provided for alterations, extensions, and redecorations. The firm of McKim, Mead, and White, architects, effected the changes at a cost of about $500,000. The East Gallery was rebuilt. By the removal of a private stairway at the west end of the central corridor, room was made for the enlargement of the State Dining Room. The public reception rooms were made structurally sound. The Executive Office Building was completed in 1902, but it was enlarged to twice its original size under President Taft in 1909-10.

The west garden was set out with roses by Mrs. Taft. President Wilson planned a straight-line arrangement of the bushes, and had high hedges and walks put along the base of the south portico on the west side, for the "President's Walk" and the "President's Rest."

The office building was damaged by a fire on Christmas Eve in 1929, but was restored the following year. Machinery for cooling the offices was introduced in the spring of 1932. In 1934 the increasing burdens of the Presidency required another overhauling of the Executive Office Building. With the advice of the Commission of Fine Arts, the President developed a plan that tripled the available office space, without any apparent increase in the mass of the building. This was done by excavating the basement and extending it beyond the office to the south, making a new story of the former attic, and extending the first story to the east in the form of terrace. In 1942 the East Gallery was extended to East Executive Avenue.

In the summer of 1936 the archaic electric wiring system was found to be inadequate and dangerous. The White House was closed for several weeks while the old wiring was torn out and a complete modern system installed, including the lead wires from the State Building into the White House. A complete automatic fire-alarm system was installed throughout the building. Much antiquated, worn-out plumbing was reconditioned at the same time.

Through the years there has developed a system of White House etiquette, although details are changed from time to time in accordance with the wishes of the President and the First Lady. The President receives calls but returns none except to royal visitors. Acceptance of invitations to formal dinners at the White House is considered obligatory, unless absence from the city or illness prevents. Dinner guests are always expected to arrive at the hour stated in the invitation. The President is always attended at state gatherings by his military and naval aides. The order of precedence is based partly on official standing and partly on the ranking age of the officers involved—rather than on personal titles, as in Europe. The President, naturally, always comes first; then the Vice President; ex-Presidents; foreign ambassadors; the Chief Justice of the Supreme Court. The order beyond this point is left to the discretion of the State Department. Dinner guests enter by the east entrance, where they are shown a plan of the seating arrangements. A junior aide then escorts them to the East Room and introduces them to their dinner partners. The guests then take their places in line according to rank.

At state dinners today the table is set with china purchased by the Franklin D. Roosevelts. Ivory tinted, with a gold edging and an inner band of blue containing 48 gold stars, it bears the Presidential seal and a formal design in light gold tracing, which includes the rose and triple feathers of the Roosevelt coat of arms. The Monroe gold service, or a silver set including as centerpiece a great silver boat on a plate-glass sea, often supplies service plates, although some First Ladies have preferred that these match the dinner set. The small silver is marked "The President's House." There is one butler to each four guests.

State dinners generally consist of six rather than eight courses as formerly, and no longer include caviar and terrapin, popular in the White House some years ago. Dinner ended, the ladies usually retire to the Green or Red Room, where they are joined by the gentlemen after coffee and cigars. A musicale may follow in the East Room, in which case, by 11:30, the host and hostess rise to indicate the end of the evening's entertainment. Less formal dinners are sometimes followed by dancing.

Despite the earlier formalities, life in the White House was much simpler a century ago. The First Lady was likely to keep a close eye on domestic affairs and, more than once, exchanged recipes with her predecessor. William Henry Harrison, as late as 1841, was given to going to market with a basket on his arm. Whereas Jefferson had about a dozen servants, under President Taft the staff totaled about 100 persons. Mrs. Taft eliminated the office of steward and abandoned having caterers to serve large dinners. She appointed a housekeeper, and all meals were thereafter prepared in the White house.

The White House staff today includes the chief usher and his assistants, the housekeeper, ladies' maids, the President's valet, doormen, engineers and maintenance men, telegraph and telephone operators, butlers, cooks, chambermaids, secretaries, garden help, chauffeurs for the White House automobiles, police, Secret Service men, and personal, military, and naval aides to the President; all these in addition to the Executive Office staff. Extra waiters and kitchen help are hired for large dinners. Some 3,000 guests are entertained at meals each year.

At the diplomatic reception, which heads the list of annual functions traditionally held in the White House, the guests assemble in the East Room, wearing their uniforms. They place themselves in order of precedence, each Chief of Mission being immediately followed by his staff and their ladies. The Secretary of State enters with the aides of the President. They escort the dean of the Diplomatic Corps—the oldest ambassador in the point of service—to the Blue Room, where the President awaits with his wife. The President's senior military aide presents the dean to the President, and then to his wife. The rest of the Diplomatic Corps follow and are presented individually. Then the entire company goes to the State Dining Room for refreshments.

Indiscriminate public receptions now are part of the past. Even the traditional New Year's Day and inaugural receptions were abandoned a few years ago, because of the great strain put upon the President by the number of persons who came to shake his hand.

The one Federal employee who does not receive a salary check from the United States Treasury is the President. He has no superior officer to certify him, so a claim for services rendered has to be filed with the

General Accounting Office, which prepares a claim for the amount to be recovered from the Treasury.

STATE DEPARTMENT BUILDING

The gray-granite State Department Building (*open 9-5:30 Mon.-Fri., 9-1 Sat.*), SW. corner 17th Street and Pennsylvania Avenue NW., flanking the White House on the west, in many ways epitomizes an epoch in American architecture. The transitory taste for French neoclassicism, fostered by the École des Beaux Arts in Paris, has few more striking expressions. The baroque complexity of the structure is produced by the broken lines of its central and corner pavilions, extended porches, sharp dormers thrusting out from mansard roofs, veritable cascades of 900 small plain columns, and tall chimneys capped by overweighted chimney-pots. At the center of each façade is a six-story pavilion, approached by a broad flight of steps and faced with two-story porticos and superimposed colonnades. The four corner pavilions, also designed with superimposed colonnades, are adorned with small one-story porches or loggias. The numerous windows on the three principal floors are crowned with hooded pediments.

Each main entrance is flanked by old-fashioned cannon, four of those at the Pennsylvania Avenue entrance, cast between 1693 and 1779, having been captured at Santiago in 1898. A bronze howitzer here was surrendered by Cornwallis at Yorktown in 1781, and one piece was taken by Union troops at Fort Sumter late in the Civil War. The most-used entry, at Pennsylvania Avenue, is a curious example of Victorian monumentality. The flagstone sidewalk at this point is almost on a level with the north entrance, but there are steps down to a paved court and the traditional monumental steps up again to the first floor level.

The interior is in the taste of the period, with marble halls, granite stairways with bronze balusters, and antiquated fixtures recalling the grandeur of the 1870's. The two miles of corridors and other portions of the immense and complex interior require a large force of charwomen to clean it each night. A simple bronze plaque on the wall facing the Pennsylvania Avenue entrance lists with cold brevity the names of 66 diplomatic and consular officers who lost their lives under heroic or tragic circumstances while on active duty. The first name is that of William Palfrey, lost at sea, 1780. The next is that of Joel Barlow, exposure, Zarnowics, Poland, 1812. The last entry (1941) is that of J. Theodore Marriner, murdered, Beirut, Syria, 1937. In addition to serving as a roll of honor, this plaque, in its listing of many foreign towns and cities, is an indicator of the Nation's widespread interests. A bronze tablet left of the entrance commemorates the "services and sufferings" of 243,135 horses and mules used by American forces in the First World War.

The ANTECHAMBER OF THE SECRETARY OF STATE, on the second floor, south corridor, contains portraits of former Secretaries, including such historic and contemporary personages as Thomas Jefferson, James Madison, Henry Clay, Elihu Root, William Jennings Bryan, and Charles Evans Hughes. Other portraits, notably that of Daniel Webster, hang in the diplomatic reception room near by. By special permission the visitor may be shown the treaties of the United States since 1906; the older treaties have been transferred to the National Archives Building.

The State Department, organized in 1789 primarily to conduct foreign affairs, occupied the southern front of this building in 1875, though the entire structure was not completed until 1888. A. D. Mullet, architect of the Treasury Department, was in charge of constructing this huge edifice, which cost $10,405,850. When General Grant returned from his round-the-world tour in 1877, the building was sufficiently advanced for him to remark that it climaxed all the curious constructions he had seen elsewhere in the world. Henry Adams acidly referred to it as "Mr. Mullet's architectural infant asylum." In general, however, it was much praised, and it stands today as a period piece representative of its time.

The FIRST DIVISION MEMORIAL, a 60-foot monolithic column in the park directly south of the State Department Building, is surmounted by a 15-foot gilt Winged Victory facing south. It was erected in 1924 at a cost of about $175,000 to commemorate the campaigns and battles of the Army's First Division in the World War. The heroic statue is by Daniel Chester French, and the base was designed by Cass Gilbert. Names of 5,500 First Division men are on bronze plaques imbedded in the granite base of the column.

Almost due south of this monument, across the Ellipse grounds near Constitution Avenue and 17th Street, stands the SECOND DIVISION MEMORIAL, by J. E. Fraser, consisting of a colossal bronze hand gripping an upthrust flaming sword, also of bronze. This composition is set against the opening of a blocked arch of pink marble.

Facing the State Department on the west, at the SW. corner of 17th and F Streets, stands an old four-story brick building housing the National Council for Prevention of War. It was occupied, in 1865, as headquarters by General U. S. Grant.

TREASURY BUILDING

The four-story Greek Revival sandstone-and-granite Treasury Building (*open 9-2 Mon.-Fri., 9-12 Sat.*), SW. corner 15th Street and Pennsylvania Avenue NW., flanking the White House on the east, was built in 1838-42, after the burning of a previous building in 1833. The fact that it blocks L'Enfant's Pennsylvania Avenue vista of the Capitol from the White House is said to have been on account of the impatient disposition of President Andrew Jackson. The committee appointed by "Old Hickory" had intended to preserve this view, but Jackson was exasperated by their interminable meetings and delays. Early one morning, the story goes, Jackson walked out of the White

House with a group of officials, examined the grounds, planted his cane in the ground near the present northeast corner of the building, and said, "Right here is where I want the cornerstone."

The building exemplifies the national taste for Hellenic architecture during the first half of the nineteenth century. It is constructed as a huge rectangle around an inner court and divided by a central office corridor. A T-shaped unit designed by Robert Mills constitutes the middle portion of the present east wing; the north, south, and west units were designed by Thomas U. Walter. Ionic columns and pilasters rise through three stories in support of the main entablature and balustrades. Behind the balustrades is a set-back fourth story. There are two basement floors, the upper forming a rusticated base for the superstructure.

The main approaches are through three pedimented porticoes on the north, south, and west fronts. James E. Fraser's bronze statue of Alexander Hamilton, first Secretary of the Treasury (1789-95), stands in a paved terrace opposite the south entrance. The north or Pennsylvania Avenue entrance is approached by steps leading down from the sidewalk to a sunken court in which stands a pedestal to support a statue (also by Fraser) of Albert Gallatin, Secretary of the Treasury from 1801 to 1809, and by monumental steps to the portico. The east or 15th Street front is adorned by a loggia with Ionic columns, terminating at each end with pedimented pavilions.

In the WEST LOBBY is an exhibit of original warrants and Treasury drafts, including the draft for $7,200,000 given Russia in 1860 as payment for the Territory of Alaska, warrants issued in payment for the rights to the Panama Canal, and a $200,000 warrant issued to General Lafayette "in consideration of his services and sacrifices in the War of the Revolution." Exhibits of damaged money redeemed by the Treasurer include notes mutilated by mice, charred by fire, and torn by the wheels of a streetcar. Treasury experts can often identify notes from three or four pieces the size of a fingernail. Changing exhibits include such displays as the 1940 "Know Your Money" show, demonstrating methods of detecting counterfeit bills and forged Government checks.

The two-story CASH ROOM, entered from the north lobby, is executed in varicolored marble panels and trim, decorated with Corinthian pilasters, and the two floor levels are separated by a bronze balustrade. Within this building are money vaults containing a portion of the Nation's gold and silver reserve. The vaults are built of reinforced concrete and encased in plates of chilled steel, impervious to every known cutting tool and torch. Access to them is accomplished by such a complex system of combination locks that it would take specialists three or four days to penetrate them if the combinations were lost. Passages under the vaults permit guards to inspect for tunneling. Microphones connect with a general alarm system, and all locks close automatically with the sounding of an alarm.

The Secret Service Division of the Treasury, with offices in the west wing facing the White House, guards this building, the Bureau of Engraving and Printing, and other structures having to do with Government exchange, and is in charge of the White House Police, which safeguards the President and his family. Originally created in 1860 to suppress counterfeiting, the duties of the Secret Service have since extended to many fields.

The TREASURY ANNEX, across Pennsylvania Avenue north of the main building, a six-story neoclassic structure designed by Cass Gilbert and completed in 1919, is connected with the main building by an underground tunnel.

LAFAYETTE SQUARE

Flanking the White House grounds on the north, Lafayette Square, bordering Pennsylvania Avenue between Madison Place on the east and Jackson Place on the west, and extending through to H Street on the north, is many things to many people. To the millions of tourists who visit Washington, the landscaped rectangle is one of the most favored spots for a view of the porticoed north façade of the White House. To the student of trees and shrubbery it presents a fascinating array of native and exotic plants—ancient boxwoods, southern magnolia, bald cypress, bronze beech, Chinese paulownia, English yew, American elm, and dozens of evergreens, to mention only a few. For those who go into the parks laden with bags of peanuts or popcorn it is full of panhandling pigeons, English sparrows, and pert, inquisitive squirrels, some of them tame enough to perch on shoulders or nuzzle into pockets. For those with an interest in statuary and the history it represents, the park is centered by an equestrian figure of Andrew Jackson, first avowed "man of the people" ever elected to occupy the White House opposite, and at each of its four corners are statues of men of foreign lands who contributed to American liberty—the French Lafayette and Rochambeau, the Polish Kosciuszko, and the German von Steuben. Historically the Square and its flanking houses have played many an important role in the Nation's development.

When George Washington proposed to acquire this site as a public park in 1791, it had been owned by the Pierce family since 1685. The Pierce farmhouse stood at the northeast corner of the Square, and the Pierce apple orchard occupied most of the remainder, except a family burying ground between the present Jackson statue and the White House. North of the White House, when it was built, stretched rural land, dotted here and there with scattered farmsteads. Except for the Pierce farmhouse, the White House was the first building on or facing the Square. The Blair House, on Pennsylvania Avenue opposite the State Department Building, was built about 1810, and St. John's Church was erected in 1816. The Decatur House was opened three years later, and a diplomatic and official social group began to take form with Lafayette Square as its center. During Monroe's "era of good feeling" the Square was a focus of constant dinners, "drawing rooms," dances, and receptions. The death of Decatur in 1821 disrupted the social season, but the following year the Russian Baron Van Tuyl reopened the Decatur House to hospitality. "Washington," said this epicure, "with its venison, wild turkey, canvasback ducks, oysters, and terrapin furnishes better viands than Paris and needs only cooks."

Henry Clay occupied the Decatur House after Van Tuyl, and put in a great deal of time planning a conference of South American republics. Mrs. Clay later conducted from this house the vendetta against Peggy Eaton which nearly disorganized the Jackson administration for three years. In 1825 a public reception to Lafayette was held here. At Jackson's inauguration four years later an immense hilarious mob overwhelmed the Square, the White House grounds, and the White House itself. Tubs of liquor were sent out to the Square in the frail hope of relieving the pressure on the presidential mansion. With the departure of Jackson, the Square settled down to its old aristocratic placidity, with Dolly Madison ruling Washington society from the Cutts homestead. By 1845 the Square was surrounded by the homes of statesmen, diplomats, literary figures, and wealthy Washingtonians. Called "the lobby of the White House," it was also a congregating place for office seekers.

Dedication of the Jackson Monument in 1853 was the occasion for a great celebration. All Washington, with every band instrument and uniform it could muster, swarmed over the Square. Congress later ordered it fenced in, first using the official name, Lafayette Square.

Throughout the Civil War the Square was the scene of great military activity. The Dolly Madison House, the Blair House, the Ewell House, and others became military headquarters or emergency offices. The White House was heavily guarded. Soldiers camped on the square and reduced its gardens to quagmires. It remained muddy and undrained until restored as a part of the civic-improvement campaign in Grant's administration. The last of the many old-time public receptions here took place in 1877, when Grant returned from his world tour, but there was another large gathering when the Lafayette statue was unveiled in 1891.

Since the beginning of the twentieth century Lafayette Square has been the scene of three formal ceremonies, each connected with the unveiling of a statue. Descendants of Lafayette and Rochambeau attended the unveiling of the Rochambeau statue in 1902. There was a great gathering of Polish-American citizens for the unveiling and presentation of the Kosciuszko statue in 1910, and later in the same year the von Steuben statue was unveiled in the presence of President Taft, the staff of the German Embassy, and representatives of German-American societies. In latter years, an annual outdoor art exhibit has been held in a corner of the Square.

The centrally placed equestrian STATUE OF ANDREW JACKSON, by Clark Mills, the first equestrian figure in the United States, was cast in 1853, from bronze cannon captured by Jackson in the War of 1812. Mills, born in New York State in 1815, was a self-taught artist, acquiring most of his knowledge in South Carolina, where he discovered a method of making life masks, and thence, by methods he himself laboriously worked out, he began to work in marble. His bust of John C. Calhoun, pronounced the best of its time, resulted in Mills receiving a gold medal from the Charleston city council. When asked to do an equestrian statue of Jackson he refused, having never seen either Jackson or an equestrian statue. However, the problem interested him, and he worked for nine months to produce a miniature, which introduced the principle of balancing a rearing horse on its hind feet, which were brought under the center of the body. The story, perhaps apocryphal, is that he obtained the use of a Virginia thoroughbred and trained it to rear in the position held by the bronze steed, and that he kept a miniature on his desk, with a removable rider, to prove how well it balanced.

Mills signed a contract for $12,000, and spent two years on his plaster model, working from contemporary portraits to obtain a literal likeness of Jackson and to produce correct anatomical features of man and horse. There were no sizable bronze foundries in the country, and Mills erected his own at Bladensburg, using such information as he could gather from books and conversation, filling the gaps with his own ingenuity. Congress delayed in appropriating the cannon to provide him with bronze, and there was a series of disasters. Cranes broke, furnaces burst, and the statue was cast only after five failures on the body of the horse. Mills' feat of equestrian equilibrium filled Congress and the public with delighted amazement—and Congress voted Mills an additional $20,000 for the job. The sculptor took an order for a duplicate statue to be erected in Jackson Square, New Orleans, at a cost of $30,000. The statue was cast in 1856, but only after a tornado had destroyed the studio and the foundry had been razed by fire and rebuilt.

The STATUE OF LAFAYETTE, in the southwest corner of the square, is a heroic bronze figure by Alexandre Falguière and Antonin Mercie on a copper-stained white marble pedestal. On the east side of the base Comte d'Estaing and Comte de Grasse are represented as offering French naval support to Lafayette, and on the west side Comte de Rochambeau and Chevalier Duportail are shown tendering military aid. A seminude female figure on the south is handing his sword to the French hero, and nude infants on the north represent the gratitude of later generations to the French leader for his aid in the cause of liberty.

At the southwest corner of the square is the STATUE OF ROCHAMBEAU, a copy by Ferdinand Hamar of the memorial at Vendôme, France, to the compatriot who assisted Lafayette in the cause of American freedom. The heroic figure, holding a chart in one hand, is pointing with the other. A militant feminine Liberty, bearing a sword and two flags, and accompanied by an eagle, is on the south side of the pedestal. The statue was unveiled in 1902, when it was accepted by Theodore Roosevelt as a gift from France.

The THADDEUS KOSCIUSZKO STATUE, in the northeast corner, is

a tribute in bronze, designed by Anton Popiel, to the Polish general who fought with American colonists in the Revolutionary War. Supporting figures on east and west sides of the tall pedestal, by the same artist, illustrate an American and a Polish soldier giving aid to the wounded in battle. Quarter-spheres or globes representing North America and eastern Europe, surmounted by eagles, are placed on north and south sides of the pedestal to symbolize the fight for freedom on two sides of the world. The pedestal is engraved with a line from Thomas Campbell's "Epic of Pleasure"—"And Freedom shrieked as Kosciuszko fell."

The STATUE OF BARON VON STEUBEN, in the northwest corner, is Albert Jaegers' conception of the caped and tricorned Frederick William Augustus Henry Ferdinand Baron von Steuben, drillmaster of the Revolution and General Washington's aide through and after the dark days at Valley Forge. A bas-relief plaque on the back of the high pedestal contains portrait heads of Colonel William North and Major Benjamin Walker of von Steuben's staff. Flanking figures in bronze show the warrior teaching youth in the practice of arms, and commemoration of valorous deeds is symbolized by a seminude woman and a nude boy in the shadow of a growing laurel.

Historically, the square includes the land occupied by the TREASURY ANNEX (*see Treasury Building*), NE. corner Pennsylvania Avenue and Madison Place, which remained open until 1836, when Dr. Thomas S. Gunnel, a dentist, built an elaborate residence there. Gunnel became a part of Washington history by responding one morning, with the tools of his profession, to an emergency call from the White House. An hour later he returned as postmaster of the District of Columbia. During the Civil War this house was headquarters for the military department of Washington.

The BELASCO THEATER, north of the Treasury Annex on Madison Place, was built in 1895 as the Lafayette Square Opera House, which opened with Lillian Russell in *The Gypsy*. Ten years later it became the Belasco, opening with Blanche Bates in *The Girl of the Golden West,* and on its boards, in 1923, Julia Marlowe made her last appearance in Washington playing in *Romeo and Juliet*. During the 1920's and 1930's the building was used occasionally as a motion picture theater; it is to be razed to make room for an addition to the Treasury Annex. Commodore John Rodgers built a 30-room house on this site in 1831, having traded a prize Andalusian jackass to Henry Clay for the ground. As an elite boarding house thereafter, it included among its guests such notables as John C. Calhoun while Secretary of War, Henry Clay while Secretary of State, and Chief Justice Roger B. Taney, who handed down the Dred Scott decision. During the Civil War it was the home of William H. Seward, Lincoln's Secretary of State. As a part of a widespread plan for the assassination of Union leaders, Lewis Payne broke into the house on the night Lincoln was shot by Booth, and severely stabbed Seward in the throat. The house was later occupied by Secretary of War W. W.

Belknap and by Secretary of State James G. Blaine, before its demolition to clear a site for the opera house.

The buff-brick TAYLOE-CAMERON HOUSE, 21 Madison Place, built in 1828 by Benjamin Ogle Tayloe, is used as an annex to the Cosmos Club. Its most distinctive architectural features are a two-story circular bay, the Palladian window at the third-floor level directly above it, and an ironwork balcony at the second floor, probably a later addition. The Tayloe House is at its best when the wisteria trails its spikes of lavender flowers across the balcony. The house was occupied for a time by Don Cameron, Senator from Pennsylvania, and was known as "The Little White House" when it was occupied by Mark Hanna during the McKinley administration. The Cosmos Club later took over this building, but sold it to the Government for office use, effective July 1, 1941.

The COSMOS CLUB (*private*), SE. corner Madison Place and H Street NW., a buff stucco building used by the social club for men distinguished in science, arts, and letters, was erected by Richard Cutts, brother-in-law of Dolly Madison, in 1818. Possession passed to James Madison a few years later, and after his death in 1836, Dolly Madison devoted the proceeds from the sale of the Madison papers to restoring the mansion, which she occupied until her death in 1849. During this period her home was again a center of Washington social life, and it was customary on New Year's Day to go directly from the White House to Dolly Madison's House for a ceremonial call. The house later had several eminent occupants, including Commodore John Wilkes, leader of the Nation's first naval expedition to the Antarctic in the early 1840's. During the Civil War it was one of the headquarters of the Army of the Potomac under General George B. McClellan. The Cosmos Club purchased it following its organization in 1886. The club reshaped this and the Tayloe House to their needs, connecting them by a modern annex. This building, like the Tayloe-Cameron House, has been sold to the Government.

The FEDERAL LOAN AGENCY BUILDING (*open 8:30-5:30 Mon.-Fri., 8:30-12:30 Sat.*), NE. corner Vermont Avenue and H Street NW., designed by A. R. Clas of Washington, assisted by Holabird and Root of Chicago, was completed in 1940 at a cost of about $5,500,000. It is a modern-style, functional office building, rising sheer for 10 stories to a short setback behind which are two additional floors, and the building is capped by a penthouse story. The southwest corner is a concave section facing a modest flagpole plaza. Built of Indiana limestone on an ebony granite base, the floor plan, containing 9 acres of office space, is built around a triangular central court and an open court on the southeast side. The main entrance, on the Vermont Avenue side, is a composition of four two-story glass portals set in a frame of polished ebony granite. The interior of the air-conditioned building is finished in Alabama white marble with black marble trim. The elevator foyers, providing access to the 12 high-speed elevators, are finished in black marble and lighted by fluorescent tubes and translucent glass. Drinking fountains are set in circles of black marble. Aluminum Venetian blinds provide shading for the many wide windows.

Two rooms for board meetings, on the eleventh floor, are the most richly furnished in the building. The larger room, paneled in bleached walnut, and the smaller in Appalachian oak, are practical meeting rooms, rich in their decorations but not ostentatious. Parking space for the cars of executives is provided on the first floor, and there is added parking space in the first basement. In this building, occupied by the Reconstruction Finance Corporation and other Government lending organizations under the general supervision of the Federal Loan Agency, large and small financial transactions are made that affect the economic life of a large part of the Nation's population.

The VETERANS ADMINISTRATION BUILDING (*open 8:15-4:45 Mon.-Fri., 8:15-12:15 Sat.*), NW. corner Vermont Avenue and H Street NW., is a ten-story cast stone structure designed by Wyatt and Nolting and completed in 1918. Frankly an office building, devoted to handling benefits for veterans of the Nation's armed forces, it is sparingly decorated. Over the central three-door entrance on Vermont Avenue is a colonnade of 9 fluted Doric pilasters, almost the only embellishment on a practical building. One of the stricter Government agencies, the Administration does not encourage visitors, except those on business.

Several historic private dwellings stood on this site, in which lived such notables as Reverdy Johnson, onetime Minister to England and Attorney General under President Taylor; William D. Marcy, Secretary of State under Pierce; Lewis Cass of Michigan, Secretary of War under Jackson and Secretary of State under Buchanan; Senator Charles Sumner, New England abolitionist leader; and Senator Pomerene of Ohio. From 1869 to 1912, the old Arlington Hotel stood here, a distinguished hostelry that accommodated almost every President from Grant to McKinley while awaiting their inaugurations.

West of the Veterans Administration Building on H Street is the four-story brownstone ASHBURTON HOUSE (*private*), which was the British Legation at the time the Webster-Ashburton Treaty, adjusting the Canadian boundary line, was worked out by Secretary of State Daniel Webster and the British Ambassador, Lord Ashburton, in 1842. The two diplomats spent many hours together, dining and wining while they worked out details incident to the treaty. The house became the British Legation again in 1849, when England's diplomatic representative was Sir Henry Bulwer, uncle of the novelist Bulwer-Lytton.

ST. JOHN'S EPISCOPAL CHURCH, NE. corner 16th and H Streets NW., designed by Benjamin Latrobe and built in 1816, is known as "the Church of the Presidents." Many changes have been made in the original structure, but St. John's remains a notable example of Federal architecture. Latrobe planned it in the form of a Greek cross with flat dome and lantern cupola. After a few years the nave was carried to the building line on 16th Street, and the Doric portico, the side vestibule, and the cupolaed tower were added. The dignity of the colonnaded front reflects the architectural sobriety of the period, and the mellow texture of the yellow walls, the white trim, and the restrained classic detail contribute to this effect. The interior was originally paved with brick and lined with box pews. The latter were removed in 1842, and in 1883 James Renwick made radical alterations that included the addition of the chantry to the rear, and the installation of numerous stained-glass windows. The crossing remained unchanged, however, except for the removal of the massive columns supporting the domical ceiling. A gallery extends over the north and south transepts and nave.

A faded entry on the minutes of the vestry states that in 1816 a committee was formed to "wait on the President of the United States [James Madison] and offer him a pew in this church, without his being obliged to purchase same." Madison chose Pew 54, but insisted on paying the annual rental. The next five Presidents—Monroe, Adams, Jackson, Van Buren, and Harrison—occupied this pew, and since then it has been set aside for Presidents. Ten in all have occupied it, including Franklin D. Roosevelt. James Madison's vivacious Quaker wife, Dolly, was baptized and confirmed an Episcopalian in this church, and Presidents Harrison and Taylor were buried from it.

The HAY-ADAMS HOUSE, a modern hotel, occupies the site at the NW. corner of 16th and H Streets NW. where Henry Hobson Richardson in 1885 built a double house for the historian Henry Adams and John Hay, Secretary of State under McKinley and Theodore Roosevelt. Here Hay and Nicolay wrote their monumental biography of Lincoln; here Adams wrote the histories on which his reputation rests, and *The Education of Henry Adams,* which made him famous. Visitors at these houses included the architect Richardson, the sculptor Saint-Gaudens, the painter John LaFarge, and many political and administrative figures of half a century.

The UNITED STATES CHAMBER OF COMMERCE (*open 9-5 weekdays*), NE. corner Connecticut Avenue and H Street NW., is a four-story Indiana limestone structure with three-story Corinthian colonnades on the south and west façades, surmounted by a decorative balustrade. Designed by Cass Gilbert, the building was completed in 1925 at a cost of about $3,000,000. The entrance hall and corridors are walled in Belgian rose marble and floored with Italian travertine. Around an enclosed court is a series of chambers suitable for gatherings of various sizes. The largest is the Council Chamber, a lofty room with teakwood floors, high walls of French Crazanne marble, and a ceiling decorated by Ezra Winter. Between the beams are bas-relief panels and inscriptions commemorating explorers who blazed the paths of trade. Replicas of house flags carried by early explorers are placed at intervals along the walls. The upper floors house administrative and research staffs and the editorial offices of *Nation's Business,* official publication of the Chamber. A mahogany desk used by Daniel Webster is in the office of the Chamber's president. The U.S. Chamber of Commerce occupies a co-ordinating position with respect to State and local commercial organizations and State and national trade associations numbering nearly 1,700.

On this site stood the Corcoran House, built in 1822 and presented to Daniel Webster when he became Secretary of State in 1841. He lived here during the negotiations for the Webster-Ashburton Treaty, but finding his gift house too expensive, sold it to W. W. Corcoran, founder of the art gallery. The house was later occupied by Chauncey M. Depew, Senator from New York.

The DECATUR HOUSE (*private*), SW. corner Jackson Place and H Street NW., a three-story red-brick mansion with tall windows, delicate iron balconies, and high chimneys, was built in 1819 after the design of Benjamin H. Latrobe. The massive main structure, almost square, has the dignity of plainness and solidity, preserving, with low slave quarters and service wing in the rear, its Georgian character essentially unaltered.

The interior reproduces faithfully the subtle proportions, carved moldings, and other characteristics of the Adam style. Rooms of great dimensions, separated by graceful archways, are lighted by crystal chandeliers suspended from high frescoed ceilings. From the classic entrance hall a circular stairway ascends to the salon on the second floor. The library, south of the ground-floor hall, extends through two large rooms with windows at front and back. Here, and in the dining room north of the hall, the woodcarving and mantels are excellent. In the smaller of two drawing rooms on the second floor, Heppelwhite and Chippendale furniture, long mirrors, and a fine Adam mantel harmonize with the architectural detail and the frescoed ceiling, having a design of green palm leaves on a gray background. The great salon, forming an L across the front and along one side, is floored with parquetry of California woods, and slender sprays of bamboo extend almost the full length of the ceiling.

Commodore Stephen Decatur, builder of the house, was appointed naval commissioner in 1815, and returned to Washington from a brilliant campaign against the Tripolitan corsairs. Preparing to enjoy his wealth and fame while he and his gifted wife were still relatively young, they built a house suited to entertainment on a lavish scale. They occupied it scarcely more than a year, when Decatur was killed in a duel with Commodore James Barron in a disagreement growing out of a court martial ending the historic *Chesapeake-Leopard* incident. Mrs. Decatur retired to Georgetown (*see Georgetown*) and for a quarter of a century thereafter the Decatur House was occupied by a succession of foreign and American statesmen. They included three Secretaries of State—Clay, Van Buren, and Livingston—and Judah P. Benjamin, who was later Secretary of State for the Confederacy; Foreign Ministers Baron Van Tuyl from Russia, Baron Hyde de Neuville from France, and Sir Charles Vaughn from England; and Representative Howell Cobb, Speaker of the House and later Secretary of the Treasury. John Gadsby, Alexandria tavern keeper, took over the house in 1844 and penned slaves in the attic and in the long brick ell that extends along H Street behind the mansion. "At night," says a contemporary, "you could hear their howls and cries." He conducted auction sales in the high-walled enclosure beside the mansion, and shipped many slaves to Georgia.

The house was commandeered by the Government during the Civil War, after which it was purchased by General Edward F. Beale, under whose grandfather Decatur once served as an ensign. General Beale had himself contributed to a little-known incident in American history, when he led an experimental camel corps across the desert from Texas to California in 1857. The property was inherited by Truxton Beale, former Minister to Persia and Greece, who lived in it until his death in 1936; it has been owned since then by other members of the Beale family.

Many of the old houses that formerly lined the west side of Lafayette Square have been replaced by limestone-front structures, housing associations and foundations. The eight-story building at 740-44 Jackson Place, containing offices of the American Council on Education, and the Association of University Professors, occupies the site of the walled garden adjoining the Decatur House. The mid-nineteenth-century dwelling at 736 Jackson Place, occupied by the Women's City Club, was the home of Theodore Roosevelt and his family in 1902, while the White House was being repaired.

BROOKINGS INSTITUTION (*open by appointment*), 722 Jackson Place, occupies a nine-story limestone building designed by Porter and Lockie, Washington architects, and erected in 1931 at a cost of $720,000. The exterior details, Greek in spirit, are modern in treatment, with a liberal use of aluminum in the entrance decorations. The building, devoted to administrative and research rooms and the library, is joined in the rear by an arcade to a club and residence building occupied by fellows of the institution.

Brookings is a nonprofit corporation devoted to research and training in economics and government, in keeping with the belief of its founder, Robert S. Brookings, that the perpetuation of democracy depends upon an increasing diffusion of knowledge in these fields. The institution was formed in 1928, bringing together three separate organizations. The Institute for Government Research, established in 1916 "to conduct scientific investigations into the theory and practice of governmental organization," continues under the same name as a part of Brookings. The Institute of Economics was organized in 1922 with a ten-year grant from the Carnegie Corporation "to ascertain the facts about current economic problems and to interpret these facts for the people . . . in the most simple and understandable form." The institution also conducts super-graduate training in the social sciences, with work similar to an internship in medicine for selected research fellows. It has produced (1942) 84 volumes dealing with economic issues, 46 volumes on government administration, 66 monographs on Federal bureaus and departments, and 34 pamphlets on economic and governmental problems. It pursues its work independently of special interests and carries out studies that are of timely interest and importance. Its endowments in 1941 approximated $1,600,000, and its annual operation costs about $350,000.

The institution site was once occupied by the Stockton-Sickles House, in which, between 1824 and 1834, three Secretaries of the Navy lived—Smith Thompson, Samuel L. Southard, and Levi Woodbury.

The three-story red-brick house at 712 Jackson Place was occupied by Henry R. Rathbone at the time of the Lincoln tragedy in Ford's Theater. Rathbone and his fiancee, a daughter of Senator Ira Harris, were members of the box party at the theater, and Rathbone grappled with Booth after the assassin fired at Lincoln. Booth stabbed him and escaped.

The Carnegie Endowment for International Peace occupies the three-story red-brick building at the NW. corner of Jackson Place and Pennsylvania Avenue. The International Bureau of American Republics, precursor of the Pan American Union, occupied this building from 1906 to 1910.

The BLAIR HOUSE (*open 9-5 Mon.-Fri., 9-1 Sat.*) 1651 Pennsylvania Avenue NW., a four-story yellow stucco building with white stone lintels over the broad windows, white quoining at the corners, and paneled green shutters, was built about 1810 by Surgeon General Joseph Lovell. A simple Ionic portico, with iron railings, shelters the fanlighted entrance door, with its paneling and polished brass knocker. Originally a two-story structure, a third story was added by Francis Preston Blair, who purchased it about 1830, and the fourth story, treated as an attic parapet above a classic cornice, was built by Montgomery Blair in the late 1850's.

Blair came to Washington from Kentucky, at the behest of President Jackson, to establish the *Washington Globe* as a mouthpiece of "Old Hickory" in political matters. Members of Jackson's "kitchen cabinet" often gathered here—Levi Woodbury, Amos Kendall, Silas Wright, Martin Van Buren, and others. Blair later leased the house to John Y. Mason, Tyler's Secretary of the Navy, and to the historian George Bancroft, who lived here when, as acting Secretary of War under Polk, he gave Zachary Taylor the order for the invasion of Mexico in 1845. Blair willed the house to his son Montgomery, who was Postmaster General under Lincoln and one of the President's most trusted confidants. At a private dinner in this house, following the outbreak of the Civil War, Blair sounded out Robert E. Lee on taking command of Union forces in the war. Lee protested conflicting obligations to the Union and to his native Virginia, and later accepted command of the Virginia troops.

Northwest Rectangle

Streetcars: Potomac Park (to 18th and Virginia Ave.), 19th & F Sts. NW.
Busses: Riverside Stadium (to 26th and D), Lincoln Memorial, 23rd & Constitution, Hains Point.
Taxis: First and second zones.

Architects and city planners are accustomed to refer to the area between 18th and 23rd, C and F Streets NW., as the Northwest, or Federal, Rectangle, excluding the buildings along 17th Street and Constitution Avenue because many of them house non-governmental or quasi-governmental agencies. Extension of the building area to include the old Naval Medical Center and the grounds to the Potomac River on the west threatens to make the Rectangle no longer a rectangle, but the name is handy, and probably will stick. Since the plane figure is in jeopardy, it is perhaps not presumptuous in a guide book to enlarge the Rectangle and make it include the area west of 17th Street, north of Constitution Avenue, and south of H Street.

The U.S. Travel Bureau, at the northeast corner of the Rectangle, dispenses information of local and wider-than-local value. The L of white marble buildings looking east across 17th Street to the landscaped Ellipse, and looking south across Constitution Avenue to the landscaped Mall, includes an art gallery, the national headquarters of the Red Cross and the D. A. R., the Pan American Union, two Government buildings, and two scientific institutions. Within the elongated square are the monumental but frankly functional War Department Building and the two Interior Department Buildings, three institutions of higher education, and the Naval Medical Center, which, according to plan, will give way to a Navy Department Building. The Octagon House, one-time residence of Dolly Madison, indicates the section's importance as one of the earliest residential parts of Washington. There are many other old houses, having the same architectural flavor as those in Georgetown and Alexandria, some of them maintained as residences, some taken over by George Washington University, Washington College of Law, and the American University School of Social Science and Public Affairs. Judged by these campus sectors alone, Washington would be a brisk and youthful place—a college town. Wide-plank cottages in some portions of the Rectangle, occupied by Negroes, are of the same period as the brick mansions; the Negro name for lower levels of the Rectangle is "Foggy Bottom."

Apart from its hedge-clipped and gleaming-marble parts, the Rectangle is an area of ponderous brick apartment houses with windows at the corners, row-houses with tourist rooms to let, a few churches, a

Negro school, a huge Victorian auditorium occupied by Government offices, small eateries and retail establishments, Negro houses without benefit of quaintness, a gas works, a brewery, a commercial stadium, riding academies, close-packed parking lots, and a white cottage standing alone on a hill above the Potomac, as dissociated from Coastal Plain Washington as if it were thirty miles out.

U. S. TRAVEL BUREAU

The United States Travel Bureau (*open 7:45-4:15 Mon.-Fri., 7:45-11:45 Sat.*), 1702 F Street NW., is a service agency administered by the National Park Service. Its counter service distributes literature on the National Parks and that issued by States, transportation agencies, boards of trade, and so on, though its mail distribution is confined to Government publications. Visitors to Washington may obtain information by mail in advance of their visit, information at first hand after their arrival, and help in planning further travels from this point.

The counter room and hallway are decorated with vivid posters—pictures of Jasper National Park, Zion and Yellowstone, skiing in Sun Valley and Maine, touring in Mexico, Caribbean cruises, winter sports in the Poconos, New Orleans Mardi Gras, aviation in Argentine—which are changed in relation to seasonal interest and to a discerning eye for effect.

The Bureau was established in 1937, with additional legislation in 1940 to make it a co-ordinating agency for the promotion of travel by the Federal Government, the States, and private organizations. It issues a monthly *Official Bulletin* (a trade journal for distribution to travel organizations), while its regional offices in New York City and San Francisco publish monthly bulletins for public use—*Eastern Travel Today* and *Travel West.* The Bureau also issues technical pamphlets, such as the 1941 *Recreational Travel and Land Use.*

CORCORAN GALLERY OF ART

The Corcoran Gallery (*open, free, 12-4:30 Mon., 9-4:30 Tue.-Sat., 2-5 Sun., and holidays*), 17th Street between New York Avenue and E Street NW., containing the art collections of William Wilson Corcoran, Washington philanthropist and banker, and William Andrews Clark, metal magnate and Senator from Montana, is a restrained neoclassic structure designed by Ernest Flagg and built in 1879 of white Georgia marble. The façade is severe—the Corcoran Gallery is one of the few public buildings in the vicinity of the White House that has no ornamental columns—though somewhat relieved by an elaborate stone grillwork at the cornice. The original structure consisted of a large central section flanked by end pavilions. The north pavilion, designed as a semicircular bay, contains the offices and studios of the Corcoran School of Art; the central section and south pavilion house the Corcoran Collection. In 1928 a west wing, designed by Charles A. Platt, was added L-wise to contain the Clark Collection.

The principal entrance on 17th Street is flanked by bronze lions cast from the originals modeled by Canova for the tomb of Pope Clement XIII in St. Peter's, Rome. Steps inside the entrance lead to a central colonnaded hall or atrium, around which are disposed the galleries devoted to the CORCORAN COLLECTION. On the main floor of the atrium are plaster casts of Greek, Roman, and Renaissance sculpture, including such time-proved art-school favorites as Michelangelo's *Pieta, The Dying Gaul,* the *Venus of Melos,* Donatello's *David,* the Samothrake *Victory,* and Myron's *Discobolos.* Against the north wall is a bronze-toned cast of Ghiberti's doors to the Baptistry at Florence, the originals of which were termed by Michelangelo "worthy to be the gates of paradise." The galleries adjacent to the atrium on the main floor are chiefly devoted to original sculptures in marble and bronze, including a *Paolo and Francesca* and an *Eve* by Rodin, a portrait bust of Epstein, Paul Manship's bronze group *Dancer and Gazelles,* bronzes by Munier and Frederick Remington, and marbles by Saint-Gaudens and Daniel Chester French. The best organized and most important group in the Corcoran Collection of sculpture are the 108 bronzes of the nineteenth-century French sculptor Antoine Barye, who stood in much the same relation to sculpture as the Barbizon School to painting. This is possibly the most comprehensive collection of Barye ever assembled, and it affords an excellent opportunity to evaluate his straightforward and vigorous modeling of animal subjects.

The second-floor galleries, containing the Corcoran Collection of paintings, are reached by a wide marble stairway, which leads from the atrium, right and left, to an encircling balcony where the larger canvases in the collection are normally hung. The Corcoran Collection, though it includes many European works, is chiefly significant as a record of the development of American painting; indeed, the institution is dedicated to the furtherance of American art and its purchasing policy has been consistently directed toward the encouragement of contemporary American works.

The American works begin with examples of the early portraitists— Copley, Stuart, Malbone, Neagle, the Sullys—and include Samuel F. B. Morse's *Old House of Representatives* (with a key) and Rembrandt Peale's *Washington Before Yorktown.* The Hudson River School of landscape is represented by the works of Doughty, Cole, Durand, Church, Kensett, and others, and the first rush of Barbizon influence in America is exemplified in the works of Inness and Wyant. Of the school of genre painters that arose in America in the mid-nineteenth century, the collection includes works by Mount, Wylie, Bonham, and Eastman Johnson, and of early American impressionists, works by Theodore Robinson, Twachtman, Hassam, Metcalf, Weir, De Camp, Reid, and Mary Cassat. Winslow Homer is represented by *A Light on the Sea,* Ryder by two excellent seascapes, Eakins by

The Pathetic Song, and Sargent by *Oyster Gatherers of Cancale.* Of the moderns, the collection includes works of Gari Melchers, Arthur B. Davies, Maurice Prendergast, E. W. Redfield, Jonas Lie, George Luks, Robert Henri, George Bellows, Eugene Speicher, Alexander Brook, Maurice Sterne, Bernard Karfiol, Henry Lee McFee, Frederick Frieseke, Rockwell Kent, and Robert Philipp.

In Gallery 60, with American paintings, is the second of Hiram Powers' many marble copies of *The Greek Slave,* a chaste (and simpering) nude which in the modest 1840's was much criticized for its frank nakedness. The most popular painting in the gallery is Emile Renouf's oft-reproduced *Helping Hand;* the most popular piece of sculpture, Giuseppe Croff's *Veiled Nun.*

The entrance to the CLARK COLLECTION is on the first floor in Gallery 43, off the southwest corner of the atrium. It includes a Louis XVI salon, purchased intact by Clark from the Paris mansion of the Duc de la Trenaille, assembled in his Fifth Avenue apartment, and transferred to Washington upon his death. The harpsichord was once the property of Marie Antoinette. Four Gobelin tapestries hang in one room furnished with a suite of eighteenth-century furniture, designed by the Adam brothers and painted by Pergolese. Four Gothic tapestries, outstanding among their kind in the world, portraying hunting scenes of the Duke of Burgundy, are ascribed to fifteenth-century *tapissiers* of Arras, France. An important collection of Ispahan (Persian) rugs, principally of the sixteenth and early seventeenth centuries, includes an unusually large specimen, measuring 14 by 44 feet. Rare laces number about 50 pieces—seventeenth and eighteenth century French, Italian, and Flemish works. Faïence includes majolica of the fifteenth and sixteenth centuries, Delft ware of the seventeenth and eighteenth centuries, and de Palissy tablework and ornaments of the sixteenth century. The Urbino majolica is especially notable for its opalescent luster. Among the antiquities are funerary figurines, household figurines, and household ware ranging in age from the tenth to the second century B. C., and including Grecian, Egyptian, and Etruscan specimens.

The Clark Collection of paintings includes two Rembrandts—*An Elderly Man in an Armchair* and *Man with a Hat, Holding a Scroll*—three Van Dycks, a Rubens, and a Franz Hals, in addition to an entire gallery devoted to Dutch and Flemish painters of the seventeenth century—Cuyp, Van Goyen, De Hooch, Maes, Ostade, Ruisdale, and others. Eighteenth-century England is represented by two Gainsboroughs, a Raeburn, a Hogarth, a Lawrence, and two Reynolds. In a single gallery are 22 paintings by Corot, perhaps the largest collection of Corots outside the Louvre, revealing all phases of his art. Other representatives of the Barbizon School are Monticelli, Cazin, Diaz de la Peña, Rousseau, and D'Aubigny. Modern French paintings are represented by five works of Degas, three of Daumier, two of Chardin, and others. The Jeanne d'Arc series in the gallery was specially commissioned by Clark to Boutet de Monvel, the noted illustrator. Drawings by the old masters include works by Raphael, Rubens, Murillo, Titian, Velasquez, and Leonardo da Vinci.

AMERICAN RED CROSS

The American Red Cross is housed in three green-roofed white marble buildings (*open 8:30-4:30 weekdays, 1-4:30 Sun.*) in the block bounded by 17th, 18th, D, and E Streets NW.

The EAST BUILDING, facing 17th Street, is a neoclassic structure designed by Trowbridge and Livingston, New York architects, and erected in 1913-17. A circular drive, bordered by boxwood and magnolias, leads from 17th Street to the two-story Corinthian portico with its massive pediment, balanced by colonnaded pavilions extending north and south. Bronze grilled doors lead into a broad central hall finished in white marble, with a monumental stairway leading to the second floor. On the stair landing are busts personifying *Faith, Hope,* and *Charity,* by Hiram Powers. Elsewhere in the building is a bronze group, *Spirit of the Red Cross,* by Gertrude V. Whitney; a painting by Gentile Bellini, given by the city of Venice; and a collection of water colors by Anna Upjohn. The Georgian-style ASSEMBLY ROOM, on the second floor, is lighted by stained-glass windows designed by Louis C. Tiffany, depicting St. Filomena, the Red Cross Knight, and Una of Spenser's *Faerie Queene.*

The RED CROSS MUSEUM, in the basement, opened in 1919 as a memorial to Red Cross workers in the First World War, contains a battered but complete Red Cross ambulance that served throughout the conflict, a "rolling kitchen" that served 480,000 cups of cocoa on the battlefield, models of hospital and war scenes by Dwight Franklin, flags, war medals, kits, and other memorabilia. One room displays civil relief material and models, and the remaining exhibits include the trunk-bed Clara Barton used in the Civil War, and photographs and souvenirs of Florence Nightingale. The LIBRARY, also on the basement floor, contains about 7,000 volumes on the Red Cross, including the only complete collection in the Nation on the origin in Geneva (1863) and subsequent development of the Red Cross movement.

The NORTH BUILDING, facing E Street, similar to the headquarters building, except that it has Ionic colonnades, houses offices of the District of Columbia Chapter. The building, opened in 1929 as a memorial to the women of the First World War, also has a Braille room, a workroom, a canteen in the basement, and an auditorium on the second floor.

The WEST BUILDING, facing 18th Street, in architectural harmony with the others, was opened in 1929 as an office annex to the national headquarters.

In the landscaped courtyard formed by the three buildings is Robert Tait McKenzie's bronze STATUE OF A NURSE, unveiled in 1934 as a memorial to Jane A. Delano and 296 other nurses who died during World War I.

D.A.R. BUILDINGS

The National Society of the Daughters of the American Revolution has three imposing buildings (*open 9:30-4 Mon.-Fri., 9:30-12 Sat.*) in the city block bounded by 17th, 18th, C, and D Streets NW. Founded in 1890, the D.A.R. membership includes more than 170,000 women descended from patriots of the Revolutionary period, and there are more than 2,400 local chapters. It distributes annually nearly 500,000 copies of the *D.A.R. Manual for Citizenship,* does notable work in preserving historic buildings and sites, and encourages genealogical and historical researches.

MEMORIAL CONTINENTAL HALL (*guides*), facing 17th Street, designed by Edward Pearce Casey and completed in 1910 at a cost of more than $500,000, is a white marble building with two colonnaded porticoes and corner pavilions, the larger portico or porte-cochère forming the central feature of the east façade. The 13 Ionic columns of the semicircular south portico, symbolizing the Thirteen Original States, were donated by State chapters and legislatures.

Triple bronze doors at the main entrance memorialize the founders, charter members, and heroes of Connecticut and Massachusetts. The main entrance hall, designed in the Georgian manner, is finished in marble and enriched with fluted pilasters. Oval niches contain sculptured busts of Revolutionary heroes. At the south end of the corridor ing to Thomas McKean, Delaware signer of the Declaration.

The AUDITORIUM, seating 2,000, has the formal dignity of an old meeting hall, its white walls brightened by State flags, while a replica of the Betsy Ross flag hangs from the ground-glass ceiling. Galleries extend around three sides of the room, and a roomy stage is banked with tiers of boxes. In the south gallery is a full-length portrait of Martha Washington, by E. F. Andrews. In the north gallery is Darius Cobb's *Washington on Dorchester Heights.* A table and chair on the platform are reproductions of those used at the signing of the Declaration of Independence, and Rembrandt Peale's "porthole" portrait of George Washington hangs on the stage wall. Plenary sessions of the Conference on the Limitation of Armament were held in this room in 1921.

A series of sliding doors opens from the auditorium into the north and south MUSEUM GALLERIES, with their parquet floors, coupled pilasters, and vaulted ceilings. In these rooms more than 2,000 relics of Revolutionary days are preserved—needlework, silver, glass, china, jewelry, fans, dresses, household accessories, and weapons, all antedating 1830.

Many States have individual CHAPTER ROOMS in this building, furnished in a manner typical of early American homes. Most of them represent dining or drawing rooms, but there is a music room containing harpsichord, melodeons, and flutinas; a children's attic paneled in pine by Wallace Nutting; a bedroom with a four-poster bed and bed steps; and a Colonial kitchen with an original brick fireplace and crane. The New Jersey Room has Jacobean-style woodwork and furniture made from the timber of the British frigate *Augusta,* which sank in the Delaware River in 1777; its stained-glass windows portray dramatic scenes in New Jersey history. Outstanding pieces in the chapter rooms include Sheraton, Hepplewhite, and Chippendale furniture; the drop-leaf table on which George and Martha Washington ate their bridal supper; the sea chest of John Paul Jones; the Benjamin Reeve clock; the candle stand owned by William Penn; and the sofa belonging to Thomas McKean, Delaware signer of the Declaration.

The ADMINISTRATION BUILDING, facing D Street, a two-story Kentucky limestone structure designed by Marsh and Peter, Washington architects, has housed D.A.R. administrative offices since 1923. Long glass corridors, enclosing a landscaped central court, connect it with Memorial Continental Hall. On the south lawn stands Gertrude Vanderbilt Whitney's marble MEMORIAL STATUE to the founders of the society, the draped figure of a woman with arms outstretched.

CONSTITUTION HALL, 18th Street between C and D Streets, an Alabama limestone edifice with an auditorium seating 4,000, was designed by John Russell Pope and built at a cost of nearly $1,700,000. An Ionic entrance portico, surmounted by a pediment bearing a sculptured American eagle, accents the west façade. A carriage entrance with drive ramp extends along the north side, and on the south front is an entrance with a promenade terrace.

Broad marble corridors extend around the auditorium on three sides, and the decorative scheme of the U-shaped amphitheater is carried out in buff and blue, emblematic colors of the D.A.R., adopted from the colors of Washington's staff uniforms. The walls are of old ivory and the boxes are hung with blue velvet and decorated with State seals. The wide stage platform is decorated with four painted hangings by James Monroe Hewlett—the Boston Tea Party, the inauguration of George Washington, Jefferson reading the Declaration of Independence, and Colonel Moultrie receiving congratulations on his victory at Sullivan's Island. A painted lunette over the stage portrays Revolutionary battle flags. The National Symphony Orchestra and visiting artists give concerts and recitals here; the American Folklore Festival is held annually in this great hall; and it serves many civic and patriotic uses.

The D.A.R. LIBRARY, on the second floor of Constitution Hall, approached by a stairhall in the Administration Building, has more than 20,000 volumes of rare history and genealogy books, available for research to members and prospective members.

PAN AMERICAN UNION

The white marble villa of the Pan American Union (*open 9-4:30 Mon.-Fri., 9-12 Sat.; guides*), NW. corner 17th Street and Constitution Avenue NW., houses an international organization devoted to promoting better relations among the 21 American Republics—Argentina, Bolivia, Brazil, Chile, Colombia, Costa Rica, Cuba, Dominican Republic, Ecuador, El Salvador, Guatemala, Haiti, Honduras, Mexico, Nicaragua, Panama, Paraguay, Peru, United States, Uruguay, and Venezuela. In style the building represents a felicitous combination of French and Spanish Renaissance influences, with a free admixture, particularly in the interior, of Aztec and Maya motifs. Designed by Albert Kelsey and Paul P. Cret, the main building and the Annex, in the rear, were built in 1908-10 at a cost of $1,100,000, the major portion of which was contributed by Andrew Carnegie.

The main façade, facing 17th Street, is composed of a central section having three monumental arched entrances with Spanish-style bronze gates and surmounted by a section of red-tile roof and a classic balustrade. Flanking the entrance doors are symbolic statues set against the base of a paneled section, and at each end of the building are short wings. The north statue, by Gutzon Borglum, a symbolic female figure and child, is representative of North America, and the south statue, by Isidor Konti, is a similar group symbolizing South America. High above the statues, at the roof level of the wings, are bas-relief panels depicting Washington's farewell to his generals and the meeting of Bolívar and San Martín, South American liberators. Above these, just beneath the cornice line, are high-relief figures of a North American eagle and a South American condor.

The spacious entrance hall, finished in white marble, establishes the stately scale of the interior. With its barrel-vaulted ceiling it rises through two stories and extends the full width of the central section of the building. Three high arches give direct access to the central patio, and flanking arches open over wide marble stairways to the galleried second floor. Information may be obtained at the guard's table in the entrance hall, and literature on the member countries can be purchased at nominal prices. Cases at each end of the hall display brilliantly-colored Latin American stamp issues and pamphlet materials. At either end of the hall two veined black marble columns, with bronze caps and bases, mark the entrance to office corridors. On each side of the central arches are oval gold-leaf plaques.

The skylit PATIO, the most conspicuous feature of the interior, is kept tropically warm to permit continuous growth of palms, bananas, coffee, rubber, papaya, and other exotic plants, and to provide comfort for brilliantly-hued macaws on their perches. The pink marble fountain by Gertrude Vanderbilt Whitney, in the center of the patio, embodies phases of Aztec, Zapotecan, and Mayan art. The brick courtyard around the fountain is embellished with figures of Inca and Maya deities, inlaid in black tile. A polychrome frieze beneath the patio skylight contains the insignia of various American countries and names of national heroes. Above the frieze is an overhanging wooden cornice, painted in rich colors, and a sloping tile roof. The skylight is rolled back in warm weather and the colors stand out vividly against the blue sky.

In a hallway behind the patio is the Pan American Travel Service booth, decorated with vividly colored posters, and a long table containing current Latin American periodicals in Spanish and Portuguese. At the north end of this hall is the COLUMBUS MEMORIAL LIBRARY, containing 100,000 volumes on the American republics, and thousands of maps. The library is open to the public for consultation and research. In a corridor north of the patio is an exhibit of Mexican crafts including silver, gold, ceramics, textile, and fiber products.

An EXHIBIT ROOM west of the patio contains numerous cases displaying productions of Latin America—exquisite laces from Paraguay, drawnwork from Brazil, samplers and jewelry from Mexico, hand-woven textiles and silver jewelry from Chile, and cases containing brilliantly-hued hummingbirds, butterflies, and moths. Display items drawn from the Union's library include P. Pedro Murillo's *Geographia Historica,* a treatise on the West Indies printed at Madrid in 1752; the decree of Símon Bolívar abolishing slavery in New Granada, 1827; *Historie of the World,* by Sir Walter Ralegh, printed at London in 1614; Garcilasso de la Vega's *Royal Commentaries of Peru,* London edition of 1688; and Antonio de Herrera's *Historia General de las Indias Occidentales,* printed at Madrid in 1728. Other cases in the same room show wood, straw, pottery, and textile products from the Dominican Republic; leather, silver, pottery, onyx, and textile wares from Mexico; agate, amethyst, tourmaline, opal, emerald, topaz, garnet, and lapis lazuli from various Latin American countries.

An EXHIBIT HALL on the west side of the building is centered by large-scale relief maps of Latin America and the Panama Canal. Cases around the walls show prehistoric pottery, flints, and other artifacts of ancient peoples; Latin American tobaccos in their many forms; "Panama" hats from Ecuador, made from the fibrous *jipijapa* grass and so named because Panama was once the most important market for them; copper ores from Chile; Colombian glass; *maté* from Paraguay; cabinet woods and petroleum samples from Venezuela; sugar, logwood, rice, kapok, sisal hemp, and other products of Haiti; marble from Uruguay; ramie, straw and flax from Argentine; minerals, woods, coffee, rubber, fibers, nuts, and skins from Brazil. A large case displays birds of Latin America, including such specimens as the *jabiru* stork, the scarlet ibis, the roseate spoonbill, several varieties of toucans, and the *quetzal,* the long-tailed green-plumed national bird of Guatemala. At the south end of the hall are large maps showing the North and South American sections of the partially completed Pan American highway, extending from Laredo, Texas, on the north to quadruple southern termini at Santiago, Chile; Buenos Aires, Argentine; Asuncion, Paraguay; and Rio de Janiero, Brazil.

Broad marble stairways lead from the entrance hall to the GALLERY OF PATRIOTS, running around three sides of the patio on the second floor, and containing a series of white marble busts mounted on pink-

and-gray marble pedestals. From the southeast point of the U-shaped gallery around to the northeast, the busts are as follows: José Matias Delgado (1767-1832), Vicar of El Salvador and precursor of Central American independence, by Ferraris; Francisco Morazán (1792-60), Honduras, president of the ill-fated Central American Federation for eight years after 1830, by Robert Aitken; Juan Rafael Mora (1814-60), Costa Rica, the Central American leader most responsible for defeat of William Walker's filibustering expedition of 1855-57, by Juan R. Bonilla; Tomás Herrera (1804-54), liberator of Panama from Colombia in 1840, by Chester Beach; José Gervasio Artigas (1764-1850), liberator of Uruguay from Spain in 1815 and leader of the "Great Exodus" of 1811, by J. Belloni; José Julián Martí (1853-95), Cuban soldier, journalist, and poet, who devoted his life to the cause of independence for Cuba, by A. Penucci; Bernardo O'Higgins (1778-1843), leader in the liberation of Chile from Spain in 1818; José de San Martín (1778-1850), Argentine revolutionary leader who assisted Bolívar in the War of Independence, by Herbert Adams; Benito Juarez (1806-72), Zapotec Indian, the "Mexican Lincoln" who fought for liberal reforms for 30 years; George Washington, United States, by Hiram Powers; José Bonifácio de Andrada e Silva (1763-1838), founder of independent Brazil and internationally known naturalist, by F. Charpentier; Símon Bolívar (1783-1830), *El Libertador* of Venezuela and four other republics, and Latin America's greatest soldier and statesman, by Rudolph Evans; Francisco de Paula Santander (1792-1840), Colombian patriot and collaborator with Bolívar in the War of Independence, by R. Villar; Hipólito Unánue (1755-1833), Peruvian scientist and writer, by Sally James Farnham; Juan Pablo Duarte (1813-76), first president of the Dominican Republic and liberator of that country in 1843 from Haiti, by Abelardo Rodríguez Urdaneta; Justo Rufino Barrios (1835-85), "The Reformer," president of Guatemala (1872-85), who lost his life fighting for re-establishment of the Central American Federation; Antonio José de Sucre (1795-1830), first president of Bolivia and aide to Bolívar in the War of Independence, by Sally James Farnham; Jean Jacques Dessalines (c. 1758-1806), Negro ruler of Haiti from 1803 to 1806, by Normil Ulysse Charles.

The HALL OF THE AMERICAS, opening from the Gallery of Patriots on the west, is a great salon 100 feet long and 70 feet wide, used for inter-American conferences and for various ceremonial purposes. The barrel-vaulted ceiling, two stories above the floor, is hung with huge crystal chandeliers and decorated at each end with stained glass windows. The west side of the room, looking out on the formal garden, is lighted by five great arched windows with purple hangings and colorful borders by Nicola D'Ascenzo. Twinned Ionic columns rise from the polished parquet floor, and the great white room is brightened at one end by clusters of flags representing countries in the Pan American Union. The Governing Board Room, south of this hall, centered by an oval table of Dominican mahogany around which are

matching chairs, each bearing the coat of arms of a country represented in the Union, is ornamented with a bronze frieze by Sally
James Farnham, depicting historic events of the Americas.

Through the end openings of the hall, broad balustraded marble
stairways sweep down to a flagstoned court at garden level in the
rear of the building. The landscaped AZTEC GARDEN behind the main
building is centered by a rectangular reflecting pool, at the west end
of which, on an ivy-grown base, cross-legged, sits Xochipilli, the Aztec
god of flowers. Summer concerts in this garden by the United Service
Orchestra (Army, Navy, and Marine musicians) place special emphasis
on Latin American music.

The white stucco ANNEX, with its triple-arched loggia, red-tile
roof, and iron-balconied windows, is the residence of the Director General of the Pan American Union. Blue tilework lining the interior of
the loggia, most effective under artificial light at night, represents one
of the few modern reproductions of Aztec and Maya tiles found at
Palenque, Copán, Quirigua, Mitla, and Chichen-Itzá, noted archeological sites in Latin America. Centering a frieze high above the tilework
is the head of a huge monster, reproduced from the original on the
monastery at Chichen-Itzá, and on each side are standing figures reproduced from the Temple of Jaguars there. Smaller panels throughout
the frieze represent designs from many archeological sites in Mexico
and Central America.

U. S. PUBLIC HEALTH SERVICE

In a terraced and landscaped square at Constitution Avenue between
19th and 20th Streets NW., is the four-story white marble Public
Health Service Building (*open 9:15-5:45 Mon.-Fri., 9:15-1:15 Sat.*),
designed in neoclassic style by J. H. de Sibour and completed in 1931.
The ivory-toned marble stands out against the green of the lawn, the
hollies and magnolias, giving an appropriate air of neatness to a building devoted to the public health. A surrounding esplanade partly hides
the raised basement on which the three stories and attic are built, and
the squared U-shape of the plan is broken inside the U by a two-story
wing.

The approach to the building is by a wide straight walk, broken
by a few short steps, and entrance is through aluminum doors. The
auditorium, built in the central north wing, is entered from the
ground floor directly opposite the main entrance. In the same wing,
on the second floor, is the HEALTH SERVICE LIBRARY, having a specialized collection relating to public health. Offices and laboratories
of the Service open off the three main corridors on each floor. The
simple, modern treatment of the interior reflects the same neatness as
the exterior and grounds of the building. The Public Health Service,
administered by the Federal Security Agency, is under the immediate
direction of the Surgeon General.

The NATIONAL INSTITUTE OF HEALTH, an 87-acre

tract along the Rockville Pike north of Bethesda, Md., housed in 20 three-story red brick buildings of Colonial design, is also under the supervision of the Public Health Service. The centrally placed Administration Building contains executive offices, six laboratories, the Institute's scientific library, an auditorium, a cafeteria, and a medical dispensary, in addition to a central heating plant for the entire group. The Industrial Hygiene Building is mainly devoted to laboratories. The Public Health Methods and Animal Building houses statistical and other offices and an animal breeding unit for raising animals used in experimental medicine. The Cancer Institute Building contains many laboratory and other units for research into the causes and cure of cancer, including ultra-modern chemical and electrotherapy laboratories. Special germ-free or sterility rooms have walls and ceilings of stainless steel and are ventilated with filtered air. The Infectious Diseases and Biology Building, fitted similarly to the Cancer Building, is used for laboratory study of infectious diseases and the testing of biological serums and similar preparations. The Chemistry and Pharmacology Building is equipped for specialized laboratory studies. Fourteen additional buildings are provided as living quarters for scientific personnel of the Institute. Begun in 1936, the Institute was dedicated by President Franklin D. Roosevelt early in 1941.

FEDERAL RESERVE BUILDING

Set back 200 feet from Constitution Avenue, in a formally landscaped marble-curbed plot, the four-story white Georgia marble Federal Reserve Building (*open 9-5 Mon.-Fri., 9-1 Sat.*), between 20th and 21st Streets NW. and extending to C Street, was designed by Paul P. Cret and completed in 1937 at a cost of $3,484,000. The formal garden on either side of the broad marble walk and steps approaching the simple and monumental entrance is centered by a fountain of black Coopersburg granite. The entrance is marked by a simple motif of piers surmounted by an American eagle in white marble, the work of Sidney Waugh. In contrast with the plain white surface of the building is the design of the bronze windows, separated with spandrels of polished Swedish granite, on which bronze plaques are mounted. Bronze balconies on 20th and 21st Streets reproduce the railing of a nineteenth-century Philadelphia residence. The air-conditioned building is H-shaped in plan, and the east and west courts are formally planted in such a manner as to focus attention on wall fountains facing the bronze entrance gates. Masks for the fountains were designed by Walker Hancock. The more generally used C Street entrance is flanked by pylons with figures in bas-relief by John Gregory, symbolizing the United States and the Federal Reserve System.

The Constitution Avenue entrance opens on a lobby walled with Kansas lesina stone; in the marble floor is set a bronze plaque reproducing the seal of the Board of Governors of the Federal Reserve System. The plaster ceiling is decorated with motifs of Greek coins and a relief of Cybele, Anatolian earth-mother. On the east wall is a bronze bas-relief plaque by Herbert Adams, with a portrait of Woodrow Wilson, founder of the Federal Reserve System, and a quotation from his first inaugural address: "We shall deal with our economic system as it is and as it may be modified, not as it might be if we had a clean sheet of paper to write upon; and step by step we shall make it what it should be." On the opposite wall is a companion plaque by the same sculptor, with a profile portrait of Carter Glass, "Defender of the Federal Reserve System," and a quotation from his book, *An Adventure in Constructive Finance.*

A monumental staircase leads to the second floor, notable for its mosaic-bordered marble floors and wrought iron work by Samuel Yellin. Ceilings of second-floor corridors are decorated with emblems of the 12 Federal Reserve banks, and offices representative of these banks are grouped around the stair corridor.

The BOARD ROOM, in the Constitution Avenue wing on the second floor, measuring 32 by 56 feet, has a fireplace of Tavernelle Fleuri marble with an inlaid bronze relief symbolizing stability and productivity. Statistical charts hang in bronze frames, and on the east wall is a Federal Reserve map of the United States painted by Ezra Winter. Parquet flooring bordered with marble, and painted plaster walls and ceilings contribute to the richness of the room. Harmonizing marbles in this room represent only a portion of the 28 colors and textures used in decorating the interior of the building.

The BOARD LIBRARY is in the same second-floor wing, and the Division of Research and Statistics has its own library on the third floor. The fourth floor, covering only the middle branch of the H-shaped plan, has a cafeteria and dining rooms, and an outlet to a flagstone terrace on the west wing, from which there is a pleasant view of the surrounding Mall and Northwest Rectangle.

NATIONAL ACADEMY OF SCIENCES

The three-story white marble Academy of Sciences Building (*open, free, 9-5 weekdays; closed Thanksgiving, Christmas and New Year's*), Constitution Avenue between 21st and 22nd Streets NW., was designed by Bertram Grosvenor Goodhue and completed in 1924 at a cost of $1,450,000. The façade, accented by strong window motifs in green bronze, is gracious and dignified. A quotation from Aristotle on the value of science, in the original Greek, forms a frieze below the cornice line, above which rises the green-roofed attic story. Cresting on the roof line consists of alternating owl and lynx figures, symbolizing wisdom and observation. Bas-relief bronzes by Lee Lawrie, representing a procession of the great figures of science, from Thales to Maxwell, serve as spandrels between first- and second-story windows. The striking use of bronze is repeated in the embossed entrance doors, depicting eight episodes in the history of science.

The entrance foyer is terminated at each end with bronze and glass grilles, and the AUDITORIUM, cruciform in plan, lies beyond. At the apex of the dome, which was decorated by Hildreth Miere, is a symbolization of the sun surrounded by the planets. Allegorical figures in the pendentives represent the four Greek elements—earth, fire, water, and air. In the ceilings of the arches are painted the insignia of the academy of ancient Alexandria and of the three great academies of Europe—the Accademia dei Lincei of Rome, the Académie des Sciences of Paris, and the Royal Society of London. Dome and vaulting are colored in crisp tones of blue, gold, and sienna. Behind the rostrum at the north end of the Auditorium is a mural by Albert Herter, depicting Prometheus lighting his torch at the chariot of the sun.

The Auditorium is surrounded by seven EXHIBITION ROOMS with exhibits illustrating fundamental phenomena of nature and current scientific research. The auditorium is also used for exhibits, containing among other things a striking demonstration of the rotation of the earth through the Foucault pendulum experiment. In a few minutes' time a shift of the plane of the pendulum becomes visible, proving by simple physical analysis the movement of the earth on its axis. Most of the exhibits are dynamic, revealing phenomena or experiments in action. The observer presses a button and sees an experiment performed before his eyes, visibly demonstrating current progress in research.

The second and third floors are devoted to the offices of the National Academy of Sciences, the National Research Council, and Science Service.

AMERICAN INSTITUTE OF PHARMACY

The American Institute of Pharmacy, headquarters and research center of the American Pharmaceutical Association (*open, free, 9-5 Mon.-Fri., 9-1 Sat.*), Constitution Avenue between 22nd and 23rd Streets NW., is a relatively small, shrinelike white marble building, designed by John Russell Pope and opened in 1934. Rising from a green slope above the Lincoln Memorial, the distinguished façade, lifting above a balustraded terrace, conveys a spirit of balanced charm and dignity. The central portion, with its high attic parapet, is enclosed on three sides by a series of one-story outer chambers. The paneled bronze entrance portal, with its arched, grilled transom, is flanked by allegorical bas-reliefs, the work of Ulysses Ricci—*Pharmakeutike,* symbolizing the progress of pharmacy, and *Phos Kai Elpis,* representative of Light and Hope.

The spacious entrance hall, with classic marble trim, has an inlaid floor, Ionic pilasters, and a domical ceiling. In a niche facing the entrance stands Richard Burge's STATUE OF WILLIAM PROCTOR, JR., venerated as the "Father of American Pharmacy."

East of the central hall is the LIBRARY, containing a specialized collection of technical books and periodicals, open to the public for reference, but not available for loan. Two fine old pharmacy show globes of bronze and blown glass are exhibited in the reading room.

Several rooms west of the central hall display items of interest in the history of pharmacy—manuscripts and early editions of the *U. S. Pharmacopoeia* and the *National Formulary,* mortars and pestles, glass jars more than a century old from a drugstore in Baltimore, brass scales, show globes of two centuries, and other memorabilia of the profession and of the Association. Executive offices occupy the north side of the building, and a laboratory in the basement is used for research in the standardization of drugs.

The cost of the building was met by subscriptions from 14,000 druggists throughout the Nation, and it is the headquarters of a national organization having affiliates in every State and a total membership of nearly 40,000. The Association was organized in Philadelphia in 1852, though the first effective standardization of drugs and medicinal preparations much preceded this date, with issuance of the first *Pharmacopeia* in 1830 by delegates from medical societies. Since then, a convention has assembled in Washington every 10 years to elect a committee for the preparation of a new and amended edition.

In 1888, the year in which it was chartered at Washington, the Association published the first edition of the *National Formulary,* a list of standard compounds based on the drugs and simples listed in the *Pharmacopoeia.* The prescriptions in both publications are recognized as standard by Federal and State laws. Both publications appear decennially, with occasional supplementary bulletins. Among the others the most important is the *Recipe Book,* a set of standard formulas for preparations that pharmacists are expected to have in stock. The Association works closely with Congress and various State legislatures in drafting laws to govern the preparation and sale of medicinal products, but it is supported independently by endowments, dues, and the sale of literature. Advice is provided free to individuals and organizations.

OLD NAVAL MEDICAL CENTER

The Old Naval Medical Center (*open by special permission only*), occupies an eight-block area bounded by Constitution Avenue, E Street, 23rd Street, and 25th Street NW., with its main entrance gate at 23rd and E. Wartime agencies and the U. S. Navy Blood Donors Service are housed in the Naval Hospital, Naval Medical School, Naval Dental School, and auxiliary buildings. In front of the old buff-brick NAVAL OBSERVATORY BUILDING, erected in 1843, is R. H. Perry's bronze STATUE OF BENJAMIN RUSH (1745-1813), a signer of the Declaration of Independence and founder of the first medical dispensary in the United States, at Philadelphia in 1785. The wooded and landscaped grounds have roads and winding paths, from which there are good views of the western Mall, the Potomac, and near-by Virginia.

With completion of the new Medical Center near Bethesda, Maryland, late in 1941, naval medical facilities of this institution were transferred there. Plans call for replacement of the Naval Hospital group by a large Navy Department Building, with a museum-harbor for historic naval vessels in the Potomac above Arlington Memorial Bridge.

The NEW NAVAL MEDICAL CENTER at Bethesda, completed late in 1941, consists of a central towerlike building rising 500 feet above the Rockville Pike, with 16 stories devoted to administration, dental and medical schools, and hospital facilities. A rear wing houses a 180-bed ward, and the edifice has been so designed by the architect Paul P. Cret that additional wings in harmony with the main structure may be added as the need arises. The 10 buildings, costing $4,850,000, include a power plant, additional hospital facilities, nurses' and corpsmen's quarters, a greenhouse, and officers' quarters.

WAR DEPARTMENT BUILDING

Matching or even surpassing the massive effect of the two Interior Department Buildings in the Northwest Rectangle, the seven-story buff limestone War Department Building (*office hours 8:15-5 weekdays, open by special permit only*), 21st Street between C and D Streets NW., is the first unit, or one-quarter, of a larger plan to provide something over a million square feet of floor space for administration of the Nation's military branch.

Designed by Gilbert Stanley Underwood and William Dewey Foster of the Public Buildings Administration, the huge structure, erected at a total cost of $10,800,000 for the entire project, was completed in 1941. Large six-story wings extend from each side of a central three-door entrance set in a plain two-story base. Directly above the entrance stand limestone sculptures by Henry Kreis. Four piers extend upward from the statuary through four floors to form a monumental portico. Nine square medallions above the portico provide a decorative frieze completing the east façade. Plans call for a relief plaque high up within the portico, and for two large sculptural groups to occupy cheek blocks right and left of the entrance. Windows in the two-story base are individual wall-openings, but above this, through the four upper stories, they are ranged in vertical banks, connected by spandrels of polished carnelian granite.

The edifice is representative of an architectural trend since the late 1930's to dispense with columned and sculptured edifices and to erect buildings frankly for office use, depending on the handling of masses, lines, and planes for pleasing architectural effect. Foster and Underwood have accomplished interesting results in their design for this enormous building. They have used vertical banks of spandreled windows and occasional pierced grille windows to good effect. Their combination of angles and setbacks, particularly between the wings on the north and south façades, with a seventh-story attic crowning the composition, has resulted in a maximum of light-space for offices and a design having classical proportions and rhythms in a functional modern structure. The floor plan is essentially X-shaped, with four wings extending from a rectangular central section, though this design is altered on the west façade by a truncated central extension, to connect with a future unit. More than 7 acres of floor space is provided in the present structure, but a total of nearly 28 acres of usable space is planned for the completed War Department group. An additional $15,200,000 for this purpose has been authorized by Congress.

The main entrance opens into a hall-like lobby finished in yellowish-red travertine and black marble. Facing the entrance is a great wall space, 12 by 50 feet, to be occupied by one of the largest murals in Washington. The interior of the building is finished in varicolored domestic marbles and terrazzo. Monumental stairs give access from the entrance lobby to second floor exhibition spaces on either side, where dioramas and individual objects will form a military museum which the public may visit without entering the office areas.

This portion of the building provides suites for the Secretary of War, the Chief of Staff, and other staff officers. The offices for the Secretary and the Chief of Staff are high-ceilinged rooms on the fifth floor with wood paneling from floor to ceiling. Many of the other staff offices in the air-conditioned building are also paneled.

SOUTH INTERIOR BUILDING

The six-winged seven-storied limestone South Interior Building (*open 7:45-4:15 Mon.-Fri., 7:45-11:45 Sat.*), covering the "grand square" on C Street between 18th and 19th and extending to D Street NW., is frankly expressive of the utility and efficiency underlying its conception as an office building, and its monumental scale is a direct reflection of the huge scope of the departmental activities it accommodates. The building consists of a central section with six wings on each side, making its east and west façades the most characteristic features of the structure, in the alternation of wings and bays, and the heavy regularity of shadows cast in these open courts. The two upper stories are set back, forming an attic to the building as a whole. Paired windows across the north and south fronts and on the wing-ends are separated by pilasters, and a recessed three-story portico over five-door entrances at each end of the building is supported by square piers. The only ornamental features are the seals of the Thirteen Original Colonies across the south façade. The air-conditioned building is entered through heavy bronze doors on the first floor at the south end and on the second at the north. Centering each marble-finished entrance lobby, inlaid in the floor, is a bronze "buffalo seal" of the Department of the Interior.

Designed by Waddy B. Wood, this building—Project No. 1 of the Public Works Administration, then administered by the Interior Department—was begun in August 1935 and completed in December 1936, constituting a record at the time for construction of such an enormous edifice. It has more than 16 acres of usable floor space, 2 miles of corridors, 20 high-speed elevators, escalators from the basement to the second floor, and basement parking space approached by ramps from 18th and 19th Streets. Laying the cornerstone in 1936, President Franklin D. Roosevelt said of "this serviceable new structure, I like to think of it as symbolical of the Nation's vast resources that we are sworn to protect, and this stone . . . as the cornerstone of a conservation policy." He used the same trowel that George Washington employed in laying the cornerstone of the Capitol in 1793.

The CAPITAL PARKS PERMIT OFFICE, entered only from the outside, on 18th Street just north of C, issues permits for the use of picnic sites in the National Capital Park System, in and near Washington. Permits are issued, on written application only, for picnic areas with fireplaces; tables and other facilities are available to the public without specific permission.

Within the first-floor south entrance, in the southeast corner of the building, is the AUDITORIUM, seating 900, its stage ornamented with an oil mural by Louis Bouché, depicting a desert scene centered by antelope and cacti, and incorporating in the foreground and side panels other symbols of the Department and of western lands. Left of the stage is a cast-stone bas-relief panel by Heinz Warneke, showing the explorers Lewis and Clark in the foreground, the Indian woman Sacajawea and her papoose and other members of the expedition (1804-06) in the background. Ralph Stackpole's limestone bas-relief panel of Major J. W. Powell exploring the Grand Canyon (1869-72), on the right of the stage, depicts strong blocky figures in rowboats coursing down the swift Colorado River between high canyon walls. A frieze below the gallery level, around three sides of the auditorium, consists of bronze great seals of the States and Territories.

In the main corridor, facing each other on opposite walls near the south group of elevators, are Boris Gilbertson's ruggedly stylized limestone bas-reliefs of moose and bison families.

The INTERIOR MUSEUM, occupying Wing 2 west of the main corridor, presents a visual exposition of the Department's conservation activities, through dioramas, photographs, maps, paintings, documents, models, charts, scientific specimens, craft works, and artifacts. A huge Navaho blanket, based on the design of a medicine man's sand-painting, is shown in the information bay right of the entrance. Along the central corridor are four framed oil paintings by W. H. Jackson (b. 1843), Government photographer from 1870 to 1878. They were painted when he was in his nineties and illustrate the Hayden Survey, a Government expedition, on the Yellowstone River in 1871, the King Survey of 1867-69, the Wheeler Survey of 1873-75, and the Powell Survey of the Grand Canyon in 1867-69. Jackson made the first photographs of such areas as the Yellowstone Park, the Mesa Verde cliff ruins, the Mountain of the Holy Cross, and many other western scenic areas. These and other historic Indian and pioneer photographs are in the possession of the Department (*see North Interior Building*). Lands under the jurisdiction of the National Park Service are illustrated in the next bay on the right, with photographs, color transparencies, and maps. The next two bays, right and left of the central corridor, are given over to General Land Office exhibits. Glass cases display land patents ranging from that issued by King George III to James Baird for 10,000 acres of Florida land in 1776 to a patent issued by President Coolidge for a section of Wyoming land in 1927. Other patents include those signed by John Adams, Andrew Jackson, John Tyler, James Monroe, James Madison, and John Quincy Adams. Land warrants issued for military service include those issued to von Steuben and Lafayette for their services in the Revolution, to John Paul Jones, to Stonewall Jackson and Robert E. Lee for services in the Mexican War of 1846, to Farragut, Sherman, and Scott. Other Land Office exhibits show huge wall maps, dioramas, equipment used by pioneer and contemporary surveyors, the first public land survey—a portion of the Ohio River—made in 1786, plats of Chicago in 1836, Denver in 1864, Helena in 1868.

Geological Survey exhibits, occupying the next two bays on both sides of the corridor, include aerial photographs used in making topographic maps (the visitor may look through stereoscopic lenses and see the three-dimensional effect) ; a spiral Geologic Time Chart with flanking fossil specimens of the principal eras, showing the historic period as a thin white line in the whorl of time ; cases containing U. S. Geological Survey publications ; a diorama illustrating the method of stream-flow measurement ; and many others.

The work of the Reclamation Bureau is shown by four murals painted by Wilfrid Swancourt Bronson ; by a diorama and an aluminum model of Boulder Dam ; and by many other exhibits illustrating the reclamation of land for human use. The work of the Division of Territories and Island Possessions is shown through the medium of photographs and exhibits of native arts and crafts from Alaska, Hawaii, Puerto Rico, and the Virgin Islands. Indian Office publications and craftworks illustrate the work of this bureau. The invaluable work of the Bureau of Mines in conserving mineral resources and human life is indicated by murals, a diorama of a coal mine disaster, exhibits of mine rescue equipment, dioramas of oil and artesian wells with cross-sections of geological strata below, and other exhibits. There are additional Indian Office exhibits in the second bay left of the corridor near the front of the museum. They include Santa Clara and Zuñi pottery, a collection of Indian dolls, arts and crafts of the Plains Indians, and a special collection of craftworks made by Seneca Indians in New York State. A portion of the Colburn Gift Collection of Indian Basketry occupies a case in this bay—only a part of this comprehensive collection of 300 pieces can be shown at a time.

The INDIAN ARTS AND CRAFTS SHOP, east of the main corridor and south of the central stair, offers authentic Indian and Eskimo craftworks for sale at prices guaranteeing a reasonable return to the artist and craftsman. The front room of the shop is decorated with striking oil-on-plaster murals by Apache artist Allan Houser and Navaho artist

Gerald Nailor. Articles on sale include rugs, pottery, baskets, water colors, Eskimo ivory products, hand-woven neckties, Indian and Eskimo costume dolls, woodcarvings, beaded moccasins, totem poles, Navaho silverwork and jewelry, beaded jackets, simplified Indian Office textbooks illustrated by native artists, books on Indian art, and many other items.

The GIBSON COLLECTION OF INDIAN MATERIALS, purchased by the Department in 1936, is shown in a series of alcove cases surrounding the central stair on the first, second, and basement floors. It includes such representative items as Hopi ceremonial costumes and baskets, Plains Indian clothing, baskets by Apache and California Indians, a remarkable mountain-goat wool Chilkat blanket from Alaska, closewoven Tlingit baskets, Pima and Navaho blankets, baskets of the western United States and Alaska, Pueblo and Navaho pottery.

The CAFETERIA, basement floor at the foot of the central stairway, a huge soundproofed skylit room with facilities for 1,500 diners, has oil-on-plaster murals at each end. The west mural, by James Auchiah, Pueblo artist, depicts a harvest dance, and the east, by Steven Mopope, Kiowa artist, shows a ceremonial dance. In a courtyard south of the cafeteria are two bronzes, a statue of Abraham Lincoln by Louis Slobodkin and *Negro Mother and Child* by Maurice Glickman.

A small EMPLOYEES' CAFETERIA on the eighth floor, reached from the seventh by a flight of stairs leading up from two glass doors in Wing 2 just east of the central hall, is profusely decorated with oil-on-plaster compositions by Indian artists. The south entrance lobby, reached by these stairs, is decorated by the Potawatomi artist Woodrow Crumbo. His simply and humorously stylized *Deer* on the east wall is a masterpiece of modern Indian art; other scenes include a buffalo hunt, an action-filled horsestealing episode, courting, flute-playing, and a stylized peyote bird. The south wall of the cafeteria, reaching over the lobby entrance, contains a gently humorous composition of *Animals* by the Navaho artist Gerald Nailor. On the west wall, between windows opening on a tiled roof garden, are Nailor's weaving scene and a Navaho ceremonial dance. On the north wall are two groups of *Apaches Singing Love Songs,* by the artist of that tribe, Allan Houser. On the east wall, between windows opening toward the Capitol, he shows groups doing Apache round dances. The north entrance lobby is completely decorated by the Pueblo painter Velino Herrera; principal compositions portray buffalo dance, buffalo hunt, and making pottery, but there are paintings occupying less wall-space which have merit as art and as documents of Pueblo life—women carrying water in jars on their heads, the mother and child, and the sacred clown, are notable.

The FINE ARTS GALLERY, at the south end of the main corridor on the seventh floor, administered by the Office of Education, has a series of changing exhibits, ranging from photographic art to the contemporary paintings of college students and sketches for decorations on ocean liners. One wing of the gallery has a permanent exhibit of the

National Capital Parks and Planning Commission, showing by photographs, maps, and models the present and planned development of the Capital City area.

On the sixth floor, two frescoes by Michael Newell face each other across the hall north of the last bank of elevators. They portray typical people, products, and landscapes of the Virgin Islands and Alaska.

In a corresponding position on the fifth floor are facing canvases by John Steuart Curry portraying pioneer homesteaders and an Oklahoma land rush of the eighties or nineties. At the south end of this hall are oil paintings by Gifford Beal of scenes in National Park lands of Alaska and Hawaii.

At the south end of the main corridor, fourth floor, are statuesque oil paintings by Maynard Dixon showing a characteristic Indian and soldier, representative of the period of conflict, and an Indian and his white teacher; the Indian is learning the arts of agriculture, representing the present-day Indian Office policy. Frescoes at the north end of this hall, the work of Edgar Britton, show a composite of surveyors, the laying of pipe lines, and the drilling of oil wells on one side, and on the other a refining plant in the background, with airplanes, tractors, and automobiles refueling with petroleum products.

Henry Varnum Poor's *Conservation of Wild Life* fresco, extending across the north end of the main hall on the third floor, is one of the most pleasing composite views in the building. Flanked at each end by figures in the wilderness of Thoreau, Boone, and Audubon, early conservationists, and appealing pictures of birds and animals, the scene opens in the center to show streams and sea and flying waterfowl with strong foreground figures restocking streams with fish and caring for wildfowl in Government sanctuaries. At the south end of the hall are opposite oil paintings by David McCosh, portraying in panels various scenes from the National Parks and Monuments, including Carlsbad Caverns, Yosemite, Crater Lake, Yellowstone, Bryce, Olympic, Sequoia, Mesa Verde, Death Valley, and Rainbow Bridge.

Across the south end of the second-floor main corridor is William Gropper's dramatic oil painting, *The Building of a Dam*. Between this canvas and the central stairway the walls of the corridor are lined with oil portraits of Secretaries of the Interior. At the south end of the staircase, on opposite walls, are four oil paintings by Nicolai Cikovsky, portraying the sandy desert, irrigation, and the resulting apple industry in the Northwest and date industry in the Southwest. At the north end of the staircase, in corresponding positions, are Ernest Fiene's four oil canvases showing placer mining, reforestation, control of forest fires, and grazing.

North of the South Interior Building is the narrow rectangle of RAWLINS PARK, named for General John A. Rawlins, chief of staff under General Grant and later Grant's first Secretary of War; a bronze statue of Rawlins, by Joseph A. Bailey, stands at the eastern end of the park. This is one of the few statues in Washington erected with funds provided by Congress; it was unveiled in 1874. Two long shallow pools, where Negro children "swim" on hot summer days, occupy the central axis of the flagstoned plaza, with its bubbling fountain in the middle. Rows of magnolia bushes beside the pools are resplendent with pastel blossoms for a few days in early April. Slatted benches are filled with Government employees during the noon hour on sunny spring and·fall days, eating their lunches from paper bags. Each afternoon an attendant with an extra-long-handled rake fishes watersoaked newspapers from the pools.

GIRL SCOUTS LITTLE HOUSE

The Girl Scouts Little House (*open 9-4:30 weekdays*), SE. corner New York Avenue and 18th Street NW., is a two-story stucco building with a gray slate roof and a central red chimney, green shutters, and vine-covered trellises to the level of green window-boxes below the second-story windows. In exterior design the building is a copy of the eighteenth-century saltbox-type birthplace of John Howard Payne, author of "Home, Sweet Home," at East Hampton, Long Island. It was originally erected, after plans by Donn Barber, on Sherman Square, south of the Treasury, by the American Federation of Women's Clubs as a model exhibit in connection with the "Better Homes in America" movement in 1923. The building was then presented to the Girl Scouts and moved to its present site the following year through the generosity of Mrs. Herbert Hoover, then national president of the Girl Scouts.

A green door with a brass knocker and frosted sidelights gives access to the interior, with a living room, dining room, breakfast nook, and kitchen on the first floor, and three bedrooms and a nursery on the second floor. The house is used for training Girl Scouts in homemaking and citizenship, as an educational center for scout leaders, and for public demonstrations of Girl Scout activities. Mrs. Coolidge attended a luncheon here in 1925, and since then other Presidents' wives have been guests at social functions in the building.

OCTAGON HOUSE

The Octagon House (*open, free, 9-5 Mon.-Fri., 9-12 Sat.*), NE. corner New York Avenue and 18th Street NW., headquarters of the American Institute of Architects since 1902, in spite of its name, is actually hexagonal, broken by a semicircular tower at the corner entrance. A fine example of late Georgian architecture, the three-story red-brick house was designed by Dr. William Thornton, original architect of the Capitol, and completed in 1800; it is open to the public as a historic-house museum. Oval balconies with delicate grilled railings are placed at second-floor windows, and white marble panels ornament the space between second- and third-floor windows. A sloping roof and cornice have replaced the flat-deck roof and attic parapet—

the only important changes ever made in the building—and tall rectangular chimneys rise from the roof. A high brick wall connecting with north and east walls extends out to enclose a boxwood-planted garden, and to connect on the north side with the smokehouse, stables, and slave quarters.

A worn flight of steps with delicately patterned iron-grill railings leads up to the square Ionic portico protecting the arched doorway and the heavy paneled door, built on the curve of the central tower. Within the circular entrance hall, two cast-iron wood stoves still stand in the niches prepared for them. Opposite the entrance, a graceful classic archway opens into the oval stair hall, which gives access to the drawing room on the right and to the dining room on the left. The drawing room, with green drapes, green chairs, and a long green table, has an original mantel decorated in bas-relief with a composition of putty-plaster; it was made in London in 1798. A less ornate mantel is in the dining room, and all mantels in the building are the originals. On the drawing room walls are copies of Gilbert Stuart portraits of George and Martha Washington, and early Italian etchings. In the entrance hall, stair hall, and upstairs rooms, doors and windows are curved to fit the wall surfaces. Though somewhat shrunken with age, the doors and windows still work perfectly. The spiral stair climbs in graceful oval loops from the first floor to the third.

Dr. Thornton designed the house for Colonel John Tayloe, wealthy Virginia planter, who is said to have been persuaded by his friend Washington to build here rather than in Philadelphia. After the burning of the White House in 1814, President Madison occupied this house for a portion of 1814 and 1815. In the circular front room on the second floor the "Treaty of Peace and Amity" known as the Treaty of Ghent, ending the War of 1812, was signed by President Madison in 1815, after its ratification by the Senate. The round table on which it was signed is preserved in this room, together with a facsimile of the first and last pages of the treaty. The table itself is a curious piece, having 12 drawers, each inlaid with ivory and marked "Receipts," "Bills Paid," "Letters," and a complete combination of alphabet letters for filing. In the top of the table is a book easel that could be raised at the convenience of the reader.

The Dolly Madison Room, fronting on New York Avenue at the eastern corner of the house, second floor, was occupied by the President's winsome wife while the Octagon was in use as a temporary White House. A social center of elegance under the Tayloes, the Octagon House reached the height of its social power and glamor while Dolly Madison was hostess for several months in 1814-15. Its visitors included Jefferson, Monroe, John Quincy Adams, Decatur, Porter, Clay, Randolph, von Steuben and Lafayette.

During the Civil War the house was confiscated as property owned by Southerners and used as a military hospital. In later years it had a succession of tenants, including a Catholic school for girls and a Government department. It was for years the favorite haunted house in Washington. The ghost of Colonel Tayloe's daughter who, grieving over her thwarted love for a young Englishman, threw herself down the great stairway, is said to have appeared in wavering candlelight. Legend has it that a murdered slave girl, another suicide, and the ghosts of slaves, wander screaming through the house and grounds. Underground passages to the White House and to the Potomac, now walled up, and the hidden doors and stairways give color to the legends. At midnight Dolly Madison is believed by some to hold court among the shades of pretty women and courtly men. The house was saved from ruin in 1902 by the American Institute of Architects, which purchased and restored it to occupancy.

The two-story red-brick OCTAGON ADMINISTRATION BUILDING, built to house the offices of the Institute, east of the Octagon House across the box-grown garden, was completed in 1941 and occupied by a branch of the State Department. Designed by Eggers and Higgins, New York architects, this building, in Georgian style to harmonize with the Octagon House, occupies east and northeast sides of the garden and continues the line of the stables and servant quarters around the garden. Second-story windows have the same oval balconies as the Octagon, and the semicircular entrance portico, on the east side of the garden, protects an arched doorway executed in the same spirit as that of the Octagon. Entrance to the offices is provided through an iron grillwork gate from New York Avenue, through which a classical cornice facing the northeast corner of the garden can be seen.

NORTH INTERIOR BUILDING

The seven-story limestone North Building of the Interior Department (*open 7:45-4:15 Mon.-Fri., 7:45-11:45 Sat.*), its main section fronting on F Street between 18th and 19th Streets NW., extends through the block to E Street. It was designed in the office of the Supervising Architect and completed in 1917. Having three monumental wings extending southward from the main façade, the building is an early example of a trend that was further exemplified by the completion of its neighboring South Building 20 years later and by the War Department Building nearly 25 years later—to do away with external ornamentation and to erect buildings having an obviously functional character. A carved American eagle surmounts the north central entrance door, the outer façades have a dentiled cornice and a seventh-floor attic story, and there are a few carved plaques and panels, but in the main the building has a minimum of embellishment. The seven stories of the structure rise above a basement and ground floor, and the three extended wings are joined at the bottom by two-story sections with arched entrances to the two great courts. The need for additional floor-space has produced additions in some portions of the courts.

Glass cases in the white marble north corridor display specimens gathered by the U.S. Geological Survey, including potash minerals from Texas and New Mexico, gigantic quartz crystals from Arkansas, petrified wood from Arizona and Yellowstone Park, (one specimen is "dated," not too fancifully, "10,001,930 B.C."), minerals from Indian lands and the public domain, and native ores of the strategic minerals— aluminum, antimony, chromium, manganese, mercury, mica, nickel, tin, and tungsten.

The AUDITORIUM, reached through the north corridor, first floor, is built into the court between the east and central wings. It seats about 300, and is used mainly for the showing of National Park and other educational motion pictures, and for lectures on scenic and scientific subjects. Free lectures are announced by the press.

The GEOLOGICAL SURVEY LIBRARY, occupying a like position between the central and west wings, has two collections of international importance. Specimen volumes of the George Frederick Kunz Collection on gems and precious stones—including books printed in six centuries—are shown in a glass case outside the library entrance. The most outstanding in its field, the Kunz Collection contains about 2,000 carefully selected books valued at more than $100,000. One of the most precious items is *The History of Jewels and the Principal Riches of the East and West Taken from the Relations of the Most Famous Travelers of Our Age,* printed at London in 1671; this volume was the property of Isaac Newton and many of its pages are annotated in his handwriting. The Library's own collection of 220,000 bound volumes on geology and the related sciences is the most complete in the country. It has sets of State and foreign geological surveys, with few lacunae, State and foreign mining publications, geological reports of universities and scientific academies, periodicals on engineering, chemistry, and physics, and, of course, a full collection of Geological Survey publications. In the central library catalog room is a bronze bust of J. W. Powell, explorer of the Grand Canyon and director of the U.S. Geological Survey from 1881 to 1884; it was executed by U. S. J. Dunbar.

The GEOLOGICAL SURVEY MAP ROOM, No. 1210, in the center wing, is a sales and distribution center for topographic maps covering all areas of the country where mapping has been completed. "Quad" sheets covering small areas may be purchased here for 10 cents each.

The W. H. JACKSON PHOTOGRAPHS, a collection of scenic and historic photos, is in the custody of the Geological Survey's photographic section in the central wing, first floor. This grand old man of the Geological Survey, born in 1843, took the earliest photographs of many of the great scenic areas of the West; he accompanied the Hayden Survey of the Territories (1871) as a photographer and took pictures for the Government between 1870 and 1878. Many of his clear-cut photographs showing scenic areas and geological formations have not since been surpassed in technical excellence, in spite of the advances in photographic art. He photographed pioneer towns, Indians, miners, wagon trains, and many of his pictures are the only graphic records of areas in the West in the 1870's; his photos of the Yellowstone Park country were the first ever taken. Prints are available from the photographic section at cost. Jackson's life as a photographer is told in his book, *Time Exposure* (1940), published when he was 97 years old. The North Interior Cafeteria is in the basement of the east wing.

WASHINGTON COLLEGE OF LAW

The Washington College of Law, occupying the old Underwood House, a yellow-painted brick mansion at the southwest corner of 20th and G Streets NW., offers three-year courses in law and a four-year night course, both leading to the degree of Bachelor of Laws. It was founded, in 1896, primarily to give women equal opportunity with men in obtaining legal training; the college always has been coeducational, however, and men students in 1941 outnumbered women by 218 to 48.

Two successful women lawyers, Ellen Spencer Mussey, and Emma M. Gillett, organized the college at a time when local law schools, with the exception of one established primarily for Negroes, refused to admit women as students, though lawyers of both sexes were admitted to practice before the District of Columbia courts and before the Supreme Court. Miss Gillett had taken her degree at the Negro institution. Classes were started in 1896, and the college was incorporated two years later, with Mrs. Mussey acting as dean, the first woman to hold such a position. Since then, the school has been continuously under supervision of a woman. It was chartered by Congress in 1938 and approved by the American Bar Association in 1940.

GEORGE WASHINGTON UNIVERSITY

Largest of Washington's educational institutions is The George Washington University, with most of its buildings in the city block bounded by 20th, 21st, G, and H Streets NW., and the adjacent squares. It has a coeducational enrollment of more than 8,500 and a faculty of more than 400. In addition to its regular schedule of classes, the University offers late-afternoon courses which are attended by Government employees. Administrative offices and classrooms are housed, for the most part, in 7 large buildings of recent construction —Corcoran Hall, Stockton Hall, the Biological Sciences Building, the Hattie M. Strong Residence for Women, Social Science Hall, Hall of Government, and Lisner Hall. These have replaced large, attractive old residences which the university had converted to office and classroom use. Several of these converted homes are still in use and intermingled with the modern structures. All painted light ivory, they provide an interesting link with the past, when this was the city's fashionable residential area. Denied by its urban location any extensive campus, an attractive Yard has been developed within the landscaped quadrangle. The university further added to its plant facilities in 1941-42, when construction was completed on a large auditorium.

The university consists of 13 colleges, schools, and divisions: Junior College, Columbian College, the Graduate Council, School of

Medicine, Law School, School of Engineering, School of Education, School of Government, School of Pharmacy, Division of University Students, Center of Inter-American Studies, Summer Sessions, and the Extension Divisions. The Junior College offers freshman and sophomore work, while Columbian College, the senior college of letters and science, awards bachelors' and masters' degrees in the arts and sciences. Professional research leading to the doctorate is directed by the Graduate Council, a guild of scholars to which fellows are admitted by election. The Division of University Students makes the work of the university more fully accessible to mature students and provides for special courses to meet demands arising from the students themselves. The Center of Inter-American Studies and the Summer Sessions minister to the contemporary interest in Latin America and to students continuing their work through the summer.

The idea of a university in the Capital City was sponsored by George Washington, who left 50 shares of stock in the Potomac Canal Company for the endowment of such a national university "to which the youth of fortune and talents . . . might be sent for the completion of their Education in all the branches of polite literature:— in arts and Sciences,—in acquiring knowledge in the principles of politics & good Government." He hoped that the "General Government" would extend to such an institution "a fostering hand," but Congress took no action to carry out the provisions of his will, and the canal stock became valueless when the company failed. In 1819 a group of private persons under the leadership of Luther Rice began a campaign to raise funds for an institution here to educate students for the Baptist ministry and to offer general collegiate training. Among the contributors were President James Monroe, Secretary of the Treasury William H. Crawford, Secretary of War John C. Calhoun, Attorney General William Wirt, and Postmaster General Return J. Meigs. Failing to obtain a charter for a sectarian institution, the educational leaders proposed to Congress the incorporation of "The Columbian Society for literary purposes," and Congress in 1821 chartered the Columbian College in the District of Columbia. The main building was completed in 1822, and the first commencement two years later was attended by President Monroe, John Quincy Adams, John C. Calhoun, Henry Clay, the Marquis de Lafayette, Justices of the Supreme Court, and Members of Congress.

The name of the college was changed to Columbian University in 1873. In 1898 it was placed under the control of the Baptist denomination, but an act of 1904 restored its secular character and authorized the changing of its name to The George Washington University. In 1912 the university moved to its present location. The tremendous growth of Washington during the years of World War I was reflected in the growth of the university's student body. During this period its greatest increase in enrollment was realized. In 1930, the Junior College was instituted, the Graduate Council was organized, and a controlled independent study plan was started. The Center of

Inter-American Studies was inaugurated in 1933. These advanced educational techniques have been continued since.

LISNER HALL, 2033 G Street NW., a six-story concrete building faced with brick painted a light ivory, containing the university library, is a functional structure opened in 1939. The hall, a gift of the late Abram Lisner, for 27 years a member of the University's board of trustees, forms a central unit and completes the group of buildings on the south side of the university quadrangle. It is connected by archways to the four-story buildings that adjoin it on either side—the Biological Science Building on the west and the Social Science Hall on the east. Lisner Hall derives distinction from the thrust of its vertical lines, the proportions and placement of its window areas, and harmonious landscaping. Within, there is an air of spaciousness and light, and the interior arrangement provides for efficient library service. Among other collections, the library contains that of Richard Heinzel of Vienna on Germanic philology, the Curt Wachsmuth classical library, and a Hispanic-American collection presented by governments of the Latin American countries. Additionally, the university has a medical library and a law library, with total collections of more than 125,000 volumes.

The university's bronze replica of the life-size Houdon statue of George Washington stands in the first-floor hallway of Lisner Hall. The original, done from life by the French sculptor, is in the rotunda of the Virginia State Capitol at Richmond.

The five-story SCHOOL OF MEDICINE BUILDING, H Street between 13th and 14th Streets NW., adjoins the University Hospital. This school was founded in 1825. Its chair of bacteriology was held successively by Theobald Smith, Walter Reed, and Frederick Russell, who were among the most important figures in the evolution of the science.

STOCKTON HALL, 720 20th Street NW., houses the Law School, oldest in Washington. Organized in 1826 and discontinued the following year, it was reëstablished in 1865 and offered the first graduate course in law in the city. It grants the degrees of Bachelor of Laws, Master of Laws, Juris Doctor, and Doctor of Juridical Science. The school is a charter member of the Association of American Law Schools and is approved by the Council of Legal Education, American Bar Association.

CORCORAN HALL, 725 21st Street NW., contains the Schools of Engineering and Pharmacy. Founded in 1884, the School of Engineering, in addition to undergraduate courses in civil, electrical, and mechanical engineering, offers a combined engineering and law curriculum for those planning to enter the field of patent law. The professional degrees of Civil Engineer, Electrical Engineer, and Mechanical Engineer are granted for advanced work. The school has trained outstanding engineers, including the late Arthur Powell Davis, director of the U.S. Reclamation Service, who was in charge of vast engineering projects for the Federal Government. The School of Pharmacy has trained persons for that profession since 1867. In addition to its own rapidly growing laboratory facilities, it is advantageously situated near the headquarters of the American Institute of Pharmacy, with its pharmaceutical museum, library, and research laboratories.

The SCHOOL OF EDUCATION, 700 20th Street NW., prepares teachers, supervisors, and administrators for the higher ranges of educational service. Bachelors' degrees in home economics, physical education, and the arts are granted, in addition to the Master of Arts and Doctor of Education.

The HALL OF GOVERNMENT, 708 21st Street NW., a modern building, houses the university's School of Government. In accord with George Washington's desire for study at the National Capital in "the Principles of Politics and good government," this branch trains for municipal, State, and Federal public service. Outstanding executives in the Federal Government serve as lecturers for many of the courses. The university has more graduates in Government positions than any other institution of higher learning. The Foreign Service Branch, the first such school founded, has trained and placed many graduates in the Foreign Service of the United States.

Downtown

Streetcars: Run north and south on 7th, 9th, 11th and 14th Sts., and diagonally along Pennsylvania Ave. from southeast to northwest; east and west on F St., G St., and New York Ave.
Busses: Operate north and south on 9th, 10th (during rush hours), 11th, 12th, and 13th Sts.; east and west on E St. east of 13th.
Taxis: First zone.

Downtown Washington would be indistinguishable from a similar area in any good-sized modern city, except that the main thoroughfare (F Street) swerves around the Civil Service Commission, a typically governmental building; that, a short distance south of F Street on 10th, Ford's Theater and the Peterson House recall forcibly a great tragic event in national history; and that (especially when Government pay day falls on Saturday) the streets and stores are overrun by Government employees, as typical in the mass as is the Civil Service building. These marks of the Capital City, however, and many minor, less obvious, characteristics give this otherwise conventional array of department stores and restaurants, smart shops, theaters, beer joints, burlesque houses, and shooting galleries, business buildings, hotels, churches, and newspaper offices an atmosphere subtly in harmony with the rest of the city.

The principal shopping district of Washington lies in this area between 7th and 14th Streets, bordered roughly on the north by K Street and by E Street on the south. Here, mainly along F Street, are the largest department stores, festive and beautiful during holiday seasons, and here are the specialty shops—jewelry, men's and women's clothing, footwear, furniture, and millinery; florists' shops, book stores, and music houses; and here flourish the fascinating bazaars inaugurated by Frank Winfield Woolworth. As in other metropolitan centers, gay flower stands, corner newspaper vendors, and occasional itinerant musicians and walking advertisements animate the streets. Telegraph messengers, picketing union members, traffic officers, and legislators, often in carefully characteristic costume, are reminders of other aspects of city life. But constant in its monotony and variety is the moving crowd of tourists and residents, absent-mindedly obeying traffic rules or climbing from the omnipresent taxis, universally preoccupied with shopping.

NEW YORK AVENUE PRESBYTERIAN CHURCH

On a small triangular plot at the intersection of New York Avenue and H Street (at 13th Street NW) is the historic New York Avenue

Presbyterian Church. This is another "church of the Presidents"—
its history so interwoven with that of the city and the Nation that
successive Presidents, as a matter of tradition, have worshipped in it
and contributed to its support. The graceful Lincoln Memorial
Tower, with its lofty steeple, makes the church one of the outstanding
landmarks of downtown Washington.

The congregation lays claim to being the first Protestant organization in the Federal city. It originated with a group of Scotch-Irish
dissenters, the Associated Reform church, who came to Washington
with the transplanted Government. The congregation, with Reverend
James Laurie as pastor, met in a section of the original Treasury Building, then later established themselves in a church on the site of the
present Willard Hotel. In 1860 they united with the Second Presbyterian Church of Washington, and in 1861 the expanded congregation
moved to a new church on the site of the present one and under the
same name. In the 137 years of its history, the church has had only
8 pastors.

John Quincy Adams delivered from the pulpit of this church his
memorable "farewell to Lafayette." Andrew Jackson was a com-
municant, and the Peggy Eaton controversy caused the resignation of
the pastor and the withdrawal from the congregation of the President
and many Eaton sympathizers. President Pierce was a devout member,
and Presidents Buchanan, Johnson, Fillmore, and Cleveland also worshipped here.

It is as the "Lincoln Church," however, that the New York Avenue Presbyterian has its most significant place in American history.
Lincoln's pew, just as it was when he last occupied it, is in the main
body of the church. The side room where he frequently sat alone
during prayer meetings has been made into a small reception room and
chapel. The pastor, Reverend Phineas D. Gurley, conducted Lincoln's
funeral services. On the hundredth anniversary of its founding, in
1903, the Robert Todd Lincoln family gave the church the chimes
now in the memorial tower. They were cast in a foundry the family
of Nancy Hanks had helped to establish.

The red-brick structure, with classic silhouette, Corinthian portico, and lofty steeple, typifies the ecclesiastical edifices of the Classic
Revival period. Its heavy bracketed cornice and the molded trim of
the long arched windows are painted a bright buff, in pleasing contrast
to the wine-colored walls. The front portico is approached from either
side by a long flight of steps.

NATIONAL UNIVERSITY

National University, 816-22 13th Street NW., is a coeducational
institution, with a student body drawn largely from among Government employees. The School of Economics and Government grants
the degree of Bachelor of Arts and, in its junior college, the Associate of Arts certificate. The undergraduate division of the Law School

grants the degrees of Bachelor of Laws and Doctor of Jurisprudence; its graduate division confers the degrees of Master of Law, Master of Patent Law, and Doctor of Juridical Science.

The university was incorporated in 1869, mainly through the efforts of Professor W. B. Wedgewood. In 1896, Congress by a special act granted a broad charter to Justice Arthur MacArthur, Justice Charles C. Cole, Justice Alvey, at one time Chief Justice of the Court of Appeals of Maryland, and their associates, 13 in all, with full power "to grant and confer diplomas and the usual college and university degrees." Among the other incorporators were Eugene Carusi, at that time dean of the law faculty, Howard H. Barker, dean of the Medical Department (no longer existent), and John Goode, attorney general of Virginia and at one time Solicitor General of the United States. From its beginning, National University has been looked upon by those in charge as an institution intended for national service. During its early years, it had, as ex-officio chancellors, five Presidents of the United States: Grant, Hayes, Garfield, Arthur, and Cleveland.

PUBLIC LIBRARY

The main Public Library of the District of Columbia (*open 9-9 weekdays; Reference Room open 2-6 Sun.*), stands in Mount Vernon Square, at the intersection of Massachusetts and New York Avenues between 7th and 9th Streets NW. The marble structure, in a setting of exceptionally fine old shade trees, shrubbery, and winding walks, is an excellent example of the neoclassic architecture popular for civic buildings early in the century.

In the early 1890's a group of citizens presented to the city a collection of more than 12,000 books to form the basis of a public library, but it was not until 1898 that Congress made its first appropriation for such an institution, to be financed equally by the District and Federal Governments. The following year an Andrew Carnegie grant of $375,000 was obtained for the building, which was opened in 1903. The library now has a collection of more than 600,000 volumes, with an annual circulation in excess of 3,000,000; it maintains 7 branches and 5 sub-branches in the residential districts and a large number of special loan stations in public schools and other institutions. Use of the library is free, and residents of the District, on proper certification, may withdraw books for outside use.

The District Library has commodious reference and research rooms in its main building and branches, and in the main building is kept a comprehensive collection of Washingtoniana: literature, maps, pictures, and valuable documentary material on District history and folklore.

The massive rectangular building, somewhat heavily ornamented with decorative sculptures and Ionic columns, has a broad central section and flanking wings. Within the entrance portal, classic marble stairways lead from a narrow foyer to the second and basement floors. On the first floor are the service desks, catalog, and main reading and reference rooms, administrative offices, and stacks. The children's room occupies the second floor of the east wing; the west wing is largely devoted to literature on the arts and to the Washingtoniana collection. Technology and engineering reading rooms are in the basement. From time to time the library exhibits notable collections of books, prints, and paintings.

WASHINGTON HEBREW CONGREGATION

The gray-granite temple at 816 8th Street, between H and I Streets NW., was dedicated in 1898 by the Washington Hebrew Congregation, the oldest Jewish congregation in the city. Strong Byzantine and Eastern influences are evident in the architecture, especially in the design of the two front towers, with their onion-shaped domes, and in the choice of decorative detail. At the top of each tower is an arcaded belfry, surmounted by an octagonal cupola with extended arcades, as in the minaret of a mosque. The large rose window over the main entrance is ornamented with the Star of David. Some distance back from the front façade, a low Byzantine dome rises above the auditorium, pierced at the base with bull's-eye windows and topped, as are the domes of the towers, by the six-pointed Star of David.

In 1852 the first synagogue in Washington was organized with 25 members, mostly of German Orthodox origin. Through the efforts of Captain James P. Levy, a Federal charter was obtained for the group, under the name of the Washington Hebrew Congregation, enabling it to hold property. This charter, signed by President Franklin Pierce, hangs in the Temple office. Services were held in private homes until 1863, when an old Methodist church was acquired, where the congregation met until the dedication of the temple in 1898. President McKinley and his Cabinet officiated at the laying of the cornerstone. A schism in 1870 left this a reformed congregation, while the more conservative members withdrew and formed the Adath Israel.

The work of the Hebrew Congregation includes various social activities and the administration of the school adjoining the temple. The temple sisterhood was organized in 1906. Among the distinguished rabbis who have led the congregation are Rabbi Louis Stern, who died in 1920 after 45 years of service in Washington, and Rabbi Abram Simon, at one time president of the Washington School Board, of the Columbia Hospital, and of the Association of American Rabbis.

CIVIL SERVICE BUILDING

The Civil Service Commission, personnel agency of the Federal Government, occupies one of the oldest buildings (*open 8:45-5:15 Mon.-Fri., 8:45-12:45 Sat.*) in Washington, the former Patent Office, fronting on F Street between 7th and 9th Streets NW. The building, on the site reserved in L'Enfant's plan for a national church, was constructed in several sections between 1837 and 1867. From the completion of the first section in 1840 until taken over by the Civil Service Commission in 1932, it was occupied by the United States Patent Office, except that from 1852 to 1917 the east wing was used by the Department of the Interior.

Designed by William P. Elliott and constructed of Virginia freestone and Maryland marble, the building is an outstanding example of early Federal architecture. A rusticated ground story provides an appropriate base for the superstructure, which is adorned with Doric pilasters extending from the first-floor level to the crowning entablature. Each of the four façades is dominated by a projecting colonnaded portico crowned with a simple pediment. The massive fluted columns are of the Doric order.

The scope of the Civil Service Commission has widened considerably in recent years, with the growth in the number of employees and with the extension of the service over many new types of positions. In 1883 there were 13,924 positions under civil service. At the end of June, 1941, out of a Federal employment of more than a million, 990,218 positions were under civil service. The Commission, in addition to its own staff, functions through about 5,000 local boards of examiners throughout the country. Theodore Roosevelt served on the Commission from 1889 to 1895, and the desk and chairs he used are in the second-floor lobby, F Street side.

UNITED STATES TARIFF COMMISSION

Directly across from the Civil Service Commission is the United States Tariff Commission, F Street between 7th and 8th Streets NW., in the old General Land Office Building (*open 8:45-5:15 Mon.-Fri., 8:45-12:45 Sat.*), one of Washington's historic landmarks. The south half of the building covers the site of Blodgett's Hotel, opened by Samuel Blodgett of Philadelphia shortly after Washington was selected as the Capital City. The site and the hotel, the cornerstone of which was laid in 1795, were prizes in a lottery. In 1810 the hotel was purchased by the Government to house the City Post Office, the Post Office Department, and the Patent Office. Escaping destruction when the British invaded Washington in 1814, it became temporarily the hall of Congress. The old hotel was destroyed by fire in 1836.

Work on the south wing of the building was begun in 1839, and the construction of the north wing about 1855. Until 1897 it housed the Post Office Department and the City Post Office. The General Land Office, created in 1812 and once one of the busiest of governmental agencies, occupied it from 1897 until 1917, when it was transferred to the Department of the Interior. At present (1942) the United States Tariff Commission, a branch post office, and a part of the United States Employees' Compensation Commission occupy the fine old building. The Tariff Commission's chief duty is to investigate tariff questions and furnish accurate and comprehensive reports to the President, to Congress, and to other policy-making Government agencies. The Employees' Compensation Commission administers workmen's compensation benefits for civilian employees of the Government, for longshoremen and harbor workers, and others. The first public telegraph office in this country was opened by Samuel F. B. Morse in a building that stood on 7th Street; the site, now covered by the eastern section of the present structure, is marked by a bronze plaque on the E Street façade and by a wooden marker on the 7th Street side.

The beautifully proportioned marble building was designed in the Classic Revival style by Robert Mills and T. U. Walter, architects of the Capitol. Since its completion in 1866, the exterior has not been remodeled. Rising three stories above a rusticated ground story, the massive walls enclose an interior courtyard, 95 by 194 feet. The recessed portico in each façade is supported by delicate Corinthian columns. The entablature and parapet are simple and finely molded.

FORD'S THEATER

Ford's Theater (*open 9-4:30 weekdays, 12:30-4 Sun. and holidays; adm. 10¢*), 10th Street between E and F Streets NW., houses one of the largest existent collections of Lincoln relics. Little is left of the interior of the theater as it stood on the night of April 14, 1865, when John Wilkes Booth assassinated Abraham Lincoln. Stage, balconies, and seats have been removed or floored over.

At the end of the war, thousands of Union troops were quartered in the city or near by, but Washington had few theaters to provide entertainment. One of the first to take advantage of the boom was John T. Ford, who had managed theaters in Baltimore and Philadelphia. Ford bought the abandoned First Baptist Church on Tenth Street and converted it into a theater.

The play, on the night of April 14, was Tom Taylor's *Our American Cousin,* which had been performed for more than a thousand nights in New York and other cities. The reputation of the play and of the actress, Laura Keene, brought a crowd to the performance, "to be honored by the presence of President Lincoln."

The President arrived early, and was escorted to his box on the south or right side of the theater, with Mrs. Lincoln and two guests, Major Henry R. Rathbone and his fiancée. The box was decorated with a large American flag. Booth, a well-known minor actor of the time, had no difficulty in getting into the theater. Through the darkened aisles, he made his way to the President's box, slipped into the small foyer, and, in the absence of the bodyguard, crept close to President Lincoln and shot once, at his victim's head. There was a short struggle with Major Rathbone, but Booth stabbed his way clear and jumped from the box with the cry, "Sic semper tyrannis." In his leap a spur caught on the draped flag and hurled him to the stage, breaking an ankle. The stunned audience saw him limp to the rear of the stage and disappear.

When the audience realized that Lincoln had been shot, there was a rush to the box. Dr. Charles D. Gatch, an Army surgeon, made the first examination. Booth had used a small derringer pistol, and the wound, on the left side of the head behind the ear, bled very little and was almost imperceptible. Surgeon General Barnes, who arrived as Lincoln was being carried from the theater, advised against the rough ride over cobblestone streets to the White House, and the President was carried across Tenth Street to the house of a Mr. Petersen, where he died at 7:22 the following morning without regaining consciousness.

Booth, after breaking away from someone who tried to seize him in the rear of the theater, escaped on horseback. His first stop was at the house of Dr. Samuel Mudd, some miles south of the District of Columbia. The physician set Booth's leg, thereby involving himself. He was later arrested, tried, convicted, and sentenced to life imprisonment. After many years he was pardoned. Nothing was known of Booth's further movements until the night of April 25, when a body of cavalry found him hiding in a barn near Fredericksburg, Virginia. Booth refused to surrender, asking a chance to fight for his freedom. The barn was fired and, when Booth was seen within, a sergeant shot and killed him, in violation of orders from his superiors to take the assassin alive.

The assassination is fully described by newspapers, photographs, and other relics contained in the Oldroyd collection of the museum. O. H. Oldroyd, a great admirer of Lincoln, began the collection in 1860 and, until the time of his death in 1930, continued to care for and add to it. Although he served with the Union Army throughout the Civil War, he never saw President Lincoln. After being housed in the Lincoln home in Springfield for 10 years, the great assemblage of furnishings, pictures, and relics was brought to Washington and placed in the Petersen House, across Tenth Street. In 1931 the greater part of it was removed to the Museum and opened to the public.

Among the relics are the flag and the spur that caused Booth to break his leg, the play bill for the night of the murder, fragments of Lincoln's clothing snatched as he lay wounded in the theater, photographs of the building, and letters relating to the tragic evening. A large case contains an account of the murder conspiracy and the pursuit and capture of the conspirators. Detailed photographs in another exhibit present the executions of Payne, Herold, Atzeroth, and Mrs. Surratt. The collection includes several books from Lincoln's law library, his well-worn copy of Parson Weems' *Life of Washington,* the old Lincoln Bible with entries in the hand of Lincoln's father, and an early copy of *Pilgrim's Progress.* Other personal mementos are Lincoln's silver-plated shaving mug, his shawl, a number of walking sticks, and a collection of letters and documents relating to his career as a lawyer. In the museum is a collection of furniture from Lincoln's Springfield home.

Among the most interesting political exhibits are those associated with Lincoln's campaign for the Presidency in 1864, a collection that includes campaign songs, election buttons and badges, and a series of newspaper cartoons of the day. An extensive series of cartoons from *Punch* shows the British attitude to Lincoln—deeply hostile before, genuinely sympathetic after, his assassination. In a large case are several masks of Lincoln, including a life mask made by the sculptor Clark Mills.

PETERSEN HOUSE

The narrow red-brick house at 516 10th Street NW., opposite Ford's Treater, purchased by the Government in 1896, has become a national shrine (*open 9-4:30 weekdays, 12:30-4:30 Sun. and holidays; adm. 10¢*). Here on the morning of April 15, 1865, six days after Lee's surrender at Appomattox, Abraham Lincoln died. His life ended with symbolic appropriateness in a room similar in size and shape to the one-room cabin in which he was born. William Petersen, its owner, was a tailor of Swedish birth, whose lodgings were popular with soldiers of the Union Army.

The visitor is fortunate who goes at one of the less popular hours, possibly the noon hour. Ringing the bell, he is admitted to the house as to any private residence, and is free to walk about unhindered. Probably he will pause in the little entrance hallway and go first into the parlors that lead from it; the front parlor where Mrs. Lincoln sat during the night of April 14, and the adjoining room in which Edwin M. Stanton, Secretary of War, took testimony and wrote a full account of the assassination. The Bible, given Lincoln by Nancy Hanks, his mother, is on the center table in the rear parlor.

Various women's patriotic societies, under the direction of Lieutenant Colonel U. S. Grant, 3d, have restored the rooms, as much as possible, to their original appearance. Lincoln's favorite high-backed chair is in the front parlor. This and the marble-topped tables, corner whatnots, and many other pieces were once used in the Lincoln home in Springfield and are part of the Oldroyd collection.

On the threshold of the room at the rear of the hallway, the realization of Lincoln's death comes with an immediate and profound shock. The human intimacy of the chamber is disturbing and, for a moment, forbids intrusion. Everything has been restored or reproduced, so that the room is almost exactly as it was when the unconscious Lincoln was brought here to die. White dotted curtains shade the windows, and wallpaper, similar in pattern to the original, covers the walls. The bed, a copy of the original, a low walnut four-poster of the spool type, stands in the corner by the door. On the blackwalnut bureau is a tumbler, probably used by the attending physicians, and the original water pitcher and bowl are on the marble-topped stand at the foot of the bed. Two pictures, Rosa Bonheur's *Horse Fair,* above the bed, and *The Village Blacksmith,* hanging over the washstand, emphasize the permanence of inanimate objects.

The restoration of the room, begun in 1928, was greatly aided by a picture, now hanging in the Lincoln room, which appeared originally in *Leslie's Weekly*. The picture shows the furnishings in careful detail, and the group of notable people around the bed. According to James Tanner, who was called in to take shorthand notes of the testimony, practically every man of prominence in national life, who was then in the Capital, came at some time during the night. Pauline Petersen Wenzing, to whom the bedroom originally belonged, gave advice and help in selecting and placing the pictures and other articles. At the time of the tragedy, she was away from home in a boarding school.

Beyond the Lincoln room are two small rooms, also restored; and, at the rear of the house is a wide parlor, added later for housing part of the Oldroyd collection of Lincoln relics and furnished by the National Society of Dames of the Loyal Legion. Here are Little-field's picture of the death scene, the sketch for which was made in the room on Sunday, April 15, 1865; a copy of the New York *Herald* announcing the tragic event, and many interesting pieces of furniture and engravings.

ST. PATRICK'S ROMAN CATHOLIC CHURCH

St. Patrick's, the oldest Catholic Church in Washington proper, stands at the SE. corner of 10th and G Streets NW., its bluestone walls and Gothic architecture in strong contrast to its commercial surroundings. Designed by the architects Wood, Donn, and Deming, it is built of Potomac bluestone with limestone trim. The main façade of the church, with its deeply recessed, arched entrance and large rose window, is flanked by stair towers. The northern end of this façade is separated by an octagonal baptistry from the rectory on the corner, connecting with St. Patrick's Academy for Girls on G Street. The heavy stonework with its buttresses, the deep fenestration and entrances, narrow stair windows, and small-paned bays of the secular buildings are all characteristic of the Tudor style.

The plot was purchased in 1794 for 80 pounds sterling, and the poverty of the young parish is suggested by the difficulties it experienced in paying even this modest sum. It was not completely paid until 1804, when the property was deeded to Bishop Carroll by Father Caffery, who properly may be called the founder of the church. The church bell was hung from a wooden standard in the yard. By 1810 the congregation was housed in a brick building, which, though it had few pews, was the first Washington church to possess an organ, purchased from an Episcopal church at Dumfries, Virginia. The cornerstone of the present structure was laid in 1872, and the church was dedicated in 1884 during the pastorate of Reverend Jacob Ambrose Walter. After the brief pastorate of Father Caffery, Father William Matthews presided over the congregation for more than half a century. Father Matthews, the first Marylander elevated to the priesthood, was at one time the president of Georgetown University.

GENERAL ACCOUNTING OFFICE

The General Accounting Office (*open 8:45-4:15 Mon.-Fri., 8:45-12:45 Sat.*), 5th and G Streets NW., is housed in the old mid-Victorian red-brick Pension Office Building. Designed by General Montgomery C. Meigs and erected in 1883, it occupies the long block north of Judiciary Square, bordered by ginkgo trees at the east and west ends. This massive three-story building, containing more than 15,000,-000 bricks, has a gabled clerestory section rising three stories above the outer roof. The walls, broken by numerous windows, are decorated between the first and second floors with a faded yellow terra-cotta frieze 3 feet high, running around the entire structure. The building, a memorial to veterans of the Civil War, was occupied by the Pension Bureau until 1926, and then was taken over by the General Accounting Office, which controls Government funds. It sees that money is expended in the exact manner determined by Congress and is responsible only to Congress.

The bas-relief frieze, designed by C. Buberl, a Bohemian artist, portrays branches of the Union forces in action during the Civil War. Starting on the west side of the building, the frieze depicts the activities of the Quartermaster Corps, coming to a climax in a plaque which gives the name to the central entrance—the Gate of the Quartermaster. In the spandrel over the doorway are symbolic figures of Mars and Minerva, representing War. The frieze on the north façade portrays the medical forces, emphasized in the Gate of the Invalids, with figures in the spandrel of Justice and Truth, personifying Peace. Naval scenes are carried out on the yellow band, east wall, centered in the Naval Gate, with a spandrel identical with that over the west doorway. Infantry, cavalry, and artillery actions are illustrated in the south frieze, terminating at the main entrance to the building, the Gate of the Infantry, with over-door symbolic figures like those on the north side.

This entrance leads into a great hall, more than a hundred feet high and covering an approximate floor area of 30,000 square feet. Two rows of four mammoth Corinthian columns, each made of more than 55,000 bricks, and painted to simulate Siena marble, divide the hall into three sections. A superimposed arcaded gallery runs around all four walls, supported by a lower tier of Doric and an upper tier of Ionic columns. Of this interior hall the architect Roderick Seidenberg has said that "nothing short of an inaugural ball or a thunderstorm could possibly fill the immense void." The people who bought tickets to the inaugural balls of Presidents Cleveland, Harrison, McKinley, Theodore Roosevelt, and Taft, filled this Victorian great hall to overflowing. For President Cleveland's ball, the massive pillars were wound with white muslin and decorated with broad wreaths of evergreens.

JUDICIARY SQUARE

Judiciary Square, an area of two blocks between Indiana Avenue and F Street and 4th and 5th Streets NW., contains five Federal and District court buildings, three statues, an old brick ventilating tower, and a small park. The first building erected on this site is that occupied by the United States District Court of the District of Columbia, a mellowed limestone Federal structure, one of the finest examples of Greek Revival architecture in the city. Its classic style has influenced the architectural design of the other buildings on the Square. Informal lawns surround the dignified courthouses, with benches under the fan-shaped leaves of the ginkgo trees, where excited lawyers may regain their poise, anxious litigants cool off, and where the man in the street may rest undisturbed. On the west side of 5th Street, facing the Square, is a ragged row of frame and brick houses, with gilt lettering on the front windows, advertising the services of lawyers and bondsmen.

The UNITED STATES DISTRICT COURT BUILDING (*open 8:45-4:15 Mon.-Fri., 8:45-12:15 Sat.*), Indiana Avenue between 4th and 5th Streets NW., is a finely proportioned three-story structure of restrained classic architecture. In the court before the weathered façade stand the Lot Flannery STATUE OF ABRAHAM LINCOLN, the first public monument to his memory, erected by local subscription on April 15, 1868. The central portion of the building, with a graceful Ionic portico, is flanked on the east and west by wings, with colonnaded loggias projecting beyond the main section. Two arched doorways pierce the southern façades of the wings, at the ground floor level. A broad flight of steps, decorated at the terrace level with an iron railing, surmounted by old-fashioned street lamps, leads to the main entrance. Designed by George Hadfield, a young English *protégé* of Benjamin West and one of the architects of the Capitol, the central section was completed in 1820. The east and west wings were finished in 1826 and 1849 respectively, and the north extension was added in 1881. It was the City Hall until 1873, when the title passed from the District to the Federal Government.

The principal entrance leads into a buff-walled lobby, floored and wainscoted with marble. In the center of the hall are two marble columns, on either side of which is a stairway, with marble steps and brass-railed iron balusters. The stairs ascend half a story to landings, branch and rise again to meet in a central balcony on the top floor. Courtrooms and judges' chambers occupy the first and second floors, while the ground floor houses the clerical and administrative offices. The court has local jurisdiction over the inferior courts of the District of Columbia. Many famous trials have been held here, including that of Charles J. Guiteau, assassin of President Garfield, who was sentenced in this courthouse to be hanged from a near-by gallows. The Teapot Dome case, in which Harry Sinclair and Edward L. Doheny were charged with the bribery of Albert B. Fall, former Secretary of the Interior, was tried before the District Court.

The JOSEPH J. DARLINGTON MEMORIAL FOUNTAIN, in the corner west of the District Court and south of the Court of Appeals, is a memorial to a distinguished member of the Washington bar, erected by members of the local bar association. It is a gilt bronze nude shielding a deer, with thin streams of water spouting from the sides of the central pedestal into a shallow encircling pool. According to the sculptor, Carl Paul Jennewein, the nude woman symbolizes the perfect divine work, "direct from the hand of God instead of from the hands of a dressmaker." The deer she is protecting symbolizes the weak. The story that the statue was found one morning clothed in gingham cannot be verified, but the figure's nudity originally aroused a storm of controversy.

East of the fountain is an abandoned brick tower 15 feet high and 6 feet in diameter, covered with English ivy. It is a relic of the old ventilating system used in the Court of Appeals building, when fans sucked the air down through the tower and forced it into the court-room.

The UNITED STATES COURT OF APPEALS BUILDING (*open 9-4:30 Mon.-Fri., 9-1 Sat.*), 5th and E Streets NW., is a severely plain classic structure, with limestone walls weathered a dark gray. The main façade, with its Ionic central portico, faces north on Judiciary Square. Entrance to the ground floor is through three arched doors set under the steps leading to the main first floor entrance. Designed by Elliott Woods, assisted by W. D. Kneessi and August Eccard, it was erected in 1910.

The first-floor entrance leads to a lobby, floored with white and black marble, with plaster walls painted buff. Through the doorway to the left is the skylit two-story courtroom, occupying the center of the building. On the gray walls of the room hang portraits of former judges, and behind the judges' bench are dark green plush draperies. The outer shell of the building, on the first and second floors, is occupied by the judges' chambers.

The JUVENILE COURT BUILDING (*open 9-4:30 Mon.-Fri., 9-1 Sat.*), 4th and E Streets NW., designed by Nathan C. Wyeth, municipal architect, and erected in 1939, conforms to the early Federal classic style of the Square. It is a three-story building, having a granite base and limestone walls, with a pedimented Ionic portico in the central portion of the front façade. Under the flight of steps leading to the main entrance are the doors at the street level, entering the building on the ground floor. The interior hall and corridors are paneled with Indiana marble and floored with terrazzo, and the doors are trimmed with aluminum. Administrative and clerical offices are on the ground floor, with waiting, hearing and courtrooms on the first and second floors.

The MUNICIPAL COURT BUILDING (*open 9-4:30 Mon.-Fri., 9-1 Sat.*), 4th Street between E and F Streets NW., is a three-story-and-attic limestone structure, designed in the Office of the Municipal Architect and erected in 1939. The plain front façade faces west across a small park. With recessed Ionic porticos at the north and south extremities, the main entrance is through a bright green door with similar doorways on the other three sides. The floor plan of the building is that of a cross, with corridors running in the cardinal directions. The building houses inferior courts of the District.

In the center of the park is a bronze copy of the Dumont equestrian STATUE OF GENERAL JOSÉ DE SAN MARTIN, *libertador* of Argentine. On the east and west sides of the pedestal are bronze plaques depicting scenes from the Latin American hero's life.

The POLICE COURT BUILDING (*open 9-4:30 Mon.-Fri., 9-1 Sat.*), 5th Street between E and F Streets NW., faces the park from the west, and in size, architectural style, and interior arrangement is similar to the Municipal Court Building.

MUNICIPAL CENTER

The EAST BUILDING (*open 9-4:30 Mon.-Fri., 9-1 Sat.*), of the projected Municipal Center Group, Indiana Avenue and C Street between 4th and 5th Streets NW., designed by N. C. Wyeth and erected in 1941, is the first of a group of buildings to house municipal agencies and the Central Public Library. It departs from the accepted classicism of the old District Court Building by the use of modern materials and motifs, coupled with the functional architecture of an office structure. The foundation walls are of pink granite and the exterior walls of Indiana limestone rising six stories, with setbacks at the third, fourth, and fifth floor levels. The façades are broken by recessed windows connected by ornamental spandrels, extending from the street grade to the first setback.

The west entrance, facing the Central Plaza that will occupy the space between this and the West Building when the latter is completed, has a three-story portico supported by four square columns with grooved lines suggesting a classic capital. A broad flight of steps leads to the entrance on the north side, containing three doorways trimmed in aluminum bearing the monogrammed MP of the Metropolitan Police. The east or rear entrance is a simplified version of the north, with vehicular ramps on either side of the steps leading down to the basement.

The south, or main, entrance, similar to that on the north, leads into a lobby paneled in Tennessee marble, with black marble wainscot and terrazzo floors. In the middle of the hall, dividing the lobby into three wide aisles, are two massive square columns. A tile mosaic map of the District, in green, blue, pink, yellow, and neutral shades decorates the forefront of the lobby floor. A rectangular court faced with buff-colored brick, provides light and air for the inner rooms, separated by a corridor from the outer shell of offices. The building is equipped to house the Metropolitan Police, the Traffic Bureau, the

Health Department, and the Board of Public Welfare, with space in the basement for parking cars and an air-conditioned jail.

The proposed Central Public Library Building is to be erected between C Street and Pennsylvania Avenue, west of Sixth Street.

North and East Washington

Streetcars: Lincoln Park, Kenilworth, Seat Pleasant, Calvert Bridge via Fla., Beltsville, Brookland, Catholic University, Georgia & Alaska, Takoma, and Soldiers Home.
Busses: Riverdale, East Riverdale, Cheverly, Trinidad, 22nd & Shepherd NE., Riverdale via Hyattsville, Catholic University, and Rock Creek Cemetery.
Taxis: Second to fourth zones.

About two or three miles north of the Capitol, an unusually interesting section of Washington lies between the Anacostia River and New Hampshire Avenue, extending to the District Line and bordered on the south and west by Benning Road and Florida, Georgia, and New Hampshire Avenues. Within these limits are some of the most important Roman Catholic shrines and schools, the noted Howard University for Negroes, the National Arboretum, two of the District's well-known cemeteries, Soldiers' Home, and the National Guard Armory and East Washington Sports Center (under construction).

The terrain varies from the marshlands and wild rice swamps of the Anacostia to the softly rolling hills north of the city, including some of the highest in the District—Howard Hill, Mount Hamilton, Mount Saint Sepulchre, and Hickey Hill. Wooded tracts, with enormous trees, tiny lakes, and flowering slopes, have been made into grounds of rare beauty—gardens and parklands such as those of the Franciscan Monastery, Soldiers' Home, Gallaudet College, and Rock Creek Cemetery.

NATIONAL GUARD ARMORY AND SPORTS CENTER

The first unit of the District National Guard Armory, completed in 1941, stands at the foot of East Capitol Street on the banks of the Anacostia River. Grouped about this unit, which houses drill hall and heating plant, will be the necessary regimental buildings, scheduled for completion in 1942.

The area between the Armory and Kingman Lake has been graded for an immense athletic field and a large outdoor stadium is to be built west of the Armory. The field and stadium, with a combined seating capacity of about 100,000, and a swimming pool and boat house, to be constructed on the river, will make a sports center capable of accommodating huge athletic events, pageants, parades, and large-scale ceremonials. The grounds in the whole of this area will be landscaped, and rail and highway facilities will be provided, to serve the center without conflicting with regular traffic.

The Armory is strictly functional in design, with walls of lime-stone and arched roof of steel, rising 90 feet above the floor. The balcony provides permanent seating accommodations for 3,500; the total seating capacity varies with the nature of the event to be wit-nessed, but the maximum will be 12,000.

The total project, the cost of which will be $750,000, is under the direction of Nathan C. Wyeth, municipal architect. The Armory and the proposed East Washington Sports Center will be connected directly with the Capitol buildings by way of East Capitol Street. Federal and State buildings are planned to occupy the space north of the Armory and west of Eastern High School.

NATIONAL ARBORETUM

Extending from the lowlands of the Anacostia to Bladensburg and Hickey Roads on the north and west is the National Arboretum, an experimental forest preserve purchased by the Government in 1927. In 1899, Secretary of Agriculture Wilson recommended the reservation of an area "in which can be brought together for study all the trees that grow in Washington . . . furnishing complete material for the investigations of the Department of Agriculture and so managed as to be a perennial feast of botanical education." The site includes Mount Hamilton and Hickey Hill, the land between these heights, and the upper Anacostia marshes. Its 32 distinct types of soil permit the growth of many varieties of trees that are not indigenous to the District. The Arboretum is administered by the Secretary of Agricul-ture and an advisory council of men and women prominent in forestry, landscaping, and science.

The tract, called the "Inclosure," was patented to Ninian Beall in 1687. Some distance to the south of the Arboretum are the Cool Spring acres that Washington ordered left out of the original "ten-mile square." This tract ran roughly along present Benning Road to the Anacostia River. Near the corner of the tract, on the east side of Bladensburg Road, is a service station, marking the site of the old toll road, built in 1820 when the country road to Baltimore became a turnpike.

MOUNT OLIVET CEMETERY

About a mile out on the historic Bladensburg Road and just opposite the National Arboretum, the monuments and mausoleums of Mount Olivet Catholic Cemetery mark the crest of a hill overlooking the city. A wrought-iron fence encloses the 75-acre tract, and a gray-stone lodge marks the entrance near the intersection of Mount Olivet and Bladens-burg Roads.

In 1858, the Roman Catholics of Washington purchased Fenwick Farms, intending to provide a single large burying ground. Soon afterward, in compliance with a city ordinance of 1852 prohibiting interment within city limits, the dead in all the Catholic burial grounds were removed to the new Mount Olivet Cemetery.

Here are buried James Hoban, designer of the White House, and many notable members of the military and naval services who died before the opening of Arlington National Cemetery. In an unmarked grave is the body of Constantin Brumidi, fresco painter of the Capitol. A small stone almost hidden by shrubbery and bearing simply the name, "Mrs. Surratt," marks the grave of the woman who was hanged for complicity in the assassination of President Lincoln.

NATIONAL TRAINING SCHOOL FOR BOYS

Bordered on the south by South Dakota Avenue and extending for some distance along Bladensburg Road are the grounds of the National Training School for Boys. The institution is a Federally operated rehabilitation school for boys from any part of the United States who have violated Federal laws. The buildings are grouped upon a pleasant hillside. On the ridge to the north, Commodore Joshua Barney stationed his battery for the defense of Washington, August 1814, and the Battle of Bladensburg was fought over the terrain between this point and the town of Bladensburg (*see Bladensburg and Greenbelt*). Half a century later, one of the Civil War defenses of the Capital was built on the same site, and some of the trenches and breastworks of Fort Lincoln are still visible.

FORT LINCOLN CEMETERY

Just beyond the District Line, between the road to Baltimore and the Anacostia River, Fort Lincoln Cemetery extends over 240 acres of rolling woodland, the onetime field of the Battle of Bladensburg. Commodore Barney was shot from his horse and taken prisoner near the spot now occupied by the cemetery lodge.

The tract was part of the original grant from Lord Baltimore to George Conn, whose descendants held it for more than 200 years, until it was made a cemetery in 1914. The early Italian lodge and chapel with circular cloister stand among simply landscaped grounds like an Italian mission in its garden.

COLUMBIA INSTITUTION FOR THE DEAF

With its entrance at Florida Avenue and 7th Street NE., the Columbia Institution for the Deaf, administered by the Federal Security Agency, occupies 103 acres of campus, farm, woodland, and playground in the area known as Kendall's Green. The Institution is proprietor of the tract, and the United States Government acts as trustee. There are three separate departments—Kendall School, a normal department, and Gallaudet College, the only school of higher learning for deaf mutes in existence. Gallaudet attracts students from all over the world, and its annual enrollment averages between 200 and 250 students, with a faculty of more than 30 teachers.

The Columbia Institution for the Instruction of the Deaf and Dumb and the Blind was incorporated by Congress in 1857, and opened the same year under the superintendency of Edward Miner Gallaudet, son of the world-famous teacher of the deaf, Dr. Thomas Hopkins Gallaudet. A small school for the deaf, dumb, and blind had been forced to close its doors, and a trustee of this defunct school, Amos Kendall, local philanthropist and Postmaster General under President Jackson, assumed guardianship of five of the pupils. Determined that the education of these handicapped children should continue, Kendall was a moving force in organizing a new institution, donating a plot of land on which stood several houses, and later erecting at his own expense a substantial brick building.

The act of incorporation provided for an annual appropriation from Congress of $150 for each indigent pupil of the District. Congress increased this sum until it has assumed almost complete financial responsibility for the institution. At the same time admission requirements were broadened, so that children whose parents were connected with the Army and Navy might be accepted.

Not satisfied to stop with the training of children, Gallaudet called the attention of Congress to the need for a college. In 1864 President Lincoln signed an act authorizing the institution to confer degrees in the liberal arts and sciences. The new department was named the National Deaf Mute College, and 30 years later, Gallaudet College. In 1865 the blind students were transferred to the Maryland Institution in Baltimore. In 1867, women students were admitted, and in 1891 a normal department was inaugurated, in order to raise the standards of teaching the deaf. Only white persons are admitted, as the Negro deaf of the District are taught at Overlea, Maryland. The District pays the tuition of its residents, while Federal appropriation supplies tuition for pupils from States and Territories who are unable to pay. Students are received also on a paying basis, and many foreign countries are represented.

The institution gradually added to the original plot of land and, after Amos Kendall's death in 1865, purchased the Kendall country seat. The grounds were laid out in 1866 by Frederick Law Olmsted, landscape architect. Twenty acres in the southern part of the tract comprise the campus. Here, the opening of the collegiate department started a period of building activity—a chapel, men's dormitory, and homes for the faculty members being erected. Later, dormitories for the boys and girls of Kendall School, a shop, heating plant, greenhouses, a large gymnasium, chemical laboratory, garage, school building, and dairies were added. One of the most recent structures is a dormitory for women. A 40-acre farm supplies produce for the school.

Before Chapel Hall, the main building of the institution, stands a bronze group erected in memory of Dr. Thomas Hopkins Gallaudet, the work of Daniel Chester French and a gift from the deaf mutes of the country.

HOWARD UNIVERSITY

Howard University, 6th Street between W and Fairmont Streets NW., is about 2 miles north of the Capitol, on one of the city's highest hills. Howard Hill overlooks McMillan Reservoir, the Soldiers' Home grounds, and McMillan Park to the north and east, Freedmen's Hospital and Griffith Stadium to the south, and Banneker Center to the west. From the upper stories of Founders Library are fine views of the hills of Anacostia, the Potomac, and the Virginia shore.

Howard University, largest and most completely developed Negro university, started as a local training school for ministers. It is now national and international in the scope of its work, its student body, and its influence. Although it has a private endowment, its chief support comes from congressional appropriations, administered by the Federal Security Agency. The student body, drawn from all over the United States and from many foreign countries, numbers approximately 2,600. There have been and are a few whites, orientals, West Indian and African Negroes, but most of the students are American Negroes. The faculty, numbering 260, is biracial, although Negro members are in the majority.

In 1866 a white visitor at Wayland Institute, an early seminary for Negroes (in what is now the Meridian Hill Park section), was so impressed by the theological students that he gave an enthusiastic report to the First Congregational Church. A plan was made immediately for a theological seminary to train Negro men. Major General Oliver Otis Howard, Civil War veteran in charge of Federal funds for establishing Negro schools, led the movement for founding this seminary, and the school was named in his honor. In 1867, the institution was granted a charter by the Federal Government, and the anniversary of this day is one of the few ceremonial days at the university. The normal and preparatory departments (discontinued in 1919) opened in 1867, with five students and no funds. The Freedmen's Bureau rallied to its support, and a large tract of land, one of the most attractive sites in the city, was secured. During the panic of 1873, when the Freedmen's Bureau was discontinued, the financial support of the university sharply declined. In 1879 Congress was prevailed upon to appropriate $10,000 for the institution.

Presidents of the university generally have been white Congregationalist ministers. One Negro, John M. Langston, an ex-Congressman and a lawyer of distinction, served briefly as acting president. In 1926 Dr. Mordecai W. Johnson, a Baptist minister, became the first Negro president of Howard. Congressional appropriations increased from $218,000 in 1926-27 to $747,000 in 1940-41. Howard University's physical plant is valued at $1,560,000. Howard has graduated more than 10,000 students, whose influence upon the life of their race and upon American life has been considerable. Howard graduates make up a large percentage of the Negro professional class.

The dominant architectural note of the 25 buildings on the campus is Georgian. A central group includes the President's House, the Founders Library and Andrew Rankin Memorial Chapel on the south; on the west, the School of Religion and Frederick Douglass Memorial Hall, a $960,000 structure constructed with PWA funds; Clarke Hall, Cooke Hall, and the gymnasium, on the north; Spaulding Hall, the Applied Science Building, devoted to the School of Engineering and Architecture, and Miner Hall, on the east.

The ivy-covered ANDREW RANKIN MEMORIAL CHAPEL was built in 1894 as a memorial to Andrew E. Rankin, brother of the president, J. E. Rankin. It has fine stained-glass windows and a steeply pitched gable roof. The pipe organ, installed in 1934, is one of the finest instruments in Washington. The lower floor of the chapel holds an art gallery, opened in 1930. Each year, generally in the spring, an exhibition of Negro art is held here.

FOUNDERS LIBRARY houses 135,000 volumes, 880 periodicals, and 23 newspapers. Those relating to the Negro are in the Moorland Room, in which the most valuable collection is that given by Dr. Jesse E. Moorland, a member of the university's board of trustees. Additional collections make this the most complete library of Negro Americana in existence.

Other buildings include the School of Music group, comprising the Conservatory, the Conservatory annex, and Howard Hall; the School of Religion (Johnson Hall); the Home Economics Building, mostly occupied by the School of Law, Thirkield Science Hall, and the Chemistry Building (erected in 1936). The university stadium seats 10,000. The three women's dormitories are named in honor of Sojourner Truth, former slave and antislavery crusader; Prudence Crandall, New England abolitionist and educator; and Julia Caldwell Frazier, alumna of Howard, distinguished in education.

The Colleges of Medicine, Dentistry, and Pharmacy are in buildings at 5th and W Streets NW., facing Freedmen's Hospital. Freedmen's Hospital operates in connection with the School of Medicine, employing a staff composed largely of the faculty of the School of Medicine.

Howard University's 9 schools and colleges are: College of Liberal Arts, School of Engineering and Architecture, School of Music, Graduate School, School of Religion, College of Medicine, College of Dentistry, College of Pharmacy, and School of Law. The university publishes the *Howard University Bulletin,* the *School of Religion News,* and the *Journal of Negro Education,* a quarterly review. Student publications are *The Stylus, The Hilltop,* a weekly newspaper, and *The Bison,* a year book.

Student activities at Howard University include athletics, debating, dramatics, and music. There are State, literary, scientific, liberal, and scholarship clubs and Greek-letter fraternities and sororities. A unit of the ROTC qualifies graduates for commissions as lieutenants in the reserve officers' corps. Student government is invested in a student council.

TRINITY COLLEGE AND CHAPEL OF NOTRE DAME

Trinity College, Michigan Avenue and Franklin Street NE., is one of the largest women's colleges in the vicinity of Washington. Since its establishment in 1897 by the Sisters of Notre Dame, it has been an outstanding Catholic institution, with an enrollment of 300 to 400 students.

At the north side of the grounds is the CHAPEL OF NOTRE DAME, completed in 1924 at a cost of more than $500,000. The architects, Maginnis and Walsh, were awarded the American Institute of Architects' gold medal for general excellence in ecclesiastical design. The spirited architecture of the chapel combines the simplicity of the later Classic style with a refinement of Byzantine art. It is distinguished by its graceful basilican mass and the low segmental dome over the crossing, surmounted by a slender lantern cupola and decorative bronze cross. On the south façade, a colonnaded portico screens the main entrance. The sculptures of the pediment, representing the Mother of God and the Divine Child, are the work of Sidney Woollett, of Boston.

Among the noteworthy features of the singularly delicate interior are the domical mosaic ceiling of the sanctuary, by Bancel LaFarge; the transept altars, dedicated to the Sacred Heart and to the Blessed Julie Billiart, the work of Woollett; the canopied shrines on each side of the sanctuary, representing the Immaculate Conception and St. Joseph holding the Child Jesus; the medallions of the transept and nave windows, by Charles Connick, and a series of small windows around the central dome, devoted to the Angelic Hosts.

CATHOLIC UNIVERSITY OF AMERICA

On Michigan Avenue, in the highest part of Northeast Washington, Catholic University and affiliated institutions occupy a tract more than 150 acres in extent. This university is the only academic center in the country that receives the direct patronage of the Pope and of the Catholic hierarchy. Originally founded as a school of theology, it is now open to Catholic and non-Catholic alike, and its graduate school is open to men and women. The annual enrollment is about 5,000, with a faculty of 300.

In 1866 the Catholic bishops of the United States expressed their desire to have a university under Catholic auspices, but not until their third plenary council at Baltimore in 1884 did they finally decide to establish a *seminarium principale* as the nucleus. Pope Leo XIII gave his formal approval of the project in a letter to Cardinal Gibbons, April 10, 1887, and on March 7, 1889, approved the constitution of the university and granted it full power to confer degrees. Meanwhile the council had accepted a gift of $300,000 from Miss Mary Gwendoline Caldwell of Newport, Rhode Island, for the proposed institution. The James Middleton estate, called Sidney, of 60 acres in the section now known as Brookland was selected for the site, and the Right Reverend John J. Keane, S.T.D., formerly Bishop of Richmond, was chosen rector. The cornerstone of Caldwell Hall was laid in 1888, President Cleveland and his Cabinet attending the ceremony, and the next year the School of the Sacred Sciences was housed in this structure. In 1891 the university came into properties given by the Very Reverend Monseigneur James McMahon for the founding of schools of philosophy, letters, and science.

Associated with the university are the autonomous houses of study, or scholasticates, belonging to various religious orders. About 20 buildings belong to the university proper, while more than twice this number are owned by the seminaries and brotherhoods. These stone buildings represent an expenditure of more than $25,000,000.

Fronting Michigan Avenue are three college dormitories; Gibbons Hall with its two towers; Graduate Hall, in the same Tudor Gothic style, and the oldest dormitory on the campus; Albert Hall, a narrow red-brick structure with Flemish gables. In line with these, but at the extreme southeast corner of the grounds, is the Maloney Chemical Laboratory, the gift of Martin Maloney of Philadelphia.

The road running north from Albert Hall passes the white marble JOHN K. MULLEN MEMORIAL LIBRARY, Romanesque in style, and the most distinguished building on the campus. It contains nearly 500,000 volumes, about half its capacity. Included among its collections are the State library, gift of E. Francis Riggs, a repository for Biblical literature; the Bouquillon sociological library; and the Ibero-American Library. The Knights of Columbus contributed the Gymnasium, at the rear of the library, where in 1933, President Franklin D. Roosevelt received his degree of LL. D. McMahon Hall, a large Romanesque building about the center of the campus, contains several laboratories and lecture rooms. To its left is the Music Building, a U-shaped brick structure with low-pitched roof and corbeled eaves. Caldwell Hall, the administration building, is farther north.

Center of the religious life of the university is the NATIONAL SHRINE OF THE IMMACULATE CONCEPTION, the crypt of which serves as the university church. "Designed to be the greatest church edifice in the Western Hemisphere and one of the most magnificent basilicas in the world," the Shrine is being built on an elevation to the left of the main driveway. The finished crypt represents more than 10 years of labor and the expenditure of $1,500,000. The cost of the whole is estimated at $7,000,000 to $8,000,000. As far back as 1846 it was proposed to build in Washington a Roman Catholic church that would rank in splendor with those of Europe. The first step was taken in 1913 by Bishop Shahan, rector of the Catholic University, when he appealed to Catholic women to co-operate in the undertaking. Three Popes and Catholics from all over America contributed to the building fund. For the laying of the foundation in 1920, more than 10,000 people thronged the campus, among them Cardinal Gibbons and Cardinal O'Connell, ambassadors of 24 foreign countries, and more than 70 bishops. During Holy Week in 1926, the crypt was opened for services.

Based on examples of Byzantine and Romanesque architecture, the building is basilican in mass, with an overall length of 465 feet and a transept of 238 feet. The dome, 90 feet in diameter, will rise 254 feet above the crossing, while the campanile will be still more lofty. Maginnis and Walsh are the architects, with Frederick V. Murphy, professor of architecture at Catholic University, as associate. In the completed apse crypt, the low-vaulted ceilings and massive walls are decorated with ornate ceramics and multicolored marble. Onyx, granite, and marble from more than 50 countries compose the columns supporting the powerful arches. The Mary Memorial Altar, gift of Catholic women of America, is a great block of golden onyx upon steps of travertine white marble. It has a central position under a colorful ceramic ceiling design representing "God, the Holy Ghost." Each of the three semicircular bays around the main altar contains five recessed wall chapels, those of the central bay adorned with mosaic panels by Bancel LaFarge. The 15 symbolic lunette windows are the work of Charles Connick. A reproduction in mosaic of Murillo's *Immaculate Conception,* made of 35,000 pieces of colored enamel, was given to the Chapel by Pope Benedict XV and Pope Pius XI. The Memorial Chapel and a chapel dedicated to Bishop Shahan occupy important crypts. In the west transept is a miniature Grotto of Lourdes.

Academically, the university functions under 10 schools and colleges, immediately governed by the rector and academic senate. Summer sessions are held in Iowa, Texas, California, and New York, as well as on the Washington campus. Courses are available at the university in practically every branch of secular learning, and the College of Arts and Sciences offers unusual courses such as those in the Hebrew, Syriac, Egyptian, and Coptic languages. Undergraduate courses are open to men only, but women are admitted to the Graduate School. Included among the schools are those of law, engineering and architecture, social work, nursing, and social science (opened in 1935). Emphasis is put upon theological training through the School of the Sacred Sciences, the School of Canon Law, the School of Philosophy, and the Seminary. Theater work at the university has attracted national notice (*see Music and the Theater*). Among the university's important publications are the *Catholic Educational Review,* the *Historical Review,* and the *Ecclesiastical Review.*

The university maintains affiliations with schools throughout the country, but the largest group is in the immediate vicinity. This group includes the Marist College and the Holy Cross College, at the northwest corner of the university grounds; St. Paul's College, the College of the Immaculate Conception, Sulpician Seminary, the Augustinian College, Foreign Mission Seminary, Chaminade College, Capuchin College of St. Francis, St. Anselm's Priory, Carmelite College, Pallottine House of Studies, Claretian College, and the Dominican House of Studies. The Franciscan Monastery is probably the most frequently visited building. An integral part of the university is the Catholic Sisters' College, 1000 Bates Road NE., at the northeast corner of the Catholic University grounds. It was established in 1911 as the first institution in the world to train Sisters for teaching in parochial schools.

FRANCISCAN MONASTERY

About one-half mile northeast of Catholic University, on the wooded hill of Mount Saint Sepulchre, is the Franciscan Monastery Memorial Church of the Holy Land, with its adjoining cloister (*open, free, 8:30-5:30; guides*), 14th and Quincy Streets NE. Within the monastery church and grounds are facsimiles of the chief shrines of the Christian religion, among them the Bethlehem Manger, the Garden of Gethsemane, the Grotto of Lourdes, the Holy Sepulchre, and the Catacombs of Rome.

This 44-acre tract, part of a large original grant from George Calvert, first Lord Baltimore, to an early colonist, was probably a part of the Turkey Thicket or Cuckold's Delight area. The deserted estate had fallen to ruin when Father Godfrey Schilling of the Order of St. Francis visited it in 1897. He saw the possibilities of the land as a setting for an institution that would interest the American people in support of the holy places of Jerusalem, the guardianship of which had been entrusted to this order by the Roman Catholic Church for more than 700 years. Two years later, in 1899, an apostolic delegate from Rome, Archbishop Martinelli, dedicated the monastery, which was officially made the Commissariat of the Holy Land for the United States, the Holy See having sanctioned the transfer from New York City. Catholic University welcomed the new institution as an affiliate. Twenty years later Cardinal Gibbons selected this church as the scene of the jubilee commemorating his fiftieth year as bishop and his twenty-fifth as cardinal. On September 17, 1924, the Feast of the Stigmata of St. Francis, the church was consecrated at an impressive ceremony.

The friendly character of this retreat is in harmony with the traditions of monastic architecture and the simplicity of the Franciscan Order. The monastery church is approached by a road that winds past the Monastery Pilgrimage Hall, a building designed in the style of early Franciscan missions in California. Surrounding the church is a cloisterlike enclosure, called the Rosary Portico, with a double gateway giving entrance to the grounds. The cloistered arcades of the Portico, with their sloping tile roofs, tinted walls, graceful colonnades, and series of chapels, form a pleasing architectural frame around the broad front lawn and the flower gardens. Close to the entrance is a heroic statue of St. Christopher bearing the infant Christ upon his shoulders.

To the left stands Rosignoli's bronze figure of St. Francis and the Doves. A little farther along is the stone chapel of Saint Mary of the Angels, a copy of the Chapel of Portiuncula near Assisi where St. Francis, after casting aside his wealth, founded the order.

The church and the adjoining monastery quadrangle were designed by Aristides Leonori of Rome, a member of the Third (or laymen's) Order of St. Francis. The architecture of the group is Byzantine in character, with elements drawn from the classic Italian Renaissance. The plan of the church is that of the Five-fold Cross of the Holy Land. The exterior, with the exception of the disproportioned cupola over the central dome, conforms to the classic basilica with gabled roof and lofty clerestory. Its buff-brick walls are adorned with Corinthian pilasters and pierced with graceful arcaded windows.

The light within the church is tempered by brilliant, stained-glass windows, representing the Saints of the Three Orders of St. Francis. The Byzantine theme is particularly evident in the entrance to the four corner chapels through the triple arcades of which can be seen the high altars, dedicated to St. Joseph, St. Francis, St. Anthony, and the Blessed Virgin. In the extended west arm of the cross are the Shrine of the Crowning with Thorns and the Shrine of the Scourging.

Entering the sacristy at the southeast corner and passing through the Chapel of St. Joseph, the visitor is drawn to the main altar and lofty baldachino beneath the great central dome. This altar canopy is supported by four columns, symbolic of the Four Evangelists, and 12 lamps honor the Twelve Apostles. Other features of the vast interior are: the Altar of Thabor, dedicated to the Transfiguration; the Shrine of the Holy Sepulchre, a copy of the one built in Jerusalem in the fourth century; the Sanctuary of Calvary with its Altar, a facsimile of the Greek altar in the basilica in Jerusalem, giving a realistic panorama of the Crucifixion; the Altar of the Holy Ghost; and the Sacred Heart Altar. Two broad marble stairways in the transepts lead down to extensive underground catacombs, where numerous chapels and shrines reproduce portions of the passages beneath the city of Rome where early Christians found refuge. Among these underground chapels are the Martyr's Crypt, the Purgatory Chapel, the Chapel of St. Sebastian, the Chapel of St. Cecilia, and the Grotto of Bethlehem.

In June the monastery garden is in its splendor, displaying many of the world's finest roses. Among the trees and flowers are shrines dedicated to persons and events associated with the life of Jesus. The Garden of Gethsemane, reproducing the original in Jerusalem, is halfway down the hill. Of special interest are the outdoor Stations of the Cross, and the copy of the Grotto of Lourdes in the Pyrenees. The Way of the Cross, as a devotion, is of Franciscan origin.

Though the order is not cloistered in the strictest sense, their cloister is not open to the public. The building is in the form of a large quadrangle enclosing a flower-set courtyard, with an arched ambulatory. In the cemetery, below the cloister on the slope of the hill, is the grave of Father Godfrey Schilling, founder of the monastery.

SOLDIERS' HOME

The oldest soldiers' home in the United States is situated in a partially wooded tract of 500 acres, about 3 miles north of the Capitol, Rock Creek Road and Upshur Street NW. (*grounds open at all times; buildings open 9 a.m. to sundown*). The main entrance is Eagle Gate, on the northwest, but there are several entries to the grounds.

Although administered by the War Department, Soldiers' Home is organically a separate institution, financed outside War Department appropriations and directed by a board of governors whose office is based on their status in local units of the Military Establishment. The home was founded in 1851 by act of Congress, largely at the instance of General Winfield Scott and Captain (later Major) Robert Anderson, Civil War hero. Scott had transmitted to the War Department in 1848 the $100,000 tribute levied on Mexico City, with the suggestion that it be used for an Army asylum. Success in starting the Soldiers' Home, soon afterward to furnish a haven for Federal soldiers, was primarily due to Jefferson Davis of Mississippi. As head of the Senate Committee on Military Affairs, Davis pushed through the Soldiers' Home Bill, which he had introduced in 1848. The main building, started in 1852, was completed in 1891.

Requisites for admittance to the Home are 20 years' service in the Army, or disablement from wounds or disease acquired in line of duty, with an honorable discharge from service. Accommodations are provided for 2,000 inmates.

Soldiers' Home is one of the most attractive estates in the District. Ten miles of macadamized roadway wind through groves of beautiful trees, many of great age, with lanes and paths leading to quiet retreats. The southern acreage is utilized as a truck farm. Eight thousand chickens supply eggs for the institution, while a herd of 200 Holsteins furnishes milk. East of Eagle Gate, to the left, is the small marble Administration Building. Directly ahead, past a circular water tower, stands the Scott Building with its castellated clock tower, on one of the highest points (320 feet) in the District of Columbia. Joined to this by a central annex is the Sherman Building, designed by B. S. Alexander in Norman-Gothic style and constructed of unfinished white marble. Historically, the most interesting of the buildings is the Anderson cottage, the gray stucco homestead just west of the Scott Building. It supplied the first lodgings for the members and was used by Presidents of the United States as a summer residence. Lincoln stayed in the Anderson cottage in the summer of 1864.

Northwest and northeast of the Sherman Building are the Sheridan Building (1883), a three-story brick dormitory, and Stanley Hall (1897), the recreation center. North of these is the Grant Building (1911), used as a mess-hall and barracks. A heroic bronze statue of General Scott, by Launt Thompson, was erected in 1874 on a bluff affording a sweeping view of the city. Below is the 500-bed hospital.

All members of the home are entitled to military burial in the small national cemetery just east of the home. Memorial Gateway, at the northwest corner, just opposite the entrance to Rock Creek Cemetery, gives access to this soldiers' burial ground.

ROCK CREEK CEMETERY

Just north of Soldiers' Home are St. Paul's Church and Rock Creek Cemetery, the oldest church and burying ground in the District. The red-brick Colonial church, thrice restored, is surrounded by 100 acres of gently rolling park land, with many ancient trees and a diminutive lake. At the entrance, Webster and 3rd Streets NW., diagonally opposite the north gates of Soldiers' Home, is a small Tudor lodge. An Ionic granite cross in front of the lodge is dedicated to Colonel John Bradford, who gave to the Chapel of Ease in 1719 a quantity of tobacco and 100 acres of land for the establishment of a glebe. Within a year of the donation, the little chapel that had been founded in 1712 was expanded into St. Paul's Church. The Glebe Oak, 14 feet in circumference, marks the site of this church, which was rebuilt in 1775, remodeled 89 years later, and, following a fire in 1921, again restored.

The ivy-covered red-brick building, with its square central tower, white cupola with its surmounting cross, and tall round-arched windows, is one of the most charming examples of church architecture in Washington. An arched white doorway in the base of the tower and round windows piercing the tower below the cupola add interest to the simple and well-proportioned plan of the building.

Interments in the cemetery began in 1719. These early graves, almost exclusively local in interest, are grouped about the church. A number of prominent people, however, are buried farther within the grounds, among them William Windom, Secretary of the Treasury under Garfield and Arthur; Hugh McCullough, Secretary of the Treasury under Lincoln and Arthur; Alexander Shepherd, second and last governor of the District, who attained fame for his work in rebuilding Washington; Elisha F. Riggs, founder of the Riggs National Bank; Francis P. Blair, editor of the *Globe*; and Peter Force, early publisher.

The road running west of the church passes imposing vaults on the way to the tiny lake, which lies to the left. Around it are numerous sarcophagi, that of Levi Z. Leiter, wealthy Chicago merchant, being one of the most elaborate. The fine texture of the Italian marble and the delicate chiseling of the bas-reliefs are protected by glass. To the right of the road is the Hitt Monument by Laura Gordon Fraser, a simple block of polished pink granite with bronze high-reliefs.

Farther along is the Kaufmann Memorial by William Ordway Partridge. Almost due east is the Ffoulke Memorial by Gutzon Borglum. The draped figure of a woman portrays Mary Magdalene beside the tomb from which Christ has risen. Mary's cry of "Rabboni," meaning "My Master," is used as the inscription.

The road bears right until it crosses a gravel path, a shimmering white section of which leads toward the church. About halfway along its length a circular grove of evergreens and holly screens from view the most noted of the memorials—the figure by Augustus Saint-Gaudens, above the grave of Mrs. Henry Adams. Its hexagonal platform, designed by Stanford White, supports granite benches that face the shrouded figure of bronze, seated upon a boulder and backed by a polished granite block—a figure so impressive that Gaston, famous French critic, said, "I know of no work so profound in sentiment, so exalted in its art, and executed by methods so simple and broad." Henry Adams called it *The Peace of God*, and Saint-Gaudens referred to the memorial as *The Mystery of the Hereafter*, "beyond pain and beyond joy." A remark attributed to Mark Twain, that the enigmatic figure embodied all human grief, led to its being known quite generally as *Grief*.

Close to the southeast corner of the church, under the Glebe Oak, is the Boardman Memorial, by James Earle Fraser. In this *Journey Through Life*, bronze figures of a man and a woman stand against a simple granite block.

South of the Mall

Streetcars: Bureau of Engraving (on 14th Street), 7th St. Wharves (on 7th Street), 17th & Penna. SE., and Navy Yard (on 7th Street and Independence Avenue).
Busses: S. Capitol & O (S. on 4th Street from Pennsylvania Avenue), Congress Heights and Bolling Field via Portland (Pennsylvania Avenue and 2nd Street).
Taxis: First and second zones.

Government buildings south of the Mall are grouped in two widely separated sections. The western group, at Independence Avenue and 14th Street SW., includes the Bureau of Engraving and Printing, the Agriculture Department, and the Central Heating Plant. Those in the eastern corner, formed by the Mall and 1st Street SW., are the Social Security Building, the Railroad Retirement Building, and Federal Office Building No. 1. Standing between, and equidistant from either, is the Procurement Building. In architectural design, the buildings on this side of the Mall are examples of classical design greatly modified and modernized when compared with the massive types in the Federal Triangle. The use of vertical planes and lines, with a minimum of exterior ornament, has unashamedly brought out the plain purpose of the buildings—to provide suitable office quarters for Government employees. The Central Heating Plant is an outstanding example of this forceful style of functional architecture. In developing the area south of the Mall, the Government has removed from this section the stigma, "on the other side of the tracks," and has diverted some Federal offices from the overcrowded northwest section of the city.

BUREAU OF ENGRAVING AND PRINTING

The Bureau of Engraving and Printing (*conducted tours 9-11 and 1-2:30 Mon.-Fri.; closed to visitors in 1941 for duration of national emergency*), 14th and C Streets SW., is the greatest money-making plant in the world. The front façade of the main building, with its Doric colonnade and corner pavilions, first occupied in 1914, faces west across the Tidal Basin. The east or 14th Street side, with its four factory-like wings, of which 60 per cent of the wall area is given over to windows, has 43,000 panes of glass through which can be seen, especially at night, the spreading ghostglow of many mercury tube lights. The entrance, used by 5,800 employees and 1,700 visitors daily, is over the enclosed bridgeway extending from 14th Street to the midsection of the great structure. Across 14th Street is the modern ANNEX,

317

erected in 1938; its multiple skylights in serrated ranks shut out all but the north light.

Production of national currency is the most familiar function of the Bureau, but it is only one of the 70 main items on the work schedule. Four types of paper money are issued: United States notes, silver certificates, gold certificates, and Federal Reserve notes. Gold certificates, in denominations of $100 to $100,000, are printed only on special order and are used to pay for gold delivered by banks into Federal custody. The daily average for all notes is about 4,237,000, with a face value of $15,000,000. Thirty-two denominations of stamps are needed for ordinary postage, but 100 kinds are made at the rate of 66,000,000 daily. Billions of revenue stamps are printed annually. Other items include bonds, treasury warrants, customs stamps, "duck stamps," patent certificates, and currency (peso notes) for the Philippines.

When the Bureau was started in 1862, it was housed in the attic room of the Treasury. Printing was done under contract and sent to the Treasury for signing, sealing, and separating. In 1880 the Bureau moved to a newly equipped building one block north of its present location, where all operations on national currency were centered. In 1894 it took over the production of postage stamps.

Designs for currency originate in the ENGRAVING DIVISION. Highly skilled engravers, each a master in his field—portraiture, lettering, or decoration—do their work on a soft steel plate after the Secretary of the Treasury has approved the design. By the retransfer process the original engraving is impressed in the printing plate, and then is kept as a die for making other plates. The Bureau also uses the electrolytic process for making plates. After an engraved plate is made, it is placed in a special bath, and by means of electrodeposition a plate, called an "alto," is built up to a required thickness. The master plate is then removed from the bath, and the alto separated from it. The engraved plate being intaglio (cut below the surface), the design on the alto is in relief. After another bath a layer of chromium is deposited on the plate to prolong its life. The alto can be used repeatedly for making additional plates.

The flatbed press equipment of the PLATE-PRINTING DIVISION totals 313 units. Each is operated by a printer and two assistants, one of whom has exclusive responsibility for all stock drawn for production each day. Four identical plates are used, and inking, wiping, polishing, and printing go on continuously. Polishing is done by hand, for no machine has been invented to perform this delicate operation satisfactorily. Backs are always printed first, and fresh sheets, packed so that the impressions cannot be injured, are delivered to the EXAMINING DIVISION for counting and checking. At the end of the workday, the plates on the presses are locked under steel covers. Plates not in use, with stock and printed sheets, are stored in vaults.

Extra safeguards are necessary in the last phase of production, since the notes are negotiable as soon as a seal and number are affixed. Special multipurpose presses, by a continuous automatic process, perform all the final operations except packing. The finished notes are packaged, bound with welded steel bands, and stored to await shipment. Currency production cost is $1 per 140 notes. The major work of the CURRENCY DIVISION is replacing $1 bills, the life of which is only 8 to 9 months. Five- and ten-dollar bills last 1 to 2 years; twenties, 5 years; ten-thousand-dollar bills, the highest denomination, much longer. Mutilated and worn-out currency redeemed by the Treasury and spoiled currency sheets are macerated and reduced to pulp. Ten million pounds of pulp are disposed of annually.

Nearly all postage stamps are printed from curved intaglio plates on rotary presses in one continuous process, from wetting the stock to drying the gum and rolling the printed product into coils. Precanceling devices are attached for use as required. The rolls are then fed automatically into perforating machines. The unit capacity is 1,800,000 to 3,000,000 stamps a day, and production cost is about 1 cent for 140 stamps.

Typographic and offset processes of the SURFACE PRINTING DIVISION are employed in printing such items as Government checks, liquor and tobacco stamps, naturalization certificates, several types of licenses, and revenue stamps. This Division also overprints currency, bonds, certificates, and securities in general. It maintains nearly 100,000 electrotypes and more than 5,500 numbering machines.

The ACCOUNTING DIVISION keeps final check on production against unused and damaged stock. There are few actual losses, but occasional misplacements are charged against the employees of the Division where they occur. No employee is bonded, but carelessness and neglect are virtually unknown. Bureau employees may not leave the building during working hours unless granted a special pass; the Bureau has a cooperative lunchroom, an emergency hospital, and recreational facilities within the building.

DEPARTMENT OF AGRICULTURE BUILDINGS

The massive Administration Building and huge extensible South structure of the Department of Agriculture (*open 9-5:30 Mon.-Fri., 9-1 Sat.*), fronting on the Mall and Independence Avenue respectively, between 12th and 14th Streets SW., testify to the all-important role of agriculture in the life of the Nation.

With a gleaming white portico facing the Federal Triangle across the Mall, the ADMINISTRATION BUILDING, designed by Rankin, Kellogg, and Crane, of Philadelphia, conforms to the classic tradition, except that the variety of detail suggests a more composite scheme. The five-story central section with its broad Corinthian colonnade and high attic story in flanked by four-story wings, and, on the north side by sculptured pediments, the work of A. A. Weinman, showing stylized fruits, cereals, flowers, and forests. The two widely separated wings were erected in 1905, and 25 years later the imposing central section was added to bridge the gap.

A two-story inner court or patio occupies the center of the building, and corridors walled in tan marble and floored with travertine lead to spacious lobbies.   Through an arched glass ceiling the warm glow of sunlight falls on a central fountain, gay flower boxes, and on the arcaded brick walls.   Here the 26 bureaus of the Department place exhibits to illustrate the widespread activities of this great service agency and research institution.   On the wall above the circular stairway is a mural, *Agriculture,* by Gilbert White.

In the basement, near the west wing, the Welfare and Recreational Association has a grocery store for Department employees and the public, specializing in meats and dairy and poultry products from the Government's experimental farm at Beltsville, Maryland.

The seven-story SOUTH BUILDING, designed in the offices of the Supervising Architect of the Treasury, contains 4,500 office bays, and is connected to the Administration Building by two single-span bridges at the third floor level over Independence Avenue.   Bas-relief portrait plaques of James Wilson, Secretary of Agriculture from 1897 to 1913, and of his special agent, Seaman A. Knapp, who made important contributions in the battle against the boll weevil, embellish the 14th and 12th Street Bridges respectively.   The plaques are by Carl Moseo.   The exterior of the building is finished in variegated tan brick and decorated with terra-cotta, except the 12th and 14th Street wings, which are faced with limestone.   Metal spandrels between third and fourth floor windows are ornamented with conventionalized heads of horses, bulls, rams, and turkeys, the work of Edwin Morris.   The principal entrance on 14th Street is approached · through a central pavilion with a Corinthian colonnade.   Six inner courts afford light and air to this huge office building, occupying three city blocks.

The DEPARTMENTAL LIBRARY, serving all bureaus and containing more than 250,000 volumes on agriculture, natural science, forestry, economics, sociology, and engineering, is housed in Room 1051, main floor.   The AUDITORIUM, also on this floor, is on the Independence Avenue side, between the 5th and 6th wings.   The main CAFETERIA is on the sixth floor, C Street side.

CENTRAL HEATING PLANT

The buff-brick Central Heating Plant (*ordinarily open 9-4:30 Mon.-Fri.; 9-12 Sat.; closed to the public during national emergency*), C and D Streets between 12th and 13th Streets SW., is a forceful example of functional design adapted to the rigid height requirements of the zoning law and the architectural style of Federal buildings.   The outer walls of the structure rise sheer to a setback 92 feet above the street, above which its massive octagonal smokestacks rise 42 feet.   The front façade is broken into vertical planes by a series of longitudinal windows set deep into the wall.   Designed by Paul Philippe Cret and completed in 1934, the building and its equipment cost approximately $4,000,000.

The boiler room is a great space finished in buff brick and floored with red quarry tile, in which heat and dust are noticeably absent, and the maze of pipes, the array of gauges and recording instruments, are spotlessly clean. Six giant furnaces, each five stories high, burning 100,000 tons of coal a year, have auxiliary apparatus for conveying and stoking the coal. Jets of water under pressure sluice the ashes from the grates into a pit where heavy machinery grinds them into cinders for paths and fills in city parks. Each boiler is capable of converting 215,000 pounds of water (more than 25,000 gallons) into steam every hour at a pressure of 200 pounds a square inch. One cold day in January 1937, 15,000,000 pounds of steam were made, representing the conversion of 1,800,000 gallons of water and the consumption of 700 tons of coal. Although soft coal is used, the smoke is reduced to a steam-like vapor before it escapes—electric precipitators attract the carbon particles to diversion pipes, which convey them to ash bins at the base of the building.

PROCUREMENT DIVISION BUILDING

The huge white-painted concrete structure of the Procurement Division of the Treasury (*open 8:30-5 Mon.-Fri., 8:30-12:30 Sat.*), occupying two blocks between 7th and 9th and C and D Streets SW., is composed of two seven-story buildings of modern structural design, joined together and functioning as a single unit. The Main Building, with tunnel and railroad siding, was constructed in 1932, and the Annex, with light bays for the convenience of Treasury architects, was completed in 1935, at a total cost of $2,600,000. The interior of the building is used as a warehouse and the outer shell is occupied by offices.

In the main lobby, 7th Street entrance, murals illustrate the work of this central Government purchasing agency, including the drawing of architectural plans, the buying of materials, and the supervising of Federal buildings under construction. The LIBRARY OF THE SUPERVISING ARCHITECT (*open to serious students*), sixth floor, south side, contains photographs of buildings and construction processes, architectural plans and blueprints, technical books and periodicals. Eight rooms on the fifth floor, each finished in a different type of material, ranging from metals to plastics, exhibit a great variety of building materials and their uses. Here are displayed tiles, bricks, building stones, woods, lighting methods, casement and sash windows, chromium and nickel decorations, engravings on glass, and plastics in polychrome, to mention only a few. In the corridors on the fourth floor, the ART BRANCH exhibits paintings available for hanging in public buildings.

SOCIAL SECURITY BUILDING

The Social Security Board Building (*open 9:15-5:45 Mon.-Fri., 9:15-1:15 Sat.*), Independence Avenue between 3rd and 4th Streets SW., completed in 1940, is the only Government building of modern classical design fronting on the southeastern end of the Mall. Rectangular in plan, the limestone and buff-brick building has five stories and an attic, with a series of spandreled windows rising from the second through the fifth floors, breaking the horizontal mass of the structure with vertical lines. The central section of the floor-plan runs east and west, from which five wings extend north and south, forming two bays and two enclosed courts south of the main axis and two bays on the north. The treatment of the bays is unusual, with the cornice line carried across the end of the open court on supporting piers above the first floor, and the openings into the courts are in harmony with the window design.

The main lobby, entered through bronze doors paneled with glass, is finished with marble walls and terrazzo floors. A new development in air-conditioning controls the temperature of the offices in accordance with the position of the sun. When the sun's rays beat upon the eastern face of the building, rheostats increase the flow of cool air in that area, and throughout the day the air-conditioning system follows the sun in its westward course.

A ramp for freight and mail enters the basement from C Street, and a tunnel connects this building with that of the Railroad Retirement Board across the street.

RAILROAD RETIREMENT BUILDING

The building of the Railroad Retirement Board (*open 8:45-4:15 Mon.-Fri., 8:45-12:45 Sat.*), C Street between 3rd and 4th Streets SW., is similar to the Social Security Building in architectural style and in the use of building materials. The main section fronting on C Street has two entrances, and from the rear six wings extend to D Street, with the south wall of each wing broken by a single high window. The interiors of the two buildings are also alike in design and decorative treatment. The three-member Railroad Retirement Board administers retirement pensions and unemployment insurance for railroad employees.

FEDERAL OFFICE BUILDING NO. 1

Federal Office Building No. 1 (*open 8:30-5 Mon.-Fri., 8:30-12:30 Sat.*), D Street between 2nd and 3rd Streets SW., is a modern utilitarian structure, erected in 120 days to house 1940 Census activities and other Government agencies in need of office space. The floor plan is divided into three long parallel units connected by a central section, forming three wings and two bays on the north side, and a wing, a bay, and an enclosed court on the south. The main façade, fronting on 2nd Street, has 280 office windows and rises sheer for six stories from a high basement. The exterior walls are faced with buff brick, with cornice and trim of stone. From Virginia Avenue a ramp leads to a large ground floor space for loading and unloading materials and for parking automobiles.   Designed in the Office of the Supervising Architect, Public Buildings Administration, the building and site cost about $3,500,000.

The lobbies at the 2nd and 3rd Street entrances have terrazzo floors, marble wainscots, plaster ceilings and cornices, and wood doors and trim.   A large cafeteria, storage, and utility rooms occupy the ground floor.   The various wings contain floor areas which can be divided by movable partitions into offices of the required size.

Along the Water Front

Streetcars: Seventh St. Wharves, Navy Yard, and Bureau of Engraving.
Busses: Bureau of Engraving.
Taxis: Second zone.

Washington's water front, along Maine Avenue east of 14th Street SW., on the north bank of the Washington Channel, is, after the ponderous monumentality of the Mall and the impounded elegance of posted parks, a realm of welcome small things and the reassuring clutter generated by humans going about their essential business. The buildings are modest, inclined to dinginess, and take character from the kind of merchandise that is handled in them; craft along the wharves and in the slips are usually small—pleasure boats, oystermen up from Chincoteague and Tangier, heavily-laden melon boats from the Carolinas, a topheavy river steamer or two, and squat potent tugs. Trespass signs are interpreted liberally, and "gamming" (salt-water gossip) is honored for its own sake. There are excellent sea-food restaurants, wholesale and retail markets for fish, poultry, vegetables, and groceries, yacht clubs, yacht brokers, boat chandlers—in short, the water front, apart from the potentially lethal truck traffic, is probably just about as Pierre L'Enfant visualized it.

Immediately east of 14th Street, Maine Avenue dips under southbound railroad tracks separating Washington Channel from the Tidal Basin. In this blind end of the Channel are Government-built slips, complete with fresh-water and electrical outlets, which can be rented by owners of self-propelled craft. Across Maine Avenue from the public wharves are a series of busy wholesale markets where barrels, sacks, baskets, and boxes are perpetually shifted by stevedores from trucks into high piles, into warehouses and out again. Immediately east of the public wharves are fish markets, where the customer may name it and get it fresh. Or he may go out on the whitewashed wharf and bargain first hand for "SALTY WATER OYSTERS AND CLAMS" with fishermen who hawk from the decks of their boats, and who offer samples of raw oysters shucked on the spot.

Down channel from the fish-markets are the berths of the Capital Yacht Club, the long blank wall of the District of Columbia Penal Institution, wharves, commercial boatyards and slips, where houseboats as well as sail and power craft may berth. At the foot of L and K Streets is the disembarkation point for the overnight steamer to Norfolk, and for excursion steamers, charter boats, and an occasional windjammer. At the foot of N Street are the wharves and buildings of the District Harbor Police, with their eight motor launches and a Diesel-powered tugboat. Near by is the harbor of the *Firefighter,* the District's fireboat, capable of pumping 6,000 gallons of water a minute. Just east is a municipal pier, completed in the summer of 1941. Below, on the point dividing the Potomac from the Anacostia River, the buildings of the Army War College wall off the water front from civilians. Up the Anacostia a few blocks is the huge institution of the Washington Navy Yard, and back of it the block-square Marine Barracks.

For those who have not the fever of boats or of fishing, the cuisine of almost any of the water front restaurants is ample magnet. Maine or Florida lobster, Maryland terrapin, bluepoints on the half-shell, scallops, soft-shell crab, crabflakes sauté, or any of the delicacies that come up from the sea are served here. Below the balcony dining room of one restaurant, darky boys dance for coins if the law is benign. From the water front there is a panorama of transportation— two-wheel carts pulled by Negroes, multicolored trucks, southbound streamliners, boats under power and under sail, sleek airliners from the airport beyond Hains Point, speedy airfighters from the military airports across the Potomac, and over everything the constant wheeling and shrilling of gulls.

ARMY WAR COLLEGE

The War College (*open in normal times 9-2:30 Mon.-Fri., 9-12 Sat.*), 4th and P Streets SW., the ranking school in the Army's educational system, stands on the grounds of a beautiful old army post of 87 acres, fronting on the Washington Channel and the Anacostia River, extending east along Canal Street to 4th Street. The red-brick War College Building, of Colonial design, at the south end of the long parade ground near Greenleaf Point, is an imposing structure occupying a sentinel-like position. Smaller buildings of similar design flank the parade ground and house officers and enlisted men and the work of army units on duty at the post.

The lower portion of this quadrangular area was reserved by L'Enfant for a great military works to secure the city from naval invasion by way of the Potomac River. In 1794, a one-gun battery was established on Greenleaf Point, and three years later the site became a military reservation. The Washington Arsenal was started here in 1803, and in 1826 the buildings for a Federal Penitentiary were erected north of the arsenal limits, with a brick wall extending east and west across the peninsula, separating the two institutions. During the Civil War convicts were removed and the prison buildings were taken over by the expanding arsenal. The greatest change came in 1903 when the site was selected for the College, and McKim, Mead, and White, architects, designed the present main building. Finally, in 1938, the name of the post was officially changed from Fort Humphreys to Army War College.

Entrance to the College is through the iron gateway at the foot of 4th Street, where a sentry is always on guard. Barracks stand on either side of an arch of towering trees. The building on the left is occupied by the Army Band. At the end of the row of trees stands a flagpole beside the gun that is fired at the raising and lowering of the flag in the traditional manner at sunrise and sunset.

To the west is a long row of quarters for officers, and to the east another row for married enlisted men. Also on the east is the SIGNAL CORPS PHOTOGRAPHIC LABORATORY, where films used for publicity purposes and for training the Army are developed.

In the center of the parade ground are two buildings that link the present post to its historic past, when the reservation was the first United States Arsenal and the first United States Penitentiary. The north building, a 44-foot section of the eastern end of the old prison, has been remodeled into apartments for officers. In the northeast corner room, third floor, a military court tried the conspirators after Lincoln's assassination. On July 7, 1865, four of the prisoners—one, Mrs. Mary E. Surratt—were hanged in the prison yard, at the spot now occupied by the tennis court. The body of John Wilkes Booth was secretly buried in a room of the penitentiary, where it remained until 1867, when the central portion of the building was torn down. The other large square structure to the south, now occupied by officers, was the old Arsenal Headquarters Building.

In front of the entrance to the WAR COLLEGE BUILDING are 12 spaces intended for statues of famous military leaders who have materially contributed to the art of war. Eleven of the spaces are empty. A statue of Frederick the Great, by T. Uphues, donated by Kaiser Wilhelm II before the building was completed, stands alone.

In the ROTUNDA of the College are oil portraits of Generals Pershing, Bliss, Foch, Field Marshal Haig, and Baron von Steuben at Valley Forge. The LIBRARY is the largest on military science in the world. Since 1914, it has included the War Department Library and ranks second to that of the State Department as the oldest Government library in the country. The building contains an auditorium and classrooms for advanced instruction in tactics and allied subjects, attended by one hundred officer-students selected annually.

NAVY YARD

The Navy Yard (*working hours 8-4:30 weekdays; closed during national emergency*), 8th and M Streets SE., occupies a site of 115 acres on the west side of the Anacostia River between New Jersey Avenue and 11th Street, enclosed within a high wire fence, a line of red-brick walls, and a fringe of buff-colored barracks. The main entrance, with its iron-grille gates, was designed by B. H. Latrobe and built at the inception of the Navy Yard between 1801 and 1805. The superstructure, a later addition, contains a marine barrack room. Within the Yard, to the left of the entrance, are officers' quarters and the residence of the Commandant and Yard Captain, also designed by Latrobe. Specializing in the production and testing of naval ordnance, the Navy Yard, with its orderly rows of immense shops and correct little parks, is a modern steel plant, operated with the neatness and precision of a battleship.

Most of the buildings are of the factory type, and the few dating from the Civil War have been remodeled to meet the requirements of modern ordnance manufacture or have been converted into offices and storehouses. Large steel and brass foundries prepare the raw materials for manufacture. The Navy Yard also has a school which instructs sailors in diving and submarine work, and a fire-control division to teach the technique of range-finding and the control of heavy guns in action. During World War I, 14-inch guns were produced here in the shadow of the SAIL LOFT, a relic from the days of sailing ships.

Around Leutze Park, the broad green vista between overhanging trees in the center of the Yard, are guns captured by the Navy in every war in which it has participated. At the southwest corner of the park is "Long Tom," a 42-pounder that saw service in the navies of Great Britain, France, and the United States, and was finally recovered from the harbor at Fayal, Azores, where the American privateer *General Armstrong* went down in 1814. Scattered around the small parks are guns and projectiles of many nations and eras, from the round stones used in ancient catapults to the projectiles used in World War I.

The MUSEUM contains, in historical order, the most comprehensive collection in America of the rifles used by the Navy. It also has small trophies and mementoes of the Navy's past, including a table from the *Constitution;* a fragment of the stem of the *Niagara,* Oliver Hazard Perry's second flagship in the Battle of Lake Erie; relics of two of the Navy's polar expeditions; a collection of small arms; and sentimental reminders taken from famous warships.

MARINE BARRACKS

Marine Barracks (*normally open 11-12 Tues., 8-9:30 Wed., 3-4 Fri.; closed during national emergency*), 8th and I Streets SE., headquarters of the Marine Corps in Washington, occupies a small rectangular plot selected by Thomas Jefferson in 1801.

The COMMANDANT'S HOUSE, two and one-half stories high, erected in 1805, is the only building of the original group still standing. The interior, remodeled several times, contains 23 rooms for the accommodation of commandants and their families. Flags captured by United States troops in Mexico, Samoa, Cuba, Puerto Rico, China, and the Philippines are exhibited in the various offices.

During the occupation of Washington in 1814, British troops under Major General Ross made the barracks their headquarters and upon leaving the city destroyed some of the buildings. Aaron Burr was confined here pending his trial on charges of treason for his colonization schemes in the Southwest. The Confederate naval officer, Raphael Semmes, commander of the *Alabama,* was imprisoned in the barracks in 1864.

SOUTHWEST PUBLIC HEALTH CENTER

The Southwest Public Health Center (*open 9-4:30 Mon.-Fri., 9-1 Sat.*), Delaware Avenue and I Street SW., is the first public health unit established in Washington for the benefit of a particular section. A branch of the Health Deparment of the District of Columbia, the Center occupies a modern three-story building, completed in 1940.

It maintains clinics for maternity cases and treatment of children's diseases, dental clinics, and others specializing in the treatment of venereal diseases and tuberculosis. It also has an X-ray laboratory, biological laboratories, and a dozen reception rooms.

Anacostia

Streetcars: 17th & Penna. SE. cars connect with eastbound busses at Sousa Bridge. Navy Yard cars connect with southbound busses over Anacostia Bridge. Kenilworth and Seat Pleasant cars cross Benning Bridge and serve the northern Anacostia area.
Busses: Anacostia, Hillcrest, and Kenilworth Jct. busses operate eastward from Sousa Bridge, 17th St. and Pennsylvania Ave. SE. Congress Heights, Bolling Field via Portland, and Barry Farms-Garfield busses operate southward across the Anacostia Bridge. Benning busses operate eastward from Benning Bridge.
Taxis: Second, third, and fourth zones.

Anacostia, reputedly visited by Captain John Smith in 1608, is the eastern slice of Washington, on the far side of the Anacostia River from the Capitol, extending from the Maryland Line to a point opposite Alexandria and occupying one-fifth of the District of Columbia. It is further separated from the rest of the city by a reclaimed strip of land running along the river from north to south, forming Anacostia Park, Bolling Field, the Naval Air Station, and the Home for the Aged and Infirm. The Anacostia, Sousa (Pennsylvania Avenue), and Benning Road bridges span the river to connect the two parts of the city.

Divided from the rest of Washington by a meandering river and swamps, and having few Federal institutions, Anacostia developed slowly and independently. The present population, with an increasing proportion of Government workers, lives on the heights above the river. The older section is occupied by small stores and shops, creating the atmosphere of a small town going its own way with little consciousness that it is a part of the Nation's Capital.

St. Elizabeths Hospital, one of the leading psychiatric institutions in the country, occupies a large area in the southern part of Anacostia. West of it, stretching along the river, are the Army and Navy flying fields, and to the south on Blue Plains overlooking the river is the District's Home for the Aged and Infirm. Points of interest in Anacostia include the outstanding Kenilworth Aquatic Gardens and the Frederick Douglass Home, a memorial to an outstanding leader of the Negro race.

ANACOSTIA PARK

Anacostia Park, newest of the larger park systems, begun in 1912, extends for about 5 miles along the eastern shore of the Anacostia River from Bolling Field to the Maryland Line. South of the Sousa (Pennsylvania Avenue) Bridge, the Park is landscaped and developed for recreational use, having golf links, baseball and football fields, tennis courts, croquet and quoit grounds, a field house with locker rooms, and a refectory. A concrete driveway follows the edge of the river under Anacostia Bridge to the boundary of Bolling Field. On the north side of the Pennsylvania Avenue Bridge, with the exception of a golf course, the upper reaches of the river have been left as largely as possible in their natural state.

In the northeast corner of the Park are the KENILWORTH AQUATIC GARDENS (best approach, north on Kenilworth Avenue to Douglas Street, branching west), containing probably the greatest collection of water lilies, lotus, iris, and sub-aquatics in the world. Formerly known as the Shaw Lily Ponds, the Gardens contain 40 pools in an area of 90 acres, acquired by the National Park Service in 1938. W. B. Shaw started the gardens as a hobby in 1882 by transplanting some of the hardy wild varieties of water lilies from the ponds of Maine, gradually adding pools for other domestic and exotic imported varieties, and for new types produced by hybridizing. The best time to view the display is in the morning, from 8 o'clock to noon. Beginning in June the hardy day bloomers appear, followed in mid-July and August by the tropical varieties. Among the hundreds of distinct varieties are the Giant Victoria Regina, whose leaves often reach 6 feet in width; the Nelumbium, the lotus of history, with its large flowers beautifully tinted and delicately fragrant; the Egyption lotus (*Nelumbium speciosum*), reputed favorite of Cleopatra, deep rose in color; Oriental and American varieties ranging in color from carmine to pale yellow; and tender tropical night-blooming lilies.

The whole of Anacostia Park is a wildlife sanctuary, and in the gardens and adjacent wild-rice swamps are blue herons, snowy egrets, osprey, wild ducks, other kinds of waterfowl, and numerous songbirds common to the area.

FREDERICK DOUGLASS MEMORIAL HOME

The Frederick Douglass Memorial Home (*open, free, 9-5 daily*), 14th and W Streets SE., a 20-room white Colonial-style brick and stucco house, sheltered by tall oaks and cedars, occupies the crest of a hill with a commanding view of the Potomac River and Washington. The home, called Cedar Hill, commemorates the life of a man who freed himself from slavery and rose to a position of public trust before the Civil War.

Frederick Douglass was born Frederick Augustus Washington Bailey in 1817 at Tuckahoe, Maryland, of a slave mother and a white father. His youth was spent working on plantations, but somehow he learned to read and write. In 1836 he attempted to escape, but was captured and apprenticed as a ship caulker to Hugh Auld of Baltimore. Two years later he made good his escape, reached New York City by train and went to New Bedford, Massachusetts, where he worked as a day laborer under the name of Douglass.

A moving speech against slavery led to his appointment as an agent of the Massachusetts Anti-Slavery Society in 1841, and his autobiography, *Narrative of the Life of Frederick Douglass, an American Slave,* published in 1845, brought him recognition as a forceful abolitionist writer. Fear of recapture drove him to England, where he lectured for two years on the movement against slavery in the United States. Before his return a subscription was raised to purchase his manumission. For the next 13 years he conducted a weekly antislavery journal, the *North Star,* later called *Frederick Douglass' Paper,* and spoke frequently at meetings in which he advocated the more conservative abolitionist principles. He suggested the use of Negro troops during the Civil War, and two of his sons served in the Union Army. His popularity as a lecturer increased after the war, and he received several public and diplomatic appointments—as assistant secretary of the Santo Domingo Commission, as marshal and then recorder of deeds for the District of Columbia, and as Minister to the Republic of Haiti.

A man of wide interests and friendships, Douglass acquired considerable wealth through his writing and lecturing. He purchased Cedar Hill in 1889 from a former slave owner and lived there until his death six years later. His second wife, a white woman, acquired it from the heirs and, in her will, left it to the Frederick Douglass Memorial Association, which was incorporated by Congress. Financial difficulties constantly beset the association until it was affiliated with the National Association of Colored Women in 1917.

The house has much of the original Douglass furniture, paintings, silver, glass, and a LIBRARY (*open to research workers, 10-4*), containing 2,000 books, many of them relating to anti-slavery and woman suffrage. There are also several first editions, autographed copies, periodicals, and Douglass' personal correspondence arranged in chronological order. Among the exhibits are the flag carried by John Brown at Harpers Ferry; Lincoln's favorite walking stick, the gift of Mrs. Lincoln; a set of gold coffee spoons received from Queen Victoria at the time of Douglass' second marriage; letters from Presidents Lincoln, Cleveland, and Harrison; and a chair and table from Harriet Beecher Stowe.

Annual memorial services, attended by Negro school children, are held at Cedar Hill on February 14, the probable date of his birth. Each year, on the Friday nearest February 12 and 14, the Musolit Club, an adult organization, observes a combined Lincoln and Frederick Douglass Memorial Day.

ST. ELIZABETHS HOSPITAL

St. Elizabeths Hospital (*grounds open 8-6 daily; buildings open 9-11, 1-4 daily*), Nichols Ave., between Pomeroy Road and Lebaum Street SE., is internationally known for its work in mental diseases and for pioneering the malaria treatment of paresis. The Hospital, housed in 168 buildings scattered over a rectangular 800-acre tract on both sides of Nichols Avenue, overlooks the Anacostia River and the city.

Established by Congress in 1855 to give the most enlightened curative treatment to the mentally ill of the armed services, residents of the District of Columbia, wards of the Government, and citizens of some of the Territories, St. Elizabeths was known until 1916 as the Government Hospital for the Insane. Since 1940 it has been administered by the Federal Security Agency.

Entrance to the Hospital, the largest Federal institution of its kind, with more than 6,000 patients and 1,500 employees, is at the main gate on Nichols Avenue. The grounds are laid out in spacious lawns, landscaped with shrubbery, flowers, and trees. The ADMINIS-TRATION BUILDING is a brick and stone structure, with a central section, two wings, and a three-story Colonial-style portico. The MEDI-CAL LIBRARY (*open to students*), housed in the Administration Building, first floor south, contains 12,000 volumes dealing chiefly with psychiatry, reprints of medical papers, periodicals, and medical journals. For the patients there is a circulating library of 18,500 books and numerous magazines purchased by the institution and augmented by the Library of Congress from its surplus stock. The other buildings vary in size and detail of design. In addition to the numerous psychiatric wards, the Hospital has a Medical and Surgical Building for the care of patients who are physically ill.

Wards are equipped with radios and loudspeakers, controlled from the central office, and have spacious day rooms and porches furnished with card tables, magazines, and other means of entertainment. The Red Cross has a "hut" at the Hospital and supervises social and recreational activities, including trips to the American League ball park and the circus, river excursions, automobile rides, and such field sports as tennis, basketball, and baseball. Vaudeville performances, operettas, musicals, and dances are held in HITCHCOCK HALL, with a seating capacity of 1,300.

The Hospital carries on agricultural, trade, and industrial activities; improved patients are encouraged to participate in the work in the willow shop, the shoe shop where all the shoes furnished the patients by the Hospital are made, the ice-cream plant, bakery, sewing rooms, broom and brush factories, and the print shop. The effort at St. Elizabeths is to restore as many patients as possible to useful lives.

BOLLING FIELD

Bolling Field (*normally open 8-3 Mon., Tues., Wed., Fri.; closed during national emergency*), entrance at South Capital and Portland Streets SE., is an army air field covering an area of 835 acres.

The original Bolling Field, a tract of 340 acres, was purchased by the Government when the air field was proposed in 1918. It was named for Colonel Reynal C. Bolling, who was killed in the First World War. The newer section of 495 adjacent acres was added in 1929. During the Civil War, part of the reservation, Giesboro Depot, was used by the Army of the Potomac as a remount station.

NAVAL AIR STATION

The Naval Air Station (*normally open 8:30-3:30 daily; closed during national emergency*) occupies 50 acres of ground, surrounded by Bolling Field. The station, established in 1918, stands on land that was formerly a swamp, and was used by the Army in 1916 as a target range.

HOME FOR THE AGED AND INFIRM

The Home for the Aged and Infirm (*visiting hours 10-4 daily*), Nichols Avenue SE., occupies a sloping, partly wooded 200-acre tract at the southern end of Anacostia, overlooking the Potomac River. The Home, commonly called "Blue Plains," contains 64 red-brick buildings, joined together in an E-shaped plan, with dormitories, recreation rooms, and cafeterias. The ADMINISTRATION BUILDING, a plain white-painted frame house, is at the point of the central wing. Administered by the District of Columbia Board of Public Welfare, the Home, established in 1906, cares for more than 600 elderly, indigent white and colored people, two-thirds of whom are men.

Entrance to the grounds is from Nichols Avenue, east of the reservation. The institution operates a farm, dairy, and piggery, where employees and the more able men share the work, producing more than half of the products consumed at the Home.

Potomac and Rock Creek Parks

Streetcars: Bureau of Engraving cars (on 14th St. to Maine Ave. SW.) approach nearest to the Tidal Basin. Mt. Pleasant cars connect (by transfer) with Zoo Park busses at 16th and Harvard NW.
Busses: Hains Point busses operate on Riverside Drive from the Lincoln Memorial to Hains Point and return around the north shore of the Tidal Basin to 17th and Constitution NW. Lincoln Memorial busses leave 17th and K Sts. NW. for the Memorial. No busses operate in Rock Creek Park, but many lines run to or beside it. Zoo Park busses run in season from 16th and Harvard NW. • All Connecticut Avenue busses pass the main entrance to the Zoo. Busses marked Georgia & Alaska, or 16th & Eastern, provide transportation to the Rock Creek golf course west of 16th St. at Concord Ave.
Taxis: Second to fourth zones.

Washington's most impressive chain of public parks is that including the artificially created East Potomac Park between the Potomac River and Washington Channel, West Potomac Park between the Potomac and the Mall, Rock Creek and Potomac Parkway, winding along beneath the bridges to National Zoological Park, and, north of that, the unspoiled recreation ground of Washington—Rock Creek Park, reaching 4 miles north of the Maryland Line. The thirty-mile park area is joined by bridle paths, footpaths, rustic bridges, winding automobile roads, and fords through swift-flowing Rock Creek. It has views that range from the marine and nautical atmosphere of the broad Potomac and Washington Channel to intimate nooks of native woodland in Rock Creek Park. Its picnic grounds, its cool green-shaded roads, its windblown river margins, its golf courses, bicycle lanes, tennis courts, playgrounds, and other recreational facilities are used by thousands upon thousands of Washington people during the three seasons of "open" weather. The Zoo, arranged and presented with a maximum of showmanship, attracts nearly 3,000,000 visitors a year.

EAST POTOMAC PARK

East Potomac Park, first section of Washington parks to be reclaimed from swampland, is a 329-acre tract somewhat in the shape of a water-bird's head, between the Tidal Basin on the west, the Potomac River on the south, and Washington Channel on the north. It is reached by a side road from 14th Street SW., or along a continuation of Riverside Drive from West Potomac Park. A one-way drive encircles the Park, entered on its south side.

Between the ramparts of the Highway (or 14th Street) Bridge and the Railroad Bridge are the WASHINGTON ROSE GARDENS, where more than a hundred varieties of roses bloom throughout the summer, in formally landscaped and fountain-centered grounds. At the 14th Street entrance to these grounds is a display of more than a million pansy blossoms. The Cuban Urn, chiseled from a fragment of the Havana Memorial to the *Maine,* which was destroyed in a tropical storm, stands in the garden. The urn was presented to President Coolidge by President Morales of Cuba.

An underpass beneath the embankment of the Railroad Bridge gives access to the WASHINGTON TOURIST CAMP, operated by the Welfare and Recreational Association, and having furnished cabins, trailer and tent sites, and a pavilion with beds for rent at a nominal charge. Bed linen and blankets are available at small cost; visits are limited to two weeks. This Government-owned and -inspected camp is popular with visitors, and it is advisable to make reservations in advance.

DOUBLE-BLOSSOM JAPANESE CHERRY TREES line the inside of the drive, which has an outer row of weeping willows along the sea wall. Fugenzo trees, bearing light pink blossoms, are intermingled with Fukurokuju and Kwanzan varieties, bearing large, deep pink flowers. These cherry trees, perhaps less generally appreciated by outsiders than the single-flowering varieties around the Tidal Basin, blossom about two weeks after the Tidal Basin trees, when the ceremonials of the Cherry Blossom Festival are over and most of the hundreds of thousands of visitors have departed. Washington people, however, may appreciate them more, because they can be seen with less traffic congestion. The double-flowering trees, since 1938, have blossomed as early as April 14 and as late as May 1. Like those around the Tidal Basin, they were presented to the United States Government by the city of Tokyo.

A railed walk extends along the sea wall, and fishermen with hand-lines or poles are almost constantly at the railing during the season. Horsemen go posting by along the bridle path north of the driveway, sometimes singly or in pairs, sometimes in the attenuated line of a conducted class.

At Hains Point, the eastern tip of the park, is a Municipal Tea House (*closed for "the duration"*), from which there is a magnificent view of the spreading lower Potomac with its traffic of tugboats and barges, sailing craft, steamers, launches, and, occasionally, the long gray lines of a naval vessel. Aviation activity can be seen on the east bank of the river—the daring maneuvers of military and naval planes from Bolling Field and Naval Air Station—and the more sedate movement of silvery civilian airliners landing and taking off at Washington National Airport on the Virginia side. There is always a breeze at Hains Point, and it is a favored place during the hot Washington summers. Speedboat, rowing, canoe and sailboat races are run in the Potomac Channel off Hains Point, culminating in the great September event—the President's Cup Regatta.

The willow-bordered highway on the north side of the park skirts the WASHINGTON CHANNEL with its slips for the Norfolk steamer and excursion boats, and all manner of pleasure boats moored in the protected harbor (*see Along the Water Front*). This channel is, in part, responsible for the formation of East Potomac Park. Work on it was begun in 1890 by Army Engineers, who pumped mud from the river to make an artificial peninsula serving a triple purpose—to clear the channel, to form a bulwark for protection of the newly created harbor, and to provide spacious recreational grounds.

The 36-hole EAST POTOMAC PARK GOLF COURSE (*see Recreation*), with its natural and artificial hazards, is entered from this portion of the drive. The clubhouse has lockers, showers, and clubrooms available with the purchase of a small number of playing tickets. A midget course, also occupying a portion of the land in the middle of the park, is open in summer.

The drive reenters 14th Street SW. through an underpass in the railroad embankment opposite the Jefferson Memorial.

JEFFERSON MEMORIAL

The white marble, Pantheon-style Jefferson Memorial, surrounded by a peristyle of Ionic columns, faces across the Tidal Basin, which serves it as a reflecting pool, at the southern end of the Mall cross-axis, in line with the White House and Washington Monument. Designed in the office of John Russell Pope and his surviving partners Otto R. Eggers, Daniel Paul Higgins, and associates, New York architects, it was substantially completed in the summer of 1942. The Thomas Jefferson Memorial Commission was created by act of Congress in 1934; two years later Congress authorized the expenditure of $3,000,000 for the structure, and President Franklin D. Roosevelt broke ground for the Memorial in 1938. Frederick Law Olmsted is retained as landscape architect.

The Memorial is an adaptation of spherical architectural types, of which the Jefferson-designed Rotunda at the University of Virginia is the best example in this country. It also bears a close kinship to the low dome and pedimented portico of Monticello, Jefferson's home of his own design near Charlottesville, Virginia. The low, rounded dome and the portico with its classic pediment are remarkably like the central features of the National Gallery of Art, on the Mall, also designed by Eggers and Higgins.

In keeping with the general design are the two circular terraces around the Memorial. The outer terrace is 420 feet in diameter and 64 feet wide, with a light gray Georgia granite retaining wall. The inner terrace is 290 feet in diameter and 53 feet wide, with a wall rising above it to support the floor of the Memorial. The main floor of the building is 22 feet above grade, and its diameter to the outer face of the columns is 180 feet. There are three broad flights of steps, with intervening terraces and platforms, leading from the edge of the Tidal Basin to the great portico.

Twelve columns, eight of them across the front of the portico, support the pediment, which will be decorated with a symbolic group in high relief. From the portico, which is 93 feet long and 23 feet deep, other monumental structures of the Mall axis and cross-axis can be seen—the Washington Monument and the White House due north, the Lincoln Memorial over the treetops to the northwest, and the Capitol dome rising above other Government buildings to the northeast. The colonnade surrounding the structure has 54 columns, each 43 feet high and weighing about 45 tons. The building rests on a foundation of steel cylinders filled with concrete and driven to depths of 80 to 135 feet, then countersunk in bedrock. Since the land is filled earth and has no binding power, the cylinders are tied together at grade with concrete beams.

The towering main entrance is framed by pilasters, and there are three other monumental entrances, each facing in one of the cardinal directions. The circular memorial room, 82 feet in diameter, has floors of pink-and-gray Tennessee marble, walls of Georgia white marble, and a coffered dome of Indiana limestone. Sixteen columns of Vermont marble, 41 feet high, circle the room. Four marble panels will be inscribed with appropriate passages from the works of Jefferson. A circular interior frieze is inscribed, in letters two feet high, with a quotation from a letter Jefferson wrote Dr. Benjamin Rush in 1800— "I have sworn on the altar of God, eternal hostility to every form of tyranny over the mind of man." Above the frieze rises the interior self-supporting dome, resting on the interior walls and so mathematically perfect that it is in error less than $\frac{1}{16}$ of an inch at any point. The outer marble dome is unconnected with the inner at any point. A heroic bronze statue of Jefferson, by Rudulph Evans, will dominate the room. The statue is expected to be completed for a formal dedication on April 13, 1943, the 200th anniversary of Jefferson's birth.

When the Tidal Basin site was selected for the Jefferson Memorial, women crusaders vehemently protested the removal of cherry trees in the vicinity. Some of the more militant tree-savers chained themselves to trees, others sat in the holes where trees had been uprooted. To the clicking of newsreel and news cameras, they mourned the lost glory of the flowering Japanese cherry trees. The rebuttal of the Memorial Commission, less photogenic as a news subject, finally appeared in its own report, pointing out that there were 1,700 cherry trees in the Potomac Parks, that 83 of those removed would be transplanted later, that 88 were cut because they had reached their natural age of 30 years and could not be moved, and that 1,000 additional cherry trees would be planted as part of the completed landscaping plan.

The Memorial building has elicited many criticisms. There are those who find its architecture "sweet," and not of the times. Because of the liberal use of columns, some have called it a cage for Jefferson's statue, while more virulent critics have dubbed it "Jefferson's muffin." When millions are being poured into a cold memorial, there are always those who could find more social usefulness in a Jefferson library or a

Jefferson hospital, or some manifestation more suited to the ideals of the living man. "I desire as my monument," Jefferson wrote, "a plain die or cube of 3 f., without any moldings, surmounted by an obelisk of 6 f. height, each of a single stone." Such a modest monument was erected to him in the family graveyard at Monticello, but something more grandiose was inevitable when the Capital City set about to honor the third President. The structure has many admirers, who find it fitting that a monument to Jefferson should follow the basic scheme of a type of architecture he admired.

WEST POTOMAC PARK

West Potomac Park, separated from East Potomac Park as a matter of administrative convenience, has as one of its outstanding features the Tidal Basin, a scenic as well as a sanitary adjunct to the Capital City. With the gradual building up of reclaimed land that forms the two Potomac Parks and provides a harbor in Washington Channel, it was decided that a flush-basin was needed to clear the debris from the harbor at low tide. One floodgate connects the eastern end of the basin with the Washington Channel and another, at the southern end, connects with the Potomac River. As the tide rises the Potomac River gate is opened and the Channel gate is closed; as the tide recedes the operation is reversed, periodically flushing the Channel. At the northern tip of the Basin is a public boathouse and a landing for "swan boats" that take passengers for leisurely tours of the basin. The enclosed waters provide good fishing, from boats or from the masonry sea wall.

The SINGLE-FLOWERING JAPANESE CHERRY TREES, planted around the periphery of the Tidal Basin, are known to millions of people at first hand and through photographs, picture postcards, newsreels, and paintings. These Yoshino trees furnish the setting for the annual Cherry Blossom Festival, usually held during the first week or ten days of April. Hundreds of thousands of visitors come to Washington each year for the blossoming of the Tidal Basin trees, and enjoy the exotic experience of wandering among the trees as their pale pink petals flutter to the ground. There are scores of basin-mirrored views of the Washington Monument, the Lincoln Memorial, the Jefferson Memorial, and the more distant Capitol, seen through a screen of blossom-laden branches. The trees remain in flower ten or twelve days, and this display is usually followed in about two weeks by the blossoming of the double-flowering varieties in East Potomac Park. Seasonal variations make a great deal of difference in the time of blossoming—since 1938 the trees have bloomed as early as March 20 and as late as April 15—and the date of the festival is set about two weeks in advance, on advice of Department of Agriculture horticulturists. The trees bear no fruit.

The first cherry tree, planted by Mrs. William Howard Taft in 1912, is several hundred yards west of the John Paul Jones statue, which stands at the south end of 17th Street NW. A bronze tablet set in concrete at the base of the tree commemorates the occasion, and a similar tablet near by memorializes the planting of the second tree, on the same occasion, by Viscountess Chinda, wife of the Japanese Ambassador. The first shipment of trees reached Washington from Tokyo in 1909, during an era of warm good-feeling with Japan. The Department of Agriculture inspected the trees, found them infected with insect pests and fungus diseases, and required them to be burned. The situation called for careful diplomatic handling. Secretary of State Philander C. Knox sent a polite note to Japanese Ambassador Yasuya Uchida, regretting that so handsome a gift, and one so deeply appreciated by the people and officials of the United States of America and the city of Washington, should have had to be destroyed. Count Uchida suggested that the city of Tokyo be requested to send another consignment, taking necessary precautions to prevent infection. The offer was accepted, and the Okitsu Imperial Horticultural Station undertook to provide the plants. Scions were taken from trees on the river bank near Tokyo, grafted on wild cherry roots, and set out for a time in a special nursery. The trees were lifted in 1911 and reached Washington in excellent condition early in 1912. Shorty after, the simple ceremony of planting, attended by very few people, was held.

Early in the week after the Japanese attack on Pearl Harbor, Hawaii, Sunday, December 7, 1941, vandals lopped off three or four of the Tidal Basin cherry trees. The act was generally regarded as a poor specimen of military retaliation, and no one came forward, in the style of the George Washington legend, to accept responsibility.

One-way drives encircle the Tidal Basin, on the south side of which is the POLO FIELD, where Army and civilian teams play occasional games in summer. Also on the south side of the park are two golf courses, one of them for Negro players (see Recreation). An inner lane on the loop around the polo field is reserved for bicycle riders, and giant weeping willows, with tips dragging the ground, grow inside the sea wall. At the north tip of the Tidal Basin, and at the south end of 17th Street, is the bronze JOHN PAUL JONES STATUE, the work of Charles Henry Niehaus, unveiled in 1912 to commemorate the naval hero of the Revolution. Along a road south of the Lincoln Memorial Reflecting Pool is the DISTRICT OF COLUMBIA WORLD WAR MEMORIAL, a circular white marble Doric band pavilion, where free concerts are sometimes given in summer. In a circle on Riverside Drive, due south of the Lincoln Memorial, stands the JOHN ERICSSON MEMORIAL, the work of James E. Fraser, a sculptured group carved from pink Milford granite to memorialize the designer of the Civil War ironclad, the *Monitor*. The seated figure of the inventor is backed by a shaft of granite on which are sculptured three allegorical figures—a nude woman, *Vision;* a Norse seaman, *Adventure;* and an iron moulder, *Workmanship*—grouped around the gnarled trunk of the "Tree Yggdrasill," the Tree of Life in Norse mythology. The memorial is, in part, a gift of Scandinavian-American citizens.

Riverside Drive continues along the water front, under an abutment of the Arlington Bridge, and around the Water Gate (*see Along the Mall*).

ROCK CREEK AND POTOMAC PARKWAY

Rock Creek and Potomac Parkway is a landscaped, winding, relatively narrow park area connecting West Potomac Park with National Zoological Park. Georgetown and Northwest Washington residences along its edges peer out over the tree-filled ravine.

At the NE. corner of Constitution Avenue and Riverside Drive stands Gutzon Borglum's bronze STATUE OF WILLIAM JENNINGS BRYAN, portraying the statesman in the characteristic pose of an orator. On the landscaped river bank at the intersection with New Jersey Avenue stands the TITANIC MEMORIAL, sculptured by Gertrude Vanderbilt Whitney in tribute to the men who responded in 1912, when the "non-sinkable" *Titanic* went down, to the age-old cry of "Women and children first." The idealized male figure, with arms outstretched, was donated in 1927 by the Women's Titanic Memorial Association.

Between the Memorial and the K Street Bridge are several riding academies, where horses can be rented for rides northward into Rock Creek Park or southeastward through the Potomac Parks. Negro fishermen find the sea wall here a convenient place for angling, and this open stretch of riverside provides a view of Washington's most concentrated industrial area, across Rock Creek in Georgetown. Smokestacks, elevators, derricks, and aluminum-painted structures resembling chemical laboratory appliances, against a background of red-brick buildings and the spires of Georgetown University, make this industrial complex a favored place for artists and photographers. Against a background of the many-arched Key Bridge and the river, busy little tugs ply, pushing and towing buff-cargoed barges in and out of this area, which includes a sand and gravel plant.

The low-arched fieldstone K STREET BRIDGE, opened in 1941, gives access to lower Georgetown by a series of "cloverleaf" approaches, whereby all turns are to the right. This is the southernmost of a series of eight bridges under which the Parkway passes as it follows the banks of Rock Creek to the Zoo. It is a curious experience to drive under these bridges in a dashing rain, which completely stops for a moment as the car passes under each span. The arched PENNSYLVANIA AVENUE BRIDGE and the perfectly flat M STREET BRIDGE are passed in quick succession, followed by the flat-arched fieldstone P STREET BRIDGE and the more ornate round-arched Q STREET (or DUMBARTON) BRIDGE (*see Georgetown*) with its row of war-bonneted Indian heads on the keystones, and its transverse arcade of lesser arches running through the piers.

Opposite R Street, on the west side of the Parkway, are the gravestones, ornate monuments, and elaborate family mausoleums of OAK HILL CEMETERY (*see Georgetown*). Between Q and R Streets,

Waterside Drive branches to the right, giving access to Massachusetts Avenue.

At Massachusetts Avenue the highway passes under the massive, high-arched single-span MASSACHUSETTS AVENUE BRIDGE, completed in 1941.

A steep road climbs westward out of the Parkway opposite Belmont Road, a branch of which goes under an arch of the Taft Bridge and an arch of Calvert Bridge to connect with Cathedral Avenue, and the other, leading into Calvert Street, gives access to Connecticut Avenue. Two towering spans in succession arch over the Parkway north of this —TAFT BRIDGE, carrying Connecticut Avenue, and CALVERT STREET BRIDGE. Within a block the road crosses through a paved ford (*5 m.p.h. speed limit; test brakes after fording*). South of this point, to Constitution Avenue, the Parkway is a one-way thoroughfare during rush hours each day—southbound in the morning, northbound in the evening. The narrow road crosses a stone bridge and enters the Zoo.

NATIONAL ZOOLOGICAL PARK

National Zoological Park (*gates open daily 7:30 a.m. to dark; buildings open daily 9-5 in summer, 9-4:30 in winter; adm. free*), commonly called Rock Creek Zoo, is a roughly oval 176-acre tract with 7 main exhibition buildings and many outside exhibits, connected by automobile roads, paved walks, and bridle paths. Most-used approaches are from Connecticut Avenue (north of Cathedral Avenue) on the west, from Harvard Street and Adams Mill Road on the east, and from the Parkway north or south. The Zoo maintains about 2,500 specimens representing more than 750 species of birds, mammals, reptiles, amphibians, fishes, and invertebrates. Births, deaths, purchases, and exchanges make constant alterations in the exhibits.

The animals are fed on a definite schedule: Lions, tigers, and jaguars, 1:30 p.m. Monday to Saturday—they fast on Sunday; foxes and coyotes, 1 p.m. Monday to Saturday; monkeys, 9:30 and 2:30 daily; orangutans and gibbons, 9 and 3 daily; grain-eating animals in Antelope House, 8 and 2:30 daily; bears, 8 and 3 daily; seals and sea otters, 8:30 and 3:15 daily; animals in Small Mammal House, 9 and 3 daily; animals in Large Mammal House, 8 and 2:30 daily; deer, buffalo, zebras, and similar animals, 8 and 2:30 daily; seed-eating birds, 8 a.m. (feedings last all day); meat- and fish-eating birds, 2:30 daily.

The Park, which is under the direction of the Smithsonian Institution, was opened in 1890, when a few animals were moved from the scientific institution on the Mall, where they served as models for taxidermists. William T. Hornaday, noted American naturalist and conservationist, was the first animal curator, while the collection was still in the Smithsonian area. S. P. Langley, the pioneer in aviation, while secretary of the Institution, urged the establishment of a zoological park. Circus showmanship was introduced with the appointment of William H. Blackburne of Barnum and Bailey's as the first head keeper. The Zoo had lean years, during which it solicited gifts to build up its collection, and in the years preceding 1930 raised pigmy hippos to exchange for other animals. Buildings and specimens have increased enormously since that time.

A choice herd of American bison is under fence near the Connecticut Avenue entrance, and there are wild horses, wild asses, and zebras in the next enclosures to the east. Across the roadway are paddocks occupied by several species of hardy deer. In the oval FLIGHT CAGE below the deer paddocks, many species of birds nest and rear their young under natural if somewhat restricted outdoor conditions. The BIRD HOUSE, near by, ordinarily has about 400 species of birds within and occupying adjacent cages. They vary from humming birds, the tiniest species, to Andean condors, the largest of flying birds. Backgrounds in this building were painted by artists of the Public Works of Art Project. There are large flightless birds—ostriches, emus, rheas, cassowaries—and a refrigerated room in which penguins live in comfort.

The LARGE MAMMAL HOUSE, down the hill from the wild horse paddocks, accommodates giraffes, hippopotamuses, pigmy hippos, African rhinoceroses, the rare Indian rhino, African and Asiatic elephants, tapirs, and other large mammals. Figurine restorations of prehistoric pachyderms in this building were executed by Charles R. Knight. Animals, principally of the sheep and antelope tribe, are exhibited in outdoor paddocks on the opposite side of the road south of the Large Mammal House. One choice specimen, shown in a paddock here, is an albino bison, one of two known to exist (the other is in the National Bison Range near Moiese, Montana).

The SMALL MAMMAL HOUSE boasts what many authorities consider the finest collection in the world, including the tiniest mice and other furred animals to the size of the great apes. This building, among the best of its kind, is outstanding because of its freedom from odors, made possible by forced ventilation. Behind the Small Mammal House are enclosures containing yaks, bears, panthers, raccoons, and other animals.

The ANTELOPE HOUSE, directly south of the Small Mammal House, is an old frame structure accommodating mammals that require shelter, such as the anoa, a dwarf water buffalo, the barking or ribbed-faced deer, warthogs, and antelopes.

The REPTILE HOUSE, designed by Albert Harris and erected in 1931, is a modified Italian Romanesque building, with many of its details executed in designs suggested by reptiles. Stone corbels beneath the eaves are carved with reptilian heads. Twisted columns flanking the principal entrance rest on the backs of stone turtles, and the capitals are carved in lizard motifs. The doorway is framed with glazed mosaics and surmounted by a pictorial fresco of a prehistoric reptile by Charles R. Knight. The interior presents theatrically the various reptiles and amphibians, each of the 100 cages having a simulated natural environment and a background painted by Public Works of Art Project artists. A compound heating system provides temperatures ranging from 70° to 86° within the cages and 63° in the corridors. The reptile collection ordinarily includes a choice group of alligators, crocodiles, gavials, and caymans; many species of turtles, including giant sea turtles and the great tortoises of Galápagos; tiny ring-necked and other harmless local snakes, venomous king cobras, giant pythons and anacondas; lizards ranging from the "horned toad" of the Southwest to the giant Komodo "dragon" of the Dutch East Indies; and amphibians including salamanders, newts, frogs, and toads of many kinds and colors.

The MONKEY HOUSE, south of the Reptile House, usually contains at least 30 species of various sizes, in addition to other medium-sized mammals. The monkeys range from the weirdly-colored mandrills to the long-tailed little capuchin monkeys with their wrinkled foreheads and monk's cowls.

The LION HOUSE, southernmost in this group of buildings, has 22 cages occupied by lions, tigers, leopards, jaguars, cheetahs, sloths, and other middle-sized mammals. The big cats are permitted outside, in barred pens, when the weather is warm. A fieldstone RESTAURANT is across the road from the Lion House. WATERFOWL PONDS, below the restaurant, accommodate some 30 to 40 species of American waterfowl throughout the year. A recalcitrant Canada goose prefers the outside of the pens, but shows no disposition to run away.

The BEAR PITS, westward and around the hill from the restaurant, are ranged in a semicircle along the side of a hill. Barred outdoor cages permit a good view of the bears, which inhabit man-made rock caves on the inside of the semicircle. There are polar bears, giant Kodiak bears from the Alaskan peninsula, Himalayan bears, and others. The Zoo has three specimens that are thought to be unique—the product of mating by a polar bear and a Kodiak bear. Light-cinnamon in color, they are larger than the average polar bear, but have physical resemblances to the polar variety. One of them waves his paw for peanuts, and all three sit up and beg, and carry their ponderous bodies about endlessly for an occasional peanut.

The DIRECTOR'S OFFICE sits on a wooded hill west of the Adams Mill Road entrance. This charming old building, erected in 1805, was a favorite summer refuge of Andrew Jackson, as diamond-scratched legends on an upper window testify. The room from which this window looks out was once used by S. P. Langley, the aviation pioneer, as an observation post from which to study the flight of birds.

ROCK CREEK PARK

Rock Creek Park, set aside by Congress in 1890 as "A pleasuring ground for the benefit and enjoyment of the people of the United States," is an area of 1,800 acres extending northward from the Zoo, along the wooded Rock Creek valley to a point 4 miles north of the Maryland Line. Most of the area is undisturbed native woodland, where dogwoods and redbuds blossom in spring, and where wildflowers bloom through three of the seasons. It has groves of smoke-colored beeches, areas of oak and the omnipresent native cedar, tangles of fragrant native honeysuckle, and open meadowlands. Tastefully improved by the addition of dozens of picnic sites, fireplaces, rustic tables and benches, water outlets, footpaths, bridges, and other facilities, the park has been so handled that it retains a maximum of its native wildwood character. There are sandpiles and swings for children, baseball diamonds, tennis courts, two 9-hole golf courses, 30 miles of bridle paths, and a practice ring and hurdles for horseback riders. On the hottest summer day or night the park is always cool, and thousands avail themselves of it, if for nothing more than a cooling drive in the evening.

The road goes through another ford a short distance south of the point where Klingle Road crosses the Park, near the upper end of Zoo Park. Apparently nobody tries to enforce the five-mile speed limit at fords, but those who go faster promptly drown their engines, and the warning is generally heeded. To dry the brakebands after a crossing, it is wise to travel a short distance with the brakes applied lightly.

A road crosses the Park from Tilden Street on the west to Park Road on the east, where the driver may take his choice between bridge and ford. Just west of the intersection is the bridge, and northward from it is a ford, crossing the creek above the millpond; another road branching diagonally northeast from the ford connects with Blagden Avenue and Sixteenth Street. At the Tilden Street intersection is PIERCE MILL, a three-story-and-attic dressed stone building. One of the finest examples of an early water-power mill in this section, it is one of the eight mills that formerly operated with power derived from Rock Creek. Having an undershot wheel, it grinds flour and meal as a public demonstration of pioneer milling methods; its products are on sale. Reconditioning was accomplished in the late 1930's by means of a PWA grant. A flock of white domestic ducks swims in Rock Creek in the vicinity of the mill.

Beach Drive is the principal thoroughfare through the Park, but there are many branching roads, leading to higher areas. Where Military Road crosses the Park east and west, there is a Park Police Lodge, a stone building of Colonial design, playgrounds for children, and a collection of representative picnic sites. Military Road connects with Connecticut and Wisconsin Avenues on the west and with 16th Street on the east.

About a third of a mile north of Military Road, on the west side of Beach Drive, is the JOAQUIN MILLER CABIN, originally built and occupied in the eighties by the "Poet of the Sierras," on 16th Street near the Henderson Castle. The cabin retains its great stone chimney and rough-hewn beams, but the newspaper clippings and rejected manuscripts that papered its walls were torn down and its bearskin rugs removed when the California State Society purchased and moved it to the Park. It is, apparently, the only log cabin in Washington.

At MILK HOUSE FORD, just above the Miller Cabin, the driver

again has a choice between using the ford or crossing a closely parallel bridge.

Winding Beach Drive continues through woodland and meadow, with abundant picnicking and recreational facilities, to the Maryland Line and its junction with the East-West Highway. Meadowbrook, in this immediate vicinity, is the scene of international horse shows, and there are practice and other equipment in the area, near the riding academy. Bridle paths in the four miles of Rock Creek Park north of the District are popular with those riding out from nearby stables.

Georgetown

Streetcars: Cabin John, Friendship Heights, and Rosslyn cars.
Busses: Glover Park, Potomac Heights, and 35th and O NW.
Taxis: Second and third zones.
All Georgetown houses are private unless otherwise indicated in the text.

Along the north bank of the Potomac, west of Rock Creek, lies historic Georgetown, now a quiet suburb of the National Capital. In the commercial section, the old houses have been given new shop fronts, the streets are smoothly paved, and sidewalks evenly laid. But in the residential areas, with their small fine homes, occasional quaint cottages, and many pretentious mansions, here and there a shaded street is still laid in ancient cobblestones, and a sidewalk in smooth, worn brick. Gabled roofs, tiny dormers, and inviting doorways with brass knockers are reminders of the past. Formal mansions on terraced lawns with stately trees contrast with the smaller houses set flush with the walks. Along the river, old warehouses—relics of a once extensive commerce— crumble away beside railway sidings and modern industrial plants.

From the Yellow House on 33rd Street, built before 1733, through the progression of Georgian mansions and town-houses, early Federal and Classic Revival homes, to the florid structures of the post-Civil War era, Georgetown houses are an interesting record of American architecture. In recent years, the smaller homes have been bought by artists, newspapermen, moderately well-to-do Government employees, and others who appreciated the charm that lay beneath dilapidation. With the restoration of these homes, a cultured and intelligently lively community began to develop. Families of wealth and position purchased and renovated the larger mansions, and with them returned the brilliant social life for which Georgetown was once famous.

In the last quarter of the eighteenth century and in the early nineteenth, the busy seaport of Georgetown had the finest of America's gun factories, a flour mill that shipped to a world-wide market, and a fleet of locally owned ships carrying on an international trade in tobacco. At that time the homes of wealthy merchants were beginning to dot Georgetown heights, and four- and six-horse Conestoga wagons rumbled through the streets, piled with farm produce for sale or barter. Most of Georgetown's imports went out by overland trails. Friendly inns were centers of a vivid, lusty life, especially during "Fair days" when all persons "within the bounds of the town" were free from arrest "except for felony or breach of the peace." Along the new Potomac Canal came inland trade, and out upon it went pioneers to the West.

Mechanical progress ended the merchants' dream of a commercial

346

metropolis. The coming of steam navigation about 1816, with its need for deeper harbors, and, later, the competition of railroads, disregardful of strategic waterways, gradually destroyed Georgetown as an industrial center. Finally, the old town was absorbed by the Federal city that arose beside it.

Long before this, at an indeterminable date, the site of Georgetown was chosen by the Anacostan Indians for their village of Tohoga, established at the fall line. From here, they could navigate the Potomac in either direction. In 1632, Henry Fleete visited the region around the falls. A letter written by him in June of that year is the earliest extant description of the Georgetown-Washington area. Fleete remained near the falls and set up a trade with the Indians. Other trading posts developed, and then towns, notably Saint Mary's, the capital of the new Province of Maryland.

For many years the Indian town of Tohoga was abandoned and forgotten, but, around 1700, several grants of surrounding land were made to individuals, and the beginnings of Georgetown were laid. Quaint names were given many of these old patents, doubtless expressing the owner's reaction on seeing his wilderness grant: The Widow's Mite, Poor Tom's Last Shift, Knave's Disappointment, Conjurer's Disappointment, and the more optimistic Plain Dealing, Success, and Fortune. The most famous of all is the Rock of Dunbarton grant, which included the greater part of the land later occupied by Georgetown.

In 1703 Ninian Beall obtained his patent for the Rock of Dunbarton, a tract of 705 acres. Then George Gordon took up his patent near by and, within a few years, acquired Knave's Disappointment from the original patentee, James Smith. Gordon named his land Rock Creek Plantation and established on it Inspection House, a "rolling house" for tobacco, in which there was a rapidly growing trade. A town grew up around Gordon's Inspection House. Rolling roads stretched away into the back-country plantations, and over them lumbered great casks of tobacco that served as containers and carriers, since each cask had an axle through its center and shafts for men, horses, or oxen. Wharves were built for shipping tobacco, the "meat, drink, clothing, and money of the colonists."

When disturbed conditions in Scotland in 1715, and again in 1745, sent tides of immigrants to America, many settled in tolerant Maryland, but others chose to build a home in the undeveloped areas around the falls of the Potomac or farther south. The Scottish settlement on the Potomac developed into a thriving community, the western frontier of Colonial civilization, and in 1751 it was authorized by the Maryland Provincial Assembly, under the name of George. Henry W. Crabb, James Perrie, Samuel Macgruder, John Claggett, Josias Beall, David Lynn, and a few other men with stout Scottish surnames were deputized, as commissioners of the new town, to buy, or to condemn and seize, for incorporation purposes, 60 acres of land belonging to George Gordon and George Beall, son of Ninian Beall. The owners refused to sell but accepted payment for the land in accordance with the act of incorporation. They evidently became reconciled to the plan of a new town and helped to forward its development to such an extent that, in 1791, it was judged by George Washington the greatest tobacco market in the State, if not in the Union.

The Potomac was the gateway to the fertile Ohio Valley, technically British but actually still in the possession of the French. To open the way for English trade, young George Washington was sent in 1753 to order the French out of the valley, and again in 1754 he was sent on the same mission, this time with military force. Both these attempts having failed, General Edward Braddock brought his troops to Alexandria in 1755; here he divided his forces, some to leave by way of the town of George through Maryland, others to proceed up the Virginia side of the Potomac, for the ill-fated campaign against Fort Duquesne. Finally, in 1763, punitive expeditions against the French and Indians cleared the way for westward expansion.

The men of George, for the next decade, were busy with the rapidly growing trade. Robert Peter and Thomas Richardson established stores, and a large flour mill was built by Amos Cloud. A ferry across the Potomac was put in operation to the Virginia shore in 1748. Simon Nickols erected the first wharf. Joseph Beall, John Orme, and Cornelius Davise operated a race track. George Washington continued to agitate for a canal to the West, along the Potomac.

Then came the Boston Tea Party. The town of George supported the Revolution, contributing men, supplies, and munitions to the first company that marched in defense of Massachusetts. John Yoast, a local gunsmith, offered the use of his plant to the newly formed government and, from there, turned out many of the muskets carried by the Colonial army. Throughout the war, the inland seaport remained a base of supplies and munitions.

At the close of the war, George Washington's suggestion of a canal was considered with respect. To finance the project, a lottery was held, under the management of Patrick Henry, Peyton Randolph, Richard Bland, Benjamin Harrison, William Byrd, George Wythe, and other outstanding men. George Washington, Charles Carroll of Carrollton, and other men of wealth subscribed to the fund. The Potomac Canal was completed by the end of the century, and, before it was superseded by the Chesapeake and Ohio Canal, carried nearly $10,-000,000 worth of freight. It opened the region to trade with points as far north as Lake Erie and as far south as Mobile, carried on by way of the Monongahela, Ohio, and Mississippi Rivers and several overland portages.

The city of George Town, incorporated in 1789, grew rapidly, and its flourishing trade drew the attention of men with capital to invest. Thomas Corcoran, journeying south in 1788, saw a harbor with 10 square-rigged vessels and decided to stop here and put his small fortune to work. His son, W. W. Corcoran, increased that fortune until he became one of the wealthiest men of his time and a noted philanthropist. Francis Dodge and his brother formed an important shipping concern. Richard Parrott, E. M. Linthicum, Joseph Middleton, John Peter, Washington Bowie, and other founders of well-known George Town families, built or bought ships for foreign trade. More than 80 of these ships, bound for Europe with freight brought overland or down the canal, were registered out of the customhouse at George Town.

The building of the new Federal city did not immediately affect the commercial development of George Town. A new canal, the Chesapeake and Ohio, was begun in 1828, and further expansion of trade was anticipated. The railroads, however, first threatened and then destroyed the usefulness of canals. The city of Washington soon overshadowed the older town, whose residents had invested much of their wealth in ill-advised real estate developments. In 1871 the separate governments of George Town (referred to as "Georgetown") and Washington were abolished by Act of Congress. Georgetown then gave up its original charter, which it had kept even after inclusion in the District of Columbia, and became a pleasant suburb of the Capital, a reminder of an earlier day.

There are several equally attractive approaches to Georgetown, but perhaps the most obvious is by way of Pennsylvania Avenue. A few blocks west of Washington Circle, the Avenue crosses Rock Creek over a bridge that is built completely around and over another bridge.

POINTS OF INTEREST

ROCK CREEK BRIDGE extends between 24th and 27th Streets NW. The inner of the two bridges is a tubular arch 200 feet long. The two 48-inch pipes that form the span once served as conduits for part of the Washington Aqueduct, which connected the reservoirs at Dalecarlia and Great Falls with the city water system of Washington. In 1913 Congress appropriated funds for the new bridge, which was completed around the main arch of the older one in 1916. The superstructure of the first bridge was removed, but the cast-iron pipes of the arch are still part of the District water system.

From M Street, one block north, may be seen a concrete bridge, erected on the site of the first bridge to connect Georgetown with eastern Maryland, built in 1788. Washington traveled over the original structure in 1791, to bargain for his Federal city. Over it in 1814 the British pursued the pitiable remnants of the Army defeated at Bladensburg. Not long after, the bridge collapsed during a storm, carrying with it a coach with horses and driver.

M street, now a busy commercial thoroughfare, was once Bridge Street, with comfortable houses and fine mansions, mud roads and wooden walkways, stepping stones, and wooden pumps along the way.

At 2921-29 M Street NW., a series of whitewashed flats occupies the SITE OF UNION TAVERN, the famous inn where many notable Americans and Louis Philippe, later King of France, and Jerome Bonaparte were entertained as guests. The tavern, with a main section three stories high (facing Bridge Street), was opened in 1800 by John Suter; it was destroyed by fire in 1832 and rebuilt in 1836. In 1936 all but the west wing of this second structure was torn down.

In the two-storied east wing of the original building (facing 29th Street) was Pompeian Hall, an elaborately decorated ballroom. Here, before the tavern was formally opened, George Washington's Birthnight Ball was held, February 22, 1799, believed to be the last public function attended by the President.

The SITE OF OLD PRESBYTERIAN CHURCH, SE. corner 30th and M Street NW., is across the street from Union Tavern, where the Gospel Mission now stands. The church was founded in 1780 by the Reverend Stephen Bloomer Balch (1747-1833), pastor for more than half a century. The first church, built in 1782 on "Conjuror's Disappointment," was enlarged in 1793, with Thomas Jefferson, Secretary of State, as a subscriber. A new church, built in 1821, was demolished in 1873. Reverend Mr. Balch, who taught in the Columbian Academy at 3241 N Street, drilled the boys of Georgetown and led his youthful company at the Battle of Bladensburg.

INITIAL POINT, ORIGINAL SURVEY, NW. corner 30th and M Streets NW., marks the point where Alexander Beall, clerk of the town, began his survey of the 60 acres of George, in 1751. Shortly after making the survey, he went off to the French and Indian War with another young surveyor, George Washington.

JOHN ABBOTT AND JOHN MOUNTZ HOUSES, 3012 and 3016 M Streets NW., two dilapidated old houses now used as stores, were the homes of John Abbott, an official who moved with the Government from Philadelphia in 1800, and John Mountz, second clerk of incorporated George Town (1791). The window keystones of the Mountz House are marked with the Federal eagle, symbol of the owner's authority. The upper floors retain much of their original eighteenth-century character, particularly in the long 18-light windows, the single attic dormer, and the remnant of a finely molded cove cornice.

A half-block south is MASONIC LODGE NO. 5, at 1056 Jefferson Street, built in 1810. Members of this lodge officiated at the laying of the cornerstone of the Capitol in 1793.

WASHINGTON'S ENGINEERING HEADQUARTERS, 3049 M Street NW., stands almost opposite the end of Jefferson Street. The tiny story-and-a-half stone house is typically pre-Revolutionary in style, with its two entrances, one on street level and one from the raised stoop, its little sash window and low eave lines; inside, the ceilings are low, the halls narrow, and the rooms small. The house, built in 1764 by Christopher Lehman (or Layman), on land forfeited by John Boone (a relative of Daniel Boone, it is believed), has been a matter of controversy for many years. Efforts have been made to have it preserved as a national monument, but the facts concerning its original use have never been established. According to tradition it may have been Washington's headquarters when he planned the Federal City, or headquarters of Pierre L'Enfant and, later, of Major

Ellicott, or headquarters of the Commissioners of the Federal City during its early years. The Goddard family, who have been owners for more than 50 years, have preserved the little stone house, or it would long ago have become one of the innumerable little shops of M Street.

The SITE OF CORCORAN'S COMMISSION HOUSE, NE. corner 31st and M Streets NW., where the three Corcoran brothers, James, Thomas, and William Wilson, once conducted their commission and auction house, is now occupied by a grocery store. Across the street, on the southeast corner, was the Farmers' and Mechanics' Bank, founded in 1814. This institution funded the war debt after the war with Mexico. At 3119 M Street is the site of the home of Thomas Corcoran, leather merchant, who settled in Georgetown in 1791. Here his youngest son, William Wilson Corcoran, was born in 1798; and here Christ Church was founded in 1817.

The SITE OF LINTHICUM'S HARDWARE STORE is on the NW. corner of Wisconsin Avenue and M Street. At old High Street (now Wisconsin Avenue), Bridge Street became Falls Street; and at this corner Edward M. Linthicum conducted a hardware store with such success that he became the owner of the large estate of Dumbarton Oaks. The lower end of old High Street (south from M Street) was called Water Street, as it led to the docks and water front of Georgetown. A few old warehouses remain among modern industrial plants.

VIGILANT FIREHOUSE, 1066 Wisconsin Avenue, a gray-painted brick building, once housed the Vigilant Fire Company, organized in 1817, the second oldest volunteer brigade in Georgetown and the first to have a steam fire engine (1868). Subscription to a volunteer fire brigade was a form of fire insurance, and the houses of subscribers were marked with the company's insignia on iron plaques, a few of which remain. Membership in a company was also a minor social distinction, and a captaincy a local honor. Rivalry between companies was keen, and pride in equipment great. Set in the wall of the Vigilant Firehouse is a memorial plaque to Bush, the dog who was the company's mascot until he was poisoned.

South of the firehouse is a small granite obelisk commemorating the building of the Chesapeake and Ohio Canal. The marker was discovered in an old mill in 1889 and erected here in 1900 by H. P. Gilbert, at his own expense. The century-old masonry of the canal may be seen from the bridge just beyond.

Somewhere near the bridge, probably just south of it, is the SITE OF SUTER'S TAVERN, built in the late 1700's by Robert Peter, the first mayor of Georgetown. Here John Suter operated his one-story frame Fountain Inn, better known as Suter's Tavern. In 1800 he sold this building and bought at auction the more commodious Union Tavern. For more than a decade the tavern was the gathering place of "gentlemen," while Sailors' Tavern flourished about a block to the south, City Tavern for commercial travelers, a block to the north, and, a little farther north, farmers gathered on market days in Montgomery Tavern.

On March 29, 1791, George Washington and the commissioners of the proposed Federal City met at Suter's with the landowners of the newly surveyed "Territory of Columbia," and the next day the 19 "original proprietors" signed the agreement, permitting the tobacco farms and frog ponds to be converted into the Nation's Capital. John Lockwood opened the first lending library of the District in the tavern in 1792. According to tradition, it was here also that the disputed Jefferson-Adams election was settled in 1801, in favor of Jefferson.

Within half a block of the water, just south of the present Grace Church, was Sailors' Tavern, and on the river's edge stood George Gordon's Warehouse, center of Georgetown's commercial activity. Built on Conjuror's Disappointment grant in the early 1730's, this warehouse, for the inspection and sorting of tobacco, was also virtually a bank. Tobacco was the general medium of exchange, and the destinies of farmers for miles around were controlled by Gordon's Warehouse.

Along the water front, some of the old warehouses are recognizable by their Flemish bond, or brick stretcher-and-header walls. Here, east of Wisconsin Avenue, was a busy, noisy world, with ships at the wharves, sailors in peajackets swaggering along the board walks, and well-dressed merchants conferring with shipping masters. To the west and north were the homes of men of growing wealth and distinction. Until the merchants began to build on the heights, Cherry Lane (now Grace Street) was the social center of the town.

At the foot of Wisconsin Avenue was MASON'S FERRY. In 1748, a ferry was licensed to run to the Virginia shore. By 1805 the ferry ran only between the Maryland shore and ANALOSTAN ISLAND (Theodore Roosevelt Island), about midway between the Arlington Memorial and Key Bridge; a causeway had been built by John Mason from the island to the Virginia shore. Some time in the 1790's General John Mason, son of George Mason, bought the 75-acre island, variously known as Analostan, or Anacostan, My Lord's Barbadoes, and Mason's Island. He built a summer residence there and entertained lavishly. Nothing remains of Mason's fine house. The island was bought by the Roosevelt Memorial Association in 1931 and presented to the Government as a park site, to be known as Theodore Roosevelt Island. After CCC boys had drained the swampy shore and built paths and trails to make the woods accessible, the park was opened to the public in 1936. It can be reached only by boat, since no provision was made for vehicular traffic on the island.

A modern drygoods store masks the front of the WILLIAM THORNTON HOUSE, 3221 M Street, where the architect lived while supervising work on the Capitol. Thornton designed the Capitol, the Octagon House, and Tudor Place.

Across the street is the SITE OF THE BANK OF COLUMBIA, 3208 M Street, chartered in 1793 and one of the first in the District.

A few doors west, at 3214 M Street, is FIREHOUSE NO. 5, from which engines rushed gallantly to the great Baltimore fire of 1905. At 3222 M Street are the car barns, on the former Warehouse Lots, once high-piled with casks of tobacco and bales of cotton, or cleared off for fair days and circuses. The MARKET, 3276 M Street, is on the site of the Butcher's Market of Revolutionary times.

The FORREST-MARBURY HOUSE, 3350 M Street, a large gaunt building, now a garage and restaurant, was built about 1791-92 by General Uriah Forrest, Revolutionary soldier and statesman, who lost a leg at Brandywine. In 1800, the house was sold to William Marbury, made famous by the *Marbury* vs. *Madison* case in 1803, in which Chief Justice Marshall established the right of the Supreme Court to determine the constitutionality of Federal statutes. The massive dignity of the former town house remains, despite much remodeling and the third story with heavy bracketed cornice, added by Marbury.

FRANCIS SCOTT KEY MANSION, 3518 M Street, was built by the author of "The Star Spangled Banner" in 1805, as a home for his bride. Considerably altered and dilapidated, it looks little like a mansion now. Eleven children were born here, "the usual number for that time," as one historian points out. In this house, on the night of September 12, 1814, the young attorney agreed to rescue Dr. Beane, who had been taken prisoner by the British. Key sailed down the Potomac in a small boat and boarded the flagship of the British fleet, anchored before Fort McHenry. While negotiations with the officers were pending, the attack began, and Key was forced to remain on board and watch the bombardment. When, at dawn, he saw the American flag still flying above the gallant fort, the idea for his great poem came to him. He wrote a rough draft on his way to Baltimore and later completed it in a tavern room. Key was actively interested in social problems; he founded in 1811 the first Lancaster Free School in America and helped to organize the American Colonization Association in 1816. This movement to send free Negroes to a self-governing colony in Africa eventually resulted in the establishment of Liberia.

FRANCIS SCOTT KEY BRIDGE was designed and erected by United States Army Engineers under Colonel W.L. Fiske, to replace the earlier Aqueduct Bridge and to connect Washington with Arlington and other towns of Fairfax County. The Virginia end is in the small industrial town of Rosslyn. The bridge, built of reinforced concrete, is 1,650 feet long and carries a 70-foot roadway and sidewalks on its 7 arches. Each of the arches is composed of a series of inner arches, providing strength and lightness in the structure. The remains of the Old Aqueduct Bridge may be seen across the Potomac from behind the Key Mansion. Its 8 piers of masonry were built by Army engineers, to support a bridge designed to connect a canal from Alexandria with the Chesapeake and Ohio Canal. On the piers rested a wooden, water-filled trough, through which boats crossed the river from one canal to the other. Above was a wooden bridge for vehicular traffic. Opened in 1843, the canal-bridge was never a great success: the wooden structure required such frequent repair that the company finally went into bankruptcy. An iron bridge was opened in 1888 and served until Key Bridge was opened in 1923. The ironwork and upper part of the piers were removed by CWA workers.

From M Street, 34th Street (old Frederick Street) rises on a steep hill, from which may be seen the retaining wall of the old Stoddert terraces and part of the STODDERT HOUSE, 3400 Prospect Street (side entrance at 1212 34th Street). A cigar-store Indian perched on a Georgian rail; an Italian gate screening an early American doorway; a fragment of cornice, a classic pediment; rusty nondescript lamps, urns, and busts; iron balconies of Southern Colonial style—all have been added to the stately home of Benjamin Stoddert, first Secretary of the Navy. The southern façade and terrace gardens are little changed; some of the boxwood is probably more than 150 years old. Stoddert, wounded at Brandywine, served as Secretary of the War Board until 1781. He retired to George Town and, in 1788 or 1789, built his home "after the manner of some of the elegant houses I have seen in Philadelphia." During the early negotiations for the Federal city, he acted as Washington's agent and was one of the 19 "original Proprietors" who signed the agreement for the "ten-mile square." He lost his fortune in land speculations in the new city.

The WORTHINGTON-KEARNEY HOUSE, 3425 Prospect Street, at the other end of the block, a weather-beaten house with white trim and shutters, was once the home of Dr. Charles Worthington, Washington physician during the War of 1812 and after. Built by John Thompson Mason in 1799, the house is of brick laid in Flemish bond, still discernible beneath layers of gray paint. The Colonial doorway, with slender colonnettes and unusual pediment, is of particular interest. The main cornice, designed with small modillion brackets and fluted frieze, extends in a line with the eaves across the two gables. The interior paneling and woodwork are finely done. The floors are sealed with river sand, an early example of soundproofing.

The MORRIS HOUSE, 3508 Prospect Street, restored to its former dignity, presents a well-proportioned front, with trim brick walls and fine Georgian detail. The west wing has been remodeled into a garage. It is certain that the house was built by John Templeman prior to 1800, because, in that year, his "next neighbor," Benjamin Stoddert, then Secretary of the Navy, wrote Templeman of the proposed visit of President John Adams to the new Capitol; he urged his neighbor "to set bashfulness at defiance and urge the President to go to the balls . . . and ride with you in your coach." The house was inherited by Lieutenant Commander George Upham Morris, whose daughter eloped with W.W. Corcoran, an unknown drygoods clerk at the time. The octagonal watchtower overlooking the river terraces may have been built by Templeman, so that he might watch his merchant ships, or later by Morris, to keep a lookout over his fleet. The galleries, also looking down upon the terraces, were added later, and their beautiful iron grillwork, in leaf-and-grape design, are in the manner of the New Orleans French Quarter.

The SOUTHWORTH COTTAGE, 3600 Prospect Street, a weathered frame house in dilapidated state, was the home of the popular novelist, Mrs. E.D.E.N. Southworth, until her death in 1899. Mrs. Southworth, who was born in Washington, is buried in Oak Hill Cemetery. The first novel ever published serially in America was Mrs. Southworth's *Sylvia Brotherton,* which ran through seven issues of *The National Era,* a Washington antislavery paper.

GEORGETOWN UNIVERSITY HOSPITAL occupies the block between Prospect and N (old First) Streets, on the west side of 35th (old Fayette) Street.

CONVENT OF MERCY, 3525 N Street, has the brick façade and belfry of the old Convent of Mercy, built in 1787-92 as Trinity Church, the first Roman Catholic church in the District. The church, founded by Francis Neale, a brother of Leonard Neale, first president of Georgetown University, was built on land acquired from John Threlkeld for five shillings. Many communicants had to bring their own stools or chairs, and the few pews provided were rented out by the contractor. Later, he turned these pews over to Georgetown College (now University), with instructions that the rents collected were to pay for his sons' education. During the Civil War, the church was converted into a Federal hospital. The Sisters of Mercy are teachers in the adjacent parochial schools. The two large modern school buildings, erected in 1918, one for boys and one for girls, are on the east side of 36th Street.

GEORGETOWN UNIVERSITY has its Administrative Office and Foreign Service School at 37th and O Streets, Medical and Dental Schools at 3900 Reservoir Road, Astronomical Observatory on Georgetown Heights, and Law School at 506 E Street. The university, on the bluffs of the Potomac, occupies one of the most advantageous sites in the District, with a fine river view for miles. Founded in 1787, it is the oldest Catholic college in the United States. Since 1805 it has been under the direction of the Fathers of the Society of Jesus, but, unlike Catholic University, it is sustained by private philanthropy and student tuition and not by church funds. Approximately 2,500 men students are enrolled.

John Carroll, who was the first American bishop and first Archbishop of Baltimore, founded the modest Georgetown Academy, from which the university developed. Carroll, born in Maryland, was educated as a Jesuit at Liége, Belgium, but returned to the United States shortly after suppression of the Jesuit order in 1773. To spread the ideals of the order, Carroll opened an academy to students of "every Religious Profession." The first building was erected in 1788, but 1789, the date on the original deed of property, is generally considered the year of founding. Carroll chose the site on the "old Potomak" bluffs in preference to present Capitol Hill, which he regarded as "too far in the country."

In 1815, Congress granted the university the right to confer degrees, and in 1833, the Holy See empowered Georgetown College to confer degrees in philosophy and theology. Formal incorporation took place in 1844. The School of Medicine was opened in 1851, the School of Law (one of the oldest in the District) in 1870, the University Hospital in 1898, the Dental School in 1901, and the Training School for Nurses in 1903. In 1909, the Seismic Station was established, and, ten years later, the School of Foreign Service. Within the last few years, the Chemo-Medical Research Institute has attracted widespread attention; its avowed purpose is the development of tests to aid in the diagnosis of cases of cancer.

Georgetown's history, from the early days when students followed a rigorous regimen designed "to implant virtue and destroy . . . the seeds of vice," has been enriched by many vivid personalities. Noted among these are Father Tom Mulledy, president in 1829; Father Matthews, the sixth president and a friend of Andrew Jackson; Father Algue, the "typhoon tamer," who invented the barocyclonometer; and Father Tondorf, of seismological fame.

Beyond the main gate to the 78-acre campus, opening from 37th Street, stands a large bronze STATUE OF JOHN CARROLL, by Jerome Connor. To the west is the HEALY BUILDING, administration headquarters, a somber gray-granite structure with a Victorian Gothic tower of slate and stone, illuminated at night and visible from all high points in Washington.

The Healy Building forms the eastern boundary of the quadrangle, an open plot of lawn and garden almost surrounded by buildings of red brick and stone, appearing as one tremendous structure with a frontage of 1,200 feet. To the right of the Healy Building stand two newer stone structures—Copley Hall and the White-Gravenor Building, both in Collegiate Gothic style. Maguire Hall, Ryan Hall, Mulledy Hall, and the Infirmary form the south boundary of the quadrangle. Ryan Hall, the gift of Mrs. Thomas Fortune Ryan, stands upon the site of the Old South Building, the first hall of the original Georgetown Academy. The third side of the square is composed of the New and Old North Buildings. From the porch of the latter, it is said that George Washington made a brief address in 1796. The Chapel of the Sacred Heart, standing alone on the west side, is used for important ecclesiastical events; it was the gift of Mr. and Mrs. John Vinton Dahlgren in memory of their infant son, who is buried there.

Between the quadrangle and the Medical Center to the north is an oak grove, part of the famous woodland "walks." The Medical School and Dental School occupy a Colonial-style H-shaped structure. The Astronomical Observatory's white walls and dome stand out sharply at the extreme southwest of the grounds.

The buildings of the Law School are downtown, half a block from Judiciary Square.

The university owns many works of art and relics of historical

interest, most of which are in the Healy Building. In the PHILODEMIC
.ROOM, meeting place of the oldest college debating society in the United
States, hang portraits of Chief Justice Edward Douglas White, James
Ryder Randall, Bailey K. Ashford, and other distinguished members
of the society. In the CARROLL PARLOR, which contains the Leonard
Calvert dining table, is a portrait of Archbishop John Carroll, by
Gilbert Stuart, a portrait of the Archbishop's mother by Stuart pupils,
the *Call of St. Matthew,* by Luca Giordano, an *Annunciation* ascribed
to Fra Angelico, and copies of Veronese's *St. Aloysius Gonzaga,* Rubens'
Descent from the Cross, and Raphael's *Madonna della Sedia.*

The university archives in the basement of the same building hold
a set of 800 pontifical medals, tracing the history of the Roman Catholic Church through nearly five centuries. Glass cases display vestments from Mexico and Europe. Two rear parlors are devoted to the
DUBUISSON LITURGICAL MUSEUM, formed around the Dubuisson collection of relics. Of special interest is the large iron cross made from
horseshoes and scrap iron by Calvert pilgrims during their first days
in the New World. Here also are sets of fourteenth- and fifteenth-
century vestments, one of which is purported to be the oldest of those
in actual use in America. The Beauchamp-Hughes art cabinet com-
prises a collection of rare laces, pictures, manuscripts, and china.

The Reliquary in the basement of Copley Hall holds the bones of
St. Vincentius, a Spanish martyr of the fourth century, and of St.
Aelius and St. Theophilus, Roman soldiers. This same building houses
the Coleman Museum, with its excellent collection of rocks and fossils,
including specimens from the District.

The libraries of the university, which include the RIGGS MEMORIAL
LIBRARY and the HIRST LIBRARY, contain more than 220,000 volumes;
they are in the Healy Building. Among the rarities are 100 volumes
printed between the years 1472 and 1520. The collections are particularly rich in Americana and ecclesiastical chronicles. Items of
interest are facsimiles, one of which is the Duke de Loubat's reproduction in photochromography of ancient Aztec manuscripts. Probably
the university's most valuable single literary item is the original script
of *Tom Sawyer,* written by Samuel Clemens (Mark Twain) in long-
hand and valued at $45,000. It was the gift of Mrs. Nicholas Brady
of New York. The ground floor of the Riggs Library is devoted to
Maryland Colonial history and the history of the District, made
possible by the Morgan Maryland Colonial History Endownment. A
section of the Riggs Library holds the collection of Dr. John Gilmary
Shea, valuable for its Americana and works in the Indian languages,
and for the collections dealing with Georgetown University and the
scientific and literary treatises of its professors and scholars.

The ASTRONOMICAL OBSERVATORY was founded in 1843 by the
Reverend J. Curley, S.J. Its equipment has been much enlarged, and
the purpose changed from student instruction to scientific research.

The SEISMOLOGICAL OBSERVATORY, in the basement of Maguire
Hall, was founded by the Reverend Francis A. Tondorf, S.J., and has

attained Nation-wide recognition.   As the official seismological station at Washington, it is closely associated with the United States Coast and Geodetic Survey.   The Observatory, a member of the Jesuit Seismological Association, records and interprets teleseisms and prepares two monthly publications, one a digest of reports on earthquakes and volcanic disturbances.

The university consists of the College of Arts and Sciences, with a graduate school, undergraduate school, and the observatories; the School of Law, the School of Dentistry, the School of Medicine, and the School of Foreign Service.   The teaching is guided by the *Ratio Studiorum*.   The School of Foreign Service, the first in the country devoted entirely to this field, is one of the best known of such schools and one of the few to give courses in Chinese.

Extending all along the west side of Georgetown University grounds is FOUNDRY BRANCH PARKWAY, 25 acres of virgin woodland in a narrow gorge-like valley.   It is named for Foundry Branch, a stream that runs into the old Chesapeake and Ohio Canal to the south, and upon which Foxall Ordnance Foundry was established in 1797.

Across Reservoir Road, which bounds Foundry Parkway on the north, is GLOVER-ARCHBOLD PARK, a 100-acre tract of irregular shape extending northward to Massachusetts Avenue.   The park was presented to the Distrcit in 1924 by Charles C. Glover and Mrs. Anne Archbold.   Throughout this woodland area, within the watershed of the Foundry Branch, are some of the finest trees in the District; tremendous beech groves are interspersed with great old elms and oaks and broad stretches of grassland.

WHITEHAVEN PARKWAY, a narrow strip of land broken by many intersecting streets, leads eastward at V Street from Glover-Archbold Park.   It is planned to continue this parkway, through a wooded area already used as a park, to meet the Montrose Park extension of Rock Creek and Potomac Parkway (*see Potomac and Rock Creek Parks*).   Westward, Glover-Archbold Parkway sends out a spur to connect with Fort Drive, which extends southward to Conduit Road and then west to Weaver Place, opposite Palisades Park (*see Two Ways to Great Falls*).

From the O Street entrance of Georgetown University, the tour continues to N and 34th Streets.

In COX'S ROW, 3327-3339 N Street, are the houses that remain of a row built in 1790 by John Cox, mayor of Georgetown.   Two still show distinctive traces of the early Federal period, especially in the proportions, the detail of doors and windows, set flush with the outer walls, and in the delicately carved wall plaques.   Cox entertained Lafayette at Number 3337 during his last visit to America in 1824-25.

BODISCO HOUSE, 3322 O Street, is a large cream-colored brick house of severe lines and massive proportions, typical of late Federal architecture.   Under a pedimented portico, a graceful twin stair leads up to the transomed entrance.   The door, with its narrow sidelights, and the large double-hung windows, with slender mullions and paneled shutters, is of considerable interest. The garden, open only during Garden Week, is entered through an arched and pedimented gate in the enclosing wall. Baron Alexander de Bodisco, Russian envoy to the United States (1837-54), married Harriet Williams of Georgetown, a girl in her teens. The reception following their wedding in 1840 was an elaborate affair, attended by a brilliant company of diplomatic and governmental officials. For many years the Bodisco House was the Russian Embassy.

The WAGGAMAN HOUSE, 3300 O Street, now (1942) the residence of Jouett Shouse, a prominent figure in national politics, was once the home of John S. Waggaman, real estate operator and art collector.

The YELLOW HOUSE, 1430 33rd Street, has been known by that name for more than two centuries. Built before 1733, it was willed on that date to John Gorden, then a young man in the British East India service. It is believed to be the oldest house in Georgetown, having been built on the Knave's Disappointment grant; the north wing of the Mackall Place may be older, but the date of its building has not been authenticated.

A two-story-and-attic structure of brick painted yellow, the house gives little exterior indication of great antiquity. It has characteristic arched dormers and wide chimney, green-shuttered windows, and a green door with a brass knocker, under a graceful arched transom. The door opens into a stair hall with its original stair-rail, rounded to fit the hand, and slender banister spindles, each with a carved motif. The newel post, unfortunately, has been replaced by a later piece. The spacious drawing room, north of the hall, has a graciously curved Colonial mantel and a generous fireplace. This room opens into the living room by a wide-arched door, and the rooms thus connected suggest the two centuries of hospitality the house has enjoyed. In the living room is a smaller fireplace, fitted with a miniature of the drawing-room mantelpiece. The master bedroom, over the drawing room, is a spacious room with its own fireplace, and there are other rooms at different levels, charmingly fitted into an interior arrangement that extends out on an angle in the rear and looks down on an intimate small garden on the south side of the house. Several doors are the traditional "witch doors" of Colonial pattern, paneled to form the "double cross," flat on one side and full-paneled on the other. The Yellow House, not as well known as it deserves, has on occasion been included in Georgetown garden tours.

The GREGG HOUSE, 3245 O Street, faithfully restored, is a small house of fine proportions and simple Colonial style. On the adjoining site is the old CURTIS SCHOOL, which contributed much to nineteenth-century Georgetown culture and at one time housed the Peabody Collection, now in the Georgetown Branch of the Public Library.

ST. JOHN'S CHURCH, SE. corner O and Potomac Streets, is the oldest Episcopal church in the District. The congregation, established in 1794, met in the Reverend Mr. Balch's Presbyterian Church until erection of the present structure in 1807-09, from plans drawn by William Thornton, architect of the Capitol. The building was dedicated in 1809 by the Right Reverend Thomas Claggett, first Protestant Episcopal bishop consecrated in America. Efforts have been made to remove from the church the neo-Gothic additions made in later years and to restore Thornton's design. The cupola of the front tower has been reconstructed twice. When research disclosed an octagonal tower under a square overstructure and steeple, these architectural overlays were removed, and Thornton's three-tiered cupola restored, with a dome replacing the upper tier.

At the street intersection, a boulder with a bronze tablet was placed in 1910 by the Society of Colonial Wars, commemorating Ninian Beall (1625-1717), patentee of the Rock of Dunbarton and commander-in-chief of Provincial forces of Maryland.

The SITE OF MONTGOMERY TAVERN is at 1363 Wisconsin Avenue. The rambling Montgomery Tavern, with a stableyard accommodating 300 teams, catered to farmers in the early days. Their tobacco and other produce sold, their teams and Conestoga wagons in the inn yard, the farmers could look over and bid with Scottish caution for John Beattie's "hands" (slaves), quartered near by.

The FOXALL-McKENNEY HOUSE, 3123 Dumbarton Avenue, built by Henry Foxall for his daughter, about 1800, is a notable example of Federal architecture. A low stone wall and white picket fence enclose the spacious front yard. The pillared porch, with wooden handrails and gabled pediment, has a blue vaulted ceiling conforming to the curve of the late-Georgian door. The long lintel stones over the windows are decorated with corner blocks, a characteristic feature of the period. It is said that Commodore Perry refused to start for the encounter on Lake Erie until his ships were fitted with guns from Henry Foxall's foundry, and to destroy this important gun factory was one of the objectives of the British attack on Washington in 1814. The attempt failed.

The small store on the NW. corner of Wisconsin Avenue and N Street was once W. W. CORCORAN'S STORE, the "Thread and Needle" shop. On the NE. corner, Mitchell's Boys School was in operation in the early 1800's.

FORREST HALL, 1262 Wisconsin Avenue, an ante bellum social gathering place, is now a commercial garage. Forrest Hall was converted into a Union hospital during the Civil War, and here Lincoln came frequently to cheer his soldiers.

The JOHN LUTZ HOUSE, 1255 Wisconsin Avenue, with a modern red-brick front, is now a home for elderly women. From the 1830's to the 1860's this was the home of Francis Lutz, whose son, John Lutz, married the actress Laura Keene. This John was the son of the earlier John Lutz, Revolutionary War soldier and bodyguard to Washington. It was Laura Keene's performance of *Our*

American Cousin that brought President Lincoln to Ford's Theater on the night of April 14, 1865.

The CONGRESS STREET METHODIST CHURCH, 1238 31st Street, completed in 1830, has been somewhat remodeled. In 1772, Francis Asbury passed through Georgetown as a missionary for the Methodist faith. His little group grew slowly, but the struggle was hard. When the church land was sold for taxes, W.W. Corcoran bought it and restored it to the congregation.

The ROMULUS RIGGS HOUSE, 3038 N Street, a narrow two-storied brick house with fine attic dormers, is notable for the corbeled brick cornice and the delicate craftsmanship of doors and windows. It was purchased by Romulus Riggs in 1812. Years later, Mrs. Johnston, granddaughter of Abraham Lincoln, lived here. Romulus Riggs was a brother of Elisha and a half-brother of George W. Riggs, founders, with W.W. Corcoran, of the Riggs National Bank.

The BEALL MANSION, 3033 N Street, is one of the oldest brick houses in the District. The central portion may have been built by George Beall with money received when he was forced to sell part of the Rock of Dunbarton for platting the town of George in 1751. The plans for the Beall mansion called for a 12-foot hall on the east side, with two rooms opening from it on the east, each 20 feet square. The second story had the same plan, and a dormered third story was finished with two rooms. The wings have been added. The house may have been built by one or other of George Beall's sons. Thomas Beall inherited the property in 1780 and in 1786 gave it to his brother George Beall, Jr., "for the affection I bear." Contrary to general opinion, the property was described in the deed as "Rock of Dunbarton," and it was not until about 1800 that the spelling "Dumbarton" began to appear.

Ninian Beall fought at the battle of Dunbar for King Charles I and was exiled by the triumphant Cromwell. He was sold into "servitude" as a political prisoner, but whether he was sent to Barbados, to Ireland, or directly to Maryland is not certainly known. His name is recorded in Maryland as early as 1658, and he became commander of Maryland's provincial forces under the restored monarchy. His grant of more than 700 acres of land he named "Rock of Dunbar-ton," a sly pun on the celebrated Rock of Dumbarton in Scotland.

At 3017 N Street is the residence of Major William E.P. French, U. S. Army, retired, a cousin of the late Daniel Chester French, sculptor. This massive buff-painted three-story brick house has many features typical of seacoast mansions of the Federal period: heavy detail and overhanging cornice, low-pitched roof and lookout tower, and long service wing at one side. It was built as an investment by Thomas Beall in 1794-96, and the first "genteel family" to occupy it was that of John Laird. Later it was bought by Major George Peter, known as the organizer of the "Flying Artillery," famous in the War of 1812 and a forerunner of present-day light field artillery.

The central section of the long red-brick DUNLOP-LINCOLN

HOUSE, 3014 N Street, was built by John Laird, about 1799-1800, and inherited from him by his son-in-law, Judge Dunlop, who was deposed from the Supreme Court bench by Lincoln because of his Southern sympathies. Robert Todd Lincoln, eldest son of President Lincoln, bought the house after Dunlop's death and lived there until he died in 1926.

The surface arches framing the doors and 20-paned windows of the first and second stories of the original house are unusually interesting. The transomed doorway is set behind a pillared portico of fluted columns. The detail of the added wings conforms to that of the main section. In the garden, one of the showplaces of the Garden Club, is a small stone marker, the second of the survey stones set out by Alexander Beall in 1751, and the only one remaining.

Colonial Apartments, 1305-1315 30th Street, occupy the site of Mr. Rodger's Academy, opened shortly after the Revolution, where many potential statesmen were educated. Later, the buildings of Miss Lydia English's Female Seminary were erected. The school was used as a Union hospital during the Civil War. The present apartments include some of the old seminary buildings, altered to suit modern needs.

The EDES HOUSE, 2929 N Street, stands in the place of one of the seminary units, which was torn down to make way for a "home for indigent widows of Georgetown," according to a bequest made by Miss Margaret Edes. Many residents think that "widows" may have been a clerical error, and that Miss Edes intended a home for "indigent women."

At 1239 30th Street is Georgetown's narrowest house, scarcely 11 feet wide and not quite two complete stories high. With its oriel window and three skylights on the second floor, the house is livable and attractive.

The FOXALL HOUSE, 2908 N Street, one of the four connected with the name of Henry Foxall, is a charming nineteenth-century house, with detail and proportions on an intimate scale. Tiny shuttered windows look over a high brick wall, and the basement entrance has small, double, wrought-iron gates.

The ADMIRAL WEAVER HOUSE, 2923 N Street, is a pre-Revolutionary house, except for the south front, added in the early 1800's, and the two-story gallery at the rear of the oldest portion, extending north along 29th Street. For a time this was the home of Admiral Aaron Ward Weaver, commander of the *Mahopac* at the capture of Fort Fisher and the surrender of Richmond.

The SUSAN WHEELER DECATUR HOUSE, 2812 N Street, was for many years the home of the widow of Stephen Decatur, hero of the Tripolitan War. Susan Wheeler Decatur, not wishing to meet the man who had been her husband's opponent in the fatal duel, nor his second, whom she blamed in part for the tragedy, withdrew from society to this house, a three-story brick structure designed with the restraint in detail and large-scale treatment of masses characteristic

YELLOW HOUSE (BUILT *c.* 1730), OLDEST IN GEORGETOWN

TUDOR PLACE (1815), GEORGETOWN

Photos by W. Lincoln Highton

OCTAGON HOUSE (1800)

BLAIR HOUSE (1824-27)

W. Lincoln Highton

DUMBARTON HOUSE (*c.* 1790), GEORGETOWN

Washington Daily News

SWETNAM HOUSE, 815 FRANKLIN STREET, ALEXANDRIA

COTTAGE AT 1222 28TH
STREET, NW.,
GEORGETOWN
*Historic American Buildings
Survey, Library of Congress*

LOCKHOUSE (*c.* 1830), SENECA, MD.

ALLEY DWELLER

NEGROES REHOUSED IN HOPKINS
PLACE ALLEY DWELLING DEVELOPMENT

ROOM TO PLAY, GREENBELT, MD.

TYPICAL SUBURBAN DEVELOPMENT (1941), BETHESDA, MD.

APARTMENT HOTEL

ROW-HOUSE, BOARDING-HOUSE WASHINGTON

of the Federal style. Mrs. Decatur became a Roman Catholic and was greatly interested in Georgetown University. She left several mementoes of her husband to the school, including his portrait by Gilbert Stuart, his ivory chessmen, and a jeweled toothpick box, such as was carried by every gentleman of that day.

The GUNBARREL FENCE, NW. corner of P (old West Street) and 28th Streets, is made of a hundred musket barrels. The most plausible of the three stories about the origin of the fence is that Reuben Daws, a merchant, obtained from the Navy Yard a lot of discarded and antiquated muskets; by imbedding the stock end of the barrel of each gun in a low wall and adding spikes at the muzzles, he made the fence.

The MILLER COTTAGE, 1524 28th Street, is unmistakably New England in style, thrown into sharp relief by the architecture of so Southern a city as Georgetown. Its white clapboarded walls, small porch, casement windows with louvered shutters, six-panel door with delicate transom, and even the wooden benches on the porch, painted green to match doors and shutters, are reminiscent of New England. Benjamin Miller, who built the cottage about 1840, came to Georgetown as designer and engineer of the Aqueduct Bridge.

In contrast to the Miller house is the ROBERT DODGE HOUSE, SW. corner Q and 28th Streets, an early example of Classic Revival architecture, popular in the District in the first quarter of the nineteenth century. The large yellow house of stucco-covered brick has many characteristic features: the large square piers of the corner porch, the plain cornice, gable pediments, large arched windows, and low attic parapet.

Diagonally opposite is the home of Mrs. Thomas Bradley, 1601 28th Street. In the garden, open only during Garden Week, is one of the original survey stones of Evermay.

EVERMAY, 1623 28th Street, on one of the most commanding elevations in Georgetown, but almost hidden by a high brick wall, is an eighteenth-century Georgian manor house, now considerably altered. When the stucco, applied many years ago, was removed, the mellow texture of its rose brick walls was revealed. From the gate lodge, a formal approach leads through unusually beautiful grounds to the Georgian entrance doorway. The fine paneled door, with solid fan transom, opens on a low stoop, with iron handrails and newel lamps. Dark boxwoods, evergreens, and azaleas, a classic summer house, fountain statuary, and formal paths make the garden a show place.

Samuel Davidson, a successful speculator in Federal city real estate, bought the property in 1792 and built the manor house shortly thereafter. Davidson, an eccentric bachelor, so feared intrusion that he inserted advertisements in the newspapers advising all persons "to avoid Evermay as they would a den of devils or rattlesnakes." He left the estate to his nephew, John Grant, on condition that he take the name Davidson. John Grant Davidson's daughter, Eliza, married Charles Dodge, June 12, 1847, in a quadruple wedding at the old Dodge farm.

The ceremony, during which three Dodge sons and a daughter were married, took place at four o'clock in the morning, so that the young couples might travel on the early stage to Baltimore. Thus Evermay became another Dodge home, of which there are several in this section of Georgetown.

MACKALL PLACE, 1623 29th Street, hidden from view by dense foliage, occupies the entire square. The northern wing of the house may be the oldest structure in Georgetown, believed to have been built about 1717. The Mackalls retained the original wing when the present brick house was built. The stables are of comparatively recent date.

TERRACE TOP, 1642 29th Street, is interesting mainly because it was at one time the home of E.H. Sothern and Julia Marlowe.

The entrance to OAK HILL CEMETERY (*open 7-5 weekdays; 8-5 Sun. and holidays*) is at 30th and R Streets. The cemetery, studded with large oaks, extends along the western bank of Rock Creek, just above Dumbarton Bridge. The 25-acre tract rolls across four plateaus, separated by terraced ravines, then drops almost to creek level. East of the yellow-brick lodge of the superintendent is the Gothic chapel, designed by James Renwick.

When William Wilson Corcoran purchased the 12½-acre plot and founded the cemetery in 1848, he made provision for retaining the woodlands. The present informal landscaping follows plans made at that time by George F. de la Roche. Eleanor, daughter of Elizabeth and George Corbin Washington, from whom the land had been acquired, was the first person buried in Oak Hill Cemetery, on April 13, 1849.

Between the lodge and the chapel is the grave of John Howard Payne, author of "Home, Sweet Home." The identifying monument and bust stand in a clearing on the first plateau, and near by is the flat tombstone from Payne's original resting place, a gift of the city and of the Kingdom of Tunis. Payne was United States Consul in Tunis for 4-years, and, in 1852, he died and was buried there. Thirty years later, W.W. Corcoran, a friend of Payne, had the body brought home and interred at Oak Hill.

On the northeast slope of the same plateau is the memorial stone to the Reverend Stephen Balch, militant pastor of the Old Presbyterian Church. A flight of steps on the north side leads to the grave of Mrs. E.D.E.N. Southworth, romantic novelist. Around the terrace curve to the east, a shaft of granite commemorates Alexander de Bodisco, Russian envoy to the United States for 17 years.

This first plateau is one of three that curve to the southeast. On a fourth plateau, to the north, is a circular Greek temple of white marble, the tomb of W.W. Corcoran (1798-1888), founder of the Corcoran Gallery of Art. West of the Corcoran tomb, an octagonal shaft stands over the grave of John H. Eaton, Secretary of War under Jackson, and Minister to Spain. Beside him lies his wife, Peggy O'Neale, the tavern-keeper's daughter whose spectacular career divided Washington society. Her burial is only referred to indirectly, on the stone she had erected to the memory of her daughter and grand-daughter.

On the second plateau, east of the chapel, a white granite obelisk marks the grave of Edwin M. Stanton, Secretary of War during Lincoln's administration, and, northeast of it, a Celtic cross stands above the grave of James G. Blaine, Secretary of State under Benjamin Harrison.

In the hollow to the east is the grave of General John A. Joyce, marked by a monument and bronze bust by Jerome Connor, erected before the poet's death. On the stone is inscribed the well-known line, "Laugh and the world laughs with you, weep and you weep alone." The authorship of this quotation, claimed by Joyce and also by Ella Wheeler Wilcox, was the subject of considerable dispute; the two writers carried on their controversy for some time in the newspapers.

Still farther to the east is a square granite block dedicated to Joseph Henry, first secretary of the Smithsonian Institution. On the easternmost heights is the Van Ness Mausoleum, designed by George Hadfield, architect of the old City Hall, after the Temple of Vesta in Rome. Here are buried Marcia Burnes Van Ness, principal founder of the Church of the Ascension; her husband, General John Peter Van Ness; and their daughter, Ann.

DUNBARTON, 1647 30th Street, the eighteenth-century home of the Bealls and Washingtons, stands on spacious grounds among giant shade trees and dark evergreens. The mansard roof is a later addition. The massive central portion, of buff-painted brick, is set off by an eastern service wing and a western octagonal bay. The mansion was built by Thomas Beall in 1784, shortly after he inherited the Rock of Dunbarton from his father, George Beall, Sr. It was given as a wedding present to Thomas Beall's daughter, Elizabeth Ridley, when she was married to George Corbin Washington, great-nephew of the President. Their son, Lewis Washington, was captured by John Brown at Harpers Ferry and held as hostage until rescued by troops under Lieutenant Colonel Robert E. Lee. Lewis sold the estate to Elisha Riggs.

MONTROSE PARK, across the street from Dunbarton, is part of the Government-owned system of District parks. It was purchased in 1911 for $110,000 and named for former owners of the estate. Originally this tract was known as Parrott's Woods, for Richard Parrott, who owned this land and a ropewalk, where cordage was made by hand. Parrott named the place Elderslie when he built a home there about 1806-09. In 1812, the grounds of the estate accommodated the large crowds who came to the funeral of General James Maccubin Lingan, a victim of mob violence in Baltimore. George Washington's war tent was spread over the bier, and the President's adopted son, George Washington Parke Custis, delivered the oration. Lingan and a number of Revolutionary soldiers had long contended that President Madison's vacillating policies would lead to war. When Madison finally allowed himself to be forced into a declaration of war, these Federalists published a stinging rebuke in their Baltimore organ. Madison followers attacked the newspaper plant, and Lingan, General "Light-Horse Harry" Lee, and others, went to Baltimore to defend their political position and the freedom of the press. Mob violence broke out; Lee was injured, and Lingan was killed by a stone.

In 1837, Mrs. W.M. Boyce, of the same family as the Earls of Montrose, bought the estate and named it Montrose. Her rose gardens were always open to the public.

Immediately west of Montrose Park is Lovers' Lane, officially recognized by that name in 1900. At one time it was a stage road, part of the long route to Baltimore. Today it is closed to vehicles and makes one of the pleasantest walks in Georgetown, from Rock Creek Park to the heights.

Almost facing the entrance of Lovers' Lane is the HURST HOME FOR THE BLIND, 3050 R Street, a long yellow-gray brick building with a colonnaded portico. Braille and Moon type, basket weaving, chair caning, and other manual arts are taught to the blind of the District in the Hurst Home. The institution was founded in 1899 by private subscription. The downtown property was sold in 1915, the new site purchased, and an 18-room building erected. The present home was built when Henry and Annie Hurst bequeathed the institution an estate of $500,000. It stands on the site of the home of Harriet Williams, who married Baron de Bodisco.

DUMBARTON OAKS, 3101 R Street, one of largest remaining late-Georgian estates in the District, was, until 1940, the home of Robert Woods Bliss, former Ambassador to Argentina, noted art collector, and Castoria manufacturer. Mr. and Mrs. Bliss gave Harvard University their house, with its tapestries and other art objects, the surrounding grounds, and their research library and famous collection of Byzantine and early Christian art. Twenty-seven acres of the estate were turned over to the Government to be developed into Dumbarton Oaks Park. The Bliss family retained a small tract, east of the Naval Observatory Grounds.

In a special number of Harvard's *Bulletin of the Fogg Museum of Art* (March, 1941), the purpose of the gift and the plans of the University in connection with it are concisely stated:

> They [Mr. and Mrs. Bliss] have done this in the hope that Harvard University may carry forward in the field of Byzantine and Mediaeval Humanities the serious and imaginative work initiated by them with such skill, developed by them with such care and with such singleness of purpose, and given direction by them with such far-seeing vision.
>
> This gift opens for Harvard University a new path of intellectual endeavour, a new stimulus for creative work in Research. We plan to invite to Dumbarton Oaks each year a few senior research scholars of international reputation, and to associate with them a small group of junior investigators who can devote themselves to extending knowledge in the Early Christian, Byzantine, and Mediaeval fields. We shall cooperate with the other educational institutions in Washington and elsewhere; we shall offer seminars to small selected groups of scholars, and series of lectures concerned particularly with our special field, to larger groups.

We recognize the high purposes and ideals of the founders of the Dumbarton Oaks Research Library and Collection. It is our ideal to make of Dumbarton Oaks a research centre worthy of its founders and of the best traditions of Harvard University.

The Research Library, built up by Mrs. Barbara Sessions, contains some 10,000 volumes related to Byzantine and early Christian art. Special emphasis has been placed on publications in the Russian language dealing with phases of Byzantine Art, numismatics, and history. Among the valuable reference material are copies of the *Princeton Index of Christian Art* and the catalogue of the Hyvernat Semitic Library in the Catholic University of America. With the assistance of museums and other institutions and private collectors, the *Dumbarton Oaks Census of Early Christian and Byzantine Art in America* has been compiled, a work of inestimable value to research students.

The Dumbarton Oaks Collection is one of the finest in the world in the field of Byzantine art. The greater number of the exhibits are from the early, middle, and full Byzantine periods, and especially from the fifth and sixth centuries. Included are examples of pre-Byzantine art, early art of the Mediterranean world, the arts of Greece and Rome, and a few from Western medieval culture. The exquisite taste of the Byzantines, as well as their love of precious stones, is richly represented by jewelry in the collection—rings, bracelets, necklaces, and earrings—and by other objects in stone, jewels, gold, silver, bronze, and mosaic. From the tenth, eleventh, and twelfth centuries, the period of highest development, comes the fine relief in ivory of the *Holy Virgin Between the Two Saint Johns* and several excellent examples of small carving. In the collection are also many rare examples of Scythian art, and of the workmanship of the Avars, the Huns, the Visigoths, and the Merovingians. What is said to be the finest Merovingian monument in America is the chalice of Saint Chrodegang (d. 775), a chalice of copper with silver incrustation and niello. Romanesque sculpture is illustrated by a few choice marble reliefs and an ivory altar. Two of the largest surviving Coptic textiles are among the Dumbarton tapestries.

The Dumbarton Oaks estate was originally part of Ninian Beall's Rock of Dunbarton grant. The mansion was built about 1800 or 1891 by William H. Dorsey, first judge of the Orphan's Court established by Jefferson. Dorsey sold his Acropholous, or Grove on the Hill, to Robert Beverley, whose son transferred it to James Edward Calhoun. John C. Calhoun lived here during his terms as Secretary of War, Vice President, and Senator from South Carolina. In 1846, Edward Linthicum bought Acropholous and gave it the name of Monterey, in memory of his son-in-law, who was killed in that battle of the Mexican War. The next owner, Colonel Henry M. Blount, renamed the property The Oaks, for its magnificent trees.

Within the 27 acres donated to the Government, and now developed as Dumbarton Oaks Park, is the Branch, with its old waterwheel, fish pond, arched bridges, and flowering banks. The grounds, adjoining Montrose Park, may be entered from Massachusetts Avenue or Lovers Lane.

The main house, its Georgian style somewhat altered by a mansard roof and other changes, stands in a grove on a high knoll. Surrounding it are the 16 acres now belonging to Harvard University, containing great stretches of lawn, terraced gardens, many varieties of trees; tennis courts, swimming pool, the formal Ellipse, and the lovely Star Garden, with the signs of the Zodiac inlaid in the flagstone terrace.

The interior has been much altered, although the library, paneled in Jacobean oak, is much as it was, and a few steps down from this room is the original orangerie, now used for research material. On the walls of the various rooms are fine paintings of different periods, among them the *Répétition du Chant,* by Degas, and El Greco's *Visitation.* Tapestries, sculptures in wood and bronze, and other art objects, included in the gift to the University, are in the drawing room and in the two-story Renaissance music room. On the upper floor are the quarters of the Executive Officer and rooms available to research scholars in residence and other scholarly visitors. On the lowest floor are the working quarters, the Rare Book Room, and the Slavic Library.

The two new wings, added by Mr. Bliss to house the Byzantine Collection and Research Library, adjoin the music or lecture room and are connected by a loggia, with small patio. The entrance is on 32nd Street. Among other buildings are the Superintendent's House, the bindery, and the living quarters of Junior Fellows.

The ROUSSEAU HOUSE, 3238 R Street, is the home of Mrs. Rousseau, landscape architect and widow of Rear Admiral Harry M. Rousseau. Her garden is notable for its old trees, rock garden, and iris-bordered walks. The square bright-red-brick house, with white trim, is crowned with a low-pitched roof and cupola and is embellished by elaborate iron balconies, console brackets, a large octagonal bay window, and the entrance portico and vestibule beneath a great Palladian window at the principal floor. It is sometimes called the General Grant House, though Grant only lived here a short time as guest of General Halleck. General John A. Joyce, colorful soldier-poet of the nineties (*see Oak Hill Cemetery*), also lived in the Rosseau house.

On the corner of Wisconsin Avenue and R Street is the Georgetown Branch of the PUBLIC LIBRARY (*open 5-9 Mon., Thurs.; 2-6 Tues., Wed. 9-12:30 Fri.*). The library is on the site of the dismantled Georgetown Reservoir, on Lee's hill, and the retaining wall of the terrace was formerly the reservoir wall. Two tridents are still to be seen in the wall, and a third is on exhibit in the Peabody Room. The George Peabody Collection of Georgetowniana (imprints of the nineteenth-century, early maps of the region, and works of Georgetown authors), is in the custody of the library.

The three other corners at Wisconsin Avenue and R Street are occupied by the pre-Civil War homes of the Dougal and Marbury families and Mount Hope, former home of Colonel William Robinson.

MACKALL-WORTHINGTON HOUSE, 3406 R Street, in a grove of fine shade trees, is a great symmetrically built house of gray-painted brick, with bracketed cornice and mansard roof. Across the main façade is a heavy white balcony, which is carried on consoles above the head of the door. The house was built about 1800 by Leonard Mackall, who had received the land as a dowry when he married a daughter of Brooke Beall. In 1867, John Worthington, son of Dr. Charles Worthington, bought the estate.

SITE OF THE CEDARS, the wooded acreage on the west side of 35th Street, formerly the estate of Colonel John Cox, now belongs to Western High School. The land was part of Burleith, the Threlkeld estate. Jane Threlkeld brought the land as a dowry to her husband, John Cox, who built a manor house there. In order that Cox might accept nomination for mayor (a position he held for 22 years), the city limits of Georgetown were extended to include his property. His large house was later converted into a "female seminary," conducted by the Misses Earle.

Along the west side of 35th Street from Reservoir Road to P Street are the 40-acre grounds and the red-brick buildings of the CONVENT OF THE VISITATION OF THE HOLY MARY, 1500 35th Street, and of the girls boarding school conducted by the Sisters of the Order of the Visitation. Behind the Academy Building, the first on the north, housing classrooms and laboratories, are the school dormitories and infirmary. Next is the Chapel of the Sacred Heart, erected in 1821, the oldest structure on the grounds. Facing 35th and P Streets is the convent itself. A gymnasium, built in 1934, the May Seep Fennessy Memorial Hall of the graduate school, and an old slave house, restored and made into recreation quarters by the Alumnae Association, complete the quadrangle on the west. While excavating for a tennis court foundation in 1939, workmen unearthed what are believed to be the ruins of Burleith, home of Henry Threlkeld, built in 1716. The pecan trees in the convent garden were a gift from Thomas Jefferson to Threlkeld's son John, who married Elizabeth Ridgely. The original Burleith was burned shortly after the Revolution, and another house was built.

The convent is the oldest of the Order of the Visitation in this country and is considered the mother convent of 20 others. The order was founded in 1610 by St. Francis de Sales. The Right Reverend Leonard Neale, first president of Georgetown College and second Archbishop of Baltimore, founded the Georgetown convent in 1799 for Miss Alice Lalor and two other young Georgetown women, who had become interested in taking the vows through study with Poor Clare nuns, exiled during the French Revolution and staying at Burleith. Under Father Picot Clorivière, exiled nobleman and priest, the convent was recognized in 1816 by Pope Pius VII as the Order of the Visitation; Miss Lalor, as Sister Theresa, became Mother Superior.

In the chapel, erected with part of Father Clorivière's fortune, are gifts from Charles X of France, a marble altar, and an altarpiece, *Martha and Mary*, by Madame LeBrun. In the chapel crypt are interred the bodies of Archbishop Neale, Father Clorivière, Sister Theresa, and many other early members of the order. Two small cemeteries are within the grounds.

VOLTA BUREAU, 1537 35th Street, is headquarters for the American Association to Promote the Teaching of Speech to the Deaf and a clearing house for new scientific information and medical aids. Helen Keller, on May 8, 1893, turned the first sod for the present structure, which replaced the original home of the bureau on Connecticut Avenue.

Volta Bureau was established by Alexander Graham Bell in 1880, with the $10,000 Volta prize he received for inventing the telephone and with the returns from his patents on the disk-record graphophone. The Volta prize was created by Napoleon I in honor of Count Alessandro Volta, Italian physicist and inventor of the electric battery. Alexander Melville Bell, father of the inventor, was an Edinburgh professor of physiology who perfected a system of "visible speech." Alexander Graham Bell, while teaching his father's method in Boston, married a deaf pupil, Mabel Hubbard, daughter of Gardiner Greene Hubbard, founder of the National Geographic Society. Bell discovered the principles of electrical reproduction of sound while working on an electrical apparatus for the deaf.

Across Volta Place and facing the Convent of the Visitation is the ALEXANDER MELVILLE BELL HOUSE, 1525 35th Street, a large pre-Civil War structure of dark-gray stucco. Here Alexander Graham Bell maintained the laboratory, now used as a garage, where he perfected the disk-graphophone.

CONVERTED SLAVE QUARTERS, 3410 Volta Place, behind the Melville Bell House, are now picturesque cottages, with rambler roses and many-paned windows.

YELLOW TAVERN, 1524 33rd Street, is a small house of brick in Flemish bond, painted bright red, with white trim and shutters. The graceful arched doorway, its threshold level with the sidewalk, is of exceptionally fine detail. The Yellow Tavern, sometimes called the White Horse, was one of the better-class inns that sprang up during the period of Georgetown's commercial importance and declined as Washington grew up beside the older town.

On the NW. corner of Volta Place and Wisconsin Avenue is the church of the oldest congregation in Georgetown, the gray-stone Gothic GEORGETOWN EVANGELICAL LUTHERAN CHURCH. About 1769, the Lutherans built a log church on this site, taking advantage of a deed made for this purpose by Beattie and Hawkins, for the development of Georgetown. The present church, built in 1914, is the fourth erected on the site.

Set back from the road, at 3215 Q Street is the red-brick building of the JEWISH FOSTER HOME, where more than 50 children are given a home and vocational training. Each child has a bank account, membership in the Jewish Community Center, and the privilege of attending the Home's summer camp.

The BOWIE HOUSE, 3124 Q Street, is set so high on its terrace as to be almost unnoticed from the street. The two-story brick mansion, in late Georgian style, was built about 1800 by Washington Bowie, godchild of George Washington, and of the same family as Colonel James Bowie, hero of the Alamo, and Colonel Rezin P. Bowie, inventor of the Bowie knife. Bowie lost his home in bankruptcy after the British had seized his large shipping interests during the War of 1812. In the central portion of the house, which is flanked by twin two-storied wings, is a baronial hallway with double staircase. Delicate plaster friezes, mahogany doors, marble mantels, and other interior furnishings and decorations represent the period. Mrs. John Sevier, the present owner (1942), intends the home to be a public museum after her death. She is the widow of John Sevier, direct descendant and namesake of the hero of King's Mountain, John Sevier, who became the first g 'ernor of Tennessee.

TUDOR PLACE, 1644 31st Street, aloof and beautiful on Georgetown Heights, is closely associated with the Washington family. Here Martha Parke Custis came in 1805, shortly after her marriage to Thomas Peter. In this great yellow-stucco mansion were entertained Lafayette, in 1825, on his last visit to America, the defeated General Lee in 1869, and all the notable families of the neighborhood. Designed by William Thornton, it is today, as it has been for more than a century, a house of individual charm, one of the finest early Federal houses in the District.

The twin two-story wings were built about 1794 by Francis Loundes, who intended to erect the main house between them later. In 1805 Martha Parke Custis purchased the unfinished house with money George Washington had left her. During the erection of the central portion, the family lived in the east wing, and, it is said, from a window in this wing Mrs. Thornton and Mrs. Peter, in 1814, watched the burning of the Capitol.

Thornton, an intimate friend of the family, redesigned the wings and designed the main house to fit between them. Before construction began, Thornton changed his original plans, which included a large oval room on the major axis of the house, a main entrance opening from the south portico, a grand stairway on the west side of the central hall, and a low third story behind an attic parapet. As finished in 1815 and as Tudor Place now stands, a small entrance hall takes the place of the oval room, the main entrance is on the north, the stairway is on the east side of the central hall, and there is no attic parapet.

The most prominent feature of the house, visible from Q Street, is the "temple" porch of the south entrance, a domed circular portico two stories in height. Half of this "temple" extends in a graceful semicircular colonnade in front of the building, and the other half, in the form of a niche with a triple French window, is recessed into the wide central hall.   The exterior of the house as a whole is characterized by Thornton's skillful handling of form and detail.

The north façade, overlooking the circular carriage drive and garden, set with boxwoods, is more severe than that of the south. Here, the main entrance door, framed by an untrimmed arch and surmounted with a delicate transom and wrought-iron lamp, is the most conspicuous feature.   At the east end of the house, formerly used as a stable, is a minor entrance with flanking iron railings and newel-post lamps.

The north entrance opens into a central hallway and a transverse hall across the north side.   In the angles of the T thus formed are spacious living rooms, the doors of which are of curly maple, polished to satiny sheen by more than a century of hand rubbing.   The delicate plaster friezes, the marble mantelpieces, and the wide plank flooring of these rooms remain unchanged.

Martha and Thomas Peter's daughter, Britannia, who inherited Tudor Place, married Commodore Beverly Kennon, who was killed in the explosion aboard the *Princeton*.   She died in 1911 at the age of 96.   Her daughter, Martha Custis Kennon, married a distant cousin, Dr. Armistead Peter, bringing the family name back to the old home, which has remained in the family for more than a century and a quarter.

The huge brass locks of Tudor Place have protected for generations a notable collection of the Washington family relics, among them Martha Washington's seed-pearl wedding dress and jewelry, a set of china made for President Washington by the French Government, a bowl presented him by the Order of the Cincinnati, his camp trunk used during the Revolution, and numerous paintings, miniatures, and letters.

A fairly modern house at the SE. corner of Q and 31st Streets stands on part of the FRANCIS DODGE FARM SITE. Here was the home of Francis Dodge, Sr., founder of one of Georgetown's prominent families, who controlled many of the city's large commercial interests.   Hammond Court, the gray stucco apartment on the SE. corner of Q and 30th Streets, was remodeled around the home of the oldest Dodge son, Francis, Jr.   At 28th and Q Streets is the Robert Dodge house.

DUMBARTON HOUSE, 2716 Q Street, maintained as head-quarters of the National Society of the Colonial Dames of America, is the only house of historical interest or architectural merit in Georgetown that is open to the public the year around (*open, free, 10-5 weekdays; 2-5 Sun.*).

A short distance west of the bridge that spans Rock Creek at Q Street, Dumbarton House stands on a rise of ground well above sidewalk level, a fine brick mansion trimmed in white, with a pillared porch approached by a long flight of recessed steps.   The central portion of the structure is symmetrically flanked by service wings.   Due to uncertainty as to its history, and because of the alterations and restorations that have been made, complete fidelity to any period is not claimed for Dumbarton, but many architectural and decorative forms, inside and out, are excellent examples of Georgian and early Federal styles. The reconstruction, as effected by the Colonial Dames, recreates domestic life in the United States between 1790 and 1810, in a characteristic house with authentic furniture.

The date of the building is uncertain, probably somewhere between 1780 and 1795; although a coin bearing the date 1805 was found imbedded in the wall of the main hall, a mason's record difficult to reconcile. Dumbarton is not on its original site; the name of the builder is in question; the house has been known as Bellevue, Rittenhouse Place, Dumbarton. Yet, for 100 to 150 years, it has preserved its identity and has been associated with many noted American families. The first owner of the site was Ninian Beall, who came to this country late in the seventeenth century and, in 1703, was granted a tract of land, which he named Rock of Dunbar-ton. Both spellings, Dunbarton and Dumbarton, occur in records of the Beall family. The plantation was willed by Ninian Beall to his son George in 1717 and remained in Beall ownership until 1796. It was then sold to Georgetown's Mayor, Peter Casanave, who resold it almost immediately to General Uriah Forrest. Samuel Jackson bought it in 1798, improved and enlarged it, and in 1799 sold it to Philip Fitzhugh. In the next decade, it changed hands several times; in 1805, it was sold for taxes to Gabriel Duvall, who resold it to Joseph Nourse, first Register of the Treasury. Nourse made several improvements and then sold the property to Charles Carroll, a relative of a signer of the Declaration of Independence. During his years of residence, the new owner proudly called himself "Carroll of Bellevue," and the house carried that name for a century. About this time, Latrobe designed a front portico for the house. Dolly Madison "tarried" at Bellevue for a time during the British raid in 1814. Passing from the Carroll family in 1841 to Mrs. Lydia Newbold Whital of Philadelphia, the estate was inherited by her daughter, a Mrs. Rittenhouse, and was known as Rittenhouse Place until 1890. The next owner, Horace Hinckley, sold it to the Newbold family, who made it their home until 1928, when it was purchased by the Colonial Dames and named Dumbarton.

For more than a century, the old house blocked the way from Q Street to Rock Creek. When, in 1915, it was decided to open Q Street and span the creek, John Newbold, the owner, had the house moved to its present site. The two wings and connecting corridors, having no cellars, were taken down and rebuilt in the course of the moving. In the reconstruction, the central portion of the structure was lowered and second stories added to portions of the wings, thus materially changing the original architectural composition.

Investigations by Fiske Kimball, consultant, showed that the house was much enlarged and improved during the late eighteenth and early nineteenth centuries, mainly by Samuel Jackson and Joseph Nourse. The Beall sale price to Mayor Casanave, $600, indicates that the house was not elaborate at that time, but, when sold for taxes in 1805, Government advertisements described "a very elegant house with two round rooms in the rear." In the restoration by Architect Horace W. Peaslee, Victorian mantels, French windows, wood quoins, and other incongruous elements of interior and exterior decoration were removed, and an approximation of the original porch and balconies achieved. The cornices of the main house were retained as milestones of its development. The Colonial Dames opened Dumbarton as a public museum of Colonial Americana during the Washington Bicentennial in 1932.

Dumbarton, as restored by Mr. Peaslee, is a typical late-Georgian building, with a central hall extending through the house and, on either side, two large rooms opening into each other and upon the hall, the front room nearly square, and the rear looking into the garden from circular bays—the two round rooms of the "very elegant house." The terraced garden contains flowers characteristic of Georgetown gardens of 1800. Its high brick wall with plastered panels features a terminal niche adapted from an English garden of the period. The interior has been furnished gradually under the supervision of Mr. and Mrs. Luke Lockwood and Mrs. Stephen Bonsel. Especially noteworthy are the delicate plaster cornices, revealed by tedious scrapings from their many coats of paint, and the fine collection of carved wood mantelpieces acquired during the restoration from various sources. All furnishings in the main part of the house are authentic Colonial pieces made between 1780 and 1810, gifts of members of the society and associated with many of the oldest families in the United States. On the second floor are displayed china, bric-a-brac, and costumes that belonged to General and Mrs. Washington, Mrs. Thomas Law, Dolly Madison, George Mason of Gunston Hall, Lord Fairfax, and other notable persons. Portraits by Peale and Stuart hang in the dining room and parlor.

The National Society of Colonial Dames of America, organized in 1891, is an association of women who trace their descent from a resident in an American Colony before 1776. The work of the society includes the restoration of the old church at Jamestown, Virginia, building of the granite-columned canopy over Plymouth Rock; restoration and maintenance of Sulgrave Manor in England, home of the Washington family; erection of a memorial in Arlington National Cemetery to American soldiers of the Spanish-American War; and custody of Gunston Hall in Virginia, home of George Mason.

From Dumbarton House, the shortest route back to Washington is by way of Q Street over DUMBARTON BRIDGE. The 5 full-center arches of the bridge, the series of corbeled arches that support the overhanging walks, the solid stone balustrade, and the solidity of the reinforced concrete construction are all reminiscent of a Roman aqueduct, as the designers, Glenn Brown and his son Bedford, intended.

The 35-foot roadway has a 7-foot walk on either side. Four massive bronze bisons, the work of A. Phimister Proctor, stand guard at the approaches. On the Washington side, the bridge enters the residential section, only a block from Massachusetts Avenue and Sheridan Circle.

Pennsylvania Avenue

Streetcars: Eastbound—Kenilworth (on Pennsylvania Ave., 29th NW. to 15th NW.), Union Station (29th NW. to 1st NW.), 17th & Penna. SE. (29th NW. to 17th SE.), Navy Yard (14th NW. to 8th SE.), Navy Yard via N. J. Ave. and Navy Yard via Fla. Ave. (1st SE. to 8th SE.). Westbound—Rosslyn (15th NW. to 29th NW.), Cabin John, and 36th & Prospect NW. (15th NW. to 29th NW.), Washington Circle (15th NW. to 23rd NW.), Friendship Heights (17th SE. to 29th NW.), 14th & Colorado and 14th & Decatur (8th SE. to 14th NW.), Calvert Bridge via N. J. and Calvert Bridge via Fla. (8th SE. to 1st SE.).
Busses: Operate between 1st and 13th Streets, NW. and between 15th and 19th Streets NW.
Taxis: First to fourth zones.

Pennsylvania Avenue extends in a northwesterly direction from the District Line, across the Anacostia River on the John Philip Sousa Memorial Bridge, and then, through its famous central section between the Capitol and the White House, to a point in Georgetown just west of Rock Creek—a distance of about 7 miles. The Anacostia section, between the District Line and the river, has developed as an attractive residential area, especially upon the Anacostia heights.

The steel-arch bridge, dedicated to the "March King," was constructed by the District and completed in 1940. The $2,000,000, six-lane structure, designed by Parsons, Klapp, Brinkerhoff, and Douglas, architects, is 1,590 feet long and has an overall width of 72 feet. Its broad sweep, with 6-foot walks on either side, and illuminated by a line of lights by night, is in harmony with the upper stretches of the Avenue.

Between the White House and the Capitol, connecting the executive with judicial and legislative branches of the Government, Pennsylvania Avenue is rich in historic association, traditions, and sentiments; no other mile of American roadway has provided the setting, over so long a period, for such a pageant of national pomp and ceremony. The inaugural parade of every President since Jefferson, and the funeral processions of the four Presidents who died in office, have followed this course; Lafayette and Kossuth and many other distinguished foreign guests, the King and Queen of England and other crowned rulers, have been acclaimed here; the homecoming armies of three wars have received tumultuous welcome as they marched along the Avenue.

Thomas Jefferson, in a letter written in November 1791—3 months after L'Enfant had drawn up his plan for the "Federal City"—is believed to be the first to refer to Pennsylvania Avenue under that name. In L'Enfant's plan, the main diagonal avenue was to ex-

376

tend from the Anacostia River to Georgetown along the line of three chief points—the "Federal house," the "President's palace," and a "grand square" at what is now Washington Circle. In his report of 1791, accompanying the L'Enfant plan, President Washington wrote: "The Grand Avenue connecting both the palace and the federal house will be most magnificent & most convenient." But at the time when this report was written and for several years thereafter, the "Grand avenue" was no more than a footpath cut through a tangled growth of trees and bushes along the marshy border of Tiber Creek. During the winter of 1800-01, a clearing the full width of the projected avenue was made through this wooded morass, from the Capitol to 15th Street; and the city commissioners began construction of a flagstone walk along the north side of the clearing, with ditches to carry off the water from side streets and a stone bridge over Tiber Creek where it crossed the avenue at Second Street. A rude "corduroy" road was later built in the center of the avenue, with logs "piled in to fill up the mudholes and miry places along the route."

Jefferson, during his second term as President, planted four rows of Lombardy poplars, through which the roadway ran in three lanes. Under foot it remained a veritable slough until 1833, when Congress provided for grading and macadamizing an 80-foot central roadway, removing for this purpose the inner rows of Jefferson's poplars and substituting elm trees for those in the outer. A stone arch replaced the earlier bridge over Tiber Creek, and this remained until the stream was confined to an underground tunnel.

The early development of the "Grand avenue" was chiefly residential until about 1825. Then the substantial red-brick dwellings began to be converted into boarding-houses and shops, while hotels sprang up all along the thoroughfare. After the middle of the century, Pennsylvania Avenue from the Capitol to 9th or 10th Street steadily deteriorated into a blighted region of saloons, gambling dens, lodging houses, quick-lunch rooms, cheap-jack shops, and catch-penny amusement places. Then came the great regeneration in the first quarter of the present century. Most of the old buildings on the south side of the Avenue between the Capitol and the Treasury, and for several blocks on the lower north side, were demolished; park areas were laid out, and the ambitious Triangle development begun (*see Federal Triangle*).

Within the original city limits, Pennsylvania Avenue began at Commodore Barney Circle SE., named for the officer who made a valiant stand against the British at the Battle of Bladensburg. The Sousa Bridge, which carries the Avenue eastward over the Anacostia River, replaced an older one erected in 1890.

POINTS OF INTEREST

Just northeast of Barney Circle is the CONGRESSIONAL CEMETERY, or old Washington Parish Burial Ground, 18th and

E Streets SE., about 30 acres on the north bank of the Anacostia. It was established in 1807 by a group of private citizens, who, five years later, turned it over to Christ Church. In 1816 a committee selected 100 burial sites for the interment of members of Congress, and the grounds were known thereafter as the Congressional Cemetery.

Near the main entrance on E Street is the superintendent's lodge, and just to the east are some of the oldest graves. Among those buried in the cemetery were Elbridge Gerry, a signer of the Declaration of Independence; George Clinton, first governor of New York; Secretary of State Abel Upshur; Attorney General William Wirt; Major Generals McComb, Brown, and Gibson; Commodores Ridgley, Patterson, Tingey, and Rodgers; diplomats from foreign countries; 16 Senators and 68 members of the House. (The remains of 12 Congressmen and of Governor Clinton have since been removed to their home States. President Zachary Taylor, John C. Calhoun, and Dolly Madison also were temporarily buried here.) Push-Ma-Ta-Ha, Choctaw Indian chief who fought under Jackson in the Pensacola campaign, died of diphtheria in Washington in 1825, while negotiating a treaty between his people and the United States. His grave is near those of William Thornton, George Hadfield, and William Elliott—three figures prominent in the architectural history and general development of the Capital. Here, too, lie the bodies of 21 young women who perished in the explosion of the Federal Arsenal during the Civil War, and the bodies of victims of the disastrous fire aboard the steamer *Wawaset* on the Potomac in 1873.

The memorial to Elbridge Gerry, one of the most striking in the cemetery, is a truncated pyramidal shaft surmounted by an urn and flame, the work of W. and J. Frazee. A shaft resembling an Indian totem pole commemorates Major General McComb. A small but exquisitely proportioned exedra stands above the grave of John Philip Sousa, native of Washington, who died in 1932. Between 1838 and 1877 the Government erected memorials to Senators and Representatives who had died in office, and this group of ungainly sandstone cenotaphs is conspicuous. After Senator Hoar of Massachusetts, in 1877, told the Senate that the prospect of being interred beneath one of these atrocities added a new terror to death, Congress decided against erecting any more.

Between 9th and 10th Streets SE., on the south side of Pennsylvania Avenue, stands the OLD UNITED STATES NAVAL HOSPITAL, built in 1861, and which, from 1911 to 1922, served as headquarters for the Naval Reserve. Since the later year it has been used as a temporary lodging place for veterans of the naval and military services.

At the southwest corner of 9th Street is the SITE OF TUNNICLIFF'S TAVERN. The date of its erection is uncertain, but it was operated as a tavern in 1793, and William Tunnicliff seems to have acquired the place in 1796. It was torn down in 1932.

Pennsylvania Avenue traverses an open square between 9th and 7th

Streets SE., intersecting with South Carolina Avenue at its center. On D Street facing the north side of the square is the Wallach Public School, built during the Civil War and still in use. Two blocks south of the Avenue, between 8th and 9th and G and I Streets SE., are the MARINE BARRACKS (*see Along the Waterfront*). A block west of the barracks, on G Street between 6th and 7th, is the Protestant Episcopal CHRIST CHURCH. The building, erected in 1807, has been much restored.

The MAPLES (*open*), 619 D Street SE., a rambling white-painted brick house, was built in 1797, by William Wayne Duncanson, "during whose residency General George Washington was his guest." Since 1937, the old house, with numerous additions, reconstructions, and changes, has been known as "Friendship House," a day nursery for children of employed mothers.

At the close of the Revolution, a woodman's cabin stood on some part of Maple Square. William Wayne Duncanson, a tobacco planter, acquired a plantation extending far beyond its borders and built a frame house, which was enlarged in 1796. Lavish entertainment, brought Duncanson to poverty, and in 1809 the estate passed into the hands of trustees, one of whom was Francis Scott Key. Owner then succeeded owner. In 1846, Captain A.A. Nicholson gave up the house after the suicide of his wife. Under the next owner, Senator John M. Clayton of New Jersey, extensive alterations were made in 1858. It is thought that the original frame house still stands encased within the thick walls erected about this time. The east wing was added for use as a ballroom. Brumidi, the Italian artist whose frescoes in the Capitol were perhaps the first painted in America, decorated the high ceiling and walls, but much of the plaster covered with his work has fallen.

Mrs. Emily Edson Briggs, a relative of George Mason of Gunston Hall and distinguished as the first woman admitted to the White House Press Room, bought the Maples in 1871 and added a few more rooms. Mrs. Briggs had won her reputation as a war correspondent, writing under the name of "Olivia," during the administration of President Lincoln.

Facing the southwest corner of Seward Square, between 6th and 4th Streets SE., is TRINITY METHODIST CHURCH. As successor to the Ebenezer M. E. Church, organized in 1802, this is the oldest Methodist congregation in the city.

At its junction with B Street, between 3rd and 2nd Streets SE., opposite the Library of Congress Annex, Pennsylvania Avenue temporarily loses its identity. From this point its traffic is carried on Independence Avenue to 1st Street SW., then north on this thoroughfare a short distance to the Peace Monument (*see Along The Mall*), where it resumes its northwesterly course.

The most important section of Pennsylvania Avenue begins just opposite the northwest entrance to the Capitol grounds, at 1st Street, NW. Two blocks north, at 101 Indiana Avenue, is the HOME

OWNERS LOAN CORPORATION BUILDING (*open 8:30-5:30 Mon.-Fri., 8:30-12:30 Sat.*), where Albert Stewart's eight sculpture reliefs on the building trades are an attraction to visitors. From 1st Street to the old Ford Building on the right and the National Gallery of Art on the left, nothing but park space adjoins the thoroughfare on either side. This denuded region was long one of the most thickly settled portions of the city. The earliest building erected here, a coachmaker's two-story frame shop and home, put up about 1799, stood just east of 2nd Street, on the north side of the Avenue. Washington's first railway station was built on the northwest corner of 2nd Street in 1835, when the Baltimore & Ohio Railroad entered the city.

Most of the city's earliest inns and hotels were on the Avenue between the Capitol and 7th Street. Notable among these was the St. Charles, known in later years as the New Capitol Hotel, on the northeast corner of 3rd Street. It was built soon after the British invasion in 1814, and some columns from the burnt Capitol went into its 3rd Street entrance. In addition to sheltering a number of noted statesmen—Jackson, Calhoun, Clay, Webster, Van Buren, and others—it was a favorite rendezvous for Indian chiefs on missions to "the great white father."

Two other old hostelries also stood at the 3rd Street intersection. That on the northwest corner was one of three early hotels known as Gadsby's, its proprietor in the forties being a son of the John Gadsby who founded the National Hotel. Made's Hotel, on the southwest corner, was opened in 1848 by a Swiss immigrant.

Jacksons' Hall, a three-story brick building wherein President Zachary Taylor's inaugural ball was held, stood from 1845 until the late 1930's on the north side of the Avenue, west of 3rd Street; the *Congressional Globe,* forerunner of the present *Congressional Record,* was published in this building. Nearly adjoining it was the United States Hotel, popular around the middle of last century; and across the Avenue was Brenner's boarding-house, where Chief Justice Roger B. Taney and two Associate Justices of the Supreme Court lived for several years.

The next intersection west of 3rd Street was at the thoroughfare which long bore the designation of Four-and-a-half Street, later John Marshall Place, and now a part of the Municipal Center development. The land centering on old John Marshall Place, between Third and Sixth Streets, from Pennsylvania Avenue north to Indiana Avenue, is all to be occupied by the Municipal Center (*see Downtown*).

From about 1834 to 1855, a "select boarding house" stood at the northwest corner of John Marshall Place and was patronized by Clay, Calhoun, Justice Story, Chief Justice Marshall, and other notables of the time. Later it was remodeled and occupied by Fritz Reuter's restaurant, noted for its German cooking and its wines.

Farther along in the same block was the Rockendorff House, a famous gambling resort; it was torn down in 1860. At the end of the block, on the northeast corner of 6th Street, stands the last surviving structure of the central Avenue's early years—the old National Hotel, a square five-story building of whitewashed brick, marked by two commemorative tablets. Among its distinguished guests were Horace Mann, Alexander H. Stephens, Thaddeus Stevens. Henry Clay died here in 1852. The first proprietor of the National, largest hotel of its time in Washington, was John Gadsby, whose name is associated with the old Franklin House, two or three other local hostelries, and the noted tavern in Alexandria.

Across 6th Street, just beyond the northwest corner, is a site devoted to hotel purposes for a century and a quarter. Here, as early as 1802, stood Woodward's Center Tavern, torn down a few years later to make way for Davis' Hotel—rechristened the McKeown Hotel about 1815, and the Indian Queen in 1820. Under the latter name, derived from a colorful portrait of Pocahontas on its signboard, it flourished for several decades as the city's most popular hostelry. At the Indian Queen (or Brown's Hotel), John Tyler was sworn into office as President after William Henry Harrison's death in 1841; and here the Hungarian statesman, Louis Kossuth, and his retinue of armed guards were guests in the winter of 1851-52. A later hotel, the Metropolitan, stood on this site for about 75 years.

In the narrow triangular plot between Pennsylvania and Constitution Avenues, from 7th to 6th Streets NW., is the Apex Building, which houses the Federal Trade Commission. The southeast corner of the Avenue at 6th Street, long occupied by the St. James Hotel, lies within the end of the Triangle (*see The Federal Triangle, for descriptions of all governmental buildings on the south side of the Avenue from the Apex Building to Fifteenth Street*).

The block east of 6th Street was the scene of a famous conflict on July 28, 1932, when World War veterans in the "Bonus Army" billeted in the vacant buildings here were driven out by United States troops. In one of these old buildings on the north side of the Avenue, Walt Whitman occupied a wretched third-floor bedroom for several months in 1864. Here also was the most popular of Washington's mid-century gambling places, conducted by one of the Virginia Pendletons.

At 7th Street, Pennsylvania Avenue enters a plaza formed by the intersection of several thoroughfares. A canopied Victorian "temperance fountain" stands at the right of the Avenue, where C Street enters; and a little to the north and west of this is a memorial (J. Massey Rhind, sculptor) erected in 1909 by the Grand Army of the Republic in honor of that organization's founder, Dr. B.F. Stephenson. Just across 7th Street stands Henry Ellicott's equestrian statue of General Winfield Scott Hancock.

For more than 125 years the south side of this plaza, between 7th and 9th Streets and extending back to B Street, was the site of the Center Market—demolished in 1931 to make way for the National Archives Building.

The Department of Justice Building fills the entire block between 9th and 10th Streets NW. Near the 9th Street corner, from Civil War days until the 1930's, stood a theater building known most recently as "the old Bijou." Just beyond 9th Street on the opposite corner was the Iron Hall, another old theater, later called Metzerott Hall.

At 10th Street, where the Avenue also intersects D Street NW., is an open area, with a STATUE OF BENJAMIN FRANKLIN, by Ernest Plassman, standing at its center. On the northeast corner of 10th and D Streets was once the home of Peter Force, publisher, editor, historian, and mayor of Washington from 1836 to 1840; his garden was a beauty spot of old Washington.

Opposite the 10th Street plaza, a wing of the Internal Revenue Building extends from 10th to 11th Streets, and just west of this, between 11th and 12th Streets, is the Old Post Office Building.

The Washington Theater, built by public subscription, was opened in 1805 at the northeast corner of 11th and C Streets, just north of the Avenue. After its partial destruction by fire 15 years later, the building was remodeled and opened in 1822 by Louis Carusi as a dancing academy, with a public ballroom and dining room, under the name of Carusi's Assembly Rooms or the City Assembly Rooms—a later designation being Carusi's Saloon. For a third of a century this was the smartest of the Capital's public social resorts. Most of the inaugural balls from John Quincy Adams' in 1825 to James Buchanan's in 1857 were given here. Soon thereafter, the building was reconverted to use as a theater.

On the northeast corner of 12th Street is the RALEIGH HOTEL, erected in 1893. The block on the south side between 12th and 13th Streets is occupied by the Post Office Department Building. At 13th Street, the Avenue enters an open area officially bounded, both north and south, by E Street. In a triangular bit of park near the 13th-Street side, somewhat above street level, is the bronze equestrian STATUE OF COUNT PULASKI, Polish hero of the American Revolution. The statue, erected in 1910, is the work of the Polish sculptor, Casimir Chodzinski.

The NATIONAL THEATER, 1325 E Street NW., Washington's oldest theatrical institution, has occupied six successive buildings on this site since 1835. On the southern side of the plaza, just west of 13th Street, is a large brown-brick building housing the Farm Credit Administration. Two hotels have stood on the site of this building: one, the old Prescott House, where political prisoners were held during the Civil War, and the other, the Globe Hotel, dating from about 1827.

In a small triangular plot between E Street and the Avenue and between 13th and 14th Streets, stands a bronze statute of the second and last governor of the District and a prime mover in Washington's physical regeneration, Governor Alexander R. Shepherd. His statue, done by U.S.J. Dunbar, was unveiled in 1909.

At the northwest corner of 14th Street is the WILLARD HOTEL, a relatively new building on a site occupied by Willard's since 1850. The best known of the hostelries that stood here between 1818 and 1850 was Fuller's or the City Hotel, the favorite resort of prominent visitors to Washington in the 1840's. Then Henry Willard and his brother took over the management, and their name has been identified with the hotel ever since. Close to Willard's is the well-known OCCIDENTAL HOTEL, with its autographed collection of photographs of distinguished patrons. On the northeast corner at 15th Street is the WASHINGTON HOTEL, near the site of a much earlier hotel of the same name. The 10-story structure was designed by Carrère and Hastings.

At 15th Street, opposite the south end of the Treasury, Pennsylvania Avenue makes a "jog," then continues from the north end of the Treasury. Carl Rohl-Smith's equestrian STATUE OF GENERAL WILLIAM T. SHERMAN stands in the square of parkland between 15th Street and the White House grounds.

From the point where it resumes its course at the north end of the Treasury, Pennsylvania Avenue runs due west to 17th Street. Along this section are the Treasury, the White House, and the State Department Building, on the left, and Lafayette Square on the right (*see President's Square*). Inaugural parades are reviewed from a stand on the south side of the Avenue, in front of the White House.

At the 15th Street corner, the Old State Department Building stood on the site now occupied by the north wing of the Treasury. The opposite or northwest corner was the site, early in the nineteenth century, of the Bank of the United States; and just west of this stood the first Department of Justice Building. The Treasury Annex occupies the northeast corner at Madison Place, opposite Lafayette Square.

On the north side of the Avenue beyond the square, the first building is an old residence housing offices of the Carnegie Endowment for International Peace. Then come the historic Blair House and the Lee Mansion, No. 1653, where Andrew Johnson lived during his term as Vice President. On the northeast corner at 17th Street is the original Corcoran Art Gallery, where from 1873 to 1897 the art collection of W.W. Corcoran was on public display; the mansarded red-brick building, notable for a certain Victorian dignity, is now occupied by the United States Court of Claims.

At 17th Street, the Avenue resumes its diagonal northwesterly course to the neighborhood of Washington Circle, traversing what was for a long time the city's most select residential neighborhood— the old "west end." The State, War, and Navy Departments had their first separate Washington headquarters on this upper section of Pennsylvania Avenue. At the southwest corner of 17th and H Streets, is the METROPOLITAN CLUB, for many years the wealthiest and most fashionable of Washington's social clubs. The fine old mansion at 1710 H Street NW., just west of the Metropolitan Club, was built by Dr. Benjamin Rush, a signer of the Declaration of Independence; among its later occupants was Rear Admiral David D. Porter.

The modern building on the southeast corner of Pennsylvania Avenue at 18th Street was formerly occupied by the Interstate Commerce Commission. The modern building of similar size on the southwest corner is occupied by the Federal Power Commission. Across the Avenue is the Roger Smith Hotel, formerly known as the Powhatan.

Between 18th and 19th Streets, with H Street as both northern and southern boundary, is a large square. On the southeast corner of 19th and H Streets is a small brick building, the museum and meeting place of the ASSOCIATION OF OLDEST INHABITANTS, organized in 1865. Once used by a volunteer fire-company house, the building still bears the inscription "Union Engine Institution— 1815." It was assigned by act of Congress to the Association of Oldest Inhabitants and to the Volunteer Firemen's Association, but, since the death of the last volunteer fireman in 1935, it has been the property of the Oldest Inhabitants. The Museum contains fire-fighting equipment and the surveyor's chain used in laying out the streets of Washington. Visitors are welcome, but the building is closed during most of the winter.

Beyond 19th Street, from 1901 to 1913 Pennsylvania Avenue NW., still stand the timeworn and much-remodeled "Seven Buildings," dating back to about 1800. Many prominent Government officials, foreign ministers, and private citizens have lived in this row. The corner building housed the State Department when John Marshall was Secretary; Vice Presidents Elbridge Gerry and Martin Van Buren were later occupants; and Major General George B. McClellan had headquarters here in 1861.

From 20th to 21st Streets are two small triangular parks, where L'Enfant intended to have one of his "five grand fountains." The old Western Market, one of Washington's busiest trade centers from 1802 until it was destroyed by fire in 1852, occupied the northeast corner of this area, facing 20th and I Streets. Near this intersection stood the Union Chapel Hospital of Civil War times. At the southeast corner of 21st and K Streets is the present Western Market, erected in 1893.

Peggy O'Neale, of Jacksonian days, lived at 2007 I Street for several years after her marriage to John H. Eaton. A few doors beyond, at 2017 I Street NW., is a large three-story house where James Monroe lived while Secretary of State, later while Secretary of War under Madison, and for the first 6 months of his own Presidency. Charles Francis Adams, Minister to Great Britain 1861-68, and Dr. Cleveland Abbe, a founder of the United States Weather Bureau, were later residents of this house, which now serves as headquarters for the ARTS CLUB. The house, in the late Georgian style, red Flemish-bond brick with white stone trim, is well preserved and its architectural detail unchanged, except for the dormer windows of the attic story. The arched entrance doorway, a reproduction of which is the Arts Club insignia, is of exceptional merit, crowned by a finely molded keystone and architrave. The solid paneled door, painted a light blue-green, is accompanied by narrow sidelights and surmounted by a delicate transom rail and large fan transom. At the rear is a walled garden, bright with flowers in the summer, where club members often dine.

The land on which the building stands was part of the Widow's Mite, a large tract patented by John Langworthy in 1664. In 1802, Timothy Caldwell bought a small strip facing I Street and built a house here, well back from the street and facing east. On an additional frontage, Caldwell built, probably between 1805 and 1808, the house now occupied by the Arts Club. The older house serves as a wing for the I Street house.

At the northeast corner of 21st and I Streets NW., facing Pennsylvania Avenue, stood one of the Capital's most prominent early hostelries, the Franklin Hotel, built in 1812 by William O'Neale, who for some 15 years had conducted a tavern in the same block. It was during their frequent stays at this hotel that Andrew Jackson and Senator Eaton came under the spell of O'Neale's daughter, Peggy, the beautiful and romantic girl Eaton afterward married and Jackson gallantly defended during his Presidency. Among other distinguished Southern guests of the house were John C. Calhoun and John Randolph of Roanoke; Lafayette stayed here while on a visit to the Capital in 1824, when the hotel was owned and managed by John Gadsby. The building was converted into dwellings in 1828, and known as Gadsby's Row or McBlair's Row until torn down about 1905.

Across 21st Street, at the northwest corner of the Avenue and extending westward, is the site of a historically important row known as the "Six Buildings," erected late in the eighteenth century and torn down in the early 1930's. The "Six Buildings" comprised the numbers on Pennsylvania Avenue from 2107 to 2117. The first Washington offices of the Navy Department and the first separate offices in Washington of the State Department were in this row. Among the distinguished residents here were James Madison (while Secretary of State under Jefferson) and General Sam Houston, hero of San Jacinto and the first Senator from Texas. Nearly opposite, on the Avenue's south side, stood the first Washington headquarters of the War Department.

WASHINGTON CIRCLE, at the intersection of Pennsylvania and New Hampshire Avenues with K and 23rd Streets, is one of the most attractive of the city's smaller "breathing areas." At its center stands a bronze equestrian STATUE OF GEORGE WASHINGTON, designed by Clark Mills and unveiled in 1860; the face was modeled from Houdon's celebrated bust, and the uniform was copied from one known to have been worn by Washington. The region of Washington Circle was known in early days as "Round Tops"—"a misnomer for the octagon cupolas surmounting the high roofs of two brick dwellings northwest of the present Circle." A part of the building now occupied by ST. ANN'S INFANT ASYLUM and Maternity Hospital, on K Street between the Circle and 24th Street, dates back to the early 1820's. Just west of Washington Circle, at K and 24th Streets, was the Circle Hospital of Civil War time.

The building and grounds of COLUMBIA HOSPITAL FOR WOMEN occupy the block between 24th and 25th Streets facing L Street, close to its intersection with Pennsylvania Avenue. Just north of the hospital, facing on M Street, is the Administration Building of the UNITED STATES WEATHER BUREAU, which houses various units of the bureau.

ST. STEPHEN'S CHURCH (Roman Catholic), established in 1865, stands on the southeast corner of the Avenue at 25th Street. At 2618 and 2620 K Street NW., a block or so south of the Avenue's intersection with 26th Street, stand two attached three-story dwellings that were prominent in the city's early social and political life. They were built about 1795 for Thomas Peter, who married Martha Washington's granddaughter, Martha Parke Curtis. Mr. and Mrs. Peter resided at No. 2618, the PETERS MANSION, for several years, and George Washington was a guest here on the last night he spent in the Capital (Aug. 5, 1799). In 1803 the buildings were leased to the British minister, Anthony Merry, with whom the poet Thomas Moore stayed while on his visit to the city in 1804. Merry's two immediate successors in the British diplomatic service, David Erskine and Francis Jackson, also resided here.

Just beyond the 26th Street intersection, Pennsylvania Avenue crosses Rock Creek and Potomac Parkway into Georgetown and continues to its western terminus at M and 29th Streets (*see Georgetown*).

Massachusetts Avenue

Streetcars: Operate for short distances only on Massachusetts Ave.; parallel or cross-routes provide transportation to or near points between 9th St. NW. and 14th St. NE.
Busses: 18th & Penna. NW. (eastbound) and Wis. & Fessenden (westbound) busses operate on Massachusetts Ave. between Connecticut Ave. and 49th St., except between Wisconsin and Nebraska Aves.
Taxis: First to fourth zones.

Massachusetts Avenue, the longest of Washington's thoroughfares, extends entirely across the District—a distance of 10 miles—with the exception of about three-fourths of a mile, where its course is broken by Anacostia River and Park and the grounds of Gallinger Hospital. East of the Anacostia stands Fort Dupont with baseball and horseshoe pitching grounds, and a growing residential area, with apartment houses and shopping centers.

For at least half a century, Massachusetts Avenue was the "farthest north" of anything that could properly be called the city of Washington. "An act to Prevent Swine from Going at Large," passed by the city council in 1809, confined its interdiction to "any part of this city south of Massachusetts Avenue." The greater part of the Avenue within the city limits long consisted of a rough wagon track, with stepping-stones at the intersections of cross streets. By 1850 the section between Stanton and Mount Vernon Squares was fairly well built up, and there was an occasional dwelling west of 9th Street NW. After Alexander R. Shepherd's herculean grading, sewer-installing, and tree-planting operations of the early seventies, the Avenue began to share the marked northwestern trend of fine residential building. By the nineties the section above Thomas Circle was a popular site for wealthy home builders, and for embassies and legations. Though it has suffered from the trend of fashion toward other districts, the upper half of the Avenue remains one of the most distinctive and beautiful of Washington's residential thoroughfares.

West of the Anacostia River, Massachusetts Avenue begins at 19th Street SE., opposite the grounds of Gallinger Hospital, a municipal institution for the care and treatment of indigent patients, psychopathic and contagious cases. Within the same grounds, to the north, stands the antiquated red-brick building of the District Jail, where Charles J. Guiteau was hanged in 1882 for the assassination of President Garfield. Adjoining the Gallinger Hospital grounds on the southwest is the old Congressional Cemetery (*see Pennsylvania Avenue*).

POINTS OF INTEREST

From 19th Street the Avenue runs westward between neat rows of small houses until interrupted by LINCOLN SQUARE, extending from 13th to 11th Streets, and centering on East Capitol Street. Developed about 1870, the square is notable for trees and shrubs. Near its center stands the EMANCIPATION MONUMENT, a bronze figure of President Lincoln holding in his right hand the Proclamation, his left hand resting on the shoulder of a crouching Negro whose shackles have been broken. The statue, executed by Thomas Ball and unveiled in 1876, was paid for by the voluntary subscriptions of emancipated Negroes.

Massachusetts Avenue continues through a section of small apartment houses and residences, past the Ingram Memorial Congregational Church at 10th Street NE., and the Casualty Hospital at 8th Street. One of the city's more important social service agencies, the Christ Child Society has its headquarters and maintains a settlement house at No. 608.

From 6th to 4th Street, the Avenue is interrupted by STANTON SQUARE (named for Lincoln's Secretary of War), which, though smaller than the one dedicated to Lincoln, has almost as much variety in its planting. A bronze equestrian statue of GENERAL NATHANAEL GREENE, Revolutionary hero of Rhode Island and presiding officer at Major André's trial, stands at the center of the square. The work of Henry Kirk Brown, it was erected in 1887.

At 1st Street NE., the Avenue enters a spacious semicircular plaza, before UNION STATION (*see Capitol Hill*).

A little north of the Avenue, the historic group of red-brick buildings known as DOUGLAS ROW stands on the NW. corner of 2nd and I Streets NW. The houses, built for Stephen A. Douglas, Henry M. Rice, Senator from Minnesota, and John C. Breckenridge, Vice President in Buchanan's administration, were taken over by the Government during the Civil War and used for hospital purposes. Number 201, originally occupied by Douglas, was later the Papal Legation. Numbers 205-207 were occupied at various times by Douglas, and after the Civil War by Ulysses S. Grant, William T. Sherman, and Matthew G. Emery, the first mayor of Washington after Governor Alexander R. Shepherd's term expired.

Between 2nd and 7th Streets NW. are rows of old and more or less shabby buildings. At the intersection with K Street, Massachusetts Avenue is interrupted by MOUNT VERNON SQUARE, in which stands the white marble Public Library (*see Downtown*). The square is the site of the old Northern Liberties Market, scene of the bloody "Know Nothing" riots of 1857. During Alexander R. Shepherd's drastic clean-up in 1872, the market stalls were demolished.

The seven-story building on the NW. corner at 9th Street houses the central offices of the AMERICAN FEDERATION OF LABOR. Beyond 10th Street, on the north side of the Avenue, is the bronze

GOMPERS MEMORIAL, designed by Robert Aitken and erected in 1933 by the Federation in tribute to its former president. The MOUNT VERNON PLACE METHODIST CHURCH, facing the Public Library (in the triangle formed by the junction of the Avenue and 9th and K Sts. NW.), was built in 1917 to replace the old church erected during the Civil War. The present stone structure, with broad steps leading to a high colonnaded portico, was designed by Sauginet and Staats, architects of Fort Worth, Texas. It was completed at a cost of $500,000—most of which was raised by Southern Methodists throughout the South. The congregation was formed in 1869 from a group of small churches and missions established between 1851 and 1863 to promote the doctrines of the Southern branch of the Methodist Episcopal church. The Southern branch had been organized following a schism on the slavery question. Mount Vernon Place Church, the South's Representative Church, has the largest membership among Protestant churches in Washington, and one of the finest choirs. The Education Building, just west of the church, completed in 1940, contains classrooms, a social hall, and the chapel in which the "Children's Church" is conducted Sunday mornings at 11 o'clock.

Just east of 12th Street, among the trees of a small triangular park, is the EDMUND BURKE STATUE, presented to the United States by the Sulgrave Institute of England; the bronze figure is a copy of one by Havard Thomas in Bristol, England. At the NW. corner of 12th Street rises the great limestone mass and soaring spire of the CHURCH OF THE ASCENSION (Episcopal), erected in 1874.

The neighborhood around the intersection of Massachusetts Avenue and 13th Street NW. was long known as Nighthawk Hill, possibly because of the number of nighthawks killed here in early days. Number 1312 Massachusetts Avenue is the headquarters of the National Catholic Welfare Conference, established in 1919.

At 14th Street, where the Avenue intersects Vermont Avenue and M Street, is THOMAS CIRCLE, with J.Q.A. Ward's spirited bronze EQUESTRIAN STATUE OF MAJOR-GENERAL GEORGE H. THOMAS in its center, and four Camperdown elms within the circle. The memorial was erected in 1879 by the Society of the Army of the Cumberland. The Thomas Circle underpass, completed in 1940, was built at a cost of $530,000 to relieve traffic congestion at an intersection crossed daily by 50,000 automobiles. The tunnel is 420 feet long, and with the approaches the total length of the underpass is approximately 1,000 feet.

The NATIONAL CITY CHRISTIAN CHURCH, of the Disciples of Christ, looks down upon the circle from the NW. corner of 14th Street and the Avenue. This fine structure, faced with Indiana limestone, was designed by John Russell Pope and completed in 1930 at a cost of $1,000,000. Rising above the gabled pediment of the Ionic portico, the well-proportioned tower, 200 feet above street level, culminates in a lantern cupola surmounted with a gilded finial. In the tower are automatically controlled Westminster chimes of a four-manual organ.

Arched piers and Tuscan columns support the richly coffered ceiling and frame the tall, gracefully arched windows. Two of these are memorial windows by Nicola D'Ascenzo, with a border of colorful medallions offset by an area of clear glass. The semicircular chancel of marble, choice fabrics, and softly burnished wood, is under a half-dome supported by columns of St. Genevieve marble. To the left is the pulpit, set with inlaid panels of Italian Cremo marble and at the right is the baptistry of marble matching that of the pulpit. In the center of the chancel is the communion table, with a carved walnut screen as a background. The screen, which conceals the console organ, portrays *The Last Supper,* carved by Alois Lang.

On the opposite side of 14th Street is the spired red-sandstone LUTHER PLACE MEMORIAL CHURCH, built a few years after the Civil War in thanksgiving for national peace and unity. In front of the church and facing Thomas Circle stands a bronze STATUE OF MARTIN LUTHER, a copy of the figure by Rietschel in the Reformation Monument at Worms. The old, red-brick, flatiron-shaped Portland Hotel, on the south side of the circle, the oldest of Washington's apartment hotels, has had many distinguished residents. A much older landmark, the Judge Andrew Wylie house, stands east of the Circle between M Street and Vermont Avenue.

Along the north side of the Avenue, between 14th and 15th Streets NW., there is a decided rise, and this block is known as Highland Terrace (the houses bear Massachusetts Avenue numbers). Between the houses and the stone wall that borders the sidewalk is a narrow roadway. The red-brick GERMAN EMBASSY stands near the middle of the block, No. 1439. Many distinguished persons have lived on both sides of the Avenue between 14th and 15th Streets, including Lucius Q.C. Lamar and Samuel F. Miller, Associate Justices of the Supreme Court, and Thomas F. Bayard, onetime Ambassador to Great Britain.

The LOUISE HOME, a red-brick building on a rise of ground at the SW. corner of 15th Street, was established a few years after the Civil War by W.W. Corcoran, as a residence for indigent aged gentlewomen of Southern birth. The home is a memorial to Corcoran's wife and daughter, both of whom were named Louise.

The BELL-MORTON HOUSE, around the corner at No. 1500 Rhode Island Avenue NW., was occupied by Alexander Graham Bell, who sold it in 1889 to Levi P. Morton, Vice President under President Benjamin Harrison. From 1903 to 1907, as the residence of Count Cassini, Russian Ambassador to the United States, it was the scene of some of the most lavish entertainments in the city. Elihu Root, Secretary of State under President Theodore Roosevelt, occupied it from 1907 to 1909, and John Hays Hammond lived here for two years. Thereafter Morton reoccupied the place until his death in 1920, when it was taken over by his daughter, Mrs. Edith M. Eustis. It was occupied by Ogden L. Mills, Secretary of the Treasury under President Hoover, until 1931, when Mrs. Eustis again lived here for five years. In 1936 the National Democratic Club rented it as District of Columbia headquarters. In 1940, The National Paint, Varnish and Lacquer Association bought and took possession of this famous old house, the scene of so many gay social events and political gatherings.

Centering treeless SCOTT CIRCLE, at the joint intersection of Massachusetts and Rhode Island Avenues and 16th and N Streets NW., stands the bronze equestrian STATUE OF GENERAL WINFIELD SCOTT, by Henry Kirk Brown. The figure, erected in 1874, was cast from cannon captured in the Mexican War. In a triangle just east of and facing the circle is the HAHNEMANN MEMORIAL, designed by Charles Henry Neihaus in collaboration with Israels and Harder, architects. It was erected in 1900 by the American Institute of Homeopathy in honor of S.C.F. Hahnemann (1775-1843), founder of the homeopathic school of medicine. A STATUE OF DANIEL WEBSTER stands among the trees of a small triangular park on the west side of the circle; the bronze figure was designed by Gaetano Trentanove and cast in Italy. This statue was presented to the city in 1900 by Stilson Hutchins, who lived for many years in the house at 1603 Massachusetts Avenue, just across from the Webster statue. An underpass carries 16th Street traffic under the Circle (see Sixteenth Street).

The red-brick PERUVIAN EMBASSY, on the northwest corner of 16th Street NW., was formerly the home of William Windom and James G. Blaine. On the west side of the circle, at No. 1615 Rhode Island Avenue, is the home of Gifford Pinchot, chief of the Forest Service during the Taft administration. At No. 1746 Massachusetts Avenue is the stone and brick CANADIAN LEGATION, and at 1780 is the handsome BELGIAN EMBASSY, with its Chancery across the street at No. 1777. Next to the Canadian Legation is the old FORCE SCHOOL attended by the sons of Theodore Roosevelt; in the schoolyard is a tree planted in memory of Quentin Roosevelt, killed in France during the World War.

Of special interest to the literary student are the first Washington homes of Thomas Nelson Page, at 1708, later occupied by the composer Reginald DeKoven; and the house at 1770, built by Mrs. Frances Hodgson Burnett in the late eighties, with the book and play royalties from Little Lord Fauntleroy. Fairmont School, at 1711, one of Washington's older finishing schools for girls, was once the home of Henry A. Dupont, Senator from Delaware. At No. 1719 is a Roman Catholic day school for boys and girls, conducted by the Convent of the Sacred Heart. Henry Cabot Lodge, Senator from Massachusetts, made his home for 25 years at No. 1765.

At 1801 Massachusetts Avenue NW., filling most of the triangular area between P Street west of 18th, is the Sulgrave Club, a women's organization with a limited associate membership of men. The large red-brick house at the southwest corner of 18th Street was once the home of Melville W. Fuller, Chief Justice of the Supreme Court

(1888-1910), and later of Charles W. Fairbanks, Vice President under Theodore Roosevelt. At 1535 18th Street is the PANAMA EMBASSY.

DUPONT CIRCLE, at the joint intersection of five important thoroughfares—Massachusetts, Connecticut, and New Hampshire Avenues, and 19th and P Streets—was originally called Pacific Circle. The name was changed in 1884 when Launt Thompson's bronze statue of Rear Admiral Samuel F. Dupont was erected by Congress at the center of the circle. The statue was replaced in 1921 by a stone fountain, a gift of the Dupont family. In the niches on the three sides of the marble shaft, supporting a shallow upper bowl, are sculptured seminude figures—symbolizing Sea, Stars, and Wind—the work of Daniel Chester French. The composition is , completed by three streams of water from the surmounting bowl.

The first important residence in this once supremely fashionable area was that of Senator William M. Stewart of Nevada, built in 1874-75 on the site now occupied by a branch of the Riggs National Bank, between Massachusetts and Connecticut Avenues at the west side of the circle. This was popularly known in its time as "Stewart's Castle" or (because of its then rather remote situation) "Stewart's Folly." It served as the Chinese Legation for some time before its demolition in 1901. Among the few remaining old houses on the circle, the three most imposing are on the northeast side. At 15 Dupont Circle is the mansion designed by Stanford White and erected in 1902 for Mrs. Robert Wilson Patterson, whose daughter, Mrs. Eleanor Medill Patterson (owner of the Washington *Times-Herald*) now lives there; President Coolidge and his family occupied the house for a few months in 1927, while the White House was undergoing repairs. Next to it, at 1501 New Hampshire Avenue, is the residence of Mrs. Robert R. Hitt, widow of the Illinois Congressman; it was designed by John Russell Pope and built in 1909. At 1500 New Hampshire Avenue is the home of Mrs. Joseph Leiter, widow of the Chicago "Wheat King." Streetcar tracks were laid west of the circle, local people say, so that the noise would not disturb the occupants of these palatial houses.

At 1521 New Hampshire Avenue is the NICARAGUAN LEGATION. Number 1526, formerly the home of John W. Weeks, Secretary of War under Harding and Coolidge, is occupied by the WOMEN'S NATIONAL DEMOCRATIC CLUB; the ARGENTINE EMBASSY is at 1600; Rear Admiral William T. Sampson, of Spanish-American War fame, lived and died at No. 1613; No. 1618, once the home of O.H.P. Belmont, onetime Minister to Spain, is used as international headquarters of the Grand Chapter, Order of The Eastern Star.

Just east of Dupont Circle on P Street NW., at the northwest corner of 18th, is the residence of Miss Mabel Thorp Boardman, for many years secretary of the American Red Cross. To the northeast and diagonally across 18th Street stands ST. THOMAS CHURCH, a granite structure with central tower and spire. President and Mrs.

Franklin D. Roosevelt are members of this Episcopal congregation, organized in 1891. A little farther north on 18th Street, at No. 1614, is the GUATEMALAN LEGATION.

The first thoroughfare crossing Massachusetts Avenue west of the circle is 20th Street. On the NW. corner are the local headquarters of the Junior League, housed in a modern building, with a bookshop on the street floor. On the opposite corner is the once-impressive JAMES G. BLAINE MANSION, erstwhile home of the "plumed knight" of American politics; it was later occupied by Levi Z. Leiter and George Westinghouse. The nineteenth-century elegance of the house (now occupied by Government offices) is emphasized not only by the functional little building opposite but more crudely by the grocery store against its rear wall. Number 2009 Massachusetts Avenue was the home of Nicholas Longworth, Speaker of the House from 1925 until his death in 1931; Mrs. Longworth, the former Alice Roosevelt, is in residence there.

Another of Washington's former show places is the WALSH MANSION, 2020 Massachusetts Avenue NW. Built in 1902-03 by Thomas F. Walsh, of Colorado, at a cost of $835,000, this house was for a long time the acme of luxury and ostentation. King Albert and Queen Elizabeth of Belgium were entertained here by Vice President and Mrs. Thomas R. Marshall. Now its grandeur is the setting for the activities of the Red Cross Roll Call, the Red Cross Surgical Dressing Unit, and, more appropriately, of the Washington Civic Theater.

Just north of the triangle formed by the intersection of Q and 21st Streets is the PHILLIPS MEMORIAL GALLERY (*open, free, 11-6 weekdays, 2-6 Sun., Oct. to June*), 1600 21st Street NW. The gallery, installed in the former home of the family for which it is named, retains an atmosphere of comfort and hospitality. The collection of modern art is one of the best in America. The gallery was incorporated in 1918 by Duncan Phillips to commemorate the lives of his mother, father, and brother. From the start the purpose of the gallery has been educational. Works of art are not simply exhibited, but are interpreted by contrasts and comparisons. The four-story brick mansion is entered from a small porch and doorway opening into a reception hall. To the right is the main gallery and to the left are smaller galleries. Opposite the entrance a staircase leads to exhibition rooms on the second floor and in the basement. In the Gallery School of Art, instruction is based on the principles and resources of the Phillips collection.

The record of development in art begins, in the Phillips collection, with a limestone head from the ruins of Tel-el-Amarna, a holy city of the Eighteenth Dynasty in ancient Egypt. Its significance is explained by Director Phillips: "Our exquisitely sensitive and realistic portrait in stone is not out of place in the midst of modern paintings, no less marked by sensibility and simplification. It was a challenge in its day to the Academies of Egypt just as these paintings are a challenge to our arbiters of art."

Another major influence on modern art is El Greco, represented in the collection by *The Repentant Peter*. In this masterpiece El Greco's conception of the Biblical narrative is expressed in a composition of somber hues, brilliant interplay of light and dark, and sharply distorted forms. Modern artists, claiming him as one of their own, accept his imaginative space relationships, and draw upon his devices of arbitrary lighting, dissonant tones, and exaggerated shapes. Here, too, in one of the largest groups of Daumiers in the world is the *Uprising*, the weighty image of an oppressed people at their moment of attack against tyranny. More reflective in conception and more expressive of his humor and tenderness are *On a Bridge at Midnight* and *Three Lawyers*. Vincent van Gogh, another artist who opposed the Philistinism of his day and startled the art world with his blazing broken colors and crude rhythmic patterns, is represented by his *Garden at Arles*. Two men from whom Van Gogh drew heavily, Delacroix and Monticelli, may be seen respectively in *Paganini* and *As You Like It*. Impressionism, based on theories of light refraction, is represented by Manet's *Ballet Espagnol* and other works. Claude Monet, another impressionist, is represented by his *Basket of Fruit*. Renoir, with the grand-scale *Le Déjeuner des Canotiers,* one of his most important canvases, and Bonnard, with *Le Midi* and *The Palm,* have a significant place in the collection.

Cézanne's *Mont Saint Victoire* and *Self Portrait* exemplify the artist's epoch-making structural handling of color and space. Indebted to Cézanne is the work of that many-sided and prolific genius, Pablo Picasso; the gallery has his cubist *Abstraction,* with its angular planes in a two-dimensional pattern, and his poetic *Early Morning*. Allied to the painting of Picasso are abstractions by George Braque, *Still Life* and *Round Table,* and the arrangement of simplified forms in low relief, called *Plums, Pears, Nuts, and Knife*.

Akin to these European moderns are the works of Maurice Sterne, of which the gallery has *The Reapers, Afternoon at Anticoli,* and *Still Life*. Two other outstanding artists represented in the collection are Ryder and Marin. To the world of his day Albert Pinkham Ryder was an eccentric gentleman in miserable circumstances who toiled years on end over small and unprepossessing canvases. But later generations have acclaimed him for his poet's imagination and his original grasp of plastic design. The work of Ryder has been critically compared by Director Phillips with that of the important French realist and romantic, Courbet. Comparison in the gallery might begin with the *Rocks at Ornans* and *Mediterranean,* by Courbet, studied in relation to Ryder's *Moonlit Cove, Fishermen's Huts,* and *Resurrection*. John Marin, in his *Sunset, Rockland County* and *Back of Bear Mountain,* shows his original handling of the problems of design. His water colors, which may seem at first sight capricious and obscure, reveal themselves as architecturally constructed and of undeniable clarity.

The purity of his wash has been praised by Virgil Barker, the critic, as worthy of ancient Chinese masters.

Matisse, whose aim has been to paint with the unspoiled vision of a child and whose technical bases are the color and calligraphy of the Orient, is represented by *Torso, Poppies and Mirror,* and *A Path at Nice.* Here also are the mystical conceptions of Redon and Tack, romantic figure and landscape paintings of Eilshemius, an example of the chromatic vision of Constable, a portrait head in bronze by Maillol, and one in plaster by Despiau. Other fine pieces are the luminous *Ballet Rehearsal* by Degas; *The Pink Candle* by the Parisian primitive, Rousseau; the *Landscape in Southern France* by Derain; a monumental color composition, the *Circus Performers,* by Rouault; an emotional color pattern developed from a landscape view by Dove; color and tonal arrangements by O'Keefe; sensitively colored compositions by Knaths, and paintings by Burchfield, Segonzac, Weber, and a number of younger Americans.

A series of lectures on the appreciation of art is delivered each season by Duncan Phillips and others. Phillips publications and collections of prints are available for further study.

The house at Q and 21st Streets, directly opposite the Phillips Gallery, was once occupied by Theodore Roosevelt, Jr., former Governor of Puerto Rico and of the Philippines; later it was the home of Dwight Morrow, Ambassador to Mexico (1927-28), and Senator from New Jersey at the time of his death in 1931.

At 2121 Massachusetts Avenue NW. is the town house of Sumner Welles, Under Secretary of State and owner of the historic estate, Oxon Hill, in Maryland. The town house, reminiscent of an eighteenth-century chateau in its spacious grounds, was designed by Carrère and Hastings of New York. The large stone house at 2118, once the residence of Lars Anderson, Minister to Belgium and Ambassador to Japan, is the national headquarters of the Society of the Cincinnati, an order formed by officers of the Revolutionary Army in 1783.

Florida Avenue, which long marked the city's northern limits, enters Massachusetts Avenue from the northeast and terminates here at the 22nd Street intersection. The historic Kalorama section extends north and west from this point to Rock Creek (*see Connecticut Avenue*). Beyond 22nd Street the avenue swings around SHERIDAN CIRCLE, which is entered by R Street from the east. At the center of the circle, set low in a ring of Norway maples, is the bronze equestrian STATUE OF GENERAL PHILIP H. SHERIDAN, designed by Gutzon Borglum and erected in 1909. On the north side of the circle, at 2247-49 R Street NW., is the SWEDISH LEGATION; at 2221 Massachusetts Avenue is the GREEK LEGATION; at No. 2301, the EGYPTIAN LEGATION; and at 2315, the IRANIAN (Persian) LEGATION. The TURKISH EMBASSY occupies a large mansion on the southwest corner of 23rd Street; opposite, on the southeast corner, is the RUMANIAN LEGATION. At 2349 Massachusetts Avenue is the CZECHOSLOVAKIAN LEGATION. The LUXEMBOURG LEGATION is at 2200 Massachusetts Avenue.

At 23rd and Q Streets is the eastern entrance to DUMBARTON (or Q STREET) BRIDGE over Rock Creek into Georgetown, sometimes called the "Buffalo Bridge." A pair of bronze bison, designed by A. Phimister Proctor, stands at each end of the bridge.

East of the circle on R Street NW. are several notable residences: No. 2223 is the home of Charles Evans Hughes, former Chief Justice of the Supreme Court; at 2131 Franklin Delano Roosevelt made his home while Assistant Secretary of the Navy under Wilson; and No. 2101 was the home of William Jennings Bryan while he was Secretary of State under Wilson.

The TEXTILE MUSEUM OF THE DISTRICT OF CO-LUMBIA (*open, free, 2-4 Mon., Wed., Fri.; adm. by card only*), 2330 S Street NW., was founded in 1925 by George Hewitt Myers, to house his collection of textiles. The museum, formerly a private house, contains a remarkable collection of Persian (eleventh to eighteenth centuries) and Egyptian (fourth to thirteenth centuries) tapestries and textiles; Indian (sixteenth to ninteenth centuries) and Peruvian (pre-Columbian) textiles and printed cloths; Greek Island and Asia Minor embroideries (sixteenth to nineteenth centuries), and Spanish textiles (thirteenth to sixteenth centuries). The exhibits are changed from time to time.

On S Street NW., at No. 2340, a short distance from the avenue, is the WOODROW WILSON HOUSE, where the ex-President lived for nearly three years before his death in 1924. From the balcony of this house he made a brief speech on Armistice Day in 1923, three months before his death. The DANISH LEGATION is at No. 2343. The house at 2300 S Street was the residence of Herbert Hoover during his term as Secretary of Commerce under Harding and Coolidge.

The former home of Mary Roberts Rinehart is at 2419 Massachusetts Avenue NW., and at 2445 Massachusetts Avenue is the modernistic VENEZUELAN EMBASSY.

The JAPANESE EMBASSY, 2514 Massachusetts Avenue NW., was designed by Delano and Aldrich in neoclassic style. With the exception of the conventional decoration above the first-floor windows, the exterior suggests in no way the architecture of Japan. The interior, while designed in the spirit of the French Empire, reflects the Far East in the ancient wall hangings, in the effectual use of flat surfaces, and in sharp color contrasts. The interior has a transverse corridor with a spiral stairway, a walnut-paneled smoking room, and a state dining room with walls of robin's-egg blue.

A short distance west of the Japanese Embassy the Avenue crosses Rock Creek over the one-span stone MASSACHUSETTS AVENUE BRIDGE, completed in 1941, and, passing through a park-like area the greater part of the way, rises gradually to Wisconsin Avenue. The BRAZILIAN EMBASSY (office at 3007 Whitehaven Street), at No. 3000, is a good example of modified Italian Renaissance design. At

No. 3003 Massachusetts Avenue NW. is the residence of Alanson B. Houghton, former Ambassador to Germany and to Great Britain; and at No. 3012 is the home of James J. Davis, Secretary of Labor under Harding and Coolidge and now (1942) Senator from Pennsylvania.

The BRITISH EMBASSY, 3100 Massachusetts Avenue NW., largest of the foreign diplomatic establishments in Washington, was designed by Sir Edwin Lutyens and completed at a cost of approximately $1,000,000. Standing in a characteristically English setting, the Embassy with its red-brick walls trimmed with white stone, its steep roofs and towering chimneys, recalls an English manor of the Queen Anne period. Within, eighteenth-century baroque architecture is effectively combined with the appointments of a modern country house. Portraits of British monarchs, crystal chandeliers, marble pilasters and cornices, beautifully paneled woodwork, cabinets of rare Chinese objects, and chintz draperies and chair covers contribute to the general effect.

Almost opposite the British Embassy is the LEGATION OF THE UNION OF SOUTH AFRICA. One of the most imposing structures on the Avenue is the three-story APOSTOLIC DELEGATION, at No. 3339, designed in modified Italian Renaissance style.

The Avenue takes a long curving course around the grounds of the United States Naval Observatory on the left, with the wooded ravine of Normanstone Parkway on the right. Near the end of this arc, at No. 3401, stands the NORWEGIAN LEGATION. East of the Parkway, at 2881 Woodland Drive, is the BULGARIAN LEGATION.

The NAVAL OBSERVATORY (*closed during national emergency; ordinarily open 10 a. m.-2 p. m.; adm. at night by card only; children under 10 not admitted*), operated under the Bureau of Navigation of the Navy Department, is the official Government establishment charged with the collection of data for navigational astronomy, the determination of standard time (the Observatory stayed on Eastern Standard Time even when the Nation changed to War Time in 1942), and the repair of navigational instruments. More than 50 buildings, including many one-room instrument houses, are scattered over the wooded 72-acre plot. The clock vaults, occupying the center of the 1,000-foot Observatory Circle, are amply protected from noise disturbances. The two-story Administration Building, near the Massachusetts Avenue entrance, houses offices, library, and laboratory; adjoining it are a shop and quarters for astronomers and an observatory housing the 26-inch telescope. The other instrument houses, including that for the 40-inch telescope, are detached structures. In the northeast section of the circle is the residence of the Chief of Naval Observation; the rest of the personnel, including naval officers and civilians, have quarters off the grounds.

William Lambert, an amateur astronomer, urged Congress to establish a national observatory in 1809, but nothing came of the effort. A naval depot of charts and instruments, started in 1830, formed the base on which the Naval Observatory grew. With borrowed instruments and those furnished by naval astronomers themselves, the "observatory" continued unofficially until it was first named as such in the Secretary of the Navy's report in 1841. Finally, seven years later, Congress made an appropriation, and the first observatory was built at the present site of the Old Naval Medical Center. By the time it removed to its present site in 1893, the Observatory had taken rank with other international institutions such as the Greenwich Observatory in England and the Russian Observatory at Pulkowa—a rank it has since maintained. The LIBRARY of the Naval Observatory contains the best collection of astronomical works in this country.

Beyond the Observatory grounds, Massachusetts Avenue resumes its gradual ascent and, one block before reaching Wisconsin Avenue, it skirts the grounds of the CATHEDRAL CHURCH OF SS. PETER AND PAUL—also known as Washington Cathedral, and the National Cathedral.

Inspired by the precepts of fourteenth-century Gothic architecture, the Cathedral Church, seat of the Protestant Episcopal Diocese of Washington, ranks even in its present unfinished state among the great ecclesiastical structures of the country. Situated on a magnificent site, 400 feet above the Potomac, its towering silhouette dominates the northwestern section of the city. After 35 years of construction the cathedral is not half completed; yet the strength and power of the whole are already manifest. The scale of the work, the sense of sound construction and carefully studied detail, are evident in the great choir and the side chapels with their pinnacled buttresses and huge masonry walls. Few churches other than its prototypes of medieval France and England will surpass it, when completed, either in beauty of design and workmanship, or in sheer magnitude. Commanding an almost unrivaled view of Washington, Mount St. Alban, a tract of 58 acres, affords a superb setting for the cathedral. The Cathedral Close, containing the Bishop's house, a memorial library, and a number of schools and other buildings, is artistically landscaped.

In 1893 Congress granted a charter to the Protestant Episcopal Cathedral Foundation, empowering it to establish and maintain a "cathedral and institutions of learning for the promotion of religion and education and charity." The Right Reverend Henry Yates Satterlee, first Bishop of Washington, chose the present location on Mount St. Alban in 1898. In 1907 preliminary plans for the Cathedral, drawn by George F. Bodley of London and his pupil, Henry Vaughan of Boston, were accepted, and the foundation stone was brought from Bethlehem and laid at a ceremony during which President Theodore Roosevelt delivered the address of dedication. Vaughan continued the work alone upon Dr. Bodley's death soon after. Ground was first broken in 1908. After Vaughan's death nine years later, the work was carried on by the architects, Frohman, Robb and Little, who have made necessary revisions. Guided by the principles and traditions of fourteenth-century Gothic architecture, they have employed the methods of construction developed during the Middle Ages and introduced in the rich carvings and stained-glass windows the symbolism and artistry that reached its height just before the Renaissance. Following the traditional cruciform plan, the apse, choir, and nave form the shaft of the cross, while the north and south transepts serve as the arms.

Built on a somewhat larger scale than was originally contemplated, the Cathedral will take its place among the ten largest ecclesiastical structures in the world. Two square towers, 220 feet high, will flank the main entrance on the west (Wisconsin Ave.) façade, while a taller central tower will rise 285 feet above the crossing. The total length of the building, is 525 feet; the total width, at the transepts, is 275 feet. The west façade, with its deeply recessed porch, will resemble the front of Canterbury Cathedral. The large rose window above the main west portal represents the *Seven Days of Creation*. A large octagonal bapistry, one of the outstanding features of the Cathedral, will be erected at the northwest corner. This baptistry with its radiating buttresses will open from the west end of the north aisles and is to contain the Jordan Font.

The north and south transepts will be virtually identical. Each will have a great portal, a triforium or gallery above the side aisles, and a rose window. The north transept entrance is protected by a deep arcaded porch, while the south transept entrance, set between two massive turrets, will be framed by a deeply recessed arch with rich carving. The latter will form a monumental entrance to the Cathedral from the Pilgrim Steps. On the north side a long Gothic cloister will connect the Cathedral with the future Chapter House and Administration Building.

The design of the interior will embody the same lightness, grace, and richness of detail which characterize the general mass of the exterior. Like the latter, the rectilinear character and treatment of its details will conform to the English Gothic. In addition to the major elements of the plan—the great apse with its sanctuary, the choir with its long side chapels, the transepts, the nave, and the baptistry—there are numerous memorial chapels and others set apart for private prayer and devotion. Three chapels are in the crypt and four others are completed on the main floor. There will be 32 side aisle niches down the length of the nave. The nave, with its double side aisles, triforium galleries, and lofty clerestory walls above, with long stained-glass windows, will extend 9 bays west of the crossing and will measure 100 feet from floor to ceiling vault.

The entire eastern end of the Cathedral is structurally complete, as are the north transept, the north transept porch, the crossing, the crypt and foundations of the whole Cathedral, the east aisle of the south transept, and part of the north cloister. An architect's model of the finished Cathedral is in the curator's office at the west end of the Cathedral foundations.

The Bethlehem Chapel, dedicated to the Nativity, was the first portion of the building completed. Begun in 1908, it has been used for daily service since 1912. The chapel is entered by way of the south crypt aisle and outer south portal—the Benedictus Doorway. Under the stained-glass windows, which depict the Messianic prophets, are many historic stones: one from a tomb in the Appian Way, presented by St. Paul's Church in Rome; another from the church built when Columbus, on his second voyage, established the city of Isabella on the Island of Santo Domingo. In niches of the south wall are memorial tablets to Henry White, a trustee of the Cathedral and former Ambassador to France, and his wife. They are the work of Daniel Chester French. The interior of the chapel, designed in Norman-Gothic style, offers in the simplicity of its slender columns and vaulted ceiling a striking contrast to the highly ornamental chancel and altar executed in the later Perpendicular mode. The decorative sculptures of the reredos screen behind the altar and the stained-glass windows of the ambulatory or vaulted passage behind the chancel, both of exceptionally fine workmanship, tell the story of the birth of Christ.

Following the precedent established in Westminster Abbey, many of the Nation's illustrious dead will be entombed in the Cathedral. In the ambulatory is the alabaster tomb of Bishop Satterlee, to whose memory the chapel was dedicated. The tomb was designed by W. Douglas Caroe, resident architect of Canterbury Cathedral. A marble slab in the center of the chapel floor marks the burial vault of Woodrow Wilson, Admiral Dewey and his wife, Bishop Claggett, Melville Stone (founder of the Associated Press), and others. The cenotaphs of Admiral Dewey and President Wilson are placed in deep wall niches in the north and south chapel aisles.

The Chapel of St. Joseph of Arimathea, under the great crossing of the Cathedral, is an impressive twelfth-century crypt-chapel, dedicated in 1929. Its walls are formed by four giant corner piers, 26 feet in diameter, which rise through the vaulted ceiling to support the proposed central tower. The design of this chamber, with its heavy Norman columns and massive ribbed arches, is expressive of the simplicity and vigor of early English medieval architecture. The chapel altar and the communion rail are of Celtic design. A mural painting on the east wall by John Hendrick De Rosen, *The Entombment of Christ,* symbolizes the Good Friday message. Under the chapel floor is a vault which holds the body of Dr. William H. Wilmer, noted ophthalmologist of Johns Hopkins University. This chapel has been allocated by the Cathedral Chapter as a memorial to Canon Walden Meyer and his sister, Gertrude Walden Meyer.

The Chapel of the Resurrection, a stylized Norman chapel completed in 1929, in the crypt of the south transept, has been set apart for private devotions and is approached through a long thirteenth-century antechapel, the windows of which reveal the 9-foot thickness of the outer walls. The simple massive interior produces an effect of seclusion and solemnity. To the right of the chancel arch is the elaborately carved cenotaph of the Right Reverend Alfred Harding, second Bishop of Washington.

The Nave Crypts, two of the longest crypt corridors in the world, extend 275 feet under the north and south aisles. Stairways at the west end of the corridors lead to the north and south nave aisles on the main floor.

The Apse, which includes the sanctuary, was the second portion of the Cathedral completed. Its octagonal plan and radiating or chevet vaulting, reflecting French influence, are the most radical departures from the English Gothic in the entire Cathedral. The walls at the east end, rising 147 feet above the Bethlehem Chapel, form a magnificent screen behind the altar and reredos. Below their high clerestory windows are the traceried arcades of the triforium gallery. The angels carved on the arcades are by Sichi and Fanfani. Two long windows in the north and south walls are designed with the theme of the *Te Deum,* the work of Earl Edward Sanborn. The high altar, called the Jerusalem Altar because it is built of 12 stones from Solomon's quarry in Jerusalem, is inscribed with words from the New Testament recording the Crucifixion, Burial, Resurrection, and Ascension. A gift from 70 dioceses, missionary jurisdictions, and congregations of the Episcopal Church, it was consecrated in 1902 before any building had begun. The lofty *Ter Sanctus* (Thrice Holy) reredos, rising behind the high altar, is richly carved with a delicate cresting and canopies and about 100 niched figures, by Angelo Lueldi.

On the north side of the sanctuary is the Glastonbury Cathedra, or bishop's chair, made of stones from Glastonbury Abbey, the church in which, according to legend, King Arthur and Queen Guinevere were buried.

The Choir, the third part of the Cathedral to be completed and opened to the public since 1932, consists of five bays lying to the west of the Apse. The clerestory windows, by Earl E. Sanborn and Lawrence B. Saint, depict the *Apparition of the Angels.* The sculptured angels on the choir arch at the west end are by John Earley. The choir furnishings include carved oak stalls with accommodations above for a concealed orchestra, the principal organ, a carved choir screen, and the Canterbury Ambon or pulpit made from stones of Canterbury Cathedral and sculptured under the direction of W. Douglas Caroe. The pulpit is the gift of the Archbishop, Dean, and Chapter of Canterbury.

In the north choir aisle is the Chapel of St. Mary, set apart for women. A soft light enters the chapel through the fine stained glass of the parable windows, by L.B. Saint. The five corresponding bays of the south choir aisle are occupied by the Chapel of St. John, dedicated as a memorial to Norman Prince, a young American aviator who founded the Lafayette Escadrille and later met his death on the Western Front in 1916.

The Chapel of the Holy Spirit, a small corner chapel between the Chapel of St. Mary and the north transept, was completed in 1936. Enclosed by an exceptionally fine grille, it has been designated as a place of private prayer and devotion. The chapel contains a colorful wood reredos in the form of a triptych portraying the figure of Christ and the descent of the Holy Spirit. The painted and gilded panels were executed by N. C. Wyeth. The chapel window, designed by Nicola D'Ascenzo, recalls the story of Christ talking to the woman of Samaria.

Corresponding to the Chapel of the Holy Spirit, but on the south, is the Children's Chapel, completed in 1936, one of the two Cathedral chapels in the world designed especially for children. Of intimate scale and appropriately decorated, it provides a friendly atmosphere for young people. The symbolic decorations and statues were chosen to arouse a child's interest—the statue of Christ standing with open arms, the colorful figures in the reredos, and the carved squirrels in the molding.

The north transept is structurally complete. Above the transept gallery are a traceried arcade, three memorial windows, and a magnificent rose window, by L.B. Saint, which tells the story of the *Last Judgment*. The south transept, only partially completed, corresponds in plan and general detail with the north transept. The rose window above the portal will represent the *Church Triumphant*.

The Cathedral Close is being developed in harmony with the medieval atmosphere of the whole, with cloisters and old world gardens set with ivy, boxwood, yew, thorn, holly, cedars of Lebanon, rare Norman and Gothic fragments from ruined monasteries.

From the Lych Gate, Wisconsin Avenue entrance, a road curves past St. Alban's Church to the Bishop's House. St. Alban's Parish Church, one of the earliest buildings erected on Mount St. Alban, recalls in its low rambling mass the parish churches of rural England. The Bishop's House, erected in 1913, was designed by Henry Vaughan, in the Tudor manner.

At one side is the Bishop's Chapel of the Annunciation. A little farther along is the Cottage Herb Garden, its box-bordered plots fragrant with hundreds of tiny flowerpots containing herbs, ivy, slips of famous shrubs and trees, to be sold to visitors for the benefit of All Hallows Guild. Near the Herb Garden is the Bishop's Garden, enclosed by a high stone wall in which is set a twelfth-century Norman arch brought from France. Through the gate is a view down the terraced southern slope, broken by flagstone walks and boxwood hedges into several inner gardens—the Rose Garden, the Perennial Walk, Hortulus, the Spring Garden, the Yew Walk.

The Pilgrim Steps, a stately flight of 51 steps, 40 feet wide, broken by three broad landings, descend from the south transept of the Cathedral to the Amphitheater and woods below. The copings are overhung with huge boxwoods more than 200 years old. The massing of the colors is held here each year on the Sunday before Memorial Day under the auspices of the Military Order of the World War. In the Sylvan Amphitheater, south of the Bishop's Garden, as many as 7,500 persons can attend the outdoor services. Up a slight rise from the Amphitheater is the Peace Cross, erected in 1898 to mark the site of the Cathedral and commemorate the ending of the Spanish-American War.

The College of Preachers, fronting on Woodley Road, erected in 1929 and designed by Frohman, Robb, and Little, is the only institution in the church for post-ordination training of clergy. The irregular mass of the building, with its turreted tower, spacious refectory, and long dormitory wing, introduces an informal note at the north approach to the Cathedral. The Memorial Cathedral Library ultimately will adjoin the College of Preachers, and these two buildings, with the adjacent Chapter House, Administration Building, and Guest House, will form a harmonious architectural group at the east side of the Apse.

St. Alban's School for Boys, at the southwest corner of the Cathedral Close, is a boarding and day school, established in 1909 by the Protestant Episcopal Cathedral Foundation of the District of Columbia. It was founded through a bequest of President Buchanan's niece, Mrs. Harriet Lane Johnston, and is administered by a committee of which the Bishop of Washington is president. The Lane-Johnston Building, erected in 1904, and the Lower School Building, added in 1929, form with a connecting cloister, an impressive group of rustic stone buildings of English medieval architecture. The school offers an 8-year preparatory course for college. Athletic fields extend south of the lower school.

The main building of the National Cathedral School for Girls, in the northwest corner of the close, was erected in 1894. The school was founded by the first Bishop of Washington as an integral part of the Cathedral Foundation. The neoclassic design of the building is related to the original scheme for the National Cathedral, which was classic in conformity with the early architecture of the Federal City.

West of Wisconsin Avenue, Massachusetts Avenue begins a gradual descent through a district of apartment houses and Colonial-type dwellings. For a short distance, just before and beyond its intersection with Arizona Avenue, it forms the northern boundary of Glover-Archbold Park.

The CHILDREN'S MUSEUM OF WASHINGTON (*open 3-5 Tue.-Fri., 11-5 Sat., 2-5 Sun.*), 4215 Massachusetts Avenue NW., is housed in a square three-story pink-stucco mansion with a red-tile roof, set in landscaped grounds. A sign on the north side of the avenue indicates the entrance, which is not conspicuous in a tree-grown expanse.

Exhibits are placed in first- and second-floor hallways and in spacious upstairs rooms. Not entirely in cases, they are informally arranged, at a level where they can be seen and touched by children, as a mounted Andean condor, largest of flying birds, whose plumage may be stroked. Changing exhibits include dolls, figurines, carvings, pottery, stamps, models of native houses of foreign lands, minerals, textiles, art work by and for children, and whatever else is in demand by the young patrons of the museum. Small loan cases can be borrowed and taken home for a week's study, like books from a library. The museum is perhaps most refreshing because its program has not crystallized, still depending on the requests and suggestions of child patrons for exhibits and instruction. A class in tinning has been organized, and other classes—in nature study, astronomy, stamps, plastic arts—will be started as the need develops for them. A balustraded terrace at the second-floor level is used for showing motion pictures.

Opened on Washington's Birthday, 1942, the museum is the spiritual descendant of the Brooklyn Children's Museum, first in the country, organized in 1899, and of the WPA Children's Art Gallery of Washington, first in the Nation, which existed from 1937 to 1942.

From WARD CIRCLE (with its bronze STATUE OF ARTEMAS WARD, the Revolutionary general, by Leonard Crunelle), at the intersection with Nebraska Avenue, to WESLEY CIRCLE, at 46th Street NW., the avenue skirts the 90-acre campus of the College of Liberal Arts of AMERICAN UNIVERSITY. The university, which has a downtown center at 1901-07 F Street NW., is coeducational and has a total enrollment in all departments of nearly 1,900, with a faculty of more than 100. Though historically connected with the Methodist church and maintaining church affiliation to the extent that two-thirds of its board of trustees must be members of that denomination, the university is free from sectarian bias in teaching and administration. In 1891, Bishop John Fletcher Hurst began the campaign for funds that made possible the purchase of the Nebraska Avenue site. The University was incorporated by act of Congress in 1893, and under Bishop Hurst's leadership a board of trustees was organized. Five years later the first building, Hurst Hall, was erected on the campus, and in 1902 a second structure, McKinley Hall, was begun. Both stood vacant until America entered World War I, when the university officials turned over to the Government the disused campus to serve as a training base for the Gas and Flame Division of the Army. Here chemists discovered the deadly lewisite gas. Graduate instruction at a temporary downtown center was inaugurated on May 27, 1914, with an address by President Woodrow Wilson. Dr. Albert H. Putney, who had been Chief of the Near Eastern Division of the State Department, was in charge of organization. To house this fast-growing graduate school, a group of buildings on F Street, between 19th and 20th Streets, was purchased in 1920 with funds allocated to American University by the Federal Government as reimbursement for its wartime services. In 1925 the College of Liberal Arts was opened in various buildings on the uptown campus.

The campus buildings and equipment have been appraised at approximately $3,500,000. The original plan for the university, calling for 26 magnificent white-marble structures, was abandoned as over-ambitious. Two buildings carry out this scheme, Hurst Hall, completed in 1898, a neoclassic three-story building, and McKinley Building, completed in 1917 and now being used as the Fixed Nitrogen Research Laboratory of the Department of Agriculture. Other buildings are: The Women's Residence Hall (1925) accommodating 400; the heating plant (1925); the chancellor's house (1925); the gymnasium (1926); the Batelle Memorial Library (1926); and Hamilton House (1930), which is the first unit of a dormitory group for men. The college library contains more than 52,000 volumes. One of its finest collections is the mathematics library that formerly belonged to Artemus Martin, librarian of the United States Coast and Geodetic Survey.

The College of Liberal Arts is a typical American undergraduate school. The School of Social Science and Public Affairs grants the degrees of Master of Arts and Doctor of Philosophy in the fields of history, economics, economic history, international affairs, political science, social economy, and public administration. Experts in Government service supplement the regular staff, and day and evening classes are held. This school provides primarily an in-service program for Federal employees and courses for teachers and students of the social sciences who desire a first-hand acquaintance with Governmental methods in dealing with current problems. Similar in-service courses have been developed in co-operation with the Graduate School of the Department of Agriculture, the Census Bureau, the Farm Credit Administration, and the Bureau of Labor Statistics.

A little north of Ward Circle, on the east side of Nebraska Avenue, is MOUNT VERNON SEMINARY, founded in 1875, the District's oldest nonsectarian boarding school for girls. Immediately north are the grounds and buildings of Hillcrest "Children's Village," incorporated as the Washington City Orphan Asylum.

At a point about 150 yards west of the Nebraska Avenue intersection stood Fort Gaines, one of the defenses hastily constructed around Washington after the battle of Bull Run in 1861. There are indications that part of the fort stood on what is now Massachusetts Avenue, which passes through the high ground here in a deep cut. The fort was dismantled soon after the close of hostilities. Near the same point, at a much earlier day, stood the manor house of William Murdock, a delegate to the Stamp-Act Congress of 1765 and onetime owner of a huge tract of land in this vicinity.

Beyond WESLEY CIRCLE, the Avenue passes through a partly developed district to the Massachusetts Avenue Portal, on the northwest District Line. This is its western terminus within the District, but Massachusetts Avenue Extended continues to Glen Echo, Maryland.

Connecticut Avenue

Streetcars: Northbound—Mt. Pleasant (on Connecticut Ave. from K St. to California St.). Southbound—Lincoln Park, and 13th & D NE. (California St. to K St.).
Busses: Northbound—Chevy Chase Circle (M St. to Chevy Chase Circle). Southbound—4th & E NW. (Chevy Chase Circle to K St.), Calvert Bridge (Chevy Chase Circle to Calvert St.).
Taxis: First to fourth zones.

In the L'Enfant plan, what is now Connecticut Avenue appears as a principal diagonal thoroughfare running from Lafayette Square in a northwesterly direction to "Boundary Street" (now Florida Avenue). This is but a small segment, however, of the broad avenue which today extends in a nearly straight northwesterly course of 5 miles from Lafayette Square to the northwest District Line at Chevy Chase Circle—and continues for several miles, under the same name, through the Maryland countryside.

Although its lower end, in the immediate vicinity of Lafayette Square, was fairly well built up at an early date, the development of Connecticut Avenue, even within L'Enfant's original city limits, occurred largely in the last 60 years. Until well after the close of the Civil War, the section above M Street was considered "out in the country." The erection of "Stewart Castle" (Senator William M. Stewart's home) at Dupont Circle in 1873 and of the British Legation Building at N Street in 1875 stimulated building on what was then known as the "upper avenue." New and pretentious houses began to supplement the scattered earlier residences below Dupont Circle, and by the late eighties this section of Connecticut Avenue had become the most fashionable of Washington thoroughfares.

The commercial invasion, which has transformed the lower avenue into something similar to New York's 57th Street, began in the late nineties, but was greatly accelerated just after World War I. With this transformation of the lower section came the extension and development beyond Florida Avenue; today, the long upper section, with the exception of an occasional vacant tract on either side of the Avenue north of Zoological Park, is built up all the way to Chevy Chase Circle.

POINTS OF INTEREST

Connecticut Avenue begins at H Street NW., just across from the northwest corner of Lafayette Square. The impressive building of the

UNITED STATES CHAMBER OF COMMERCE (*see Lafayette Square*) stands at the northeast corner of the Avenue and H Street. The old Rochambeau Apartment building (now occupied by the Social Security Board), just beyond the Chamber of Commerce, was long a favored residence for Army and Navy officers, Government officials, and some of the South American legations. The ARMY AND NAVY CLUB, an organization for officers of both services, stands on the northeast corner at I Street.

Headquarters of the AMERICAN ASSOCIATION OF UNIVERSITY WOMEN is in the former home of Benjamin F. Tracy, Secretary of the Navy under Benjamin Harrison, at 1634 I Street. Number 1720 is the former home of Oliver Wendell Holmes, Associate Justice of the Supreme Court (1902-32). The house at No. 1731 has been the residence successively of Theodore Frelinghuysen, Senator from New Jersey in 1866 and after; William M. Evarts, Secretary of State under Hayes; William C. Whitney, Secretary of the Navy under Cleveland; and John Wanamaker, Postmaster General under Harrison. The last Washington HOME OF JEFFERSON DAVIS was on I Street, at No. 1736.

FARRAGUT SQUARE, between I and K Streets NW. (bounded both east and west by 17th Street) contains several rare varieties of shade trees. Near the center of the square stands the heroic bronze figure of Admiral David G. Farragut, by Vinnie Ream (Hoxie); the statue, cast of metal from Farragut's flagship, the *Hartford,* was unveiled in 1881. Mrs. Hoxie lived at 1632 K Street, facing Farragut Square.

At the northwest corner of K and 17th Streets NW. is the YWCA BUILDING. The WASHINGTON CLUB, organized in 1891, the oldest existing women's club in the city, occupies the house opposite the YWCA, on the northwest corner, the former home of Vice President Charles W. Fairbanks and Leland D. Stanford, Senator from California (1885-93). Facing the east side of Farragut Square, at 919 17th Street NW., is the building of the AMERICAN FORESTRY ASSOCIATION, an educational organization and publisher of the monthly magazine *American Forests.*

On Connecticut Avenue between K Street and Dupont Circle are many of Washington's finer shops—high-class markets, shoestores, bookstores, art dealers, antique shops, dress and specialty shops. Of the many old dwellings converted to business use, the most conspicuous is a house on the northeast corner of the Avenue at K Street, facing Farragut Square; built in 1875, it was occupied for four years by Alexander R. Shepherd. Later occupants were Senator Don Cameron of Pennsylvania, the Chinese Legation, the Russian Embassy, Mrs. Washington McLean (who turned the house over for a time to Admiral George Dewey after his return from the Philippines), and William F. Draper, Minister to Italy. This mansion was the scene of the "butterfly wedding" of Draper's daughter to Prince Boncampagni of Rome, in 1917. After the marriage ceremony, thousands of butterflies, imported

for the occasion, were released among the guests.   The Stoneleigh
Court apartment building, erected in 1902 by John Hay, Secretary of
State under McKinley and Theodore Roosevelt, fills the rest of the
block between K and L Streets on the east side of the Avenue.

The huge Mayflower Hotel, on the southeast corner at De Sales
Street, is a fashionable center of Washington life, the residence of
prominent Government officials and foreign diplomats.

A bronze STATUE OF LONGFELLOW, executed by William Couper
and unveiled in 1909, stands in a triangular area on the west side,
just north of M Street.   At the apex of a triangular plot between M
Street and Rhode Island Avenue is the so-called "NUNS OF THE BAT-
TLEFIELD" MONUMENT, commemorating the "various Orders of Sisters who gave their services as nurses on battlefields and in hospitals
during the Civil War"; designed by Jerome Connor, it was erected in
1924 by the ladies' auxiliary of the Ancient Order of Hibernians.

On the northeast corner at Rhode Island Avenue NW. is the
LONGFELLOW BUILDING, an 11-story structure of reinforced
concrete and brick, with modernistic canopy front and continuous
windows.   Designed by William Lescaze, New York architect, it was
constructed in record time between June 1940, and January 1941.
The building is occupied by Government agencies.

Before the erection of this modern structure, ST. MATTHEWS
ROMAN CATHOLIC CATHEDRAL, 1725 Rhode Island Avenue
NW., was clearly visible from Connecticut Avenue, a great red-brick
edifice; its handsome green-topped dome is one of the city's conspicuous
landmarks.   Named in honor of St. Matthew, the Cathedral also pays
tribute in its name to Father William Matthew of St. Patrick's (see
Downtown), the first native Marylander to be ordained a priest.   Property donated by Father Matthew was sold to provide the first funds
used in building the church.   Designed by Grant La Farge and begun
in 1893, the edifice is still incomplete.   Its exterior, imposing in mass
and courageous in color, follows the traditional simplicity of early
church architecture in northern Italy, particularly of Bologna, with its
cruciform plan, classic silhouette, colorful detail, and imposing dome.

Its massive walls rise comparatively unadorned to support a low-
gabled roof.   The high green dome, directly over the crossing, springs
from an octagonal drum pierced by long arched windows and enriched
with columns of red terra cotta.   A slender lantern, terminating in a
small gilded dome and Latin cross, surmounts the ribbed-copper dome.
A broad flight of steps along the principal façade leads up to three
bronze portals flanked by engaged columns and enriched with delicate
arabesques in bas-relief.

In striking contrast to the external simplicity, the interior presents
an air of sumptuous richness.   What little light enters the interior
through the translucent windows reveals the majestic lines of great
structural piers and arcades, supporting an ornate vaulted ceiling.
The walls are decorated with bright mosaics and faced with Italian
marble of varying shades and textures.   Behind a delicate alabaster

rail is the chancel sanctuary, with its gleaming white altar set with intarsia. To the left of the altar is a raised choir, gallery, and organ, and to the right a large pedestaled pulpit with hooded canopy.

On either side and to the rear of the Cathedral is St. Matthew's Court, or Alley, lined with attractive old residences made into studio apartments. The atmosphere of the court is agreeably like that of artists' quarters in older cities.

On the east side of Connecticut Avenue at N Street stands a bronze STATUE OF JOHN WITHERSPOON, signer of the Declaration of Independence and president of Princeton University. The work of William Couper, it was unveiled in 1909.

The gray stone CHURCH OF THE COVENANT (First Presbyterian), notable for its tall square tower with open arches, is at the southeast corner of N and 18th Streets NW., facing the Witherspoon statue. James G. Blaine, one of the founders of this church, and President Benjamin Harrison attended services here. The great stone tower's collapse in 1889, as the church was nearing completion, delayed the dedication ceremonies for several months.

The house at 1910 N Street NW., a little west of the Avenue, was occupied by Theodore Roosevelt during his term as Assistant Secretary of the Navy under McKinley. At 1215 19th Street, in the block south of N, is still another of his Washington residences.

Connecticut Avenue just south of Dupont Circle derived distinction for more than half a century after 1875 from the British diplomatic residence (the first in Washington to be built and owned by a foreign government), which stood at the northwest corner of N Street. As Legation, then as Embassy, this was a prominent diplomatic-social center until 1930, when the Embassy moved to its present quarters on Massachusetts Avenue. James Bryce, author of The American Commonwealth, lived here during his term as British Ambassador to the United States (1907-13).

From 1897 to 1900, the Austro-Hungarian Government maintained a diplomatic residence at 1307 Connecticut Avenue, opposite the British Embassy; farther north, at No. 1355, stood for many years the home of Alexander Graham Bell. Beyond DUPONT CIRCLE (see Massachusetts Avenue), Connecticut Avenue resumes its northwesterly course. Its acutely angled intersection with 20th Street NW. permits a tiny triangular park. Close by is the COLOMBIAN EMBASSY, 1520 20th Street. A few blocks off the Avenue, at 1816 Corcoran Street, is the ARGENTINE EMBASSY.

The land on the east side of the Avenue, for two blocks north of Q Street, was known in Washington's early years as O'Neale's Farm; the farmhouse stood on Connecticut Avenue a little south of R Street. After O'Neale's death in 1834, the property passed to his daughter, Mrs. Margaret Eaton—the famous Peggy O'Neale.

Florida Avenue ("Boundary Street" in L'Enfant's plan) crosses Connecticut Avenue a little north of S Street. At No. 2154 is the CHILEAN EMBASSY. The block north of S Street, between 19th and 20th Streets, was long the old Holmead Burying Ground, established in 1798 on land originally owned by Anthony Holmead. It ceased to be used as a cemetery about 1860; 20 years later the bodies were removed and the land subdivided. At 2101 Connecticut Avenue is the LEGATION OF THE DOMINICAN REPUBLIC.

From Florida Avenue north to Columbia Road, Connecticut Avenue is the western boundary of Temple Heights, an undeveloped tract of more than 9 acres, originally part of the Holmead estate, which derives its name from the fact that it was purchased as the site for a proposed Masonic Temple. This project was abandoned, and an ultramodern residential community, "Crystal City," is planned, to be built under the direction of Frank Lloyd Wright. Across from Temple Heights, on the northwest corner of the Avenue and Bancroft Place, is ST. MARGARET'S PROTESTANT EPISCOPAL CHURCH.

A bronze equestrian STATUE OF GENERAL GEORGE B. McCLELLAN, executed by Frederick MacMonnies and unveiled in 1907, occupies a commanding position in an open triangle at the junction of Connecticut Avenue and Columbia Road. The Avenue, continuing a gradual upward slope, enters a select residential neighborhood, where large apartment houses border its course for the three blocks to Rock Creek and Potomac Parkway.

Kalorama Road, which intersects Connecticut Avenue near the parkway, derives its name from the historic Kalorama tract, lying south and west of this intersection within a deep horseshoe curve of Rock Creek, with Connecticut Avenue and the lower end of Florida Avenue for its approximate eastern boundary. This tract was originally a part of the Holmead estate; and the Holmead manor house, built about 1750, stood near the present intersection of S Street and Phelps Place. Joel Barlow, a noted political and literary figure of his time, purchased the tract in 1807, named it Kalorama (Greek, "beautiful view"), and had the house remodeled under Benjamin Latrobe's supervision. After his death in 1812 the house had several owners and was used as a Government hospital during the Civil War. What remained of it, after a destructive fire, was torn down in 1889. The Barlow family mausoleum once stood near the east end of Decatur Place; here the body of Commodore Stephen Decatur, after his fatal duel with Captain Barron in 1820, was temporarily interred.

The Kalorama tract is now a fine residential section, especially favored by high Government officials. Five Presidents have lived here, before or after their terms in the White House: Woodrow Wilson (for 3 years preceding his death in 1924) at 2340 S Street; William Howard Taft at 2215 Wyoming Avenue; Warren G. Harding at 2314 Wyoming Avenue; Herbert Hoover at 2300 S Street; and Franklin D. Roosevelt (as Assistant Secretary of the Navy) at 2131 R Street. At 2223 R Street is the residence of Charles Evans Hughes, Chief Justice of the U.S. Supreme Court (1930-41); at 2205 California Street is the home of Louis D. Brandeis, formerly Associate Justice of the

Supreme Court; and Harlan Fiske Stone, appointed Chief Justice in 1941, lives at 2340 Wyoming Avenue.

At 2200 Kalorama Road is the BOLIVIAN LEGATION, and, since early in 1936, the FRENCH EMBASSY has occupied the palatial residence at 2221, formerly owned by John Hays Hammond. Close by, at No. 2300, is the THAI (SIAMESE) LEGATION, and to the south is the IRISH LEGATION, at 2310 Tracy Place. The FINNISH LEGATION has quarters at 2144 Wyoming Avenue. Several legations in the Kalorama region are on or near Massachusetts Avenue (*see Massachusetts Avenue*). At 2128 Bancroft Place is the COSTA RICAN LEGATION.

The FRIENDS MEETING OF WASHINGTON, 2111 Florida Avenue, reflects the simple tastes and practices of the Quaker sect. The building was designed by Walter H. Price, Philadelphia architect, with the restrained good taste and integrity of early eighteenth-century rural architecture in Pennsylvania. The building, completed in 1930, is of rough quarry stone, with a slate roof. The stone wall around it, the broad terrace, flagstone walk, and rustic steps contribute much to its charm. Interesting details are the entrance portals, white-trimmed windows with tiny panes and paneled shutters, solid doors with strap hinges, and small pillared porch at the right entrance. A sundial on the upper terrace bears the inscription: "I mind the light, dost thou?"

The house at 2401 Kalorama Road (*private*), a fine example of Georgian architecture dating from 1754, was removed in sections from its original site in Danvers, Massachusetts, and reconstructed here in 1936. It was long known as the Gage House, because it had been occupied for a time by General Thomas Gage, British Colonial governor of Massachusetts.

Curving rather sharply westward from Kalorama Road, Connecticut Avenue crosses TAFT BRIDGE, high above Rock Creek and the wide parkway on either side. The bridge, designed by George S. Morrison and Edward P. Casey and opened in 1908, is of solid concrete, with a pair of lions, by R. Hinton Perry, flanking either end. In 1930, the year of William Howard Taft's death, the structure was given its present official name. A little to the north and east is the CALVERT STREET BRIDGE, designed by Paul Cret and completed in 1935.

Just beyond Taft Bridge are two large hotels—the SHOREHAM, opened in 1930, between Rock Creek Parkway and Calvert Street; and the WARDMAN PARK, on a high terrace facing Woodley Road. The URUGUAY LEGATION has quarters in the Shoreham. The Wardman Park, opened in 1918, houses the PORTUGUESE LEGATION and the PARAGUAY LEGATION, and many United States Senators live here while in Washington. At 2611 Woodley Place is the HONDURAS LEGATION.

Cathedral Avenue, the next intersecting thoroughfare beyond Woodley Road, leads directly to the Cathedral of SS. Peter and Paul (*see Massachusetts Avenue*), about three-fourths of a mile west. On the right-hand side is the western entrance to the National Zoological Park. A little farther north, just beyond the huge KENNEDY-WARREN APARTMENTS on the right, a modern steel-arch bridge, designed by Paul Cret and erected in 1932, carries the avenue over KLINGLE VALLEY PARKWAY.

The Government of Switzerland in 1941 purchased the estate known as SINGLE OAK, at 2920 Cathedral Avenue, and the Swiss Legation staff moved in after the house was remodeled. The estate, 6 acres of landscaped grounds and gardens, was owned by Lawrence Phipps, former Senator from Colorado; the house, last occupied as a residence by A. A. Berle, Jr., Assistant Secretary of State, was the home of Josephus Daniels, Secretary of the Navy, during the World War period.

West of Connecticut Avenue are two select residential areas: Woodley Park, to the south of Cathedral Avenue, and Cleveland Park, to the north: The latter was named for President Grover Cleveland, whose summer home was in the neighborhood. Both areas originally were part of the great Rosedale tract acquired by George Beall in 1720, as an addition to the Rock of Dunbarton grant patented by his father, Ninian Beall. In the 1790's, Benjamin Stoddert and General Uriah Forrest, hero of Germantown, acquired the 990 acres between Wisconsin Avenue and Rock Creek and gave the property the name of Pretty Prospect. General Forrest erected a frame house, and named the estate Rosedale, for the Forrest family estate in England; he died here in 1805. The present ROSEDALE, 3501 Newark Street, consists of this eighteenth-century dwelling (*private*), an addition made in 1805, and the "new house" built in 1860. The wide, yellow-painted Colonial house, set well back on a rise of ground, is surrounded by a considerable acreage, in which the outbuildings and wooded spots are artfully disposed to give the effect of accidental arrangement. The house itself has the simplicity and balanced construction characteristic of its period.

General Forrest's daughter married John Green in 1814, and they came to Rosedale in 1827. Through the marriage of their daughter Alice in 1855, the old house became associated with one of the most picturesque figures in North American history—Don Augustin Iturbide, first and last native Mexican Emperor, 1822-23. Alice Green married Don Angelo de Iturbide, second son of Don Augustin, and it is believed they made their home at Rosedale for a time. Alice's son Augustin, born April 2, 1863, was adopted by Emperor Maximilian, but the parents later regained possession of their child.

The history of WOODLEY (*private*), 3000 Cathedral Avenue, is inseparable from that of Rosedale. A few years after General Forrest had built his house, he sold 250 acres to his brother-in-law, Judge Phillip Barton Key, who built the present house at Woodley. Here the judge's nephew, Francis Scott Key, spent considerable time. On a reduced estate of 18 acres, the old Georgian manor house of Woodley stands among immense oak and chestnut trees, a luxuriant woodland behind it. The large central structure, of stucco-covered brick, with classic portico at front and rear, arched windows and fanlight doorways, is much as it was at the end of the eighteenth century, and the few additions are in character with the original building. It is said that four Presidents made Woodley their summer home: Van Buren, Tyler, Buchanan, and Cleveland. Pretty Prospect, later known as Red Top, the country home of President Cleveland, was in the near neighborhood. Redwood, where Jefferson Davis lived, and Kalorama and other famous houses were not far off. Woodley was also for a time the home of Baron Gerault, German Ambassador and, during President Wilson's first term, Colonel E. M. House lived here. It is now (1942) owned and occupied by Henry L. Stimson, Secretary of War.

At 3225 Woodley Road, in this same area, is TWIN OAKS (*private*), the residence of Dr. Hu Shih, Chinese Ambassador. Twin Oaks was formerly the home of Gardiner Greene Hubbard, first president of the National Geographic Society and father-in-law of Alexander Graham Bell.

At 3120 Cleveland Avenue, near the western edge of the area, is WHITE OAKS, the residence of the Right Honorable Richard G. Casey, Australian Minister.

The Broadmoor, a large apartment building at No. 3601, is the most conspicuous feature of Connecticut Avenue between Klingle Bridge and the National Bureau of Standards, some two-thirds of a mile north.

The NATIONAL BUREAU OF STANDARDS (*closed during national emergency*), Connecticut Avenue at Upton Street NW., resembles a university more than a large Federal agency. A quadrangle, with four principal buildings, dominates the crest of a hill. Fifteen other structures are scattered over the 68-acre hillside among footpaths and winding roads, well-kept lawns, flower beds, and magnificent old shade trees. The Bureau of Standards, of the Department of Commerce, is the country's authority on measurements, the world's largest diversified testing laboratory, and an outstanding institution of pure scientific research.

In purchasing this property in 1901 the Bureau acquired a hill of solid rock, the ideal foundation for high-precision instruments. In later years the Bureau added several adjacent lots to protect itself from the encroachment of the city and to provide space for expansion. The three- and four-story red-brick structures, standardized in external appearance, were designed to meet special requirements; more money was spent on laboratories and equipment than on the buildings. The operation of the Bureau of Standards in the suburbs has been cited by the National Capital Park and Planning Commission as an outstanding example of successful Government-agency decentralization.

"The Congress shall have the power . . . to fix the standards of weights and measures." In this brief Constitutional provision, the

Bureau had its origin. For forty years Congress took no action, though Washington repeatedly called attention to the importance of the subject, and Jefferson proposed the adoption of the metric system, then gaining popularity in France. Congress examined the plan and pigeon-holed it for 71 years. In 1821 John Quincy Adams submitted his classic report to Congress, showing that the Massachusetts pound was almost a quarter of an ounce lighter than the Maine pound, and that it took 100 bushels of grain in New York to equal 96 bushels in South Carolina. Finally, in 1830, the Treasury Department at the Senate's request directed Ferdinand Rudolph Hassler, first superintendent of the Coast and Geodetic Survey, to investigate standards used in the various ports. The standards of length, mass, and capacity used in making these comparisons were obtained in England and conformed closely to British standards then in use. The Office of Standard Weights and Measures was established in 1832, and four years later replicas of the standards adopted were supplied to governors of the States. The functions of the Office were taken over by the National Bureau of Standards in 1901.

The Metric Act of Congress in 1866 legalized the use of the metric system, defining the meter as equal to 39.37 inches, though the inch had never been legally fixed. Following an international conference in 1875, at which the United States was represented, the International Bureau of Weights and Measures was established at Sèvres, near Paris, and proceeded with the construction of platinum-iridium meters and kilograms. Of these, one meter and one kilogram were chosen as international standards, while the others were distributed among the supporting nations by lot. In 1889 the United States received meter bar No. 27 and kilogram No. 20, and by order of the Secretary of the Treasury (1893) designated these two prototypes as its primary national standards. In the field of weights and measures the Nation operates on a two-system plan: the so-called "customary" system for everyday use, and the metric system in science and increasingly in industry.

At the turn of the century Congress passed the organic act creating the National Bureau of Standards, charged with the development, construction, custody, and maintenance of the reference and working standards used in science, engineering, industry, and commerce; with the comparison of these standards; with theoretical research, including determination of physical constants; and with the determination of the properties of materials. Since the organization of the Bureau in 1901 no change in the fundamental law has been required. In addition to the 1,000 employees, two-thirds of whom are scientifically and technically trained, there are many research assistants (at times more than 100), supported by industrial groups to work on basic problems of mutual interest to Government and industry.

More than half of all the tests and measurements made by the Bureau are for the Government, the largest individual purchaser in the country. The Government buys materials and supplies on specifications, and the Bureau sees that these meet requirements. The Bureau also seeks to eliminate unnecessary variations in sizes and shapes of commodities. Until the early 1920's, for example, beds were made in 72 different sizes; today they come in one length and four widths. As an aid to the retail buyer, the Bureau encourages manufacturers to label products meeting Government specifications with a Bureau of Standards certification, and many have done so.

The SOUTH BUILDING, erected in 1904, contains administrative offices and numerous laboratories of weights and measures. It has heavy walls set deep in solid rock, to eliminate vibration. High-precision instruments are also set on rock, in air-conditioned underground vaults. In a first-floor room are even-arm balance scales, like the statue-of-justice scales, scientifically improved for comparing pounds and kilograms. A balance for 50-pound weights is accurate to 1 part in 20,000,-000, and a kilogram balance to 1 part in 100,000,000. In another first-floor room are three large fused-quartz disks, which are the standards for plane-surface measurements. Fifteen years were spent in grinding and polishing these disks, and they are accurate to 1 part in 5,000,000.

In a room on the second floor is a watch and clock clinic, where manufacturers' products are tested and certified. This laboratory cooperates with the Horological Institute of America in raising standards of watch repairing. The institute grants certificates to workmen who show high proficiency.

In a fourth-floor room, fluorescent light is used to reveal some of the impurities in materials. In an adjoining room the Bureau, as custodian of the standard railway-signal colors, has a set of colored glass disks against which the standards belonging to manufacturers of railway-signal lamps are checked before use. The Bureau also fixes the colors of the American flag, and manufacturers must meet the specifications before the Government buys a flag. In cabinets along the corridors are some of the old weight and capacity measures once standard in this country.

Laboratory and clinical thermometers are tested in the WEST BUILD-ING. At the end of the test the clinical thermometers are placed in a rotary device, which exerts the same amount of force as a doctor does in shaking the mercury back into the bulb.

The purity of sugar is also determined in this building, through use of a saccharimeter, a special form of the optical instrument known as a polariscope. Sugar in solution has the property of rotating a beam of polarized light, and the saccharimeter measures this rotation. The Customs Service levies duties on sugar shipments according to readings made on this device. The Bureau developed levulose, the sweetest of all sugars, from the Jerusalem artichoke, and worked out a commercial method for its production.

The SOUND OR REVERBERATION CHAMBER, in a small individual building, has double walls and ceilings separated by dead air space. It has no windows, and the entrance is protected by a series of four doors. A six-foot-square sample of acoustical material to be tested is placed on the floor, and the duration of echoes from it reveals its sound-absorption quality.

In the DYNAMOMETER GROUP of buildings, the performance of internal-combustion engines, fuels, and lubricants is investigated.

A small-scale experimental foundry is housed in the high-windowed NORTHWEST BUILDING. On the second floor is the BUREAU OF STANDARDS LIBRARY, containing some 42,000 volumes, and, in addition, almost all domestic and foreign periodicals in the fields of physics, chemistry, and engineering. The library serves the needs of the Bureau and is open to students.

The CHEMISTRY BUILDING, erected in 1916, down the hill from the quadrangle, is a modern alchemist's shop. Its efficient ventilating system sucks out chemical fumes, deodorizing the laboratories. The equipment of the Electrochemistry Laboratory, in this building, includes a small electroplating plant, which was used in working out the process for plating steel and other metals with chromium, one of the hardest metals known. Through this discovery the Bureau was able to prolong the life of engraving plates and to sharpen the outlines of pictures on paper currency. In a fourth-floor room the artificial weathering of paint accomplishes in weeks the processes that normally require years. A mimeographed guide to the chemistry laboratories may be obtained in Room 215.

The EAST BUILDING, erected in 1914 to house electrical tests, was constructed for the most part of nonmagnetic materials. When it became necessary to measure the ohm more accurately, stray magnetic fields caused errors in the calculations. The walls had to be torn down, because the sand used in mixing the cement contained particles of magnetite.

Other activities in this building include the burning out of approximately 6,000 electric light bulbs each year, to spot-check the supply of 3,000,000 lamps purchased annually by the Government; the measurement of the total amount of light given off in all directions by any electric lamp; and the testing and measurement of radium, results of which are watched through a telescope by an observer at some distance from the radioactive material.

In the main hall and museum of the RADIO BUILDING are various types of electron tubes, French and American radio sets used in the First World War, apparatus developed for research work, and publications of the radio section. The Bureau's station, WWV, at Beltsville, Maryland, broadcasts the standard frequency of radio. For musicians and laboratory workers, it also broadcasts the standard of musical pitch, A above middle C, and time intervals exactly one second in length.

The HYDRAULICS BUILDING, on the southeast edge of the grounds, contains supply and measuring basins, flumes, and pumping and metering equipment for every variety of hydraulic investigation. Problems of flood control, irrigation, and power generation are solved in this laboratory.

In the INDUSTRIAL BUILDING the work of measuring structural strains ranges from girders to girdles, and from breaking cups and saucers to extensive research in organic plastics. The Bureau tests 35,000 samples of concrete annually, representing the 5,000,000 barrels purchased by the Government. Its vertical machine has the greatest capacity of any hydraulic press in the world. One of the finest instruments owned by the Bureau is a high-precision testing machine with a capacity of 2,300,000 pounds compression and 1,150,000 pounds tension. It is so nicely adjusted that it can crumple a steel girder or hold an egg without cracking the shell.

The building contains many special machines for testing textiles. A robot leg wears out women's stockings, while scientists study the problems of runs and durability. Another machine, with leather-covered wheels, wears down samples of carpet. Here the Bureau helps to draw up specifications for 1,100 paper items purchased by the Government. It increased the life of $1 and $5 bills by changing the specifications from 100 per cent linen to 80 per cent linen with 20 per cent cotton. The resulting paper, less brittle, can be folded many more times than the old, before wearing through. There is an ingenious device, of adjustable wheels, weights, speeds, and hydraulic brakes, to test the endurance of automobile brake linings. Constant investigations are carried on in leather, tanning solutions, and the causes of leather deterioration. An eight-footed robot, each foot in a different style of shoe, plods over an endless belt; at intervals the shoes are examined for extent of wear.

In the FIRE RESISTANCE GROUP of buildings the ability of structural materials to withstand fire is determined. Full-sized walls are exposed to fires of varying duration and intensity, and the temperatures on the unexposed sides are measured. When these become high enough to ignite cotton waste, the wall is considered to have failed. Roofs, safes, and filing cabinets are also tested.

The X-RAY PLANT, in the High Voltage Building, is capable of generating 1,500,000 volts; it was built in 1940. The huge room contains X-ray generators and tubes about 30 feet tall, so connected that any desired voltage can be obtained. The room, 65 by 132 feet, with a height of 60 feet, is lined with copper sheeting to imprison the high voltage, which would disrupt other electrical experiments. A periscope, from another room, is used for observing experiments, to guard the observer from the rays. X-rays from this plant have the power to penetrate an armor-plate section 12 to 14 inches thick. In the same building tests are also carried out on high-voltage equipment.

A little east of the Bureau of Standards, at 2935 Upton Street NW., is the ACADEMY OF THE HOLY CROSS, a Roman Catholic school for young women. Soapstone Valley, a narrow wooded ravine extending eastward from Connecticut Avenue, just beyond Yuma Street, is the site of an ancient soapstone quarry.

There is little of special interest in the remaining stretch of Connecticut Avenue to Chevy Chase Circle, with the exception of the buildings and grounds of the METHODIST HOME FOR THE AGED, in the block between Ellicott and Fessenden Streets.

A half-mile detour west from the avenue on Fessenden Street leads to RENO (at or near the present intersection of Ellicott and 39th Streets), where stood Fort Reno, one of Washington's defenses during the Civil War.

CHEVY CHASE CIRCLE, at the northwest District Line, marks the upper terminus of Connecticut Avenue within the District— although the Avenue, bending somewhat to the east, continues due north beyond the circle for several miles into Montgomery County, Maryland.

The land hereabouts on both sides of the District Line was originally the proprietory estate known as Cheivy Chace, held by Joseph Belt (1680-1761), member of the Maryland House of Burgesses and colonel of militia in the French and Indian War. A boulder bearing a bronze plaque in commemoration of Belt, placed here in 1911 by the Society of Colonial Wars, stands just west of the circle, on the grounds of ALL SAINTS' EPISCOPAL CHURCH.

Chevy Chase Circle is adorned with a simple stone fountain spouting a central jet of water that can be seen for a mile or so along the Connecticut Avenue approach. This fountain was erected as a memorial to Senator Francis G. Newlands of Nevada, for several years a resident of the Chevy Chase district. Facing the circle, at the southeast corner of Connecticut Avenue and Chevy Chase Parkway, stands the CHEVY CHASE PRESBYTERIAN CHURCH, a large stone structure of Gothic type. The CHEVY CHASE CLUB occupies an extensive tract of land between Connecticut and Wisconsin Avenues, a little north of the District Line; and about a mile farther north is the COLUMBIA COUNTRY CLUB, the grounds of which lie between Connecticut Avenue and Jones Bridge Road, in what is known as the Chevy Chase Lake region. The CHEVY CHASE WOMAN'S CLUB is at Connecticut Avenue and Dunlop Street.

Sixteenth Street

Busses: Northbound—Chillum and Petworth (on 16th St. from Eye St. to Harvard St.); Georgia & Alaska (K St. to Alaska Ave.). Southbound—8th and Penna. NW. (Harvard St. to Eye St.); 14th & Colorado (Eastern Ave. to Kennedy St.).
Taxis: First to fourth zones.

The most important of Washington's numbered thoroughfares, 16th Street is laid out along the exact north-south axis of the White House, and only a little east of the north-south axis of the District of Columbia, stretching some 6½ miles. It is a street of impressive churches, of national organizations, of hotels and apartment houses, and of fine private residences. It borders one of the most interesting small formal parks and one of the most beautiful natural parks in the country.

After the Civil War, 16th Street from L Street north to Meridian Hill was in large part given over to small dwellings inhabited by Negroes. As late as the eighties young people skated over a stretch of low swampy ground near the U Street intersection. Until the nineties, Meridian Hill and Mount Pleasant were rather sparsely settled suburban areas. "Henderson's Castle" was built in 1888 at the corner of Florida Avenue, but 16th Street's development into a metropolitan thoroughfare has taken place chiefly within the present century. The most important personal force in that development was Mrs. John B. Henderson, widow of the United States Senator who built the "Castle." Between 1906 and 1929, under the architectural guidance of George Oakley Totten, Mrs. Henderson constructed nearly a dozen costly residences on or near 16th Street, most of them in the Meridian Hill district and designed to house foreign embassies or legations. Largely as a result of Mrs. Henderson's persistent lobbying, 16th Street was officially renamed "Avenue of the Presidents" by Congressional Act in 1913, but the awkwardness and inappropriateness of this designation caused Congress to restore the old name the following year.

POINTS OF INTEREST

Sixteenth Street begins at the north or H Street side of Lafayette Square. Directly south, through the trees of the square and beyond the Jackson Monument, appears the columned north portico of the White House (*see President's Square*).

On the southeast corner of I Street is the Lafayette Hotel. Diagonally opposite, on the northwest corner, is the former home of Horace Gray, Supreme Court Justice (1881-1902), and of John Barton Payne,

419

Secretary of the Interior under Wilson and later head of the American Red Cross.

The Carlton Hotel, at the southeast corner of K Street, is one of the most fashionable Capital hostelries and the Washington home of several high Government officials. Admiral George Dewey, naval hero of the Spanish-American War, died in the house on the northwest corner.

Adjoining the Dewey home on the west, at 1603 K Street, is a house occupied by William Howard Taft while Secretary of War under Theodore Roosevelt. Nearly opposite, at 1608 K Street, are housed the District of Columbia headquarters of the American Legion and the offices of the National Legislative and Rehabilitation Committees of the American Legion. Hoke Smith, Secretary of the Interior under Cleveland, lived for a time in the house at 1623 K Street.

On the east side of 16th Street, between K and L Streets, construction of a 1,000-room Statler Hotel began in the spring of 1941. As planned it will be the largest hotel in the city, costing $8,500,000.

North of L Street is the EMBASSY OF THE UNION OF SOVIET SOCIALIST REPUBLICS, at 1119 16th Street. The stone mansion, built in 1910 by Mrs. George M. Pullman, widow of the sleeping-car magnate, was never occupied by her. It served as the Czarist Russian Embassy for several years before the revolution of March, 1917. Then it was taken over by the Kerensky provisional government, which was officially recognized by the United States for five years. From 1922 until this country's formal recognition of the Soviet Union twelve years later, the mansion was unoccupied. It was reopened by the Soviet Government in 1934. The UNIVERSITY CLUB occupies a large building immediately north of the Soviet Embassy, at No. 1135.

The HEADQUARTERS OF THE NATIONAL GEO-GRAPHIC SOCIETY (*open 9-5, Mon.-Fri.*) occupy adjoining buildings at 16th and M Streets. Hubbard Memorial Hall, now the Library Building, was erected in 1902 by the heirs of Gardiner Greene Hubbard, first president of the Society. The Administration Building, designed by Arthur B. Heaton, was completed in 1932. Both are buff-brick structures with limestone trim. The society is supported by more than a million members who receive, as privileges of membership, the *National Geographic Magazine,* wall maps, and pictures reproduced by the society.

The National Geographic Society was founded in 1888 by a group of scientists in Washington, who began with a lecture series and a technical bulletin. At the time of Dr. Hubbard's presidency the membership was small, but when his son-in-law, Alexander Graham Bell, inventor of the telephone, became president of the organization in 1899, a policy of popularization was determined upon. Bell invited the general public to join and brought to the editorial chair of the *National Geographic Magazine* Gilbert Grosvenor, then a young teacher. As editor and as director and president since 1920, Dr. Grosvenor treated geographical investigation as a high adventure. By 1905 subsidies for publishing were discontinued; geography had become popular reading, and the magazine, no longer a technical journal, was definitely progressing toward a circulation of 1,000,000.

The society occupied Hubbard Memorial Hall from 1902 to 1913, built the first unit of the Administration Building in the latter year, and expanded its headquarters to present dimensions in 1932. Its control rests with a self-perpetuating board of trustees, on which individuals serve for life. All administrative and editorial business is handled at the 16th Street address, and the routine of publication in the clerical and records building at 3rd Street and Randolph Place NE. Dues of subscriber-members provide sufficient income for publication of the magazine and for explorations and expeditions undertaken by the society.

The National Geographic Society has explored, mapped, and photographed hitherto unknown areas, has uncovered archeological remains in many countries, and has gathered information about the stratosphere and the deep sea. It pioneered the study of Alaska and extended aid to the polar expeditions of Peary and Byrd. Its expeditions have investigated earthquakes and volcanic eruptions at Mont Pelée, Messina, and in the Mount Katmai region in the Alaska peninsula, where one of the several expeditions discovered the Valley of Ten Thousand Smokes, since set aside as a national monument.

Other expeditions discovered Machu Picchu, the ancient city of the Incas in Peru; found in the Valley of Mexico a city buried under lava like Pompeii; and penetrated regions along the Chinese-Tibetan border previously untraversed by white men. A series of expeditions to northern New Mexico unearthed and restored Pueblo Bonito, a vast communal dwelling in which existed a high pre-Columbian Indian civilization. The Society sponsored the tree-ring researches of Andrew E. Douglass, which have dated Pueblo dwellings of the Southwest and pushed back the historic horizons in that part of our country to a period nearly eight centuries before Columbus.

In 1934 and 1935 the society sponsored and managed an expedition into the stratosphere, under trained balloonists of the United States Army, which ascended to the world record altitude of 72,395 feet, and obtained, among other data, the highest altitude photograph ever made of the earth. Captain Albert W. Stevens was in charge, and Captain Orvil A. Anderson was pilot. In 1934 the society also shared in the deep-sea explorations made by William Beebe off the Bermuda Islands, to a depth of 3,028 feet, the greatest ever reached by man.

Members of the society in Washington have attended in large numbers the lectures given each winter by the men distinguished for these and other contributions to science, and have witnessed the award of medals to Commander Robert E. Peary, Captain Roald Amundsen, Captain Robert A. Bartlett, Grove Karl Gilbert, Sir Ernest Shackleton, Vilhjalmur Stefansson, Commander Richard E. Byrd, Colonel Charles A. and Anne Morrow Lindbergh, Dr. Roy Chapman Andrews, Colonel

George W. Goethals, Floyd Bennett, Dr. Hugo Eckener, Amelia Earhart, Major Albert W. Stevens, Captain Orvil A. Anderson, Lincoln Ellsworth, and Dr. Thomas C. Poulter. The society has granted funds amounting to $65,000 to the United States Astrophysical Observatory of the Smithsonian Institution, and purchased for the Nation more than 2,000 acres of redwood forest for inclusion in Sequoia National Park.

The largest public room in the Administration Building is the HALL OF EXPLORERS, in which are displayed enlarged photographs made by explorers and photographers of the society. In the lobby, near the register for visitors, is a necklace of turquoise beads, an adornment of the women of the Pueblo Bonito in New Mexico eight centuries before the *conquistadors* set foot in the New World. There is a sun compass used by Admiral Byrd, an instrument invented by the chief cartographer of the society, Albert H. Bumstead; a model of Lincoln Ellsworth's airplane *Polar Star,* his sextant, chronometer, parka, and other equipment used on his flight across Antarctica in 1935; and the chronometer used by Sir Ernest Shackleton on his expedition of 1908-09. Also shown are the instruments and a scale model of the gondola used in the 1934 stratosphere flight of Captain Stevens and the bathysphere equipment used by William Beebe.

In Hubbard Memorial Hall are three large mural paintings by N.C. Wyeth, illustrating discovery and exploration, and Wyeth maps ornament the staircase. The library collection includes records of exploration and 15,000 volumes on geography and travel.

The NATIONAL EDUCATION ASSOCIATION is housed in a red-brick building at the northeast corner of 16th and M Streets. In front of the 16th-Street entrance is a section of a giant redwood tree, nearly 2,000 years old when it was felled in 1915. Notable epochs in history are indicated by labels, placed at intervals on the ring-growths, making the display a graphic yardstick of historic time. The section was brought from Sequoia National Park and presented to the association through the courtesy of the Department of the Interior. The lobby, on the M Street side, is dominated by a statue of Horace Mann, educational reformer and organizer of the public school system of Massachusetts.

The association, with a membership of 200,000, is a voluntary organization of active educators and others interested in the promotion of education. Its purpose, according to the charter, is "to elevate the character and advance the interests of the profession of teaching in the United States." The association was organized at Philadelphia in 1857 by a small group of educational leaders, under the name of the National Teachers' Association. In 1870 the American Normal School Association and the National Superintendents' Association were merged with it. By act of Congress in 1906 the association was incorporated under its present name, and headquarters were removed to Washington in 1917. Work is carried on by individual members and by local and State associations affiliated with the national body. There are 27 specialized departments, the governing bodies, and the head-quarters staff in Washington of more than 200 members. The association publishes the monthly *Journal,* five *Research Bulletins* each year, an annual volume of *Addresses and Proceedings,* and many other jour-nals, bulletins, and yearbooks.

In the four-story building at 1212-14 16th Street are the HEAD-QUARTERS OF THE CHARLES LATHROP PACK ORGANI-ZATIONS: The American Tree Association, founded in 1922, pub-lishes *Forestry News Digest* and numerous educational pamphlets. Membership is open, without dues, to anyone who has planted a tree. The American Nature Association, also founded in 1922, publishers of the monthly *Nature Magazine,* has a subscriber-membership of more than 75,000. The Charles Lathrop Pack Forestry Foundation, incor-porated in 1930, has established forestry fellowships and endowed chairs of forestry; it conducts special studies and contributes to the maintenance of demonstration forests.

At No. 1227 is the building of the NATIONAL SOCIETY OF THE SONS OF THE AMERICAN REVOLUTION. A "George Washington bicentennial tree," planted in 1932, and a transplanted seedling from the Washington Elm in Cambridge, Mass., stood for a time in front of the building; they were dug up when way was being made for the Scott Circle Underpass (*see below*) and have been re-planted in the grounds of the Chevy Chase Woman's Club (*see Connecticut Avenue*).

Across 16th Street, at No. 1232, is the former residence of Eliphalet Frazer Andrews, director of the Corcoran School of Art, 1877-1902, and painter of various portraits now in the White House. At the joint intersection of 16th and N Streets with Massachusetts and Rhode Island Avenues is Scott Circle (*see Massachusetts Avenue*).

The SCOTT CIRCLE UNDERPASS, completed in 1942 at an estimated cost of $460,000, has a tunnel 230 feet long and an over-all length of 800 feet, to carry traffic under the circle on 16th Street. Ramps and tunnel extend between M and O Streets on Sixteenth.

The FIRST BAPTIST CHURCH, a red-brick structure built in 1890, stands at the southwest corner at O Street. This church was organized in 1802 with six members and, for several years after 1833, occupied the site on 10th Street where Ford's Theater was later erected. Elihu Root, Secretary of State under Theodore Roosevelt, was at one time a resident of No. 1333, on the southeast corner; and No. 1401, on the northeast corner, was successively occupied by Rus-sell A. Alger, Secretary of War under McKinley, and Vice President James S. Sherman.

Prominent at the P Street intersection is the administration building of the CARNEGIE INSTITUTION OF WASHINGTON (*open 9-5 weekdays*), a classic structure housing one of the leading founda-tions devoted to research in natural science. This is the only one of the Carnegie philanthropies that directly carries on scientific research. The building, designed by Carrère and Hastings, and constructed of

Indiana limestone, was completed in 1910 at a cost of approximately $250,000. The principal façade is dominated by an Ionic portico approached by a broad flight of steps; a bronze door leads into a circular rotunda or foyer two stories in height. The walls of the rotunda are adorned with engaged variegated-marble columns of the Corinthian order, and the floor is paved in marble inlay.

Established originally by Andrew Carnegie in 1902 with an endowment of $10,000,000, the institution has received additional funds until its endowment is now $35,000,000. It maintains eight departments, two of which—the Geophysical Laboratory and the Department of Terrestrial Magnetism—are in Washington. The Department of Terrestrial Magnetism, with headquarters on a 9-acre tract near Rock Creek, maintains observatories in several countries; its high-voltage and vacuum-tube equipment for studying atomic physics and magnetism is probably unrivaled in the world.

As early as 1930 a need was felt for an annex to the administration building to house conference rooms and offices, and in 1931 Elihu Root, then chairman of the board, established a fund for the building. Under the direction of William Adams Delano, architect, construction of Elihu Root Hall was completed in 1938. The building, with auditorium and encircling offices, conference rooms, and exhibition corridors, is considered one of the most beautiful in Washington. The auditorium is decorated with heroic figures of astronomers, geographers, and other scientists. Photographic transparencies of the moon and sun in the ceiling of the hall are its most conspicuous feature.

Research units outside Washington are the Department of Embryology in Baltimore; Department of Genetics, Cold Spring Harbor, Long Island; Nutrition Laboratory, Boston; Division of Plant Biology, Stanford University, California; Mount Wilson Observatory, Pasadena, California; and the Division of Historical Research, Cambridge, Massachusetts. Through a system of research associates, the institution maintains contact with other organizations.

In December, when annual meetings of the trustees are held, popular exhibits are placed in the administration building. There is also a series of popular lectures during fall and winter months (*tickets free upon application*).

The house on the northwest corner of 16th and P Streets, once the home of Joseph B. Foraker, Senator from Ohio, is now the John Cowen Letts Educational Building, owned by the FOUNDRY METHODIST CHURCH, dedicated in 1904. This graystone edifice stands immediately to the north of the house. In an apartment building at 1424 16th Street is the chancery of the HUNGARIAN LEGATION, and at No. 1520 is the YUGOSLAV LEGATION.

The JEWISH COMMUNITY CENTER, a limestone building on the southeast corner at Q Street, contains a fine auditorium, gymnasium, music rooms, community rooms, and offices. Of chief interest in the block north of Q Street is the CHURCH OF THE HOLY

CITY, Swedenborgian, designed by H. Langford Warren and dedicated in 1896.

The HOUSE OF THE TEMPLE (*open weekdays 8:30-4:30*), at the southeast corner of 16th and S Streets, is the headquarters of the Supreme Council of the Southern Jurisdiction of the Thirty-third Degree of the Ancient and Accepted Scottish Rite of Freemasonry. Organized in 1801, at Charleston, S. C., it was the highest authority in the Scottish Rite in America until 1813, when a Supreme Council for the Northern Jurisdiction was established in Boston, and another for the Southern Jurisdiction in Washington.   The cornerstone of the House of the Temple was laid in 1911; the Bible, candlesticks, silver trowel, and gavel used by George Washington at the laying of the cornerstone of the Capitol were used on this occasion.   Designed by John Russell Pope, with Elliott Woods as consultant, the building was completed at a cost of $1,800,000 and dedicated in 1915.

Within and without, the Temple is designed and decorated with bronze inscriptions expressing the spirit of Freemasonry.   The exterior is a development of the design of the Tomb of Mausolus—one of the Seven Wonders of the ancient world.   A towering superstructure in the form of a square granite podium is surmounted by a limestone peristyle of 33 columns, 33 feet in height, terminating in a pyramidal roof.   On either side of the superstructure is a low wing.   The bronze entrance door is approached by granite steps, rising in groups of three, five, seven, and nine—numbers of symbolic significance.   On both sides of the upper flight are sphinxes, the one at the north side symbolizing Power and expressing determination and activity, while the one at the south side symbolizes Wisdom through contemplation.   Bronze grilled doors open from the vestibule into the Atrium, or main hall. The colorful decorations of this vast hall repeat Egyptian and Greek ornamental forms.   The walls are of limestone; the heavy oak beams in the ceiling are richly embellished, and the floor is of Tavernelle and Tinos marbles.   Along the side walls are four great Doric columns of polished green Windsor marble.

A grand stairway leads from the eastern end of the Atrium to the Temple Room occupying the entire upper portion.   The lower part of the room is kept dark and massive, with walls of Botticino marble, furniture of Russian walnut, and floor of black marble and white mosaic border; the upper part, leading to the polygonal dome of painted plaster, has walls of limestone.   The glass in the windows grades upward from rich orange to pale yellow.   In the center of the room is the great altar of black and gold marble.   The Executive Chamber on the main floor receives exterior light only through a skylight; artificial light is diffused through alabaster bowls.   This room, the most highly decorated in the Temple, has dais, columns, altar, and other features of Botticino marble.   The furniture of walnut consists of three officers' chairs under a throne-like canopy of black velvet in the east of the room, two chairs at the opposite end, and a series

of 33 connected side seats for the 33 active members of the Supreme
Council.

On the main floor is the LIBRARY, containing one of the largest
collections of Masonic literature in the world. On the ground floor
directly below the Atrium is the Banquet Hall, with accommodations
for 400. South of this hall is the BURNSIANA ROOM, containing the
largest American collection of books, busts, and portraits of Robert
Burns, the first poet laureate of Freemasonry. In the room on the
north side, the books are general in character, but five cases are devoted
to the works of Goethe, the poet, who was also a Freemason. Other
rooms on this floor are for committees of the Supreme Council, but one
room especially noteworthy is the PIKE ROOM, containing portraits and
busts of General Albert Pike, prominent in Freemasonry, together with
nearly all books written by or referring to him. In the southwest corner of this floor is the office of the *New Age,* official publication of the
Supreme Council.

Diagonally opposite the Scottish Rite Temple, on the northwest
corner at S Street, is the UNIVERSALIST NATIONAL MEMO-
RIAL CHURCH, designed by Allen and Collins of Boston and completed in 1930. The high-buttressed Tower of World Peace, dominating the façade, is "dedicated to the ideal of international justice and
world peace in loving and grateful tribute to Owen D. Young."
The church proper, a massive structure of light-buff stone and brick,
an adaptation of medieval Romanesque design, stands to the right
of the tower. The heavy buttresses flanking the main entrance portal
rise to the full height of the tower, which is crowned with an arcaded
belfry. The deeply recessed portal is enriched with finely carved
ornament and a sculptured lunette bearing the figure of Christ. At the
street corner another entrance leads into the long east vestibule. The
large rose window in the broad front gable is designed with delicate
tracery.

Inside, the massive walls and heavy arcades are enriched with carvings symbolic of ancient Christian liturgy. The three chancel windows,
unified by the great chancel arch, symbolize Faith, Hope, and Love,
while the lofty clerestory windows represent episodes from the life of
Christ; the lower aisle windows illustrate the progress of Christianity.
The timber ceiling is ribbed with heavy hewn beams, supported at the
clerestory walls by richly carved stone corbels. On the raised platform
is set the chancel with its carved rail. At the left is an octagonal
pulpit on a colonnaded pedestal, and at the right a delicately carved
lectern. A stone communion table takes the place of the usual altar.
In the central arch of a high wall screen is a sculptured cross, set
in a field of colorful mosaic. The right aisle of the church is arranged
as a small chapel; in its octagonal bay is a font, reproducing, in part,
an Italian Romanesque wellhead.

On the northeast corner, between U Street and New Hampshire
Avenue, is the WOMEN'S CONGRESSIONAL CLUB, erected in
1914. The organization, founded in 1908, provides a center for social

gatherings and activities of the wives of Senators, Representatives, Supreme Court Justices, and Cabinet members.

The house on the northwest corner at V Street was the home of Charles Evans Hughes at the time of his nomination for the Presidency in 1916; it was later occupied by John W. Weeks, Secretary of War under Harding and Coolidge. At the northwest corner of V Street and New Hampshire Avenue is ST. ANDREWS CHURCH, Episcopal, erected in 1915.

North of W Street on the east side, and Florida Avenue on the west side, 16th Street begins a rather steep ascent through the Meridian Hill district. Originally a part of the Robert Peter landholdings and known as Peter's Hill, this district later acquired the name of Meridian Hill, because one of the first stones marking the zero meridian of the United States was placed on the line of 16th Street, a little north of Florida Avenue. Roughly, the district includes the land between 14th and 17th Streets, north of old "Boundary Street" (Florida Avenue) to Columbia Road. For some 40 years after 1803, when this was included in the Holmead estate, the racing grounds of the Washington Jockey Club occupied a part of the Meridian Hill district, north of Euclid Street. The southwestern part, including what is now Meridian Hill Park, was purchased for $13,000 by Commodore David Porter in 1816. Thirteen years later, the house Porter built on this estate was leased by President John Quincy Adams, and here Adams retired immediately after leaving the White House in 1829. In 1869 a large part of the region was laid out in building lots, but active development did not begin until much later.

On a high knoll at 16th Street, a little north of Florida Avenue, is a turreted red-stone mansion, now a boarding house, formerly known as HENDERSON'S CASTLE. It was built in 1888 by John B. Henderson, Senator from Missouri (1826-69), who drafted the Constitutional amendment abolishing slavery, and whose widow was a prominent social figure and successful real-estate operator in Washington.

Crescent Place and Belmont Street, like short curving canyons, cut through the high land here to connect with 17th Street. Two fine private houses, designed by John Russell Pope, occupy most of the ridge between. The first, west of 17th, was built for Henry White, former Ambassador to France, and is now the residence of Eugene Meyer, publisher of the Washington *Post*. Here Marshal Joffre, Premier Viviani, and other members of the French Commission were guests in May 1917. The second house is occupied by Irwin Laughlin, former Ambassador to Spain. The log cabin occupied for three years in the early eighties by the poet Joaquin Miller stood on the slope below the Meyer house until 1912, when it was removed to Rock Creek Park (*see Potomac and Rock Creek Parks*).

On the east side of 16th Street, extending from W Street north to Euclid and east to 15th Street, is MERIDIAN HILL PARK, a great public garden. The architect responsible for its final plan and structural development is Horace W. Peaslee of Washington, who made a special study of European parks and in 1917, as architect of public buildings and grounds, succeeded George Burnap, landscape architect, author of preliminary studies for the project. Vitale, Brinckerhoff, and Geiffert prepared the general planting scheme that was carried out by landscape architects of the National Park Service. A new type of decorative concrete, with exposed aggregates variously graded for size and color, was developed from experiments begun with John Earley and continued over a 20-year period with the Tompkins and Drew construction organizations, all of Washington.

Two-thirds of the acreage is high land, made level and usable by massive retaining walls. Long promenades and a mall in the French manner, bordered with heavy planting masses and winding walks, culminate at the break of the hill in an elm-crowned terrace with terminal fountains, offering distant vistas of the Virginia and Maryland hills across the Potomac and Anacostia Rivers.

The outstanding feature of the park is its lavish use of water in terrace and wall fountains; in jets large and small; in a cascade of Italian inspiration, with 13 falls of graduated size; and in a broad reflecting basin with an enclosing seat-coping modeled after a pool in Zurich, Switzerland. The cascades and fountains are kept in operation during the summer season by a recirculating system, with underwater illumination for special occasions. Temporary provisions have been made for music and pageantry in the upper terrace concert grove and in the lower hedged garden, but completion of the park program awaits a permanent concert pavilion, lighting installation, and organization of recreational facilities. The park site, comprising nearly 12 acres, was purchased by the Government in 1912 for $490,000, and the total development has cost more than $1,156,000.

A bronze ARMILLARY SPHERE, 16 feet in circumference, designed by Carl Paul Jennewein, stands centrally within a semicircular exedra between a reflecting pool and the south wall of the park. Opposite the eastern end of the pool and facing 16th Street, is the bronze STATUE OF JAMES BUCHANAN, the work of Hans Schuler. A bronze STATUE OF DANTE, a copy of the original by Ettore Ximenes in New York City, stands a little to the north of the Buchanan Memorial below the grand terrace; the statue, unveiled on the 600th anniversary of the poet's death, was a gift by Carlo Barsotti "in behalf of the Italians of the United States."

The bronze equestrian STATUE OF JOAN OF ARC, near the south end of the upper terrace, is a copy of the statue by Paul Dubois which stands in front of Rheims Cathedral. It was unveiled in 1922. Near the west walk on the upper level is José Clara's marble SERENITY, purchased by Charles Deering at the Paris Exposition of 1900, and, after more than two decades placed here as a memorial to Lieutenant Commander William H. Scheutz, a naval officer in the Spanish-American War.

The three buildings designed by George Oakley Totten and erected by Mrs. John B. Henderson face the park on the 16th Street side. Of these, Hotel 2400 (named for its number on 16th Street) is an apartment-hotel building about midway along the park's western side; it houses the LEGATION OF EL SALVADOR. North of the park, at the northwest corner of Euclid Street, is the "PINK PALACE," once the home of Mrs. Marshall Field. This, the earliest of the buildings designed by Totten in this neighborhood, is constructed of pink stucco, with white marble trim and a red roof. The first occupant after its completion in 1906 was Oscar S. Straus, Secretary of Commerce and Labor under Theodore Roosevelt. It is now headquarters for the District of Columbia Order of the Eastern Star.

The next few blocks along 16th Street justify the name of "Embassy Row." At No. 2622 is the LITHUANIAN LEGATION; at No. 2630, the CUBAN EMBASSY; and at the southwest corner of Fuller Street, the POLISH EMBASSY. The ITALIAN EMBASSY, at No. 2700, was designed by Warren and Wetmore of New York City in Italian Renaissance style; it contains many rare and beautiful examples of medieval Italian craftsmanship and has a formal walled garden. At No. 2801 is the SPANISH EMBASSY, built in 1923. To the rear, facing on 15th Street, is the Chancery, built by the Spanish government. The MEXICAN EMBASSY, 2829 Sixteenth Street, was formerly occupied by Breckinridge Long, at one time Ambassador to Italy and now (1942) an Assistant Secretary of State. King Albert and Queen Elizabeth of Belgium, with their son, Prince Leopold, were guests here in 1919.

North of the Italian Embassy is the SCOTTISH RITE TEMPLE, at 2800 16th Street, headquarters of the District of Columbia Jurisdiction of the Ancient and Accepted Scottish Rite of Freemasonry. The temple was designed by the Washington architects Porter, Lockie, and Chatelaine. The cornerstone was laid in June 1939, and dedicated with Masonic ceremonies on May 12, 1940. It was completed at a cost of $500,000. Steps leading to the entrance are in groups of three, five, seven, and nine. Around the Great Portal are 33 massive square stones, one for each degree in Scottish Rite Masonry. The Portal, in mosaic and bronze, depicts life and the virtues.

The main entrance lobby has walls of black marble and a vaulted ceiling of 14-carat gold leaf, reflecting the light issuing from six bronze double eagles on marble pedestals. At the north end of the lobby is the office of the Secretary of the Washington Jurisdiction. From the main lobby, corridors lead to the Tiler's Lobby, its gray walls creating a subdued atmosphere as an approach to the Auditorium or Great Hall.

The GREAT HALL, in the form of an amphitheater, seats nearly 600. Its walls are draped with hangings decorated with Masonic motifs; from the proscenium arch gleam the 29 jewels of Scottish Rite Masonry. Just off the Great Hall is a spacious MASONIC LIBRARY, and above it are recreation rooms. On this floor also is a small lodge room for business meetings of the co-ordinate bodies of the Rite. On the street-level floor are the banquet hall and the lodge room of the Robert Le Bruce Chapter, Order of De Molay, of Washington.

Between the intersections of Harvard Street and Columbia Road with 16th Street is an open area of considerable size, dominated by three of the city's most impressive churches. On the west side, on one of the highest elevations in the city, rises the WASHINGTON CHAPEL of the Church of Jesus Christ of Latter-day Saints (Mormon), with its spire surmounted by the Angel Moroni, the equivalent of Gabriel in Mormon cosmogony. The structure, completed in 1933, was designed by Young and Hansen, of Salt Lake City, to reflect the spirit of the great Temple there. Simplicity, directness in form and line, and extreme verticality are emphasized. Above the entrance portal a brilliantly colored mosaic depicts the Sermon on the Mount. Beyond the spacious lobby is the Chapel, arranged as an amphitheater with rostral platform, organ console, and choir seats in the east end. In the ceiling above the organ console are grilled openings to the organ in the tower. The high windows are decorated with Mormon historical symbols. The Chapel is noteworthy as being practically perfect acoustically.

The Washington Chapel demonstrates the Mormon ideal of relating religion to social life. By means of a sliding panel, the chapel and recreation hall, with stage, projection room, and gallery, can be converted into a great auditorium; on the lower floor are classrooms, relief society room, Scout room, and banquet hall with modern kitchen; a gymnasium is in the basement. The offices of the chapel and congregational authorities are on the Columbia Road side of the church, and above is a modern apartment for the Chapel Director.

At the corner of Harvard and 16th Streets is ALL SOULS' UNITARIAN CHURCH, successor of the First Unitarian Church, which stood for more than half a century at 6th and D Streets. The congregation, organized in 1821, erected a new church at 14th and L Streets in 1877, changing the name to All Souls'. The magnificent church on the present site was designed by Coolidge and Shattuck and erected in 1924 at a cost of nearly a million dollars. From its very beginning many distinguished Americans have been identified with All Souls', among its earliest members being Presidents John Quincy Adams and Millard Fillmore. President Taft was long a member; his funeral services were conducted by the present pastor, Dr. Pierce, in 1930. Other prominent members were Senators Webster, Sumner, and Calhoun. From the pulpit was heard the eloquence of Edward Everett Hale, Ralph Waldo Emerson and William Ellery Channing, who was pastor here for a time. Here also was delivered the famous pro-slavery sermon of the acting pastor, Moncure D. Conway, who was practically forced to resign when his utterances were reported in the New York *Tribune* by its editor, Horace Greeley, then a member of Congress (filling a vacancy for three months in 1848-49).

The design of All Souls' is based on that of St. Martin in the Fields, London, one of the great works of James Gibbs. The exterior, of mellow red brick and white-stone trim, is adorned with Corinthian columns and pilasters, and crowned with a balustraded parapet. The pedimented door headings, stone quoins, keystones over the arched and segmental windows, and occasional wall niches are all characteristic of the English prototype. The lofty clock tower, with its lower belfry, crowning lantern and white spire, topped with a gilded weather vane, is the most distinctive feature of the building. The classic influence prevails in the all-white interior, where Corinthian columns support a vaulted ceiling and carry the sweeping lines of a continuous entablature. An octagonal walnut pulpit, on a platform at the eastern end, stands against the folds of a red wall hanging.

The parish house, in the rear of the church, is in the form of a quadrangle enclosing the open "Court of the Founders." In the right wing is Pierce Hall, containing a small stage and projection room; in the left wing is the Hale Parish House, with the Ida May Gale Memorial Library.

At the northeast corner of 16th Street and Columbia Road stands the modern white-limestone edifice of the NATIONAL MEMORIAL BAPTIST CHURCH, formerly known as the Immanuel Baptist. Designed by Egerton Swartwout, New York architect, it was constructed as a national memorial to religious liberty through the united efforts of the Northern and Southern Baptist Conventions, and dedicated in 1933. The distinctive architectural feature is its massive, round corner tower, whose classic silhouette is derivative of late seventeenth-century examples. The interior of the tower forms a circular chancel in one side of the hexagonal auditorium. The main entrance, in the façade fronting 16th Street, is crowned by a classic balustrade, behind which the low dome of the auditorium is visible.

Adjoining the main building on the east (completed in 1941), is the BIBLE SCHOOL BUILDING, in architectural harmony with the main building and extending through to 15th Street.

Harvard Street, west of its intersection with 16th, leads to a principal entrance to National Zoological Park, about a half-mile distant. The little triangular park between 16th and Mount Pleasant Streets has the bronze equestrian STATUE OF FRANCIS ASBURY, pioneer Methodist bishop of America. The statue, the work of Augustus Lukeman, was erected in 1891.

The CENTRAL PRESBYTERIAN CHURCH stands close to the eastern side of 16th Street at its intersection with Irving Street. Close to its western side, between Irving and Lamont Streets, is the FRANCIS ASBURY METHODIST CHURCH. A little west of the intersection of 16th and Lamont Streets, the Mount Pleasant branch of the Washington Public Library occupies a gray stone building.

On the triangular site, between 16th Street and the library at this intersection, stands a MEMORIAL STATUE TO GUGLIELMO MARCONI, inventor of wireless telegraphy, erected in 1941 by the Marconi Memorial Foundation. The sculptor was Artillio Piccarilli and the architect Joseph Freedlander, both of New York. The base of the statue is of Stony Creek granite, supporting two pedestals of the same material. A bronze bust of Marconi tops the smaller pedestal, while the larger supports a bronze figure symbolizing electricity, carried on a half-globe suspended in clouds.

The Mount Pleasant region is a somewhat indeterminate area of high land east of Rock Creek, more or less centering on Sixteenth Street, between Columbia Road and Piney Branch. Its development as a residential section dates from Civil War times. A writer of the early seventies characterized it as "perhaps the most healthy suburb of Washington" because of its exemption from the malarial chills and fevers "which frequently prevail in the city."

The Roman Catholic SHRINE OF THE SACRED HEART, at the southeast corner of 16th Street and Park Road, was erected in 1921-22 from designs by Murphy and Olmstead of Washington. It is notable, not so much for its structural design, which has the basilican mass and cruciform plan of the seventh-century churches of northern Italy, but for the elaborate symbolism and richness of its interior decoration. Viewed from a short distance, the Shrine stands severely white against the green of a small park before its west front. In this triangular plot is the bronze STATUE OF CARDINAL GIBBONS, by Leo Lentelli, erected in 1932 by the Knights of Columbus.

The plan of the church, with nave and transepts of equal breadth, its large segmental dome and graceful half-dome over the apse and transept chapels, is readily discernible from the exterior. A continuous colonnaded portico adorns the 16th Street façade; a cartwheel window in the broad front gable is flanked by niched figures of St. Joseph and the Virgin Mary. A wealth of decorative display, colonnades and Byzantine archways, inlays of gold and colored mosaic, sculpture and rare marbles, mark each of the three entrance portals. The walls, done in modern mosaic by John J. Earley of Washington, picture symbolically the Catholic liturgy and lives of martyred saints. The high main altar, of Italian marble with brilliant mosaic inlays, is surmounted with a massive canopy, on which the Paschal Lamb is portrayed against a background of floral arabesques. At either side is a peacock, symbol of eternal life. In a chapel to the left of the main altar is the Altar of the Sacred Heart, with a processional of angels above its canopy. The Altar of the Blessed Virgin, to the right, holds a charming canopied figure of Botticino marble. Part of the wall treatment are the Stations of the Cross in resplendent mosaic.

At the southwest corner of Newton Street is the GUNTON-TEMPLE MEMORIAL CHURCH, and a little east of 16th on Newton Street is the Episcopal CHURCH OF ST. STEPHEN AND THE INCARNATION.

The FOURTH CHURCH OF CHRIST, SCIENTIST, between Meridian Place and Oak Street, designed by Howard L. Cheney of Chicago and completed in 1929, is distinguished by its simple mass and classic detail. The variegated limestone walls are adorned with finely molded architraves and cornices, an attic frieze, delicate anthemion crestings, and paneled arabesques. The central portion of the church encloses an inner dome and is carried well above the surrounding structure in the form of an attic setback. The curved front portico, with its fluted Greek Doric columns, is approached by a broad flight of steps, the curved line of which is recalled in the end bays of the north and south transepts. The auditorium, seating 1,000, is designed with great restraint; along its soft beige walls are Ionic columns and pilasters, supporting a coffered dome with a medallion skylight. On the raised platform, with delicate iron rail, in the east arm of the cross, are the readers' desks and organ console. The great organ loft behind it is concealed by grilled screens of classic design. On the floor below are readers' studies, reception room, church offices, and Sunday-school room.

Just south of Piney Branch Bridge, MARTHA WASHINGTON SEMINARY, a nonsectarian finishing school for girls founded in 1905, occupies several buildings set far back from the street in extensive grounds. Below the southern slope of Piney Branch Parkway is a deep and wide wooded ravine extending eastward from Rock Creek Park. The concrete bridge, erected 1907-10, which spans this ravine at 16th Street is sometimes referred to as "Tiger Bridge" because of the bronze tigers, by A. Phimister Proctor, at either end. Piney Branch was once a considerable stream, flowing from the northeast into Rock Creek. It appears on L'Enfant's map of 1791 as Pine Creek, "whose water, if necessary, may supply the City, being turned into James White's branch"—a small tributary of Tiber Creek. What a Smithsonian Institution report characterizes as "the greatest aboriginal boulder quarries known, and their most important implement shops yet observed on the Atlantic slope" have been found along the banks of Piney Branch and the hillsides above it. Construction of the parkway, as an extension of Rock Creek Park, was authorized by act of Congress in 1907.

GRACE LUTHERAN CHURCH stands a few blocks north of the Piney Branch Bridge, at the northwest corner of Varnum Street; two blocks beyond, at the northeast corner of Allison Street, is the HAMLINE METHODIST CHURCH, organized in 1866.

From Upshur Street northward to Alaska Avenue, a distance of more than 2 miles, 16th Street is bordered by 507 memorial trees planted in 1920, each with a bronze marker bearing the name of a resident of the District of Columbia who died in military or naval service during the First World War. Baskets of flowers are placed beside each marker on Memorial Day.

At the intersection with Colorado Avenue is also the terminus of Iowa Avenue, which enters from the southeast, and of Gallatin Street, from the east. At 5017 16th Street is the HAITIAN LEGATION. On the northeast corner at Gallatin Street is the CHRIST EVANGELICAL LUTHERAN CHURCH; and in the next block, at the southeast corner of Kennedy Street, stands the SIXTH PRESBYTERIAN CHURCH.

From the Colorado Avenue intersection for most of its remaining northward course, 16th Street forms the eastern boundary of Rock Creek Park; one block south of Colorado Avenue is the Blagden Avenue entrance. Just inside the park, a little beyond the intersection, is the SITE OF THE BRIGHTWOOD RESERVOIR, built in 1901 and used for 30 years. Tennis courts now occupy the site.

East of 16th Street and northward for about a mile is an indeterminate area known as Brightwood, centering approximately at the intersection of Georgia and Concord Avenues. Before the Civil War, this region was a suburb of Washington, where many prominent residents maintained country estates. Long since subdivided and absorbed into the urban area, it retains its original designation. In the Brightwood area are the remains of FORT STEVENS, where General Early and a force of Confederate troops were turned back from an attack on the Capital in July 1864. They may be reached from Sixteenth Street most directly by following Fort Drive for two blocks eastward. Grass-grown earthworks and restored palisades mark the old battlefield.

Half a mile northeast of Fort Stevens, a plot of ground of one acre, on the east side of Georgia Avenue, constitutes BATTLE-GROUND NATIONAL CEMETERY (*open, summer, 6:30 a.m.-7 p.m.; winter, 7:30-4:30*), the smallest national cemetery. Here are buried the Union soldiers who fell during the engagement at the fort July 12, 1864. Two of the smooth-bore cannons used in defense of Fort Stevens guard the entrance at 6625 Georgia Avenue. Beyond the rubble wall, to the right, is the two-story superintendent's lodge, erected in 1865, a neat square building of dressed fieldstone, with a gray-slate mansard roof; two ancient boxwoods stand at the entrance to the circular plot of 41 graves, each with its marble headstone. To the east of the graves is a marble rostrum where Memorial Day services are conducted. Four granite shafts on the Georgia Avenue side commemorate the volunteer regiments that fought at Fort Stevens. Near by is the 200-year old cherry tree under which President Lincoln stood when he dedicated the cemetery.

Just north of the Brightwood Reservoir, in 1859, a half-mile race course was laid out between Rock Creek and Colorado Avenue (then part of Piney Branch Road). Known as the Crystal Spring Track and later as the Piney Branch Track, the course was operated by the Brightwood Driving Club at the time of the closing in 1909. Here, in 1894, "General" Coxey's army of unemployed made its camp before marching to the Capitol.

North of the Brightwood district, the ARMY MEDICAL CENTER, including the Walter Reed General Hospital and Army Medical School, occupies landscaped grounds between 16th Street and Alaska Avenue on the west and northwest and Georgia Avenue on the east. The grouping in a single military reservation of all the District's scattered medical facilities was urged from Civil War days until 1892, when a plan began to take shape; but it was not until 1898 that the post hospital at the Washington Barracks was established by a general order as the Army General Hospital. A "company of instruction" for training recruits to the Hospital Corps was later transferred to the control of the hospital, and the Army Medical School was opened in 1901. In 1905 Congress appropriated funds for a more adequate hospital; the present grounds were selected, and the hospital named for Walter Reed, the noted surgeon whose death in 1902 was hastened by his researches into the cause of yellow fever. An administration building, with hospital accommodations for 60 beds, was the first building erected in 1908, and in 1909 the hospital was opened, having a capacity of 120 beds. Functioning on a small scale for eight years, it underwent enormous expansion in 1917-18, the temporary wards at one time having 2,500 beds. At the close of the First World War Congress appropriated $3,000,000 to increase the facilities, and with the erection of the Army Medical School Building in 1923 at a cost of $500,000, the hospital became the Army Medical Center. Seventeen red-brick barracks and two wards were completed in 1941 in the northeastern corner of the grounds.

To the right of the Georgia Avenue entrance, just beyond Whittier Street, is Delano Hall, the nurses' quarters, a rambling Georgian building of brick. The Service Club is near by, and on an eminence to the left of the entrance is the Army Medical School, a huge plain brick building screened by a grove of oaks. Near the west entrance are the officers' quarters, two white-porticoed brick buildings in shaded lawns. About midway between the 16th Street and Georgia Avenue entrances, the Administration Building of Walter Reed Hospital dominates the park from its imposing site among wards, laboratories, warehouses, and quarters, and its notable gardens and terraces. Close by the hospital buildings is the Red Cross recreation center. The term "general" is applied to the hospital to distinguish it from post hospitals; it signifies that patients are admitted under special regulations from the Army at large. More than 1,200 beds are available. Instruction in physiotherapy and occupational therapy supplements medical and surgical treatment. The gardens, which contribute to the therapeutic program, can be reached directly from the Administration Building or from an adjacent parking space hidden by clipped hemlock borders. In these elaborate and beautiful grounds the hospital staff and patients gather on Easter morning for sunrise services. Three greenhouses supply flowers for the hospital; in a fourth, tropical plants flourish—palms, rubber trees, and pandanus with aerial roots.

At 12th and Dogwood Streets, opposite the obstetrical ward, is the Post Exchange cafeteria. Except for a few officers' quarters and the gray-stone Memorial Chapel, most of the buildings are south of Dogwood Street. Toward the north are tennis courts and an athletic field (west of 13th Street).

The grounds of the Medical Center embrace the site of the Confederate battle line in the attack on Fort Stevens. President Lincoln was exposed to fire during the battle; his presence is commemorated by a bronze plaque near the east entrance to the reservation. The old Sharpshooter's Tree, used for reconnoitering, and from which it is said an attack was made upon the President, stood here until destroyed by a storm in 1919.

Opposite the southwest corner of the Army Medical Center grounds is the Sherrill Drive entrance to Rock Creek Park. The area north of the Center and adjacent to Rock Creek Park is known as Sixteenth Street Heights. Here are many distinctive houses—stone Norman "castles," tile-roofed Spanish-type houses, English houses with pitched roofs and half-timber gables, Colonial mansions, square modern dwellings with round windows—among tastefully landscaped gardens and lawns. The 10-acre campus of the MARJORIE WEBSTER SCHOOL FOR GIRLS, founded in 1920, extends from 16th Street west to 17th, just south of Kalmia Road.

BLAIR PORTAL, at the District Line, marks the northern terminus of 16th Street. Here the thoroughfare connects with the East-West Highway leading to Silver Spring, Maryland, on the east and to Chevy Chase, Maryland, on the west. Blair Portal is a circular plaza around one of the original boundary stones set out soon after the District was surveyed in 1792. Groups of detached two-story brick apartment units (the Falkland group), built in the late 1930's, occupy wooded grounds to the north of Blair Portal.

PART III
In the Environs

Arlington

Busses: Fort Myer, Washington National Airport (10¢ fare), and sightseeing busses and limousines.
Taxis: Extra-fare prices for travel outside the District; fare to airport 60¢.

Visitors to Washington by the thousands every year make the pilgrimage to Arlington National Cemetery, visit historic Arlington House, and drive along the landscaped Mount Vernon Memorial Highway. History comes alive along much of the route, but there is also a great deal of contemporary interest—an Army cantonment; an airport; a wildfowl refuge where snowy egrets, herons, and wild ducks congregate within sight of the road; a marine memorial of unusual spirit; a harbor-channel where small boats and little seaplanes moor; and the landscaped highway itself, which courses beside tidal creeks and offers broad vistas of the Potomac.

The approach to Arlington House and Arlington National Cemetery extends southwest from the Lincoln Memorial across the Arlington Memorial Bridge (*see Arlington Memorial Bridge*). Part of a development to afford a broader vista across the river to the white-columned Arlington House, a short bridge spans the Boundary Channel of the Potomac, connecting Columbia Island with the south shore of the Potomac. The small bridge, designed by McKim, Mead, and White, is in the style of the Arlington Memorial Bridge, having four 35-foot terminal pylons surmounted with eight-foot eagles carved by C. Paul Jennewein. This bridge leads to the Memorial Parkway flanked by formal planting, which ends in the Arlington Memorial Gate. The Gate takes the form of a court of honor, enclosed at the end against the sloping hill by a high semicircular wall, or exedra, and on two sides by an iron fence set between massive pylons, repeating those on Arlington Bridge. At the center of the exedra is a semicircular niche with a fountain, framed by a triumphal arch bearing medallion seals of the United States, the Army, and the Navy. The broad driveway leading into the court splits right and left into branching drives through heavy iron entrance gates on which are the seals of the Army, Navy, Marine Corps, and Coast Guard. A stairway at each side leads to a balustraded promenade above the exedra. The entrance highway at the right leads to Arlington House; that on the left, to the Tomb of the Unknown Soldier and the Arlington Amphitheater.

ARLINGTON HOUSE

Standing on the brow of the hill, an outstanding landmark visible from many parts of Washington, Arlington House (*open daily 9-6 Apr.*

*through Aug., 9-5 during Sept., 9-4:30 Oct.-Feb., 9-5 during March;
adm. 10¢)* has a portico of eight heavy Doric columns supporting a
massive buff pediment. The building of stuccoed brick, painted buff
and trimmed with white, has balancing wings on either side of the
central section. The portico is 60 feet wide and 25 feet deep, and the
entire front of the building measures 140 feet.

Entrance is usually made from the rear where parking space is
provided in the courtyard. The road curves around the shoulder of
the hill, and the domestic life of another century suddenly presents
itself—the main structure of the mansion with its welcoming doorway,
vine-covered outbuildings, and servants' quarters about the once busy
courtyard with a great Himalayan cedar in the center. From the
eastern terrace the great columns of the portico can be seen in unusual
perspective, and from this vantage there is a sweeping view of the
Potomac, the Lincoln Memorial, and the city of Washington. The
refurnished smokehouse and summer kitchen are low, brick-and-stucco
buildings flanking the rear of the mansion. The square yellow building beyond the original kitchen garden to the north was the ice house,
now used as a tool house for Arlington Cemetery. Across the ravine
among the trees is the brick stable, with a portico like that on the
house; the building which houses offices of the cemetery, was accurately
restored after a fire had destroyed the original.

Arlington estate was originally part of a 6,000-acre tract, including
what is now Alexandria, Virginia, granted in 1669 to Robert Howsen,
a ship captain, for bringing colonists to Virginia. The Alexander
family, for whom Alexandria was named, later acquired the acreage
for six hogsheads of tobacco. In 1776 John Parke Custis, son of
Martha Washington and Daniel Parke Custis, purchased 1,100 acres
of this area and named it Arlington, for an older Custis property on
the Eastern Shore. He and his wife, Eleanor Calvert, did not live
here, however, residing at Abingdon. When John Custis died, his only
son, George Washington Parke Custis, and his youngest daughter,
Nellie, were adopted by the Washingtons and went to Mount Vernon
to live.

After the death of Martha Washington in 1802, George Custis
came into his inheritance and began plans for the mansion; some say
that work began on it that year. Two years later, however, when he
married Mary Fitzhugh Lee, they took up their residence in a four-
room cottage near the river, about a mile from Arlington. Foundation
stones and timber for the mansion came from the estate, and bricks
were made by slaves from native clay. It is believed that George
W. P. Custis designed and supervised the original building, which was
not completed, apparently, until after the War of 1812. The building
was remodeled about 1820 under the direction of George Hadfield.
One of the memorable events at Arlington during its early history was
the entertainment of the aged General Lafayette during his visit to
America in 1824-25.

In 1831 Mary Ann Randolph Custis, only child of the house, was married to Lieutenant Robert E. Lee, son of "Light Horse Harry" Lee, a friend of Washington. Arlington was their home for 30 years and their seven children were born here. During much of this time Lee was absent from home as a cavalry officer during the Mexican War and while stationed at distant army posts. During one of his brief periods at Arlington in 1859, Lee, now a lieutenant colonel, was called upon to capture John Brown and his raiders at Harpers Ferry. Later, after a brief interlude along the Texas border, he was again called to Washington to make the critical decision of his life. At the request of President Lincoln he was offered the field command of the United States Army, which appeared certain to invade Virginia in the event of the outbreak of the threatened Civil War.

In his study at Arlington, April 20, 1861, after two days of deep thought, Lee wrote a brief formal letter to the Secretary of War, resigning his commission as colonel of the First Regiment of Cavalry. To General Winfield Scott he wrote intimately: "I can anticipate no greater calamity than the dissolution of the Union. . . . Still a union that can only be maintained by swords and bayonets . . . has no charm for me. . . . If the Union is dissolved . . . I shall return to my native state and, save in defence, will draw my sword no more." Soon after, he rode out of the plantation enclosure in civilian clothes to offer his services to Virginia.

When Federal forces crossed the Potomac, one of the first positions occupied was Arlington, a key situation in the defense of the Capital. Mrs. Lee, taking such possessions as she could hastily assemble, fled to Ravensworth, near Fairfax. Later, General McDowell, commander of Union forces, sent to the Patent Office as many Washington heirlooms as could be collected, but many had disappeared. No Lee lived at Arlington after 1861. Three years later title passed to the United States in lieu of taxes illegally levied. A decade later a Supreme Court ruling restored the estate to its rightful heir, but meantime it had become more than a military post and more than a house. Union soldiers were buried in the grounds of the former Confederate leader's home. Recognizing that it had become public property in sentiment, if not in fact, the heir, George Washington Custis Lee, sold Arlington to the Government for $150,000. During the next half century the house stood untenanted and untended, except for the one wing that housed offices of the cemetery.

Restoration was approved by act of Congress in 1925. Most of the furnishings had gone back to Mount Vernon, to the National Museum, or to the Lee heirs. Some were returned, but for the most part the furnishings of Arlington are copies of the originals, or genuine period-pieces suited to the house. Brought back from a state of crumbling decay, Arlington House is a home reflecting a period of gentle and gracious living rather than a museum. In 1934 its care passed from the War Department to the National Park Service.

Within the house, entered from the west or rear courtyard, a long hall traverses the central building and wings. Lofty ceilings, wide arches, and broad cornice moldings preserve the scale of the exterior. On the north side of a well-proportioned central hall are the family dining room and parlor; on the south, an exceptionally long drawing room. A stairway at the west end of the central hall leads to the second story. In the south wing, beyond the drawing room, is the state dining room, with a study and conservatory adjoining. The bedroom and sitting room used by the Custis family are in the north wing, at the end of which is a small sewing and schoolroom. A service hall in the north wing gives access to a stairway into the basement with its commodious winter kitchen and wine cellar.

In the main hall is a copy of the painting, *Washington at Yorktown,* which George Washington Parke Custis considered his masterpiece. In the drawing room, which he used as his studio, hangs the *Washington at Valley Forge,* believed to be an authentic Custis. Most of the paintings at Arlington are copies of originals that hang in the library at Washington and Lee University, Lexington, Virginia. General Lee was president of that institution, then known as Washington College, from the Civil War until his death in 1870, when it was renamed Washington and Lee University. An original water color, *Arlington House in 1853,* by Benson J. Lossing, hangs in the drawing room at Arlington, which also contains a music case believed to have been the property of Nellie Custis.

In the state dining room, south wing, the chairs are reproductions of a Sheraton set willed by Martha Washington to her grandson. In the study beyond is a desk used by Lee from 1848 to 1852. In the parlor and family dining room, north of the main hall, are twin mantels of Carrara marble, said to have been imported by Custis from Italy. The Duncan Phyfe chair is an original piece. The Heppelwhite dining-room chairs are reproductions of a set originally here. Under the archway between the two rooms, Mary Custis and Robert E. Lee stood in 1831 for their wedding ceremony. Aside from the few original pieces and many excellent reproductions, gifts and loans have provided Chippendale and Sheraton pieces, old silver and china, draperies, nineteenth-century needlework and kitchen utensils, and a rare Sèvres vase decorated and signed by Pascaut.

ARLINGTON NATIONAL CEMETERY

Largest and most noted of American national burial grounds, Arlington National Cemetery (*open daily 7-5 Jan.-Feb., 7-6 March, 7-7 April, 6 a. m.-7:30 p. m. May-July, 6 a.m.-7 p.m. Aug., 6-6 Sept., 7-5:30 Oct., 7-5 Nov.-Dec.*) is a landscaped 409-acre tract, roughly semicircular in shape, on rolling Virginia hills southwest of the Lincoln Memorial. Ten gates, nine of which are open for public use, give entrance to the burial ground, in which 49,927 burials had been made to January 1, 1941. Arlington provides a beautiful and impressive setting for memorial celebrations and for military funerals. As in other national burial places, interment here is principally reserved for officers and enlisted men of the Army, Navy, Marine Corps, and Coast Guard, though wives, unmarried daughters, and minor sons are frequently buried in the same plot with officers, and wives of enlisted men are often buried in the same grave with their husbands.

In 1861 the land now constituting Arlington National Cemetery was occupied by Union forces, the old Arlington estate having been converted into an armed camp.   On the site of the present Fort Myer, Fort Whipple was hastily built, one of the strongest in the cordon of forts that encircled Washington.   Fort Whipple, completed near the close of the war, was never manned; its grass-grown ramparts remain in the southwestern part of the cemetery.   In 1864, 210 acres in the immediate vicinity of Arlington House were set aside as a national cemetery for Union soldiers and sailors.   The first man buried, however, was a Confederate prisoner who had died in a local hospital; last rites for him were held on Friday, May 13, 1864.   The slopes below the mansion were set aside for the interment of officers, while the rank and file were buried in the "Lower Cemetery" at the northeast of the enclosure.   Of 5,199 burials made in old parts of the cemetery, 3,802 were refugee Negroes who attached themselves to the Union Army at the beginning of the war.   In 1889 and 1897 the grounds were extended by the addition of 142 and 56 acres, bringing the reservation to its present size.

The unknown dead of the Civil War were commemorated in 1866; those of the Spanish-American War in 1902; and the dead of the *Maine* disaster in 1915.   The bronze monument to the Confederate dead in Jackson Circle was dedicated in 1914.   Canadian memorials to American dead in the World War were erected in 1920.   The Memorial Amphitheater was completed the same year, and the Tomb of the Unknown Soldier was finished in 1931.

The history of Memorial Day has an intimate connection with that of Arlington.   The custom irregularly followed throughout the country of decorating the graves of Civil War soldiers on a certain day, was fixed in 1868 by General John A. Logan, commander in chief of the Grand Army of the Republic.   First official services on May 30 were held on the portico of Arlington House.   Increasing crowds made the portico inadequate, and the Old Amphitheater was built.   Many years later the Arlington Amphitheater provided additional accommodations for the crowds.

On the slopes east and south of Arlington House is the TOMB OF GENERAL PHILIP HENRY SHERIDAN (1831-88), who was outstanding as a Union cavalry leader during the Civil War; and, near the flagstaff, the TOMB OF ADMIRAL DAVID DIXON PORTER (1813-91), naval officer in the Mexican and Civil Wars and superintendent of the U. S. Naval Academy from 1865 to 1869.   Around them stand many other granite monuments bearing names distinguished in the military annals of the nineteenth century.   The GRAVE OF PIERRE L'ENFANT (1754-1825), original designer of Washington, is marked by a granite slab on six granite legs; the monument, designed by W. W. Bosworth, was erected after the city planner had been given the belated honor of an Arlington burial in 1909. The GRAVES OF ROBERT TODD LINCOLN and PRESIDENT WILLIAM H. TAFT are down the slope toward the Memorial Gate. The GRAVE OF MAJOR GENERAL GEORGE H. CROOK, farther south of Arlington House, is marked by a monument bearing a bas-relief showing the surrender of the Apache chief Geronimo; the surrender took place, however, after Crook had asked to be relieved of the command in the Apache campaign.

On high ground just south of the mansion is the TEMPLE OF FAME, a round-domed arbor with 12 eminent names inscribed on its 8 columns and cornice. West of it is the MONUMENT TO THE UNKNOWN DEAD OF THE CIVIL WAR, a granite tomb in a cluster of oaks, above a single grave containing the bodies of 2,111 unidentified soldiers killed at Bull Run and on the route to the Rappahannock. Farther west is the OLD AMPHITHEATER, a vine-covered pergola once used for Memorial Day services. Opposite its west portal is the CANADIAN MEMORIAL, a bronze sword bound to a granite cross, given by the Canadian government to memorialize Americans who served with Canadian forces in the World War. The equestrian STATUE OF GENERAL PHILIP KEARNY (1814-62), one-armed commander of cavalry in the Union Army of the Potomac, who was killed in action, stands at the point where Lee, Wilson, and Meigs Avenues intersect; the statue is the work of Edward Clark Potter.

West of the Old Amphitheater, on Meigs Avenue, is a crowded section of officers' graves. The GRAVE OF QUARTERMASTER GENERAL MONTGOMERY C. MEIGS, who first suggested to President Lincoln the appropriateness of Arlington as a national cemetery, is marked by a sarcophagus of dressed marble. Other graves in this area include those of Major General Abner Doubleday, who was among the defenders of Fort Sumter in 1861; Brigadier General W.S. Harney, a noted Indian fighter; Brigadier General James B. Ricketts, veteran of 27 Civil War battles; Dr. Alexander T. Augusta, major and surgeon of the Seventh United States Colored Troops; and Captain Orindatus S.B. Wall, of the 104th U. S. Colored Infantry Volunteers.

A sharp left turn to McPherson Avenue leads to the FIELD OF THE DEAD, where lie thousands killed in the Civil War. Near the curve of the hill are the GRAVES OF GEORGE WASHINGTON PARKE CUSTIS AND MARY CUSTIS, the builders of Arlington House, marked by simple shafts and shaded by three giant oaks. The baroque bronze MONUMENT TO THE CONFEDERATE DEAD, the work of Moses Ezekiel, stands in the center of Jackson Circle, near the intersection of McPherson and Farragut Avenues. The central female figure symbolizes the South in Peace, and a circular frieze on the base portrays the women of the South sending forth their men to fight for the Confederacy. Confederate dead were removed from the original Lower Cemetery and reinterred here in 1901. The statue, given by the Daughters of the Confederacy, was dedicated by President Wilson in 1914.

East of Jackson Circle, beyond a Negro section, is the SPANISH-AMERICAN WAR MEMORIAL, a conventional Corinthian-style granite shaft surmounted by an eagle, around which are 600 graves of soldiers who fell in Cuba, Puerto Rico, and the Philippines. A MEMORIAL TO THE ROUGH RIDERS is surrounded by the graves of those who were killed in this noted cavalry regiment. Army and Navy nurses of this war are buried in a plot to the southwest, marked by another memorial. On higher ground, north of the eagle-topped column, is the MAST OF THE U.S.S. MAINE, with its conning tower still in place. Raised in 1912 from the sunken battleship in Havana Harbor, the mast with shrouds attached was set in a circular granite base inscribed with the names of the 253 men who lost their lives in the explosion. The large anchor, similar to those on the *Maine*, was brought from the Boston Navy Yard.

West of McPherson Avenue, a quarter of a mile south of Jackson Circle, are the seemingly endless white headstones of the World War dead, each a simple cross, precisely ordered and aligned, with equal intervals between. The graves of Gentiles are marked with a Latin cross, the graves of Jews with the Star of David. A white Argonne Cross stands at the end of a narrow open field between two sections of Argonne dead.

Far to the southeast, beyond the Fort McPherson earthworks, is the GRAVE OE WILLIAM JENNINGS BRYAN (1860-1925), three times candidate for the Presidency and Secretary of State under Woodrow Wilson, and the GRAVE OF REAR ADMIRAL ROBERT E. PEARY (1856-1920), accredited as the discoverer of the North Pole in 1909. Peary's tomb is marked by a marble globe, given by the National Geographic Society. Near by is the COAST GUARD MEMORIAL, a bronze seagull poised before a stone pyramid.

Northeast of the *Maine* Memorial, in landscaped grounds, stands the white marble ARLINGTON MEMORIAL AMPHITHEATER, built in 1915-20 as a memorial to the Army, Navy, and Marine Corps dead at a cost of $825,000. The elliptical amphitheater, seating 4,000, is surrounded by a stately colonnade having an outer wall penetrated by an arcade, providing several thousand additional seats. At the east and west ends are pavilions, the east pavilion constituting a separate building, with a reception hall, trophy room, and stage on the main floor, a museum on the second floor, and a chapel in the basement. The architects, Carrère and Hastings, modeled the structure on the design of Greek and Roman theaters, and, except for a few interior details, finished it entirely in white Vermont marble. The east façade overlooks Washington and the Potomac 210 feet below. On the wall of this entrance portico, behind a Corinthian colonnade, is a paneled frieze symbolizing War and Peace.

The reception hall of the TROPHY ROOM is divided by a colonnade of Ionic columns into three parts, the central area being in the form of an atrium which permits a view of additional exhibition halls on the second floor. Within the Trophy Room are the decorations conferred on the Unknown Soldier by the Allied nations, and in the same room stands the bronze and gold-leaf figure of *Victory* by Augustus Saint-Gaudens. Beneath, in the vaulted Mortuary Chapel, is a simple shrine and altar on a low platform. From this chapel a long circular hall runs under the main-floor colonnade, with 48 crypts spaced along its walls, intended originally for the interment of one man from each State who had distinguished himself in the service of the Nation; this memorial plan was later dropped, and the 48 crypts are empty.

There is a fine view of the Amphitheater from the colonnade at the Trophy Room door—the curved marble benches enclosed by the colonnade, the rim of which stands clear against the sky. At the far end is the simple western portal bearing a Latin inscription, which in translation reads, "It is sweet and seemly to die for one's country." On the outer walls of the portal are the names of 44 battles in American wars. From the interior of the western pavilion the semicircular, domed stage looks out over the amphitheater. The rostral platform is arranged in three levels, and in the center of the lower level is the simple marble dais and chair used by the President at official ceremonies. On either side are niches containing sculptured urns, and above them are honor rolls of the Army and Navy. The stage is framed by a Palladian proscenium, the trim of the arch bearing a passage from Lincoln's Gettysburg Address. A quotation from Washington is inscribed below the dome.

East of the Amphitheater, set in a paved formal terrace, is the TOMB OF THE UNKNOWN SOLDIER, rising above a green lawn bordered by clipped beech hedges. Dark clumps of boxwood and groves of cedar add to the atmosphere of solemnity and repose surrounding the Tomb, before which a lone sentinel stands and paces his beat across the terrace. The tomb is cut from a single rectangular block of white marble, 16 feet long, 11 feet high, and 9 feet wide. Erected in 1931 over an older, uncompleted cenotaph that stood for ten years, it is the work of Thomas Hudson Jones, sculptor, and Lorimer Rich, architect. Carved pilasters and sculptured wreaths lessen the austerity of the tomb, and the front panel is adorned with three figures symbolic of Victory through Valor attaining Peace. The rear panel bears the inscription, "Here rests in honored glory an American Soldier known but to God."

Lying in a sarcophagus beneath the tomb is the body of an unidentified soldier brought from France. The body lay in state in the rotunda of the Capitol before it was interred with an Armistice Day ceremony at which President Warren G. Harding officiated. The United States honored the soldier with the Congressional Medal of Honor, and the Allied Powers bestowed upon him their highest military decorations. One of the best known memorials in the Nation, the Tomb of the Unknown Soldier stands today as a memorial to all American soldiers and sailors who lost their lives in the First World War.

FORT MYER

The neat brick barracks and quarters of Fort Myer (*open, in normal times, 9 a. m. to sundown*), standing at attention among well-trimmed and tree-planted lawns, represent a typical post of the United States Army. In addition to quarters for troops, the military establishment has a post office, chapel, hospital, post exchange, and fire house. A red-brick mansion within the cantonment is occupied by the Army's chief of staff. On Grant Avenue are the houses of fort officers, and opposite them is a broad lawn with a flagstaff and salute gun, where daily ceremonies are held at the raising and lowering of the flag.

The FORT MYER PARADE GROUND has an important place in aviation history. After their private experiments at Kitty Hawk, North Carolina, and at Dayton, Ohio, the Wright brothers held their first public demonstration on this parade ground in 1909. Using facilities offered by the Army, they carried out a number of test flights, during one of which Lieutenant T. E. Selfridge was killed while flying with Orville Wright; a small monument on the spot commemorates this early martyr to aviation, for whom Selfridge Field, Michigan, is named. The first planes owned by the United States were accepted after demonstration here.

Fort Myer provides guards of honor, escorts, and squads for firing volleys at military funerals in Arlington National Cemetery. Negro soldiers, with other Fort Myer units, before the outbreak of World War II participated in most of the great parades in Washington. An annual horse show and occasional polo games are held at the post.

Visible from Fort Myer, and a landmark on the skyline south of Washington from the time they were built in 1912 until the summer of 1941, stood three orange-painted steel towers of the Naval Radio Station, the tallest 600 feet high and the flanking structures 450 feet high. A pioneer in high-frequency broadcasting, it was in its time the world's most powerful sending station. In 1941 the Navy awarded a contract to a New York firm to demolish the towers for and in consideration of a contract price of $1. Removal of the towers improved the safety of air navigation to and from the Washington National Airport.

FEDERAL OFFICE BUILDING NO. 2

As part of a program for the decentralization of Government office structures, Federal Office Building No. 2 (*office hours 8–4:30 weekdays*) was completed in 1941 and occupied by some offices and divisions of the Navy Department. Standing on a suburban 17-acre tract at the intersection of N. Arlington Ridge Road and Columbia Pike, south of Arlington National Cemetery, the four-story buff-brick structure, with an office capacity of 7,000 employees, was designed by the Public Buildings Administration for general office use as needed by governmental agencies. The extended north façade, 781 feet long, has three entrances leading to elevator foyers within. Seven wings, having a depth of 421 feet from the face of the building, extend south from the main structure. Spaces between the wings are set aside as parking lots, and the seven parallel wings are connected at the second and third stories by service bridges. The fire-proof, sound-conditioned, and air-conditioned office building has a cafeteria on the ground floor. It was constructed under a congressional allotment of $3,200,000.

COLUMBIA ISLAND TO ROACHES RUN

The traveler crossing Arlington Memorial Bridge westward from the Lincoln Memorial is scarcely conscious that the Virginia end of the bridge rests on an island rather than on the mainland. Columbia Island is an attenuated strip of land about a mile and a quarter long, less than 300 feet wide at its narrowest point and not more than 1,000 feet at the widest. Boundary Channel of the Potomac separates it from the mainland. A traffic circle at the west end of the bridge is flanked at each end by longer ovals, around which one-way traffic flows; this plaza was opened to public use in 1941. Three bridges connect Columbia Island with the mainland—the short bridge on the Arlington Memorial Parkway, a bridge at the north end of the island on the US 50 route to the town of Arlington, and the arched stone bridge at the south end of the island, carrying Mount Vernon Memorial Highway. Planted with clumps of trees, the island presents a pleasant park area, with views on the east of the Potomac and its occasional traffic of tug and pleasure boats, and, when the leaves are off the trees, of the new War Department Building on the west.

Mount Vernon Memorial Highway, which extends from Arlington Bridge to Mount Vernon, was opened to traffic in time for the birthday pilgrimage to Washington's home in February 1932. The broad four-lane boulevard, landscaped on both sides, is maintained by the National Park Service.

The NAVY AND MARINE MEMORIAL, at the southeast end of Columbia Island, is a striking sculptured composition of seven seagulls in flight, rising from the crest of a breaking wave. The sculptor, Ernesto Begni del Piatti, achieved an unusual effect of flight by joining his gulls wing-tip to wing-tip, and his conventionalized breaker is interesting. Cast in aluminum and given a green-bronze finish, the memorial was dedicated in 1930. The green granite base, arranged in concentric terraces and extending to Boundary Channel on the south and to the Potomac River on the east, was completed as a WPA project in 1941.

BOUNDARY CHANNEL HARBOR, a snug little mooring place west of the Marine Memorial, is best viewed from the bridge across the channel at this point. Brightly painted motor launches, sailboats, and outboards rock gently on the waters of the Channel. Two or three small red or yellow seaplanes are usually tied up here; they taxi in and out under the stone bridge and take off and land on the roomy waters of the Potomac.

An underpass carries the Memorial Highway beneath HIGHWAY BRIDGE, often called the 14th Street Bridge. A "cloverleaf crossing" at the bridge, which carries truck traffic on US 1, permits access from one highway to the other without crossing traffic lanes and always by right-hand turns. The name is applied to this type of bridge approach because, seen from the air, it strikingly resembles a four-leaf clover.

The OLD WASHINGTON AIRPORT, south of Highway Bridge, was, until 1941, the principal commercial airdrome in the Washington area. It was used for a time by private planes, but, after construction began on the New War Department Building, its Terminal Building and hangars, some still bearing the insignia of airlines, were abandoned as aviation facilities.

The War Department's PENTAGON BUILDING (*open to passholders only*), a huge three-story reinforced concrete structure, faced with Indiana limestone, looms up southwest of the Old Washington Airport. Scheduled for completion late in 1942, it is believed to be the largest office building in the world. It will have almost 92 acres of usable space, and will accommodate 30,000 employees. Construction is expected to cost $31,110,000.

Designed by George Edwin Bergstrom of Los Angeles, this enormous utilitarian structure is built in the shape of a pentagon, each of its five outside faces measuring 921 feet. Concentrically placed within the outer structure is another pentagonal building, with a 40-foot space between them. The two connected buildings, each averaging about 170 feet in width, are built around a six-acre court measuring 360 feet on each of its five sides. Air-conditioned and acoustically treated, the building will have only one passenger elevator; communication between floors will be by stairways, ramps, and escalators. Two parking spaces are planned for 8,000 cars, and there will be a large bus terminal and taxicab stand in the basement; bus fares will be paid at turnstiles. On the first floor will be such facilities as a cafeteria, drugstore, barber shop, and newsstand, to meet the needs of a swarm of employees equal in number to the population of a sizable town. The construction job is so big that three large contracting firms are engaged in it, and the problems of air-conditioning, heating, handling of sewerage, water supply, and other corollaries are stupendous. A "garden of Versailles" is to extend from the north front of the building to Boundary Channel, and the Washington Memorial Parkway will eventually run in front of the building. All in all, this vast building promises to equal or even excel the Commerce Building as a good place in which to get lost.

A flat-arched fieldstone underpass carries the Memorial Highway under the Railroad Bridge, on the south side of which is the lagoon-like ROACHES RUN WATERFOWL SANCTUARY. Hundreds of wild ducks use these waters as a feeding ground in winter, and during the summer months there are often flocks of snowy egrets wading near the borders of the sanctuary or roosting in near-by trees. A parking space and picnic area is provided about midway of the lagoon, which is most appealing at sunset, when pastel colors, deepened by their transmission through smoke from passing railroad trains, are reflected in the quiet waters.

WASHINGTON NATIONAL AIRPORT

The 750-acre Washington National Airport, commonly called the Gravelly Point Airport, occupies a block of dredged land along the Mount Vernon Memorial Highway south of Washington. Within a driving radius of 10 minutes from the business section, the airport is nearer the heart of the city than most others serving American metropolitan areas; the taxi fare is 60¢ each way, and bus service to the city, on regular schedule, is 10¢. Nine-tenths composed of hydraulic fill, this $12,500,000 airport went into full operation without the fanfare of a formal dedication in 1941.

The airport has long runways, providing for landings and takeoffs in eight directions. The surrounding terrain, with the Potomac River on three sides and the valleys of Hunting Creek and Roaches Run extending west and northwest from the landing field, permit landings and takeoffs at extremely flat angles. Paved areas, including runways, taxiways, and aprons in front of the Terminal Building and hangars, total nearly 140 acres. The port has exceptional facilities for spectators, with a spacious restaurant and terraced parking areas that eventually will accommodate 5,000 cars; there are also facilities for "flight-seeing" trips by airplane and blimp. Around the circumference of the airport will be constructed a bridle path more than 2 miles long. Washington National Airport is already the third busiest in the Nation, and three airlines in addition to the three now operating from Washington have applied for an extension of their services to the Nation's Capital.

On the upland above the dredge-filled airfield proper are the red-brick buildings of the Public Roads Administration, partly occupied by the Civil Aeronautics Administration, and the ruins of Abingdon, historic mansion of the Washingtons and Custises.

Ever since aviation became a practical reality, Washington has been plagued by the need of an adequate airport commensurate with its stature as the National Capitol. The question had been argued in and out of Congress, and discussed pro and con in the public prints. Army Engineers and Congressional committees had recommended the Gravelly Point site since all but two small parcels of land and the underwater rights were owned by the Government. Many actual flights were made over the site by practical pilots, members of the Air Line Pilots Association, and year-round studies by the U.S. Weather Bureau showed that the airport, though subject to river fogs, would be usable at least 90 per cent of the time. President Franklin D. Roosevelt in 1938 assigned the task of building the airport to the newly created Civil Aeronautics Administration. On November 19 of that year he witnessed the ceremony as the *Talcott,* a Government dredge, dumped the first bucket of gravel on the site. Two days before, the PWA had allocated $8,747,500 for work on the airport, and the WPA had made the first of a series of allocations which later totaled more than $1,400,000.

Workmen swarmed over the area. At times there were more than 4,500 WPA men at work building the 2¼ miles of levees and revetments around the fill, grading, draining, stabilizing the bases of the runways, installing gas and water mains, sewers, laying concrete, making telephone connections. There was a constant clutter and clatter of heavy-duty trucks, busses loaded with workmen, graders, bulldozers, concrete mixers, as America's peacetime army applied its mechanized blitzkrieg to reshape a span of earth to the civilian, peacetime needs of commercial aviation. Clusters of searchlights blazed at night, as work went on in shifts. Powerful dredges, lighted at night like showboats, pumped 24 hours a day, their jointed pipe lines extending snakewise in from the river on floats, to spout dirty horizontal geysers of gravel and water upon the site. In spite of all the mechanical equipment, with not a horse on the pay roll, signs at each end of the project warned, "Keep Horses Under Control." A poster opposite the Roaches Run Waterfowl Sanctuary remained standing with its caption, "Bird Refuge," long after the waterfowl had fled and long before the remote descendants of birds—the aviators—found it safe to set down on the runways.

Construction of the airport posed interesting problems for the engineers. Gravelly Point, well-named, has a firm base of gravel and sand, but on the airport site it was silted over to a depth of 10 to 20 feet. Once the encircling levee was completed, and the water shut out, mud was removed from the runway sites, and the construction project took on the appearance of a canal-building enterprise, with ditches intersecting oddly, like the "canals" on Mars. Sand and gravel were then pumped into the canals from the riverbed, directly on a sand-and-gravel base, to obviate settling. Long ridges of pumped-in sand and gravel were raised 15 feet above the proposed runway level, and the surplus was later pushed to the sides to provide shoulders for the broad runways. When the water was finally drained off, the mechanized army went to work tearing down and landscaping the hill on the west side of the airport to complete the job of filling the airfield proper, and to relocate the Mount Vernon Highway.

President Roosevelt dedicated the Terminal Building in September 1940, when the first airplane, an official ship of the Civil Aeronautics Authority, landed on the long north-south runway and taxied up to the Terminal. It was followed by planes of American Airlines, Eastern Air Lines and Pennsylvania-Central Airlines. After this ceremonial landing, a military airshow began, with more than 400 Army and Navy planes maneuvering in one of the most impressive air spectacles ever seen over Washington. Perfect timing and a clear day contributed to this "flexing of the military muscle," as the President phrased it. Planes came from such distant points as Selfridge Field, Michigan, New Orleans, New York, and from an aircraft carrier off Norfolk, to cross and recross the airfield, sometimes at four different levels and from four different directions. A later and more grandiose dedication of the airport itself, with guests of international importance, was foregone because of the disturbed world situation, and the airport was gradually put into service in a workaday manner in June 1941.

The TERMINAL BUILDING, an arc-shaped cast-stone structure four stories high, occupies a west-central position in the airport, at the base of the terraced upland. Designed by Howard Cheney, Chicago architect, it represents the most up-to-date developments in air terminal design, control of air traffic, and smooth handling of all activities incident to airport operation. The floor plan is laid on a curve, and the building itself, with a three-story central section and each oval-ended floor set back somewhat from the one below, appropriately enough suggests an airplane motif. The surmounting glassed-in control tower, and the radio aerial, add a navigator's touch to a building designed to guide pilots in traversing the upper ocean of air.

The concave west facade, facing the traffic circle at the entrance, has a two-story recessed portico supported by eight square pillars and flanked by bas-relief Great Seals of the United States and the Civil Aeronautics Administration. The building is rather sparsely windowed on this side, but second-floor offices are abundantly fenestrated. Wing-like canopies extend over platforms for car and taxi passengers at the ground level. The convex east façade, however, is almost solidly windowed, to allow every facility for observing the operation of a busy airport. The field-side wall of the central two-story waiting room, with its eight slender columns, is solidly filled with 30-foot windows. First- and second-story wings are covered entirely with glass, as is the surmounting central story above the waiting room. On the crescent-shaped concrete apron fronting the Terminal Building, the numerous loading points have "built-in" service connections, doing away with the succession of trucks that normally clutter an airport. Hand trucks, mechanics' ladders, and gangways are kept on the ground floor except when in actual use.

Visitors and passengers leave their cars at the traffic circle and enter the building at the first-floor level. Two vestibuled entrances lead into the two-story waiting room, with its long ticket and information desk, telegraph and telephone facilities, and its sweeping view of the airport. There is an outer observation terrace, a passengers' coffee shop, and passengers' concourse on this floor, the southern wing of which is occupied by offices. Visitors are not encouraged to enter the waiting room, since it is possible for them to walk around the building on an outside railed deck to view the operations of the airport from this higher level and look into the waiting room from its windowed east front. They can also obtain a more general view of the waiting room through windows from the floor above and return to the motor-car level without crossing the path of passengers or airline operations.

The south wing, at the first-floor level, also occupied by offices, has a wide glass-enclosed observation terrace on the side facing the airport. A second-floor inside balcony provides an opportunity for visitors to observe activities in the waiting room below. The north wing at this level is occupied almost entirely by a huge dining room, 40 by 120 feet, with a windowed east wall through which arrivals and departures of planes can be seen, in addition to a general view of the airport, the Potomac, and the city of Washington. An open-air dining terrace, 20 feet wide and 200 feet long, on the east and north sides of the wing, is open in favorable weather. Combining a pleasant scenic view with leisurely dining and observation of airport activities, this wing, with its bar, café, and private dining rooms, constitutes a social center of a new kind for the Nation's Capital.

The third floor, a many-windowed setback section atop the central waiting room, is given over to offices for airline and airport operations. The automatic "progress board" in the Airways Operations Office reveals at a glance the position along the airlanes of every arriving or departing plane. Each flight has a number, and each pilot reports general conditions and the expected time of arrival at the next point of report. This information, received by earphone at the terminal, is written in code on a special teletype machine and flashed automatically on the progress board, which resembles electric boards used by stock brokers. It was developed by the Civil Aeronautics Administration after several years of study.

The ground floor, below the waiting room level, is the airport's working and utility area, so designed as to keep baggage, postal, express, trucking, and other services separated from passenger movement. A truckway runs under the building, and truck roads, for speedy movement, are distinct from passenger routes. A tier of outer offices, just off the airport apron, accommodates dispatchers and crews, servicing and equipment units, field attendants, utility rooms. A special reception room, at the south end, is used for the reception of distinguished visitors. Between parallel truckways west of these offices are the post office; lockers; facilities for handling baggage, which is chuted down from the waiting room; mechanical equipment and storage space; a cafeteria for airline and terminal employees; and an air express office, in addition to other facilities.

Southwest of the Terminal Building, along an extension of the concrete apron, are the six flat-topped steel-and-concrete hangars, built wall-to-wall, each 181 feet wide, 193 feet deep, and 55 feet high, with sliding doors measuring 30 by 175 feet. Together, they cover 10 acres of floor space, including office, garage, and shop areas; 5.2 acres of space is available for airplane storage. The ever-present blimp, which is almost as much a part of the Washington skyline as the Capitol, operates from this airport. Ground crews can occasionally be seen in action, holding the blimp to earth with ropes while it loads and unloads passengers taking lighter-than-air sightseeing tours over Washington.

The red-brick RUINS OF ABINGDON, on a knoll northwest of the Terminal Building, are all that remain of a Colonial mansion built in 1677 by John Alexander, one of the original patentees of Alexandria.

John Parke Custis, Martha Washington's son, bought the house in 1776 from the Alexander family for his bride, Eleanor Calvert, daughter of the fifth Lord Baltimore—a deal in real estate that for some reason greatly displeased George Washington. Custis served as Washington's aide during the Revolutionary War, and Washington became reconciled to him. When Custis died at Yorktown in 1781, of camp fever, Washington adopted his two children, Nellie and George Washington Parke Custis, and took them to Mount Vernon, returning Abingdon to the Alexander family. Nellie, who was born here, married Lawrence Lewis, son of George Washington's sister. By 1829 the house was owned by the Hunter family and was a retreat for President Andrew Jackson, who threatened to shoot office-seekers who invaded Abingdon while he was there. During the Civil War the mansion was the property of Major Bushrod Hunter and his son, both of whom served in the Confederate army and their property was confiscated. James A. Garfield, as an attorney before he became President, obtained a part of the estate as his fee for regaining the property for the Hunters. The old house was owned by the Richmond, Fredericksburg & Potomac Railroad when, long empty, it was ignited by a brush fire in 1930 and burned. The foundations, part of a wall, and a chimney were reconditioned by the Society for the Preservation of Virginia Antiquities, and a bronze plaque erected on the grounds, which were purchased by the Government during the development of the Mount Vernon Highway.

The red-brick PUBLIC ROADS BUILDINGS *(open 8:45–5:15 Mon.-Fri., 8:45–12:45 Sat.)*, west of the Terminal Building, used for several years as a laboratory for the study of road-building materials and their behavior and use, are (1942) being gradually turned over to the use of the Civil Aeronautics Authority.

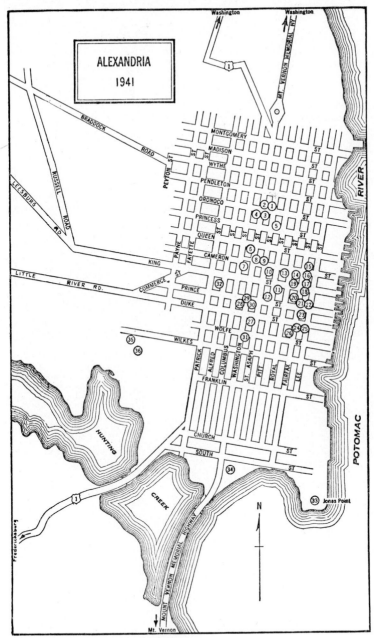

See over for key to points of interest.

ALEXANDRIA. Points of Interest.

1. Robert E. Lee House
2. Hallowell School
3. Fendall House
4. Edmund Jennings Lee House
5. Alexandria Jail
6. Lloyd House
7. Christ Church
8. General Henry Lee House
9. Lord Fairfax House
10. Site of Washington's Town House
11. Marshall House
12. Washington's Tenement Houses
13. Gadsby's Tavern
14. City Hall and Public Market
15. Ann Lee Memorial Home for the Aged
16. Bank of Alexandria
17. Carlyle House
18. Ramsey House
19. Alexandria Gazette Building
20. Stabler-Leadbeater's Drugstore
21. Elisha Cullen Dick House
22. George William Fairfax House
23. William Brown House
24. Craik House
25. Coryell House
26. Old Presbyterian Meeting House
27. Lafayette House
28. Old Lyceum
29. Confederate Monument
30. Alexandria Post Office
31. Alexandria Academy
32. Friendship Engine House
33. Jones Point Lighthouse
34. St. Mary's Roman Catholic Cemetery
35. U. S. Military Cemetery
36. St. Paul's Cemetery
37. George Washington Masonic National Memorial Temple

Alexandria

Busses: Alexandria, Barcroft, & Washington line; Alexandria-Washington fare 15¢, 8 tokens for $1.

On the west bank of the Potomac, between Four Mile Run and Hunting Creek, 9 miles south of Washington on the Mount Vernon Memorial Highway, stands Alexandria (alt. 50, pop. 33,523), retaining much of its eighteenth-century Colonial flavor and many landmarks associated with the formation of the Nation. Old Alexandria lies principally on the east, or river, side of Washington Street (Mount Vernon Highway), though there are numerous fine old houses on the west side. The older portion of the town is laid out on a gridiron pattern, with some blocks more extended than others. King Street, the main commercial thoroughfare, intersecting Washington Street at right angles near the center of town, is one of several bearing royal names— Queen, Prince, Princess, Duke, Duchess, and Royal. Others, such as Washington, Franklin, Pitt, Wythe, Patrick, and Lee, reflect the bearing of later history on the layout of the Colonial and Revolutionary town.

The streets are lined with brick and clapboard houses of Colonial and early Federal types of architecture, with green shutters, transomed doorways, and brass knockers. Most of the houses are set flush with the sidewalk, and, presenting the narrow side to the street, give a deceptive appearance of diminutiveness. Typical houses have boarded or brick-walled gardens in the rear, of which there are charming glimpses from the sidewalk through arched wooden gates. Many of these gates give access to gardens through tunnels between connecting houses. Every street and alley has its series of intimate views, with angles, chimneys, gardens, trees, exuberant vines, to give it charm and character. Most houses have Venetian blinds, and it is one of the town customs to leave these partially open, affording glimpses of roomy interiors, hallway arches, delicate stairs, oil paintings of ancestors, ship models on bookcases, fireplaces with carved mantels, and crystal chandeliers. Many well-preserved exterior details contribute to an authentic feeling for Colonial and Revolutionary style and type—iron footscrapers set in stone beside fanlighted doorways, carved eavestones set under copper downspouting to carry away the water from roofs, oval plaques painted with a fire hydrant and hose and marked "F A" (Fire Assurance), recalling a time when fire companies were operated by insurance groups, delicately executed iron-grille railings at stoops and windows, dormers of a dozen different types and degrees of gentility.

455

Frequently seen in Alexandria is the "flounder house," a type not too common elsewhere, though it apparently originated among the Quakers of Philadelphia, where several exist (numerous Quakers settled in early Alexandria). Set back from the street, and presenting a narrow end to it, the flounder house is essentially half a house, with a perfectly blank and unwindowed wall on the side where its lean-to roof is highest, and a porch extending out from the other side. Various theories have been advanced to account for this type of construction, one being that it was cheaper to build a shed-roof type, another that they were designed to fit narrow lots, still another that this was an attempt on the part of owners to avoid taxation on an "unfinished" house. The name, quite descriptive, was undoubtedly applied, in a seaport town, by sailors to whom the phrase "flat as a flounder" was part of the common vocabulary.

A curious chain of circumstances has operated over a period of nearly 200 years to preserve Alexandria's original character. Built by European city-dwellers desirous of a genteel privacy within their walled back gardens, the older portion of the town was well suited to its time, when maritime trade with Europe and domestic trade in tobacco and wheat from the hinterland made the city a prosperous seaport. Completion of the railroad to Baltimore in the 1840's, however, diverted much of the inland trade to the Maryland city, a growing port, and Alexandria went into decline as a seaport. It was spared the ravages of the Civil War, being taken over by Union forces at the beginning of the conflict. It went through several decades of sluggish economic development and was largely spared the eras of porch-building, Victorian towers, and bungalows. Washington officialdom "discovered" Alexandria shortly after World War I, and when the Roosevelt administration, in 1932, brought many habitual commuters from other metropolitan areas, Alexandria's nearness to Washington and the revived interest in early American houses quickly produced a "Foreign Legion" that is quietly resented by original Alexandrians, thankful though they may be for the added prosperity. The cycle was complete, and residents of crowded cities were again thankful for the seclusion of back-yard gardens. Many Alexandrians, however, find it more pleasant to move their rockers out to the sidewalks on hot summer evenings, where they can observe, sociably, the comings and goings of their neighbors.

Alexandria's water front has an attractive utilitarian air about it, represented by the long pier of the fertilizer plant, cone-shaped piles of sand and gravel, a few rickety wharves where freighters dock, a historic boat club or two, warehouses, an automobile assembly plant, fish markets, and the pier for the Norfolk steamer, the whistle of which Alexandrians note unconsciously at seven in the evening. In a few eating places, some likeness can still be found to the jolly barrooms and taverns that once clustered around the port of Alexandria.

Governor Berkeley, in 1669, made a grant of 6,000 acres of land to Robert Howsen "on the freshes of the Potomac, for bringing into the

Colony of Virginia one hundred and twenty persons to inhabit." In February of the following year, Captain John Alexander, whose grant lay in Stafford County, bought the Howsen grant and built a house on the patent.   The tobacco trade flourished in Virginia, and the old Indian Trail became the "rolling road" along which hogsheads of tobacco from the Oronoco fields were drawn by oxen to warehouses along the King's Highway.   A group of Scottish merchants built a tobacco warehouse at the foot of this road—the Hunting Creek warehouse.   Finished in 1732, it became the nucleus of a small settlement at West's Point, with a ferry to the Maryland shore.   The village, largely settled by Scottish people, was called Belhaven; it was incorporated in 1748 under the name of Alexandria, being founded on Alexander property.   In 1749 George Washington assisted John West, Jr., in surveying the streets for the new town.

Situated on the great King's Highway from Williamsburg to New England, and possessing one of the most favored natural ports, Alexandria became one of the most important and thriving towns in the Colonies.   Taverns, caring for weary stagecoach passengers, became centers for lavish entertainments and royal birthnight balls.   The Lees, Custises, Washingtons, Fairfaxes, Masons, Blackburns, and other wealthy plantation owners built their fine mansions in or near the town.

The neat Colonial jail was built and measures were taken to keep the town orderly, clean, and healthful, and to protect it against fire. From this time on, and until after the Civil War, Alexandria flourished.   The market square was the center of activity, where fairs, political assemblages, and other meetings took place.   Here George Washington drilled the Virginia Rangers, and later, the Virginia militia, before and after the defeat of Braddock in 1755 in his campaign against the French.   The royal governors of five Colonies met in the Carlyle House to arrange this campaign, and, at the same time, recommended the tax levies on the Colonies which later led to the Revolution.   The famous "Fairfax Resolves," drawn up by George Mason of Gunston Hall, were adopted by a convention in Alexandria at Gadsby's Tavern in 1775.

Alexandria sent many famous men and many more, unnamed in history, to follow George Washington into the Revolution.   On his way to inauguration in New York as first President, Washington stopped in Alexandria to be addressed by Colonel Dennis Ramsay on behalf of his townsmen.

When the District of Columbia was laid out in 1791, all of Alexandria was included within its borders.   Virginia became dissatisfied, however, with the bargain struck with Maryland, by which all public buildings were to be erected on the north side of the Potomac.   Alexandria hoped, by reuniting with Virginia, to receive help in paying for the expensive Alexandria Canal.   Retrocession of this territory was realized in 1846.

During the War of 1812, Alexandria purchased immunity from attack by a payment to the British equivalent to about $100,000.   During the Civil War, Alexandria became the capital of the "Restored Government of Virginia," the constitutional fiction by which West Virginia gave itself permission to secede from the mother State, and remained in that capacity until the end of the war.

One of the great heroes of the Civil War, Robert E. Lee, grew up in Alexandria. The General Henry Lee House, at 611 Cameron Street, was for a time the home of his father, the brilliant "Light Horse Harry" Lee, and the Lee House on Oronoco Street was later the home of his widowed mother. Robert E. Lee owned a pew in Christ Church, where his name is engraved beside that of Washington.

After the Civil War the prosperity of Alexandria declined. Other ports were opened and the fast clipper ships from Baltimore cut into Alexandria's profitable trade. During recent years there has been considerable industrial growth and Alexandria stands as the eighth city in Virginia, with a population of 33,000. Aside from ordinary industries in a town of this size, Alexandria has a large fertilizer plant, a plant for the construction and repair of refrigerator cars, iron works, brick kilns, refineries and one of the busiest freight yards in the Nation.

POINTS OF INTEREST

The ROBERT E. LEE HOUSE *(private)*, 607 Oronoco Street, became, after the death of "Light Horse Harry" Lee in 1818, the home of his wife and children, among them the 11-year-old Robert E. Lee. From this house, as a young man, Lee rode over to Arlington to pay court to Mary Custis. He was prepared for West Point at the Quaker School next door, conducted by Benjamin Hallowell. It is not known exactly when the house was built, but it was owned by John Potts in 1795. Lafayette visited here in 1824, and met young Robert.

The HALLOWELL SCHOOL *(private)*, 609 Oronoco Street, opened by Benjamin Hallowell in 1825, was attended by boys from some of the most distinguished families in the neighborhod. The Lee House and the Hallowell, architectural counterparts, are good examples of the late Georgian style, designed with unusual restraint. The severity of the main facade of each is relieved by a fine classic cornice, broken at the center by a steeply-raked, beautiful pediment. The entrance doorways are noteworthy for their classic moldings and delicate fan transoms.

The FENDALL HOUSE *(private)*, 429 N. Washington Street, built before 1791 of frame over brick in Federal style, was the home of Philip R. Fendall, an attorney, who married two members of "Light Horse Harry" Lee's family. In 1792, Richard Bland Lee came into possession of the house, and for the next 50 years it was owned by the Lee family. John L. Lewis, president of the United Mine Workers of America, has lived here since the mid-1930's.

The EDMUND JENNINGS LEE HOUSE *(private)*, 428 N. Washington Street, built in 1799 by the brother of Robert E. Lee, is a late Georgian town house of individuality, departing from the formal symmetrical style and having its beautifully executed doorway at the corner, rather than in the center, of the principal façade. Its owner, Edmund Lee, was an eminent lawyer.

The ALEXANDRIA JAIL, Princess and St. Asaph Streets, is a simple whitewashed brick building, scarcely distinguishable as a jail. Its original portions date from the time when the city was part of the District of Columbia, but the building has been considerably enlarged.

The LLOYD HOUSE *(private)*, 220 N. Washington Street, since 1832 the residence of the Lloyd family, was built in 1793 by John Hooe. It is one of the largest and, for simplicity and dignity, perhaps the finest house in the Federal style in Alexandria. The fine brickwork and formal detail of the exterior are matched by the graceful proportions and beautiful woodwork of the interior. Robert E. Lee received word, in this house, that he had been chosen to command the Army of Northern Virginia.

CHRIST CHURCH *(open 9–5 weekdays, services Sun.; adm. 10¢)*, Cameron and Columbus Streets, built 1767-73, was attended by Washington and Lee; the pews they owned are marked, and marble tablets commemorate both men. Here Lord Bryan Fairfax was rector for two years. This fine church, designed from plans submitted by James Wren (reputed descendant of Sir Christopher), is typical of the Georgian Church architecture of the pre-Revolutionary period. The tower and cupola were built as an afterthought in 1818. The simple square building, of subdued red brick in Flemish bond accented by the white stone quoins and keyblocks, stands quietly in a shaded churchyard. The delicate formality of the well-lighted interior is emphasized by the pure white woodwork of its walls and furnishings. The sky-blue ceiling, simple white box pews and gallery, and the pedestaled and canopied pulpit approached by a narrow flight of steps and supported by inscriptions of the Creed and the Lord's Prayer, are all typical of this charming style. The wrought-brass and crystal chandelier was brought from England in 1818.

There are a number of early gravestones in the churchyard, and a monument to 36 Confederate soldiers. Washington's family Bible (presented in 1804 to G. W. Parke Custis) and the vestry book containing his signature are in the possession of Christ Church, but not on view.

The GENERAL HENRY LEE HOUSE *(private)*, 611 Cameron Street, was occupied by "Light Horse Harry" Lee in 1811, after he moved here from his ancestral home, Leesylvania, to educate his children. He died in Georgia 7 years later, and his family occupied a house on Oronoco Street.

The LORD FAIRFAX HOUSE *(private)*, 607 Cameron Street, with its imposing square brick facade, cut sharply by two white belt courses, portrays a curious blend of the northern and southern Federal styles. The three full stories are reminiscent of a Boston town house of that era, while the white stuccoed surface arch and deeply recessed vestibule are distinctly southern. It was erected in 1816 and purchased by Thomas Lord Fairfax, ninth Baron of Cameron, in 1830.

The SITE OF WASHINGTON'S TOWN HOUSE, in the 500 block of Cameron Street, is marked by a bronze plaque in a little opening cut in the hedge, behind an iron fence.

The MARSHALL HOUSE, SE. corner King and Pitt Streets, its lower floor occupied by a retail store, is notable as the scene of the first casualty of the Civil War. A young colonel, named Ellsworth, tore down the Confederate flag from the house, then a tavern. The proprietor, J. W. Jackson, shot and killed Ellsworth and was in turn shot down by Union soldiers.

WASHINGTON'S TENEMENT HOUSES *(private),* stand on the NW. corner of Pitt and Prince Streets.

GADSBY'S TAVERN *(open 9–5 weekdays; adm. 25¢),* Royal and Cameron Streets, a noted old inn, occupies two adjacent brick buildings erected in 1752 and 1792. The earlier building (the old City Tavern), in its diminutive scale and in the delicacy of its classic detail, accurately portrays the characteristic Georgian architecture of Colonial Virginia. The later and larger building was used during the nineteenth century as the City Hotel.

The City Tavern served as Washington's military headquarters in 1754, when he was lieutenant-colonel of the Virginia militia, and when he returned from his defeat at Great Meadows. Here was held the celebration of Washington's birthday in the last year of his life, and, from the steps of the tavern in the same year, he reviewed his troops for the last time, thereby ending his military career where it started. The tavern was used again for a military purpose in 1940, when young men registered here for military training under the Selective Service Act.

George Mason's "Fairfax County Resolves," one of the most important statements of human rights ever made, was drawn up here in 1775. John Paul Jones, Lafayette, and de Kalb met accidentally in the courtyard of the inn, at the beginning of their life-long friendship. In 1824, on his last visit to America, General Lafayette was entertained here by the people of Alexandria.

The City Tavern was rented to John Gadsby in 1795 and was known as Gadsby's during the many years of festivity and popularity that followed. Ann Warren, the English actress, died here in 1818 while engaged at the Alexandria Theater; she is buried in Christ Churchyard. And here, in 1816, the lovely "Female Stranger" came to die. Her tomb, in St. Paul's Cemetery, has a tragic and universally applicable inscription.

CITY HALL AND PUBLIC MARKET, Royal and Cameron Streets, with its clock-tower and spire, only faintly suggests its Georgian prototypes. The remainder of the building, covering a city block, is stamped with the crude detail and unharmonious proportions of post-Civil War buildings. In the roomy courtyard on the south side of the building a public market is held, with long stalls of flowers and produce, and other commodities are for sale within the market space in the building.

The ALEXANDRIA-WASHINGTON LODGE OF MASONS *(open 9–5 weekdays)*, in the central part of City Hall on the Cameron Street side, was organized in 1783 under the Grand Lodge of Pennsylvania. In 1788, as Alexandria Lodge No. 22, it was chartered under the authority of Masons of the jurisdiction of Virginia, and George Washington was its first Worshipful Master. A few years after the death of Washington, the name was changed to Alexandria-Washington Lodge.

Among the unbroken records of the lodge are reports of the various ceremonies attended, including the laying of the cornerstone of the Capitol. The important collection of portraits and relics now housed in the MUSEUM *(adm. 10¢)*, will eventually be moved to the Memorial Temple. At the entrance is a set of weights and measures sent from England in 1774 and used in the market for weighing ducks, venison, grain, tobacco, and other products. This is one of the few complete sets of English standards in this country.

The ANN LEE MEMORIAL HOME FOR THE AGED, NE. corner Fairfax and Cameron Streets, occupies the two Herbert houses, built shortly after the Revolution. The corner house was originally a hostelry, known at separate times as the Bunch of Grapes and Wise's Tavern. George Washington halted here on the way to his first inauguration, to be addressed publicly for the first time as President, and to reply formally in that capacity.

The BANK OF ALEXANDRIA, 133 N. Fairfax Street, organized in 1792, was the first authorized bank in Virginia. Washington was a depositor and stockholder.

The CARLYLE HOUSE *(open 9–5 weekdays; adm. 15¢)*, 123 N. Fairfax Street, entered through the Wagar Building, was erected in 1752 by John Carlyle, one of the Scottish merchants of Belhaven and a founder of Alexandria, who married Sarah Fairfax of Belvoir. The stately Georgian architecture of the house has been much altered, but it contains a good collection of early American furniture; it was opened as a historic house museum in 1914. Dungeon cells under the house are believed to be part of an old stone fort used for protection against the Indians.

Here, in 1755, General Braddock and the five royal governors planned the campaign against the French and Indians and, while in conference, decided to tax the Colonies. At this meeting Washington's advice was asked but rejected by Braddock, who marched from the Carlyle house to his death. The conference between delegates from Maryland and Virginia was begun here, in 1785, and continued, at Washington's invitation, at Mount Vernon, to settle the problem of intercolonial tariff duties. From this meeting evolved the Constitutional Convention in Philadelphia in 1787. Many other famous men gathered at the Carlyle House, including Lafayette, Lee, Mason, Jefferson, Franklin, Burr, and John Paul Jones.

The RAMSEY HOUSE, NE. corner King and Fairfax Streets, its ground floor open as a tavern, is the oldest house in **Alexandria.** Built in 1749–51 by William Ramsey, who came from Galway, Ireland, in 1749 and settled in the village of Belhaven, the old frame-over-brick house is typically Colonial. The roof, a modification of the "salt box" type, has a long slope to the rear and a gambrel front with three short dormers.

The ALEXANDRIA GAZETTE BUILDING, 317 King Street, houses offices of the oldest continuously published newspaper in the United States. Founded as the weekly *Virginia Journal and Alexandria Advertiser* on February 5, 1784, its name underwent many sonorous changes before the *Alexandria Gazette* was adopted in 1834. Suppressed because of its Southern sympathies in 1861, the paper continued to publish, surreptitiously, a one-sheet *Local News* until the *Gazette* was revived the following year. In 1940, after 156 years of existence, the *Gazette* began publication of a suburban edition for distribution in neighboring Fairfax County.

STABLER-LEADBEATER'S DRUGSTORE *(open, free, 10–4:30 weekdays)*, 105 S. Fairfax Street, was operated from its establishment in 1792 until 1933, when it was declared by the American Pharmaceutical Association to be the most typical and least-altered store of its kind in the United States. Six years later, the store was restored and opened by the Alexandria Landmarks Association, with the sponsorship of the American Pharmaceutical Association. Old bottles, mortars and pestles, and scales are among the old-fashioned equipment displayed in the store. Ledgers preserved here show accounts with many families noted in American history—Washingtons, Fairfaxes, Custises, Lees, and others. Robert E. Lee was in this store in 1859 when he was handed his orders to suppress the John Brown uprising at Harpers Ferry.

The ELISHA CULLEN DICK HOUSE *(private)*, 209 Prince Street, was the home of Dr. Dick, who attended George Washington in his fatal illness and cut the pendulum cords of the bedroom clock, marking the exact time of his death; the clock is owned by the Alexandria-Washington Lodge of Masons.

The GEORGE WILLIAM FAIRFAX HOUSE *(private)*, 207 Prince Street, another of the restored Prince Street dwellings, was built by the last master of Belvoir in 1752.

The WILLIAM BROWN HOUSE *(private)*, 212 Fairfax Street, was built by Dr. Brown about 1775, when he was Washington's family physician. His son, Gustavus, was one of the consulting physicians during Washington's last illness.

The CRAIK HOUSE *(private)*, 210 Duke Street, was the home of the Scottish physician, Dr. James Craik, who served Washington in every campaign from Great Meadows to Yorktown and attended him before his death. The three-story red-brick house was built about 1790.

The CORYELL HOUSE *(private)*, 208 Duke Street, is a "flounder" house leaning against the Craik House. It was the home of George Coryell, who ferried Washington across the Delaware River on Christmas Eve, 1776.

The OLD PRESBYTERIAN MEETING HOUSE *(open 9:30–5 daily, Apr. to Oct.; adm. 10¢),* 321 S. Fairfax Street, completed in 1774 with the subscription of John Carlyle, was attended by the descendants of most of the original Scottish settlers until 1886. This austerely simple Early Georgian structure, with its broad gabled mass and "regimental" windows, the square tower and balustraded cupola at one end and the double entrance stoop at the other, is characteristic of the public halls of its period. The beautifully proportioned interior is notable for a severity commoner in New England than in the South. Its furnishings include the original pews and the organ with an "Egyptian trumpet." In the churchyard are the graves of many distinguished citizens and patriots of the early days of Alexandria and an Unknown Soldier of the Revolutionary War.

The LAFAYETTE HOUSE *(private),* 301 S. St. Asaph Street, was built in 1795, by Thomas Lawrason and, in 1824, was lent by Mrs. Lawrason to General Lafayette during his farewell visit to America. Of exceptional beauty is the doorway with wide fan lunette transom, a wreathlike arch within an arch.

The OLD LYCEUM, Washington and Prince Streets, open as the headquarters of the Alexandria Chamber of Commerce, was built about 1825 by popular subscription as the home of a literary club. Benjamin Hallowell, besides conducting his school on Oronoco Street, frequently addressed the townspeople in this building, and many traveling lecturers stopped here. The calm, stately structure is a fine instance of Greek Revival architecture. The two-story portico, with Doric columns and the Doric cornice decorated with regular triglyphs, is in perfect Greek style. A finely paneled doorway in natural wood is set in the deeply recessed doorway.

The CONFEDERATE MONUMENT, standing in a circle at Washington and Prince Streets, is the bronze figure of a Confederate soldier atop a column, facing the South. Erected by Confederate veterans, it memorializes Alexandria men who lost their lives in the Civil War.

ALEXANDRIA POST OFFICE is a square red-brick building on the SE. corner of Washington and Prince Streets.

ALEXANDRIA ACADEMY, Washington and Wolfe Streets, had its cornerstone laid with Masonic ceremony in 1785. Washington was a trustee and, in his will, bequeathed $1,000 in stock of the Bank of Alexandria for the establishment of a free school in connection with the Academy. Robert E. Lee attended school here, "a most exemplary scholar," before he entered Benjamin Hallowell's school in 1824.

FRIENDSHIP ENGINE HOUSE *(open irregularly; adm. 10¢),* 107 S. Alfred Street, is a small red-brick building with a tall octagonal cupola. The company was organized 1774 and in 1775 Washington purchased for it the finest type of fire engine then available, a replica of which is on view, the original being in Baltimore. The brass nozzles and leather hose that went with it are exhibited, as well as a miscellaneous collection of relics.

A walk south on Lee Street leads to the marshy shores of Hunting Creek, where, on the northern point at the mouth of the inlet, stands the old JONES POINT LIGHTHOUSE, at the south end of the Alexandria water front. This property, including the south cornerstone of the District of Columbia, placed in 1794, is owned by the Mount Vernon Chapter of the D. A. R.

ST. MARY'S ROMAN CATHOLIC CEMETERY, SE. corner Washington and South Streets, contains burials made since St. Mary's Church, the first Roman Catholic Church in Virginia, was established in 1795. Along the cemetery fence, and generally forgotten, is the temporary stone used in marking the southern corner of the District in 1791.

The U.S. MILITARY CEMETERY, near the west end of Wilkes Street, established in 1862, contains the bodies of 3,570 Union soldiers. Thirty-six Confederate soldiers, originally buried here, were removed in 1879 to Christ Churchyard.

GEORGE WASHINGTON MASONIC NATIONAL MEMORIAL TEMPLE (*open, free, 9-5 daily*), is a gray pyramidal mass rising 400 feet above the town of Alexandria on Shooters Hill (the site once proposed for the Capitol), a mile north on King Street, at the junction with Russell Road. Intended as a lasting tribute to Washington the Mason, the lofty structure was designed by Harvey Wiley Corbett, and $5,000,000, contributed by 3,000,000 Masons, have thus far gone into its construction. From a square base with a Greek-temple portico, rises a series of three cubical units capped by a steep pyramid. Eventually the Alexandria-Washington Lodge of Masons will move to the temple, with its relics and pictures, a remarkable collection including the Reynolds portrait of Lord Thomas Fairfax, the trowel used by Washington in laying the cornerstone of the Capitol, and the clock that was stopped at the moment of his death. From the steps of the temple there is a sweeping view east, north, and south, commanding Alexandria, Washington, and the District and Virginia shores for many miles. The quiet old town is spread out below.

ALEXANDRIA TO MOUNT VERNON

Six-tenths of a mile south of the Richmond Highway (US 1) intersection in Alexandria, the Memorial Highway crosses the HUNTING CREEK BRIDGE, commanding a wide view of the Hunting Creek marshes, where Colonial gentlemen once gathered for the duck season. At the more favorable periods of the year, flocks of snowy egrets and white and blue herons can be seen feeding in the marshes, now part of a Federal bird sanctuary. Paths lead from the highway into the marshes, where rare plants grow.

WELLINGTON, 4.2 *m.,* with its remodeled Colonial buildings and modern additions, approached by a cedar-bordered drive on the east (L) side of the road, was erected in 1760 as part of the Mount Vernon Estate. The farm was given for life tenure to Tobias Lear, who was George Washington's confidential secretary for 16 years. After Lear's death in 1816 it remained in the Washington family two generations, and has been in private hands ever since. Lear's second wife was a Washington, and his third a Dandridge, niece of Martha Washington. As consul, Lear negotiated with the Barbary pirates in 1805, and held numerous other Government posts.

ARCTURUS, 4.7 *m.*, is a small settlement around a once noted watering place.

FORT WASHINGTON VIEW, 5.8 *m.*, is directly across the Potomac River from historic Fort Washington, on the Maryland side, occupying a site chosen by George Washington in 1795. Fort Warburton was built here in 1808. Following its abandonment without a shot during the British invasion in the War of 1812, Pierre L'Enfant, original designer of the city of Washington, planned a star-shaped medieval fortress, which was built in 1822. One of the few remaining examples of this type of architecture in the Nation, it has a moat (now dry), a drawbridge that no longer lifts, and many other details of interest. It is approached, in Maryland, by State Highways 224 and 549, and is 7.7 miles southwest of Oxon Hill. The site is being improved and preserved by the National Park Service.

The Memorial Highway curves gently between formally landscaped areas, through native woods where dogwood and redbud bloom in spring. There are driveouts to stone-walled springs, picnic sites, and lookouts across the wide Potomac.

RIVERSIDE PARK, 7.6 *m.*, is a picnic reservation on a bluff overlooking the Potomac.

The traffic circle at 8.9 *m.* is at the entrance to Mount Vernon.

Mount Vernon

Busses: Mount Vernon and sightseeing busses.
Taxis: Extra-fare prices for travel outside the District.
Boats: Round-trip to Mount Vernon, on boats leaving 7th Street Wharves, 50¢; children 25¢.

Mount Vernon *(open, summer, 9-5 weekdays, 1-5 Sun.; winter, 9-4 weekdays, 1-4 Sun.; adm. 25¢),* the home of George and Martha Washington, 15 miles south of Washington on the Virginia side of the Potomac, has more universal appeal than any other shrine of American history. Restored and maintained by the Mount Vernon Ladies' Association, a "nonprofit" organization, the historic estate is visited by more than half a million people a year, at 25 cents a head. The Association has been scrupulously exact in its restoration, following George Washington's own plans of detail and furnishings. It has collected, to a large extent, the original equipment, furniture, books, paintings, and accessories of Washington's day. The grounds are landscaped according to Washington's records and notations to his estate manager. Modernization, such as heating, lighting, and fire control, have been subordinated or concealed.

The land including Mount Vernon estate, 5,000 acres along the Potomac between Dogue Creek and Little Hunting Creek, was first patented in 1674 to Nicholas Spencer and John Washington, first of the name in America, and great-grandfather of George Washington. When the two families divided the property in 1690 the Washington land, 2,500 acres of Little Hunting Plantation, went to Lawrence, son of John, and then to his daughter Mildred, who sold it to her brother, Augustine, the father of George.

Here in 1735 Augustine built a home, and removed from Wakefield, the old family estate at Bridges Creek, where George was born in 1732. Shortly after, in 1739, the Little Hunting home was destroyed by fire, and the family moved to Ferry Farm, near Fredericksburg. The Hunting Creek grounds were given to Lawrence, the oldest son, with the proviso that, should he die without issue, they would go to his half brother, George. Lawrence in 1743 built a home for his bride, Anne Fairfax, of Belvoir, probably on the foundations of the old house, and called it Mount Vernon, for his old commander, Admiral Edward Vernon of the British navy. Richard Blackburn, of Rippon Lodge, designed the new home after Belvoir, home of Colonel William Fairfax.

George Washington spent much of his youth visiting the two houses and romancing with the younger Fairfax daughters. While at Mount Vernon, young George was commissioned to survey the Northern Neck properties of Lord Fairfax. In 1752 Lawrence died during a trip to Barbados and Bermuda with George (the only time George Washington ever left his country). Lawrence left the estate to his only daughter, who was dying of consumption, and named her uncle, George, as administrator and heir to Mount Vernon. When she died, two years later, the estate went to George Washington, who then purchased the old Spencer tract, combining them in a single estate. For several years afterward he was busy surveying the outlying parts of the Fairfax lands, and, during 1753, 1755, and 1758, he was engaged in campaigns against the French and Indians.

George Washington, in 1759, married Martha Dandridge Custis, a wealthy young widow. During that winter he caused the house to be renovated. The following spring he brought his wife to their home and began to develop the estate. He enlarged it considerably, creating five large farms, each with separate buildings and management, but he remained their personal supervisor. In 1773 he added a story to Mount Vernon House, and drew plans for two extensions, one north and one south, now the banquet room and library. A group of outbuildings was decided upon, but the outbreak of the Revolution and his appointment as commander in chief of the American forces prevented him from personally directing the work. During the six years he was away a distant cousin, Lund Washington, managed the estate and completed the additions and remodeling. In 1783, on Christmas Eve, Washington once again settled on his estate. One of his ambitions was to become the "first farmer in the country." On one occasion he was given a silver cup by the Agriculture Society of South Carolina "as a premium for raising the largest jackass." He laid out the bowling green, the serpentine drive, the gardens, the deer park, and the "ha-has" (sunken walls with a deep ditch outside to prevent cattle from straying on the lawn). He supervised the gristmill on Dogue Run and put the farms and buildings in order.

Reluctantly, in 1789, he accepted the Presidency, and again left his farming, returning only for occasional visits, but keeping in close touch with weekly reports, and sending regular advices. In 1797 he finally returned home, to devote himself to his wife's two grandchildren whom he adopted, George Washington Parke and Nelly (the spelling used in George Washington's letters) Custis. Washington died in 1799 and was buried in an old tomb under a bluff overlooking the Potomac. In 1802 Martha Washington died and was buried beside him. The main estate and home went to Washington's nephew, Bushrod Washington, and the remainder to grandnephews. Nelly Custis and her husband, Lawrence Lewis, Washington's nephew, had already received 2,000 acres, where they later built Woodlawn.

Bushrod Washington, Justice of the Supreme Court, lived but little on the estate. On his death in 1829, the house and immediate grounds went to his nephew, John Augustine Washington, and from him to his wife, Ann. Their son, John Augustine Washington, Jr., was the last private owner of Mount Vernon, which he received as a wedding gift in 1843. He attempted to have the United States or the State of Virginia take it over as a memorial, but failed.

In 1853 Ann Pamela Cunningham of South Carolina began the promotion of a society to purchase the estate. Organized in 1856, the Mount Vernon Ladies' Association finally bought the house and grounds for $200,000, raised by private subscription. Edward Everett, writer and lecturer, contributed the largest sum, $68,000, and the society took possession in 1860.

THE HOUSE

Mount Vernon is typically Georgian in style, with a carriage entrance on the west connecting through a spacious central hall with the colonnaded portico overlooking the river. The hipped roof with dormers and cupola form the attic story, which Washington added in 1773. At the same time the clapboard siding was covered with sand-finished wood, cut to give the appearance of stone blocks. Long windows, with numerous small panes, on the first floor were originally there, and the shorter windows of the second story, characteristic of the period, were installed with the additional story. Sandstone blocks which pave the portico, the family gathering place in mild weather, were imported by Washington in 1786 from St. Bees Head in Cumberland, England. A duplicate set has been obtained from the same quarry for replacements.

The BANQUET HALL, a story and a half high, across the north end of the mansion, was one of the two 22-foot additions planned by Washington in 1773 and finished under Lund Washington, although the general returned from Yorktown in time to supervise the decorating of the Adamesque ceiling with its agricultural symbolism. The marble mantel, allegedly by Canova, and the two vases were a gift from Samuel Vaughn, of London. Among the exhibits in the room are a Gobelin rug, gift of Louis XVI, which arrived after donor and recipient were dead; portraits of Washington as general, by Charles Willson Peale, and as President, by Gilbert Stuart; and such original pieces as the silver bracket lamps, the clock, the candle stands, and two landscapes in oil. The "hurricane" candle lamps, here and throughout the house, not original, are typical of the period.

The WEST PARLOR, adjoining the banquet hall, has a fireplace with an iron back, in which are cast the initials "G. W.," and above, in a broken pediment, is the Washington coat of arms. The curtain cornices, mirror, oval tea tray, and inlaid Sheraton-type table are original. The engraved portrait of Louis XVI is a contemporary copy of one presented to Washington.

The MUSIC ROOM, overlooking the river, was especially fitted out for Nelly Custis. Washington admitted that "I can neither sing one of the songs, nor raise a single note on any instrument," though his flute is in his room. Nelly's harpsichord, which Washington imported from London for her, and which she later took to Woodlawn, was the first item restored to Mount Vernon in 1860. On it are some of Nelly's music books and a sitar or guitar belonging to a Washington cousin. The mirror and brackets supporting cut-glass lusters, an urn-shaped lamp, and a small china figurine, date from Washington's time. A portrait of Nelly Custis Lewis, by Trumbull, is of later date.

Wide stairs at the west end of the spacious CENTRAL HALL sweep around and over the eight-paneled carriage entrance door, with its massive locks and H and L hinges. The colors of the paneled walls, following the removal of a center partition in 1775, have been restored. The clock on the stair landing, the marble-topped table, the hall lantern (gift of Admiral Vernon to Lawrence), and two gifts from Lafayette, a hunting horn and the key to the Bastille, are part of the original furnishings. Here, encased in glass, are four of Washington's swords; one used during the Braddock campaign; his dress sword, now damaged by rust; a sword presented by a German admirer; the silver-mounted blade he wore when he resigned as commander-in-chief in 1783 and at his inauguration in 1789. With the swords are two of his military sashes, one the gift of General Braddock. Washington willed his swords to his nephews, cautioning them "Not to unsheath them for the purpose of shedding blood except in self-defence or in the defence of their country and its rights, and in the latter case, keep them unsheathed and prefer falling with them in their hands to the relinquishment thereof."

The FAMILY DINING ROOM, south of the main hall, contains eight original ladder-back chairs of Chippendale style, and a portrait of Lawrence Washington, by Wollaston. The mirror-topped dining room table was used on formal occasions during Washington's Presidency. Always a generous host, Washington kept his house open at all times. He wrote once in his diary, "Mrs. Washington and myself will do what I believe has not been done within the last twenty years by us,—that is sit down to dinner by ourselves." Nelly Custis' high chair stands in a corner. The sideboard, believed to have been a Fairfax piece, was inherited by the Custises and taken to Arlington, and was later turned over to Mount Vernon by Mary Custis, wife of Robert E. Lee. The Venetian blinds here and throughout the house are modern adaptations of one, "such as draws and closes and expands," ordered by Washington about 1775, "that others may be made by it at home."

MARTHA WASHINGTON'S SITTING ROOM, with windows opening on the river view, was the scene of the domestic education of her daughter, Martha (Patsy) Custis, and her granddaughter, Nelly. The armchair, three occasional chairs, the Heppelwhite center table, and the Chippendale card table are original pieces. The rug, not a part of the Washington furnishings, was hand woven more than 200 years ago by two English ladies whose names are worked into the border.

The LIBRARY, or Washington's Study, from which he directed the activities of several farms, wrote letters, made daily entries in his diary, and sought retreat from the continuous flow of guests, is an intimate shrine of the master of Mount Vernon. Two maps in the bookcase, and a few of the original volumes, including a set of Gibbon, are all of Washington's library that has been restored to Mount Vernon. He willed to Judge Bushrod Washington "all papers in my possession which relate to my civil and military administration of the affairs of the country" and "my library of books [884 volumes] and pamphlets of every kind." Partitions among Bushrod's heirs scattered the library, a large portion of which was collected by the Boston Athenaeum. Official papers and many military books were acquired by the Government in 1834. The inventory of Washington's executors was used to compile the present library, largely composed of contemporary duplicates.

Two thermometer-barometers are on Washington's desk, indicative of his husbandman's interest in the weather. One of the instruments apparently came in response to a letter to a northern friend: "Pray get me one of those thermometers that tell the state of the mercury within the twenty-four hours." The desk and a chair in his study were mentioned in Washington's will: "To my compatriot in arms and old and intimate friend Doctor Craik I give my Bureau (or as the Cabinet makers called it Tambour Secretary) and the circular chair, an appendage of my study." They were purchased by the Mount Vernon Association from the Craik heirs and restored to their original position. Other genuine Washington articles are the globe, the mahogany bookcase, and a pair of spectacles. The round table is said to have belonged to Robert E. Lee.

The BUTLER'S PANTRY contains silver pitchers inscribed "G.W. 1776," said to have been the gift of Governor Sessions of Rhode Island. The wine chest beneath the window is described in the bill from Washington's London agent: "A neat mahogany square chest with 16 Gall'n Bottles in Ditto with ground stoppers, Brass lifting handles and brass Casters." The china, copper, and pewter utensils are typical of those used during Washington's lifetime.

The NELLY CUSTIS ROOM, on the second floor, overlooks the bowling green and gardens. Nelly and her husband, Lawrence Lewis, lived here before the completion of Woodlawn, and their first two children were born here. The cradle was a gift at the birth of their eldest. The upholstery of the footstool is a sample of Nelly's needlework.

The LAFAYETTE ROOM, on the same floor, where the marquis stayed, contains the bed in which he slept.

The GUEST ROOM was used by young George Washington Parke Custis, brother of Nelly and builder of Arlington House.

The YELLOW CHAMBER was used by the Washingtons before the additions of 1775.

The WASHINGTON ROOM and dressing rooms, occupying the whole of the south addition on the second floor, are almost completely furnished with original pieces. In the large wing chair Mary Ball Washington nursed the infant George. The bed on which Washington died is covered with a spread copied from one worked by Martha; the tester and valances to match are also copies of her needlework. (The originals are in the Museum). The clock is in the Alexandria-Washington Lodge of Masons. The walls of this room are covered with wallpaper of rare design copied from the original, which was discovered under a layer of plaster during the restoration.

When Washington died, his room, according to custom, was closed until the next male heir should take over the property, and Mrs. Washington retired to a small room directly above, from whose window she could view his tomb.

MARTHA WASHINGTON'S ROOM, under the third-story eaves, is furnished mainly with contemporary duplicates; only the rocking chair, dressing glass, and corner wash stand are original. Neither this room, nor any of the other five guest rooms on this floor, is open to the public. Mount Vernon has no closets, except in Nelly Custis' room. Clothes were hung on pegs. Mount Vernon, of course, had no bathrooms. Among the earliest bathrooms in America were two in the Van Ness mansion, built about 1815. The White House had none until about 1840.

GROUNDS AND OUTBUILDINGS

The front lawn, sloping toward the Potomac, is surrounded by a ha-ha designed to keep deer within bounds of a private park, which Washington laid out but soon abandoned. The restored walls are made of brick taken from a Colonial Virginia house. The pecan trees on the lawn were planted by Washington and were probably gifts from Thomas Jefferson.

The original approach to the mansion was by the West Lodge Gate, about a mile west of the present entrance. The drive passed through the west ha-ha walls and ended in the pear-shaped serpentine drive at the carriage entrance of the house. The serpentine drive encloses the bowling green and a lawn protected by posts and chain. A sundial set up by Washington is near the center of "my Court Yard."

The numerous outbuildings, where the work of the estate was carried on, constituted a self-sustaining village. Cotton, wool, and even silk, were grown, spun, and woven on the estate. Corn and wheat were milled; eggs, butter, milk and cheese were home products; wine was pressed and whisky distilled; tobacco was raised and cured for home consumption. Wood was hewn to beams and planks; bricks were molded and fired in kilns. It took 66 servants to operate the home estate and 150 more to keep the four outlying farms going; most of these latter were field hands.

The OFFICE, north of the west approach, is connected by a curved arcade to the main house. Originally the headquarters for domestic activities, and sleeping quarters for white servants, it is now the office of the superintendent. To the west, across a walkaway, is the GARDENER'S HOUSE, now occupied by Mount Vernon guards. North of that are the STOREHOUSE; the SPINNING HOUSE, completely reequipped with original spinning and weaving machinery; and the MUSEUM, a modern reproduction, replacing old slave quarters, housing a notable collection of Washingtoniana, including the original bust of Washington, made by Houdon from Mount Vernon clay. It is the only sculptured likeness of the first President made from life, and has served as a model for nearly all later statues of him.

West of these buildings is the FLOWER GARDEN, arranged approximately as Washington planned it, with the same varieties of old-fashioned flowers. The delicate perfume of the garden, more than the roped-off rooms of Mount Vernon House, seem to carry over to the present an authentic air of gracious eighteenth-century living. The dwarf-box maze is original. At the west end of the garden is the SCHOOLHOUSE where G.W.P. and Nelly Custis received their early education. North of the gardens are the long greenhouses, where potted plants and ivy can be purchased, and the servants' quarters, reconstructed after a fire in 1835.

The KITCHEN, south of the oval, is also connected to the house by a symmetrical curved arcade. The interior is furnished with authentic Colonial Virginia kitchen equipment, but only the crane and iron mortar are original Washington pieces. A part of the kitchen is now a souvenir and information booth. Directly west is the BUTLER'S HOUSE, and, southward along a brick walk, are the DAIRY, on the east, and the "SMOAK HOUSE" (Washington's spelling), on the west. Next is the WASH HOUSE, and the reconstructed COACH HOUSE, in which there is a coach of Washington's period by the maker of the President's vehicle. Across from this building is a brick barn built in 1732. At the end of the barn is a large kitchen garden which furnished Mount Vernon with vegetables. Along the north wall are fig bushes planted by Washington and still bearing.

A path continues south and west along the terrace to Washington's Tomb.

THE TOMB

At the end of the walk stands the ivy-covered tomb of the Washingtons, with an open outer vault containing the two simple marble sarcophagi of George and Martha Washington. Both were originally buried in the old family vault on the slope overlooking the river. This old tomb was built in 1745 by Washington for his brother Lawrence. Later Washington, his wife, and his nephew, Bushrod, were buried there. Although Washington had left express instructions in his will that a new brick tomb be built, even naming the site, the work was not undertaken until 1831.

Congress made several efforts to have the body of the first President entombed in the city of Washington, even constructing a crypt in the Capitol. The Virginia State Legislature, in 1816, also made efforts to have his body enshrined in Richmond.

Shortly after the death of Judge Bushrod Washington, John Augustine Washington, the elder, took over the management of Mount Vernon. Early in 1830 he discharged an employee, who, in a drunken rage, returned by night and broke into the old tomb, intending to steal the skull of George Washington. He was caught with the skull of Washington's nephew. John Augustine then set about building the new tomb. It was completed in 1831, and the bodies from the old tomb were removed. In 1837 the open outer vault was built and the two sarcophagi set in it. The last person buried in the inner vault was Jane Washington, in 1855. The doors were then locked and the key thrown into the Potomac.

In such veneration is this spot held that on every ship of the United States Navy, while passing the spot, the flag is lowered to half-mast, the bell tolled, and the crew drawn up at attention. During the Civil War, this ground was held neutral by both sides.

Bladensburg and Greenbelt

Busses: East Riverdale and Cheverly busses, operating on Bladensburg Road, go by way of Bladensburg School. Bladensburg busses operate from 17th St. and Penna. Ave. SE.

Two towns of sharply contrasting character exist almost side by side in near-by Maryland, both within half an hour's drive from the Nation's Capital. Bladensburg, noted as a battle site during the invasion of Washington in 1814 and for its historic dueling grounds, but perhaps less known for its fine old historic houses, is 8 miles northeast of downtown Washington. Greenbelt, a modern suburban housing development, is 4 miles beyond.

The simplest approach to Bladensburg and Greenbelt is via US 1, northeast from the Capitol on Maryland Avenue and Bladensburg Road, travelling beyond the National Arboretum and the National Training School for Boys *(see North and East Washington)*.

On the northeast portion of the National Training School grounds is the SITE OF THE BATTLE OF BLADENSBURG, where Commodore Joshua Barney's battery, manned by sailors, gallantly but futilely attempted to defend the Capital on August 25, 1814. Barney had blown up his little ships on the Patuxent the previous day to avoid capture and had marched his 300 sailors to this position. During the tragic rout of the Americans, Barney's Battery stood firm, but Barney was wounded and captured with the remnants of his force. The battle was fought over the ground between this point and Bladensburg, with President James Madison in command of the American forces. He was the first President to take part in actual fighting while in office, and the first and only one to go into action as Commander in Chief.

BARNEY'S SPRINGS, where the wounded Commodore was treated by British surgeons, is bricked up, under the porch of the private house at 3041 Bladensburg Road. Wounded combatants of early duels at the Bladensburg grounds were often brought here to have their injuries washed and dressed.

The RIVES HOUSE *(private)*, late Federal in design, is hidden by a high fence almost opposite Barney's Springs. It was built about 1830 by John C. Rives, partner of James Preston Blair in ownership of the *Globe,* the political organ of Jackson's administration. Rives was a member of Jackson's "Kitchen Cabinet."

The DUELING GROUND, SW. corner Bladensburg Road and Bunker Hill Road, where a nursery now stands, was for many years the fashionable field of honor where gentlemen of Washington settled their political and personal differences. In 1820 the former Commodore James Barron shot and killed Commodore Stephen Decatur on this ground. More than 30 duels were fought here. The bloodiest challenge was that made by Brigadier General Armistead Mason to his cousin, Colonel John McCarty. The latter, as the challenged party having the choice of weapons, first proposed that both leap from the dome of the Capitol. This being refused, McCarty next suggested that both sit on a keg of gunpowder and be blown up. A third proposal to fight with dirks hand-to-hand being likewise rejected, the Colonel next proposed shotguns at 10 paces, which was accepted but modified to "rifles at 12 paces." Mason was killed and McCarty wounded.

The MEMORIAL CROSS, more generally called the Peace Cross, occupies a plaza at the intersection of US 1 and US 50 (Defense Highway). Erected in 1925, the blocky cast-stone cross, 30 feet high, is a landmark in this area, and often enters into local directions. It is a memorial to the men of Prince Georges County, Maryland, who died in World War I. South of the cross is the tree-lined stream, the upper waters of the Anacostia River, which was, unbelievably, once deep enough to provide a spacious harbor for sailing ships.

BLADENSBURG

Bladensburg (20 alt., 1,220 pop.), at the junction of US 1 (Baltimore-Washington Boulevard) and US 50 (Defense Highway), is a suburban town from which Government workers commute to Washington, but its history reaches back to pre-Revolutionary days. On the Baltimore-Washington Boulevard side, filling stations and barbecue stands have almost obliterated its character as a historic town, and soot from the railroad has disguised many of its Colonial homes in the area along the Defense Highway. Finely proportioned old mansions, however, peep out from among the more recent architectural increment, giving a genuine feeling for the place Bladensburg once held as stage station, tavern site, and residential area for the wealthy of a bygone period. Little that is convincing remains to recapture the aroma of Bladensburg as a seaport town.

Bladensburg was a commercial center for half a century before the Capital City was conceived. This trading post at the head of navigation on the Anacostia prospered through its tobacco trade. Charles Calvert, descendant of the Lords Baltimore, acquired the land around the headwaters through marriage, and Calvert's daughter, Eugenia, sold 60 acres in 1742 for the creation of a town at Garrison's Landing, to be called Bladensburg, in honor of Sir Thomas Bladen, then royal governor of Maryland. By the middle of the eighteenth century the new town enjoyed two sources of revenue—its trade as an inland port, and its coaching custom—for the town was on the main coach road between the northern and southern Colonies. Its taverns were famous and its citizens wealthy.

Early in the nineteenth century the Anacostia began to silt up and larger ships could no longer navigate the stream. The coming of rail-roads robbed the town of its distinction as a coaching center and ruined the rest of the shipping trade, so that dredging the stream was unprofit-able. The new Capital was absorbing the town's citizens and their money. Bladensburg settled into suburban insignificance and there it remained for a century, except for that brief moment of fame, the Battle of Bladensburg, which preceded the burning of Washington by the British in the War of 1812.

The railroad was not at first allowed to enter the Capital, so that, for a brief time, Bladensburg was the western terminus for the Balti-more & Ohio Railroad and the station for all Washington passengers. In 1835, Congress reluctantly permitted the "iron horse" to snort into Washington, to the very foot of Capitol Hill, and Bladensburg, losing its position as a railroad terminus, again lapsed into obscurity.

Proceed L. from the Peace Cross on US 1 (Baltimore-Washington Boulevard).

GEORGE WASHINGTON TAVERN (L), again open as a roadside "tavern," was built in 1732, the year of Washington's birth. Here in 1774 Washington and other southern delegates stopped overnight on their way to the First Continental Congress. On March 27, 1790, Washington again stayed at the tavern, breaking the journey that resulted in the agreement for a National Capital near by. Later, the tavern's name was changed to the George Washington House and many distinguished guests mention stopping "at the sign of the George Wash-ington." The inn was a coaching house and relay station when stage lines flourished, and many gentlemen spent the night here so that they might meet at dawn on the Bladensburg dueling ground.

SPA SPRINGS, just off the highway (R), was once a famous watering place. The iron waters were considered so healthful that a bill was introduced in Congress to have them piped to hospitals in Washington; the bill, however, did not pass.

Continue over the curving bridge above the Baltimore & Ohio tracks through Hyattsville to the suburban town of Riverdale.

RIVERDALE *(private),* on Arthur Avenue, also known as the Calvert Mansion, is a cream-colored Georgian house with massive central sec-tion and low symmetrical service wings. The house, when completed in 1803 by George Calvert, descendant of Lord Baltimore, was one of the most elaborate mansions in Maryland. It was built and lavishly furnished largely through the financial aid of Calvert's father-in-law, Henri Stier, a wealthy merchant of Antwerp. In the garden behind the house stands a cannon, said to be one of the four brought to Maryland on the *Ark,* in 1634. Suburban development has encroached heavily on the once spacious grounds.

Return to the Peace Cross, and proceed east on US 50 (Defense Highway).

The ROSS HOUSE *(private),* 0.2 *m.* from the Peace Cross, set back from the road (L) amid shabby surroundings, was built in 1749 by Dr. David Ross, distinguished soldier and purveyor of supplies during the French and Indian War. The old house, though much dilapidated, still preserves the sturdy lines of early Georgian architecture.

The MAGRUDER HOUSE *(private)*, on a grassy knoll opposite the Ross House, is named for a former owner. Little is known of its early history. Legend has it that the two-and-a-half-story house of typical Dutch Colonial architecture was built in 1743 and that at one time, just prior to the Revolution, it was owned by a Doctor Harvey. Washington's diary of the period refers to a visit to "the Doctor's house in Bladensburg", probably meaning this one. The doorways, woodwork, mantels, and flooring, including H-strap hinges, and locks stamped with the British lion and unicorn, are very old and remarkably well preserved. Antique furnishings and equipment add interest to the interior. In the cellar is a slave "dungeon" fitted with an iron ring, to which unruly slaves were fastened.

At 0.2 m. east of the Ross House, turn R. (south) on River Road.

The SHIP BALLAST HOUSE *(private)*, is concealed from the road by trees and shielded by more modern dwellings. The entrance (R) is by a footpath from an arched opening in the picket fence. The diminutive house, with its small casement windows, low roof, and stone chimney, is reminiscent of a cottage in Wales or Ireland. The stone used in its construction was presumably brought in ships as ballast to be replaced by heavy return cargoes of tobacco. It was built in 1750 for the master of the market, which lay along the wharves of the Anacostia River.

The BOSTWICK HOUSE *(private)*, high on a series of neat grass terraces (L) was built by Christopher Lowndes, early shipping magnate, American member of the English firm of Edward Lowndes Co. "C. L. 1748" in wrought iron is imbedded high in the south chimney. To sustain the south wall, which sagged in the course of construction, a hollow buttress of brick was built. It contains two rooms, which served as a jail for disobedient slaves. Benjamin Stoddert, Lowndes' son-in-law, found refuge in this home after he lost his fortune, dying here in 1813.

The drawing room on the south side has a fireplace 7 feet high and 10 feet wide and is paneled in black walnut. In this room Lafayette received his admirers during a visit in 1824 to Judge John Stevens, who had bought the house after the death of Stoddert. The house remained in the Stevens family for more than a century, when it was purchased by James H. Kiner, distinguished Civil War veteran. It still belongs to his heirs.

Return to US 50 (Defense Highway) and continue east.

PARTHENON HEIGHTS *(private)*, 0.4 m. east from the junction with River Road, is set high on a wooded bluff (R). Built about 1769 by Christopher Lowndes as a wedding gift for one of his daughters, the frame house is similar to the central exterior portion of Mount Vernon. The interior arrangement, however, is quite different. The living room, contrary to custom, faces the entrance door from an ell at the rear of the central hall. This plan gives the hall and living room great depth and perspective.

Landover Road forks R., 0.6 m. east of Parthenon Heights.
BEALL'S PLEASURE (*private*), 1.6 *m.* from the fork, is visible from
the main road, up a narrow private road (L). This fine example of
Georgian architecture was built about 1795 by Benjamin Stoddert,
first Secretary of the Navy, and Washington's confidential agent in
securing rights for the Capital City. It was built of brick burned at
clay pits still visible on the grounds.

GREENBELT

Greenbelt, the Government-owned housing development for low-
income families, is reached by the Edmonston Road, which branches L.
(north) from US 50 about a mile east of the Peace Cross. The route
is clearly marked by signs. (Greenbelt may also be reached by turning
R. from US 1, 1.9 *m.* north of Riverdale.)

Established by the Resettlement Administration, now the Farm
Security Administration of the Department of Agriculture, Greenbelt is
one of three demonstrations in providing low-rental housing for rural-
industrial communities. The name is derived from the general plan of
a community surrounded by a "green belt" of park and farm land. Similar projects have been initiated at Greenhills, near Cincinnati, Ohio,
and Greendale, near Milwaukee, Wisconsin.

The purpose of these land-utilization projects is "to create a community protected by an encircling green belt; the community to be
designed for families of predominantly modest income, and arranged
and administered so as to encourage that kind of family and community
life which will be better than they now enjoy." The large area of
land, which serves as protective belt and belongs to the community, prevents encroachment of industrial or commercial activities such as so
often destroy the rural advantages of privately constructed housing
developments. Within this area are garden plots for the use of
residents.

In addition to providing satisfactory living conditions for their
residents, Greenbelt and the other green-belt communities are a practical
demonstration in low-cost housing which can be liquidated within a
reasonable time. Officials hope that similar communities will be developed by private, municipal, or State enterprise.

All construction work at Greenbelt was done by men on relief
rolls. Units for housing nearly 900 low-income families have been
completed on the great horseshoe-shaped plateau. The outer rim of the
plateau is utilized for home and apartment units and the concave central
section contains stores, shops, a motion picture theater, a school, and a
recreation center with swimming pool, baseball diamonds, and tennis
courts. To the northwest of the community, a creek has been dammed
to form an artificial lake, with boating and fishing privileges.

The residential section of the community is divided into super-
blocks. The relatively few motor roads skirt these blocks, with the
housing units on the outer edges of each block, so that the homes are

easily accessible. Within the center of the super-blocks are landscaped play areas for children. Traffic hazards are further reduced by underpasses.

The community is composed entirely of families within the income group receiving $1,200 to $2,500 per year. There is a long waiting list of prospective tenants for the units, which rent from $20 to $45 a month, including light, heat, and water. Each unit is of sound construction, durable, and fire resistant, and is soundproofed (in the case of row houses) from its neighbor; it is also equipped with modern plumbing and ventilation. Each block of units is centrally heated. The design and conveniences of the dwellings are modern in treatment and conception, and the blocks and individual units are pleasingly landscaped.

For the sake of economy of construction surface materials have been limited to brick and cinder block with flat or pitched roofs. By alternating the use of these materials, and of the roof types, considerable variety has been attained. Some of the houses are further differentiated by novel color schemes. Finally, pitched- and flat-roof structures have been planned not only to afford variety within a section, but also to create interesting patterns for the sections as a whole.

The community has a municipal government comparable to other Maryland towns of the same size. It makes payments in lieu of taxes to the State of Maryland and to Prince Georges County. The management of the town is vested in the Resettlement Division of the FSA until it can be turned over to a local non-profit corporation. It is estimated that the rents will pay the taxes, the maintenance and replacements, the interest on the investment, and amortize the Government subsidy within 60 years. Thus the community will eventually be self-supporting.

Greenbelt now (1941) has 885 dwellings and provision for expansion to about 3,000. Only 217 acres of its 3,600 have been developed; 2,633 acres are to be preserved as a protective belt, in line with the original scheme for the community, and the remaining 750 acres will be utilized for expansion of housing units and additional recreation space.

To meet the needs of wartime housing, 1,000 new dwellings are being constructed; these new units will conform to the present housing standards of the community and the new tenants will probably be drawn from income brackets comparable to those of residents already living in the community.

Two Ways to Great Falls

Streetcars: Rosslyn cars go as far northwest as 35th and M Sts., a convenient Georgetown approach to the canal. Cabin John cars serve the Maryland shore as far up as Cabin John Bridge.

Busses: Potomac Heights busses operate northwest on MacArthur Blvd. to Norton St. Charter busses make trips to Great Falls on the Virginia side in summer.

Canoes, Rowboats: For rent at nominal hourly rates along the Georgetown water front, at Fletcher's Boathouse, Canal and Reservoir Rds., and at Great Falls. Locks do not operate, but equipment is being installed to aid in portaging.

Horse-drawn Barge Trips: The National Park Service operates 4-hour Sunday afternoon barge trips on the canal in season, covering different sections on different trips. Barge fare $1, bus fare 50¢ to $1.

Hiking: Canal towpath on Maryland side provides an easy water-level route of 11.2 miles from Key Bridge to Great Falls, or a shorter route of 6.7 miles from the end of the Cabin John trolley line to Great Falls.

Fishing: Catfish, perch, bass, and other fresh-water species. Maryland laws apply to fishing in canal and in Potomac River, which is under the jurisdiction of Maryland above the District Line; no license required in the District.

Prohibited along Canal: Swimming, hunting, horseback riding, use of power boats, building fires, except at established picnic sites by holders of permits, which are granted free by Park Police at Room 1211, South Interior Building.

Precautions: Three-leafed poison ivy and the painful but not dangerous nettle grow in the woods on both sides of the river. Insect pests include mosquitoes, ticks (examine body for ticks, which should be removed within two to four hours to avoid the dangerous Rocky Mountain fever), and "chiggers," which some say can be avoided by dusting the legs with flowers of sulphur before entering the woods. Hikers should carry a stick in case of an encounter with a poisonous copperhead snake.

Great Falls, where the Potomac River tumbles in a broken series of cataracts and rapids over the edge of the Piedmont Plateau, is less than 15 miles from the Key Bridge in Georgetown, whether approached from the Maryland or Virginia side. The view of the falls is more advantageous from the Virginia shore of the Potomac, but the Maryland approach has added interest because of the historic Chesapeake and Ohio Canal, which was operated under this and another name between 1802 and 1924. Purchased by the Federal Government in 1938, it is being reconditioned as a memento of the canal period in American history. The only major waterfall in this part of the country, Great Falls is visited by thousands each year, and is a pleasant cool spot even at the height of Washington midsummers.

THE MARYLAND APPROACH

Paralleling the old canal, the motor car route to Great Falls on the Maryland side of the river is in many respects disappointing. The hiker, fisherman, and canoeist, meeting the canal on its own level, and on its own leisurely terms, have the better of it in exploring this historic route. The road offers a number of points of access to the canal, and there are opportunities for shorter or longer hikes, and for canoe trips on extended stretches between locks for distances of three or four miles each way. Bird students with their binoculars find the canal route a splendid place for songbirds, especially in early spring before the foliage fills out. Herons and ducks can be seen in several areas along the river. Wildflowers bloom through three seasons, and the riverside is splendid for outdoor plant study, with its marsh plants, great tall sycamores, elms arching over the canal, water beeches, flowering locusts, and tangles of vines, including native honeysuckle and trumpet vine, and dozens of less frequently found species. The fine masonry of locks and lockhouses of the 1830's, the leisurely flow of water in the canal, and the generally even tempo of life beside canal and river carry their own appeal.

The natural route provided by the Potomac River Valley had much to do with the Nation's history, and was a prime consideration in the location of Washington as the Nation's Capital. Before the Revolution, transportation in America was mainly on tidewater, and George Washington, while still in his twenties, saw the advantages of a canal-and-river system that would link the eastern seaboard with western lands in the Ohio River drainage. This same young surveyor, nearly 40 years later, was called upon to choose a site for the "Federal City." That the planner he chose, Pierre L'Enfant, should have designed a city suited to canals (*see The L'Enfant and Later Plans*) was only natural.

Washington organized the "Patowmack" Canal Company in 1785 and served as its first president. He supervised workmen engaged in clearing the river of obstructions, and in building skirting canals around the falls in the river. The company's route consisted primarily of river-lanes to carry small raftlike boats, and a number of canals, with locks, around the principal falls. Washington died three years before the "Patowmack" Canal was completed, in 1802. The principal canal and locks, around Great Falls on the Virginia side, carried traffic nearly three-quarters of a mile, through a series of five locks with a lift of 76 feet. Some of the locks were carved from solid rock, and the canal-and-lock series was considered a great engineering feat. Furs, flour, farm produce, and lumber began to move down the Potomac to Georgetown. In succeeding years, however, it became apparent that the river development was inadequate, and that the Potomac could be used for navigation only in times of high water. Half a million dollars were poured into the enterprise, but it was impractical in the end, and the company went into bankruptcy in 1828.

Completion of the Erie Canal in 1825, and its immediate success, prompted the organization of another company, the Chesapeake and Ohio concern, to complete canalization of the Potomac to Pittsburgh. President John Quincy Adams turned the first shovel of earth at Little

Falls on Independence Day, 1828. (On the first attempt, his shovel struck a root; on the second, the ceremonial earth-turning was successful.) Within three years water was flowing in the first 22 miles of canal, between Georgetown and Seneca, the section now restored. In 1833 navigation was opened to Harpers Ferry; to a point near Hancock, Maryland, in 1839; to Cumberland, Maryland, 185 miles above Georgetown, in 1850. Growing financial difficulties, legal tangles, and the competition of the nearly parallel Baltimore & Ohio Railroad, caused the company at that time to abandon its plan to extend the canal to Pittsburgh—the railroad had reached Cumberland 8 years ahead of the canal, and was pushing on to Wheeling, on the Ohio River, with which it established connection in 1852.

The canal carried a heavy load of traffic during the last half of the nineteenth century, reaching its height in the 1870's, with the transportation of coal for a growing industrialism in the East. In that decade there were as many as 540 boats navigating the canal, the standard model being 92 feet long and 14½ feet wide. Black boys exercised their native art in "skinning" the two or three mules needed along the 12-foot towpath to keep the boats in motion. An extra or relief team was carried in a stable in the forward house on the boat; there was a hay-house amidships, and the captain and his family lived in a little cabin aft. Canal traffic gradually dwindled thereafter, being superseded by other forms of transportation, and in 1924 the last boatload of goods was carried on the Chesapeake and Ohio water route. The canal company continued to exist, selling water to industrial firms in Georgetown, and renting lands and houses along the canal route. Floods damaged and filled canals and locks, and the channel filled with water plants, muck, and stagnant water. In 1938 the Government purchased the canal, and the National Park Service began immediate restoration of the stretch between Georgetown and Seneca, 8.5 miles above Great Falls. In the following years much of this work was accomplished.

Twenty-three of the original 74 locks are on the restored portion of the canal, and at many of the locks are the original dressed-stone lockhouses, which were begun in 1828 and built a few years later. Along the original length of 184.5 miles between Georgetown and Cumberland there was a lift of about 600 feet. Along the restored 22-mile section there is a lift of about 190 feet.

Within Georgetown, once a busy tidewater shipping point, there are four lift locks joined by narrow canal basins, and the old canal bridge across Wisconsin Avenue.

KEY BRIDGE, 0 *m.* (*see Georgetown*), is a convenient starting point for visits to Great Falls on both the Maryland and Virginia sides of the river. The abutments of the OLD ALEXANDRIA AQUEDUCT, 0.1 *m.* (*see Georgetown*), where a branch of the Potomac Canal was carried across the river, are just above Key Bridge. A footbridge at this point gives access to the towpath.

M Street leads into Canal Road, which winds along just above the canal, but a concrete wall and, farther up, a stone wall effectively cut off the view of the placid channel from the road. Several boathouses stand on the river bank, below the canal, within the first half-mile above Key Bridge. River and canal are lined with towering sycamore trees, which have been preserved because their wood is fortunately uneconomic as lumber. There are soft green willows, tall slender poplars, flowering locusts, wild cherry, and many other species of trees and smaller plants.

At 1.8 *m.* there is a view of a wet-weather WATERFALL across the Potomac River on the Virginia side, a charming cataract that can be seen from the road when the foliage is not too dense. A full-bodied waterfall after a hard rain, it makes a pattern of white in the darkness of a ravine on the Potomac cliffs.

FLETCHER'S BOATHOUSE, 2.4 *m.,* at the intersection of Canal Road and Reservoir Road, occupies a two-story white-painted stone house and subsidiary buildings. A well-known intermediate point on the canal and river, it rents boats and canoes. Access to the towpath is provided at the boathouse.

At 2.7 *m.* a B. & O. RAILROAD BRIDGE spans canal and highway; at this point the stone wall is low enough to see the grass-bordered canal from an automobile. A road sign indicates the right turn on a road to Potomac Heights. At 3 *m.* is a left turn on MacArthur Blvd., which is followed for the greater part of the distance to Great Falls.

Right from MacArthur Blvd. on Little Falls Road 0.2 *m.* is the NATIONAL TRAINING SCHOOL FOR GIRLS, with four buildings on 20 acres of land and a staff of 23 teachers having the care of about 75 girls committed there by the juvenile court.

BROOKMONT, 4.7 *m.,* a suburban settlement built mainly during the 1930's, stands on a bluff above the C. & O. Canal and the Potomac River. A road (left) enters the subdivision between lighted posts. A sharp right turn, after crossing the Cabin John trolley tracks, leads (bearing left) down a steep second-gear hill to reconditioned LOCK 6 beside a diminutive, two-story, white-painted, cut-stone lockhouse. Below the canal is "the feeder," a swift canal-size channel drawing water from the river and discharging it into the canal at Lock 5, four-tenths of a mile below. To raise the level of the river, a rubblestone feeder dam was built by Potomac Company engineers across the river a short distance above Lock 6. Its center is on Snake Island, a low wooded area about midway across the Potomac, which was literally split in two by the floods of 1936 and 1938. Between the feeder and the turbulent main river channel below the dam are two islands—Low Island, often inundated by floods, and High Island, lifting its rocky tree-grown crest far above high water level, offering a fine upriver view.

GLEN ECHO PARK, 6.6 *m.,* is the usual amusement park, with thrill rides, swimming pool, dance floor, and shooting galleries, open from May to September.

At 6.7 *m.* is the western end of Massachusetts Avenue Extended, indicating another of the several routes by which the upper canal and Great Falls may be reached.

CABIN JOHN BRIDGE, 7.3 *m.*, of sandstone and granite, is one of the longest masonry arches in the world. The single arch with a span of 220 feet rises 57¼ feet above Cabin John Creek. The roadway is too narrow for comfortable passing by motor cars, but it was sufficiently wide for the carriages of the 1850's and 1860's, when it was built. Steel doors, long since locked, in each of the abutments, gave access to the hollow interior, with its spandrel arches above the main arch.

Captain Thomas Meigs of the U. S. Army designed the bridge, and work was begun in 1857, while Jefferson Davis, later president of the Confederacy, was Secretary of War. A dam was built across the creek, with a lock to enable barges to deliver building material. There was a shortage of funds, contractors were slow in making deliveries, and the span was first used late in 1863. During construction a controversy arose over the proper credit on the inscription, and there was a ludicrous cutting and recutting of names. One was finally engraved, naming Meigs as engineer and Davis as Secretary of War. During the Civil War, Davis' name was chiseled off. Forty-six years later, in 1908, President Theodore Roosevelt ordered it restored.

Court records show that, as far back as 1750, Cabin John Creek was known as Captain John's Branch, for a mysterious hermit who lived in a log cabin near the stream. In one legend he is an Indian; in another he is a pirate with hoards of stolen riches. So seriously was the latter story taken that until about 1930 purchasers of land in the neighborhood were required to sign an agreement to surrender half of any buried treasure found on the property.

The Cabin John trolley line has its terminus at the eastern end of the Cabin John Bridge. A trail down Cabin John Creek leads to the canal, about midway in the four-mile stretch between Lock 7 and Lock 8. Up the canal, the stretch from Lock 8 to Lock 14 is known as Seven Locks Road, all being built within a distance of 1.3 miles.

CABIN JOHN, 7.9 *m.*, a residential village scattered along both sides of the broad highway, has a post office, a fire house, a school, a church or two, a store or two, and residences set back in tree- and flower-planted lawns.

BRIDGE NO. 3, 8 *m.*, a sandstone arch recalling the masonry of Cabin John Bridge, spans a hollow to the right of the present highway. Carrying an abandoned curve of the road, it bids fair to be preserved as an example of fine mid-century masonry.

CARDEROCK, 8.8 *m.*, a section of broad meadows on the canal side, lies a little above the upper end of Seven Locks Road. The tow-path can be reached from this area.

In the MUSEUM of the David W. Taylor Model Basin, near Carderock, are six panels of "plastic mosaic," portraying ships that typify progress in propulsion and hull design of American vessels: Donald McKay's 2,421-ton *Sovereign of the Seas,* one of five or six swiftest clipper ships in history, built in 1852, made a record 82-day Honolulu-

New York run in 1853, carrying 8,000 barrels of whale oil. The *Sovereign* soon made another record trip, New York dock to Liverpool dock, in 13 days 23 hours. The fast steam cruiser *Wampanoag,* displacing 4,215.5 tons, built by the U. S. Navy in 1868, was the first to incorporate structural principles similar to those of the modern destroyer. Her first trial run, under adverse weather conditions, showed an average speed of 16.75 knots over 630 nautical miles. The 20,000-ton battleship *Delaware,* equipped with the "bulb bow" below water line (since copied by naval and merchant ships generally), was completed in 1910, after tests in the original model basin at Washington Navy Yard. The 10,826-ton heavy cruiser *Salt Lake City,* 32.6 knots, incorporating lessons learned in World War I, with a highly developed "bulb bow," slid down the ways in 1929. The 1,979-ton Coast Guard cutter *Itasca,* completed in 1930, with "typical body lines for weatherliness and speed," was designed by Coast Guard engineers for general work on the open sea. The torpedo boat destroyer *Worden,* displacing 1,726 tons and having a speed of 36.5 knots, was built after several years of post-World War experimentation in ship models.

The OLD ANGLER'S INN, 12.1 *m.,* under the trees at a turn in the road, is about a half mile from WIDEWATER, a broad stretch of the C. and O. Canal where early engineers made use of an inactive river channel and blocked it from the river by towpath embankments. Widewater has the appearance of a little mountain lake, with rugged areas of rock rising from the water's edge. A foot bridge crossing the canal near the old inn leads to Widewater.

At 13.3 *m.* is the intersection (right) with Potomac Road, indicating still another approach to Great Falls, via River Road and Potomac Road from Georgetown.

A left turn at this intersection leads through a wooded area to GREAT FALLS TAVERN, 14.6 *m.* This rambling stuccoed brick structure of Colonial design, with low porches and green shutters, was built between 1828 and 1831 and restored in 1942. For many years the steam packet *Louise* carried excursionists from Washington to the hotel. Potomac floods have twice entered the building—in 1889, the year of the Johnstown flood, and in 1936, when there was 18 inches of water on the first floor. Behind the tavern stands a pioneer log cabin, which, however, is not as old as the hostelry. Cabin and tavern stand beside reconditioned LOCK 20; water in the canal at this point flows about 170 cubic feet a second.

A pedestrian CABLE BRIDGE (*toll 10¢*) spans a Potomac channel to Falls Island. The plank bridge, supported by cables moored in bedrock, runs in roller-coaster dips across a series of triangular piles built of log cribbing and filled with stones. During the flood of 1889 the water level rose 16 feet above the crest of Great Falls Dam, which is a short distance above the cable bridge.

A sanded path runs between the metamorphic boulders of Falls Island, which is dotted with wildflowers, and a five-minute walk leads to the top of the cliff overlooking GREAT FALLS. The 50-foot waterfall, dashing down between dark gray rocks, over and around great boulders in an intricate system of channels, cataracts, rapids, and white-water stretches, accounts for one-third of the 150 feet of drop in the Potomac River between here and tidewater. It is the most conspicuous part of the "fall line," a stretch about 10 miles wide, where waters of the Piedmont Plateau tumble down to the Coastal Plain. Washington, Philadelphia, Richmond, and Savannah are among the important cities that have been built on the "fall line," at the head of navigation on coastal rivers.

The Potomac River, draining an area of 11,460 square miles—larger than Rhode Island, Delaware, and Massachusetts—discharges over Great Falls an average of 11,900 cubic feet of water a second, representing a force equal to 232,050 horsepower. The amount of water tumbling over the dam varies enormously. A water-supply study made by the Federal Government from 1896 to 1919 shows that the volume varied from 653 cubic feet per second to 248,000 cubic feet per second—considerably greater than Niagara's average flow of 205,-000 second-feet. These figures did not include the high levels of 1889 and 1936. In the latter year, according to eye-witnesses, the water rushed down in such a torrent that the falls were obliterated and the river was one broad level of racing muddy water. The Virginia Geological Survey, making a study of hydroelectric possibilities in 1920, estimated that by harnessing the falls an even flow of 6,000 cubic feet a second could be maintained by a system of upriver reservoir dams, and as much energy could be produced in a year as by burning 356,000 tons of coal. Fortunately for the scenic beauty of the spot, the power program was never put into operation. The wild beauty of the scene varies with the water volume. There are more possibilities of flood in February and March than at other seasons, though they have been known to occur in August and October.

Scrambles up and down the rocks at Great Falls, to view the falls from below, are popular diversions in this area, which is a well-patronized picnicking ground. Towpath hikes from Great Falls Tavern include an 8.5-mile hike upstream along the remainder of the reconditioned canal to Seneca, Maryland, or a 6.7-mile hike downstream to the Cabin John trolley terminal. For a short water-trip on the canal, boats and canoes may be rented at Great Falls Tavern for the 2.3-mile trip upstream to Lock 21.

THE VIRGINIA APPROACH

A tour to Great Falls on the Virginia side of the Potomac may logically begin at the same place—KEY BRIDGE in Georgetown, 0 m.—and follow Canal Road to CHAIN BRIDGE, 3.3 m., which was rebuilt in 1937 and 1938 following damage to the old bridge in the floods of 1936 and 1937. The first bridge built at this point, in 1797, was destroyed in 1804. Another and still another was built; the latter, supported by chains, has given its name to subsequent bridges at this

HORSE-DRAWN BARGE, ON A SUMMER SUNDAY TRIP ALONG
THE C. & O. CANAL, ENTERING LOCK 5 ABOVE CHAIN BRIDGE

BICYCLE BUILT FOR TWO — A RIDE AROUND THE TIDAL BASIN

HUNT RACE AT NEAR-BY MIDDLEBURG, VA.

HORSEBACK RIDING IN ROCK CREEK PARK

©H. H. Rideout

GREAT FALLS FROM THE VIRGINIA SIDE OF THE POTOMAC

PICNICKING IN ROCK CREEK PARK

CANOEISTS' CAMPFIRE ON THE UPPER POTOMAC

National Park Service

PRESIDENT'S CUP REGATTA

SWIMMING AT TAKOMA PARK POOL,
ONE OF MANY IN WASHINGTON

Washington Post

WPA: Wilson
HANDLINE FISHING ALONG THE SEAWALL BELOW GEORGETOWN

Donald C. Kline

AFRICAN ELEPHANT AT THE ZOO

HYBRID BEAR, HALF POLAR, HALF KODIAK, ONE OF A UNIQUE LITTER AT NATIONAL ZOOLOGICAL PARK
Washington Star

point. A fourth span was erected in 1811 and operated as a toll bridge for 22 years. The predecessor of the present structure was put up in 1874.

LITTLE FALLS, a series of rapids above Chain Bridge, was one of the obstructions to navigation around which engineers of the old "Patowmack" Canal Company built a skirting dam, on the Maryland side of the river. The section of canal was later incorporated in the Chesapeake and Ohio system, for which President John Quincy Adams turned the first spadeful of earth on July 4, 1828, somewhere near Chain Bridge. Little Falls is at the head of navigation on the Potomac, and represents the lower portion of the "fall line" in this vicinity. The Chain Bridge area is a popular fishing spot, with bait for sale and poles for rent at both ends of the bridge. It is within the District, and no license is required for fishing in these waters. Crowds of anglers assemble on the rocks below the bridge at the time of the shad run each spring, which comes so near the blossoming of the redbuds each year that many in this vicinity call these trees "shadbush."

PALISADES PARK, an undeveloped wooded lowland between the canal and the river, extends for about 7 city blocks down-stream from Chain Bridge and for three blocks above it, to the District Line.

At 3.4 m. is a right turn on the Leesburg Road toward Great Falls.

NOTRE NID (*private*), a residence on the bluff above Chain Bridge, is on the site of the former High View Hotel. President Franklin D. Roosevelt, viewing the 1936 flood from this point, said that in former years he had come here on "bacon bats," picnics with broiled bacon. Near here, in 1826, after John Randolph of Roanoke called Henry Clay a "blackleg" in a speech, the two men fought a duel. Randolph's coat was pierced by a bullet, but the duel was bloodless.

LANGLEY, 6.2 m., is a rural community with numerous fine old Virginia mansions set back from the road. A local custom is that of building miniature houses over rural mail boxes; one is a convincing miniature of a Colonial house, another is a Christopher Wren church.

Left on State Highway 9 at Langley, 0.6 m., to RIDGELAWN (*private*), a stone house formerly owned by Percy Crosby, cartoonist creator of "Skippy." At 0.9 m. on State Highway 9 is the entrance (left) to SALONA (*private*), a 208-acre estate upon which is a red-brick mansion built in 1801 for the Reverend William Maffitt. The Smoot House, as it is known in Langley, provided temporary shelter for President and Mrs. Madison after the burning of the White House in 1814. Dolly Madison, carrying the Declaration of Independence and the Gilbert Stuart portrait of George Washington among the possessions she had hurriedly salvaged, arrived here by carriage over Chain Bridge. Joined later by her husband and members of the Cabinet, they stood on the lawn to watch the fires that ruined several public buildings in Washington.

Leesburg Road continues in roller-coaster fashion through woodland and farmland. At 10.7 m. (right) is the entrance to MISS MADEIRA'S SCHOOL, enclosed in a white plank fence. The 11 Georgian Colonial buildings of this exclusive school for girls are set back from the road on the bluff overlooking the Potomac.

At 11.8 *m.* (left) is a wire-enclosed Virginia prison camp, from which men go out to work on the maintenance of secondary roads.

At 12 *m.* is a right-angled turn with a sign indicating Great Falls Park. The graveled woodland road goes past a rock quarry at 12.6 *m.* and at 13.4 *m.* enters GREAT FALLS PARK (*25¢ parking fee, adm. 10¢ for hikers*). From the tree-grown, boulder-dotted grounds of the park, Great Falls reveals itself in full-face view as a turbulent cataract that divides the river into two principal channels, one of which later divides into three other channels. There are lacy waterfalls complete in themselves, foaming flumes, rapids, black upthrust boulders, and nearly every variant of the waterfall, including the swirling gorge below the rocky bluff.

Dining pavilion, dancing floor, carrousel, and over-the-counter lunchroom are included in the equipment of the park. The skirting canal of the "Patowmack" Canal Company can be traced for its entire length, about seven-tenths of a mile, through the grounds of the park. The foundations of one of George Washington's mills can be seen on the grounds, and water still runs in the upstream portion of the canal, finding an outlet through the old millrace. At the lower end of the park, reached by a woodland trail along the canal, four of the five locks of the old canal can still be seen. One of them, carved from solid rock, represented a new engineering development at the time. Here also, beside the locks, is the site of the ghost town of Matildaville, conceived by Washington as a potentially important milling and foundry center. It is marked only by the ruins of the jail, supposed to have been erected about 1820. Through the Potomac canal, now a grass-grown ditch, it is estimated that $10,000,000 worth of merchandise passed during the 26 years of its existence (1802-28). Matildaville, never more than a project, collapsed with the Potomac Company.

A three-story wooden lookout stands on the edge of the bluff, with a coin-slot telescope on its first floor, for observation of the falls, which can be seen in all their intricate detail from this shore. The Maryland State Line runs along water level at the base of the Virginia cliffs.

Trees on the grounds are marked to show the high-water level in the flood of 1936—signs nearly 8 feet above ground, giving some indication of the terrific inundation on that date.

Great Falls Park is a cool and shaded spot, with well-kept lawns under the trees, and its picnic tables and amusement areas are well patronized in summer.

PART IV
Appendices

The Negro in Washington

★

EDITOR'S NOTE:
This chapter is reprinted in its entirety from the original Federal
Writers' Project Guide to Washington, D.C., published in 1937. In the
1942 edition, this material was substantially cut, and much of what was
most interesting about it was lost. We include it here to show the full
breadth of the original.

THE NEGRO
IN WASHINGTON

THE history of Washington so far sketched has been a chronicle of events from the city's distant beginnings to its indelible present, concerning itself mainly with the white population. But the story would remain incomplete without a discussion of the Negro in Washington who, from the start, exerted a profound influence upon the city's destiny. Aside from the fact that at the present day the Negro population constitutes more than one-fourth of the city's total, the Negro's subtler influences are by far greater than might be apparent on the surface.

Chronologically this subject lends itself to treatment in three distinct periods.

I. FROM THE BEGINNINGS TO THE CIVIL WAR

Benjamin Banneker, a Negro mathematician, was appointed by George Washington to serve on Major L'Enfant's commission for the surveying and laying out of the city. Though this might be considered symbolic of the Negro's later participation in Washington life, the lot of Banneker's fellows, even in our times, has hardly been so auspicious. Viewing Washington in its early years Thomas Moore found

> Even here beside the proud Potowmac's streams . . .
> The medley mass of pride and misery
> Of whips and charters, manacles and rights
> Of slaving blacks and democratic whites . . .

Though spoken by a pro-British son of Erin, his indictment is substantiated by other sources.

It was not alone the shabby contrast between the profession of democracy and the practice of slavery that struck the observer, nor was it chiefly the brutality of the working and living conditions of slaves in the District of Columbia. Although conditions hardly deserved to be called ideal, still the cook, coachman, and artisan, in Alexandria, Georgetown, or Washington, or the truck-farmer in the rural areas surrounding these towns was generally better off than the field hand in the deep South and Southwest. What brought ill-fame to the District was the extensive slave trading conducted here. Because of its location, the District served as a natural outlet for both the coastwise slave ships and the overland coffles and was rightly called the very seat and center of the domestic slave traffic.

The District of Columbia, too small for slave rearing itself, served as depot for the purchases of interstate traders, who combed Maryland and northern Virginia for slaves. Since the slave jails, colloquially known as "Georgia pens", and described by an ex-slave as worse than hog holes, were inadequate for the great demand, the public jails were made use of, accommodations for criminals having to wait upon the more pressing and lucrative traffic in slaves. There were pens in what is now Potomac Park; and one in the Decatur House, fronting on what is now Lafayette Square. More notorious were McCandless' Tavern in Georgetown; in Washington, Robey's Tavern at Seventh and Maryland Avenue, and Williams' "Yellow House" at Eighth and B Streets SW. In Alexandria, the pretentious establishment of Armfield and Franklin, who by 1834 were sending more than a thousand slaves a year to the Southwest, was succeeded and surpassed by the shambles of the much-feared Kephart.

In 1819, when Miller's Tavern at Thirteenth and F Streets NW. was on fire, a bystander, William Gardiner, refused to join the customary bucket brigade and loudly denounced the place as a slave prison. The resulting controversy conducted in newspaper columns revealed the tragic past of the tavern. A Negro woman, about to be sold South apart from her husband, had leapt in frenzy from an attic window, breaking both arms and injuring her back, but surviving. This focused attention upon the local slave trade. Humanitarian Jesse Torrey came to Washington shortly after the attempted suicide, visited the injured woman, and discovered two kidnaped Negroes in the attic. He began suit in the circuit court for their freedom, the expenses being defrayed by a group of persons headed by Francis Scott Key, who gave his legal services gratis. It is highly probable that the stir attendant upon this celebrated case urged the slave owner John Randolph to that bitter invective in which he said:

You call this the land of liberty, and every day that passes things are done in it at which the despotisms of Europe would be horror-struck and disgusted.

. . . In no part of the earth—not even excepting the rivers on the Coast of Africa, was there so great, so infamous a slave market, as in the metropolis, in the seat of government of this nation which prides itself on freedom.

A chorus of voices rose in harmony with Randolph's. The sight recorded by Torrey, and engraved as the frontispiece of his *Portraiture of Domestic Slavery*, of a coffle of manacled slaves, like a butcher's drove of hobbled cattle, passing along the east front of the ruined Capitol, became a familiar figure in the many orations attacking the traffic. The struggle for abolition in the District recruited such men as Benjamin Lundy, Salmon P. Chase, Charles Miner, Charles Sumner, William Lloyd Garrison, Henry Wilson, William H. Seward, and Abraham Lincoln when serving as Congressman. John Quincy Adams' famous fight for free speech and against the "gag rule" in Congress was prompted by the refusal of the two Houses to hear petitions for the abolition of slavery in the District of Columbia. But the forces commanded by men like Calhoun were too great, and while solicitude was expressed by Northerners and Southerners, Congress, which had the power to abolish, refused to act. The District, wedged in between two slave States, was kept slave territory, and the slave trade prospered until the Compromise of 1850. The black code of the District was even more severe than the codes of Maryland and Virginia of which it was the reenactment, and the "stealing" of free Negroes was shamefully widespread. William Wells Brown, in *Clotel*, the first novel by a Negro, has one of his heroines jump into the Potomac to escape slave catchers.

The Negroes of Washington, both free and slave, at times took matters into their own hands against these flagrant abuses. The Underground Railroad had important stopping places in Washington; ex-slaves today remember churches whose basements served as layovers, and out-of-the-way Georgetown homes that were specially marked for the fugitives. One of the famous trails started at a cemetery skirting the stage road leading north from the city. It is probable that Harriet Tubman, "the Moses of her people", the greatest underground agent, worked around Washington as well as on the Eastern Shore. Legend has it that she was discovered by her friends asleep in a local park beneath a sign advertising a reward for her capture, which meant nothing to her, as she could not read.

In 1848, 77 Negroes under slave and free Negro leadership, took advantage of the relaxed patrolling of Washington while it was celebrating the liberty of the new French Republic, and escaped on board Captain Drayton's *Pearl*. But at Cornfield Harbor, 140 miles from Washington, contrary winds forced the schooner into shelter and an armed steamer captured the runaways and the crew. The manner of flight had been betrayed by a Negro hackman. Captain Drayton was mobbed (an Irishman cutting off a piece of his ear), sentenced to a fine of $10,000, and imprisoned until Sumner prevailed upon President Fillmore to intercede. For captured Negroes there was only occasional intercession. Emily and Mary Edmondson, long coveted by the trader Bruin, were sold South, but later were redeemed through Henry Ward Beecher and other sympathizers. Another Emily, who had hoped to reach her mother in New York, met with a different fate. Said to be the "finest looking woman in this county", and destined as a "fancy article" for New Orleans, she died from exposure on the overland trek. Her mother, who had bought herself free by labors over the washtub, thanked God.

In 1830 there were 6,152 free Negroes in the District of Columbia compared with 6,119 slaves; in 1840, 8,361 compared with 4,694 slaves; and in 1860, 11,131 compared with only 3,185 slaves. Thus, in 30 years, the free colored population was nearly doubled, while the slave population was halved. It would be inaccurate to infer from this that there was any wholesale manumission or that the District was a haven for free Negroes. The free Negroes were of several classes: Those whose antecedents had never been slaves, such as descendants of indentured servants; those born of free parents, or of free mothers; those manumitted; those who had bought their own freedom, or whose kinsmen had bought it for them; and those who were successful runaways. These free Negroes were an ever present "bad example" to the slaves of the District and of the surrounding slave States, and the more they prospered, the "worse example" they became.

Especially stringent regulations affecting free Negroes were added by the District Common Council to the slave codes. Every free Negro was required: (1) to give the mayor "satisfactory evidence of freedom", plus $50 for himself, and $50 for each member of his family; (2) to post a bond for $1,000 and to secure five white guarantors of good behavior. It was necessary to show manumission papers in order to remain free; even so, gangs bent on kidnaping could and frequently did seize and destroy them. No Negro, slave or free, could testify against whites. The jails were crowded with captured free Negroes and suspected runaways; there were 290 of these in the city jail at one time. Many were sold for prison fees, ostensibly for a fixed period, but really for life. Meetings for any other than fraternal and religious purposes were forbidden. After

Nat Turner's insurrection in Virginia in 1831, colored preachers were banned. Curfew rang at 10 o'clock for all Negroes, free or slave.

In spite of all this the class of free Negroes increased and, in the main, advanced. Though forbidden by law to do so many succeeded, through the connivance of friendly whites, in opening and running such businesses as hotels, taverns, saloons, and restaurants. In the District, as in so many southern cities, they had a monopoly of barbering and free colored boys were porters and bootblacks. Waiters were numerous and, in the gay hospitality of a southern city, were comparatively well paid. There were many skilled carpenters, bricklayers, shoemakers, stonemasons, wheelwrights, blacksmiths, plasterers, printers, cabinetmakers, cab drivers, and draymen. For free colored women the opportunities were limited to dressmaking, laundry work, nursing, and general housework.

With chances for a livelihood scanty, many Negroes were driven to petty larceny. The newspapers, as is their custom, interpreted this frequently as grand larceny. The Old Center Market was the resort of plundering marauders. Many Negroes ignored or violated the laws, particularly the curfew. Race riots developed in spite of the fact that the penalty for striking a white man was the cropping of the ears (exacted in the District until 1862). Mulattoes sometimes set up invidious self-defeating distinctions against their darker brothers. Frequently the blacks retaliated. There were unfortunate examples of Negroes serving as informers, as catchers of runaways, as hat-in-hand seekers of personal favors, and ex-slaves still speak with hatred of one Stonestreet, a Negro slave-kidnaper. But more often there was co-operation, the Resolute Beneficial Society being founded for concerted action toward the betterment of conditions. Occasionally free Negroes owned slaves. However, they were usually wealthier Negroes buying kinsfolk for liberation.

The free Negro was avid for education. In 1807, shortly after the first two white schoolhouses had been built, three recently freed Negroes who could not read or write hired a white teacher and set up the first school for Negroes. More successful were the ventures of such pioneers as Louisa Parke Costin, Mary Wormley, Arabella Jones, Father Vanlomen, and Maria Becraft. John F. Cook, a shoemaker, set up a school in 1834, 8 years after his aunt, Alethia Tanner, had purchased his freedom. The Snow Riot gave a set of hoodlums the excuse for attacking his school. Cook fled to Pennsylvania, but returned a year later, doggedly intent upon his mission. Myrtilla

Miner, a white woman from New York, driven from place to place in the city in her attempt to establish a Negro school, finally purchased the entire square between what are now Nineteenth and Twentieth and M and O Streets. Harriet Beecher Stowe's donation of $1,000 helped her greatly in this purchase, and Johns Hopkins was one of the trustees. Her students were insulted and attacked by white men along the streets. The buildings were stoned and set afire. But Miss Miner stood her ground. Using some of their leisure time, she and Emily Edmondson (of the famous case of the *Pearl*) warned hoodlums of their mettle by firing pistols at a target in the yard.

The education of Negroes was frowned upon by the majority of whites in the District, especially after Nat Turner's famous uprising. Negroes paid taxes for the support of white schools, but received no consideration themselves. Private Negro schools continued to spring up and no school closed its doors for lack of "scholars." In 1860 there were more than 1,200 free colored children in school.

Church was the solace of the free Negroes. Negro Methodism in the District started in 1820 when a group of free Negroes withdrew from Ebenezer Church and formed a separate congregation. After 1831 when obvious discrimination started in most of the white churches, other Negro groups withdrew from congregations. At St. Johns Church an outside stairway leading to the gallery was called the "niggers' backstairs to heaven." But the Negro members decided that there must be other ways to get there and left the church. In 1833 the First Baptist Church, moving from Nineteenth and I Streets NW. to a new edifice which later became Ford's Theater, instituted segregation. Negro members stayed in the old home. One feature of the churches was the popularity of Sabbath schools among adults as well as among children because they furnished instruction in the three R's. Taking advantage of every chance, the free Negro frequently left Jonah waiting and the Walls of Jericho standing while he fathomed the mysteries of the alphabet.

The houses in which free Negroes lived ran the gamut from hovels to commodious homes. The first were remote from slave quarters, and crouched behind the imposing dwellings of employers, or were grouped in hidden alleyways. The homes of the well-to-do, scattered here and there, were purchased before the law forbidding free Negroes to own property was passed, or later in defiance of it. There were some separate communities, especially in Southwest Washington, "on the island" (so-called because the Tiber and the old canal cut it off from the city). Many free Negroes were poverty stricken, and gave point to the proslavery argument of the wretched freed-man, but with the odds against them, it is surprising that this im-poverished class was not larger. Many, comparatively wealthy, owned property in such a valuable section as Fifteenth and New York Avenue; many had homes on Sixteenth Street; and a feed dealer, Alfred Lee, purchased the mansion on H Street which had been the British Embassy. In 1865, when scoffers charged that Negroes did not own $40,000 worth of property in the whole city, it was proved that in one square their holdings aggregated $45,592. At the time of the Emancipation Act, Negroes in the District of Columbia were paying taxes on $650,000 worth of real estate.

II. FROM THE CIVIL WAR TO THE TURN OF THE CENTURY

In 1862, the year in which slavery was abolished in the District, President Lincoln authorized the enlisting of Negroes as part of the Army. Two regiments were soon mustered in from the District and vicinity, the First organized at Washington in May 1863, and the Second at Arlington a month later. These regiments served with honor at Fair Oaks, Petersburg, Fort Taylor, and in other battles. It is estimated that the District supplied over 3,000 colored troops of the 200,000 in the Union Army. Negro contrabands, male and fe-male, had earlier crowded to the camps, eager to serve as teamsters and road builders, laundresses, and cooks for "Marse Lincum's boys."

As early as 1862 more than 13,000 refugees had collected in Wash-ington, Alexandria, Hampton, and Norfolk. The Emancipation Proclamation in 1863 was an added stimulus to Negroes to flee to the Union lines. Washington, strategically located for slave trading, now became the favorite place toward which contrabands headed. The mustering out of Negro regiments in Washington at the close of the war further increased their number in the District. Washington became a Mecca for Negroes in the next two decades, and in 1880 there were 59,696 in the city and its immediate environs. The pro-portion to the city's population (about one-third) remained fairly constant.

The picture therefore is greatly changed from what it had been in 1867, when one-fifth of all owners of real estate had been Negroes. In the main the refugees were illiterate and penniless. At their best, these people were intelligent and eager to help themselves; at their worst they showed, in the words of a Federal chaplain, "cringing deceit, theft, licentiousness, all the vices which slavery inevitably fosters." They constituted a grave problem for the District. One

497

proposed way out was colonization. President Lincoln favored this, and Congress appropriated funds for transportation to Liberia or Haiti. Several hundred former slaves were shipped to the Island of Vache, Haiti. But when their plight became desperate, a war-ship was sent after them. They were settled in Arlington in a place known as "Freedmen's Village", very near a tract left by George Washington Parke Custis to his colored daughter, Maria Syphax. Appeals were made to encourage Negroes to migrate en masse to sections farther north, or to return to the plantations in the South. But the majority chose to remain in Washington.

The first contrabands during the war were housed in the old "Brick Capitol", on the site of the present Supreme Court Build-ing. They were then moved to what was Duff Green's Row, east of the Capitol. As the flood swept in, McClellan's Barracks housed them, and then numerous barracks were built in Washington and Alexandria. Two hundred tenements were fitted up at Campbell Hospital. Many Negroes settled in the neighborhoods of the old forts. The Fort Reno settlement in Tenleytown is one of the last of these to succumb to fine suburban developments. In the main, how-ever, philanthropic efforts did not prove equal to the housing short-age. Real-estate agents floated a project that resulted in Washing-ton's notorious "alley system." The deep back yards, and even the front yards provided by L'Enfant's plan, were found to promise more alluring rewards than lovely gardens. Lots were divided and the rear portions sold separately. The first of the ill-fated alleys, as the present day Washington knows them, were laid out in 1867. In 1897 there were 333 alleys, inhabited by approximately 19,000 people, more than three-fourths of them Negroes. Shacks costing as little as $10 proved highly profitable investments. Here, in these disease-infested sties, ex-slaves got their first taste of freedom. And it is here that, in too large numbers, their children's children still drag out their lives.

Negro communities had such suggestive names as Goose Level, Vinegar Hill, Froggy or Foggy Bottom, Hell's Bottom, Swampoodle, and Bloodfield. Cowtown, so-called because, outside of the city proper, cows and hogs and chickens ranged at will on sidewalks and streets, was the present Barry Place. Of a somewhat higher level were the communities across the Anacostia: The Flats, Hills-dale, Barry Farms (an earlier settlement of race-conscious slaves), Stantonstown, Garfield; those in the northeast at Benning, and Burrville; and Brightwood, in the vicinity of Fort Stevens and Fort Slocum. Georgetown had its goodly share of oldest inhabitants, who sat aloof, gazing with well-bred disdain at the ignorant trespassers. Other prosperous Negroes were scattered in almost all of the quiet residential sections.

For new arrivals, accustomed chiefly to manual labor in the fields, there was little employment to be found in a city predominantly governmental and residential. Pauperism forced many to eke out a living by pickings on the dumps. Many took to pilfering. It is hardly a matter of wonder that the rate of crime was high. The paths of many Negroes led straight from the alley to the workhouse. Crimes of violence were numerous. In 1891 the superintendent of police attributed much of the crime to the neglected state of the Negro child. Illegitimacy was frequent. Health conditions were wretched. The death rate in 1891 for Negroes was nearly double that for whites, and both were far too high. The death rate was largely increased by infant mortality. In spite of all this, Negroes were unwilling to go to the poorhouse. Perhaps they saw no reason merely to change addresses.

And yet the grimness of the picture is not without some relief. The Freedmen's Bureau, missionary organizations, and Negroes themselves with their lodges, churches, and schools, waged a determined though hard-pressed battle against prejudice, poverty, and ignorance. The Freedmen's Bureau was created by act of Congress in 1865, for "relief work, education, regulation of labor, and administration of justice", among the freedmen. Major General Oliver Otis Howard, who had lost an arm at Fair Oaks but had returned to serve under Sherman and as commander of the Army of Tennessee, was named commissioner. Unable to cope successfully, for all its gallant efforts, with the problems of destitution and housing, the Freedmen's Bureau exerted its greatest influence in the establishing of Freedmen's Hospital, Howard University, and a number of schools for Negroes that eventually became a part of the city school system. Some of the officials of the Bureau were connected with the Freedmen's Savings and Trust Company which, contrary to the opinions of some, was never controlled by Negroes. This company did not withstand the contagion of the Gilded Age. With its central bank in Washington and 34 branches in the South, it "received in the aggregate deposits amounting to $57,000,000 from more than 70,000 depositors, chiefly Negroes." It taught valuable lessons in thrift, but when, following the panic of 1873, the imprudence of its investments and the dishonesty of certain directors forced it to close its doors, it taught the freedmen an embittering lesson.

499

Although an act of Congress ruled that Washington and Georgetown should allocate to the trustees of colored schools a proportionate part of all moneys received, the corporation of Washington refused to do this as late as November 1867. After this Negro schools fared well. The northern missionary associations which had conducted schools in temporary barracks and basements of churches joined forces. A high school was organized in 1870. One of its frequent removals found it in Myrtilla Miner's famous building. Then in 1891, M Street High School was erected. Night schools, privately maintained for day-time workers, became part of the public-school system in 1886. George F. T. Cook, son of the militant educator John F. Cook, was appointed superintendent of schools in 1868. A heated contest was waged in 1871 under the leadership of William H. A. Wormley and William Syphax to remove all restrictions of color from the public schools, but those opposing segregation were defeated by whites and some Negroes who feared that mixed schools would return the issue to local politics, and mean the death of the progressing schools.

The old Negro preacher in Georgetown who said of the freed Negro: "Fifteen years after he came out of slavery, what did he do? Sat down by the River of Babylon and sang, 'Peace at home and pleasure abroad', and went to sleep down by the weeping willows for 25 years", was overstating the case. There was definite, if gradual economic advance. Many made their living as domestics, barbers, cobblers, grocers, dry-goods merchants, artisans, contractors, real-estate operators, hucksters, market vendors, saloonkeepers, and hotel-keepers. Others inherited property, made prudent investments, and became prosperous. Colored firemen were appointed on a full-time basis in 1870; colored policemen have been on the force since the Metropolitan Police was organized in the sixties. A colored policeman arrested General Grant for speeding; whether the culprit had set his people free or not, the law was the law.

At Fifteenth and H Streets stood one of Washington's most exclusive hotels, catering to family patronage and the congressional and diplomatic sets. This was owned and managed by a Negro, Wm. Wormley, close friend of Charles Sumner. Many Negroes found employment in the Government service, most of them as laborers, messengers, a few as clerks. Certain political plums fell to Negroes such as the positions of the fourth Auditor, the Register of the Treasury, and the Recorder of Deeds. There was an increasing professional class of doctors, lawyers, preachers, and teachers. Professors were ubiquitous, professors of music, of the dance, of the cakewalk, of algebra, and of penmanship. The title is not so comic when one recalls how rarely a Negro is granted the title "Mister."

Though politically well informed and articulate, the Negro of Washington in this period exerted little force. His newly acquired suffrage was swept away by the disfranchisement of the District in 1874, an act which was definitely influenced by the fact that Negroes comprised one-fourth of the population. Political figures among them, however, were numerous. There were over a score of Congressmen, many intelligent and able. Those whose imprint was most lasting upon Negro history were Robert Brown Elliott, John M. Langston, and John R. Lynch, who later corrected many of Rhodes' inaccuracies in reconstruction history. Representative Ransier caused a commotion during one session while John T. Harris of Virginia was declaiming: "And I say that there is not one gentleman upon this floor who can honestly say that he really believes that the colored man is created his equal." Ransier interrupted with a casual "I can." Later, Ransier, listening to a Negro-baiter who insisted that the Civil Rights Bill meant that Negroes would absorb the whites, stated with suavity that "If we are powerful, we know how to be merciful." Negro Senators were Hiram R. Revels and Blanche Kelso Bruce, both of Mississippi. P. B. S. Pinchback, after a picaresque career culminating in the lieutenant governorship of Louisiana, and Francis Cardoza, State treasurer of South Carolina, were prominent newcomers. Finally there was Frederick Douglass, justly famed fugitive and antislavery orator, later Marshal and Recorder of Deeds for the District, and Minister to Haiti, who spent his last years in the old Van Hook Mansion on Cedar Hill.

The Republican Party was favored in these years. Frederick Douglass' statement: "The Republican Party is the ship, all else the sea", was held axiomatic to such a degree, that when at the Second Baptist Lyceum (a free forum) a paper endorsing the Democrats followed one endorsing the Republicans, the audience hissed; newspapers called it "double play", and the chairman was accused of traitorous intentions against the entire Negro race. The most exciting political campaigns were contests for delegates to the Republican National Convention. The Blaine Invincible Republican Club and the W. Calvin Chase Republican Club were elaborately organized. The Cleveland administration, however, left not a few Negro Democrats in its wake.

For many years after the Civil War, Washington was said, with some justice, to have "the most distinguished and brilliant assemblage of Negroes in the world." The reputation was sustained by cultural societies such as the Second Baptist Lyceum, the Congressional Lyceum, and the Bethel Literary Society. The National Negro Academy had upon its rosters such scholars as W. E. B. DuBois, of Atlanta, the Grimke brothers, W. S. Scarborough, J. W. Cromwell, and Kelly Miller. At the close of the century Paul Laurence Dunbar, best-known Negro writer, lived here. From 1897 to 1898 he was assistant to another Negro, Daniel Murray, who held a high place in the Congressional Library. Dunbar wrote and gave readings of his poetry, reciting with gusto of the Negro peasant. Will Marion Cook, similarly distinguished in music, collaborator with Dunbar in such musical shows as *Clorindy* and *In Dahomey*, was for a number of years a resident of Washington. The two leading Negro newspapers of the period, W. Calvin Chase's Washington *Bee* ("Watch the Sting") and E. E. Cooper's *Colored American*, are not only valuable as indices to social life, but also refreshing because of the occasional highly personal combats between the editors.

Despite the destitution and the earnest fight to keep the grudged gains, there was still a gay social life for some Washington Negroes. Negro lodges were convivial as well as "mutually benevolent." Conventions of elders and bishops made Washington their Mecca. G. A. R. encampments in Washington gave excuses for lavish hospitality. The Emancipation Day ceremonies were for a long time popular turnouts, until rivalries terminated them. Two rival factions, urged by President Cleveland to reconcile their grievances, persisted in holding parades with brass bands and "queens of love and beauty" for each. The celebration did not survive this contretemps. Inaugural balls for Negroes, held on March 5 after the official ball, were likewise causes for dissension between groups claiming to represent Negro Washington. Other balls and banquets were numerous and prodigal in the dozens of hotels, buffet-cafes, and saloons. Churches and clubs had frequent excursions down the river to Marshall Hall, Notley Hall, and Chapel Point. There was a flamboyant sporting life; political dignitaries at times had to yield to a visitor like Peter Jackson, heavyweight champion of Australia, against whom John L. Sullivan drew the color line, or Isaac Murphy, noted Negro jockey of the eighties. Major Taylor, "the champion colored bicycle racer of the world", defended his title and, in spite of foul play, defeated all comers at the old Washington Coliseum.

Before the Civil War the elder Joseph Jefferson, lessee of the Washington Theater, had petitioned the city fathers to change the curfew law, as it affected "a great proportion of our audience of this [Negro] caste" and lessened his box-office receipts. This interest in drama persisted into the period under consideration. Musicals were very popular. A Negro opera company founded in 1872 gave several performances at Ford's Theater. Williams and Walker and Cole and Johnson, "in the brightest ebony offering, *A Trip to Coontown*", were viewed by Washington Negroes with only occasional disputes with the theater management over the sale of orchestra tickets. Sissieretta Jones, "Black Patti", sang in 1892 for President Harrison's White House reception; she returned in 1900 with her troubadours in *The Essence of Ole Virginny*. The biggest musical event in years was the first all-colored oratorio, *Emmanuel*, directed by Prof. J. Henry Lewis. He was versatile enough to train a chorus of 70 for "A Mammoth Cake Walk and Jubilee Entertainment in Convention Hall." The Fisk Jubilee Singers and other school choruses sang in Washington to raise funds for their institutions. Some musical organizations were the Dvorák Musical Association, the Amphion Glee Club, the Washington Permanent Chorus, and the Georgetown Musical Association.

III. THE TWENTIETH CENTURY

The first decade of the twentieth century was marked by a consolidation of some of the gains and a loss of others. Negro leaders, attracted by the period's visions of reform, turned more hopefully to the "race problem." In 1903 at Lincoln Temple Congregational Church there was a conference on "How to Solve the Race Problem." Suggested solutions were the setting up of a forty-ninth state, the conciliatory gradualism of Booker T. Washington, and the demanding of full citizenship rights. It was urged that a "Commission to Consider Every Phase of the American Race Problem" be appointed by Congress, and a "Permanent Commission on the American Race Problem" was set up. Many of the militant members of the conference, hardly to be satisfied with commissions and committees, later joined forces with liberal movements which in 1910 culminated in the National Association for the Advancement of Colored People.

With America's entry into the World War, advice came from Negro leadership to forget grievances and close ranks for the sake of democracy. In Washington this was enthusiastically heeded. The First Separate Battalion, the Negro National Guard unit, which had previously served on the Mexican border, was called upon to guard Washington. This battalion was the first in the District to be mustered to war strength. Its commanding officer, Maj. James Walker, was the first District officer to die in the line of duty. When

503

the Three Hundred and Seventy-second Regiment was formed, the First Separate Battalion was included. Overseas this regiment was brigaded with the "Red Hand" Division of the French Army. Of nearly 600 Washington Negroes in the outfit, more than 200 were wounded and 33 killed. One of the first to fall fatally wounded was Private Kenneth Lewis, a mere youngster, just out of the high-school cadet corps. He was awarded the *Medaille Militaire*. A score of Washingtonians received the *Croix de Guerre*, and the Three Hundred and Seventy-second Regiment had its colors decorated with the *Croix de Guerre* and palm for distinguished service.

In October 1917 Emmett J. Scott was appointed by Newton Baker as Special Assistant to the Secretary of War, in order to promote "a healthy morale among Negro soldiers and civilians." Attempts were made in his office to iron out cases of discrimination and injustice. A campaign was zealously initiated to obtain a separate training camp for Negro officers, since no Negro, regardless of qualifications, was permitted to enter the other camps. The spearhead of this movement was found in the newly established office and at Howard University. After much hesitation, authorization of a camp at Des Moines, Iowa, came on May 19, 1917. It is perhaps more than a coincidence that four days earlier, Henry Johnson and Needham Roberts, enlisted Negroes of the Fifteenth New York, had performed feats of valor for which they were later cited by General Pershing. From Des Moines 700 commissioned officers were sent out, the majority to serve in the Ninety-second Combat Division. Many were Washingtonians and of these several were cited for bravery, especially in the Argonne offensive. Over 5,000 Negroes from the District came into service through the operation of the selective draft law. World War veterans were organized in the James Reese Europe Post No. 5, and the James E. Walker Post No. 26 of the American Legion.

The hopes expressed "that the American people will be disposed more and more to remove such handicaps and to right such injustices as we now struggle against after the settlement of this great emergency which now faces our common country" turned barren in the post-war years. A bloody riot had taken place in East St. Louis during the war; on July 19, 1919, the Washington riot started. Inflammatory headlines announced a wave of assaults on white women by Negroes; several of these earlier publicized attacks were shown to be false, and later ones were definitely invented as whips for the mob. A number of white soldiers, sailors, and marines proceeded to southwest Washington and beat up several innocent Negroes.

Negroes retaliated and beat up several innocent whites. Street fighting was fierce, if sporadic. On July 21 a newspaper announced a "mobilization of every available service man stationed in or near Washington or on leave . . . the purpose is a clean-up." Negroes mobilized likewise, alley dwellers and most respectable burghers, side by side, and there was no clean-up. The bitter resistance of Negroes, the calling out of regular troops (officially this time), and a rainstorm helped the authorities to disperse the mobs. A year later, a Negro charged with murder confessed to the attacks for which two Negroes (positively identified by the women in the cases) were serving undeserved long-term sentences in penitentiaries.

The great forces opposed to the Negro, however, were not mobs that could be stopped at a brick barricade at Seventh and M Streets. These were, as they have always been, poverty, ignorance, disease, and crime. The extensive migration from the South, accelerated in the years of the war because of the cutting off of European immigration, the demand for industrial labor in the North and Midwest, and a growing resentment at conditions in the South, stranded many Negroes in Washington. Other cities were prepared for the mass invasion of industry, but Washington, even though it was growing

ALLEY DWELLERS IN WASHINGTON

505

by leaps and bounds, had little work for the newcomers to do. There was an aggravation of the post-Civil War problems of housing, health, and employment. At the collapse of the boom period, Negroes preferred the word "panic", depression being what they had experienced in the days of "prosperity."

Negroes of Washington total 27 percent of the population. At one time as many as 4 out of 10 were unemployed. Over 70 percent of the relief cases in 1935 were Negro, almost in inverse ratio to the racial distribution of the population. Many of these unemployed live in the 200 alleys which remain in the slum sections of Washington. An Alley Dwelling Elimination Act was enacted June 12, 1934, contemplating the riddance of inhabited alleys before July 1, 1944. Until then it is likely that these alley dwellings, for which exorbitant rents are charged, will continue to breed vice, crime, and disease.

Negroes who are able to make a living do so generally in domestic and personal service, and in manufacturing and mechanical pursuits (generally unskilled labor). A large number are in various departments under Civil Service; only a few of them, in spite of their capabilities, ranking as clerks or foremen. About 4,000 are listed in trade, and about 3,500 in the professions. The New Negro Alliance was founded in 1933 to demand equal working opportunity for Negroes in Negro areas. One of its slogans is "Don't Buy Where You Can't Work." But in spite of its picketing and boycotting, there has been no large gain in jobs. The struggling Negro business concerns cannot furnish much employment. Regardless of qualification, the Negro worker meets with definite discrimination. Many American Federation of Labor unions exclude him; even more than the white worker, he remains poorly led and unorganized. The Joint Committee on National Recovery, with headquarters in Washington, was active in focussing attention upon and fighting Nation-wide discrimination against, and exploitation of, Negroes.

Many of the slum streets are close seconds to the alleys in squalor, and a mushroom shanty-town at Marshall Heights on the outskirts of the city is much like the camp of the bonus-marchers, with "shelters" made out of pieces of tin, cast-off lumber and beaverboard. Prosperous Negroes live in all sections of the city and Negro expansion into areas of better homes has been bitterly, and at times unscrupulously, contested. "Covenants" to bar Negroes from certain sections were upheld by the Supreme Court in the Curtis case. But the "covenant", while a powerful weapon, frequently cuts both ways. During this century the fastnesses of Le Droit Park were penetrated and transformed to a Negro section. Newer additions to Deanwood and Burrville in the northeast are Kingman Park, Capitol View, and De Priest Village, pleasing, well designed communities for the Negro middle class. Langston Terrace was sponsored by the Public Works Administration to afford better housing for Negro families of low income. The bulk of the Negro population, however, is still in the northwest, where the Negro business area is located.

The health situation resulting from the crowded slums is a grave menace. Only one city in the United States has a higher death rate from tuberculosis than Washington; over half of the tubercular cases in 1935 were Negroes. Other forces playing havoc are infant mortality, social diseases, accidents in the home, and disintegrated home life. Negro patients are received in segregated wards at most of the hospitals, while some of the hospitals afford clinic service only. Freedmen's Hospital, founded by the Freedmen's Bureau and supported by the Department of the Interior, is the Negro general hospital. Its facilities are utilized by the Howard University Medical School. There are also private hospitals conducted by leading surgeons of the race. Although in comparison with the rest of the country Washington has a heavy concentration of medical practitioners, the number is still not large enough to cope with the health problem. Recognition of the socio-economic causes of the high mortality rate is becoming more apparent in recent surveys and their resultant recommendations.

Crime is correspondingly high; areas found to be dense in disease are classed in police reports as dense in crime. Some alleys are "no man's land" for any stranger, Negro or white. Knives flash and pistols bark to terminate crap games and domestic brawls. Rasped nerves and short ugly tempers are not soothed by the heavy drinking of liquor which is as likely to be "canned heat" as corn whisky. Efforts of the police to ferret out crime are not helped by the furtiveness of the alley dwellers, who consider "John Law" to be their natural enemy—with good reason, at times, in light of police brutality. The "numbers" game, an American form of gambling, is popular in the alleys as it is on the avenues. The money that dribbles away to the number "baron" and "runner" could well be used for bread, milk, and shoes, but these poor people look upon the number slip as a magic sesame to momentary affluence.

Agencies struggling to improve these conditions are few in number and lack money. The Twelfth Street Branch Y. M. C. A., erected in 1912 in Hell's Bottom, has its boys' clubs and summer camp, Camp Lichtman; fosters dramatics, athletics, and forums; and attempts

507

to aid employment. The Phyllis Wheatley Y. W. C. A., founded in 1905, aims at similar community service for women and girls, with Camp Clarissa Scott operating in the summer months. The Department of Playgrounds is coming to recognize the needs of this fourth of the city's population. Important playgrounds are the one at the historic Barry Farms, the Howard Playground, the Cardoza Playground, the Willow Tree Playground, Lincoln Playground, and the new Banneker Center. The 30 others are as crowded and active, and all are important. Community centers and settlement houses have programs of wide variety. In all of these, the paid Negro personnel is too small, and still underpaid.

Some other agencies in social welfare are the Washington Corps No. 2 of the Salvation Army and the fraternal organizations which launch occasional programs for civic betterment. Although the Police Boys' Clubs date back to 1933, plans for the inclusion of Negro boys in the surmised benefits are still in the making. The first lesson in civics for these boys seems to be their segregated status.

Athletics are, of course, popular. In the earlier years there was a strong governmental baseball league as well as many sand-lot teams. The present Washington Elite Giants, not indigenous like the old popular Le Droit Tigers, are successful in the National Negro League and therefore in good favor. Against such teams as the Pittsburgh Crawfords, the New York Black Yankees, the Homestead Grays, they put on colorful shows in the Griffith Stadium. Local basketball teams have become nationally known. Howard University and Miner Teachers College have heavy schedules in football and basketball against many of the best Negro collegiate teams, and the high schools are bitter athletic rivals. There are frequent track meets. Jesse Owens gave exhibitions at one of these. This was his only possible performance in Washington, as white colleges in the District do not allow Negroes to participate in their open meets. Tennis enthusiasts in Washington had a great deal to do with the founding of the American Tennis Association. Washington has had many Negro tennis champions, but with the paucity of the courts, public and private, tennis for a time declined. Negroes box in the District on "all-Negro cards." Negro golfers have only one inadequate golf course in the city. In spite of this, golf is increasing in popularity.

Baptists are the most numerous of the churchgoers in Washington; second to them are the Methodists, divided into several branches. There are churches of other denominations together with many independent store-front churches. The churches frequently have duplicated names, because of "splitting," or because of the shifting of population. Famous preachers of the early century were the Reverend George Lee, whose pulpit power was commensurate with his vast bulk, and the scholarly Reverend Walter Brooks and Reverend Francis Grimke. "Black Billy Sunday," the Reverend Alexander Willbanks, combined the resources of southern camp meetings with the tricks of his model. But even more spectacular have been the careers of Elder Solomon Lightfoot Michaux and Bishop "Daddy" Grace. The first of these, whose "Happy Am I" chorus and sermons are broadcast over Station WJSV, preaches to crowds in his Georgia Avenue tabernacle, with seats reserved for delegations of whites. Elder Michaux has experimented with communal ventures in lodging, and at present runs a One-Cent Cafe founded for him by Bernarr Macfadden. "Daddy" Grace, whose churches have swept from New Bedford to Augusta, Ga., has set up a House of Prayer at Sixth and M Streets NW. Store-front churches attract attention with crudely lettered signs, their unconscious humor checked by their patent sincerity. In one backward section a little church given over to noisy rousements and sing-song "gravy-giving" sermons is neighbor to a chapel of quiet, dignified services, pastored by a devoted and scholarly man who, without reaching a wide audience, has left a deep impress upon the community. That is a familiar contrast in the church life of Washington, and the less spectacular preachers who speak with quiet authority are not to be underestimated. Andrew Rankin Memorial Chapel at Howard University attracts some of the best known liberal preachers of both races, and the Howard University School of Religion aims to train a graduate ministry and to advance the admittedly backward condition of Negro preachers.

Out of more than $11,000,000 appropriated in 1936 to the public schools of the District of Columbia, approximately one-third was devoted to the colored schools. Education for Negroes in the District has come a long way from the first school founded by illiterate ex-slaves to the teachers' college, 3 senior high schools, 2 vocational schools, 6 junior high schools, and 40 elementary schools, with 1,004 teachers and 35,739 students. These schools are under the direction of Garnet C. Wilkinson, First Assistant Superintendent, divisions 10 to 13. Two other Negroes serve as second assistant superintendents, there is a Negro examining board and there is proportional membership on the Board of Education. The teaching force is unusually well prepared and the salaries are on the same scale as the salaries of the white teachers. The fact of segregation, however, must still be reckoned with. The theory of equal, though separate, accommodations breaks down into the fact of unequal facilities and equipment. Negro high schools are badly overcrowded and too often, instead of new structures, school buildings abandoned by whites are used for Negroes.

Howard University, called by some the "capstone of Negro education", is for the first time headed by a Negro, Dr. Mordecai W. Johnson. Under President Eugene Clark, Miner Teachers College, in spite of its youth, has received high rank from accrediting agencies. Frelinghuysen University, with Mrs. Anna J. Cooper as president, gives college instruction to students who must attend night classes. Miss Nannie Burroughs is the founder of the National Training School for Women and Girls, the school of the three B's: the Bible, the Bath, and the Broom, called the "nickel and dime school" because it depended for support almost wholly on contributions from Negroes who could not afford to give more.

Because of these universities there are many Negroes of ability in the humanities, and the social and natural sciences. Frequently their influence is greater than academic. At Howard University the *Journal of Negro Education* is ably edited. Carter G. Woodson edits the pioneering *Journal of Negro History* and directs the Association for the Study of Negro Life and History in this city. The weekly *Afro-American*, with a Washington edition, and the semiweekly Washington *Tribune* are the city's Negro newspapers, both tending to develop race consciousness.

These give some point to the boast of Washington's "cultural supremacy" among Negroes, but the boast is not too well founded. There is little literature even attempting to do justice to the facets of Negro life in Washington. There have been literary circles with a few poets, dramatists, and writers of fiction. The Little Theatre movement, initiated among Negroes by Alain Locke, editor of the *New Negro*, and Montgomery Gregory at Howard University, has only partially succeeded.

In 1903 the British Negro composer, Samuel Coleridge-Taylor, sponsored by a society named in his honor, conducted in Washington the first American performance of his *Hiawatha* trilogy. Other musical organizations of the century were the Clef Club and the Amphion Glee Club. The Washington Folk-Song Singers, directed by Will Marion Cook, presented as soloists Abbie Mitchell, Lottie Wallace, and Harry T. Burleigh, all later to become widely famed. The Washington Conservatory, under Mrs. Harriet Gibbs Marshall, was an important factor in musical education. Roland Hayes sang in Washington churches on his long, uphill road. Lillian Evans Tibbs, later known in opera as Madame Evanti, was one of Washington's well-known soloists. Of national popularity is the Howard University Glee Club under the direction of Roy W. Tibbs and Todd Duncan. The latter carried the role of "Porgy" in Gershwin's *Porgy and Bess*. Among jazz composers and orchestra leaders there are many Washingtonians; chief among these are Claude Hopkins and Duke Ellington, who has as one of his "hot" numbers, *The Washington Wabble*.

Although politically voluble, Negroes in Washington are still politically ineffectual. The hey-day of important political figures has passed. Oscar De Priest, Republican Congressman from Illinois, was followed by Arthur Mitchell, Democratic Congressman from the same State. There are still staunch Republicans and a Young Republican Club, and some of the old school have espoused the Liberty League; but there are many Democrats as well. The number of Negro appointees to administrative posts in the New Deal, while by no means adequate, is greater than in previous administrations. Many of these appointees are Washingtonians. Although political disquisitions may still stir the somnolence of barber shops, or break up friendships quadrennially, and although job-seekers abound, disfranchisement makes most of the Negroes politically apathetic. There is likewise a civic apathy. Civic organizations bringing grievances are often treated with scant courtesy by municipal authorities; without the vote they have little redress. There is a growing liberalism among Negroes who understand their plight, but the urging of such groups as the National Negro Congress and the N. A. A. C. P. too often meets with inertia and confusion. Segregation in Washington seems an accepted fact. Public buildings and public conveyances are not segregated, although on every southbound train Negro passengers are "jim-crowed." Negroes are not served in restaurants, saloons, hotels, movie-houses, and theaters, except those definitely set aside for them. Some stores will not accept their trade. Some governmental departments have separate accommodations, and some discriminate in the type of work offered to Negroes.

One boast, perhaps better founded than those of culture or civic status, is that Washington Negroes have a good time. Dances range in full plenty from the "house shouts" to the "bals masqués" of Washington's mythical Negro "400." Social scribes flatteringly speak of Negro "Mayfair" with no sense of incongruity. Social clubs are legion; the What-Good-Are-We Club (composed of ex-Howard students), is widely known for intensive hilarity. Though college sororities and fraternities seem to be awakening to social realities, their lavish "formals" are still the most important events on their schedules. Washington Negroes are great "joiners"; the largest orders are the Elks, Odd Fellows, Knights of Pythias, and the Masons, but some with an ancient history like "Love and Charity" linger on. The Musolit Club and the Capital City Pleasure Club have large memberships.

The movie-houses attract great crowds of Negroes. Of the chain theaters owned by the Lichtmans, three are located on U Street, the thoroughfare of Negro businesses and pleasure-seekers. The Howard Theater, something of a theatrical institution, affording both movies and fast-stepping, high-hearted shows, attracts an audience of both races. Poolrooms, short-lived cabarets, beer gardens, and eating places, from fried-fish "joints", barbecue, and hamburger stands to better-class restaurants, do an apparently thriving business. And yet, when the outsider stands upon U Street in the early hours of the evening and watches the crowds go by, togged out in finery, with jests upon their lips—this one rushing to the poolroom, this one seeking escape with Hoot Gibson, another to lose herself in Hollywood glamor, another in one of the many dance halls—he is likely to be unaware, as these people momentarily are, of aspects of life in Washington of graver import to the darker one-fourth. This vivacity, this gayety, may mask for a while, but the more drastic realities are omnipresent. Around the corner there may be a squalid slum with people jobless and desperate; the alert youngster, capable and well trained, may find on the morrow all employment closed to him. The Negro of Washington has no voice in government, is economically proscribed, and segregated nearly as rigidly as in the southern cities he contemns. He may blind himself with pleasure seeking, with a specious self-sufficiency, he may point with pride to the record of achievement over grave odds. But just as the past was not without its honor, so the present is not without bitterness.

In spite of the widespread segregation of the Negro in the District of Columbia, his story as told here has not concerned him solely. From the outset, white humanitarians have protested his enslavement and abuse, and farsighted statesmen have worked toward his integration in the total pattern. His schooling resulted from cooperation between Negroes and whites. Interracial organizations have worked toward an abolition of the injustices he faces. Governmental and municipal agencies have attempted to deal out to him a measure of what is his due. Today he is no longer asking, if he ever asked, to be considered as a ward. He asks to be considered as a citizen. But fulfillment of this hope seems still desperately remote.

The Negro has been donor as well as recipient. His contributions cannot be limited to those of menial or entertainer, as those who stereotype his character would insist. Many of the oldest inhabitants of the city who happen to be Negroes, and many newcomers, can boast of a record of citizenship as honorable as any. Culturally, the Negro has much to give, and, in spite of its being grudgingly received, has given much. No city can afford to disdain the creative potentialities of the Negro in music, drama, literature, and the arts. The scholars concentrated in Washington have a function greater than that of Negro scholars. They are American scholars who happen to be Negroes, and Washington and America have need of them. The Negro professional class of Washington, limited to service among Negroes, could contribute greatly to the advance of the entire city. The Negro has contributed. What could be a greater contribution is held in check by segregation.

From the preservation of the color-line in the District grave consequences arise. Educationally, segregation means the maintenance of a dual system—expensive not only in dollars and cents but also in its indoctrination of white children with a belief in their superiority and of Negro children with a belief in their inferiority, both equally false. Politically, it is believed by many that the determination to keep the Negro "in his place" has lessened the agitation for suffrage in the District. Economically, the presence of a large number of unemployed constitutes a critical relief problem; the low rate of pay received by Negro workers lowers the standard of living and threatens the trade-union movement. Socially, the effects of Negro ghettos are far-reaching. One cannot segregate disease and crime. In this border city, southern in so many respects, there is a denial of democracy, at times hypocritical and at times flagrant. Social compulsion forces many who would naturally be on the side of civic fairness into hopelessness and indifference. Washington has made steps in the direction of justice, but many steps remain to be taken for the sake of the underprivileged and for the sake of a greater Washington.

513

Statues, Monuments, and Memorials

There are more than 500 works of sculpture in Washington, exclusive of those in public and private collections. A general critical discussion of Washington sculpture is given in the article on Art. Many monuments, statues, and memorials are described in the accounts of individual streets and areas. The following selected list is given for convenient reference.

NAME	SCULPTOR	PLACE
Adams Memorial ("Grief")	Augustus Saint-Gaudens	Rock Creek Cemetery.
American Federation of Labor Memorial (see Gompers, Samuel)	Robert Aitken	
Ann Simon Memorial	Brenda Putnam	Rock Creek Cemetery.
Arlington Memorial Bridge Buffaloes (bas-relief)	Carl Paul Jennewein	
Arlington Memorial Bridge Eagles	C.P. Jennewein	Arlington Memorial Bridge.
Arlington Memorial Bridge groups (proposed): Valor and Sacrifice	Leo Friedlander	
Peace and Arts of Peace	James Earle Fraser	
Armillary Sphere (Noyes Memorial)	C.P. Jennewein	Meridian Hill Park.
Arsenal Monument	Lot Flannery	Congressional Cemetery.
Asbury, Bishop Francis (equestrian)	Augustus Lukeman	16th and Mount Pleasant Sts. NW.
Aztec Fountain (see Pan American Union Fountain)		
Barry, Commodore John (statue)	John J. Boyle	Franklin Park.
Bartholdi Fountain	Augustus Bartholdi	Botanic Garden, 1st St. and Independence Ave. SW.
Bryan, William Jennings (statue)	Gutzon Borglum	West Potomac Park.
Buchanan, President James (statue and ideal figures)	Hans Schuler	Meridian Hill Park.

515

NAME	SCULPTOR	PLACE
Buffaloes (see Q Street Bridge Buffaloes)		
Burke, Edmund (statue modeled from the work of Havard Thomas at Bristol, England)	Horace W. Peaslee	Massachusetts Ave. at 11th and L Sts. NW.
Butt-Millet Memorial Fountain	Daniel Chester French	Northwest portion of Ellipse, south of E St. NW.
Carroll, Archbishop John (statue)	Jerome Connor	Georgetown University campus.
Center Stone (see Jefferson Pier)		
Civil War Unknown Dead Memorial		Arlington Cemetery.
Coast Guard Memorial	George Hoover Gaston Lachaise	Arlington Cemetery.
Colonial Settlers Monument		15th St. between Constitution Ave. and E St. NW.
Columbus Memorial Monument and Fountain	Lorado Taft	Union Station Plaza.
Confederate Dead, Memorial to (group)	Moses Ezekiel	Arlington Cemetery.
Connecticut Avenue Bridge Lions	Roland Hinton Perry	Connecticut Ave. Bridge.
Corcoran, W.W., Tomb of		Oak Hill Cemetery.
Corcoran Gallery Lions	Canova (copy)	Steps of Corcoran Gallery.
Court of Neptune Fountain	R.H. Perry	Library of Congress.
Cuban Friendship Urn	From *Maine* Memorial, Cuba	West Potomac Park.
Daguerre, L.J.M. (statue)	Jonathan Scott Hartley	Smithsonian Grounds.
Dante (statue)	Ettore Ximenes (copy)	Meridian Hill Park.
Darlington (Joseph J.) Memorial Fountain	C.P. Jennewein	Judiciary Square.
D.A.R. Memorial to the Founders	Gertrude Vanderbilt Whitney	Constitution Ave. near 17th St.
D'Arc, Jeanne (see Jeanne D'Arc)		
Delano, Jane A. (ideal figure)	R. Tait McKenzie	Red Cross Bldg.

NAME	SCULPTOR	PLACE
Department of Agriculture War Memorial (plaque)	John Flanagan	Department of Agriculture patio.
Downing, Andrew Jackson (memorial vase)	Calvert Vaus	Smithsonian Grounds.
Dupont Memorial Fountain	D.C. French	Dupont Circle.
Ericsson, John (portrait and group)	J.E. Fraser	Potomac Park.
Farragut, Admiral David (statue)	Vinnie Ream Hoxie	Farragut Square.
Ffoulke Memorial ("Rabboni")	Gutzon Borglum	Rock Creek Cemetery.
First Division A.E.F. Monument ("Victory")	D.C. French	South of State Department Bldg.
Franklin, Benjamin (statue)	Jacques Jouvenal (after Plassman)	10th St. and Pennsylvania Ave. NW.
Frederick the Great (statue)	T. Uphues	Army War College.
Gallatin, Albert Memorial (proposed)	J.E. Fraser	North Entrance U. S. Treasury Bldg.
Gallaudet Teaching the Deaf Child (portrait group)	D.C. French	Columbia Institution for the Deaf.
Garfield, President James (portrait and group)	J.Q.A. Ward	1st St. and Maryland Ave. SW.
Gibbons, Cardinal James (statue)	Leo Lentelli	16th St. and Park Rd.
Gompers, Samuel (portrait and group)	Robert Aitken	Massachusetts Ave. at 10th St. NW.
Grand Army of the Republic Monument (see Stephenson, Grand Army)		
Grant, General Ulysses (equestrian and groups)	Henry M. Shrady	Union Square, foot of Capitol Hill.
Greene, General Nathanael (equestrian)	Henry Kirk Brown	Stanton Square.
"Grief" (see Adams Memorial)		
Gross, Dr. Samuel D. (statue)	A. Sterling Calder	Smithsonian Grounds.
Hahnemann (Dr. Samuel) Memorial (portrait and monument)	Charles Henry Niehaus	East of Scott Circle.
Hamilton, Alexander (statue)	J.E. Fraser	South of Treasury Bldg.

NAME	SCULPTOR	PLACE
Hancock, General Winfield Scott (equestrian)	Henry Ellicott	7th and Pennsylvania Ave. NW.
Henry, Professor Joseph (statue)	William Wetmore Story	Smithsonian Grounds.
Hitt Memorial	Laura Gardin Fraser	Rock Creek Cemetery.
Hoxie, Vinnie Ream, Memorial	C.T. Zolnay and Vinnie Ream Hoxie	Arlington Cemetery.
Jackson, General Andrew (equestrian)	Clark Mills	Lafayette Square.
Jeanne d'Arc (equestrian)	Paul Dubois (copy of one at Rheims)	Meridian Hill Park.
Jefferson Pier (center stone)		Washington Monument Grounds.
Jones, Commodore John Paul (statue and monument)	C.H. Niehaus	Potomac Park.
Journey Through Life (ideal figures)	J.E. Fraser	Rock Creek Cemetery.
Joyce, John J. (bust)	Jerome Connor	Oak Hill Cemetery.
Kaufman Memorial ("Memory")	William Ordway Partridge	Rock Creek Cemetery.
Kearny, Philip (equestrian)	Edward Clark Potter	Arlington Cemetery.
Kosciuszko, General Thaddeus (statue and groups)	Anton Popiel	Lafayette Square.
Lafayette, General Marquis de (statue and groups)	Alexandre Falguière and Antonin Mercie	Lafayette Park.
L'Enfant Memorial	Welles Bosworth	Arlington Cemetery.
Lincoln, Abraham (marble statue)	D.C. French	Lincoln Memorial.
Lincoln, Abraham (statue)	Lot Flannery	Judiciary Square.
Lincoln, Abraham (group)	Thomas Ball	Lincoln Park.
Lincoln, Robert Todd (sarcophagus)	J.E. Fraser	Arlington Cemetery.
Logan, General John A. (equestrian)	Franklin Simmons	Logan Circle.
Longfellow, Henry W. (statue)	William Couper	Connecticut Ave. at 18th and M Sts. NW.
Luther, Martin (statue)	Rietschel (copy)	14th and Vermont Ave. NW.

NAME	SCULPTOR	PLACE
Maine Memorial	Nathan Wyeth	Arlington Cemetery.
Marconi Memorial	Anton Piccarrilli	16th and Lamont Sts.
Marshall, Chief Justice John (statue)	W.W. Story	Capitol, West Terrace.
McClellan, General George B. (equestrian)	F.W. MacMonnies	Connecticut Ave. and California St. NW.
McMillan, General James (fountain)	Herbert Adams	McMillan Park.
McPherson, Major James B. (equestrian)	Louis T. Rebisso	McPherson Square.
Meade, General George Gordon (statue and group)	Charles A. Grafly	Union Square.
Navy and Marine Memorial (gulls in flight)	Ernesto Begni del Piatta	Columbia Island, SE. end.
Newlands Fountain	Edwin W. Dunn	Chevy Chase Circle.
Noyes Memorial (see Armillary Sphere)		
Nuns of the Battlefield (bas-reliefs and ideal figure)	Jerome Connor	Rhode Island Ave. and M St. NW.
Pan American Union Fountain	Gertrude Vanderbilt Whitney	Constitution Ave. at 17th St. NW.
Payne, John Howard (bust and memorial)		Oak Hill Cemetery.
Peace Monument (ideal figures)	Franklin Simmons	Pennsylvania Ave. and 1st St. NW.
Peace and Arts of Peace (groups proposed)	J.E. Fraser	Arlington Memorial Bridge.
Peary, Admiral, Memorial	Davis Sculptor Co.	Arlington Cemetery.
Pike, General Albert (statue and monument)	G. Trentanove	Indiana Ave., 3rd and D Sts. NW.
Piney Branch Bridge Tigers	A. Phimister Proctor	Piney Branch Bridge, 16th St. NW.
Pinkney, Bishop William (statue)		Oak Hill Cemetery.
"Puck"	Brenda Putnam	Folger Library.
Pulaski, General Count Casimir (equestrian)	Kasimir Chodzinski	Pennsylvania Ave. and 13th St. NW.
Q Street Bridge Buffaloes	A. Phimister Proctor	Q Street Bridge, Rock Creek.
Rawlins, General John A. (statue)	Joseph A. Bailey	Rawlins Square.
Rochambeau, Comte de (statue and groups)	F. Hamar	Lafayette Park.

NAME	SCULPTOR	PLACE
Rough Riders Memorial		Arlington Cemetery.
Rush, Dr. Benjamin (statue)	R.H. Perry	Old Naval Medical Center.
Sacrifice (group, proposed)	Leo Friedlander	Arlington Memorial Bridge.
San Martín, General José de (equestrian)	Dumont (copy of one in Buenos Aires)	Judiciary Square.
Scheutze, Lieutenant, memorial to ("Serenity")	José Clara	Meridian Hill Park.
Scott, General Winfield (equestrian)	H.K. Brown	Scott Circle.
Scott, General Winfield (statue)	Launt Thompson	Soldiers Home.
Second Division A.E.F. Memorial	J.E. Fraser	Constitution Ave. near 17th St. NW.
Shepherd, Alexander R. (statue)	U.S.J. Dunbar	Plaza, District Bldg.
Sheridan, General Philip H. (equestrian)	Gutzon Borglum	Sheridan Circle.
Sherman, General William T. (equestrian and group)	Carl Rohl-Smith and others	Treasury Place, E and 15th Sts. NW.
Sousa, John Philip (memorial bench)	Hans Voltz, architect	Congressional Cemetery.
Spanish-American War Monument		Arlington Cemetery.
Stephenson Grand Army Memorial	J. Massey Rhind	7th St. and Pennsylvania Ave. NW.
Straus, Oscar A. Memorial (statue and group)	A.A. Weinman	Grand Plaza, Commerce Bldg.
Taft, William Howard (stele)	J.E. Fraser	Arlington Cemetery.
Temperance Fountain		Pennsylvania Ave. and 7th St. NW.
Thomas, Major General George H. (equestrian)	J.Q.A. Ward	Thomas Circle.
Titanic Memorial (see Women's Titanic Memorial)		
Union Station Fountain (see Columbus Fountain)		
Unknown Soldier, Tomb of	Thomas H. Jones, sculptor; Lorimer Rich, architect	Arlington Cemetery.

NAME	SCULPTOR	PLACE
Valor (group, proposed)	Leo Friedlander	Arlington Memorial Bridge.
Van Ness Mausoleum	A. Phimister Proctor	Oak Hill Cemetery.
Von Steuben, General (statue and groups)	Albert Jaegers	Lafayette Park.
War Memorial (9-foot plaque)	John Flanagan	Department of Agriculture patio.
Ward, General Artemas (statue)	Leonard Crunelle	Nebraska and Massachusetts Aves. NW.
Washington, George (equestrian)	Clark Mills	Washington Circle.
Webster, Daniel (statue and relief)	G. Trentanove	West of Scott Circle.
Witherspoon, John (statue)	William Couper	Connecticut Ave. and N St. NW.
Women's *Titanic* Memorial	G.V. Whitney	West Potomac Park, foot of New Hampshire Ave.
Zero Milestone	Horace W. Peaslee	Ellipse, just south of Executive Drive.

Chronology

1600   Indian town of Nacotchtant, on Anacostia Flats, is first human settlement of record in the District of Columbia.

1608   First Potomac excursion—Captain John Smith sails past future site of D.C. to Little Falls. (Questioned by historians.)

1622   Henry Fleete involuntarily becomes D.C.'s first white resident. Captured by Indians and held several years.

1632   Fleete writes first description now extant of Washington region.

1662   George Thompson gets first D.C. land patent from Maryland.

1669   John Howsen gets first D.C. land patent on Virginia side of Potomac.

1741   Georgetown organized as a community.

1749   Alexandria laid out.

1787   Constitutional provision made for independent National Capital— exact location undetermined.

1788   Maryland cedes to Congress territory north of Potomac for site of Capital.

1789   Virginia cedes to Congress territory south of Potomac for Capital site.

1790   Congress authorizes George Washington to choose site of "Federal City."

1791   Washington choses D.C. site for capital. L'Enfant drafts plan for city. Congress creates first District administrative body of three commissioners. Name "City of Washington" first officially used.

1793   George Washington lays cornerstone of Capitol.

1797   John Adams (1785-1826) inaugurated. First bridge built over Potomac near site of present Chain Bridge.

1798   Construction of White House under way.

1800   Population 14,003.

       Post Office Department, first Government agency to arrive from Philadelphia, opens in Washington. Others follow. Congress begins first session in November.

       Washington Navy Yard established.

       First theater opens in Washington.

1801   First New Year's Day reception at the White House.

       Thomas Jefferson (1743-1826) inaugurated.

       Congress assumes jurisdiction over the District.

       City of Washington incorporated; mayor-council government established, with mayor appointed by the President.

       First District buildings erected; a jail is prominent among them.

1803   Council passes ordinance directing the mayor to cause lamps to be placed on most public avenues and streets, to employ lamp-lighters, and to supply oil for lamps.

1805   First school board meeting.

1806   First two public schools opened.

1807   Three Negro freedmen open first colored public school at their own expense.

1808   Tiber Creek Canal, along present Canal Street and Constitution Avenue, begun.

1809   James Madison (1751-1836) inaugurated.

1810   Population 24,023.

1814   British under General Ross and Admiral Cockburn burn the Capitol, the White House, and several other public buildings.
Curbstones and foot-pavements introduced, with paving brick and stone crosswalks at intersections.

1815   First appropriation to maintain trees in District.

1817   James Monroe (1758-1831), after inauguration, occupies reconstructed White House.

1819   Ship-of-the-line *Columbus* launched at Navy Yard.

1820   Population 33,039; three-quarters white, remainder about equally divided between slaves and freedmen. Georgetown population 7,360.
Congress authorizes popular election of mayor.
First District courthouse completed.
First White House wedding—Maria Monroe to Samuel L. Gouverneur.
Decatur-Barron duel. Decatur killed.

1824   Lafayette has grand reception on his second visit to this country.

1825   John Quincy Adams (1767-1848) inaugurated.

1826   Clay-Randolph duel—bloodless.

1829   Andrew Jackson (1767-1845) inaugurated.

1830   Population 39,834.

1832   Cholera epidemic in which 459 are known to have died.

1835   Baltimore & Ohio Railroad reaches Washington.

1837   Martin Van Buren (1782-1862) inaugurated.

1838   Captain Marryat, Royal Navy, author of sea stories, visits Washington.
Cilley-Graves duel—last important American duel over the "freedom of debate" issue.

1840   Population 43,712.
Smithsonian Institution founded.

1841   Wm. Henry Harrison (1773-1841) inaugurated, dies of penumonia 30 days later.
John Tyler (1790-1862) inaugurated.

1844   Gunboat *Princeton,* first screw steamship in U. S. Navy to visit Washington, gives an exhibition of firing its largest cannon, the "Peacemaker." The cannon bursts and kills the Secretary of the Navy, several Congressmen, and prominent citizens.
First telegraph news dispatch sent, from Washington to Baltimore.

1845   James Knox Polk (1759-1849) inaugurated.
        National Theater burns.
1846   District territory south of Potomac retroceded to Virginia.
1848   Seventy-six Washington house slaves lured on board an abolitionist vessel and carried away; they were later recaptured.
        The *National Era,* Abolitionist weekly, mobbed.
        Cornerstone of Washington Monument laid, July fourth.
1849   Zachary Taylor (1784-1850) inaugurated.
1850   Population 51,867.
        Millard Fillmore (1800-1874) inaugurated.
        Chesapeake & Ohio Canal completed.
1853   Franklin Pierce (1804-69) inaugurated.
        Jackson statue, first equestrian figure in U. S., dedicated in Lafayette Square.
1857   James Buchanan (1791-1868) inaugurated.
        National Theater burns again.
        "Know Nothing" riots; six persons killed, many injured.
1859   Shooting of Philip Barton Key by Representative Daniel E. Sickles, afterward a Civil War general, near Lafayette Square.
1860   Population 75,080.
        Albert Edward, Prince of Wales, visits Washington.
        First Japanese delegation ever to reach America visits Washington.
1861   Abraham Lincoln (1809-65) inaugurated.
        Lincoln orders Washington Militia into Federal service.
        Metropolitan Police force organized.
1862   Street railroad laid on Pennsylvania Avenue.
1863   President Lincoln proclaims Emancipation from Washington.
1864   Early's repulse in skirmish at Silver Spring, north of Washington, saves the Capital from the Confederacy; President Lincoln under fire at Fort Stevens.
1865   Victorious Federal troops take more than 12 hours to march down Pennsylvania Avenue past the White House.
        Assassination of Lincoln. Attempt on Secretary Seward's life.
        Andrew Johnson (1808-75) inaugurated.
1866   National Training School for Boys founded.
1867   Hanging of participants in the Lincoln conspiracy.
        D.C. suffrage bill passed over veto of President Johnson.
        Systematic development of Washington's park system begins, under supervision of War Department.
1868   Impeachment of President Andrew Johnson.
1869   U. S. Grant (1822-85) inaugurated.
        Treasury building completed.
        Completion of Howard University.
1870   Population 131,700.
        District of Columbia goes under territorial government.
        State, War and Navy Building begun.
        Alexander R. Shepherd begins physical regeneration of Washington.

1872   National Theater burns again.
Carnival on Pennsylvania Avenue to celebrate laying of its first woodblock pavement.
1874   Chain Bridge completed.
1877   Rutherford B. Hayes (1822-93) inaugurated.
Peace Monument unveiled.
1878   Temporary commission government, begun in 1874, becomes permanent.
Chin Lin Pin, first Chinese envoy to Washington, arrives.
1879   Old Tiber Creek canal filled in.
First electric lights in the Capital.
Colonel Robert G. Ingersoll delivers his immortal funeral oration over his brother (1402 K St., June 2).
First apartment house erected.
1880   Population 177,624.
Work recommenced on Washington Monument.
1881   James A. Garfield (1831-81) inaugurated.
Disastrous flood covers city under six feet of water from Monument to Capitol; part of Long Bridge washed away.
Roof of City Hall blown off during an unusually heavy windstorm, and 1,200 trees are blown down.
President Garfield is assassinated and dies at Long Branch, N.J.
Chester A. Arthur (1830-86) inaugurated.
1883   First long-distance telephone communication—with Baltimore.
1884   Washington Monument completed.
1885   Grover Cleveland (1837-1908) inaugurated.
Dedication of Washington Monument.
National Theater burns in February and reopens in October.
Opening of first free night school in D.C. at Franklin School.
1886   Four earthquake shocks rock Washington at the same time that a severe earthquake nearly destroys Charleston, S.C.
Grover Cleveland and Miss Frances Folsom married at the White House.
1887   Queen Kapiolani and Princess Liliuokalani, of Hawaii, visit Washington.
1888   Great blizzard closes most of Washington.
Senate passes first attempt at national prohibition amendment.
First electric street car.
National Training School for Girls established.
1889   Benjamin Harrison (1833-1901) inaugurated.
Flood reaches to level of Pennsylvania Avenue streetcar floors.
1890   Population 230,392.
Cable cars on 7th Street begin operation, first in Washington.
Development of Rock Creek Park begins. Smithsonian Zoo moves to tract on Rock Creek.
First electric lights in White House.

1891   President Harrison signs the act prohibiting the sale of liquor within one mile of Soldiers' Home; first prohibition law thus makes nearly one third of Washington dry.   .

1892   High water mark of the D. A. R.—80,000 Civil War veterans parade past the White House.

1893   Grover Cleveland's second inauguration.
Infanta Eulalia of Spain visits Washington.

1894   Coxey's Army arrives.

1895   Act of Congress merges Georgetown with Washington.
S. P. Langley's motor-driven "airdrome" has successful flight on Potomac River. Altitude 100 feet and flew half-a-mile, when fuel became exhausted (May 6).
Electric cars go into service on F Street line, from Lincoln Park to Georgetown; first third-rail trolley system.
Rudyard Kipling visits Washington.

1896   Li Hung Chang, viceroy of China, and Queen Liliuokalani of Hawaii visit Washington.
Washington Free Library, forerunner of the Public Library, opens.

1897   William McKinley (1843-1901) inaugurated.
Library of Congress Building opens.
The first Horseless Carriage inaugurates the traffic problem.

1898   McKinley's war message to Congress.
First D.C. volunteers off to Spanish-American War in May; return in October.
Admiral Pasquale Cervera of the Spanish Navy is an involuntary guest of the U.S. Navy.

1899   Great blizzard; 20½ inches of snow falls on top of a previous 15 inches; all traffic and business suspended.
Carnegie donates a building for a public library.
Consolidation of 12 street railway and 2 electric light companies accomplished.
Admiral Dewey's great reception in Washington.

1900   Population 278,718.
First public automobiles, forerunners of the taxi, are put into operation.
The city celebrates its first centennial.
Creation of the Potomac Parks begun.

1901   McKinley is assassinated in Buffalo, N.Y.; the body is brought to Washington for funeral services.
Theodore Roosevelt (1858-1919) inaugurated.

1902   Prince Henry of Prussia, brother of the Kaiser, a guest at the White House.
First complete restoration of White House since Monroe's administration.

1903   First provision for public playgrounds made.

1907   Union Station completed.
Carry Nation raids Washington.

1909   William H. Taft (1857-1930) inaugurated.

1910   Population 331,069.
1912   First fully-equipped motor fire engine goes into commission at Petworth.
1913   Woodrow Wilson (1856-1924) inaugurated.
1914   Spadeful of earth in Potomac Park marks the beginning of construction of Lincoln Memorial.
       Giant suffrage parade down Pennsylvania Avenue.
1917   Wilson's classic war message to Congress; "war population" floods Capital.
       New District Courthouse completed.
       Suffragists demonstrate before the White House; many arrested.
1918   First aeroplane mail service established, Washington-Philadelphia-New York.
       First Armistice Day; Washington revels over end of World War I.
1919   Bomb explosion at home of Attorney General A. Mitchell Palmer injures only the bomber.
       King Albert of the Belgians, Queen Elizabeth, and the Duke of Brabant visit Washington.
       Prince of Wales makes a three-day visit.
1920   Population 437,571.
       Arlington Memorial Amphitheater dedicated.
1921   Warren G. Harding (1865-1923) inaugurated.
       Unknown Soldier's body in Capitol; thousands pay tribute.
1922   Lincoln Memorial dedicated.
       Knickerbocker Theater roof collapses under 26-inch fall of snow; 98 killed, 150 injured.
       Premier Georges Clemenceau, of France, visits Washington.
1923   President Harding's body lies in state in the Capitol.
       Calvin Coolidge (1872-1933) inaugurated.
1924   Key Bridge completed.
1925   Last horse passes out of District Fire Department, by retirement.
1927   Opening of first Vocational School for Girls in Dennison School building.
       Trans-Atlantic telephone service inaugurated between Washington and London.
       Part of White House rebuilt (March 4 to September 11).
1929   Herbert C. Hoover (1874-   ) inaugurated.
1930   Population 486,869.
       Prince Takamatsu, brother of the Emperor of Japan, and King Prajadhipok of Siam visit Washington.
1931–32 Hunger Marchers "invade" Washington.
       Bonus Army driven out by U.S. Army; one killed, several injured.
       Folger Shakespeare Library opens.
       Department of Commerce Building opened in Federal Triangle.
1933   Franklin D. Roosevelt (1882-   ) inaugurated.
1935   Supreme Court and National Archives Buildings completed.
1936   Potomac River goes on rampage; more water than in 1889 flood.

1937   Second inauguration of Franklin D. Roosevelt.
       Children's Art Gallery, first in Nation, opened on the Mall.
       South Interior Building completed.
1939   King George VI and Queen Elizabeth of England visit Washington.
1940   National Defense program organized.
       Washington National Airport Terminal Building dedicated.
1941   Franklin D. Roosevelt inaugurated as first third-term President of
       the United States.
       National Gallery of Art opens.
       War Department Building completed.
       Jefferson Memorial completed.
       U.S. declares war on Japan, Germany, Italy.

Selected Reading List

DESCRIPTIVE AND GENERAL

Barbee, David R. *Washington, City of Mighty Events.* Illustrated. Richmond, Va., 1930.

Borah, Leo Arthur. *Washington, Home City and Show Place.* 20 natural color photographs, 1937.

Bulkley, Barry. *Washington, Old and New.* Illustrated. Washington, 1913.

Cooley, E. *A Description of the Etiquette at Washington City.* Philadelphia, L. B. Clark, 1829.

Ecker, Grace Dunlop. *A Portrait of Old Georgetown.* Illustrated. Richmond, Va., 1933.

Essary, J. Frederick and Helen. *Washington Sketch Book.* Illustrated. New York, 1932.

Forbes-Lindsay, C. H. *Washington, the City and the Seat of Government.* Illustrated. Philadelphia, 1908.

Gatchel, Theodore Dodge. *Rambling Through Washington: Old and New Landmarks in Our Capital City.* Illustrated. Washington, 1932.

Hutchins, Stilson and J. W. Moore. *The National Capital, Past and Present.* Washington, 1885.

Leupp, Francis E. *Walks About Washington.* Illustrated. Boston, 1915.

Monroe, Mrs. Harriet Earhart. *Washington, Its Sights and Insights.* Revised edition. Illustrated. New York, 1909.

Moore, Charles. *Washington, Past and Present.* Illustrated. New York, 1929.

Moore, Joseph West. *Picturesque Washington.* Illustrated. Providence, 1886.

Nicolay, Helen. *Our Capital on the Potomac.* Illustrated. New York, 1924.

Page, Thomas Nelson. *Washington and Its Romance.* Illustrated. New York, 1923.

Pepper, Charles M. *Every-Day Life in Washington with Pen and Camera.* Illustrated. New York, 1900.

Rainey, Ada. *The Charm of Old Washington.* Illustrated. Washington, 1932.

Roosevelt, Mrs. Franklin D. *A Trip to Washington with Bobby and Betty.* Illustrated. New York, 1935.

Shackleton, Robert. *The Book of Washington.* Illustrated. Philadelphia, 1922.

Taft, William Howard, and James Bryce. *Washington, the Nation's Capital.* (Reprinted from the *National Geographic Magazine.*) Washington, 1915.

Townsend, George Alfred ("Gath"). *Washington, Outside and Inside.* Illustrated. Cincinnati, 1874.

—— *Events at the National Capital, and the Campaign of 1876.* James Betts & Co. Hartford, Conn., 1876.

Trollope, Anthony. *North America.* Two volumes. London; Chapman & Hall, 1862. Vol. II, pp. 3-56, for Washington scenes.

Warden, David Baillie. *A Chorographical and Statistical Description of the District of Columbia.* Paris, 1816.

Weller, Charles Frederick. *Neglected Neighbors: Stories of Life in Alleys, Tenements and Shanties of the National Capital.* Illustrated. Philadelphia, 1909.

Wilson, Rufus Rockwell. *Washington, the Capital City and Its Part in the History of the Nation.* In two volumes, Philadelphia, 1901.

—— *The Capital of Our Country.* (Reprinted articles from the *National Geographic Magazine.*) Illustrated. Washington, 1923.

HISTORY

Briggs, Emily Edson. *The Olivia Letters: Some History of Washington City for Forty Years.* Washington, 1906.

Brooks, Noah. *Washington in Lincoln's Time.* New York, 1895.

Brown, George Rothwell. *Washington, a Not Too Serious History.* Illustrated. Baltimore, 1930.

Bryan, Wilhelmus Bogart. *History of the National Capital, from Its Foundation through the Period of the Adoption of the Organic Act.* In two volumes. New York, 1914-1916.

Columbia Historical Society. *Records.* Washington, 1897— .

Crew, Harvey W., Editor. *Centennial History of the City of Washington.* Dayton, Ohio, 1892.

Ewell, James. "Unwelcome Visitors to Early Washington, August 24, 1814." (In *Columbia Historical Society Records,* Vol. I, No. 2, pp. 55-118. December, 1896).

Gahn, Bessie Wilmarth. *Original Patentees of Land at Washington Prior to 1700.* With map. Washington, 1936.

Gleig, George Robert. *A Narrative of the Campaigns of the British Army at Washington, Baltimore and New Orleans . . . in the year 1814.* Philadelphia, M. Carey & Sons, 1821.

Kite, Elizabeth S. *L'Enfant and Washington, 1791-1792.* Illustrated. Baltimore, 1929.

Levasseur, Auguste. *Lafayette in America in 1824 and 1825, or a Journal of a Voyage to the United States.* Philadelphia, Carey & Lea, 1829.

McKee, Thomas H. *Presidential Inaugurations from George Washington to Grover Cleveland.* Washington, 1893.

McLane, Mary Jane. *Life in Washington.* Philadelphia, J. B. Lippincott & Company, 1859.

O'Malley, Frank Ward. *The War-Whirl in Washington*. Illustrated. New York, 1918.

Peets, Elbert. *L'Enfant's Washington*. Reprinted from *The Town Planning Review* for May, 1933.

Porter, John Addison. *The City of Washington: Its Origin and Administration*. Baltimore, 1885.

Proctor, John Claggett, Edwin Melvin Williams, and Frank P. Black, Editors. *Washington, Past and Present*. In five volumes. Illustrated. New York, 1930.

Slauson, Allan B. *A History of the City of Washington, Its Men and Institutions*. Illustrated. Edited for the *Washington Post*. Washington, 1903.

Thatcher, Erastus. *Founding of Washington City*. Washington, 1891.

Tindall, William. *Standard History of the City of Washington, from a Study of the Original Sources*. Illustrated. Knoxville, Tenn., 1914.

Todd, Charles Burr. *The Story of Washington, the National Capital*. Illustrated. New York, 1889.

Williams, John S. *History of the Invasion and Capture of Washington*. New York, Harper and Brothers, 1851.

Wilson, Edith Bolling. *My Memoirs*. Indianapolis, 1939.

THE EARLY CITY

Busey, Samuel C. *Pictures of the City of Washington in the Past*. Washington, 1898.

Ellet, Mrs. E. F. *Court Circles of the Republic, from Washington to Grant*. Illustrated. Hartford, Conn., 1869.

Gerry, Elbridge, Jr. *Diary*. (Washington in 1813.) New York, 1927.

Jackson, Richard P. *The Chronicles of Georgetown, 1751-1878*. Washington, R. O. Polkinhorn, Printer, 1878.

King, Nicholas. "Nicholas King's Reports of the Meridian Line Survey in Washington." An appendix to an article by Marcus Baker in *National Geographic Magazine*, November, 1894.

Kochka, Mary Murray. *Washington, Its Early Days and Early Ways*. Illustrated. New York, 1930.

Mackall, S. Somervell. *Early Days of Washington*. Illustrated. Washington, 1899.

Mills, Robert. *Guide to the Capitol of the United States*. Washington, 1834.

Royall, Anne (Newport). *Sketches of History, Life and Manners in the United States*. New Haven, 1826.

―――― *The Black Book, or a Continuation of Travels in the United States*. Washington, 1829.

Seaton, Josephine. *William Winton Seaton, of the National Intelligencer*. (As portrayed in contemporary letters.) Boston, James R. Osgood & Co., 1871.

Smith, Mrs. Margaret Bayard. *The First Forty Years of Washington Society.* Letters edited by Gaillard Hunt. Illustrated. New York, 1906.

Watterston, George. *A New Guide to Washington—1842.* New York, S. Colman, 1842.

ARCHITECTURE, ART, PLANNING AND DEVELOPMENT

Brown, Glenn. *The Octagon.* Illustrated. Washington, 1917.

Caemmerer, H. Paul. *A Manual on the Origin and Development of Washington.* Illustrated. Washington, 1939.

―――― *Washington, the National Capital.* Illustrated. Washington, 1932.

Cunningham, Harry Francis. *Measured Drawings of Georgian Architecture in the District of Columbia.* New York, 1914.

―――― *Development of the United States Capital.* Addresses. Illustrated. Washington, 1930.

Henderson, Helen W. *Art Treasures of Washington.* Illustrated. New York, 1912.

Paxton, Annabel. *Washington Doorways.* Illustrated. Richmond, Va., 1940.

Peets, Elbert. *Current Town Planning in Washington.* Reprinted from *The Town Planning Review* for December, 1931.

―――― *Famous Town Planners—L'Enfant.* Reprinted from *The Town Planning Review* for July, 1928.

Phillips, Duncan. *A Collection in the Making.* (The Phillips Memorial Gallery). Illustrated. New York, 1926.

Torbert, Mrs. Alice. *Doorways and Dormers of Old Georgetown.* Washington, 1930.

U. S. Commission of Fine Arts. *Reports.* Washington, 1911.

Vosberg, Frederick G. *Wonders of New Washington; effective modern structures rise in the biggest government building program since the Capital was founded in the wilderness.* Washington, 1935.

Washington Society of Engineers. *Planning and Building the City of Washington.* Edited by Frederick Haynes Newell. Illustrated. Washington, 1932.

THE CAPITOL

Brown, Glenn. *History of the United States Capitol.* In two volumes. Illustrated. Washington, 1901-1904.

Fairman, Charles E. *Art and Artists of the Capitol of the United States of America.* Illustrated. Washington, 1927.

Frary, I. T. *They Built the Capitol.* Illustrated. Richmond, Va., 1940.

Hazleton, George C., Jr. *The National Capitol, Its Architecture, Art, and History.* Illustrated. New York, 1912.

THE WHITE HOUSE

Chittenden, Cecil Ross. *The White House and Its Yesterdays.* Illustrated. Alexandria, Va., 1932.

Colman, Edna M. *Seventy-five Years of White House Gossip, from Washington to Lincoln.* Illustrated. New York, 1926.

────── *White House Gossip, from Andrew Johnson to Calvin Coolidge.* Illustrated. New York, 1927.

Hampton, Vernon B. *Religious Background of the White House.* Boston, 1932.

Hoover, Irwin Hood (Ike), chief usher. *Forty-two Years in the White House.* Illustrated. Boston, 1934.

Hurd, Charles. *The White House, a Biography: the Story of the House, Its Occupants, Its Place in American History.* New York, 1940.

Jaffray, Elizabeth, housekeeper from the days of Taft to Coolidge. *Secrets of the White House.* Illustrated. New York, 1927.

Lewis, Ethel. *The White House: An Informal History of Its Architecture, Interiors, and Gardens.* New York, 1937.

Singleton, Esther. *The Story of the White House.* In two volumes. Illustrated. New York, 1907.

Stoddard, William O. *Inside the White House in War Times.* Illustrated. New York, 1890.

Whipple, Wayne. *The Story of the White House.* Illustrated. Philadelphia, 1910.

Willets, Gilson. *Inside History of the White House.* Illustrated. New York, 1908.

POLITICS AND PERSONALITIES

Allen, Robert S. and Drew Pearson. *Washington Merry-Go-Round.* New York, 1931.

────── *More Washington Merry-Go-Round.* New York, 1932.

Anonymous. *High Low Washington.* Philadelphia, 1932.

Clark, Delbert. *Washington Dateline.* New York, 1941.

Copeland, Frances S. *Mrs. Copeland's Guest Book.* Philadelphia, 1934.

Dart, Rufus, II. *The Puppet Show on the Potomac.* New York, 1934.

Essary, J. Frederick. *Covering Washington: Government Reflected to the Public in the Press.* Illustrated. Boston, 1927.

Gilbert, Clinton W. *The Mirrors of Washington.* Illustrated. New York, 1921.

Hall, Florence Howe. *Social Usages at Washington.* New York, 1906.

McCable, James Dabney. *Behind the Scenes in Washington.* Illustrated. New York, 1873.

McLean, Evalyn Walsh. *Father Struck it Rich.* Boston, 1936.

Rosskam, Edwin. *Washington, Nerve Center.* New York, 1939.

Squire, Anne. *Social Washington.* Revised edition. Washington, 1929.

Tucker, Roy Thomas. *The Mirrors of 1932.* Illustrated. New York, 1931.

REMINISCENCES

Ames, Mary Clemmer. *Ten Years in Washington: Life and Scenes in the National Capital.* Illustrated. Hartford, Conn., 1873.

Anderson, Isabel. *Presidents and Pies: Life in Washington, 1879-1919.* Illustrated. Boston, 1920.

Andrews, Marietta Minnigerode. *My Studio Window: Sketches of the Pageant of Washington Life.* Illustrated. New York, 1932.

Crook, William H., body-guard to President Lincoln. *Through Five Administrations.* Reminiscences edited by Margarita Spalding Gerry. Illustrated, New York, 1910.

Gobright, L. A. *Recollections of Men and Things at Washington During a Third of a Century.* Philadelphia, Claxton, Remsen & Haffelfinger, 1869.

Hines, Christian. *Early Recollections of Washington City, D. C.* Washington, 1866.

Jackson, Mrs. Cordelia. "Georgetown Events of 60 Years Ago." Interview in *Washington Post,* January 3, 1932.

Jennings, Paul. *A Colored Man's Reminiscences of James Madison.* Brooklyn, George C. Beadle, 1865.

Keyes, Frances Parkinson. *Letters from a Senator's Wife.* Illustrated. New York, 1924.

Lockwood, Mary Smith. *Yesterdays in Washington.* In two volumes. Illustrated. Rosslyn, Va., 1915.

Logan, Mrs. John A., Editor. *Thirty Years in Washington: or, Life and Scenes in our National Capital.* Illustrated. Hartford, Conn., 1901.

Poore, Ben: Perley. *Reminiscences of Sixty Years in the National Metropolis.* In two volumes. Illustrated. Tecumseh, Michigan, 1886.

THE DISTRICT GOVERNMENT

Bryan, W. B. *Various Forms of Local Government in the District of Columbia.* Washington, 1898.

Schmeckebier, Laurence, F. *The District of Columbia, Its Government and Administration.* Washington, 1928.

—— and W. F. Willoughby. *The Government and Administration of Columbia: Suggestions for Change.* Washington, 1929.

Tindall, William. *Origin and Government of the District of Columbia.* Washington, 1909.

PLANTS AND ANIMALS

Cooke, May Thatcher. *Birds of the Washington Region.* Washington, 1929.

Coville, Frederick N., and O. M. Freeman. *Trees and Shrubs of Lafayette Park.* With map. Washington, 1932.

Hitchcock, Albert S. and Paul C. Standley. *Flora of the District of Columbia and Vicinity.* Illustrated. Washington, 1919.

Kauffman, Erle. *Trees of Washington, the Man and City.* Washington, 1932.
Mann, William M. *Wild Animals in and out of the Zoo.* Illustrated. New York, 1934.
Mattoon, Wilbur R. and Susan S. Albertis. *Forest Trees of the District of Columbia: How to Know Them, Where to see Them.* Washington, 1923.
Roberts, Edna Jane. *Famous and Historic Trees of the City of Washington.* Washington, 1927.
Sites, Maud Kay. *Japanese Cherry Trees in Washington, D. C.* Baltimore, 1935.

THE NEGRO IN WASHINGTON

Greene, Lorenzo J. and Myra Colson Callis. *The Employment of Negroes in the District of Columbia.* Washington, 1930.
Ingle, Edward. *The Negro in the District of Columbia.* Baltimore, 1893.
Jones, William H. *The Housing of Negroes in Washington, D. C.* Washington, 1929.
——— *Recreation and Amusement among Negroes in Washington, D. C.* Washington, 1927.
Montgomery, Winfield S. *Education for the Colored Race in the District of Columbia, 1807-1905; A Historical Sketch.* Washington, 1907.
Shannon, A. H. *The Negro in Washington.* Washington, 1930.
Tremain, Mary. *Slavery in the District of Columbia.* New York, 1892.

GUIDE BOOKS

Daughters of the American Revolution. *Historical Directory of the District of Columbia.* Washington, 1922.
Early, Eleanor. *And This is Washington.* Boston, 1934.
Gross, Alexander, Editor. *Famous Guide to Washington, D. C.,* pictorial and descriptive, with 15 maps and 85 illustrations. New York City, 1938.
Latimer, Louise Payson. *Your Washington and Mine.* Illustrated. New York, 1924.
Parton, M. F. *Your Washington.* New York, 1938.
Rand McNally. *Guide to Washington and Environs.* Illustrated, 1937.
Reynolds, Charles B. *Standard Guide—Washington, a Handbook for Visitors.* With map. Washington, 1939.
Rider, Fremont. *Rider's Washington: A Guide Book for Travelers.* Compiled under the general editorship of Fremont Rider by Frederick Taber Cooper. With maps and plans. New York, 1924.
Sullivan, Lawrence. *All About Washington: An Intimate Guide.* New York, 1932.
Works Progress Administration, Federal Writers' Project. *Washington: City and Capital.* (First Edition). Washington, Government Printing Office, 1937.

THE ENVIRONS

King. Grace. *Mount Vernon on the Potomac.* Illustrated. New York, 1925.

Lindsey, Mary. *Historic Homes and Landmarks of Alexandria.* Alexandria, Va., 1931.

Martin, Oliver. *The Chesapeake and Potomac Country.* Illustrated. Washington, 1928.

Mount Vernon Ladies Association. *An Illustrated Handbook of Mount Vernon,* 1936.

Page, Thomas Nelson. *Mount Vernon and Its Preservation, 1859-1910.* Illustrated. Published by the Mount Vernon Ladies' Association. Revised edition, 1932.

Powell, Mary G. *History of Old Alexandria, Virginia, 1749-1861.* Richmond, Va., 1928.

Shosteck, Robert. *The Potomac Trail Book.* Washington, 1935.

—— *Guide to Trails Around Washington,* with 32 travel maps. New York, 1937.

Wilstach, Paul. *Mount Vernon, Washington's Home and the Nation's Shrine.* Illustrated. New York, 1925.

—— *Potomac Landings.* Illustrated. New York, 1921.

Index

ABOUT THE AUTHORS

The Federal Writers' Project was established in 1935 as part of Federal #1, a project to provide work relief for artists and professionals under the Works Progress Administration. In the next four years the project produced works on local history, folkways, and culture in addition to the magisterial American Guide Series.

Roger G. Kennedy is Director of the Smithsonian Institution's National Museum of American History and the author of *American Churches*.

Also available from Pantheon Books

★

THE WPA GUIDE TO ILLINOIS

*With a New Introduction by Neil Harris
and Michael Conzen*
0-394-72195-0   *$9.95 (paperback)*

★

THE WPA GUIDE TO MASSACHUSETTS

With a New Introduction by Jane Holtz Kay
0-394-71581-0   *$9.95 (paperback)*

★

THE WPA GUIDE TO NEW ORLEANS

*With a New Introduction by
the Historic New Orleans Collection*
0-394-71588-8   *$8.95 (paperback)*

★

THE WPA GUIDE TO NEW YORK

With a New Introduction by William H. Whyte
0-394-71215-3   *$8.95 (paperback)*

★

THE WPA GUIDE TO WASHINGTON, D.C.

With a New Introduction by Roger G. Kennedy
0-394-72192-6   *$8.95 (paperback)*

A revised and updated version of this guide is available in hardcover from Hastings House, Publishers, Inc., 10 East 40th Street, New York, N.Y. 10016.